THE PRINCELY COURT

Frontispiece: Feast at the court of Alexander the Great, from a *Romance of Alexander*, illuminated in the Low Countries, *c.*1338-44

THE PRINCELY COURT

*Medieval Courts and Culture
in North-West Europe
1270–1380*

170201

MALCOLM VALE

OXFORD
UNIVERSITY PRESS

OXFORD
UNIVERSITY PRESS

Great Clarendon Street, Oxford OX2 6DP

Oxford University Press is a department of the University of Oxford.
It furthers the University's objective of excellence in research, scholarship,
and education by publishing worldwide in

Oxford New York

Athens Auckland Bangkok Bogotá Buenos Aires Cape Town
Chennai Dar es Salaam Delhi Florence Hong Kong Istanbul Karachi
Kolkata Kuala Lumpur Madrid Melbourne Mexico City Mumbai Nairobi
Paris São Paulo Shanghai Singapore Taipei Tokyo Toronto Warsaw
with associated companies in Berlin Ibadan

Oxford is a registered trade mark of Oxford University Press
in the UK and in certain other countries

Published in the United States
By Oxford University Press Inc., New York

British Library Cataloguing in Publication Data
Data available

Library of Congress Cataloging in Publication Data
Vale, M. G. A. (Malcolm Graham Allan)
The princely court: medieval courts and culture in North-West Europe, 1270–1380 /
Malcolm Vale.
p. cm.
Includes bibliographical references.
1. Europe, Western—Court and courtiers. 2. Civilization, Medieval. 3. Europe,
Northern—Court and courtiers. 4. Courts and courtiers. 5. Arts, Medieval. 6. Chivalry. 7.
Europe, Northern—Kings and rulers. 8. Europe, Western—Kings and rulers. 9. Material
culture—Europe, Western. 10. Material culture—Europe, Northern. I. Title.
CB335 .V35 2001   940—dc21   2001033966

ISBN 0-19-820529-5

1 3 5 7 9 10 8 6 4 2

Typeset by Graphicraft Ltd., Hong Kong
Printed in Great Britain
on acid-free paper by Biddles Ltd,
Guildford and King's Lynn

ACKNOWLEDGEMENTS

In the course of a long-term project, one incurs many debts. It is, however, one of the incidental pleasures of scholarship to acknowledge the support, encouragement, constructive criticism and generosity of so many people. Without such informal remaining vestiges of the Republic of Letters this book would not have been written or, if it had, it would have been very much the poorer.

First, I owe a great deal to Godfried Croenen, who acted as research assistant to the project under a generous two-year award from the Leverhulme Trust. His knowledge and deployment of computer techniques produced results which it would have been both difficult and time-consuming to obtain by any other means. Secondly, I am indebted to a number of colleagues and friends for their help in many and various ways: Gerard Nijsten, Rees Davies, and Janet van der Meulen, all of whom read and helpfully commented on drafts at various stages; Wim Blockmans, Dick de Boer, Marc Boone, Jean Dunbabin, John Elliott, Steven Gunn, Olga Kotková, Frédérique Lachaud, Werner Paravicini, Walter Prevenier, Gervase Rosser, Iwona Sagan, Arjo Vanderjagt, and Frits van Oostrom, all offered stimulus and support. Institutions must be thanked for their enabling roles: above all, the Leverhulme Trust and the Netherlands Institute for Advanced Study in the Humanities and Social Sciences (NIAS) at Wassenaar. The year (1997–8) which I spent at NIAS as a Fellow-in-Residence, after election by the Royal Netherlands Academy of Arts and Sciences, enabled me to draft a substantial part of the book, and subsequent shorter visits helped to complete the process. I particularly wish to record my thanks to all members of the NIAS staff, and especially to Saskia Lepelaar, who undertook the task of converting many of the tables into publishable form. St John's College and the Faculty of Modern History in the University of Oxford have been generous in granting me leave and funding for research visits to Belgium, France, and the Netherlands. The Wiener-Anspach Foundation offered me a three-months' visiting Research Fellowship in 1991, at a relatively early stage in the project, held at the Université Libre de Bruxelles, and I owe much to Alain Dierkens of the ULB for helping to make that visit profitable.

It will be apparent that this book has drawn upon a large volume and wide range of archival and manuscript material, conserved in

Great Britain, France, Belgium, and the Netherlands. The staff of many libraries and archives have proved unfailingly helpful, and it is a great pleasure to record the assistance received from the Public Record Office, the British Library, the Westminster Abbey Muniments, the Bodleian Library, the Taylor Institution Library, and St John's College Library, Oxford; the Archives de l'État at Mons, the Rijksarchief at Ghent, the Bibliothèque Royale and Archives Générales du Royaume at Brussels; the Archives Nationales, the Bibliothèque Nationale, the Archives Départementales de Pas-de-Calais at Arras, and the Archives Départementales du Nord at Lille; the Koninklijke Bibliotheek and Algemeen Rijksarchief at The Hague, the NIAS Library at Wassenaar, and the Leiden University Library.

Among publications which came to my notice too late to be included in this book, mention should especially be made of C. Allmand (ed.) *War, Government and Power in Late Medieval France* (Liverpool, 2000) and W. Blockmans, M. Boone, and T. de Hemptinne (eds.), *Secretum Scriptorium: Liber alumnorum Walter Prevenier* (Leuven/Apeldoorn, 1999).

This book has benefited immeasurably from the unfailingly constructive and supportive contributions of my wife, Juliet, and it is dedicated to our two sons, Timothy and Patrick.

M.V.

Oxford
October 2000

CONTENTS

PART TWO
Culture

LIST OF TABLES

LIST OF FIGURES

LIST OF APPENDICES

LIST OF MAPS

LIST OF PLATES

Frontispiece: Feast at the court of Alexander the Great, from *The Romance of Alexander*, c.1338–1344. Bodleian Library, Oxford, MS. Bodl. 264, fo. 188v.

between pp. 142–143

1. Palace and abbey of Westminster, engraving by Wenceslas Hollar, 1647. V&A Picture Library.
2. The Knights' Hall of the counts of Holland in the Binnenhof, The Hague, late thirteenth century.
3. The Painted Chamber in the Palace of Westminster, looking east, William Capon, 1799. Society of Antiquaries of London.
4. Register of privileges of Flanders, 1328 submission of Bruges. Koninklijke Bibliotheek, The Hague, MS 75 D 7, fo. 3v.
5. Distribution of liveries by a ruler, Pseudo-Aristotle, *Secreta Secretorum*, c.1326–1327. British Library, Add. MS 47680, fo. 17v.
6a–f. Clasps and pewter pendants. Museum Boijmans-van Beuningen, Rotterdam. Collective van Beuningen, Cohen, Inv. 1387, 1–2, Inv. 1991, Inv. 0212, Inv. 2048, Inv. 2116, and Inv. 0009.
7. The count's castle (*Gravensteen*), Ghent. Copyright: Uitg. Thill, N.V., Brussel.
8. The count's palace (*Prinsenhof*), Ghent, engraving from *Flandria Illustrata* by A. Sanders, 1641. Bodleian Library, Oxford, Meerman 81.
9a. Westminster Abbey, nave and choir, looking east. A. F. Kersting, Architectural Photographer.
9b. Amiens Cathedral, nave and choir, looking east. A. F. Kersting, Architectural Photographer.
10a. Ivory chessman. Ashmolean Museum, Oxford, A587.
10b. Ivory chessman. The Metropolitan Museum of Art, New York, 1917.190.231.
10c. Ivory chessman. Musée Antoine Vivenel, Compiègne, V347.
11a. Pewter pendant depicting a chessboard. Museum Boijmans-van Beuningen, Rotterdam. Collection van Beuningen, Cohen, Inv. 0672.
11b. Casket decorated with a scene of wildmen and a lady playing chess, c.1380. Rheinisches Bildarchiv Köln.
12. Lid of an ivory casket decorated with scenes of a tournament, the siege of the Castle of Love, and themes from romance, Paris, c.1325–1350. Wawel Cathedral Museum, Krakow.
13. Ivory box depicting lovers with sword, France, c.1325–1350. Musées royaux d'Art et d'Histoire, Brussels, Inv. 3140.

LIST OF ABBREVIATIONS

ADN	Lille, Archives Départementales du Nord
ADPC	Arras, Archives Départementales de Pas-de-Calais
AEM	Mons, Archives de l'État
AGR	Brussels, Archives Générales du Royaume
ARA	The Hague, Algemeen Rijksarchief
AN	Paris, Archives Nationales
BCRH	*Bulletin de la Commission Royale d'Histoire*
BEC	*Bibliothèque de l'École des Chartes*
BHPCTHS	*Bulletin Historique et Philologique du Comité des Travaux Historiques et Scientifiques*
BIHR	*Bulletin of the Institute of Historical Research*
BL	London, British Library
BN	Paris, Bibliothèque Nationale
Bod. Lib.	Oxford, Bodleian Library
BR	Brussels, Bibliothèque Royale
CCR	*Calendar of Close Rolls*
CPR	*Calendar of Patent Rolls*
CR	*Comptes Royaux*
EcHR	*Economic History Review*
EHR	*English Historical Review*
GBA	*Gazette des Beaux Arts*
JWCI	*Journal of the Warburg and Courtauld Institutes*
KB	The Hague, Koninklijke Bibliotheek
MA	*Le Moyen Age*
MGH	*Monumenta Germaniae Historica*
P&P	*Past and Present*
PRO	London, Public Record Office
PRS	Pipe Roll Society
RAG	Ghent, Rijksarchief
RBPH	*Revue Belge de Philologie et d'Histoire*
RCHM	Royal Commission on Historic Monuments
RHF	*Recueil des Historiens français*
RN	*Revue du Nord*
RS	*Rolls Series*
TRG	*Tijdschrift voor Geschiedenis*
WMA	Westminster Abbey Muniments

INTRODUCTION

This book departs from conventional approaches to its subject-matter on at least two counts: first, it includes, rather than isolates, England; secondly, it attempts to treat both the material and non-material aspects of later medieval princely courts within the framework of a single study. It has been a common practice of historians to treat the unambiguously concrete and tangible aspects of the subject quite separately from the manifestations of court culture which they perceive in the visual, plastic and applied arts, and in music and literature. The court at this time was intimately and inextricably enmeshed with the ruler's household, but studies of the household, its structure, organization, and personnel, tend—necessarily—to confine themselves to matter rather than mind. My aim has been to adopt a much broader definition of culture, which takes into account the material infrastructures upon which the arts rested and which, in part, could determine their nature and function. The memorable definition of culture formulated in 1871 by the anthropologist E. B. Tylor is still worthy of consideration: 'culture . . . is that complex whole which includes knowledge, belief, art, morals, law, custom, and any other capabilities and habits acquired by man as a member of society.'[1] Tylor's emphasis upon the acquisition of cultural characteristics is significant: they are not innate, but have to be learned and acquired. Courts provided a context in which such habits and modes of behaviour were both acquired and perpetuated. Thus court culture is here seen from a broad viewpoint, in which, for example, habits of consumption, religious beliefs, devotional practices, modes of dress, and other markers or tokens of status and function, as well as patronage of the arts, are integral to its nature.

---

[1] E. B. Tylor, *Primitive Culture* (London, 1871), i. 1. The anthropological literature on culture is vast and controversial, but useful discussions of the concept are to be found in A. L. Kroeber and C. Kluckhohn, *Culture: A Critical Review of Concepts and Definitions* (Cambridge, Mass., 1952), and C. Geertz, *The Interpretation of Cultures* (New York, 1973); see also G. W. Stocking (ed.), *Malinowski, Rivers, Benedict and Others: Essays in Culture and Personality* (Madison, 1986).

My adoption in the title of the book of the term 'culture', rather than 'cultures', stems from a concern to identify what was common to the various court societies of the period studied. The anthropological definition of culture, or culture(s), stressing their pluralistic and relativistic nature, is less applicable in this context than humanistic interpretations which emphasize, among other facets, the common values and expectations shared by high-status groups across territorial, linguistic, and ethnic boundaries.[2] This is not to argue that the culture, however broadly defined, of court societies constituted a discrete, self-contained, bounded system. There was little, if any, sense of ethnic or national exclusiveness in this milieu. Court culture was open to external forces: it was essentially permeable and absorptive of a wide range of influences. Although the members of these elites possessed indigenous cultural characteristics, based upon language, tradition, and perceptions of their own past, they formed part of a single social system.

The initial idea of investigating the history of princely courts in northwest Europe, from this point of view, during the century or so between 1270 and 1380, originated in my earlier work on Burgundian chivalry and culture. The spectacular nature of the court of Burgundy, and the artistic efflorescence of the fifteenth-century Netherlands, had apparently overshadowed—if not entirely eclipsed—the preceding period, and this was reflected in the relative paucity of literature on the pre-Burgundian courts of the Low Countries. We knew much more about the Burgundian court than about its precursors, and it was in an attempt to redress this balance that the present study was born. It therefore began as a Netherlands-based project. Yet the evidence from both the southern and northern Low Countries could not be treated in isolation: material from both royal France and royal England—as primary formative influences on lesser rulers and key players in the court societies of the age—had to be introduced. However, it has not been part of any tradition of historical writing, with the exception of a few ground-breaking studies,[3] to consider English evidence beside that stemming from its nearest continental neighbours.

---

[2] For cultures as ways of living, emphasizing their holistic but diverse nature, see R. Benedict, *Race and Racism* (London, 1943), 9–14; also G. Stocking, *Race, Culture, and Evolution: Essays in the History of Anthropology* (New York, 1968), 29–47.

[3] For some important exceptions, see P. Binski, *The Painted Chamber at Westminster* (Society of Antiquaries Occasional paper, n.s. 9, London, 1986), and *Westminster Abbey and the Plantagenets: Kingship and the Representation of Power, 1200–1400* (New Haven and London, 1995); and J. Vale, *Edward III and Chivalry: Chivalric Society and its Context, 1270–1350* (Woodbridge, 1982).

The later medieval English kingdom has invariably been considered by historians separately from continental Europe, often for the soundest of reasons. Political and institutional developments, such as its relatively precocious centralization, distinguished medieval England from many of its continental European neighbours. The extent and density of urbanization in England also differed markedly from that found in northern France and the Low Countries. English towns were not equivalent in size, power, and cultural influence to the great cities of Ghent, Bruges, Ypres, Arras, Douai, and their like. But, in terms of household organization, styles of court life, and cultural patronage, the English court shared many affinities with its continental counterparts in northern France and the Low Countries. It remained part of a francophone world in which French—and its variants, such as Anglo-Norman—was a *lingua franca*. Although there were differences of detail, the material foundations and infrastructures upon which the court of the Plantagenets was built, as well as the artistic and cultural products which its members patronized and purchased, were readily comparable with those found elsewhere in north-west Europe. Cultural isolationism was not to be found at this level.

The geographical area encompassed within the scope of this book coincided with no natural physical boundaries, no clearly defined linguistic frontiers, nor with any union of territories during the later Middle Ages (Map 1). This part of 'north-west Europe' was not an entity in any formal sense—except, perhaps, in terms of its economic contacts and cultural identity. The littoral regions on both sides of the English Channel and North Sea were studded with ports and trading centres which did not deal only in raw materials and commodities. There was a human traffic, of people and ideas, for which the sea served as a highway rather than a barrier. The island kingdom of England was thus closely and inextricably bound up with the kingdom of France and the principalities of the Low Countries. Tenure of continental possessions—the duchy of Aquitaine and the *comté* of Ponthieu—by the English crown further strengthened these bonds. Diplomatic intercourse between the kingdoms of England and France was constant, as it was with the principalities of the Low Countries, while the ebb and flow of alliance and antagonism between both major and minor secular powers lent an ever-shifting character to relationships of many kinds. It is therefore with contrasts and comparisons between these major—and minor—players in the dynastic politics of the region in the later thirteenth and fourteenth centuries that we are concerned. All were princes; all maintained 'princely' establishments around them, although there were important differences of rank among and between them. There were three sovereign powers: the kings of England and France, and the German emperor; and a group of non-sovereign princes: the counts of Flanders, the dukes of Brabant, the counts of Hainault, the counts of Artois, and the counts of Holland and Zeeland (Maps 1, 2). To set the political scene, as it were, each of these will be briefly considered in turn.

The dominant role often accorded to Anglo-French rivalry during this period has tended to subordinate the political behaviour of the northern French and Netherlandish princes to the power-struggle which was to culminate in 1337 with the outbreak of the Hundred Years War. The diverse principalities are seen as conducting their own essentially reactive and defensive policies against external threats from greater powers. It has, however, been observed that, in socio-economic and cultural terms 'the mutual ties' binding the principalities of the Low Countries 'were stronger than those with the outside world'.[4] But the various princip-alities lacked any sense of common political or institutional unity, and power-relationships were determined more by attempts to reduce the capacity of greater powers to intervene than by the ambitions of any single house to dominate the region. This was to change somewhat in the second half of the fourteenth century, as 'foreign' rulers, often with territorial ambitions of their own, came to replace dynasties that had died out in the direct male line—Hainault-Holland in 1345, Brabant in 1355, and Flanders in 1384. Similarly, the gradual emergence of sporadic com-binations of territories under one ruler in the Low Countries was not merely a response to Anglo-French, or franco-imperial, conflict. The expansion of the duchy of Brabant to absorb the *pays d'Outremeuse* in Limburg (1288) (Map 2), or the union of Hainault, Holland, and Zeeland under the Avesnes dynasty (1299–1345), were symptoms of a tendency among princely houses to render themselves more independent of sovereign powers and other higher authorities—above all, of the German Empire. Imperial influence over non-German vassals, such as the dukes of Brabant and counts of Hainault and Holland, for instance, declined with the collapse of the Hohenstaufen after 1250 and the inter-regnum in the Empire which lasted until 1273. The subsequent rise of the Valois dukes of Burgundy to hegemony in the Low Countries after 1384 was to some extent prefigured and anticipated, on a much smaller scale,

---

[4] W. Prevenier, 'The Low Countries, 1290–1415', in M. Jones (ed.), *The New Cambridge Medieval History*, vi. *c.1300–c.1415* (Cambridge, 2000), 570. This survey offers the most recent overview of the history of the Low Countries during this period.

by these earlier unions. Yet the fact remains, as H. S. Lucas pointed out, that the principalities of the Low Countries, 'situated where the boundaries of the Empire marched with those of the kingdom of France and opposite the island of England, were by reason of their varied economic, social and political life bound to be vitally affected by the greater political factors in the life of the states of Europe'.[5] They were also bound to be vitally affected by the cultural movements and tendencies of the age, often—although not always—emanating from the courts of greater powers such as the Papacy or the kings of France and England. There was, however, little or no discernible correlation between political stability, administrative centralization, and cultural significance at this time. Political fragmentation and the decentralized, peripatetic nature of princely rule proved to be no obstacle to artistic and literary patronage, innovation and creativity. The allegedly more centralized Burgundian 'state' of the fifteenth century is sometimes perceived as a more stable entity than it really was, and credited with responsibility for much of the artistic and cultural flowering of the Low Countries. But the more fluid and shifting political constructs of the preceding period were by no means inimical to cultural developments.

The associations and affinities between the main players on the stage of politics at this time were thus diverse and, in many cases, complex. Each power had its own particular character and allegiances. Although technically vassals of the French crown, until 1340, for their residual continental lands—the remnant of the former Angevin Empire after the losses of 1204–1242—the Plantagenet kings of England were regarded by their Netherlandish neighbours as sovereigns in their own right. Alliances were made with them as monarchs of England, not as dukes of Aquitaine or counts of Ponthieu. The dissident rebels within the *comté* of Flanders in the 1340s, moreover, endorsed Edward III's claim to the French throne against that of Philip VI of Valois, who was supported by their own count, Louis de Nevers. A heightening of tension between England and France from the 1290s onwards led to a series of betrothals and marriage alliances, some durable and some short-lived, between the Plantagenets and the Netherlandish princes during the period from 1290 to 1369. Brabant, Holland, Flanders, Hainault, and Guelders were actively sought as allies through dynastic marriages. England's wealth and military prestige drew clients and allies, but the unexpected succession crises in three

---

[5] H. S. Lucas, *The Low Countries and the Hundred Years War, 1326–1347* (Ann Arbor, 1929, repr. Philadelphia, 1976), 30–1.

of the Netherlandish principalities after 1345, together with the military and diplomatic reverses experienced by England after 1369, combined to work to its disadvantage. The introduction of the Wittelsbachs of Bavaria into anglophile Hainault-Holland after 1358, for example, was to lead to a greater degree of independence from, and neutrality in, the Anglo-French conflict. The inability of Edward III to win the hand of Margaret, sole surviving legitimate child of Louis de Male, count of Flanders and Artois, for his son Edmund of Langley in 1369 also demonstrated that English influence and prestige in the Low Countries was not what it had previously been. Yet the resources and splendour of the English court under Edward III and Richard II still made it an important cultural force and a magnet for lesser houses.

Flanders, dependent upon imported English wool for its textile production, inclined towards England, and this created a chronic tension between the Dampierre counts of Flanders—as vassals of the French crown—and many of their Flemish subjects. French intervention in Flanders, sometimes on behalf of the counts, sometimes (as in 1302) in opposition to them, was a constant theme. The massacre of French knighthood by the Flemings, at the battle of Kortrijk (11 July 1302) was an unexpected reversal of French fortunes, but the subsequent encounter at Mons-en-Pévèle (18 August 1304) proved indecisive and led to a negotiated settlement. In 1305 and 1312 the treaties of Athis and Pontoise imposed harsh financial penalties on Flanders, and annexation by the crown of French-speaking Walloon areas (Lille, Douai, Orchies). These were to be recovered by Louis de Male in the 1360s, thereby re-establishing a significant power-base for comital authority and a safe haven in times of Flemish turbulence. French interventionism was, however, carried to its extreme by the advent of Philip the Bold of Burgundy, prince of the French blood-royal, and the bloody defeat of the Flemings in 1382. The Burgundian accession to Flanders and Artois (1384), which marks the terminal date of this book, could thus be seen as the final victory of the francophile *leliaarts* over the Netherlandish-speaking population. Yet, as we shall see, political and social turbulence in much, though not all, of the *comté* of Flanders did not prevent the growth of the comital court and its culture.

The dukes of Brabant, although their territories also included Netherlandish-speaking populations, experienced no such tensions with their subjects. The dukes owed no allegiance to the crown of France, and were imperial vassals. With an estimated three thousand vassals of their own, they were princes of considerable weight and authority, whose alliance was much sought after by both the kings of England and France. Predominantly anglophile in the later thirteenth century, they had moved towards a more neutral position by the mid-fourteenth century. As in Hainault-Holland, a failure of male heirs led to the introduction, through the female line, of a German house in the shape of Wenceslas, brother of the German emperor, in 1355. A much-weakened ducal authority was subjected to attacks from Flanders and the imposition of severe constitutional restraints by its subjects. Yet none of this had discernibly adverse effects upon the cultural flowering of the Brabant court, now more closely bound to that of Hainault, in the later fourteenth century.

The counts of Hainault, neighbours of the dukes of Brabant, rose to European prominence in the second quarter of the fourteenth century. Under the house of Avesnes, a conflict—largely over rights to Zeeland—had been intermittently waged with the Dampierre counts of Flanders until a settlement was reached in 1323. But a major transformation in the position of the counts of Hainault took place with their acquisition in 1299 of Holland and Zeeland, following the premature death of the Dutch count John I. Jean d'Avesnes became count of Hainault-Holland-Zeeland, a dynastic union which was to last until the Burgundian accession to each of its constituent parts between 1428 and 1433. The resources which their territories brought them enabled the counts to engage in power-brokering on a European scale, marrying one daughter to the Emperor Lewis of Bavaria and another to Edward III of England. The court of William III (1305–37) at Valenciennes and Mons became a focal point of pro-English diplomacy and propaganda. This was not to survive the succession crisis of 1345–6, occasioned by the death in battle (1345) against the Frisians of his son, the childless William IV. None the less, the English connection was maintained through the marriage of William V, son of Lewis of Bavaria and Margaret of Hainault, daughter of William III, to Maud of Lancaster. William V's insanity after 1358 led to the advent of his brother, Albert of Bavaria, first as regent (1358–89), then as count (1389–1404), in Hainault-Holland-Zeeland. This was to have significant cultural as well as political consequences, since Middle Dutch in addition to French was once more established as an acceptable language at court. This was a resumption of a pattern observable before the accession of the Avesnes to Holland and Zeeland in 1299. Floris V, count of Holland and Zeeland (1256–96) and his nobles had patronized vernacular Dutch as well as French literature at his court.

If the Dampierre—and Burgundian—counts of Flanders were plagued by internal conflicts with their towns, the Bavarian line in Holland and

Zeeland had to contend with a long-running feud which drew both nobles and townsmen into its orbit. In May 1350, an alliance of Dutch nobles was formed with the intention of maintaining the territorial and institutional integrity of Holland. This was the origin of the faction known as the *Kabeljauwen* ('Codfish'), against which a rival grouping of nobles and towns such as Dordrecht—the *Hoeken* ('Hooks')—was to grow up. Comital authority was weakened by this division, although it was sometimes possible to play one faction off against the other and achieve a precarious balance of power. Again, however, as in Flanders, the turbulent feuding of the nobles and towns had little apparent effect upon the cultural life and artistic production emanating from the Dutch court. Although Albert of Bavaria possessed substantial resources, the dictates of *realpolitik* inhibited further expansion of his house towards hegemony in the Low Countries, challenged as that ambition was by the Flemish-Burgundian alliance between Louis de Male and Philip the Bold of Burgundy after the latter's marriage to Margaret de Male in 1369. At the end of our period, a double marriage, celebrated with great splendour at Cambrai in April 1385, linked the houses of Burgundy and Bavaria. Philip the Bold's eldest son John of Nevers (later to become Duke John the Fearless), was married to Margaret, daughter of Albert of Bavaria; Philip's daughter, also Margaret, married Albert's son, William of Bavaria. It was an acknowledgement that neither power-bloc was at that stage able to displace the other.

As a centre of court culture, the household of the counts of Artois in the thirteenth century was a formative influence upon other courts. Yet its existence as a permanent and separate entity was not destined to endure beyond the second quarter of the fourteenth century. Under Robert II (1266–1302) and the countess Mahaut (1302–29), Artois remained firmly within the inner circle of the French royal house, as the most naturally and consistently loyal of the lordships bordering the Low Countries. Robert II paid for his allegiance to the French crown and its interventionist behaviour in Flanders with his life at the battle of Kortrijk. On Mahaut's death (1329), the *comté* of Artois passed to a series of rulers—Jeanne, countess of Burgundy (1330–47); the French crown (1347–61); and Margaret of France, countess of Artois and Burgundy (1361–82). The comital household was dissolved as a separate establishment in 1329, revived in 1361 for the countess Margaret, only to be abolished on her death in 1382. The status and prestige enjoyed by the house of Artois in the thirteenth century was never regained. Economic trends made Artois and its principal towns such as Arras and St-Omer very prosperous, but its strategic position on the route from Paris to Flanders rendered it vulnerable to the effects of warfare. The magnetic attraction exercised by Paris—where the counts maintained a splendid *hôtel* and enjoyed a particularly favoured place in royal councils among the princes of the blood—served to bridle any expansionist ambitions in the Low Countries. Like their neighbours in the *comté* of Flanders, the counts of Artois remained leading vassals of the French crown but— unlike the counts of Flanders—exercised power in the Low Countries only by means of royal lieutenancies granted to them. Absorption into the Flemish-Burgundian power-bloc after 1382 finally brought the existence of Artois as a discrete and self-sufficient entity to an end. The court of Artois was subsumed into that of Burgundy.

The scope of this book is, like all studies of this period, partly deter- mined by the nature and extent of the surviving sources. As we shall see, the later thirteenth century witnessed a sharp rise in the volume of archival documentation for court life and household administration. The structure of the court was in large part determined by the type of house- hold maintained by a ruler. One means of regulating and giving fixity of form to the household of any ruler was to draw up household ordinances. An early example survives from England, the *Constitutio Domus Regis* of Henry I (1100–35). Yet there is a dearth of such evidence in the rest of north-west Europe until the second half of the thirteenth century and, even then, household ordinances are still rare. Such documents could also be prescriptive rather than descriptive in their intent, because their authors—who could be critics of a ruler's alleged extravagance—were often more concerned with things as they ought to be, rather than as they actually were. Treatises on household governance and economy, which also begin to survive from the second quarter of the thirteenth century, were similarly prescriptive. The so-called 'commercial revolution' of the thirteenth century was, however, to have far-reaching effects not only upon supply, demand, and ways of doing business, but also upon methods of accountancy. Changes associated with the economic tendencies of the 'long' thirteenth century (*c*.1160–*c*.1330) gave rise to new forms and techniques of household accounting. The period witnessed a 'transition to an economy in which money was the measure of all things, from one in which money had had a relatively minor role'.[6] This was to have marked effects upon the manner in which rulers (and others) ordered and main- tained their households, upon their levels of conspicuous consumption,

---

[6] P. Spufford, *Money and its Use in Medieval Europe* (Cambridge, 1988), 243.

and, consequently, upon the documentation which recorded and accompanied these trends. From about 1250, household accounts (*comptes de l'hôtel*) appear in much larger quantities, drawn up in such a way that their evidence for one ruler's consumption and expenditure can be compared with that stemming from another's household administration.

The survival of household and other accounts thus allows us to piece together the patterns, not only of material provision, but also of cultural patronage and artistic production, to an unprecedented degree. Increased demand for luxury goods, fuelled by the release of large amounts of coin and bullion, and sustained by the rise of credit and banking facilities, could not fail to have an effect upon courtly living. Greater liquidity had a direct impact on levels of consumption. Chronological boundaries, especially for economic movements and trends, are always artificial, but the time-span which I have chosen began in a period of widespread economic prosperity, whose benefits were admittedly enjoyed only by a minority of European society. This was to give way to an age of recession —in large part a consequence of plague and demographic crisis—from the mid-fourteenth century (1347–51) onwards. The sources used in this study tell one little about the damaging effects of epidemic and economic contraction, apart from the evident concentration of greater degrees of wealth in fewer hands. The resilience and vitality of later medieval literary and representational culture is perhaps all the more striking in the light of these sombre events.

To gain an impression of the richness and abundance of artistic, literary, and musical life at the courts of this period we cannot rely upon surviving artefacts, literary texts, and written musical compositions. What survives forms merely the tip of the proverbial iceberg. With the exception of manuscript books, surviving artefacts of 'courtly' provenance are relatively rare, although the applied arts are perhaps better represented in this respect than is sometimes assumed. Our knowledge of patronage of the visual and applied arts, literature, and music has therefore to be derived as much from the evidence of household and other accounts as from surviving works of art. To associate surviving documentary evidence with a specific surviving work is hazardous and difficult, so that the great majority of objects which have come down to us are completely undocumented. Their 'courtly' origin or provenance can often only be inferred from stylistic comparison, and by identification with similar items described in accounts and inventories.

From the perspective of princely courts, it would thus be difficult to endorse the Florentine chronicler Filippo Villani's view of his time as a 'shipwreck of a century'.[7] The court might sometimes be caricatured by satirists and critics as a ship not only of fools but of knaves as well. But there were no signs of its foundering as a vehicle of noble lifestyles, high-status cultural patronage, and political power-brokering. Before we can begin to examine these facets of court life, however, a series of fundamental problems concerning the nature of the court have to be addressed.

[7] Cited in M. L. McLaughlin, 'Humanist concepts of Renaissance and Middle Ages in the Trecento and Quattrocento', *Renaissance Studies*, 2 (1988), 135. The theme of disaster and calamity was taken up and presented—with allusions to late twentieth-century parallels—to a wider audience in B. Tuchman, *A Distant Mirror: The Calamitous 14th Century* (London, 1979), p. xiii: 'the interest of the period itself—a violent, tormented, bewildered, suffering and disintegrating age, a time, as many thought, of Satan triumphant —was compelling and . . . consoling in a period of similar disarray.'

Part One

THE MATERIAL
FOUNDATIONS
OF COURT LIFE

Chapter 1

COURT AND
HOUSEHOLD

What was 'the court' in the later Middle Ages? What did contemporaries mean by the term? Satisfactory answers to these questions are notoriously difficult to arrive at, partly because the term could carry different meanings according to the context in which it was used. There is, however, a broad measure of agreement that a ruler's household (*domus*, *hospitium*, *hôtel*) played a fundamental part in giving substance to the idea of 'the court'. The material infrastructure, or underpinning, of all princely courts—in both the medieval and modern periods—was provided by the household. Court and household were never entirely synonymous, yet courts could not have existed without household organizations behind and within them. When a ruler 'held court', for example, the resources, and resourcefulness, of his household and its officers were necessarily brought into play. The holders of household office might be required to perform domestic functions, sometimes on a hereditary basis, and these services formed an essential element in court ceremonial. Furthermore, the holding of 'full', 'solemn', or plenary courts, summoned by a ruler on specific occasions, obviously depended upon the wide range of services provided to those present by household departments—lodging, catering, provisioning, and stabling all fell within the purview of the household.

Yet there was a more fundamental and organic sense in which the household was integral to the court. The domestic establishment which met a ruler's daily needs could also provide a skeletal underpinning—in the form of household offices and departments—for the court, which would otherwise have been an invertebrate organization. As C. A. J. Armstrong observed, writing of the court of Burgundy, 'the backbone of the court was the ducal household, an administrative institution which

imparted to it discipline and durability'.[1] Yet the court was not an institution in any formal sense, and such framework as it possessed derived, in
effect, from the household. The court thus defies analysis in institutional
terms. It therefore fits uneasily into theses which concentrate upon state
formation and state-building in later medieval and early modern Europe.
The ruler's household, which formed the backbone of the court, did not
prefigure or anticipate recognizably 'modern' bureaucratic structures. Its
role in the institutional development of the modern state has therefore
either been ignored or dismissed as insignificant.

Any study of the material foundations of court life must begin with a
consideration of the nature and role of the household. In the later Middle
Ages princely households were—with very few exceptions—itinerant
and peripatetic. It was not until the late sixteenth and early seventeenth
centuries that the resident establishment, usually set up in a major
city within a ruler's domains, came to typify and represent the *ancien
régime* court. At a later period, moreover, the 'Versailles model' of the
court—self-contained, purpose-built, outside the city, subsuming both
the prince's household and administration—has, in turn, been seen as
exceptional. But wherever the prince took up residence, he was necessarily surrounded by his household, sometimes accompanied by the
subsidiary households of his dependants. Although the household, with
its various departments and offices, can be defined and described without undue difficulty, the defining attributes of the court are far less easy
to list.

Terms such as 'elusive', 'protean' or 'chameleon-like' are the standard
currency of historians when they attempt to define 'the court' in the later
Middle Ages. They are in good company. From Walter Map's *De Nugis
Curialium* (*c*.1181–93) onwards, an inability to produce a clear definition
of the court has characterized much writing on the subject. The exasperated Map wrote, 'in the court I exist and of the court I speak, but what the
court is, God knows, I know not'.[2] Such agnosticism among contemporary clerks and *litterati* has led historians to doubt the extent to which

---

[1] C. A. J. Armstrong, 'The Golden Age of Burgundy: dukes that outdid kings', in A. G.
Dickens (ed.), *The Courts of Europe: Politics, Patronage and Royalty, 1400–1800* (London,
1977), 58. For recent revisionism, and for what follows, see J. Adamson (ed.), *The Princely
Courts of Europe: Ritual, Politics and Culture under the Ancien Régime, 1500–1750* (London,
1999), esp. 9–10, 39–40.

[2] Walter Map, *De Nugis Curialium*, ed. M. R. James (Oxford, 1914), 3. A study of
contemporary use of the term 'court' and its meanings is currently being undertaken by
Dr Frédérique Lachaud.

the medieval household resembled the early modern—and the modern—
court. Until the appearance of recent critiques, the thesis of Norbert
Elias, which places the 'court society' at the centre of the 'civilizing process', claiming that by a process of *courtization* a warrior nobility was
transformed into a court aristocracy, has been very influential in shaping
such views.[3] Elias's notion (supported largely by evidence from France
alone) that the later Middle Ages and Renaissance saw the transition
from an 'agrarian feudal class to a court nobility' has been remarkably
pervasive.[4] When buttressed by the claim that 'the rise of court society
is undoubtedly connected to the advancing centralization of state power,
to the growing monopolization of . . . revenue . . . and military and police
power' the huge sweep of Elias's theorizing is apparent.[5] It fits well into a
schema which locates the transition from 'medieval' to 'modern' government, culture, and society during the period from 1450 to 1600.

But the dynamic and pace of change in the age of Renaissance and
Reformation evidently differed within the various spheres of political,
religious, social, and cultural development. Continuity and change
co-existed. A major aim of this book is, by analogy, to stress continuities
as well as changes in court life and organization in north-west Europe
during the century or so which began with the final collapse of the Hohenstaufen emperors (*c.*1260–70) and ended with the rise of the Valois dukes
of Burgundy (*c.*1370–80). These continuities, furthermore, long outlived
this period.[6] Assumptions about Renaissance innovations have recently
been tempered by the acknowledgement that continuity must also be a
major theme of court studies. Thus R. A. Griffiths has suggested that, in
an English context, 'the most fascinating question of all is whether Henry
Tudor [1485–1509] successfully restored royal control over government
and nobility by developing his court along lines mainly laid down in the

---

[3] See N. Elias, *The Court Society* (Oxford, 1983), 158–9, 186–7. The influence of Elias
may also be detected in, for example, D. Starkey (ed.), *The English Court: from the Wars of
the Roses to the Civil War* (London and New York, 1987), 3, echoed by J.-P. Genet, 'La
monarchie anglaise: une image brouillée', in J. Blanchard (ed.), *Représentation, pouvoir et
royauté à la fin du moyen âge* (Paris, 1995), 100–1.

[4] Elias, *Court Society*, 158.

[5] Ibid. 2. For recent criticism of Elias's thesis see J. Duindam, *Myths of Power: Norbert
Elias and the Early Modern European Court* (Amsterdam, 1995).

[6] The recent surge of interest in 'court studies' has led to a number of publications
which offer evidence of these continuities. See Adamson, *Princely Courts*, 10–41; J. C. G.
Röhl, *The Kaiser and his Court: Wilhelm II and the Government of Germany* (Cambridge,
1994), 70–106.

fourteenth century'.[7] D. A. L. Morgan, in a ground-breaking study of the Lancastrian and Yorkist household, wonders whether 'the three centuries [i.e. 1130–1430] which follow the first written description of the household's internal articulation—the *Constitutio Domus Regis* of the 1130s— may be as worthy (and as much in need) of the historian's attention as the two centuries [i.e. 1450–1640] which are the concern of this present work'.[8] One purpose of this book is to attempt, at least in part, to meet this perceived need. I shall argue that, in many ways, the distinction often made between medieval household and early modern, or Renaissance, court is an inherently false and artificial one.[9]

It would be a trite statement of the obvious to observe that there was a concept, or concepts, of the 'court' running through written sources— literary, descriptive, prescriptive, and archival—from the twelfth century onwards. Beyond that there were Byzantine, Carolingian, and Ottonian precedents. In the English royal household ordinance of 1445, for example, reference is made to the 'old rule of courte' and to 'bouch of court'.[10] The ordinance prescribed that there should be 24 'valletz pur la chambre, des queux soient 12 continuelment *en la court* qe continuelment soient entendantz a la persone de nostre dit seigneur le roy quant il doit chivacher'[11] ['valets for the chamber, of whom twelve shall be continually in the court, attendant upon the person of our said lord the king when he rides out']. In 1471–2, the Black Book of Edward IV's household cited the text of the oath taken by the treasurer of the household, which included the obligation to 'serche the good, old, sad, worshupfull, and profitables *rulez of the court used before tym, and them to kepe, uphold, or bettyr if ye can,*

[7] R. A. Griffiths, 'The king's court during the Wars of the Roses: continuities in an age of discontinuities', in R. G. Asch and A. M. Birke (eds.), *Princes, Patronage and the Nobility* (Oxford, 1991), 66. This excellent volume represents a recent overview of the state of scholarship concerning the later medieval and early modern court.

[8] D. A. L. Morgan, 'The house of policy: the political role of the late Plantagenet household, 1422–1485', in Starkey (ed.), *The English Court*, 26.

[9] See below, pp.56–7. For supporting evidence from Italy that 'courts pre-dated the Renaissance' see J. E. Law, 'The *Ordine et Officij*: Aspects of context and content', in *Ordine et Officij de Casa de lo Illustrissimo Signor Duca de Urbino*, ed. S. Eiche (Urbino, 1999), 32–5. He concludes that 'as far as northern Italy is concerned, the signorial courts of the later thirteenth and early fourteenth centuries appear to have been special occasions, but in the course of the fourteenth they became more permanent and institutionalized' (p. 32). This would not be out of line with developments at the same time in north-west Europe.

[10] *The Household of Edward IV: The Black Book and the Ordinance of 1478*, ed. A. R. Myers (Manchester, 1959), 63, 66.

[11] Ibid. 70–1.

as God helpe yow and by that booke'.[12] For the compiler of the Black Book, the 'old . . . rules of the court' were first formulated in the reign of Edward III (1327–77). He was eloquent in his eulogy of that sovereign:

Domus Regis Edwardi Tertii was the house of very polycye and flowre of Inglond, the furst setter of sertayntez among his domestycall meyne, uppon a grounded rule. Nothwithstanding his fader, the secunde Edwarde, made many good custumes of household.[13]

By the later fifteenth century, a fourteenth-century origin was assumed, therefore, for the establishment of the English royal household on a disciplined and organized basis. The household ordinance of Edward III—to which this passage presumably refers—is now lost, but internal evidence from the Black Book suggests that it may have been largely a re-framing and reissue of the ordinances of his father, Edward II (1318, 1323, and a lost ordinance of Woodstock drawn up in 1310).[14] The compiler makes no mention of the 1279 household ordinance of Edward III's grandfather, Edward I, preferring to see Edward III's reign as the moment at which 'a formal and a convenient custume more certayne than was used byforn his tyme' was drawn up.[15] The chance survival (or non-survival) of formal household ordinances is not, however, always the most helpful of yardsticks for the organization and practices of a court. Other sources, such as household and wardrobe accounts, supply the evidence for well-established and long-standing structures and procedures. But the compiler of the Black Book was looking for a starting-point, a foundation grounded in good precedent, upon which to base his treatise. As he himself put it: 'exemple we take to *bylde upon a more perfit new house* bycause this noble king Edward the iijd. his household varyethe gretely from the householde that kinges have kept syn that tym, and yit in thies dayes.'[16]

Awareness of difference across the century since Edward III's death reflected a certain historical sense in the compiler. Yet the changes he

---

[12] Ibid. 147. Italics mine.   [13] Ibid. 84.

[14] See T. F. Tout, *The Place of the Reign of Edward II in English History* (2nd edn., Manchester, 1936), 244–84, for Edward II's ordinances; for the lost ordinance of Edward III see *Household of Edward IV*, Appendix II, 298–9.

[15] *Household of Edward IV*, 84. Edward I's *Ordenement del Hostel le Rei* of 1279 is printed in T. F. Tout, *Chapters in the Administrative History of Medieval England: the Wardrobe, the Chamber and the Small Seals* (Manchester, 1920–33), ii. 58–63. For a recent survey of household ordinances and their nature see H. Kruse and W. Paravicini (eds.), *Hofe und Hofordnungen, 1200–1600* (Sigmaringen, 1999), especially the essays on France and England by E. Lalou and F. Lachaud respectively on pp. 91–102 and 103–16. For ordinances drawn up for dependent households see below, Appendix I.

[16] *Household of Edward IV*, 85. Italics mine.

noted were perhaps more of degree than of real substance. They involved the movement 'out of court' of certain officers and departments, and the substitution of others in their place. For example, he noted that it was now the task of knights banneret or bachelor to act as carvers and cup-bearers 'in this courte of lyke degree for the kinges person'.[17] Under Edward III, he claimed, 'worshipfull squiers did this servyse'—in effect, continental European (particularly Burgundian) practices, whereby knights performed these domestic duties, had apparently been intro-duced at the English court by the fifteenth century. But some aspects of Edward III's household—as described in the Black Book—would not have been out of place under his grandfather Edward I (1272–1307): the payment of 'wages within court or without'; the distribution of liveries, in cloth and furs, winter and summer; the payment of fees to 'all astates . . . of officers and householdes and degrees, as well of yeftes of money, feez of bestes [animals], and also feez of other stuffe perused [purveyed] or otherwise occupied within the court and towching it'.[18] What the com-piler tells us, moreover, about the more ceremonial and lavish aspects of Edward III's household accords well with later practice at the English court: 'in the festyvall dayes', he wrote 'or whan astate shuld be showed, he [Edward III] wold be servyd with iiij course or v, his lordes and gentyles with iii cors, and every messe after [all other household members eating together, usually in groups of four] ij course . . .'[19] To be served with four of five courses, even in the greater households of the fifteenth century, was exceptional, and considered to be a sign of great luxury.[20] The evidence from Edward IV's time therefore tends, sometimes despite the intentions of the Black Book's author, to emphasize and highlight similarities rather than differences, continuities rather than innovations, in household practice, at least across the fourteenth and fifteenth centuries.

It is important to discover what meaning, or meanings, lay behind the term 'court' and its various uses in medieval Europe.[21] One distinguished early modern historian, at least, has described the court as a 'basically medieval institution'.[22] It has been argued that, since at least the

---

[17] *Household of Edward IV*, 106. For the movement of departments out of court, see below, pp. 24, 30 and Tout, *Chapters*, ii. 73–8.

[18] *Household of Edward IV*, 84.   [19] Ibid. 84–5.

[20] See *A Collection of Ordinances and Regulations for the Government of the Royal Household* (London, Society of Antiquaries, 1790), 174, for the numbers of courses served in Henry VIII's household (1526).

[21] See Starkey (ed.), *The English Court*, 3.

[22] See R. J. W. Evans, 'The court: a protean institution and an elusive subject', in Asch and Birke (eds.), *Princes, Patronage and the Nobility*, 491.

Carolingian era, rulers' courts had been regarded by the clerical scholars who wrote about them as constituting an important dimension of the 'formative milieu' in which social education took place.[23] Hincmar of Reims's *De ordine palatii* of 882 saw the court as a 'school' (*scola*) which taught by example, and thereby imposed the '*habitu, incessu, verbo et actu atque totius bonitatis continentia* [the behaviour, deportment, speech, deeds, and the restraints of the good life]' upon its noble and clerical pupils.[24] Less high-minded and favourable views of the court soon emerged, and a strong tradition of anti-court literature developed. From the late eleventh century onwards the use of the terms *curia* (court) and *curialitas* (courtliness) was often pejorative and derogatory.

Courts, it was fashionably asserted, fell far short of the ideal presented by contemporary commentators and didactic writers. Some courts had a particularly notorious reputation—above all, the papal court. When Guy de Dampierre, count of Flanders, his beleaguered family, and their envoys, were attempting to plead the Flemish cause before Boniface VIII at Rome in 1298–9, they exchanged letters which not only lamented the uncertainties and privations of following the papal court, but were striking for their candour and cynicism.[25] In April 1298, Michel as Clokettes, chaplain and Flemish proctor at Rome, wrote to the count's son, Robert de Béthune, complaining that he could not reserve lodgings for him and his entourage at Rome or anywhere else, because 'we have no idea where the court will be, whether at Rome, or elsewhere'.[26] The thought of having to decamp to Anagni, Boniface VIII's birthplace, filled him with horror—it was 'a very expensive place, and very unhealthy'.[27] Such views were shared by Guy de Dampierre himself: in a letter to his sons at Rome of (?)1299, he uttered the memorable words 'the pope and cardinals are very greedy, and you can gain little or nothing from the pope, nor the cardinals, without doing them favours and giving big

---

[23] A. Scaglione, *Knights at Court: Courtliness, Chivalry, and Courtesy from Ottonian Germany to the Italian Renaissance* (Berkeley, Los Angeles, and Oxford, 1991), 47.

[24] Cited in C. S. Jaeger, 'Cathedral schools and humanist learning, 950–1150', *Deutsche Vierteljahrsschrift für Literaturwissenschaft und Geistesgeschichte*, 61 (1987), 609. For an important study of courtly literature and society in the Ottonian, Salian, and Hohenstaufen periods see also S. Jaeger, *The Origins of Courtliness: Civilizing Trends and the Formation of Courtly Ideals, 939–1210* (Philadelphia, 1985).

[25] For the political background see F. Funck-Brentano, *Les Origines de la Guerre de Cent Ans: Philippe le Bel en Flandre* (Paris, 1897), 286–9, 293–4, 303–4.

[26] ADN, B.248, no. 4059 (20 Apr. 1298): 'car nous no poons savoir ou la Court sera, ou a Rome, ou ailleurs'.

[27] B.248, no. 4054 (9 Apr. 1298): 'un treskier liu, et mau sain'.

presents'.[28] The Flemish case against Philip the Fair of France at the court of Rome was, he wrote, a lost cause because the king 'could give a hundred times more than we could'. In a final despairing letter he told his envoy, the knight Jean de Menin, that 'all these troubles are born at the court of Rome . . . it's clear that the pope, who ought to act in God's place on earth, and be the author of peace . . . is in fact the author of never-ending war'.[29] Perhaps the satirists were not so far short of the mark—the tide of complaint and criticism was to rise even higher during the Avignonese period (1309–78).

But a more positive general view of the court was never entirely absent: the rise of a concept of *curialitas* in the twelfth century which led nobles to place their children for 'nurture' in princely courts was a symptom of this enduring characteristic. The inmates of the *palatium* (palace) or *aula* (hall) became in effect members of a court. By the late twelfth century, the literary *topos* of the court is fraught with paradox, if not outright contradiction. Walter Map could on the one hand applaud Henry I of England's (1100–35) practice of admitting to his household, or *familia*, all young nobles (and presumably clerks) who wanted a good beginning to their social education.[30] On the other hand, he inveighed against the court, its vices and inconstancy, concluding:

I know . . . that the court is not time; but temporal it is, changeable and various, space-bound and wandering; never continuing in one state. When I leave it, I know it perfectly: when I come back to it I find nothing or but little of what I left there . . . The court is the same, its members are changed . . . yet the court is not changed; . . . it remains always the same . . . a hundred-headed giant . . . a hydra of many heads, . . . the court is constant only in inconstancy.[31]

At its most minimalist and reductive, Map's definition of the court, despite his professed agnosticism and clever paradoxes, points to one very important characteristic: the court is 'space-bound and wandering'.[32] The court of Henry II (1154–89), like its European counterparts, predecessors, and successors, was essentially an itinerant body, a place filled by a mobile assemblage of people. The court was where the ruler was. If, as has recently been observed, 'the court is the environment in which the

    [28] ADN, B.248, no. 4191: 'li pape et li cardenal sunt moult convoiteus, et ke peu u nient en puet besognier au pape sans biaus serviches et grans dons ne as cardenaus'.
    [29] B.248, no. 4194.   [30] Map, *De Nugis*, 235.
    [31] Ibid. 3, 511.   [32] Ibid. 3.

king [or prince] existed'[33] then any definition can only be time-bound, changing and dependent upon contingent circumstances. How that environment—or space around the ruler—was organized; who filled it; how it presented itself, and with what degree of ceremony and spectacle: these depended upon such factors as relative levels of wealth, habits of consumption, inherited traditions of princely and aristocratic lifestyle, and many others—some common to many regions, others peculiar to a given area. The court, throughout medieval Europe, was a protean place, as well as a gathering of people, often fluid in composition and (as Map observed) constantly changing. Literary usage, however, is often no more helpful than household ordinances, when the practicalities of court life are considered. The terminology used in non-literary contexts is worthy of further study.

We can again take English evidence to illustrate and exemplify more general European tendencies. In Edward I's household ordinance of 1279, the term 'court' (*curt*) is used, together with *hostel* and *sale*, simply to describe the space occupied by the king's entourage. For example, the ordinance stated that only a small number of people were allowed to sleep within the office of the wardrobe, including Orlandino of Lucca, the king's banker, 'quant il vient a la curt'. The phrase 'loinz de la curt' is also used in relation to the periodic absences of the king's chamberlains.[34] The 'court' in this context must surely describe the space, or ambiance, around the king. The ruler must be resident within that space for the court to exist. But the term does not denote an institution, department, or specific place. On the other hand, the household (*hostel, hospicium, domus*, peopled with the *familia* or *maisnie*) was the formal body which provided a permanent framework, or structure, for the court. The household's component parts—hall, chamber, wardrobe, and the other departments—formed sub-units, each one, as T. F. Tout observed, increasingly forming 'a little society of its own, dependent upon its departmental chief for its board, lodging and social life'.[35] This process was furthered by the lost statute of St Alban's (13 April 1300) *de aula non tenenda in hospicio regis*. Under the pressure of warfare against the Scots, when the household grew to the size of a small army, the statute decreed that wages in money were henceforth to be paid to certain of its members (including

[33] See R. Horrox, 'Caterpillars of the commonwealth? Courtiers in late medieval England', in R. E. Archer and S. Walker (eds.), *Rulers and Ruled in Late Medieval England: Essays presented to Gerald Harriss* (London, 1995), 2.

[34] Tout, *Chapters*, ii. 163.   [35] Ibid., ii. 51.

the wardrobe staff) in lieu of the right to dine in the hall.[36] In January 1293 the chancery had been put 'out of court' (*extra curiam*), so that the Chancellor was required *ad hospicium tenendum extra curiam regis* ['to maintain a household outside the king's court'].[37] The chancery thus became self-sufficient as far as the material needs of its staff were concerned. In all these instances, the term 'court' has an essentially spatial dimension to its meaning—it was the physical space around the ruler, occupied in part by his own and his dependants' subsidiary households.

If we attempt to survey the surviving evidence from north-west Europe, starting with England, a number of both similarities and differences in employment of the term 'court' appear. The formal administrative and financial records of England, Flanders, Brabant, Artois, and Hainault-Holland during the period from *c.*1270 to 1340 refer frequently to the 'court'. In England, the presence of household knights in or out of court is noted in the wardrobe books and accounts under Edward I. During the year which ran from November 1289 to November 1290, for instance, the Gascon knight Gaillard de Thil took a reduced fee of 6 l.st. *quia solus fuit in curia sine socio* ['because he was alone in court without a companion'].[38] Similarly, in 1307, Humphrey de Bohun, the constable, received a fee of 3s.6d.st. per day when he ate 'in court' (*in curia comederit*), 5s. when he did not (*in curia non comederit*).[39] The court in this sense was also an area of formal jurisdiction: the steward of the household exercised aulic authority over its members, empowered to judge offences committed within its precincts, or within the 'verge of the court' (*infra virgam*).[40] The treatise known as 'Fleta' gave him jurisdiction 'of life and limb' *de placitis aulae regis* ['concerning the pleas of the king's hall'].[41] The 'verge' of the court could extend beyond the strict confines of the king's immediate entourage or environment, and led to conflicts with those living within one day's journey—twelve miles radius by the early fourteenth century—from the court.[42] The term 'verge' was also applied to those holding minor offices within the household: under Edward I a series of attempts were made to reduce their number. It was asserted that there were too many *vergeours*, and references are often made to the excessive

[36] PRO, E.101/357/28; Tout, *Chapters*, ii. 49–50.

[37] Tout, *Chapters*, ii. 76 n. 3.   [38] C.47/4/5, fo. 62r.   [39] E.101/373/15, fo. 10v.

[40] W. R. Jones, 'The Court of the Verge: the jurisdiction of the steward and marshal of the household in later medieval England', *Journal of British Studies*, 10 (1970–1), 1–29.

[41] Tout, *Chapters*, ii. 33.

[42] Morgan, 'House of policy', in Starkey (ed.), *The English Court*, 32–3.

throng of *gentz qui devient de droit porter verge* [rod or wand of office] *en la court le Roi.*[43]

But, as already indicated, the most frequently found use of the term 'court' at this time in the English financial and administrative records simply refers, almost as a kind of shorthand, to the entourage or assemblage around the king. It is not the household to which men go, in which they serve, or from which they depart, but the court. Thus Patrick de Trumpington, falconer, was released from the king's service and permitted to return home in February 1297 *quia . . . impotens erat ad laborandum amplius in Curia* ['because he was unfit to work any more in the court'].[44] The presence of strangers was also recorded. Visitors, guests, and messengers—who were in no sense members of the king's household—were said to be 'in' or 'at' court. Thus François, Philip IV of France's messenger, was said in October 1307 to be 'staying at court until the king's arrival at Westminster' (*moranti in Curia usque adventum Regis apud Westmonasterium*).[45] In July 1299, during preparations for the celebrations of Edward I's second marriage at Canterbury, the clerk of the kitchen was sent ahead and paid in advance *quia procedit Curiam pro hospitiis assignandis hominibus Curie ibidem* ['because he went ahead of the court to assign lodgings to the men of the court there'].[46] The court was evidently not synonymous with the household—the latter was subsumed within it and, as Walter Map had put it, borrowing an analogy from Porphyry, provided just one of the many organisms which together formed a single body.[47]

From the second half of the thirteenth century onwards, the survival of both official and private letters, often to and from lay people, in vernacular languages, allows us to observe the use of terminology in another type of record. Contemporaries referred, rather loosely, to the 'court' in their correspondence. An exasperated and anonymous English writer (*c.*1301–2), for example, ordered his unknown addressee to send sugar for the evidently sweet-toothed queen's use:

Vueillez maunder *a la court* aucun sucre en payn et segche espicerie, car je nay point . . . e je crey bien qe la plainte sera faite a la Reigne, car elle ne ad sucre pur son euwe, ne pur sa quisine, ne pur autres viaundes.[48]

---

[43] E.101/354/17.   [44] C.47/4/6, fo. 3r (Feb. 1297).
[45] E.101/373/15, fo. 21r (Oct. 1307).   [46] E.101/355/18, m. 4r (July 1299).
[47] Map, *De Nugis*, 1; Horrox, 'Caterpillars of the Commonwealth?', 2.
[48] E.101/362/18, nos. 14, 16. Italics mine.

[You must order for the court some loaf-sugar and dried spices for I have none . . . and I know very well that complaint will be made to the queen, because she has no sugar for her water, nor for her kitchen, nor for other foods.]

Again, in a subsequent letter, he writes to his *treschier seignour* to inform him that 'sachiez qe al heure qe cestes lettres furent faites, ny avoit nule bone novelle *a la court*' ['know that at the time when these letters were written, there was no good news at court']. It was therefore common-place to refer to the environment around the king, and its location, as the 'court'. The 'people of the court' (*homines curiae, gens de la cour*) may not have been 'courtiers' in the sense understood by the sixteenth and later centuries but they were clearly not simply 'household men'.[49] Such *curiales* had a very long ancestry, going back to Carolingian times via the courts of the Anglo-Norman and Angevin kings. This did not mean that the 'court' was as yet institutionalized. It was far too fluid for that.

But this did not imply that there were not stricter senses in which terms such as *curia* or *curialitas* might be used. Since the mid-twelfth century, schooling in *courtoisie* (*hovescheit, Höflichkeit*) had been part of the social education of the secular upper classes, and there is an extensive literature on the subject.[50] Acts of generosity, magnanimity, and well-bred polite-ness earned the appellation *courtois*. In February 1298, for instance, Robert II, count of Artois, thanked the Peruzzi bankers of Florence for their loan to him of 5,000 l.p.:

lesqueles il de leur grace *et de leur courtoisie* et sanz nule autre convoitise que pour lamour de nous a nostre priere et a nostre requeste nous ont preste.[51]

[which they, by their grace and courtesy, and without any hope of gain, have lent us, for love of us and at our prayer and request.]

In similar vein, although with less optimism about the outcome, the Flemish proctor at Rome in July 1298 wrote to Guy de Dampierre telling him that the pope 'had spoken in a most courtly manner about you'.[52] The offer of what was described as *curialitas*, in the form of gifts in money or kind, to both members and non-members of a princely household was also a long-established practice. In October 1364, for instance, the

---

[49] Cf. Starkey (ed.), *The English Court*, 3, 13.

[50] See J. Bumke, *Courtly Culture: Literature and Society in the High Middle Ages*, tr. T. Dunlop (Berkeley, Los Angeles, and Oxford, 1991), 57–60.

[51] ADPC, A.2, fo. 29r, no. 172 (Feb. 1298).

[52] ADN, B.248, no. 4087 (10 July 1298): 'parla li papes moult courtoisement de vous'.

receiver of Brabant received 14 l. *pro curialitate et familia*.[53] A similar practice prevailed at the English court: payments *de dono et curialitate Regis* abound in the wardrobe and household accounts for both Edward I and Edward II—minstrels were often the recipients of such 'courteous' gratuities.[54] In 1308–9 the receiver's account for Flanders records the payment of *courtesie* to the chief usher of the German king.[55] Presence at a court therefore carried certain expectations with it—by the end of the thirteenth century appropriate styles of 'courtly' behaviour were now taken for granted.

In some cases, however, there is a clear, concrete meaning behind the use of the term 'court'. In September 1279, for example, Nicholon, the household chaplain of the count of Flanders, had a house *dedens le court de Winendale* ['within the court(yard) at Wijnendaal'], one of the count's principal residences.[56] Here the term corresponds clearly to the German *Hof* in its strictest sense. Writing at the court of Holland in the 1350s, the jurist Philip of Leyden coupled the term 'court' (*curia*) with 'palace' (*palatium*): the princes of our time, he wrote, have private treasuries 'within their courts or palaces'.[57] The court was therefore the enclosure, or precinct, around the prince, which Philip of Leyden thought should be appropriately impressive—as, he proudly declared, was the comital palace (*Binnenhof*) at The Hague.[58] The term that he used for the establishment around the prince was *hospitium* (household): but he distinguished what he called the 'palatine' offices from the household offices. The former were essentially the writing-offices—filled by notaries, scribes, and clerks who wrote letters and drew up registers—while the household offices provided the domestic services, headed by the *maître d'hôtel*.[59]

---

[53] AGR, CC, R.2692, fo. 4v (Oct. 1364).   [54] E.101/373/15, fo. 19v; 375/8, fo. 27r.

[55] AGR, Comptes en rouleaux 1, m. 23r.   [56] RAG, Gaillard 29 (Sept. 1279).

[57] Philip of Leyden, *De Cura Reipublicae et Sorte Principantis*, ed. R. Fruin and P. C. Molhuysen (The Hague, 1915), cas. xxxi, p. 116: 'Et quia hic fit mentio de privato aerario . . . quam habent principes nostri temporis, qui *in curiis seu palatiis* eorundem privatum habent thesaurarium . . .' For Philip of Leyden's life and writings, see P. Leupen, *Philip of Leyden: A Fourteenth-Century Jurist. A Study of his Life and Treatise 'De Cura Reipublicae et Sorte Principantis'* (Leiden, 1981).

[58] Philip of Leyden, *De Cura*, cas. lxxiii, p. 303: citing Justinian, he wrote that 'hi, qui provincias regunt (sicut hodie sunt reges, duces et comites) non sibi vindicent ad habitandum domos privatorum, sed sacra palatia eorum reparationi providere . . .'; cas. lxxv, p. 314: 'ad respectum multimodum aedificantis palatii de Hagha, quod consilio et cura bonae memoriae magistri Gerardi de Leyden aedificatum est . . .' See also below, pp. 63–4.

[59] Philip of Leyden, *De Cura*, cas. xxviii, pp. 105–7: 'et intellege palatinum officium notarios, scriptores, clericos epistolarum et registri . . .' (p. 105); 'observatur namque et

This may refer back to the apparent primacy of clerks and ecclesiastics—as a kind of permanent establishment—in the palatine, or aulic, ordinances of a much earlier period.[60]

Yet the most revealing usage of the term 'court' from the non-royal courts of northern France and the Low Countries is to be found in their daily, weekly, and monthly household accounts, on the occasion of feast-days. For a long time, it had been normal practice in princely and aristocratic households to celebrate the major feasts of the liturgical year (Christmas, Easter, Pentecost, but also Michaelmas, Candlemas, All Saints, and so on) in especially lavish and ceremonious style. The 'crown-wearings' of the Anglo-Norman kings, for example, took place on these occasions, although they were discontinued by Henry II. Vassals were often summoned to pay homage at these times, and such events were necessarily accompanied by increasingly elaborate ritual and ceremonial. It is in this context that the use of the term 'court' deserves particular attention, because it may serve to distinguish and differentiate court and household.

The 'court' in this setting was essentially an event or occasion. It has been argued that surviving records and regulations of royal ceremony from fifteenth-century England 'reveal the fifteenth-century court to have been a ceremonious and deferential society . . . These records of precedence and ceremony, it might be thought, reflect the very essence of the court *as a series of occasions*, a noble environment of considerable formality.'[61] The 'occasional' nature of medieval courts has also been emphasized by scholars such as Joachim Bumke who consider that 'courtly culture' received its expression only at those exceptional gatherings which marked the liturgical year or other especially important events (marriages, baptisms, and so forth) in the life of a ruling house. For Bumke, the feast at court was:

the one sphere of reality which reflects the literary image of [aristocratic] society . . . Courtly society as a historical phenomenon is best documented on these occasions, as the nobility exhibited *only in these exceptional moments*, a behaviour that was considered particularly courtly . . . if we want to compose a picture of courtly society, we depend largely on . . . literary texts and visual images.[62]

---

expedit, ut magister superior hospitii miles sit . . . (p. 106) and the *maître d'hôtel* was to be set over the kitchen, pantry, chamber and buttery staff (p. 107).

[60] See Jaeger, *Origins of Courtliness*, 26–38, 106–54.

[61] Griffiths, 'The king's court during the Wars of the Roses', 48. Italics mine.

[62] Bumke, *Courtly Culture*, 4, 6. Italics mine. While noting the existence of household account books for the counts of Tyrol (from 1288) and dukes of Upper Bavaria (1291–4),

Although this conclusion may be rather too limited (and limiting), there can be little doubt that its occasional character was one hallmark of the formal court in the thirteenth and early fourteenth centuries. The archival evidence from Flanders under the Dampierre counts, and from Hainault-Holland under the Avesnes, is notable in this respect. In December 1293, Guy de Dampierre, count of Flanders, celebrated Christmas at Petteghem. The daily account for his household tells us that a total of 415 l. 14s. 10d.p. (138 l. 12s. per day) was spent over the three days of the feast, while normal average daily expenditure ran at about 50 l. per day.[63] The account declared that the count, his household, and guests: 'i demorerent le jour dou Noeil, le jour saint Stievene, *et i tint li cuens court* et i eut grant plente de chevaliers, de dames et dautre gent'[64] ['stayed there on Christmas day, and the feast of St Stephen, and the count held court there, and there was a great crowd of knights, ladies and of other people']. The count had come from Kortrijk on 23 December, where his entourage had stabled 170 horses, a figure which rose to no fewer than 990 for the three days of Christmas. The term which normally indicated the presence of larger numbers than usual in the comital household (thereby justifying higher expenditure) was *moult de boene gent* or *grant plente de boene gent* (1, 2, 21, 22, 23, 28 December 1293; 1 January 1294).[65] But the Christmas feast was also an occasion on which the count specifically 'held court'. Similarly, at Easter 1309, many knights and others had come to Ypres, hoping to find Robert de Béthune *tenant le fieste* but were disappointed.[66] A formal court was also held in Flanders at Pentecost: in 1317, Isabella, lady of Ghistelles, widow of the chamberlain of Flanders, told the count that she was unable to come in person 'a chestui jour de Penthecouste prochain venant *en le court* de . . . mons' de Flandre pour faire le service lequel je doy faire pour le raison dou camberlenge'[67] ['on the day of Pentecost next in the court of . . . my lord of Flanders to perform the service which I am obliged to do by reason of the chamberlaincy'].

Bumke consistently underrates the value of archival and documentary sources for courtly culture and society. See below, pp. 71–2.

[63] RAG, Wyffels (chron. suppl.) 188, no. 314*bis* (June 1293–June 1294). See also Fig. 14, Table 16.

[64] RAG, Wyffels (chron. suppl.) 188, no. 314*bis*, m. 4r. Italics mine. See Fig. 14.

[65] These phrases are found on mm. 4r, 4v, and 5r of the account.

[66] AGR, CC, R.1, m. 24v (Apr. 1309).

[67] ADN, B.1569, fo. 11v. See T. Limburg-Stirum, *La Cour des comtes de Flandres: leurs officiers héréditaires*, i. *Le Chambellan et les sires de Ghistelles* (Ghent, 1868), 32–45. See also below, pp. 44–5.

A letter of 1316 also stated that the chamberlain was to attend court at Christmas and Pentecost to perform his (or her) office, as were the hereditary seneschal and constable.[68] The formal Flemish 'court', like its northern French and Netherlandish counterparts in the late thirteenth and early fourteenth centuries, was thus an occasion rather than an institution—here, too, it was the household, comprising the comital *maisnie*, or entourage, which also provided a structure, or backbone, for the court.

The non-royal, but lavishly princely, household of the counts of Artois in the late thirteenth century was in many respects closer than that of Flanders to a kingly establishment. A notion of the 'court' is found there which resembles that of the French (and English) monarchies. The counts of Artois, however, like their neighbours in Flanders and Hainault, were not sovereign princes in a formal sense. In 1918, A. de Loisne used the telling phrase 'a feudal court' when he entitled his study of Robert II of Artois's household 'Une cour féodale vers la fin du xiiie siècle', building his study upon the pioneer work on the court of Artois by J.-M. Richard.[69] Around the count, as a great prince of the blood royal, was his large household, for which extensive accounting material survives. But, as in England, the court was not entirely synonymous with the household. In the accounts, provision of wages, footwear, and so forth to knights, squires, valets, messengers, porters, and keepers of dogs and birds was said to be 'from the court'.[70] Some of them thus took footwear (*chaussement*, *calciamenta*) 'from the court' in the sense that members of the king's household in England enjoyed *bouche de court*—the provision of food and drink for themselves and, in some cases, their servants and attendants. Again, as in England, members of the count's household were said in the accounts to be 'out of court'.[71] One of the knights attached to the young Robert of Artois's establishment was said 'to have been now and then at court'.[72] To be 'at court' was, in a sense, to be on the payroll. There was therefore little doubt among the members of the Artois

---

[68] ADN, B.1569, fo. 12r; Limburg-Stirum, *La Cour des comtes de Flandres*, 125–34.

[69] A. le comte De Loisne, 'Une cour féodale vers la fin du xiiie siècle. "L'hôtel" de Robert II, comte d'Artois', *BPHCTHS* (1918), 84–143; J.-M. Richard, *Une petite-nièce de Saint Louis: Mahaut, comtesse d'Artois et de Bourgogne (1302–1329). Étude sur la vie privée, les arts et l'industrie en Artois et à Paris au commencement du xive siècle* (Paris, 1887).

[70] ADPC, A.162, fos. 26r–27r, 37v (Feb.–June 1300): 'de la court'; A.312, no. 18 (27 June 1313): 'gages ordinaires de la court madame la contesse'.

[71] A.162, fo. 39r (27 Mar. 1300): household members 'hors de la court'; A.184, no. 27 (9 May 1302): 'pas present a la court'; see Table 20.

[72] A.321, fo. 34r (July–Nov. 1314): 'a court par intervalles'.

household, and among those who drew up the household accounts, that they also formed part of a court.

This suggests that there were other, more specific and technical senses in which the term 'court' was used at this time. In May 1302, a household clerk of Artois was paid for parchment bought 'to write the court's letters'.[73] A valet of the count's kitchen could refer to 'the last account which I rendered at the court for the office of the kitchen'.[74] In this context, use of the term 'court' takes on a more specific meaning. The 'court' seems here to assume some of the functions of an office of account—as did the Burgundian Chambre des Comptes at Lille at a later date, often described as the 'court' in the receiver-generals' accounts.[75] Thus the daily household account of the young Robert of Artois for May–November 1309 tells us that 'the court owes [money] to Jean de Vilefaut, from the account rendered around Ascension 1309 at Arras'.[76] This was for extraordinary (that is, exceptional) expenses, largely incurred through the purchase of a bird-cage, a chessboard and chessmen, collars for greyhounds, cloth, and the payment of Robert's gambling debts. Here, too, there was thus a range of meanings attached to the 'court' (*cour, curia*) in various contexts, and its use by the count of Artois's clerks and scribes could often be casual or inconsistent.

That said, there can be little doubt that what men and women of this period meant by the 'court' in north-west Europe was not merely the ruler's household. The court was greater than the household and was not identical with it. It was the prince's environment, both a place, normally of unfixed location, and an assemblage of people. Where the prince was, there too was the court. The ruler's actual presence was a prerequisite for a court at this time. We are still at the stage of non-residential courts although, as we shall see, certain locations could bulk larger in prince's itineraries than others. The ruler's entourage, with attendant guests and visitors, gathered quite literally around a courtyard (*cour, Hof*), continued to provide a model of the court for later medieval princes.

Yet the princely court, at its most formal and elaborate, still possessed an 'occasional' character. What was true for Flanders and Artois was also

---

[73] A.178, fo. 74v (May 1302): 'pour faire lettres de la court'.

[74] A.185, no. 5 (15 July 1302): 'du derrenier conte que jay fait a la court pour loffice de la cuisine'.

[75] See, for a survey of the Lille Chambre des Comptes, R. H. Bautier, J. Sornay, and F. Muret, *Les Sources de l'histoire économique et sociale du moyen âge: les états de la maison de Bourgogne*, i. 2 (Paris, 1984), 32–8.

[76] ADPC, A.254, fo. 39v (May–Nov. 1309).

the case in the *comté* of Hainault. In March 1302, for example, the conditions of service of the hereditary butler (*bouteiller*) of Hainault were set out during a dispute between one of the holders of the office, Giles de Berlaimont, knight, and the count.[77] These included the duty of attending 'solemn court' (*cour sollempnelle*) within the *comté* at Easter, Pentecost, and Christmas. The hereditary butler was to serve wine before the count at those feasts from a hanaper costing 100s.t. He was also to receive hay for five horses, a supply of candles, and wages for his attendance in the comital household at those times. A similar case arose in about 1344, when the hereditary huntsman (*veneur*) of Hainault, Henri de Maubeuge, disputed his rights and duties with the receiver of the *comté*.[78] He was also obliged to attend 'full court' and received wine and candles 'at court'. As in Flanders and Artois, the great feasts of the liturgical year were lavishly celebrated, and the household accounts justify the heavy expenditure by speaking of the 'great number of people' (*grans plentes de gens*) present, often mentioning 'knights, ladies, *damoiselles*, esquires' and others.[79] But the occasions upon which 'full court' might be held were not confined to the three great feasts. In the winter of 1325, for instance, the countess's household account recorded:

dedens che terme ont este, en lostel medame, medame de Fontenielles, chevalier, escuiwier, dames et demisielles, et autres gens, *especialment a le Toussaint, ke mesire et medame tinrent court sollempnel*, et aussi a le Saint Martin.[80]

[within this term of account, there were in my lady's household: my lady of Fontenielles, knights, esquires, ladies and *damoiselles*, and other people, especially at All Saints, when my lord and lady held solemn court, and also on the feast of St Martin.]

A 'solemn court' was therefore held at All Saints (1 November) an occasion upon which liveries (*livrées*) were sometimes distributed. Again, the account for the year from 25 August 1325 to 24 August 1326 noted that exceptional expenses had been incurred, especially over Christmas and

[77] See 'Cartulaires de Hainaut (1071–1310),' ed. F. A. T. de Reiffenberg (Brussels, 1844), 469–70, no. 103; 473–4, no. 105 (15 Mar. 1302).

[78] *Cartulaire des comtes de Hainaut, de l'avènement de Guillaume II à la mort de Jacqueline de Bavière*, ed. L. Devillers, 7 vols. (Brussels, 1881–96), i, 212–14, no. 127 (c.1344); 214–16, no. 128.

[79] *De rekeningen der graven en gravinnen uit het Henegouwsche Huis*, ed. H. J. Smit, 3 vols. (Amsterdam, 1924–39), i. 90–2: Christmas, 1320 (Binche); 98–9: Easter, 1321 (Valenciennes); 101–2: Pentecost, 1321 (Valenciennes) where there were 'pluseur chevalier, dames et demizelles et autre pluseur et grand plentes de gens'.

[80] Ibid., i. 144. Italics mine. See also Table 23.

the New Year, when the countess and her daughter Philippa had been in France.[81] On these occasions, she had held *cours sollempnelz*.[82] The pattern was repeated in the following years: at the Hague during Christmas and New Year 1326–7; at Middelburg for Easter 1327; at Valenciennes for All Saints 1327, when the English envoys celebrating the betrothal of Philippa to Edward III were present; once more at Valenciennes during Christmas and New Year 1327–8; at Le Quesnoy for the same feasts in 1328–9; at Valenciennes for Easter 1329; and at Le Quesnoy for Pentecost 1329.[83] The pattern and sequence of holding 'solemn court' continued until the surviving accounts come to an end in 1336. When they resume in 1349, Christmas Day again saw the count holding court at Le Quesnoy.[84] In Hainault the holding of 'solemn court' at Christmas, New Year, Easter, Pentecost and All Saints may have reflected earlier practice in the comital household.[85] The court, in its fullest, most solemn and ceremonial form, was essentially a grand occasion. Yet, as we shall see, these 'occasional' characteristics of princely courts remained with them for a very long time.

[81] *De rekeningen*, ed. Smit, i. 145–7, 177–9, 190–214; see Tables 22, 23.

[82] Ibid., i. 169.

[83] Ibid., i. 268–9: *court solempnel* at The Hague (1326–7); 275–6: 'et y furent ausi dames, damiselles, chevaliers, escuyers au court solempnel . . . pour le feste de pasques que mesires et medame tenoient court solempnel (1327); 286–7, 374–6: 'pluseurs autres chevalier, escuyer, dames et demiselles, especialment le nuit de Toussains et le jour, que medame tient court solempnel' (1327); 377, 397, 452–3: 'le nuit et le jour de Noel, lesquelz terme mesires et medame tienrent court solempnel, et si fu mesires le samedi nuit del an' (1328–9); 461, 462: 'et pluseurs autres, allant et venant, chevalier, escuyer, dames et demiselles, especialment le jour des Pasques, que medame tient court solempnel'; 465, 466: 'et pluseurs autres chevaliers et estrange gent le jour et le nuit del Pentecouste, que mesires et medame tienrent court solempnel' (1329).

[84] See A. Pinchart, *Extraits de comptes relatifs au Hainaut antérieurs à l'avènement de Philippe le Bon* (Mons, 1884), 3: 'et ledit jour dou Noel tint mesires court de plusieurs boinnes gens' (account for 5 July 1349–19 Mar. 1350).

[85] For earlier practices at the court of the counts of Hainault, see Gislebert de Mons, *Chronicon*, ed. L. Vanderkindere (Brussels, 1904), 333–43.

Chapter 2

ORGANIZATION AND STRUCTURES

1. The household and its structure

The fundamental question of definition treated in the last chapter—what was the court?—does not repeat itself when we consider the nature and organization of the domestic princely household. It was fairly clear, from a relatively early date, that the *hôtel, hospitium,* or *domus* had a distinct and relatively well-defined structure. This was sometimes (but not always) laid down in the genre of documents known as 'household ordinances' (*ordonnances de l'hôtel, Hofordnungen, Hof-ordinatien*).[1] The *Constitutio Domus Regis* of Henry I of England (*c.*1130) provides an early example. Walter Map praised Henry I's court, because the king 'had the customs of his house and household ordained by himself, and kept in writing: of his house, to the end that it might always have plenty of all supplies, and very regular changes . . . of his household, that no one might be in want, but each receive fixed grants'.[2] Household ordinances met the need to introduce some degree of organization and discipline into an establishment which was not inherently orderly. It has recently been pointed out, by Elisabeth Lalou, when discussing the French royal household, that:

La lecture des ordonnances de l'Hôtel nous enseigne qu'elles constituent une tentative pour rationaliser sur le papier (ou le parchemin) un état de choses qui devait être assez flou et à l'organisation mouvante. La Cour, en bref, devait

---

[1] For a recent introduction see W. Paravicini, 'Europäische Hofordnungen als Gattung und Quelle', in Kruse and Paravicini, *Höfe und Hofordnungen*, 13–20.

[2] Map, *De Nugis*, 242. The *Constitutio Domus Regis* of Henry I is printed in *Dialogus de Scaccario*, ed. C. Johnson (rev. edn., Oxford, 1983), 129–35 and discussed by F. Lachaud, 'Order and disorder at court: the ordinances for the royal household in England in the twelfth and thirteenth centuries', in *Höfe und Hofordnungen*, 105–11.

ressembler à un marché, difficile à gérer, avec des va-et-vient continuels, des gens qui s'installaient où ils pouvaient pour manger ou dormir.[3]

[The reading of household ordinances teaches us that they embody an attempt to rationalize on paper (or parchment) a state of things which was very fluid and organizationally unstable. The court, briefly, resembled a market, difficult to regulate, with constant comings-and-goings, and with a personnel which lodged itself where it could to eat or sleep.]

The notion of the 'court' (that is, the greater household) as a market would not have been out of place in the mind of Walter Map.[4] Constant comings-and-goings, especially in an itinerant household, were part of its very essence. The first concern of rulers and their counsellors was therefore to attempt to limit and regulate access to its benefits and services: food, drink, accommodation, and, increasingly, privileged status. Aulic status—the privileges attaching to membership of the prince's 'hall'—was a valuable asset conferring exemption from all other jurisdictions within a certain radius of the court. The authority of the steward and marshals in England, and of the *Roi des ribauds* and his *prévôt* in France, was thus exercised over the household.[5] But rulers and their counsellors were also concerned to specify and define both the rights and the duties of the various officers within their households. This became particularly marked in the thirteenth century, when the increasing costs of maintaining an appropriately princely estate led to a heavier burden on revenues.

An early instance of an attempt to list and define the duties of officers in a non-royal household was a description of the *Ministeria Curie Hanoniensis* ('offices, or *métiers*, of the court of Hainault') composed in *c.*1212–14 by the chronicler Gislebert of Mons.[6] Gislebert was a clerk, notary, and chaplain to the counts of Hainault, canon of the collegiate church of Ste-Waudru at Mons, and served as chancellor of Hainault between 1178 and 1195. He died in 1224. The description which he drew

---

[3] E. Lalou, 'Le fonctionnement de l'hôtel du roi du milieu du xiiie au milieu du xive siècle' in J. Chapelot and E. Lalou (eds.), *Vincennes: aux origines de l'état moderne* (Paris, 1996), 146.

[4] Map, *De Nugis*, 242.

[5] See Tout, *The Place of the Reign of Edward II*, 244–50; Jones, 'The Court of the Verge', 1–12; Lalou, 'Le fonctionnement de l'Hôtel du roi', esp. 150–1; A. Terroine, 'Le Roi des ribauds de l'Hôtel du roi et les prostituées parisiennes', *Revue Historique de droit français et étranger* (1978), 253–67. See also below, pp. 58–9.

[6] *Ministeria Curie Hanoniensis* in Gislebert de Mons, *Chronique*, 333–43. The document is found in a cartulary of the church of Ste-Waudru. Gislebert described himself as *prévôt* of the churches of Mons.

up of the *ministeriales* (officials) of the count of Hainault began with a list of all those holding office on a hereditary basis (*jure hereditario possidenda*).[7] It was characteristic of the household organization of some principalities in the Low Countries during the thirteenth century (and, indeed, the fourteenth) to retain the principle of hereditary tenure of some offices, and performance of their duties, by the incumbent him-, or her-, self. In the kingdoms of France and England, these functions were discharged by their hereditary holders on an honorary or very occasional basis.[8] Thus the butler, chamberlain, and constable of France were, by the thirteenth century, fulfilling a political rather than domestic role.

In the *comté* of Hainault, however, the division and distribution of offices in the early thirteenth-century household conformed to the principality's ancient *dominationes*.[9] These were those of Mons (the Ottonian centre of government for the whole of the *comté*), Valenciennes, and Ostrevant.[10] It seems that when the court journeyed through the *comté*, some household services were provided by different officers within each of the three *dominationes*. But three higher officers served for the whole of the *comté*: the lord of Saint-Aubert as hereditary seneschal (*dapifer*); the lord of Berlaimont as hereditary chamberlain (*camerarius*); and the lord of Aulnois as hereditary butler or cup-bearer (*pincerna*).[11] There was also a hereditary *emptor escarum* (buyer of victuals), *panetarius* (pantler), *pistor* (baker), *impositor mensarum et mensalium super mensas* (layer of courses and cloths on the tables), *scultellarius* (scullion) and so on, one serving in each of the three *dominationes*. Gislebert set out their rights and duties: the heirs of Amand the chamberlain, for instance, were permitted to take cloaks and capes from all those vassals performing homage to the count, by right of their office.[12] Succession to household office was by primogeniture, and new incumbents were to be instructed in their duties by its older, more experienced members. This principle was borne out by Philip of Leyden in the mid-fourteenth century.[13] Although offices in the household of Hainault were held hereditarily, they

---

[7] Gislebert, *Chronique*, 334.

[8] Lalou, 'Le fonctionnement de l'hôtel du roi', 145; Tout, *Chapters*, i. 8–9, 19–21, 201–4.

[9] See G. Alquier, 'Les grands charges du Hainaut', *Revue du Nord*, 21 (1935), 5–31.

[10] Gislebert, *Chronique*, 334–5, 335 n. 1.   [11] Ibid. 336.

[12] 'Habet de ministerio suo pallia seu capas omnium, qui homagium faciunt domino comiti Hanoniensi' (ibid. 39). Amand was recorded as chamberlain in 1192 and 1201. For similar evidence from Flanders see below, pp. 44–5.

[13] Philip of Leyden, *De Cura*, cas. xxviii, p. 106; cf. Gislebert, *Chronique*, 342.

could, said Gislebert, be sold or given away by their holder, but only with the count's permission. Finally, the count was obliged to provide horses and wages, in certain circumstances, to the knightly holders of major offices:

si ministri curie majorum ministeriorum milites in curia fuerint, habent procurationem suam cum 2 equis; si vero milites non fuerint, cum solo equo . . . Si vero milites in armis fuerint, habent procurationem suam; id est vadia.[14]

[if the holders of the major court offices are knights, present at court, they shall be maintained with two horses; if they are not knights, with a single horse . . . If they are knights serving in arms, they shall have their maintenance, that is, wages.]

A knight holding a major household office therefore qualified for two horses *in curia*; a non-knight for one; and wages—as opposed to food, drink, clothing, and stabling allowances—were only to be paid to knights 'in arms', just as they were given to the other household knights of the count. When the count went to war, however, all his household officers, both great and small, were to be with him, to defend him (*ad corpus ipsius conservandum*) at his expense.[15] The comital household thus provided the inner core of the military forces fielded during the many conflicts in which the counts of Hainault were involved during this period.

Occasionally, disputes arose over the obligations and privileges which household offices carried: these can be valuable sources of information about their history and nature. In March and May 1184, for example, the hereditary seneschal of Valenciennes, Amand de Saint-Saulve, refused to perform his service to the count at the two great imperial courts held by Frederick Barbarossa at Hagenau and Mainz 'for lack of cloths' (*propter defectum vestium*).[16] The seneschal, *panetarius* (bread-bearer or pantler), and butler—all of them knights—also demanded the right to receive liveries of cloth from the count. Their request was adjudicated by the council of court *ministri*, and they were permitted to receive cloths and liveries 'in the manner of the count's household knights' (*ad modum commilitonum comitis*). Such cases were not confined to the twelfth century. In 1302, the hereditary butler of Hainault, Giles de Berlaimont, disputed

---

[14] Gislebert, *Chronique*, 342–3. The military dimension of these households should not be ignored. See also, for England, J. O. Prestwich, 'The military household of the Norman kings', *EHR*, 96 (1981), 4–9, and 'The place of the royal household in English history, 1066–1307', *Medieval History*, 1 (1991), 40–7.

[15] Gislebert, *Chronique*, 343.

[16] For the Mainz Pentecost feast of 1184, attended by 70 princes of the Empire, see Bumke, *Courtly Culture*, 203–7. Gislebert was apparently there in person. See *Chronique*, 343.

his duties and attempted to uphold his rights.[17] In 1344, the hereditary *veneur* (*venator*, huntsman) of Hainault, Henri de Maubeuge, set out his claims. The importance of hunting within the count's domains—especially in the great forest of Mormal—made this a significant issue, with implications for the receiver's annual income and expenditure. Henri de Maubeuge claimed to hold a fief-rente from the count for the huntsman's office: this yielded an annual income in both kind and money.[18] His claim continued:

doit il y estre delivres a court partout aval le pays u il va a ii chevaus, sans le chevaul de pourvanche, et candeilles quant il est en ville u li ostels monsigneur soit . . . Item, doit il avoir ii selles tous les ans estoffes de sellerie, et ses chevaus delivres de forge et d'ostage. Item, doit il avoir ii paires de dras l'an, ii cottes hardies, et tabart de vert drap pour estet, et de gris pour yvier.[19]

[he should receive at court, wherever he goes in the land, two horses, besides the horse for purveyance, and candles when he is in the town where my lord's household resides . . . Item, he should have two saddles every year provided with saddlery, and smithery and stabling for his horses. Item, he should have two pairs of cloths every year, two surcoats and a tabard of green cloth for the summer, and of grey (cloth) for the winter.]

The *chevaul de pourvanche* were the horses used to carry the venison from the hunt, of which Henri de Maubeuge claimed to have an unspecified number by virtue of his office. In general principle, these rights bear comparison with those claimed by the hereditary butler of Hainault in 1302, although his services in person at court tended to be confined to the great feasts.[20] The list continued with perquisites more specifically related to the hunting field—rights to parts of beasts killed, and so forth. But the hereditary huntman's *garçons* were to have surcoats (*cottez*), like the other *garchons des cottez* of the household, and the horses given him by the count for his duties were not gifts, and were to be returned, so that a new livery of horses could be given. Interestingly, the hereditary *veneur* asserted that he should not be paid wages:

Item, ne doit il mie y estre a wages, car onques ses taions ne ses peres n'i fu; ains doit y estre defraities, et il et ses garchons, des despens qu'il despendent ensi qu'il affiert a lui, pour le cause de sen offisse, aval le pays, en sen offisse faisant.[21]

---

[17] See 'Cartulaires de Hainaut', ed. Reiffenberg, i. 469–70, 473–4, and above, p. 32.

[18] See *Cartulaire des comtes de Hainaut*, ed. Devillers, i. 212–14.

[19] Ibid., i. 212.

[20] See above, pp. 32–3.

[21] *Cartulaire des comtes de Hainaut*, ed. Devillers, i. 214. The refusal of hereditary officers and other vassals to accept wages may be related to the notion that performance of such offices was an essentially honourable duty (see below, pp. 45–7).

[Item, he should not be at wages, for neither his ancestors nor his father were so; thus he should be compensated, both he and his *garçons*, for the costs he incurs by reason of his office, throughout the land, while performing that office.]

He was thus not a paid servant of the count, and fell into the category of officers who received allowances for expenses, rather than wages or stipends, in the household accounts. His cause was supported by a long list of witnesses, who made declarations in his favour.[22]

The response of the receiver of Hainault to this petition was not entirely favourable. While broadly accepting some of the huntsman's claims, he contested those relating to horses and liveries:

Item, de ses kevauls, de ses sielles, de ses cottes hardies, de ses tabars, de siellerie et de forge qu'il demande, dist li dis recheveres que tant que as kevauls il n'en doit avoir que iii, ii pour lui et i pour le brakenier, et pour les pourvanches et les venisons porter convient que plus il en ait eut empluseurs lius leur li sejours des kiens a estet ou temps passet, li quel ont estet delivret de tout au frait monsigneur.[23]

[Item, concerning his horses, his saddles, his surcoats, his tabards, his saddlery and smithery which he demands, the receiver replies that as far as his horses are concerned, he should have only three, two for himself and one for the hound-handler, and to carry purveyances and venison it was necessary for him to have more in many places where the dogs were kept in time past, which were provided with everything at my lord's expense.]

Livery of cloth was to be issued only when the count gave *plaine livrée*, that is, liveries to the whole household; otherwise not at all.[24] A similar stipulation was made when privileges were granted by the count to his cook (*keu*) in August 1338.[25] This was also the practice for offices such as the *panetier* in Hainault: in October 1316, the count stipulated that the *panetier* and his son were to receive livery 'as esquires' only when a general distribution was made.[26] The livery of cloth to the hereditary huntsman was only to be given in the hunting season, and then only at reasonable cost. The receiver, with one eye firmly fixed on domestic economy, also insisted that his claim for livery of horses, above the three allowed, was invalid: 'et s'on lui a delivret, si dist li dis recheveres que ch'a esteit de

---

[22] Ibid., i. 217–33.   [23] Ibid., i. 214.

[24] For liveries and their distribution see below, pp. 95–9. The count's receiver claimed that 'il a bien veu le tayon doudit Henry [de Maubeuge] et ses devanchiers del offisce de le vesnerie, quant messires faisoit plaine livree, avoir dras et que parmi chou, il tient bien ke il les doive ossy avoir quant messires fait livree plainne et autrement nient . . .' (ibid., i. 215).

[25] ARA, Den Haag, Archief graven van Holland, inv. nr. 218, fo. 66v, nr. 416.

[26] ARA, Arch. grav. Holland, inv. nr. 290, fo. 3r.

grasce, s'il ne le monstre souffissaument'[27] ['and if he had been given it, the receiver says that it was by an act of grace, if he could not adequately demonstrate it']. This was a refrain which was harped upon throughout the reply: many of the privileges claimed by the incumbent of this office were exercised only by the count's grace, not by right. A similar stipulation was made in 1318–19 when the duties of the hereditary chamberlain of Flanders were under discussion.[28] It seems, moreover, that the excessive claims made by incumbents of hereditary offices in Flanders under Louis de Nevers (1322–46), especially in the financially critical conditions of the period from 1322 to 1332, had led to the acquisition by the count of many, if not all, of their rights.[29] In 1330 the count thus purchased the hereditary chamberlain's office for 6,000 l.[30] The apparent grip of hereditary office-holders was gradually being undermined by such measures.

In the disputes over office, there was also an insistence—for example, by the receiver of Hainault—on proper written justification for all claims, or at least good oral evidence: 'dist li dis recheveres que se li dis Henris ne le monstre souffissaument par lettres *u par autre vive vois*, que de chou ne soit il riens . . .'[31] ['the said receiver replied that if the said Henri could not sufficiently demonstrate it by letters or by oral testimony, then it was worth nothing']. This bore out Gislebert of Mons' declaration in 1212–14 that all household officers were to account for their offices—at that time before the seneschal rather than the receiver.[32] A similar case had arisen in the duchy of Brabant in September 1293, when duke John I agreed to a rather more liberal interpretation of the rights claimed by Gerard, lord of Rotselaar, as hereditary seneschal (*dapifer*) of Brabant than that advanced in the case of the hereditary *veneur* by the receiver of Hainault in 1344.[33] The duke stated that:

[27] *Cartulaire des comtes de Hainaut*, ed. Devillers, i. 216.

[28] See Limburg-Stirum, *La Cour des comtes de Flandre*, i. 32–45; ADN, B.1569, fos. 11v–12v; and above, pp. 29–30.

[29] See P. Thomas, 'Une source nouvelle pour l'histoire administrative de la Flandre: le registre de Guillaume d'Auxonne, chancelier de Louis de Nevers, comte de Flandre', *RN* 10 (1924), 5–38.

[30] ADN, B.1569, fos. 12r, 60r.

[31] *Cartulaire des comtes de Hainaut*, ed. Devillers, i. 216. Italics mine.

[32] Gislebert, *Chronique*, 343.

[33] AGR, Cour féodale de Brabant, nr. 4, fos. 354v–355r, and see B. Minnen, 'Hertog, heer en hereboer: Een oorkonde in het "Spechtboek" van hertog Jan I aan de erfdrossard van Brabant (12 September 1293)', *De Brabanste Folklore*, 248 (1985), 325–7.

Voirt bekennen wi van rechte te ghevene den here van Rotselaer ende sine nacomelingen, van ons ende van onsen nacomelingen, twee paer cledere ende elc paer van vier stucken, te Kersavonde deen paer, ende te Schinxsenen dander, ende sinen riddere twee paer, ende elc paer van drien stucken, ten selven tiden.

Voirt, so wanneer de here van Rotselaer te hogetide tonsen hove coempt, so bekennen wi hemme ende sinen nacomelingen, van ons ende onsen nacomelingen, drie ghelten wijns, ende daer toe vyftien scellinge te sinen panden, ende daer toe gewrongene kersen, ende tortisen . . .

Voirt, wanneer ons de here van Rotselaer te hogetide dient van sinen dienste, so bekennen wi hemme sine scotele ende die silveren.[34]

[We declare that we and our successors, by right, have to give to the lord of Rotselaar and his successors two pairs of cloths (liveries), of four pieces each, one pair at Christmas, and the other at Pentecost; and to his knights, two pairs of cloths, of three pieces each, at the same times.

Item, when the lord of Rotselaar comes to the full gathering of our court he and his successors shall have from us and our successors three *ghelten* of wine, 15s. for wages, and candles and torches . . .

Item, when he does his service during the court he shall keep his plate and the silverware.]

These rights bore some similarities to those claimed by the hereditary huntsman in Hainault (especially those concerning livery of cloths) and by the hereditary seneschals of Flanders.[35] It should be remembered that the *comtés* of Flanders and Hainault were united under one ruler between 1194 and 1280, so that mutual influences could be both transmitted and reinforced.[36] The hearing of claims and counter-claims by hereditary household officers also bore witness to increasing tendencies among thirteenth- and early fourteenth-century administrations to define and prescribe the duties and benefits of household membership in written form. There were many ways in which this could be done: by the granting of specific charters relating to individual offices or by the composition of treatises on household management and procedures.[37] But the latter had

---

[34] AGR, Cour féodale de Brabant, nr. 4, fo. 355r. For an edition see A. Smolar-Meynart, *La Justice ducale du plat pays, des forêts et des chasses en Brabant (xii*ᵉ*–xvi*ᵉ* siècles): Sénéchal, maître des bois, gruyer, grand veneur* (Brussels, 1991), 539–41.

[35] See above, pp. 38–9.

[36] See D. M. Nicholas, *Medieval Flanders* (London, 1992), 75–6, 155–7. The union was, however, subject to stresses owing to the rival claims of the Avesnes family to Hainault.

[37] See, for English examples, *Fleta*, ed. H. G. Richardson and G. O. Sayles, ii (Selden Society, lxxii, London, 1955), or the treatise attributed to Robert Grosseteste, bishop of Lincoln in D. Oschinsky, *Walter of Henley and other Treatises on Estate Management and*

no formal authority and could not impose any measure of control over princely households. One means whereby this could be achieved—or at least, attempted—lay in the form of ordinances or 'establishments' (*établissements*) which set out to define the duties, privileges, and rewards of household officers and servants.

2. Household ordinances

The first surviving ordinances for the royal households of England (1279, 1318) and France (1261, 1286) sought to regulate the material conditions of court life, rather than its more formal and ceremonial aspects.[38] They are essentially concerned with the allowances and benefits in food, drink, money, cloth, and so forth to which its members were entitled—or believed they were entitled. In many cases, they also set out to establish the duties of household officers, both great and small. A primary motive for their formulation was clearly economic—receivers of finances and keepers of wardrobes were obliged to keep a close check upon expenditure and claims for allowance—but they might also embody and affirm practices of a traditional kind, which a ruler was obliged to observe. In some instances, the inspiration behind the ordinance might be a desire, and demand, for reform of the ruler's establishment—a phenomenon witnessed more often in the fourteenth century than the thirteenth.[39]

The position of hereditary office-holders in a prince's service was not necessarily a secure one. The increasing availability of able and talented administrators, often of humble birth, rising through the clerical ranks, could pose a challenge to the discharge of household functions by the noble or knightly incumbents of domestic offices. A tendency towards the suppression, or emasculation, of some ancient hereditary positions, and their conversion into 'dignities' or effectively honorary charges, is indicative of this change. For example, by the mid-thirteenth century, in neither the English nor the French royal households—nor, it seems, the household of the counts of Artois—were the principal, or even the minor, domestic offices, whose incumbents served on an everyday basis,

Accounting (Oxford, 1971), 388–407. Also Philip of Leyden, *De Cura*, 105–7, 116–18, 324–6.

[38] Tout, *Chapters*, ii. 158–63; Lalou, 'Le fonctionnement de l'Hôtel du roi', 145–6.

[39] See, for English evidence, C. Given-Wilson, *The Royal Household and the King's Affinity* (New Haven and London, 1986), 111–38, esp. 136–8.

held by hereditary entitlement. The two knightly seneschals and the two knights-marshal in England were appointed at the king's pleasure, and their heirs had no claim on their offices.[40] As in France, the ancient hereditary charges of seneschal, constable, marshal, and so on had in effect become honorary positions, exercised only on certain specified occasions.[41]

Very few household ordinances survive for the principalities of the Low Countries, however, before the Burgundian accession to Flanders and Artois in 1384. There is therefore no surviving ordinance for Brabant until 1407; nothing for Flanders before the Burgundian accession, although significant alternative documentation for its household organization exists; no ordinances for Artois or Hainault; and nothing for the counts of Holland before 1354.[42] This does not mean that household ordinances never existed for these important lordships. They may simply not have survived. But some clues as to the manner in which such hypothetical ordinances (which no longer survive) may have been drawn up could be sought. The surviving evidence from Flanders under Guy de Dampierre (d.1304) and his successors is intriguing in this respect.[43] It is clear from the household accounts for Flanders, which survive—in a broken series—from 1260 onwards, that its organization, like that of the household of the counts of Artois, closely followed that of the French royal household: beside the four greater offices—of chamberlain, seneschal, butler, and constable—were the six *métiers* (*ministeria*, *misteria*). These were the *paneterie*, *échansonnerie*, *cuisine*, *fruiterie*, *écurie*, and *chambre* or *fourrière*.[44] Just as the four greater offices had become hereditary at an earlier date, so some of the lower offices in the Flemish household were also held by hereditary succession in the mid- to late thirteenth century.

---

[40] See Tout, *Chapters*, i. 201–5; ii. 32–3, 251–3, 281.

[41] See P. Lehugeur, *De hospitio regis et secretiore Consilio, ineunte quarto decimo saeculo, praesertim regnante Philippo Longo* (Paris, 1897), 54–65; also id., *Philippe V, le mécanisme du gouvernement* (Paris, 1931), 28–40; Lalou, 'Le fonctionnement de l'hôtel du roi', 145: 'même si le sénéchal [héréditaire] tranche encore le pain, ce sont d'autres personnes qui exercent réellement les fonctions necessaires à la vie quotidienne du roi'.

[42] See Paravicini, 'Europäische Hofordnungen als Gattung und Quelle', 14–17.

[43] See below, pp. 47–8.

[44] See K. Vanderwoude, 'De hofhouding van de laatse Vlamse graaf en de eerste Bourgondische hertog (ca. 1380–1404): Bijdrage tot de kennis van het hotel van Filips de Stoute als centrale instelling', 2 vols. (unpub. thesis, Ghent, 1977–8), i. 14–20; R. Monier, *Les Institutions financières du comté de Flandre du xie siècle à 1384* (Paris, 1948), 32–4; cf. Lalou, 'Le fonctionnement de l'Hôtel du roi', 146–7. See also Table 15, Figs. 9, 11–13.

The incumbents of the higher offices received liveries at Christmas and Pentecost in cloth, or in money given them for their robes.[45] The seneschal, sub-seneschal, constable, butler, and chamberlain were all nobles, receiving wine, wages, cloths, furs, and occasional perquisites for performance of their office.[46] The chamberlain's duties and rights were set out in a letter of 1316:

quant li cambrelens venoit a le court dou conte a Noel et a le Penthecouste pour faire son office . . . il poioit avoir waiges, bouche a court por 5 personnes, 4 los de vin, 2 de le bouche et 2 dou commun, 1 turtin [torch] de 9 paumes de lonc, 20 petites candelles, 12s 6d. pour avoine . . . Item, on li envoioit au Noel 24 aunes de drap et 3 pennes de gros vair flehies, et a la Penthecouste aussi, desquels yl devoit venir, luy, tiers de chevaliers, pareis de cotes et de manteaux pour servir de son office . . . Et les li envoioit on avant les dictes fiestes a tamps, pour coy il les poioit avoir vestues as dis jours . . . Item . . . quant il donnoit leauwe au conte . . . et estoient li bachin dargent dont il servoit sien.[47]

[when the chamberlain comes to the count's court at Christmas and Pentecost to perform his office . . . he may have wages, *bouche a court* for five people, four measures of wine, 2 of the *bouche* and two in common, one torch of nine palms' length, 20 small candles, 12s 6d for oats . . . Item, at Christmas he is to be sent 24 ells of cloth and three furs of *gros vair*, and at Pentecost also, by reason of which he and three knights shall come, furnished with surcoats and cloaks to perform his office . . . And they are to be sent to him before the said feasts, so that he can wear them on the said days . . . Item, . . . when he serves water to the count . . . the silver basin with which he serves will be his . . .]

In June 1307, moreover, Robert de Wavrin, lord of St-Venant, bore witness to the count that the lord of Ghistelles, as hereditary chamberlain, was to

venir pour vous servir en cote et le mantel au col. Et sitost comme il se met en service il doit oster son mantel et luy metre en cote, et ainssi servir.[48]

[come to serve you in a tunic with a cloak at the neck. And as soon as he begins the service he should take off his cloak and wear his tunic, and thus perform his service.]

The fact that the hereditary chamberlain ritually discarded his cloak and wore his *cote* (tunic), when he commenced his service to the count,

[45] ADN, B.1569, fos. 8r–12r (so-called '9th cartulary of Flanders' compiled by Guillaume d'Auxonne, chancellor of Louis de Nevers). See below, nn. 62–3. Also see above, pp. 29–31.

[46] Monier, *Institutions financières*, 33–4.

[47] B.1569, fo. 12r; Limburg-Stirum, *La Cour de Flandre*, 414.

[48] B.1569, fos. 12r–v; also RAG, St-Genois 1365 (26 May 1319).

affords us a rare glimpse into the ceremonial of the Flemish court. It also demonstrates the long-term continuities of court life. Walter Map recounted a story about William de Tancarville, great chamberlain to Henry II.[49] The king had slighted him by not summoning him to perform his service of pouring water into silver basins, to wash the king's hands, at the Christmas feast which Henry kept at Caen in 1182. Map tells us that Tancarville angrily entered the king's hall, and 'casting off his cloak in the way proper for ministers [that is, household officers], seized the silver basins and pulled them violently towards him'.[50] Service, for these men, was not only an obligation, but an honour which, if denied or contravened in any way, gave grounds for complaint, if not outright defiance.

The giving of Christmas and Pentecost liveries of cloaks and mantles at the Flemish court must also have stemmed from an earlier epoch, as did the retention of the silver basin into which the chamberlain poured water for the count. The practice of hereditary office-holding in Flanders showed a remarkable capacity for survival. In the neighbouring duchy of Brabant, similar rights and duties were exercised by the lords of Rotselaar as hereditary seneschals.[51] But, as in Hainault, hereditary household offices in Flanders could be given away, bought or sold, with the count's permission. Not only did this offer a potential source of revenue to the counts, but it might serve to break the grip of hereditary office-holders on these functions. The obligatory attendance at 'full' or 'solemn' courts by such figures would in turn oblige the ruler to keep their company and receive their advice—both of which might be unwelcome to him, or her.[52] In 1330, for example, count Louis de Nevers bought back the hereditary office of chamberlain from its incumbents. Offices could also be exchanged. In September 1282, Guy de Dampierre had confirmed an earlier grant by Margaret, countess of Flanders and Hainault (1244–78) whereby the hereditary *huissier* (usher) of Flanders, Baudouin, lord of Bailleul, exchanged that office for the *maréchaussée* (marshalsea), to be held by himself and his heirs.[53] In turn, the holder of one of the four usherships of the comital household—Jean, lord of Belenghien—surrendered that office in November 1284, and it was purchased by Walter, son of Walter de Kortrijk, with Guy de Dampierre's permission.[54]

In Flanders, many of the lower household posts were also held by hereditary tenure in the early fourteenth century. For example, the two

[49] Map, *De Nugis*, 266–7. [50] Ibid. 267. [51] See above, pp. 40–1.

[52] See above, pp. 39–40. Monier, *Institutions financières*, 32–3.

[53] ADN, B.1569, fo. 13v. [54] Ibid., fo. 16r.

offices of marshal had become hereditary in the knightly families of Vichte and van Belle; the Belenghien held that of *panetier* from the mid-twelfth century; the van Belle also acted as ushers (*deurwaarders*), to be succeeded by the Belenghien; and the offices of cook and *saussier* were also held hereditarily.[55] The provisions relating to the services performed for the count by the hereditary officers from Bruges and his castle of Male must also have stemmed from the distant past. They bear close comparison with the duties exercised by the hereditary functionaries in the *comté* of Hainault, and within each of its three *dominationes*, as described by Gislebert of Mons.[56] When the count of Flanders and his household came to Bruges or Male, the six *héritiers*, or functionaries, performed the following tasks: laundering the table-linen and cloths from the count's chamber; lighting the fire in the great hearth of the castle; providing blankets for the household (a duty discharged by the lords of Praet); bringing peat, eels, hens, salt, eggs, and so on (the *lardier's*, or larderer's, functions); opening the doors of the comital wine-cellar; providing kitchenware (*escueles*) for the household; bringing cream and butter three times a week; while the lords of Assebroek were to provide a dish of freshwater fish for the comital table.[57] Similar functions were exercised in Hainault, for example, by the officer within the *dominatio* of Mons who acted as *lardarius* (larderer); the *scultellarius* (supplying metal-ware for the table); the keeper of the keys to the comital cellar; and the *figulus* (potter) who supplied earthenware pots to the count's kitchen and chamber.[58]

By 1335, however, some of these Flemish offices had been bought from their hereditary tenants. Not only had Louis de Nevers bought out the hereditary chamberlain's rights but, at a lower level, Guillaume de Lestanc, *bourgeois* of Bruges, had purchased the function of laundering the comital linen when the household came to Bruges or Male.[59] All these services carried corresponding privileges, of which (as in the English household ordinances) the right to eat at court, in the ruler's hall, was most common. The very fact that all these rights and duties were witnessed by named members of the comital household of Flanders in

[55] See Vanderwoude, 'De hofhouding', 15–16; ADN, B.1569, fos. 14r–16r.
[56] Gislebert, *Chronique*, 337–9, 340–2.
[57] Vanderwoude, 'De hofhouding', 16–19; ADN, B.1569, fos. 18r–19v.
[58] Gislebert, *Chronique*, 340.
[59] ADN, B.1569, fo. 20v. See also Thomas, 'Une source nouvelle', 22–3, for the transformation of the hereditary castellans of Ruppelmonde into 'simple[s] fonctionnaire[s]' in the fourteenth century.

the 1330s suggests that they did in fact correspond to reality.[60] But the incidental and occasional nature of these services, performed only when the count came to a specific location, meant that a permanent household personnel of paid, non-noble servants was also already in place at a much earlier date. In Hainault, the small body of hereditary officers who served for the whole *comté* may have, in part, provided that personnel. As in Hainault, there was a striking degree of continuity in the structure and organization of the Flemish comital household.[61]

The lack of surviving household ordinances for Flanders means that we may have to infer their existence from other sources. The so-called 'ninth cartulary of Flanders', apparently compiled between 1330 and 1337, sets out the rights and duties of many household officers, derived in part from the scrutiny of 'ancient writings'.[62] This volume is in fact what has been called a 'notebook' made by Guillaume d'Auxonne (d.1344), chancellor of Flanders, later bishop of Cambrai and, at the end of his life, of Autun.[63] But it also serves to some extent as a register of household offices, setting out their functions and privileges, just as a more formal household ordinance might do. The list (fos. 3–21) included the offices of *prévôt* of St Donatian's, Bruges; seneschal, sub-seneschal, constable, butlers, chamberlain, marshals, pantler (*panetier*), ushers, *saussier*, and the hereditary officers of Bruges and Male. Supporting documentation was included in the description of each office. The definition of the duties of the *prévôt* of St Donatian's thus reads in very much the same vein as a household ordinance:

Item, que il ne se doit mie absenter hors du province de Flandre se ce nest par cause de lestude, de pelerinage, ou de ses hostes quil doit deffendre, ou pour faire le service *de la court de Flandre* . . . Item, il doit avoir tous ses despens tant comme il est *a la court du conte* sans tauxacion.[64]

---

[60] ADN, B.1569, fo. 19v: 'Ces choses deseure dictes tiesmoignent Jehans Fautins, mess[ire] Simon Doysi, mess[ire] Bauduins dou Castiel, Biertans Petis Keus, Ghilbebiers li huissiers, Pierres le Nains et Alains le panetiers par leur lettres . . . Encoires tiesmoignent par leur lettres aucun des tiesmoigns deseure dis . . .'

[61] Vanderwoude, 'De hofhouding', 20: 'het type ambt blijft echter doorleven, ook in de Bourgondische periode' ['the basic type of office-holder remained the same, even into the Burgundian period'].

[62] ADN, B.1569, fo. 3v: where it was said of the rights and duties of the *prévôt* of St Donatian at Bruges that 'ces choses chi dessus il jure ainssinc com je trove par anciennes escriptures'.

[63] See Thomas, 'Une source nouvelle', 13–16 for discussion of the manuscript and its provenance.

[64] ADN, B.1569, fo. 3v. Italics mine.

[Item, that he should not absent himself from the province of Flanders except by reason of his studies, pilgrimage, or his guests whom he has to protect, or to perform service for the court of Flanders . . . Item, he should be paid all his expenses just as when he is at the count's court without deduction.]

Similarly, the hereditary constable was to have 'vin, wages, drap et forreures ainssi comme au seneschal' ['wine, wages, cloth and furs just as the seneschal'], and other officers' perquisites were also set out in detail.[65] Some clue as to the process whereby this information was both obtained and recorded is found in the text. Not only were 'anciennes escriptures' in the comital archive consulted, but verbal enquiries were also made. Thus the hereditary butlers' rights and allowances were established 'par enqueste dou commandement le conte Guy lan de grace 1291 *le mardi de Penthecouste* a Winendale' ['by enquiry at the order of the count Guy on Tuesday after Pentecost 1291 at Wijnendaal']. A similar note accompanied another ruling on the butlers' rights:

et ce fist messire li cuens devant dis [Guy de Dampierre] ainssi *registrer en ses registres lan de grace 1291, le mardi en Penthecouste fait a Winendale.*[66]

[and the aforesaid count had this registered in his registers for the year 1291 on the Tuesday after Pentecost at Wijnendaal.]

It appears that questions had been put verbally to Guillaume de Landrenghien, one of the hereditary butlers of Flanders, about consignments of wine and their safe-keeping. The fact that these enquiries, and consequent registrations, took place on the Tuesday after Pentecost suggests that the gatherings of the 'full' court of Flanders on the great feast days could provide suitable occasions on which to define the duties and benefits of the household officers present at those events. It does not seem impossible that such 'registrations' could have led to the formulation of household ordinances which have subsequently perished.

Even in the prevailing absence of surviving ordinances for the Low Countries, the relatively rich series of household accounts and other forms of documentation reveal a broad degree of basic similarity among princely and noble establishments.[67] Although accounting systems may have differed between England and the Continent, sufficient affinities

---

[65] ADN, B.1569, fos. 10r, 11r–v.

[66] Ibid., fo. 11r; cf. Limburg-Stirum, *La Cour des comtes de Flandre*, i. 86–94. Italics mine.

[67] See *Household Accounts from Medieval England*, ed. C. M. Woolgar, i (Oxford, 1992), 50–4.

also existed between household structures there to make comparison feasible.[68] Not only can continuities in household organization over time be found, but a certain degree of basic uniformity prevailed across north-west Europe. The structure of offices and departments (*métiers*) was fundamentally common to all princely households. Thus in England, the households of those dependent upon the king—such as his children, or those who had been committed to his care, whether as minors or because they were 'foreign' princes and nobles being brought up and educated at the royal court—not only reflected the broad traits of the king's own establishment, but shared many common features with continental households.

So the *Ordinement del hostel Jehan de Brabant* (Ordinance of the household of John of Brabant) drawn up, probably between 1284 and 1289, for John, son of Duke John I, who was to succeed his father in 1294, set out the basic features of a princely establishment, but on a smaller scale.[69] John was certainly a member of Edward I's 'court'—he slept in his own chamber there. His chamberlain, who took his livery, and all others of John's *meignie* (*maisnie* or retinue) were allowed to eat with the king's household. Rather like the household officers in Brabant or Flanders, his *chevalier* Daniel (who seems also to have acted as seneschal) took livery of wine and candles, and 'quant il gist bien loinz de court, prendra viaunde p[or] sen soper, selonc ceo qe resun sera, por lui et por les clers e por les esquiers'[70] ['when he lodges far from the court, he shall take food for his supper, according to reason, for himself and the clerks and the esquires']. John of Brabant's *genz de office* (office-holders) and *vallez de mestier* (valets of household departments) were also to eat in the king's hall. These were his cook, tailor, *panetier*, butler, and marshal. Each of these officers was also to take livery of robes and footwear 'according to the custom of the king's household'. Below these functionaries were twenty or so *garçons*, including eight assigned to John's person, all of whom discharged the more menial domestic duties. Stratification was thus already built into its organization. Another roll, listing the members of his household, tells us that one of them 'ran after John [of Brabant] in the woods and along the river banks with the dogs'—part of the small hunting establishment of

---

[68] Cf. *Household Accounts from Medieval England*, 52, where the contrasts are perhaps a little overdrawn.

[69] PRO, C.47/3/21, no. 12; for John of Brabant's residence in England see J. de Sturler, *Les Relations politiques et les échanges commerciaux entre le duché de Brabant et l'Angleterre au moyen âge* (Paris, 1936), 145–50. See Appendix I (a), (b).

[70] C.47/3/21, no. 12. See Appendix I (a).

horses, dogs and falcons which he retained.[71] *In toto*, this young prince's establishment numbered about fifty members, including the *garçons* and menial servants. As such, it compares very favourably with other dependent households, such as that of the king's two sons Thomas of Brotherton (b.1300) and Edmund of Woodstock (b.1301). Between November 1305 and November 1306, when these two boys were respectively five and four years old, their establishment numbered about forty-five members, including *garçons* and minstrels, who all received liveries of robes.[72]

At the head of the household list for John of Brabant was another young noble—his companion Humphrey de Bohun, son of the hereditary constable of England.[73] The heir to the duchy of Brabant thus received a very similar social education to the young English nobles at Edward I's court. He had a number of Brabançons (or other Netherlanders) in his service: Giles de Wynenghem, a certain Addinet, Watrelos de Ligne, Hennekin 'qi trencha devaunt Jehan' ['who carved before John'], and (perhaps) Huguenin de Reigny.[74] He also had his own chaplain, and clerk, as well as his own messenger.[75] This was a princely household in miniature—but one which any non-English contemporary would instantly recognize and which would in no way be alien to a continental noble, knight, clerk, or esquire. The 'common' culture of courts and households is a theme which will be returned to later.[76]

An even smaller establishment was that created for the young John de Warenne, Edward I's ward, at some date between 1303 and 1305.[77] An *ordeinement* (ordinance) was drawn up for it by the experts at Edward I's court: Walter Langton, bishop of Chester, the treasurer; Henry de Percy; Robert de la Warde, seneschal of the king's household; John de Droxford, keeper of the wardrobe; and John de Benstead, controller. The household numbered about fifteen members, to which the five *garçons* of Roger Mortimer, John de Warenne's companion in the king's wardship, should be added. John had two valets and an *enfaunt* to carve before him, and twice-yearly livery of robes:

Item, il meismes por son corps avera 2 foiz robes par an, dont Esmon de Mortimer serra de sa seute, et les fuiz [fils] de tieux grants seigneurs, a Noel et a Pasque, et un robe de russet por ivern a la Seynt Michel. Et ses 3 vadlez auront 2 fois robes par an as dites festes dautre seute, sicome les vadletz denfauntz de garde.[78]

---

[71] C.47/3/46/31. See Appendix I (b).   [72] E.101/368/12, fos. 5r, 6r.
[73] C.47/3/46/31. See Appendix I (b).   [74] C.47/3/21, no. 12. See Appendix I (a), (b).
[75] C.47/3/46/31.   [76] See below, pp. 165–8.
[77] E.101//371/8/97. See Appendix I (d).
[78] E.101/371/8/97. For livery distribution see below, pp. 101–5.

[Item, he shall himself have robes for his body twice a year, and Edmund Mortimer shall have the same kind, and the sons of such great lords, at Christmas and Easter, and a winter robe of russet at Michaelmas. And his three valets shall have robes of a different kind twice a year at the said feasts, just as the valets of children in wardship.]

The distinction between types of livery—of different *seutes* [sets] or types and quality of cloth—undoubtedly reflected the difference in social status between the young wards and their valets.[79] Like John of Brabant, Warenne was given three *valets de métier*—a chamberlain or *valet de chambre* and *valets* of the pantry and buttery, as well as a *vadlet keu* (cook). The structure of this tiny dependent household thus conformed to that of the grander establishments. Such evidence for the material underpinning of aristocratic culture, in both England and elsewhere, helps to explain the relative ease with which both clerical and lay members of princely and noble households passed from one court to another. It would be an exaggeration to claim that they could move from one to another without being aware of the differences.[80] But as necessary conditions for a cosmopolitan aristocratic society, these organizational similarities should not be underestimated. They provided a material infrastructure for the world of the courts which will be examined later.[81]

Although the surviving ordinances and descriptive lists of personnel are a prime source for our understanding of the structures of princely households, detailed examination of how a household actually functioned has to be grounded in analysis of the financial documentation. This will be considered in the next chapter, but it should be remembered that prescriptive evidence—of which household ordinances could often form a part—should always be treated with caution. Memoranda, treatises, and household ordinances themselves were often drawn up in response to demands for the reform or reduction of princely establishments. There is sometimes an element of bias in their composition.[82] Ordinances might describe things as they ought to be, rather than as they were. The late André Uyttebrouck, in his work on the court of Brabant, was rightly sceptical of the extent to which household ordinances reflected current reality.

Ces actes visent avant tout à mettre fin à la gabegie regnant dans les services du prince, principalement en limitant le nombre de ses officiers. C'est pourquoi sont établies les listes de personnes qui seuls devront être admises à gages à l'avenir.[83]

---

[79] See below, pp. 104–8; also Table 15(a) for comparisons.
[80] See below, pp. 282–4.   [81] See above, pp. 48–9.
[82] See Oschinsky, *Walter of Henley and other Treatises*, 390–401.
[83] A. Uyttebrouck, *Le Gouvernement du duché de Brabant à la fin du moyen âge* (Brussels, 1975), 156.

[These acts were above all concerned to put an end to the confusion which reigned in a prince's service, principally by limiting the number of his officers. That is why lists were established of those who alone could be retained with wages in the future.]

He demonstrated that the Brabançon ordinances of 1407 and 1427 were simply never implemented, at least as far as the numbers prescribed within each category or *état* of the ducal household were concerned.

More secure and reliable evidence for household organization than that from Brabant, however, survives for the court of Holland in the mid-fourteenth century. A list of household personnel, some rulings on their rights and duties, and a related list of those receiving liveries, were drawn up for the Dutch court during the period February–May 1354.[84] The list and related rulings applies only to the permanent members of the household, while the livery list refers to a much larger circle of individuals. The first document, dated to May 1354, although described as an ordinance [*ordinacie*], takes the form of a mandate from the count to his officers. It concerns the households of the new count, William V (1354–89) and his wife Maud of Lancaster, daughter of Henry of Grosmont, earl, then first duke, of Lancaster.[85] Its purpose was to regulate numbers retained in each household, and to establish what could and could not be claimed by their members. It lists a total of sixty individuals, including servants, in the count's household; fifty-four in the countess's. The relatively high figure for the latter is noteworthy. This suggests that the households of rulers' wives often tended to be as large, and often more static, than their own. Frequent pregnancies may have been in part responsible for this apparently more sedentary existence. In this *ordinacie*, those entitled to fodder and stabling for their horses are identified, and the number of horses allowed is given. The internal hierarchy of office and *métier* corresponded closely to that found in Flanders, Hainault, and Brabant. The count's household was headed by a body of *meesters* (masters) of the various departments: a master knight, master chamberlain, master squire, master butler, master pantler (*pentier*), and a master of the cooks. This structure was replicated in the countess's household. In his treatise, *De cura reipublicae*, written at the Dutch court in the 1350s, Philip of Leyden specifically endorsed this household structure. His name in

---

[84] ARA, Den Haag, Arch. grav. van Holland, inv. nr. 221, fos. 75r–v, 76r–77r. Printed in T. Van Riemsdijk, *De Tresorie en Kanselarij van de graven van Holland en Zeeland uit het Henegouwsche en Beyersche huis* (The Hague, 1908), 21–9, 399–400, 401–3.

[85] ARA, inv. nr. 221, fos. 76r–77r: 'Dese ordinacie wil mijn heer ghehouden hebben . . .'

fact appears in both the ordinance and the livery list. The master of the household should be a knight, he wrote, while his immediate subordinate should not. He continued:

unus senior et maior, alter junior et minor . . . Senes enim sint duces officiorum, et juvenes ad agilitatem eligantur, ut de cultellis et scyphis et similibus tales sunt, ut flore respirantes adolescentiae et juventutis principem eos intueri delectet.[86]

[one should be senior and greater; the other junior and lesser . . . Old men should be heads of the offices; young men should be chosen for their nimbleness as they are [so proficient] with knives, goblets and such-like that, exuding the freshness of youth and adolescence, the prince delights in bringing them forward.]

Some of these offices were certainly held by knights and squires—thus Willem van der Wateringhe served as knight to the count's body; Ghijsebrecht van Nieuwenrode as master knight; Gerard van der Wateringhe as master squire; Dieric Claeszoen as squire of the linen (*van den naape*); Gerard van Heemskerke as squire of the table (*van den messen*).[87] The countess's master knight was Gerard van der Oosteinde, her master chamberlain was Alwijn van Revel, and she had a body of *damoiselles* (*joncvrouwen*) for whom six horses were provided.

Strict injunctions were issued at the court of Holland in 1354 to limit the number of retainers and hangers-on at court:

Dese ordinacie wil mijn heer ghehouden hebben endeleken ende daer in den meysten volstaen ende daermede laten beghaen. Ende elk die knaep of knecht houden zal, die [zal] houden enen goeden harden knecht oft en ghenen ende dit zullen die meysters van der herberghe virsien . . . Ende so wi bi sinen here selve niet is ende wanneer die man selve wt is, so en sel men noch knecht noch paert leveren eer hi weder coemt.[88]

[My lord [the count] wishes this ordinance to be obeyed absolutely; and, to that end, he will assist the masters [of the household] and will let them apply it. And whoever retains a squire (*knaep*) or valet (*knecht*) will have to retain either a fit and strong one or none at all; and the masters of the household (*herberghe*) will supervise this . . . And for him who is not personally in his [the count's] company, because he is out of the household, neither valets nor horses shall be provided before he comes back.]

---

[86] Philip of Leyden, *De Cura*, cas. xxviii, p. 106. He appears among the clerks as 'Meester Philips' on the livery list (fo. 75r) and as 'Meester Phillips', one of the two clerks *van den register* in the ordinance (fo. 76r). See also Leupen, *Philip of Leyden*, 32–4, 44–5, 74–6. Cf. similar functions at the Aragonese court: see *Aragonische Hofordnungen im 13. und 14. Jahrhundert*, ed. K. Schwarz (Berlin, 1914), 142.

[87] ARA, inv. nr. 221, fo. 76r.

[88] Ibid., fo. 77r; Riemsdijk, *De Tresorie*, 403.

The new count (or his advisers) may well have been attempting to remedy past abuses. Rules were also issued to counteract the practice of taking excessive 'left-overs' or 'remainders' (*virval*) in offal, wax, and so on, by household officers. The masters of departments, garçons (*garsoen*), and valets of offices were to be paid wages of 25 and 13 *oude scilde* respectively. The ordinance thus stated:

Hiermede wil mijn heer dat nimand enich virval en hebbe die in sijnre herberghe is, mar alle dinghe, die virvallen moghen binnen der herberghen, die zellen die meysters van der herberghe nemen sonder enich wedersegghen, ende dat doen bruken toet mijns heren ere ende oerbaer.

Ende mijn heer en wille van niemand hierboven virsocht noch anghesproken, mar wes die meysters van der herberghe doen, die myn heer sinen dienst bevolen heeft, dat zal hi stede ende vaste houden sonder anders enich virsoek.[89]

[In this manner my lord [the count] wishes that no one shall have supplementary income from the 'remainders' in the household, but all the 'remainders' from within the household shall be taken by the masters of the household, without any objection, and they will put them to use for my lord's honour and profit.

And my lord does not wish to receive requests or complaints from anyone mentioned above; but whatever the masters of the household, who are called to the service of my lord, will do, the count will ensure that it is obeyed certainly and firmly, without any other request.]

The near-contemporary treatise by Philip of Leyden also referred to this practice and was emphatic about the need for princely moderation and the virtues of accurate accounting for household receipts and disbursements.[90] While advocating moderate princely liberality, Philip bore out the ordinance of 1354 in asserting that the masters of the household should ensure that 'remainders' (*remanentium*) and other perquisites should only be taken as rewards for good service, not as of right.[91] With characteristic Dutch thriftiness, he urged that the prince's clerks should know 'down to the last farthing' (*ad ultimum quadrantem*) what was needed for a balanced annual budget.[92]

Apart from their value as an account of household practice in a region for which there is relatively sparse documentation, the ordinance and livery list for Holland of 1354 are also informative about the social composition of princely households. Whereas the livery list includes six Dutch nobles or bannerets (*baenrosen*) and twelve knights, the household

---

[89] ARA, inv. nr. 221, fo. 77r; Riemsdijk, *De Tresorie*, 403.

[90] Philip of Leyden, *De Cura*, 116, 324–29.

[91] Ibid. 107.   [92] Ibid. 116, and see below, pp. 88–93.

ordinance lists only four knights.[93] The *knappen* (squires)—thirty-eight in the livery list, sixteen in the ordinance, some of whom must have been higher born than others, formed a much larger group. Names such as Hendrik and Wolfart van Borselen, Gerard van der Wateringhe, Gerard van Heemskerke, Otto van Arkel, and so on, suggest that the sons of the Dutch nobility were closely associated, as squires, with the comital household. But the discrepancy between the number of nobles, knights, squires, and clerks receiving liveries of cloth and those actually present in the household is striking. It suggests that the distinction made, for example, in Hainault, between 'ordinary' and 'full' (*plaine*) distributions of livery was also observed in Holland.[94] William V of Holland was, of course, soon to become count of Hainault (in 1356), and the two *comtés* had already been joined together under the Avesnes (1299–1345). In both Hainault and Holland a much larger body of both nobles and non-nobles received 'full liveries' from the count and countess than were retained in their households.

A distinction between regular and occasional service at court and in the household must therefore be made here. In Holland, the count and countess issued liveries of cloth (*cledinghe*) in 1354 to six nobles (*baenrosen*, bannerets), twelve knights, eleven clerks, thirty-eight squires (*knappen*), twenty-three *garcons* (*ghersone*), sixteen valets (*knechte*), two ladies (*vrouwen*), and four *damoiselles* (*joncfrouwen*).[95] Thus a total of 112 recipients of livery represented what was perhaps the *weiter Hof*: the 'broader' or 'further' court. This assembled only at especially significant times of the year—at the liturgical feasts and on particularly important occasions, or festive events, in the life of the ruling house—marriages, baptisms, knightings, tournaments, and so forth.[96] This was the occasional, 'full' or solemn court. The *enger Hof* ('narrower' court) was formed by those listed in the household ordinance, plus a penumbra of transient noble and clerical guests and visitors. The valets of the offices and the servants, plus the numerous hangers-on who attached themselves to the count's and countess's establishments, formed what was in effect a lower household, though still remaining part of the court. In effect, a small core

---

[93] ARA, inv. nr. 221, fos. 75r, 76r, 77r.

[94] See above, pp. 39–40. For comparative evidence from England, see below, pp. 99–115.

[95] ARA, inv. nr. 221, fos. 75r–v: the recipients included some English members of the countess's (Maud of Lancaster's) household, such as Sir Bartholomew de Burgersh, John Hastings, esquire, Joan Hastings, *damoiselle*, and John *dien Enghels*, clerk.

[96] See below, pp. 103–4.

or nucleus of clerks and laymen, down to the rank of squire, numbering about forty people, formed the comital court of Holland—here, as elsewhere, were the makings of an upper household.[97]

The emergence of internal divisions within princely households, whereby the *maisnie* (retinue), comprising the ruler's *familia* (household), became increasingly a kind of service department, or series of departments, responsible for the daily needs of the prince and his entourage, was already discernible in the later thirteenth century. Although the distinction between the ceremonial household (*domus magnificencie*), presided over in England by the chamberlain, and the provident household (*domus providencie*), presided over by the steward or seneschal, was not formally made before the fifteenth century, tendencies towards separation were visible much earlier.[98] The two bodies could never be completely distinct, as they existed in a sort of symbiosis. The display of the *domus magnificencie* was only made possible by the prudent accounting and provisioning procedures of the *domus providencie*.[99] But, as we have seen, the formation of a small inner, or upper, nucleus of household officers and clerks, in Flanders, Brabant, Hainault, and Holland, may have prefigured later developments. Most of the secular members of this group were knights or squires, and it was from their ranks that the later noble affinities, entourages, or retinues maintained by princes stemmed. It is here that the origins of the permanent court, which grew in size and elaboration during the fourteenth century—rather than the occasional gathering—may partly be found. That process can be traced by further consideration of changes within household organization over a much longer period.

3. Hall, chamber, and household

In the process whereby the 'court' evolved into its early modern form, much stress has been laid by historians upon the transition from warband, or retinue, to the kind of establishment, populated by courtiers, favoured by Renaissance rulers.[100] This gradual shift has been traced,

---

[97] See, for German evidence, Bumke, *Courtly Culture*, 506–7; also below, pp. 62–3.

[98] See Tout, *Chapters*, ii. 246–52; D. A. L. Morgan, 'The King's Affinity in the Polity of Yorkist England', *TRHS* 5th ser. 23 (1973), 1–25.

[99] Morgan, 'The King's Affinity', 2–4.

[100] See Morgan, 'The house of policy', 34–5, 67–70.

with varying chronologies, in most western European countries.[101] The fifteenth and sixteenth centuries are, however, seen as crucial to this evolution. In England, it has been said, one legacy of the Yorkist period (1461–85) was 'a complex of ideas and attitudes, as well as social habits and institutional forms, which had given "the court" a new or at least an acutely intensifed self-consciousness'.[102] Yet it could be argued that Walter Map's view of the court in the late twelfth century was nothing if not self-conscious.[103] The self-conscious institutionalization of upper and lower household departments in fifteenth-century England may merely represent a formalization of existing structures and procedures. For example, the very gradual detachment of the ruler's chamber (*camera, chambre*) from his hall (*aula, salle*), reflected physically in the division and distribution of space within his residences, had taken place at a much earlier date Map 3.

By the last quarter of the fifteenth century, according to the Black Book of the English household, the duties of the four household squires for the body, who were of noble status, lay in service of a personal and intimate kind to the king in his chamber:

of them alwei ij to be attendaunt uppon the kinges person to aray and unray hym, to wache day and nyght, to dresse hym in his clothes. And they be callers to the chaumbrelayn if ony thing lak for his person or plesaunce; theyre business is many secretes, som sitting in the kinges chaumbre, som in the hall, with persones of like servyse, wich is called knyghtes service . . . Oftyn tymes thees stond in stede of kervers and cupberers.[104]

They were to receive liveries of wine, ale, wax, candles, litter, clothing, rushes, and so forth, plus wages when present at court. Much of this has a familiar ring—and the compiler of the Black Book himself reminded his readers:

Thes esquiers of houshold *of old* be acustumed, wynter and somer, in after nonys and in evenynges, to drawe to lordez chambrez within courte, there to kepe honest company aftyr theyre cunyng, in talkyng of cronycles of kinges and of other polycyez, or in pypyng, or harpyng, synging, or other actez marciablez, to help occupy the court and acompany straungers, tyll the tym require of departing . . .[105]

[101] By, for example, Norbert Elias in *The Court Society*, 2–8, 158–60; also see A. Maczak, 'From aristocratic household to princely court: restructuring patronage in the sixteenth and seventeenth centuries', in *Princes, Patronage and the Nobility*, 315–27.

[102] Morgan, 'The house of policy', 68. [103] Map, *De Nugis*, 1–3, 273, 278–9.

[104] *Household of Edward IV*, 111–12. [105] Ibid. 112, 129.

How 'old' was 'of old'? This was not mere reproduction or parroting of Burgundian practice but rested upon a long-term tendency, and long-standing tradition, at the English court.[106] The activities of young squires, which in effect both reflected and shaped 'court culture', were by no means exclusive to the fifteenth century. It is clear that personal services to the ruler, as well as social and 'cultural' activities similar to those of Edward IV's squires for the body, were discharged in a broadly similar manner by their early fourteenth-century predecessors. The chamber squires of Edward I appear not to have been of 'noble condition', but a rise in their status is discernible over the following decades.[107] Edward II's reign may have been crucial in this respect.[108] But before chamber squires could play their part in the life of a household, there had to be a chamber (or chambers, as they served in 'lordez chambrez within courte') in which they could exercise their social, musical, narrative, and conversational skills. The Renaissance court, with its self-conscious emphasis upon the cultural and intellectual accomplishments of its members, was not without precursors. The need for privacy, diversion, and entertainment among rulers and their families, set apart from the communal hall, made their chambers a natural setting for 'courtly' activities.

Walter Map claimed in his character-assassination of Queen Matilda that she was a malign influence upon her son, the young Henry II, telling him that 'he ought . . . to be much in his chamber and little in public'.[109] Map alleged that Henry put this bad advice into practice: 'when he makes a stay anywhere . . . he does not allow himself to be seen as honest men would have him do, but shuts himself up within, and is only accessible to those who seem unworthy of such ready access'.[110] To retire to one's chamber may not have been politically or socially desirable in a prince. Yet the desire for privacy among twelfth-century—and later—rulers was entirely understandable. The communal life of the hall allowed very little opportunity for the prince and his family to retire from its hurly-burly and enforced sociability. The huge, noisy common table in the hall, and the constant presence of what, under Edward I, T. F. Tout described as 'the

[106] Cf. Olivier de la Marche, 'Estat de la maison du duc Charles de Bourgoigne, dit le Hardy', in *Mémoires d'Olivier de la Marche*, ed. H. Beaune and J. d'Arbaumont, iv (Paris, 1888), 16: the sixteen chamber squires of Charles the Bold kept the duke company in his chamber, where 'les ungs chantent, les autres lisent romans et nouvelletez, les autres se devisent d'amours et d'armes, et font le prince passer le temps en gratieuses nouvelles'.

[107] See below, pp. 59–61; also Table 15(a).

[108] See Tout, *Chapters*, ii. 314–60, and below, pp. 59–63.

[109] Map, *De Nugis*, 261.   [110] Ibid. 265.

monstrous crowd of riff-raff, the hangers-on of the various [household] offices, grooms, pages, boys, Welshmen, archers, messengers, women of ill-fame, and the rest whose presence made the advent of the royal household a terror to the countryside'[111] made rulers subject to almost every kind of importunity and unwelcome attention. But this was one price of personal rule. Walter Map contrasted Henry II unfavourably with his grand-father, Henry I when he claimed that the latter

would allow access to his presence, either in a great house or in the open, up to the sixth hour. At that time he would have with him the earls, barons, and noble vavasours. The young people of his household, however, were not with him before dinner, nor the seniors after it; except such as might make their way in at their own choice, either to learn or give instruction. And when this orderly method became known all over the world, his court was desired as much as others are shunned, and it was famous and frequented.[112]

Map's description, with its stress upon order, discipline, learning, and instruction at court, put forward a model which was widely influential. The part played by the 'young people' (*juvenes*) of the king's household may have made them the twelfth-century equivalents of the fifteenth-century squires to the king's body.[113]

As we have seen, it was in the chamber that the English household knights and squires were retained and where they served the king. The chamber (*camera regis*) had always been the place in which the ruler slept, and to which he might retire (Pl. 3). The very close and intimate proximity of its staff to him meant that it was often considered as his personal domain, answerable only to the prince.[114] Tout pointed out that the English household ordinance of 1279 was 'absolutely silent as to the king's chamber'. It was, he claimed, 'an excrescence, an eccentric offshoot of the wardrobe', at least until the reforming household ordinance of 1318.[115] Although Tout's interpretation of the role of administrative departments and their associated seals may not command unqualified support, his highlighting of the reign of Edward II in the 'rise' of the chamber seems entirely warranted.[116] A rise in the status of the king's chamberlain, exemplified by the high fees paid to him, was already discernible under

---

[111] Tout, *Chapters*, ii. 256–7.   [112] Map, *De Nugis*, 259.

[113] *Household of Edward IV*, 129.

[114] Edward III exemplified this view by ordering Chamber records to be burnt. See Given-Wilson, *The Royal Household*, 85–92; Tout, *Chapters*, iv. 227–348.

[115] Tout, *Chapters*, ii. 43, 332.

[116] See J. R. Maddicott, *Thomas of Lancaster, 1307–1322* (Oxford, 1970), 12–24; Tout, *Chapters*, ii. 339–40; also see below, pp. 59–61.

Edward I, while the detailed provisions for the chamber's functioning in the ordinance of 1318 endorsed its growing importance. The chamberlain was now on a par with the seneschal of the household, often holding the rank of banneret, with a knight bachelor and three squires attendant on him, all eating at the common table in the hall.[117] Piers Gaveston had already been *camerarius familiarissimus* to Edward II when prince of Wales, and his elevation to the office of chamberlain-in-chief clearly put him in a position of great influence and power.[118] The chamber also was a place in which the king would eat—served by his squires and valets (or yeomen), some of whom were from gentry families.[119] Sir John Charlton of Powys, Edward's chamberlain from 1308 to 1310, had risen from the rank of valet (yeoman) in his household as prince of Wales to squire, and then knight.[120] There appears to have been no social distinction at this period between a valet and squire of the chamber.

That the chamber provided a refuge from the hall is apparent from the supply of plate and eating utensils to it from the wardrobe. In March 1305, for instance, twenty-six plates and two bowls for washing (*lavatoria*) were delivered *pro servicio aule et camere Regis apud Westmonasterium* ['for the service of the king's hall and chamber at Westminster'].[121] In January 1307, the wardrobe delivered a quantity of plate, including twenty-two silver goblets (*ciphi*) for the chamber.[122] The chamber also received consignments of medicines and drugs for the surgeon's office: in 1322, a substantial quantity was provided by Master Étienne of Paris for the king's expedition to Scotland.[123] It also acted as a treasury for the king's plate and jewels—a function which encroached on the sphere of the wardrobe.[124] For Tout, all this—plus the use of the chamber to receive and administer the forfeited lands of rebels—constituted a 'chamber system', which was to be wrecked by political crises in the summer of 1322.[125] The lack of chamber accounts—with very few exceptions—does not allow us to penetrate very far into its working.[126] But the chamber had, by 1318, undoubtedly achieved a prominence that it had formerly lacked. Although they are not mentioned in the ordinance of that year, the existence of

---

[117] Tout, *Place of Edward II*, 244–84; *Chapters*, ii. 333.

[118] See P. Chaplais, *Piers Gaveston: Edward II's Adoptive Brother* (Oxford, 1994), 102–6.

[119] Tout, *Chapters*, ii. 334–5.   [120] Tout, *Chapters*, ii. 319–20.

[121] E.101/366/29 (Mar. 1305).   [122] E.101/370/6 (Jan. 1307).

[123] E.101/379/3.

[124] Chaplais, *Piers Gaveston*, 104–8, and see below, pp. 62–3, 67.

[125] Tout, *Chapters*, ii. 339–40.

[126] A daily account for the Chamber survives from 1324–5 (E.101/380/4).

knights of the chamber, beside the squires and valets, is attested by other evidence. Apart from the chamberlain—Sir John Charlton—Sir Hugh Despenser the younger (who succeeded him), Sir John Sturmy, Sir Edmund Darel, and Sir Giles Beauchamp were included among the *chivaliers de la chambre le roy* or *milites de camera regis*.[127] Their duties were not defined in the household ordinance, and they merged for all practical purposes into the other knights of the household, but there can be little doubt of their especially privileged status. The chamber provided its own career structure for the able and ambitious, often from well-born families: men rose from valet, or yeoman, to knight through their service there.[128]

An analogy is provided by practice at the court of the near-contemporary kings of Majorca. In May 1337, James II issued a series of *Leges Palatinae* for his household, of which a Latin version was made by Pedro IV of Aragon in 1344.[129] Although the ordinance was concerned as much with questions of protocol, etiquette, and ceremonial, the practical daily duties of the offices were also set out. The great chamberlain (*camerlingue*) was to be a baron (or banneret), assisted by two knightly subordinate chamberlains. They held sway over the kitchen and pharmacy; closed the doors of the king's apartments at night; slept armed near him; dressed and undressed him; assigned lodgings to the members of the household (the duties of the *fourrière* elsewhere); looked after his *garde-robe*, adjudicated the procedures to be followed when receiving guests and strangers, and so on.[130] Below them were six esquires of the chamber, of whom one was to be a baron, who kept watch at night, and carried the king's arms and armour behind him. There were also two *cameriers* (or valets of the chamber), who took charge of the king's plate and jewels, clothing, and footwear. They were also to prepare his next day's clothing—the traditional role of the valet or manservant. The chamber staff also included two barbers, two physicians, two surgeons

---

[127] See Tout, *Place of Edward II*, 249, 277; *Chapters*, ii. 335.

[128] Tout, *Chapters*, ii. 334–6.

[129] See A. Leçoy de la Marche, *Les Relations politiques de la France avec le royaume de Majorque* ii (Paris, 1892), 21–5. The text of the *Leges Palatinae* is printed in *Acta Sanctorum, Junii, III* (Antwerp, 1743), 1 ff.; also *Aragonische Hofordnungen*, ed. Schwarz, 142–4. For a recent discussion of the *Leges Palatinae*, from the standpoint of the organization of space within royal and princely residences, see G. Kerscher, 'Die Perspektive des Potentaten: Differenzierung von "Privattrakt" bzw. Appartement und Zeremonialräumen im spätmittelalterlichen Palastbau', in W. Paravicini (ed.), *Zeremoniell und Raum* (Sigmaringen, 1997), 156–64.

[130] For this, and for what follows, see Leçoy de la Marche, *Les Relations politiques*, ii. 23.

and apothecaries, two private secretaries, four ushers, four *nuntii virgae* (messengers), eight serjeants-at-arms, an armourer, a tailor, *fruitier*, *argentier*, *fourrier* (who prepared the king's lodgings in advance of his arrival), and a number of other minor officers.[131] This establishment certainly bore close resemblances to the chambers of the kings of England and France in the early fourteenth century. Moreover, as a result of their dissemination via Aragon and (after 1386) Castile—and the fact that a contemporary copy, subsequently to be given to Philip the Bold of Burgundy, passed into Philip VI of France's hands—the *Leges Palatinae* may well have influenced later Burgundian practice.[132]

The chamber also provided a context in which rulers attempted to live a private—or at least less public—life.[133] In England, this was demonstrated by the purpose of some large sums paid into it by the treasurer, or by the keeper of the wardrobe. In December 1312, for example, the king's Genoese banker, Antonio di Pessagno, paid out no less than 5,000 l.st. in cash *pro privatis expensis camere sue faciendis* ('to meet the private expenses of his chamber').[134] The English ordinance of 1318 tells us something about the duties of the small body of chamber squires and valets—there was a carving squire, a squire who attended to (and tasted?) the king's food, a cup-bearing squire (the equivalent of an *échanson*), as well as two squire ushers, responsible for food and litter in the office of the chamber.[135] Below them stood a body of lesser officers: cooks, 'ewerers', quarter-masters, four serjeants-at-arms, two trumpeters, two minstrels, and the administrative staff of clerks.[136] This was in effect a kind of 'lower' chamber within the greater institution, although there was a significant degree of overlap. But there was no doubt, either in the minds of the compiler of the treatise known as *Fleta* under Edward I, or of those who set out to reform the household under Edward II, that chamber and hall were distinct entities. As administrative units, the hall was regulated by the officers of the household; the chamber had its own personnel and rules. As Tout rightly pointed out: 'the chamber was to the hall as was the household to the inferior world dwelling outside the "verge" of the

---

[131] Leçoy de la Marche, *Les Relations politiques*, ii. 24; also see Kerscher, 'Die Perspektive des Potentaten', 155–86.

[132] The manuscript is now Brussels, BR, MS 9169. See Paravicini, 'The Court of the Dukes of Burgundy', in Asch and Birke, *Princes, Patronage and the Nobility*, 99–100.

[133] See below, pp. 63–7.

[134] E.101/375/8 (29 Dec. 1312). For Pessagno's role at this time see N. Fryde, 'Antonio Pessagno of Genoa, king's merchant of Edward II of England', in *Studi in memoria de Federigo Melis*, ii (Naples, 1978), 159–78.

[135] Tout, *Chapters*, ii. 334; *Place of Edward II*, 280.   [136] Tout, *Chapters*, ii. 336.

court.'[137] As we have seen, it formed an elite body of the household, a nursery in which the distinctive characteristics of courtly culture might be fostered. Here was one early precursor of the *Domus Magnificencie*, where domestic and personal service to the ruler was accompanied by courtly ceremonial and display.[138]

The distinction between hall and chamber was also expressed in architectural terms (Map 3, Pl. 7). The tenth- and eleventh-century castle, or *motte*, tended to provide rather minimal domestic accommodation. Early stone keeps, or *donjons*, might include a communal hall on one storey, with chambers and other apartments at higher levels. By the twelfth century, however, the addition of a separate hall, or *salle*, with communicating passages to the keep and chapel had become common.[139] The desire of the ruler, his immediate family, and some of the senior members of his household for greater privacy led to the provision of separate chambers, often clustering at one end of the hall. Access to the chambers from the dais or raised platform on which the ruler ate when presiding over the hall was obtained by a door, or doors, leading to passages and staircases which joined hall to chamber. The Binnenhof of the counts of Holland at the Hague, built under Floris V (1256–96), furnishes a mid- to late thirteenth-century example, with a series of chambers appended, as it were, in a turreted block, to the west end of the count's great hall (Pl. 2).[140] This arrangement was said to resemble that of Westminster Hall before Richard II's alterations, and it has been claimed that the Knights' Hall at the Hague was 'inspired' by Westminster (Pls. 1, 2, Map 3).[141] Given the close connections—political, dynastic, and economic—between England and Holland at this time, there may be some truth in this notion, although there were perhaps other parts of the palace of Westminster (such as the 'White' Hall, or the Painted Chamber), which could have influenced the

---

[137] Jones, 'The Court of the Verge', 1–8, 27; Tout, *Chapters*, ii. 335.

[138] See above, p. 56.

[139] For the Gravensteen at Ghent see D. Caillebaut, 'Le château des Comtes à Gand' in *Château Gaillard: Études de Castellogie médiévale*, xi (1983), 45–54. For the count's hall (*aula*) at Bruges and its communicating passage or gallery see Galbert of Bruges, *The Murder of Charles the Good*, ed. and tr. J. B. Ross (Toronto, 1982), 111–12.

[140] See E. H. ter Kuile, 'De bouwgeschiedenis van het grafelijk paleis op het Binnenhof', *Holland*, 10 (1978), 313–28; and H. M. Brokken, 'Het Hof in Den Haage: Grafelijke residentie en centrum van bestuur', in R. J. van Pelt and M. E. Tiethoff-Spliethoff, *Het Binnenhof: Van grafelijke residentie tot regeringscentrum* (Dieren, 1984), 13–20.

[141] See H. M. Colvin *et al.* (eds.), *The History of the King's Works*, i (1963), 42–8, 494–502, 527–33; E. Kooper, 'Introduction', in E. Kooper (ed.), *Medieval Dutch Literature in its European Context* (Cambridge, 1994), 6 n. 11.

domestic arrangements of the counts of Holland.[142] In such structures, the kitchen, buttery, and so-called 'screens passage' were at the other extremity of the hall, a practice which was to be replicated in countless examples, including the domestic arrangements favoured by the Valois dukes of Burgundy. Hence, at the Flemish counts' castle of Male, near Bruges, between Wijnendaal and Torhout, the west wing comprised the great *salle*, with the alimentary service departments; while the east wing contained the chapel, almonry, laundry, stables, and forge, as well as the moated *binnenhof* (*haute court*), the count's and countess's chambers, garden, and 'retreat'.[143]

The fundamental layout of these buildings was broadly similar to that of an Oxford or Cambridge college hall, buttery, and chapel today. Thus, in the thirteenth century, most rulers in north-west Europe possessed residences whose architectural structuring made a visual distinction between the ruler's accommodation—which could be fittingly grand—and the domestic offices of provisioning, storage, and supply. In other words, the administrative and institutional distinctions between hall, household, and chamber were reflected in the organization of physical space around the ruler. In some instances, however, the 'private' apartments could also possess a 'public' dimension. At the palace of Westminster, Henry III's (1216–72) great chamber was extensively refashioned after 1263, and its large first-floor apartment was to become known as the 'Painted Chamber' in the fourteenth century. It served as the state bedchamber, flanked by a private chapel, but was also used for audiences, meetings of the council and, in the fourteenth century, even for Parliaments (Pl. 3, Map 3).[144] The king's bed of estate was placed at the east end, against the north wall, and above its head was a large wall painting, executed in 1266–7, depicting the coronation of Henry's saintly predecessor, Edward the Confessor.[145] The Painted Chamber was, however, quite distinct from the institutional office of the chamber, as a household department, which had its own premises within the complex of buildings at Westminster

[142] See J. Cherry and N. Stratford, *Westminster Kings and the Medieval Palace of Westminster* (British Museum Occasional paper 115, London, 1995), 11–17; P. Binski, *The Painted Chamber at Westminster* (London, 1986), 9–15.

[143] See M. Cafmeyer, 'Het Kasteel van Male', *Annales de la Société d'Émulation de Bruges*, 83 (1940–6), 114–16, 119; AGR, CC, R 2090, 2091.

[144] Binski, *Painted Chamber*, 13–15, 34–5; Cherry and Stratford, *Westminster Kings*, 11–17.

[145] Binski, *Painted Chamber*, 35–6, 38–40, id., *Westminster Abbey and the Plantagenets* (New Haven and London, 1995), 49–50, and figs. 67, 68.

(Map 3). The public and private spheres of an English ruler's life were not yet completely divorced. Further chambers and inner rooms were added at Westminster during the fourteenth century, so that the king could effectively retire from public view, attended only by his immediate entourage, largely made up of the chamber staff.

In continental Europe, the evolution of the ruler's chamber, as an administrative department of his household, took different courses according to the region concerned. In royal France, although the sixth *métier* of the king's household was his chamber, its role tended to diverge, in some respects, from that of its English equivalent. Its personnel was small in number, comprising the chamberlain and the valets of the chamber. These rendered personal service to the king—and included his barber, surgeon, tailor, and *épicier*.[146] The three or so chamberlains waited upon the king and slept in his chamber by turns, taking (like their English contemporaries) meals, fees, and livery of robes. They also kept the registers in which homages performed by the king's vassals were recorded.[147] One of the chamberlains sat in the *Chambre aux Deniers* (the household's accounting office) and oversaw much of the financial business of that department.[148] The distinction between 'public' and household finance in the French kingdom at this time was not always clearly drawn, a situation echoed in part in England. This was, however, largely reflected in the unique evolution of the wardrobe, rather than the chamber, as a 'public' accounting office.

In France, as in England, a detectable rise in the status and political significance of the office of chamberlain is apparent during the early fourteenth century. Its most spectacular manifestation was the career of Enguerran de Marigny (d.1315), formerly *panetier* in the household of the queen, Joan of Navarre, where he appears in July 1298.[149] As the household officer responsible for the *paneterie* (pantry) Marigny's function was to supply the basic food requirements of the queen's entourage. The skills demanded in this office clearly served him well. His financial (and, to some extent, diplomatic) acumen was soon to be put to the test in the service of Philip the Fair. Joan of Navarre bequeathed him a legacy of

---

[146] Lalou, 'Le fonctionnement de l'Hôtel du roi', 150–1.

[147] See M. Vale, 'The world of the courts', in M. Bent and A. Wathey (eds.), *Fauvel Studies: Allegory, Chronicle, Music, and Image in Paris, Bibliothèque Nationale de France, MS français 146* (Oxford, 1998), 593; Lehugeur, *De hospitio Regis*, 43–6; for the French royal household ordinances see BN, MS fr.7852 and AN, JJ.57.

[148] J. Favier, *Un conseiller de Philippe le Bel: Enguerran de Marigny* (Paris, 1963), 80–1.

[149] See Vale, 'The world of the courts', 592–3; Favier, *Un conseiller de Philippe le Bel*, 57–71.

500 *livres* just before he moved from her household to the king's, probably in 1304.[150] In that year he succeeded his former patron and fellow-Norman, Hugues de Bouville, as chamberlain to the king. This was the decisive moment in Marigny's career—as it was in that of Piers Gaveston, his English contemporary.[151] The office of chamberlain gave direct and immediate access to the king. By 1308, Marigny, like Gaveston, had become principal chamberlain, or chamberlain-in-chief, having success-fully secured the king's favour, displaying his evident competence not only in the domestic affairs of the household but, by extension, in finance and diplomacy.[152] The subsequent careers of Marigny and Gaveston bear some similarities: both fell as spectacularly as they had risen, Gaveston in 1312 and Marigny in 1315.

But in France the function of the chamber as a household department changed markedly in the early fourteenth century. It became less of a household *métier*, or service department, and more of a financial and ceremonial office, forming one of six offices which were distinguished from the *métiers* in the ordinances of 1306 and 1316.[153] These were the *aumônerie* (almonry), chapel, chancery, *Chambre aux Deniers*, and the office of the *maîtres de l'hôtel*. Since Louis IX's household ordinance of 1261, in which it had played a significant part, the chamber had been steadily superseded by the *fourrière* (quarter-master's office) as the department responsible for the king's lodgings, and for his ushers, porters, and messengers. Again, in the early fourteenth century, the separate department of the *argenterie* was detached from the chamber.[154] By 1315, the keeper of the king's plate and jewels (*garde des joyaux*) had also left the personnel of the chamber. Thus it can be shown that

dès le début du xive siècle, la Chambre, à cause de l'importance prise par ses membres, de par leur proximité étroite avec la personne royale, n'existe plus en tant que métier: la Fourrière prend sa place.[155]

[since the beginning of the fourteenth century, the Chamber, because of its members' importance, through their close proximity to the king's person, ceased to exist as a household office: the *Fourrière* took its place.]

[150] See Favier, *Un conseiller de Philippe le Bel*, 58–60.
[151] Cf. Chaplais, *Piers Gaveston*, 102–4.
[152] Favier, *Un conseiller de Philippe le Bel*, 113–28.
[153] Lalou, 'Le fonctionnement de l'hôtel du roi', 147.
[154] See L. Douet-d'Arcq (ed.), *Recueil des comptes de l'Argenterie des rois de France* (Paris, 1851), and *Nouveau recueil des comptes de l'Argenterie des rois de France* (Paris, 1874); Lalou, 'Le fonctionnement de l'hôtel du roi', 150, 152.
[155] Lalou, 'Le fonctionnement de l'hôtel du roi', 150.

Its function was to furnish 'le feurre, les coustes et la buche', also providing a body of ushers and porters, both as permanent staff in certain royal residences, and as part of the itinerant household.

The pattern followed in the principalities of northern France and the Low Countries was a variation on this theme. In Flanders, Brabant, and Hainault, the 'chamber' remained essentially part of the domestic organization of the princely household, acting as a provisioning department whose functions were often parallel to, or merged with, those of the *fourrière*. In Flanders, the household accounts reveal the chamber to be a provisioning department, supplying spices, butter, and so on to the count, receiving purveyances of supplies, and acting as a quarter-master's office.[156] In 1293–4, it accounted for four per cent of total household expenditure—a very small percentage when compared with the kitchen and buttery. It appears to have possessed no ceremonial or other role, unlike that of the chamber in the kingdoms of England and France. But the hereditary chamberlain of Flanders certainly had ceremonial functions apparently unconnected, by the thirteenth century, with the household department whose name he bore.[157] In Brabant, the evidence suggests that the duke's chamber was again essentially responsible for commissariat and lodgings, including the purchase and hiring of beds for the *maisnie* or retinue.[158] In Artois, there was no separate entry in the household accounts for 'chamber', as the *fourrière* (following the model of royal France) performed all its domestic functions.[159] Nor is any specific entry for 'chamber' found in the Hainault household accounts, although members of its staff are recorded receiving wages, liveries, and gifts.[160] Their importance, however, seems to have grown during the Bavarian period during the later fourteenth century.[161] In both Flanders and Hainault, moreover, the chamber was also responsible for the custody of the count's plate and jewels—as it was in England under Edward II, as well as Majorca and Aragon, and France before the *argenterie* and keepership

---

[156] See the account for 1293–4 in RAG, Wyffels (Chron. suppl.) 188, no. 314*bis*. Also see above, pp. 43–4.

[157] See below, pp. 117–18. Also Fig. 13.

[158] AGR, CC, R 2420, m. 2 (1345); R 2421, 2419 (1347).

[159] See, for early examples of complete accounts for all six household departments (1300, 1302), ADPC, A.162 and A.178; De Loisne, 'Une cour féodale', 94–102, 125–34.

[160] See *De rekeningen*, ed. Smit, i. 389–93.

[161] AEM, Trésorerie, Recueil 70, no. 23 (1384–5); Recueil 71, no. 12: livery of *cottez des cambrelens* (1394).

of the jewels became detached from it after 1315.[162] Chamberlains thus became associated with the safe-keeping and security of a ruler's most precious liquid assets.

By the beginning of the second quarter of the fourteenth century, the scene had thus been set for that rise of chamberlains, chamber knights, and chamber squires which was to characterize the political life (and, in part, induce some of the political crises) of the 1380s and 1390s. In England, France, and the Low Countries, the ruler's *familiares* were now to be found, more often than not, and in greater numbers, holding office and title in his chamber. A rise in levels of household consumption and expenditure between about 1270 and 1380 was partly a product of this inflationary tendency. A growth in the size of the immediate entourage, in which the chamber formed a part of the upper household, was also evident. As a means of binding nobles to the service of princes, and enabling a more permanent dialogue to take place between them, court office-holding performed a vital function. But the maintenance of larger princely establishments made them increasingly expensive, and a ruler's resources had to be carefully deployed in order to meet that expenditure. It is to questions of income, expenditure, and accounting that we must now turn.

---

[162] For England, see above, pp. 59–63; for Majorca and Aragon, pp. 61–2; for Flanders, ADN, B.451, no. 6291 (1331); for Hainault, AEM, Trésorerie, Cartulaire 19, fo. 117v (1304); and *De rekeningen*, ed. Smit, i. 214 (1325).

Chapter 3

CONSUMPTION AND
EXPENDITURE

1. Economics and accountancy

Any study of princely courts during the later thirteenth and fourteenth centuries, as we saw in the last chapter, demands that some attention be paid to the material underpinnings of aristocratic life. The study of material culture (*Sachkultur*) is an essential tool in the analysis and interpretation of consumption, expenditure, and their place in court life. To speak of an 'infrastructure' upon which the increasingly elaborate edifice of later medieval court life was built, moreover, is to acknowledge the influence of Marxist or quasi-Marxist interpretations of later medieval culture. Yet the identification and examination of the infrastructural conditions for later medieval cultural and social developments need not necessarily be cast, as it has been by some Marxist historians, in a doctrinaire or dialectical mould. Economic forces clearly had an impact upon all forms of consumption, and deterministic interpretations can be found in such works as Friedrich Antal's *Florentine Painting and its Social Background*, Arnold Hauser's *Social History of Art*, or those of other Marxist historians of art and culture.[1] Without some consideration of the material conditions in which the court evolved, however, any picture would not only be incomplete, but distorted. Both 'material' culture (*Sachkultur*) and the patronage and cultivation of the arts rested upon a financial and economic base which can, at least to some extent, be established from our sources. The study of *Sachkultur*, as understood in Central and Eastern Europe, has certainly had a Marxist dimension and doctrinal framework. But it also has a free-standing, non-Marxist

---

[1] F. Antal, *Florentine Painting and its Social Background* (London, 1947); A. Hauser, *The Social History of Art*, 4 vols. (London, 1968).

existence, represented by such bodies as the Austrian Institute for the Study of Material Culture (Krems-an-der-Donau).[2] No study of the later medieval court can afford to neglect or ignore such approaches and their yields.[3]

The lines dividing patronage and consumption of visual and applied art from 'material' culture can often become blurred, and artificially isolating them can only have a distorting effect on any study of princely courts. A civilization which set a high price upon consumption—both conspicuous and otherwise—and display, upon material objects as symbols, and as media of exchange and gift-giving, was rooted in the material world. The study of courts has not always acknowledged this fact. A perfectly legitimate concern with 'court culture' has led historians, art historians, and literary scholars to adopt a narrower definition of 'culture' than is always desirable. A broader view might extend the field of vision beyond the 'fine' arts, literature, and music, to the applied arts, as well as to codes of behaviour, life-styles, and aristocratic *mentalités*. This wider definition need not necessarily lead to the much-criticized approach adopted by cultural historians such as Johan Huizinga (1872–1945), whose *Herfsttij der Middeleeuwen*—the *Waning* or, more correctly, *Autumn of the Middle Ages*—published in 1919, was subtitled *A Study of the Forms of Life, Thought and Art in France and the Netherlands in the Fourteenth and Fifteenth Centuries* (1919).[4] Huizinga's Hegelian intellectual formation, and his tendency to typologize, reflected in the constant use of phrases such as 'forms and modes of thought', 'ideal forms', 'poles of the mind', and above all 'spirit'

[2] See e.g. H. Appelt (ed.), *Adelige Sachkultur des Spätmittelalters. Internationaler Kongress, Krems an der Donau, 22. bis 25. September 1980* (Vienna, 1982), esp. 133–67, 195–214, 343–63 for studies of some material aspects of 'courtly' culture. Also id. (ed.), *Terminologie und Typologie mittelalterlicher Sachguter: Das Beispiel der Kleidung* (Vienna, 1988).

[3] For further instances see R. Delort, *Le Commerce des fourrures en Occident à la fin du moyen âge*, 2 vols. (Rome, 1978); F. Piponnier, *Costume et vie sociale: La cour d'Anjou, xive–xve siècle* (Paris and The Hague, 1970); F. Lachaud, 'Textiles, Furs and Liveries: a Study of the Material Culture of the Court of Edward I (1272–1307)' (unpub. Oxford D.Phil. thesis, 1992); and for a survey of methodology and recent historiography, see J. M. Pesez, 'Histoire de la culture matérielle' in J. Le Goff (ed.), *La Nouvelle Histoire* (2nd edn., Paris, 1988), 191–227.

[4] See J. Huizinga, *The Waning of the Middle Ages*, tr. F. Hopman (Harmondsworth, 1965). The best and most recent edition of Huizinga's original Dutch text is J. Huizinga, *Herfsttij der Middeleeuwen*, ed. A. van der Lem (Amsterdam, 1997). A new English translation has appeared as *The Autumn of the Middle Ages*, ed. and tr. R. J. Payton and U. Mammitzsch (Chicago, 1996). For an excellent recent study of Huizinga's masterpiece see W. Krul, 'In the mirror of Van Eyck: Johan Huizinga's *Autumn of the Middle Ages*', *Journal of Medieval and Early Modern Studies*, 27 (1997), 353–84.

(*Geest, Geist*), left the material foundations upon which later medieval civilization rested largely untouched.

The world of mundane reality is to be found in other quarters than the literary and narrative sources used by Huizinga. The pioneer work of late nineteenth-century scholars and antiquarians, such as Dehaisnes, Devillers, and the other editors of financial and administrative documents relating to both the art patronage and material existence of princely courts, was neither taken up nor exploited by Huizinga or his immediate successors.[5] Nor was the impetus given by the work of Aby Warburg (1866–1929) to the study of the material conditions in which Italian art patronage and artistic production operated during the Renaissance effectively followed up. Warburg's approach—as that of a private scholar outside the academic establishment—was regarded as too eccentric and individualistic to be incorporated into the study of either art history or *Geistesgeschichte* until long after his death.[6] Yet one means of putting Huizinga's hypotheses to the test lies in the examination of archival and documentary sources. If daily life in a later medieval courtly setting was as he described it, then where better to find evidence than in the daily documentation of courts and households? The recent surge of interest, especially in Germany, in the study of 'daily life' (*Alltag*) has meant that what was once belittled, if not despised, by professional historians as unworthy of serious attention, has been restored to its rightful place in historical writing.[7] It is to the documentation of the *Alltag* that we must turn in order to redress the balance.

[5] See *Documents et extraits divers concernant l'histoire de l'art dans la Flandre, l'Artois et le Hainaut avant le xve siécle*, ed. C. Dehaisnes, 2 vols. (Lille, 1886). Vol. i covers the period up to 1373, vol. ii the period 1374–1401. This was a pioneer work in the amassing of material, but editorial standards were not of the highest order and many documents are printed inaccurately with significant, and sometimes unrecorded, omissions. See also 'Cartulaires de Hainaut (1071–1310)', ed. F. A. T. de Reiffenberg, in *Monuments pour servir à l'histoire des provinces de Namur, de Hainaut et de Luxembourg*, i (Brussels, 1844); and iii, ed. L. Devillers (1874); *Cartulaires des comtes de Hainaut*, ed. Devillers.

[6] See A. Warburg, *Bildniskunst und florentisches Burgertum. Domenico Ghirlandaio in Santa Trinita: Die Bildnisse des Lorenzo de' Medici und seiner Angehoren* (Leipzig, 1902) and 'Flandrische Kunst und florentinische Frührenaissance', in his *Gesammelte Schriften*, ed. G. Bing, i (Leipzig and Berlin, 1932), 182–206, 370–80. Also, for Warburg's life and work, E. H. Gombrich, *Aby Warburg: An Intellectual Biography* (London, 1970), esp. 307–24.

[7] See H. Schuppert, 'Spätmittelalterliche Didaktik als Quelle für adeliges Alltagsleben?', in Appelt, *Adelige Sachkultur*, 215–57; A. A. Arkenbout, 'Das tägliche Leben des Frank van Borsselen (+ 1470)', ibid. 311–26. See also the contributions by Paravicini, Studt, Boockmann, Uyttebrouck, and Kubinyi in W. Paravicini (ed.), *Alltag bei Hofe* (Sigmaringen, 1995), 9–30, 113–36, 137–47, 149–70, 197–215.

The sources for an examination of such fundamental issues as consumption and expenditure in princely households are to be found scattered through a mass of financial and administrative documents, which often form broken series of data and can be difficult to interpret. It is to the much larger number of surviving household accounts (*comptes de l'hôtel*) that one has to go in order to penetrate beyond theoretical and prescriptive sources, as well as literary topoi, so that the realities of court life can be perceived.[8] To understand the problems involved in analysing financial documentation of this kind dating from the century between *c.*1270 and 1380, we must, first, address a number of questions, above all those concerning the forms of account and types of accounting procedure.

If the issue of household ordinances was a means whereby the costs of maintaining princely establishments were subjected to a modest degree of control, the drawing-up of household accounts was primarily determined by the need to record purchases of all kinds and to account for cash spent.[9] Although some rudimentary forms of budgetary management and forecasting were known from an early date, the major aim of household accountancy appears to have been to act as a simple check upon sums of money both received and spent over a given period of time. It also served as a means of tracing cash as it passed to the various household departments, and through the hands of those who serviced them. Household accounts assumed a variety of forms.[10] During the twelfth century, various types of written account had evolved,[11] replacing the originally oral procedures of accounting, which had been supported in some cases by written surveys or 'customaries' (texts recording and confirming rights of lordship and the exaction of dues).[12] The latter had simply listed the sums to be derived from fixed food farms (*firmae*) or renders in kind, and were monastic in origin. They might act as a yardstick

---

[8] For lists and surveys of these accounts see, for England, *Lists of Documents relating to the Household and Wardrobe. John–Edward I* (London, 1964) and *Records of the Wardrobe and Household, 1285–1286*, ed. B. F. and C. R. Byerly (London, 1977); for France and the Low Countries, R.-H. Bautier and J. Sornay, *Les Sources de l'histoire économique et sociale du moyen âge: les états de la maison de Bourgogne*, i. 2. *Les principautés du Nord* (Paris, 1984). This volume lists extant household accounts for Flanders, Artois, Brabant, Hainault, Luxemburg, and Namur.

[9] See above, pp. 51–2.

[10] See *Household Accounts from Medieval England*, i. 10–12.

[11] Ibid., i. 10–17; M. T. Clanchy, *From Memory to Written Record: England 1066–1307* (London, 1979), 55–107.

[12] See *Dialogus de Scaccario*, ed. C. Johnson, (rev. edn., Oxford, 1983), 128–35; *Household Accounts from Medieval England*, i. 10–12.

against which actual receipts and issues (expenditure) might be set and contrasted.

In England, the inflationary conditions of the period from c.1180 to 1220 may have contributed to the emergence of written household accounts, drawn up in a different format from the earlier surveys, 'extents', and customaries.[13] In both England and continental Europe, however, a more general tendency towards the compilation of formal written accounts was already well under way by 1150. As government—with its attendant clerical bureaucracy—became more complex, and as the level of sophistication and luxury with which rulers surrounded themselves began to rise, the appearance of royal and princely household accounts, rather than surveys and customaries, may have been symptomatic of more profound changes in western society.[14] The greater volume of monetary circulation, and the higher degree of liquidity in the thirteenth-century western economy also contributed to this tendency. Movements in precious metals, including the discovery of new seams of silver (especially in Bohemia) in the course of the thirteenth and early fourteenth centuries, appear to have increased the volume of coin in circulation. In north-west Europe, however, the effects of drastic currency manipulation by French kings, above all Philip the Fair (1285–1314), did not favour monetary stability. The principalities of the Low Countries, as well as royal France, felt the impact of the debasements of the 1290s and early 1300s keenly.[15] England remained exempt from such measures, and the silver pound sterling was often used as a stable base for currency transactions in the Low Countries, beside the gold Florentine florin.[16] A generally high level

---

[13] See P. D. A. Harvey, 'The English inflation of 1180–1220', Past and Present, 61 (1973), 3–30; and, for European continental evidence for a similar evolution—apparently not determined by inflation—see Fiscal accounts of Catalonia under the early Count-Kings (1151–1213), ed. T. N. Bisson, 2 vols. (London, 1984), i. 154–6.

[14] See, for the 'commercial revolution' of the 'long' thirteenth century' (c.1160–c.1340) and its effects, P. Spufford, Money and its Use in Medieval Europe (Cambridge, 1988), 240–63: 'from rural rent to courtly living, from banking and international trade to public revenue and military service, the long thirteenth century of the commercial revolution witnessed a series of fundamental transformations, each associated with a complete change in the scale of, and attitudes to, the use of money' (263). Household accountancy formed part of the response to these new conditions.

[15] See N. J. Mayhew and D. R. Walker, 'Crockards and Pollards: imitation and the problem of fineness in a silver coinage', in Edwardian Monetary Affairs, (1279–1344), ed. N. J. Mayhew (BAR 36, Oxford, 1977), 125–37; H. A. Miskimin, Money, Prices and Foreign Exchange in Fourteenth-Century France (New Haven, 1963), 6–30.

[16] See M. Prestwich, 'Edward I's monetary policies and their consequences', EcHR 2nd ser. 22 (1969), 415–16; Mayhew and Walker, 'Crockards and Pollards', 127–8.

of economic prosperity, however, prevailed in the whole region until the famines of 1315–17[17] and the outbreak of Flemish revolts after 1322, followed by the Anglo-French war (1337) and the onset of plague (1348–9).[18] But there was no dearth of commodities and services, from the most basic to the most sophisticated and luxurious, available for the provisioning—and indulgence—of princely households and their members.

The environment in which the princely court moved, during the century before Burgundian hegemony in the Low Countries, was increasingly an urban one.[19] They clearly continued to depend upon the rural economy for basic foodstuffs and supplies, as in earlier periods. But the resources of the expanding towns now strove to meet the rising needs and expectations of princes and those who surrounded them. All thirteenth-century royal and princely households were itinerant, some more so than others.[20] They began to differ from their twelfth-century predecessors, however, in the extent to which they increasingly gravitated towards towns, both great and small. Urban growth in northern France and the Low Countries, achieving spectacular results in Flanders, Brabant, and (to a lesser extent) Holland and Zeeland, made the towns natural centres of distribution, exchange, and supply to meet the demands of princes.[21] Thus the clerks and receivers responsible for household accounting became increasingly accustomed to dealing with suppliers, merchants, tradesmen, artisans, money-lenders, and bankers who operated within

[17] See H. S. Lucas, 'The great European famine of 1315, 1316 and 1317', *Speculum*, 5 (1930), 343–77; I. Kershaw, 'The great famine and agrarian crisis in England, 1315–1322', *P&P* 59 (1973), 3–50.

[18] See H. S. Lucas, *The Low Countries and the Hundred Years War, 1326–1347* (Ann Arbor, 1929, repr. Philadelphia, 1976), 1–6, 200–3.

[19] For economic explanations of this tendency see Spufford, *Money and its Use*, 249–50, where 'liberation from the necessity of living in the countryside' is attributed to the higher proportion of their incomes which rulers now received in money, not kind. This reduced the need for constant perambulation between rural estates and concentrated the flow of silver into towns, where it was increasingly spent 'at court' on 'conspicuous extravagance to emphasise political importance, or on foreign luxuries only available in such cities' (249). See also J. Le Goff, 'The town as an agent of civilisation, c.1200–c.1500', in *The Fontana Economic History of Europe: The Middle Ages*, ed. C. M. Cipolla (London, 1973), 77–86, and below, pp. 137–8, 153–4.

[20] See E. Lalou, 'Vincennes dans les itinéraires de Philippe le Bel et de ses trois fils (1285–1328)', in Chapelot and Lalou, *Vincennes aux origines de l'état moderne*, 191–212.

[21] See Spufford, *Money and its Use*, 249–52; and for an early, influential interpretation of the evidence for concentration of demand, money supply, and banking facilities in towns see R. de Roover,'The commercial revolution of the thirteenth century', *Bulletin of the Business History Society*, 16 (1942), 34–9, repr. in F. C. Lane and J. C. Riemersma (eds.), *Enterprise and Secular Change* (London, 1953), 80–5.

an urban context. Sometimes these dealings were channelled through the great fairs—St Ives' in England, or the fairs in Champagne for northern France and the Low Countries. Some of these officials developed such expertise in this respect that they rose to great heights in the service of their royal or princely masters. Enguerran de Marigny or the financial expert Geoffroi Coquatrix were not the only examples.[22] Laymen such as Marigny were flanked by clerks such as Thierry d'Hérisson, who rose in the household service of the counts of Artois to become bishop of Arras.[23] The number of English king's clerks who had served their time in the financial offices of the wardrobe and household and progressed to become canons, deans of cathedral chapters, and often bishops, is too large a subject for detailed inclusion.[24] All these men dealt with suppliers and producers whose role in the burgeoning urban economy was increasingly significant. As princely demands became more exacting and elaborate, the financial and other services provided by towns played a larger part in meeting the needs of household provision and in influencing the practice of household accountancy.

Thus the rise of banking and credit finance during the thirteenth century, dominated—though not entirely monopolized—by Italians, also had an impact upon the ways in which princes received, spent, and accounted for their incomes. At its most obvious, Italian hegemony was reflected in the steady penetration of rulers' financial administrations north of the Alps by Lombards, Florentines, and Genoese.[25] This was

---

[22] For Marigny, see Favier, *Un Conseiller de Philippe le Bel*, 57–64; for Coquatrix (d.1321), J. R. Strayer, *The Reign of Philip the Fair* (Princeton, 1980), 119–20. Coquatrix was *Maître de la Chambre des Comptes* in 1315–16 and 1319–21, and was a member of the Parisian confraternity of pilgrims to St James of Compostella. He presented a fine gold and silver-gilt reliquary statue of the saint, which survives, to the shrine there in *c*.1321. See F. Baron (ed.), *Les Fastes du gothique* (Paris, 1981), 225–6 (cat. no. 179). The figure bears a placard with the inscription: *In hoc vase auri quod tenet iste imago est dens Beati Jacobi Apostoli que Gaudfridus Coquatriz civis Parisiensis dedit huic Ecclesie. Orate pro eo.*

[23] See P. Bougard, 'La fortune et les comptes de Thierry d'Hérisson', *BEC* 123 (1965), 126–78; for accounting material relating to him as clerk of the treasury of Robert II's and Mahaut's *Chambre* see ADPC, A.135, no. 114; A.139, A.140, A.145, A.187, no. 2, A.203, A.207, no. 2.

[24] Tout, *Chapters*, ii. 14–21.

[25] See R. W. Kaeuper, *Bankers to the Crown: The Riccardi of Lucca and Edward I* (Princeton, 1973), 75–131; A. Sapori, *La compagnia dei Frescobaldi in Inghilterra* (Florence, 1947), 35–84; Y. Renouard, 'I Frescobaldi in Guyenne (1307–1312)', in his *Etudes d'histoire médiévale*, ii (Paris, 1968), 1059–68; B. D. Lyon and A. E. Verhulst, *Medieval Finance: A Comparison of Financial Institutions in Northwestern Europe* (Bruges and Providence, RI, 1967), 87–105.

helped by the rising level of anti-Jewish sentiment, often leading to expulsion of the money-lending Jews, at this time. Italian penetration also accompanied the decline of the fairs in Champagne as sources of credit and other financial services, leading to the rise of 'native' merchant-bankers and entrepreneurs in, for example, the *comtés* of Flanders and Artois.[26] The development of taxation systems during the thirteenth century also favoured this shift of economic and financial gravity towards the towns. England was a precocious pioneer in such fiscal matters (though not in the relatively limited size and growth of its towns), but by the mid- to late thirteenth century, many north European principalities were developing forms of taxation which went beyond the limited parameters of feudal aid and domain-based dues.[27] In England, France, Flanders, Hainault, and Artois, Italians are therefore found as receivers, farmers of tolls and customs, and as tax-collectors, as well as primary creditors of both princes and nobles. The names of Riccardi, Frescobaldi, Bardi, Peruzzi, Fini, Pessagno, and so on run through the accounting material of this period, and accounts, drawn up in Latin or French, are sometimes annotated in their native Italian.[28] Although they did not transform the accounting systems of the more conservative rulers, their presence was certainly felt—and sometimes resented—among the primarily clerical bureaucracies of the time.

Unlike the Italian banking houses, rulers were less concerned with the calculation of profit (and loss) than with the art of basic housekeeping. The commonest form of early household account was the so-called 'diet' account. Normally organized under the constituent departments of a

[26] See R. K. Berlow, 'The development of business techniques used at the fairs of Champagne from the end of the twelfth century to the middle of the thirteenth century', *Studies in Medieval and Renaissance History*, 8 (1971), 28–35; G. Espinas, 'Jehan Boine Broke, bourgeois et drapier douaisien [?–1310 environ]', *Vierteljahrschrift für Sozial- und Wirtschaftsgeschichte*, 2 (1904), 34–121, 219–53, 282–412; J. Lestocquoy, *Aux origines de la bourgeoisie: les villes de Flandre et d'Italie sous le gouvernement des patriciens* (Paris, 1952); and his *Patriciens du moyen-âge: les dynasties bourgeoises d'Arras du xie au xve siècle* (Arras, 1945).

[27] See J. R. Strayer and C. H. Taylor, *Studies in Early French Taxation* (Cambridge, Mass., 1939); S. Reynolds, *Kingdoms and Communities in Western Europe, 900–1300* (Oxford, 1984), 305–19; W. M. Ormrod, 'The West European monarchies in the later Middle Ages', in R. Bonney (ed.), *Economic Systems and State Finance* (Oxford, 1995), 123–60.

[28] See Kaeuper, *Bankers to the Crown*, 124–31; for the accounts of the Sienese Tommaso Fini, appointed receiver of Flanders in 1306, see E. E. Kittell, *From Ad Hoc to Routine: A Case Study in Medieval Bureaucracy* (Philadelphia, 1991), 110–31, and G. Bigwood, 'Un relevé de recettes tenu par le personnel de Thomas Fini, receveur général de Flandre', in *Mélanges d'histoire offerts à Henri Pirenne*, i (Brussels, 1926), 31–42.

household—generally the pantry, buttery, kitchen, and marshalsea or stable—the account *per dietas* (hence 'diet', meaning the nature and quantity of food consumed daily) consisted of entries for each department on a day by day, or week by week, basis.[29] The precise number of departments might vary from household to household, but the 'diet' account was a flexible vehicle for a limited purpose, well adapted to both static and itinerant establishments. All the major (and most of the minor) royal and princely houses of Europe had developed forms of this account by the end of the thirteenth century. The earliest record of domestic expenditure of this kind is that found in the archives of the count-kings of Catalonia (1156–7), followed by more formal accounts for the same rulers in the 1180s.[30] Some early thirteenth-century accounts (from the bishopric of Passau and from the kingdom of France) reveal evidence for budgetary planning and calculation, a feature apparently lacking in the earliest English household accounts.[31] The surviving accounts for daily expenses of Wolfger, bishop of Passau (1191–1204), moreover, are notable for their inclusion of payments to minstrels and entertainers, including the *minnesinger* Walter von der Vogelweide.[32] Such entries become common everywhere by the mid- to late thirteenth century.

The first diet, or daily, account to survive from England is that of an unidentified private household of the late twelfth century.[33] It is followed by the first royal accounts which concern themselves specifically with household receipts and expenditure (the *mise* and *prestita* rolls), dating from the reign of John (1199–1216).[34] These are succeeded by fragments of a diet account for the departments of the royal household under Henry III in 1225–6.[35] The fundamental format of the diet account was adopted

[29] *Household Accounts from Medieval England*, i. 7; also e.g. see Figs. 6, 7, 13.

[30] See *Fiscal Accounts of Catalonia*, ed. Bisson, i. 13, 18, 49–52, 90, 155; ii. 3–43, 101–3, 118, 120–3.

[31] See A. Hofer, 'Die Reiserechnungen des Bischofs Wolfger von Passau', *Beiträge zur Geschichte der deutschen Sprache und Litteratur*, 17 (1893), 441–549; F. Lot and R. Fawtier, *Le premier budget de la monarchie francaise: le compte général de 1202–1203* (Paris, 1932).

[32] See M. Heyne, *Fünf Bücher deutscher Hausaltertumer von den altesten geschichtlichen Zeiten bis zum 16. Jahrhundert*, i (1899), 25–30.

[33] PRO, E.101/631/1, printed in *Household Accounts from Medieval England*, i. 107–10. It is possible that the account relates to the household of Abbot Samson of Bury St Edmunds.

[34] *Rotuli de Liberate ac de Misis et Praestitis Regnante Johanne*, ed. T. D. Hardy (London, 1844); J. C. Holt, 'Praestita roll 14–18 John' in *Pipe Roll 17 John*, ed. R. A. Brown (Pipe Roll Society, n.s. 37, 1964), 69–80, 85–100.

[35] See *Roll of Divers Accounts for the early years of the Reign of Henry III*, ed. F. A. Cazel (PRS, n.s. 44, 1982), 93–102.

generally throughout north-west Europe. Alongside it, and often contained within it, ran another form of accounting—that known as the
'journal'. This was the daily record from which the diet account, usually
in summary form, might be compiled, and from which weekly and
monthly totals of expenditure were ultimately derived.

A further distinction began to be made during the thirteenth century
between the daily costs of supplying and provisioning a household with
basic necessities, on the one hand, and the disbursement of cash for other
commodities, including luxuries, on the other.[36] In England, the royal
household department which was responsible for such outlay was the
wardrobe. True to its origin, as the *garderobe* in which clothes and other
fabrics were kept, the wardrobe became the purchaser and receiver of
certain kinds of more expensive item—cloth (some of it for liveries),
luxury textiles, spices, wax, gold, silver and silver-gilt plate, jewels, and
so on.[37] Where it did not exist as a separate household office, as in parts
of continental Europe, the wardrobe's functions were assumed within
princely households by the clerk or receiver responsible for the household
accounts. Hence in Flanders, Artois, and Hainault, the account headings
known as *grosses parties, mises extraordinaires,* and *parties foraines* comprised—among other things—cash payments for commodities and
items very similar to those purchased by the wardrobe in England.[38] But
the development of the wardrobe as a major financial and accounting
office—which became a war treasury under Edward I and Edward II—
did not take place outside an English context.

However, the bald figures derived from the receipts and issues sections
of household diet accounts can mislead, when estimates of the total provisions received and consumed are attempted. These monetary sums—
representing cash received and spent—do not include the provision of
substantial quantities of items drawn from store or stock. In most cases
these are not recorded as purchases in the diet accounts, although a cash
value was sometimes given them, as in Flanders and (from time to time)
in Hainault-Holland. These were the items described as *pourvances* in
Flanders and as *pourvéances* or *pourvanches* in Hainault-Holland, equivalent in most respects to the *de providentia* section of English household

[36] See *Household Accounts from Medieval England,* i. 7–8, 50–1.
[37] See C. H. Johnson, 'The system of account in the wardrobe of Edward I', *TRHS* 4th
ser. 6 (1923), 50–72. See Appendices II–V.
[38] See Lyon and Verhulst, *Medieval Finance,* 128–39.

accounts.[39] The *pourvéances* might refer to bulk purchases, to provisions found in store at ducal or comital castles, manors, and other residences, or to the supply, by the receivers of a given area, at no monetary cost to the ruler, of items ranging (in the Hainault accounts, for instance) from wax and spices to cheeses and herrings.

Without the inclusion of commodities supplied, sometimes in great bulk, by means of *pourvéances*, our picture of the level of consumption within a great household remains incomplete. Where the records of such sources of supply are completely lacking, there is no way to make good this deficiency. In some instances, the formal household accounts do not even mention the supply or purchase of many commodities for consumption. But entries relating to these items are sometimes to be found in the accounts of receivers, *prévôts*, and other officers within a ruler's domains. Thus our knowledge of the household consumption and expenditure of Edouard I, count of Bar (1302–36), is derived from both the registers of general accounts for the *comté* and from those of its constituent *prévôtés* (Mousson, Gondrecourt, Briey, Sancy, Lamarche, and so on).[40] Similarly, some of the earliest surviving material for provisioning and other expenditure in the household of Robert II, count of Artois, is to be found in the accounts of the *baillis* and receiver-general of the *comté*.[41] In the *comté* of Hainault, some of the *baillis'* accounts, and those of officials such the *receveur* of Binche and other comital residences, contain important information about household consumption.[42] It is always necessary to remember that the figures for cash payments in the household accounts *stricto sensu* often provide only one part of a more complex story, and that any analysis which rests upon them alone is bound to distort the true situation.

There were other forms of household account besides the diet account and the journal. These included the accounts of individual departments (for example, kitchen, buttery, or pantry); and livery accounts, often in the form of rolls (as in England, Flanders, and Hainault-Holland)

[39] See, for Flanders, *Het Memoriaal van Jehan Makiel, klerk en ontvanger van Gwijde van Dampierre (1270–1275)*, ed. J. Buntinx (Brussels, 1944), pp. xxv–xxxvii; for Hainault-Holland, *De rekeningen*, ed. Smit, iii. 1–133; for England, *Household Accounts from Medieval England*, i. 20–1, 50–1. See Fig. 10.

[40] H. Collin, 'Le train de vie d'Edouard Ier, comte de Bar (1302–1336)', *BPHCTHS* (1969), 793–816.

[41] *Le Compte général du receveur d'Artois pour 1303–1304*, ed. B. Delmaire (Brussels, 1977), *passim*.

[42] See Bautier and Sornay, *Les Sources*, 555–63, 575–6.

recording the purchase and distribution of liveries in cloth, furs, and cash to both members and non-members of a household.[43] Sometimes discrete lists of all those on the 'establishment' of a household acted as supporting evidence, or *pièces justificatives*, to the accounts (for instance, in Flanders, Artois, Holland-Hainault), and separate records of wages paid to household members would often contain information about their presence or absence (England, Artois).[44] Beside all this enrolled or engrossed material (that is, recorded in rolls or registers), substantial quantities of subsidiary documents also survive, including warrants, vouchers, quittances, and receipts. These provided the accountants and auditors with justificatory evidence for disbursements, which was normally summarized in the final, formal household account. The most complete surviving collections of such subsidiary material derive from England and Artois.

The purpose for which the accounts were compiled must therefore always be kept in mind—they could furnish supporting material for accounting officers who were obliged to submit justification and authentification, often under seal, for all disbursements which they made on the ruler's behalf. It was not the aim of these documents to provide readily comparable figures, based on the calculation of average daily, weekly, monthly, or annual expenditure, so that estimates might be made and budgets drawn up. Such moves did occur, but only in exceptional circumstances, normally associated with financial and political crisis.[45] This means that we have to adapt the evidence provided by household accounts to other purposes, all the while bearing in mind that we are using them for ends for which they were never intended. The 'raw' figures they provide have thus to be worked upon and converted into meaningful units of comparison and contrast if any comparative study of courts and households is to be achieved.

2. Daily needs and expenditure

The considerations mentioned above are especially relevant when gross figures for household expenditure are examined. Difficulties in arriving

---

[43] See below, pp. 101–5. See Tables 15(a)–(c).

[44] See Tables 17, 20, 25, 26.

[45] See below, pp. 87–93. A good example (for Flanders) is to be found in ADN, B.1569, fos. 60r–71v (1332).

at precise totals for overall expenditure are often so great that we have to be content only with orders of magnitude. But in some cases, greater confidence is justified. The English evidence—the most complete and continuous of any to survive from this period—is susceptible to quantitative treatment at quite a sophisticated level. To arrive at annual totals of household expenditure is not unduly difficult: we can thus reckon that Edward I was spending about 12,860 pounds sterling on his household in the year from November 1304 to November 1305.[46] This was close to the average for annual expenditure over the last years of his reign. In 1304–5 the kitchen accounted for almost half of total expenditure. By 1307–8, however, expenditure had risen to 20,240 pounds—of which 960 pounds were spent on the kitchen, 780 on hall and chamber, and 853 on the marshalsea—whereas 1,194 were distributed in gifts and a further 1,183 spent on the purchase of horses alone.[47] By 1315–16, Edward II was spending over 21,000 pounds per year, although the deduction of wages of war from this total would bring the sum down to just over 11,000 pounds.[48] However, gross expenditure on the household during the fifteen months which covered the last year of Edward II's reign and the first of Edward III's (1 November 1326 to 24 January 1328) rose to the huge figure of 92,500 pounds, of which the costs of the new king's coronation accounted for 13,550.[49] Even without the coronation, however, annual expenditure stood at over 74,000 pounds. Such was the price of Edward II's deposition and the establishment of Isabella and Mortimer's regime.

Compared with the relatively complete English sources, the archival survivals from some other regions tend to be less substantial. The surviving material for royal France is highly unsatisfactory, as the financial and administrative documentation of the household, emanating from the Chambre des Comptes, was largely destroyed in the great archive fire of 1731.[50] A few household accounts survive from the period before 1380, some on wax tablets, but the great majority have perished.[51] For the principalities of the Low Countries, the position is better, and more readily comparable with that of England. In Flanders, the series

---

[46] E.101/367/15 and Figs. 1–3, Table 5.   [47] E.101/373/15 and Table 6.

[48] E.101/376/7 and Table 7.   [49] E.101/382/9; see Table 10.

[50] See *Comptes royaux (1285–1314)*, ed. R. Fawtier and F. Maillard, iii (Paris, 1956), pp. vii–xxix.

[51] E. Lalou, *Les Comptes sur tablettes de cire de la Chambre aux deniers de Philippe III le Hardi et Philippe IV le Bel (1282–1309)* (Paris, 1994); and 'Un compte de l'hôtel du roi sur tablettes de cire 10 octobre–14 novembre 1350', *BEC* 1152 (1994), 91–127.

of comital household accounts beginning in 1260, conserved at Ghent, Lille, and Brussels, is broken, but the material is quite dense for certain periods.[52] There are, however, notable lacunae during the reign of Louis de Nevers (1322–46) until richer accounting material re-emerges under Louis de Male during the 1370s. In Artois, extensive documentation (of almost English proportions) survives at Arras for the reigns of Robert II (d.1302) and Mahaut d'Artois (d.1329), replete with elaborate particulars of account and subsidiary documents such as sealed quittances, warrants, and receipts.[53] This remains one of the great unexplored archives of later medieval Europe. In Hainault-Holland, under the Avesnes dynasty, the extant accounting material begins in 1302, but only becomes substantial after 1319, when a more-or-less complete series of household accounts for Jeanne de Valois, countess of Hainault, and for William, son of count William III, survives until 1336.[54] For the period after 1356, a mass of particulars and subsidiary documents are to be found in the Archives de l'État at Mons (with some holdings at Lille, Brussels, and The Hague) and some of these fill the printed pages of the *Cartulaire des comtes de Hainaut*.[55] But, unlike the preceding period, there is a relative dearth of surviving complete household accounts.

Despite these deficiencies and lacunae, sufficient material survives to permit contemporaneous—or near-contemporaneous—comparison between households, in both kingdoms and principalities. The organization of the accounting material displays sufficient similarity to allow meaningful contrasts and comparisons to be made. In the *comté* of Flanders, a system of accounting had developed by the later thirteenth century which requires further elucidation. The position is made more difficult by the inadequacies of cataloguing, and by problems of identifying and dating some of these documents correctly.[56] By 1270, three types of document were in current use in the comital accounting system: first, diet, or daily, accounts (*dépenses de l'hôtel*) divided into headings representing the various household departments (*cuisine, pain, vin, cambre,*

---

[52] See Bautier and Sornay, *Les Sources*, 57–64; also see Figs. 8–14.

[53] J.-M. Richard, *Inventaire sommaire des archives départementales antérieures à 1790. Pas-de-Calais, sér. A*, i (Paris, 1878), pp. i–xv, 5–35; Bautier and Sornay, *Les Sources*, 255–63. See Figs. 15–18, Tables 20, 21.

[54] *De rekeningen*, ed. Smit, i and ii (to 1333); C. Dehaisnes and J. Finot (eds.), *Inventaire sommaire de la série B des archives départementales du Nord*, 9 vols. (Lille, 1899–1906), vii. 1–24; Bautier and Sornay, *Les Sources*, 555–64. See Tables 1, 23–6.

[55] See *Cartulaire des comtes de Hainaut*, ed. Devillers.

[56] Bautier and Sornay, *Les Sources*, esp. 58–63.

avaine, estaule, forge); secondly, lists of *grosses parties* or extraordinary expenses, comparable to the items of wardrobe expenditure recorded in England, to the *mises extraordinaires* in Artois, and to the very similar *grosses parties* in Hainault; and, finally, statements of sums received by the clerk of the household, equivalent to the receipts section of English wardrobe accounts. The *grosses parties* account was compiled specifically for auditing purposes, and the totals of the diet accounts were then added as the last entry among the overall expenses. The final total (*summa, somme*) was then balanced against the total receipts. A very similar procedure was adopted in Hainault.[57]

In the fourteenth century, these household accounts seem to have run in parallel with the separate accounts of the receiver-general of Flanders, covering complete years, with an annual audit on 24 June. The first surviving receiver's account runs from December 1308 to June 1309, for the term of office of the Italian Tommaso Fini, receiver of Flanders, soon to be disgraced for peculation.[58] But in the later thirteenth century, the household accounts were often audited after much shorter periods, such as three or six months.[59] Completely preserved sets of accounts, which include diet accounts, *grosses parties*, and lists of receipts, are rare at this time. It is apparent that the accounting system for the Flemish comital household also relied upon the submission of other types of subsidiary document, many of which have perished. Very few quittances or receipts survive from members, or suppliers, of the Flemish household before the mid- to late fourteenth century, but the occasional list of household members receiving the count's (or countess's) wages, is preserved.[60] Some of the diet accounts have such lists entered on their dorse. Where these are missing, it may be assumed that wages were paid at that time only to the regular or permanent household members. The clerk responsible for expenditure therefore only explicitly listed the names of those receiving wages while the court was travelling, or when larger numbers than usual attended it—for example, at the great feasts.[61]

One must assume that, as in the case of Artois, large quantities of subsidiary documents in the form of warrants, quittances, and vouchers once existed for the household of Flanders. The laconic nature of the engrossed accounts, however, often masks the detailed content of these

---

[57] See *De rekeningen*, ed. Smit, iii. 37–62.
[58] AGR, CC, R.1, and see above p. 76 n. 28.
[59] See, for examples, *Het Memoriaal van Jehan Makiel*, 72–4, 135–9, 139–40.
[60] For one such list see ADN, B.1266, no. 234 (*c*.1299–1300). See Table 17.
[61] See RAG, Wyffels (chron. suppl.) 188 and 314 *bis* (1293–4).

lost strips of parchment and quires of paper from us. Apart from some of
the entries in the *grosses parties*, which talk in some detail about purchases
of books, plate, jewellery, and so forth, the tendency simply to total up
payments to named individuals without describing their precise purpose
means that there are aspects of Flemish court life that remain obscure.
Similarly, the manner in which receipts and issues from stock or store
(*pourvance*) were made is not entirely clear from the accounts. When
the count or countess resided at one of their castles or palaces within their
own domains of Flanders or Namur, basic commodities such as bread,
wine, oats, litter, and so on were taken from stock (*de providentia*).[62] When
they were 'abroad', no items of *pourvance* were entered. An exactly
similar procedure was followed in Hainault-Holland.[63] When such items
were listed in the accounts, however, they appeared as entries on the diet
account, sometimes just as bulk quantities, sometimes with a cash value
given them. The *pourvances* were totalled up daily, but the sums do not
appear in the balance of the overall account. This was probably because
the daily totals were used only to check the particulars of account, and
they had to correspond with entries in the accounts of the local officers
who supplied the *pourvances*. No cash was actually transferred in such
cases, so there was no need to add the daily totals of *pourvances* to the final
diet accounts. Again, a very similar practice applied to Hainault, perhaps
unsurprisingly given the close association of the two *comtés* for most of
the thirteenth century.[64]

From an analysis of the surviving diet accounts and *grosses parties*
for the household of Flanders, it can be calculated that weekly expenses
in the 1270s averaged around 350–400 *livres parisis* (l.p.) for the count's
household.[65] The countess was spending between 30 and 75 l.p. per week,
on her much smaller establishment, during the same period.[66] The figures
rose dramatically when the comital household visited Paris, as it did
frequently, especially when other princes and nobles were entertained at
his Parisian *hôtel* by Guy de Dampierre. In 1278, the count dined with
Robert II of Artois on 13 March, at a cost to himself of 56 l. 12s. 3d., of
which kitchen expenses unsurprisingly accounted for over 40 l., when the
average daily costs of that department stood at around 6 l.[67] It should be
remembered that none of these figures included provisions derived from

[62] See RAG, Gaillard 11, 17, 25. For English evidence of similar practices see *Household Accounts from Medieval England*, 20–1.

[63] *De rekeningen*, ed. Smit, iii. 25–46; i. 32–3, 170–4.

[64] See above, p. 41 n. 36.   [65] See RAG, St-Genois 185, 209, 210.

[66] See RAG, Gaillard 25, 28, 29.   [67] RAG, St-Genois 237, m. 6r.

pourvance. Similarly, when the count was at Nieppe in August 1278, daily expenses rose to just over 100 l.p. during the three days when the count of Artois, the duke of Brabant, and the lady of Courtrai were present.[68] The highest total for daily expenses recorded at this time is found in the extremely detailed surviving diet account for 1293–4. The Christmas feast of 1293 was celebrated at Petteghem with a large company, and the stables housed no fewer than 990 horses. For the three days of the Christmas feast, 415 l. 14s. 10d.p. was spent, a daily average of 138 l. 5s.p.[69] Again, no account was taken of provisions drawn from store or stock (*pourvances*) in the calculation of these cash payments. The holding of full court, and the entertainment of guests, were expensive—but they were part and parcel of courtly existence.

Under Guy's son and successor, Robert de Béthune, a higher level of daily expenditure was maintained. If his father was spending an average of about 50 to 55 l.p. per day on his household in the 1270s and 1280s, Robert was incurring costs of between 90 and 100 l.p. in 1307–8.[70] The currency mutations and manipulations of Philip the Fair, and the inflationary surge of the later 1290s, must be taken into account, but 'good money' had been restored by 1307.[71] There were some signs that economies were being attempted, given the unsound state of comital finances in the wake of the war with Philip the Fair. One means of achieving reductions in cash expenditure lay in placing greater reliance upon *pourvances*. A surviving diet account for 15 days at Ypres between 28 August and 13 September 1309 tells us that a daily average of 44 l. 2s.p. was spent on the household.[72] Of this 36.8% was spent by the kitchen. The relatively high proportion of kitchen expenditure was not confined to Flanders. In 1293–4 Guy de Dampierre's diet accounts show that the kitchen accounted for 50.4% of total expenses (including *grosses parties*) followed by wine(*bouteillerie*) at 16.1% and bread (*paneterie*) at 10.8%[73] Kitchen expenditure in the English royal household ran similarly at 51.8% in 1304–5, followed by the stable at 17.9%, and the pantry at 13.0%.[74] During the year 1306–7, the kitchen cost Edward I 54.4% of total household expenditure, with the stable expending 14.2%, and the pantry 13.3%.[75] In Artois, however, the kitchen costs stood at only 23.1% of total expenditure during the period from 6 February to 28 June 1300; when the costs

[68] RAG, St-Genois 237, m. 10r.
[69] RAG, Wyffels (chron. suppl.) 188 and 314 *bis*. See Figs. 11, 13.
[70] RAG, Gaillard 62–3, 66–8, 70; Wyffels (chron.suppl.) 496, 505.
[71] See Spufford, *Money and its Use*, 301–3.   [72] AGR, CC, R.2040.
[73] See Fig. 12.   [74] See Figs. 1, 3, Table 5.   [75] See Fig. 4.

of the *fruiterie* are added, the figure rises to 28.6%.[76] From 1 January to 15 June 1302, the surviving account gives a figure of 20.7% for the kitchen, 25.7% when *fruiterie* costs are added.[77]

At the court of Artois, greater costs were incurred on the *bouteillerie* and stable than elsewhere.[78] In 1300, the *bouteillerie* accounted for 11.8% of expenditure; in 1302 it remained at 11%. The stable absorbed 18.1% of total costs in 1300, but that figure had fallen to 6.2% in 1302. This was partly explained by the fact that Robert of Artois's stable costs had been assumed by the French crown for part of the accounting period, and some payments relating to horses and their upkeep appeared in the *mises extraordinaires* (which reached the very high level of 34.4% in 1302). These variations between courts can partly be explained by the greater or lesser reliance of different households on *pourvances*—in the case of Artois, there seems to have been less use of this means of provisioning than elsewhere. Yet a general tendency towards inflation of household costs, detectable in most principalities, is borne out by the evidence from Artois.[79] Even smaller, dependent households, such as that of the young Robert of Artois, saw total expenditure rise from a daily average of about 4 l.p. in 1309 to 30 l. 11s.p. per day in 1314.[80] All this evidence suggests that the costs of court life were rising to meet higher expectations and demands in the fourteenth century, an aspect examined in greater detail later.

A comparable pattern can be traced in the surviving accounts for the *comtés* of Hainault and Holland under the Avesnes. Although full accounts for the count's household are largely lacking, the material for the countess Jeanne de Valois is extensive, comprising accounts for 1319–21, 1325–6, 1326–7, 1327–8, 1328–9, 1330–1, 1332–3, and 1335–6.[81] A few isolated, very summary accounts for count Jean I for 1300–1 and 1302 give average monthly totals for expenditure as 1,934 l. 19s.t. (1300–1, although the term of account included the Christmas and Epiphany feasts)

---

[76] ADPC, A.162, and see Fig. 15.

[77] ADPC, A.178, and see Figs. 17, 18.

[78] See, for 1300–2, ADPC, A.162, A.178; Figs. 15–18.

[79] See Figs. 15–18.   [80] ADPC, A.247, A.254, A.321.

[81] See *De rekeningen*, ed. Smit, i. 32–106 (1319–21), 107–242 (1325–6), 243–343 (1326–7), 344–441 (1327–8), 442–75 (1328–9), 476–542 (1330–1), 543–91 (1332–3), 592–615 (1335–6). Household accounts for the future William IV of Hainault-Holland are printed on pp. 618–51 (1332–3) and 652–80 (1333). See below, pp. 159–61 and Tables 22–6.

TABLE I. *Household expenditure of the countess of Hainault, 1319–1333*

Term of account	Total expenditure	Monthly average
24 June 1319–23 Aug. 1321	10,623 l. 14s. 4d.t.	408 l. 11s.t.
25 Aug. 1325–24 Aug. 1326	7,691 l. 8s. 4d.t.	640 l. 19s.t.
24 Aug. 1326–23 Aug. 1327	7,718 l. 17s. 5d.t.	643 l. 5s.t.
23 Aug. 1327–21 Aug. 1328	11,487 l. 10s.t.	957 l. 5s.t.
21 Aug. 1328–27 Aug. 1329	8,874 l. 4s. 4d.t.	739 l. 10s.t.
26 Aug. 1330–25 Aug. 1331	9,107 l. 15s. 1d.t.	758 l. 19s.t.
12 Jan. 1332–10 Jan. 1333	4,849 l. 0s. 4d.t.	404 l. 0s.t.[84]

and 557 l. 10s.t. (1302).[82] An account for the six months from 4 February 1302 to 17 July 1303 shows average monthly expenditure to have been 1,094 l.t.[83] We are on firmer ground for the assessment of longer-term trends when the surviving accounts for the household of Jeanne de Valois are considered (Table 1).

The pattern of rising and falling expenditure revealed by this documentation partly reflects the circumstances in which the house of Hainault-Holland found itself at this time. The marriage of count William IV's and Jeanne de Valois's daughters, Margaret and Philippa, to the emperor Lewis of Bavaria and Edward III of England respectively necessitated substantial outlay, epitomized by the exceptionally high figure for expenses between August 1327 and August 1328 which saw Philippa's wedding and the reception, entertainment, and accommodation of the attendant diplomatic missions.[85] Hainault had moved on to the centre stage of European politics and diplomacy during these years, and the countess's household accounts reflected this important development in the fortunes of the ruling house. It is also worth noting that all these accounts more or less balanced disbursements against receipts.

This cannot be said for the state of affairs in the neighbouring *comté* of Flanders. The internal turmoil which had accompanied the early years of

---

[82] *De rekeningen*, ed. Smit, i. 12–13.   [83] Ibid., i. 28–9.

[84] Ibid., i. 106 (1319–21), 169 (1325–6), 325 (1326–7), 431 (1327–8), 472 (1328–9), 540 (1330–1), 590 (1332–3).

[85] For Hainault's position in the power-politics of this period see Lucas, *The Low Countries and the Hundred Years War*, 79–101.

count Louis de Nevers (1322–46) left its mark upon the comital finances. The rebellion of maritime Flanders (1323–8), followed by hostility between Louis and Ghent and a war with Brabant, left his revenues in deficit and encumbered with debt.[86] The situation called for vigorous administrative and financial reforms, and the appointment of able men, such as Guillaume d'Auxonne as chancellor, Pierre of Douai as *maître des comptes*, and the Lombard Vane Guy as receiver of Flanders, was a step in this direction.[87] Documentary evidence was compiled to aid them in their task, including a register of the privileges and obligations of the towns and castellanies of Flanders. This large volume was adorned with an initial illumination depicting the abject submission of the burgomaster and *échevins* of Bruges to both king and count in September 1328 (Pl. 4).[88] Marginal scenes of courtly celebration accompanied this image. But the gravity of the financial situation, as it was in 1332, was set out at length in the so-called 'Ninth Cartulary of Flanders' compiled by the chancellor Guillaume d'Auxonne, apparently for his personal use.[89] The register is of great importance, as it attempts to review the count's finances—with special attention to his court and household—and to make budgetary recommendations about levels of annual expenditure.[90]

The hearing of accounts, or *renenghe*, which took place at the count of Flanders's castle of Male in March 1332 provided the material and the opportunity for action. It was calculated that between 1328 and 1330, the count's ordinary revenue stood at 10,822 l. 19s.p. per year.[91] The punitive measures taken against the towns and castellanies of Flanders in the aftermath of their defeat in 1328 increased this income substantially. A combination of perpetual rents and fines brought in an annual total of 25,934 l.p. from 1331 onwards. But of the 300,000 l.p. received by the count between September 1328 and September 1331 (an average annual sum of 100,000 l.p.) every penny had been spent.[92] A further 25,000 l.p. had been spent over the six months between September 1331 and 31 March 1332, on 'tournaments and other expenses.' The problem was

[86] See Nicholas, *Medieval Flanders*, 212–19.

[87] For the background see Kittell, *From Ad Hoc to Routine*, 156–9.

[88] Den Haag, KB, MS 75 D 7, fo. 3v.

[89] See above, pp. 47–8; Thomas, 'Une source nouvelle', 11–20.

[90] ADN, B.1569, fos. 69r–71v; Thomas, 'Une source nouvelle', 26–31.

[91] ADN, B.1569, fos. 64r–70v.

[92] Ibid., fo. 70v: 'Et yl ay recu et despendu 300,000 l.par. ens lan 1328, en Septembre que li pais se mist en obbeiessance jusques a lannee 1331 en celi mois . . .'

TABLE 2. *Budget of household expenditure, Flanders, 1332*

Item of expenditure	Amount
Ordinary expenses of household	14,400 l.p.
Grosses parties	3,000 l.p.
Ordinary livery of household	4,500 l.p.
Extraordinary livery of household	2,000 l.p.
Séjours of horses	1,500 l.p.
Purchase of palfreys and other horses	2,750 l.p.
Expenses outside Flanders	12,000 l.p.
Birds purchased	700 l.p.
Bijlokke nunnery	500 l.p.
Paris *hôtel*	3,000 l.p.
Jewels	800 l.p.
Restor of tournament horses	6,000 l.p.
Vane Guy	6,000 l.p.
Guillaume d'Auxonne	5,500 l.p.

compounded by the fact that a further 357,000 l.p. were outstanding in unpaid debts (fo. 70v), of which at least 44,000 l.p. had to be repaid in the current year. Apparently working from the evidence assembled at the *renenghe* for the year from March 1331 to March 1332, Louis's advisers produced an outline budget (fo. 69r) which set out desirable targets for household expenditure (Table 2).[93]

Some advice was given in this review, such as the desirability of a reduction in the extraordinary liveries given by the count and countess from 2,000 to 1,000 l.p. per year, and in the purchase of palfreys and other horses for the household from 2,750 to 1,000 l.p. per year.[94] Inspection of the accounts of Jakemon de Deinze, receiver in the 1290s, had revealed that annual expenses had totalled about 55,000 l.p. (fo. 70v), when there were no *faits d'armes* nor great feasts. This was a somewhat conservative estimate of Guy de Dampierre's level of expenditure.[95] But annual expenses were now in the region of 80,000 l.p. and could not be sustained, particularly in view of the fact that this sum would be unlikely to cover the costs of future wars, tournaments, and great feasts.

---

[93] ADN, B.1569, fo. 69r and Thomas, 'Une source nouvelle', 20–1, 26–31.
[94] ADN, B.1569, fo. 69r. [95] See e.g. RAG, Gaillard 54.

The final recommendations of his advisers to the apparently profligate Louis de Nevers were contained in a schedule which concluded their review of his finances.[96] A tone of admonition was adopted:

Et se il vous plaist vivre dou vostre, et a raison, si vous restraingniez petit a petit, et commenchiez a restraindre les fraiz qui sensuient.[97]

[And if you would live of your own, with reason, if you restrain yourself little by little, and begin to reduce the costs which ensue.]

Their conclusion was clearly that Louis had not even attempted to live 'of his own', nor according to the dictates of reason. If he wished to persist in his present style of life (*mener teille vie et continuer*), he would have to find other advisers and agents: 'for we do not know how to do this, nor to raise at least 80,000 *livres* for this year alone.'[98] Their schedule of recommendations detailed the results of princely extravagance, as they saw it, item by item:[99]

1. Household expenses should be kept down to 14,400 l.p. per year. This represented daily expenditure of 39 l. 9s.p. per day when both the count and countess were together in Flanders. When they travelled together outside the *comté*, a meagre increase to 40 l.p. per day was to be allowed them (cf. fo. 69r).

2. If this were done, a balance of 11,000 l.p. would remain, from which livery distributions could be met—but only once annually—at a price of 4,500 l.p. (as in 1331–2). The count and countess were to limit their outlay on their own robes to 1,000 l.p. per year, 'because everyone talks about the excess'(fo. 71v).

3. The count was to cease buying jewels, because, they claimed, 'you already have enough'. The sole exception was to be certain items at Courtrai, which he and the countess would purchase from money to be raised from his lordship of Arbois in Burgundy.

4. Louis and the countess were to refrain from taking money from the comital receivers, except in cases of *grant necessitey*, as it would redound to their dishonour if they did so in the present financial situation.

---

[96] ADN, B.1569, fo. 71v.   [97] Ibid., fo. 71v.

[98] Ibid., fo. 71r: 'se vous voulez mener teille vie et continuer, faites pourchachier par autres que par nous, car nous ne le sariens faire ne pourchachier au moins 80,000 l. pour ceste annee, et ainssi de an en an pour chescune que vous la vourrez mener sanz avoir guerre, tournoiement ne grant fieste.'

[99] ADN, B.1569, fo. 71v; Thomas, 'Une source nouvelle', 20–2, 30–1.

5. The cost of the *séjour* of horses was to be held at 2,000 l.t. (1,500 l.p.) within Flanders, to be overseen by the *maître de l'hôtel*.

6. The purchase of palfreys and other horses for the household should cost no more than 1,000 l.p. per year.

7. The costs of purchase and upkeep of hunting birds should be no more than 3,000 l.p. per year.

8. If this were done, 2,600 l.p. would remain from comital revenues for the count's frequent journeys to France, and for the *grosses parties* of the household which usually absorbed about 12,000 l.p. (as they did in 1331–2).

9. If these recommendations were carried out, a clear net balance of about 40,000 l.p. would remain. There was no other solution—except for the assignment of all revenues from lands held outside Flanders to creditors, and the raising of loans on security of these revenues.

The advisers concluded with the declaration that if war 'or other *faits d'armes*, or other costs' arose, they would be unable to give further counsel or find other solutions.[100] Such eventualties would only bring *grant peine et meschief* ['great trouble and harm']. Such was the stark truth, as these clerks, lawyers, and administrators (*gens de robe longue*) saw it. There is some evidence that their advice was taken and, to some extent, implemented. A surviving household account for the six weeks from 26 January to 8 March 1334 can be used to produce estimated, projected totals of average annual expenditure for that year.[101] If ordinary household expenses are grossed up over a twelve-month period, a figure of 10,230 l. 2s.p. is attained, well within the guideline of 14,400 l.p. set out in the recommendations of March 1332.[102] When other expenses are added, a projected figure for total expenditure of 31,382 l. 19s.p. is produced for the twelve months from January 1334 to January 1335.[103] This again would fall well within the limit prescribed by the count's advisers.[104] When the costs of war with Brabant and general expenses of men-at-arms are added, the sum reaches 34,029 l. 13s. 6d.p., but still within the budget laid down. The basis of these estimates is, of course, open to many objections, and a firmer foundation upon which to ground conclusions is to be found in the surviving account of Nicholas Gaidouche, receiver of Flanders, for the fourteen months from 7 September 1335 to 7 November 1336 (Table 3).[105]

---

[100] ADN, B.1569, fo. 71v; Thomas, 'Une source nouvelle', 31.
[101] AGR, CC, R.4 (26 Jan.–8 Mar. 1334).   [102] Ibid., m. 4v.
[103] Ibid., m. 6r.   [104] B.1569, fos. 70v–71v.
[105] AGR, CC, R.5 (7 Sept. 1335–7 Nov. 1336).

TABLE 3. *Household expenditure, Flanders, 1335–1336*

Total receipts:		74,992 l.	9s.	6d.p.
Expenditure:	Household expenses	20,323 l.	14s.	1d.p.
	Livery	4,910 l.	16s.	2d.p.
	Cloth, furs, & silk	1,049 l.	5s.	6d.p.
	Jewels & plate	2,912 l.	4s.	0d.p.
	Cash paid to count & countess	2,929 l.	10s.	7d.p.
	Horses & *restor*	2,559 l.	6s.	6d.p.
	Hunting birds	65 l.	0s.	0d.p.
	Works (*ouvrages*)	412 l.	5s.	7d.p.
	Commissaires & *procureurs*	40 l.	0s.	0d.p.
	Rieuwards & council	243 l.	7s.	7d.p.
	Castellans & *baillis*	377 l.	8s.	0d.p.
	Embroiderers & armourers	164 l.	0s.	0d.p.
	Repaid debts	16,603 l.	0s.	1d.p.
	Dykes at Beveren	11,320 l.	0s.	0d.p.
	Miscellaneous	7,354 l.	0s.	1d.p.
Total expenses:		72,497 l.	18s.	8d.p.

If these figures are notionally averaged out over twelve, rather than
fourteen months, average annual expenditure would run at 62,141 l. 17s.p.
This was certainly some improvement on the 80,000 l.p. that Louis's
advisers claimed he was spending in previous years.[106] But expenditure
on some individual items was much higher than that specified in the recommendations: ordinary household expenses, for example, totalled just
over 20,000 l.p., rather than the 14,400 l.p. which had been recommended. The costs of livery purchase and distribution, and of other textiles and
furs, were kept more or less within the guidelines, and the *restor* of horses
lost in tournaments was less than that recorded in 1331–2.[107] But there
was little evidence that Louis de Nevers was ceasing to engage in that
activity; he continued to retain knights in his service with fees and robes
for both war and tournament.[108] Nor had he stopped buying jewels and
plate, on which over 2,900 l.p. was spent in 1335–6.[109]

---

[106] See above, p. 89.   [107] See above, pp. 89–91.
[108] See, for examples, ADN, B.499, no. 6521; B.4065, nos. 145583–5.
[109] AGR, CC, R.5, m. 12v–13r.

Among those who audited Gaidouche's account at Male on 8 November 1336 were Guillaume d'Auxonne and Pierre de Douai, both of whom had made the recommendations of 1332. They may have derived some minimal satisfaction from the fact that some attempt was being made to take account of their strictures and adhere to their proposals. But there was a long way to go, and Louis de Nevers was evidently not willing to adapt his princely lifestyle to implement all their recommendations. To attempt to peg daily household expenses for the count and countess to around 40 l.p. proved unrealistic. Evidence from the few surviving complete accounts for the later years of Louis de Nevers, and for the reign of Louis de Male (1346–84), demonstrates that this aspect of the budgetary recommendations could not be implemented. Between 16 and 22 December 1345, for instance, the count and his *hosteus* (household) were at Brussels. Total household expenses for that week reached 1,389 l. 10s 6d.p., a daily average of 198 l. 10s.[110] Lodging costs (365 l.p.) were particularly high, especially in the Brussels taverns and inns, and it was, of course, the pre-Christmas period. But the notion that the household could manage on around 40 l.p. per day when staying outside Flanders, was quite impractical. Again, between 28 September and 13 December 1348, for example, the receiver of Flanders disbursed 4,204 l. 6s.p., a daily average of 59 l. 5s.p., on household expenses.[111] Between May and August 1381, Louis de Male acknowledged that he owed his *clerc des briefs* 9,548 l. 15s.p., a daily average of 85 l. 5s.p., for household expenditure.[112]

It remained patently obvious that the costs of the Flemish court and household—about 32,120 l.p. in 1335–6, out of a total expenditure of about 72,490 l.—absorbed a large proportion (44.3%) of comital income and resources. But to renounce display, to retreat from the tournament, and drastically to reduce expenditure on plate and jewels—those essential liquid assets, as well as instruments of princely gift-giving—was, at least in a prince's mind, unthinkable.

3. Liveries: status, function, and expenditure

One means whereby those in authority had rewarded and sustained the services of their vassals, clients, and servants throughout the Middle Ages was through the distribution to them of clothing and of the materials with

---

[110] ADN, B.3232, no. 111703.   [111] ADN, B.4066.
[112] ADN, B.3239, no. 111839.

which to make it. The practice of giving livery (*livrée, liberatio, librata*) in cloth and clothing was an ancient one, but it was undergoing important changes during the later Middle Ages. Our earlier examination of the organization and structures of princely households in Chapter 2 pointed to the emergence within them of inner hierarchies of both status and function.[113] One index of such distinctions was to be found in the practice of reward and gift-giving, and it is for this reason that the distribution of liveries by rulers, in cloth, furs, footwear, and money (with which to purchase clothing), is of crucial significance in the formation and evolution of court societies.

By the mid-thirteenth century, if not earlier, distinction and stratification within the princely household had developed along a number of lines—among them, discrimination according to social rank as well as functional office.[114] The emergence of both knights and squires of the chamber, for example, during the first quarter of the fourteenth century, furthered and exemplified this tendency.[115] An internal division (despite some inevitable degree of overlap) between an upper and lower household was drawn more on social than on strictly functional grounds. Some forms of domestic service to the ruler, albeit sometimes of an honorary or perfunctory character, were certainly performed by those of noble origin. But, as we have seen, the division between an upper household and a 'service' household—populated by non-noble servants—was already emerging at this time. It would be an overstatement to speak of firm and inflexible lines of demarcation, or discrimination, within the household which could not be crossed by the ambitious or simply fortunate aspirant. In some cases, ascent from lower to higher domestic office could carry social connotations, including entry into knighthood.[116] But the external signs whereby membership of a particular stratum of the household—or, indeed, membership of the household itself—could be identified merit some attention. How could one tell a member of a royal or princely court from any other lord's retainer, and how, if at all, were his or her status and function visibly expressed? Such questions carry many implications with them—above all, about the extent to which the court was 'different' from other social bodies or establishments. It is also important to consider the degree to which a prince was obliged to commit quite substantial sums of money to the expression, and promotion, of social and functional differentiation between the members of his own entourage.

---

[113] See Ch. 2, above, pp. 55–8, 68.   [114] See Morgan, 'The house of policy', 33.
[115] See above, pp. 59–61.   [116] See above, p. 60.

Princely households have often been analysed in terms of their essential distinctiveness from other forms of later medieval social organization.
The courts and court societies which formed within and around those
households have been seen as distinct social units, with lives of their own,
co-existing with their surrounding societies but not forming part of
them.[117] Robert Bartlett sets out this view: 'princely courts were, in the
best of circumstances, culturally distinct from the surrounding society,
centres of patronage, conspicuous consumption, cosmopolitanism and
fashion, and their style might easily inflame clerical, puritannical or back-
woods critics.'[118] To strengthen the point, he offers the telling example of
Edward I of England who, after his marriage to Eleanor of Castile, apparently adopted as his costume of relaxation (*esbatement*) the Spanish gown
and biretta.[119] Foreign brides—or husbands—and their entourages (if
they brought them) served to emphasize this distinctiveness of the princely
court and household from its social environment. The visible signs of
cultural and ethnic difference, or of reorientation as a result of conquest
or marriage alliance, could thus be expressed through gesture, language,
manners and, above all, clothing.

As will appear later, this view can be questioned. The court could, for
instance, be seen as a microcosm of society at large, in which hierarchical
structures—which were difficult (or indeed impossible) to maintain or
enforce outside—were more effectively kept in place. Furthermore, the
court could express, admittedly in heightened form, perceptions of social
position and status which were also prevalent far outside its boundaries.
It is in this context that the issue and distribution of clothing, or clothing allowances, in the form of regular liveries (*livrées*) in cloth, furs, or
cash, is so significant.[120] This is just one example of the ways in which

[117] See Elias, *The Court Society*, 186–7; J. Heers, 'La cour de Mahaut d'Artois en
1327–1328: solidarités humaines, livrées et mesnies', *Anales de historia antigua y medieval*,
2 (1977–9), 7–43; R. Bartlett, *The Making of Europe: Conquest, Colonization and Cultural
Change, 950–1350* (Harmondsworth, 1994), 230–2.

[118] Bartlett, *Making of Europe*, 230.

[119] See T. Tolley, 'Eleanor of Castile and the "Spanish" Style in England', in W. M.
Ormrod (ed.), *Harlaxton Medieval Studies*, i. *England in the Thirteenth Century* (Stamford,
1991), 167–92; *The Court and Household of Eleanor of Castile in 1290*, ed. J. C. Parsons
(Toronto, 1977), 23–4; Bartlett, *Making of Europe*, 230; M. Prestwich, *Edward I* (London,
1988), 122–5 for Edward's marriage to Eleanor.

[120] For a recent discussion see R. van Uytven, 'Showing off one's rank in the Middle
Ages' in W. Blockmans and A. Janse (eds.), *Showing Status: Representations of Social
Positions in the Late Middle Ages* (Turnhout, 1999), 29–34. Also, for England, F. Lachaud,
'Les livrées de textiles et de fourrures à la fin du moyen âge: l'exemple de la cour du roi

perceptions of rank and status both within and outside princely courts could be translated into visible, concrete terms. As we know today, styles of clothing and costume can send out a wide range of signals: from ideas of self-image or notions of acceptable conformity and convention, to gestures of defiance and of a desire to express a perceived sense of 'otherness'. In a later medieval context, far less freedom of expression was permitted to the individual. But dress could be a highly significant and effective means of identifying rank, function, and affiliation.

Two points must be made at the outset about the nature of our evidence. First, much of it concerns the provision to members of princely households of money or materials with which to make, trim, and line clothes, rather than the distribution of complete costumes whose specific cut, style, and colour is recorded.[121] Sometimes the issue of specific articles of clothing to individuals is mentioned in livery rolls or accounts, but these references—especially during the earlier part of the period—are exceptional and tend to relate to particular occasions, such as tournaments, marriages, or knighting ceremonies.[122] Secondly—and directly related to this point—the study of 'costume history' during this period is made more difficult by the nature of the documentary sources. These rarely refer to what was actually worn by individuals who received liveries from a prince. We have therefore to concentrate on materials, their quantity, quality, and cost, rather than on the cut and style of individual costumes.[123] Apart from a very few surviving examples of textiles from this period, our major sources for actual costumes are visual and literary—manuscript illumination, panel painting, sculpture, romances, treatises, and so forth. But this does not mean that the archival and documentary evidence for the role played by the distribution of liveries as an index and expression of status and function can be neglected by the historian.

There is another methodological consideration, however, that requires some comment. If we accept the view of some anthropologists that costume, as a 'system of clothing', is comparable to language, while clothing itself represents selected items of speech, the later medieval documentary

---

Edouard Ier Plantagenet (1272–1307)' in *Le Vêtement: histoire, archéologie et symbolique vestimentaire au moyen âge*, Cahiers du Léopard d'Or, i (Paris, 1989), 169–222.

[121] See Lachaud, 'Textiles, Furs and Liveries', 203–6.

[122] See, for an instance in which tailored robes were issued, E.101/361/19/16 (1301–2) and Table 15(b).

[123] For discussion of the problem see Lachaud, 'Textiles, Furs and Liveries', 142–4.

evidence falls largely into the former category.[124] Actual clothing uses only a few of the elements available in a system of costume. It has been rightly pointed out that 'accounts recording the purchase of materials for costume [including liveries] or particulars of accounts of tailors . . . only refer to the system of clothing, and not to what was actually worn by individuals'.[125] We can therefore only assess the role of liveries in defining and representing an individual's social rank or domestic function within a household by means of an analysis of the quality and quantity of the textiles and furs issued, and of their monetary value. Liveries of cloth were often described in terms of 'robes' issued to individuals. A 'robe' could consist of anything from three to six separate garments, not all of which were necessarily worn together.[126] Indeed, the degree of discomfort sustained if they were worn as an ensemble could well have been intolerable. A livery roll or account will sometimes tell us what a specific 'robe' consisted of, but this is by no means normal practice. Lengths, dimensions, and quantities of cloth, or the number of pelts in an issue of furs, often provide the only clue whereby the type of garment, or garments, which were actually worn as liveries can be guessed at. We can, as noted above, supplement this limited data with visual, literary, and, to a much lesser extent, archaeological sources. But the line between fiction and reality in both literature and the visual arts is often blurred and difficult to draw. Iconographical convention can sometimes mislead rather than assist as, for example, in the representation of court fools and jesters in illuminated manuscripts, although the visual arts necessarily supply costume historians with the great bulk of their material.[127]

The rare surviving specimens of clothing from this period, with the sole exception of liturgical vestments, also demonstrate the notorious

---

[124] See O. Blanc, 'Historiographie du vêtement: un bilan', in *Le Vêtement*, 7–33; J. Martinet, 'Du semiologique au sein des fonctions vestimentaires', *Vêtements et sociétés: Actes du Colloque CNRS 'Vers une anthropologie du vêtement', Musée de l'Homme (9–11 mars 1983)*, *L'Ethnographie*, 80 (1984), 141–52.

[125] Lachaud, 'Textiles, Furs and Liveries', 134.

[126] See below, p. 98 n. 132. Also Appendix VII (b) for Mahaut of Artois's robes.

[127] See S. M. Newton, *Fashion in the Age of the Black Prince: A Study of the Years 1340–1365* (Woodbridge, 1980), esp. 82–5 (representation of fools and jesters); and M. Scott, *Late Gothic Europe, 1400–1500* (History of Dress Series, London, 1980), esp. 75: 'While working from reality, artists can flatter and suppress the less attractive, be it in people or objects . . . and it is possible that we get [a] . . . too-tidy or too-frivolous impression of dress from fifteenth-century painters.'

vulnerability and fragility of textiles.[128] Not only do they represent quite exceptional survivals, but they also illustrate features of later medieval costume that do not apply to modern dress. Infrequent washing, and the daily exposure of cloth coloured with vegetable dyes to light, probably conspired to drain them of colour and necessitate their regular replacement.[129] The seasonal distribution of liveries of cloth in princely and other households may not only have been determined by tradition and by the need to provide warmer and cooler clothing. A winter livery, given at All Saints (1 November) or Christmas, might well be both faded and worn out by Easter, let alone Pentecost. Hence one important sign of social position in the later Middle Ages—and subsequently—was an ability to keep a large wardrobe, and to possess many changes of clothing. This tendency can be traced through surviving household accounts and inventories of movable goods, as they become more plentiful from the later thirteenth century onwards.[130] The sumptuary legislation of the period confirms this quantitative basis for social distinction: the French sumptuary *ordonnance* of 1294 attempted to prescribe the number of 'pairs of robes' allowed to each social rank. The *ordonnance* stipulated that knights banneret should enjoy an annual allowance of three pairs of robes, including one pair specifically for the summer livery.[131] This was rather meagre by any standards—Queen Margaret of England took twelve pairs of robes with her on a single journey to France in February 1302.[132] One of these was a green velvet 'robe' consisting of three 'furred garments', two surcoats, and a cloak in a six-piece set.

Before examining the detailed evidence, a final point should be made. It might at first sight appear somewhat paradoxical that a princely court, whose members were to some degree 'levelled' by common subservience to one ruler, should provide us with useful indicators of social rank and status. Was not one indication of their common subordinate position to

---

[128] For commentary on some surviving examples see Lachaud, 'Textiles, Furs and Liveries', 414–17.

[129] For colours, their intensity and durability, see K. G. Ponting, *A Dictionary of Dyes and Dyeing* (London, 1980), 40–3, 83; Piponnier, *Costume et vie sociale*, 188–94.

[130] See Y. Delaporte, 'Perspectives méthodologiques et théoriques dans l'étude du vêtement', *Vêtements et sociétés*, 33–57; and see below, pp. 124–5; also Appendix VII (b).

[131] *Ordonnances des rois de France de la troisième race*, i (Paris, 1723), 541–3; H. Duplès Agier, 'Une ordonnance somptuaire Inédite de Philippe le Hardi', *BEC* 15 (1854), 176–81.

[132] E.101/361/27. Cf. *Documents*, i. 137 for the robes of the countess of Nesle in Nov. 1302, which included six robes of five garments (*garnemens*) each, and three of three garments each.

be found in the very fact that they received clothing allowances? The fact none the less remained that there was a social as well as functional hierarchy within each household—although that hierarchy could sometimes be cut across, if not contradicted, by distributions of carefully graded liveries.[133] An increasing emphasis upon social, rather than functional, distinction, moreover, appears to have been made during this period.[134] But the precise context in which cloth, furs, and clothing serve, as some historians have claimed, to provide evidence for 'exhibition of estate' or 'manifestation of social position' has always to be carefully defined. How far, for example, did the wearing of clothing of a particular colour, cut, or pattern identify the wearer, and express his or her social rank, outside the relatively small circle of the princely household?[135] It is here that, as will be suggested, the fourteenth century witnessed changes in the means of identification, so that the 'language' of livery began to take on more general application outside, as well as within, court society. The following sections will consider evidence from a selection of courts and households in turn, and then attempt to draw some more general conclusions.

a. England

The practice of livery distribution at the English court, as elsewhere in western Europe, following both Roman and Byzantine imperial example, was an ancient one.[136] Although the *Constitutio Domus Regis* of c.1130 makes no reference to liveries of cloth or clothing, Walter Map tells us that Henry I 'thrice in the year . . . clad Louis, king of France, and several of his princes. He had a register of all the earls and barons of his land, and appointed for them at his coming or during the stay of his court certain presents with which he honoured them, of candles, bread and wine.'[137]

Map's reference to Henry's giving of clothing to Louis VI and his nobles can probably be interpreted to mean that these gifts were made at Christmas, Easter, and Pentecost, when liveries were given and when the

[133] See below, pp. 101–2; Table 15(a).

[134] See above, pp. 94–7 and below, pp. 101–6.

[135] See R. van Uytven, 'Cloth in medieval literature of western Europe', in *Cloth and Clothing in Medieval Europe: Essays in Memory of Professor E. M. Carus-Wilson*, ed. N. B. Harte and K. G. Ponting (London, 1983), 151–83, and 'Showing off one's rank in the Middle Ages', 20–1, 29–34.

[136] Lachaud, 'Textiles, Furs and Liveries', 186–8, for examples.

[137] Map, *De Nugis*, 258; see also F. Barlow, *William Rufus* (London, 1983), 136.

'crown-wearing' ceremonies took place.[138] It is, however, instructive that Map does not include liveries of cloth or furs among the 'presents' given to his earls and barons by Henry—like many of their continental counterparts (and inferiors) they merely received allowances of basic necessities during their visits to his court. But the fact that Henry was such an open-handed giver of largesse also attracted not only suitors and suppliants, but merchants and traders, to his court.[139] There was, wrote Map, 'a market following the king whithersoever he moved his camp, so fixed were his journeyings and his welcome stays'.[140] It would be surprising if those merchants had not included dealers in cloth, luxury textiles, and furs. Gifts of such items were de rigueur in a ruler, but regular distributions of livery were another matter.

Frédérique Lachaud has stated that, during the twelfth century, the English evidence seems to point to the fact that 'deliveries of clothes were perhaps only occasional, when need arose, and that there was no system of regular liveries'.[141] The regularization of livery distributions at the English court thus appears to have been a product of the thirteenth century. From the Exchequer Pipe Roll for Michaelmas 1204 onwards, purchases of materials for robes appear more frequently in the records.[142] From 1211 onwards, large sums for such purchases were paid out by the Exchequer, and the chroniclers also specifically draw attention to the fact.[143] The practice continued under Henry III, and the surviving documentation during the reign of Edward I (1272–1307) offers perhaps the fullest and clearest picture of regular, rather than simply occasional, livery distributions that we possess. The surviving material has been examined by Lachaud, who concludes that the systematic giving of liveries of cloth, furs, footwear, and money at fixed times of the year is clearly documented from the reign of Edward I onwards.[144] This does not mean that such distributions were not made at earlier periods—Matthew Paris was of the opinion that they had been made *ab antiquo*, although he did not specify what he meant by *antiquus*.[145]

---

[138] See above, pp. 28–9.   [139] Map, *De Nugis*, 242, 258.   [140] Ibid. 242.

[141] Lachaud, 'Textiles, Furs and Liveries', 188.

[142] See *Pipe Roll 6 John*, p. xxxiv; *Pipe Roll 10 John*, 97; cited Lachaud, 'Textiles, Furs and Liveries', 188–9.

[143] *Pipe Roll 13 John*, 39, 43, 83, 108–9, 123, 171, 176, 178, 246, 270; *Flores Historiarum*, ii. 147 (1213); 393 (1253); cited Lachaud, 'Textiles, Furs and Liveries', 189.

[144] See F. Lachaud, 'Livery of robes in England, *c.*1200–*c.*1330', *EHR* 111 (1996), 279–98.

[145] *Chronica Majora*, v. 199; Lachaud, 'Textiles, Furs and Liveries', 189–90.

If the evidence offered by livery distributions is to be used in order to identify the social status of the recipient, we have to concentrate, in the first instance, upon the cost and quality of the materials issued to the various ranks within the English royal household. In a continental context, Raymond van Uytven has used literary sources to excellent effect in order to demonstrate this point.[146] The rolls of liveries given by the English crown to new knights of the king's household for their knighting ceremonies provide a good starting-point.[147] In 1301–2, bannerets were distinguished from 'simple' knights (or bachelors) by liveries of superior cloth of gold (*in serico*), destined for the *culcitra*, or coverlet of the bed used at their vigils, and for the *cointise*, or silken ceremonial garment which they wore at their dubbing.[148] Cloth of gold *in serico* was woven in threads with a core of silk, rather than of hemp (*in canabo*). The two types were clearly recognizable by the initiated, as the clerks constantly make the distinction in the wardrobe accounts.[149] Similarly, the new knights created by Edward III in 1327–8 included two earls, six knights banneret of baronial status, and ten simple knights. The earls were distinguished from the bannerets and bachelors by their liveries of very fine diaspered, or textured, silk, forming cloth of gold *ad apparamenta sua*.[150] This had also been the case for John de Bohun, earl of Hereford, knighted by Edward II with three of the Mortimers and thirty-six other aspirants on the very last day of his reign (20 January 1327) (livery *ad apparamenta sua de panno ad aurum in serico dyasprum*', plus a scarlet robe and a green robe).[151] Diaspered silks were woven with two warps and two wefts, sometimes in two colours, creating a raised or relief effect on the surface of the cloth.[152] The bannerets were marked off from the simple knights by their *camoca* silks, as opposed to the *tarse* cloths given to the latter. Whereas the earls and barons received expensive scarlet and green robes, the bachelors—as in January 1327—were given less expensive azure (blue) and green cloths.[153] There was a significant price difference here. The

---

[146] See van Uytven, 'Cloth in the medieval literature of western Europe', 151–2, and his 'Rood-wit-zwart: kleuren-symboliek en kleursignalen in de Middeleeuwen', *Tijdschrift voor Geschiedenis*, 97 (1984), 447–70.

[147] See Table 15(b).   [148] E.101/361/17; 371/21/60; see Table 15(b).

[149] For examples, see Lachaud, 'Textiles, Furs and Liveries', 345–6.

[150] E.101/383/4 and Table 15(b).   [151] E.101/382/7.

[152] D. King, 'Sur la signification de "Diasprum"', *Bulletin de Liaison du CIETA*, 11 (1960), 14–25.

[153] See J. H. Munro, 'The medieval scarlet and the economics of sartorial splendour' in *Cloth and Clothing in Medieval Europe*, 13–70.

amounts and lengths of cloth and furs used for these liveries were very carefully graded according to social rank, and such distinctions ran throughout the court hierarchies of fourteenth-century Europe.[154]

In some cases, however, liveries did not conform to the accepted gradations of status within the social hierarchy. In 1289–90, for example, when cash sums were given for the purchase of cloth with which to make winter and summer robes, the king's surgeon received the same amount for his robes as the simple knights, together with the wardrobe clerks, the chaplains of the king's chapel, and—most significantly of all—the king's bankers (the Riccardi of Lucca).[155] Clerks of the household offices ranked lower (except for the privileged inmates of the favoured wardrobe), beside the serjeants-at-arms and huntsmen who ranked above falconers, minstrels, and squires of the king's chamber—although a rise in the latters' status was already apparent.[156] The valets of the other household offices received significantly less than the squires of the chamber—13s. 4d. rather than 2 l. sterling.[157] But to give exactly the same amount to merchant-bankers as to knights-bachelor sends out signals of caution to those who wish to use livery distributions as indicators of *social* status. The Italians—like the king's surgeon—were perhaps being rewarded here on the basis of function, rather than social rank. We know that, in 1279, Orlandino of Lucca, the king's banker, was allowed special privileges within the office of the wardrobe when he came to court.[158] It was perhaps in continued recognition of their special services that the Lucchese enjoyed more generous treatment in the livery lists than their social position might indicate.[159] Hierarchies were not entirely inflexible in this area, and such evidence suggests that, even within the somewhat artificial social milieu of the household, concepts of function and worth had as important a part to play as perceptions of rank. In any case, as will be suggested in a later chapter, the rigidity and impermeability of status distinctions and barriers during the earlier part of this period—in both an English and continental court context—may have been exaggerated by historians.

The cost of fitting-out an English household with robes could be considerable, especially in its upper reaches. Livery distributions normally encompassed most, but not necessarily all, members of the king's and

[154] See below, pp. 134–5.   [155] E.101/352/24; C.47/4/5; and see Table 15(a).
[156] See above, pp. 59–61.   [157] See Table 15(a).
[158] Tout, *Chapters*, ii. 163, and above, p. 23.
[159] See Kaeuper, *Bankers to the Crown*, 75–103.

TABLE 4. *Livery Roll, England, 1328*

Recipients	Number of names recorded
Ladies of queen Philippa's chamber	2
Damoiselles of same	5
King's bannerets	15
King's knights	36
King's clerks	41
Margaret of Daventry	1
King's squires	72
Serjeants-at-arms	27
Servants of offices	41
Falconers	6
Huntsmen	3
Minstrels	11
King's armourers	5
Valets of king's chamber	6
Valets of queen's chamber	5
Pages of queen's chamber	2
Total in receipt of liveries:	277[160]

queen's households. The reliability of any figures which purport to represent the total number in receipt of liveries during a given year, let alone their cost, has been effectively questioned.[161] But some impression of an order of magnitude can be gained from the record of those members of the household, receiving the king's wages, whose names were included on the roll of the marshalsea, and from the livery lists drawn up by the wardrobe. A list of the bannerets, simple knights, clerks, squires, serjeants-at-arms, and valets on the marshalsea roll for 1314–15 has marginal annotations noting that some, but by no means all, were also receiving robes from the king (*ad robas regis*).[162] One of the fullest livery lists, however, is to be found early in the reign of Edward III, showing liveries made on the feast of St John the Baptist (24 June) in 1328 (Table 4).

This was an exceptional livery, falling on a date at which liveries were not normally given—under Edward III the normal distributions appear to have been made at All Saints, the Purification, Christmas, Easter,

---

[160] E.101/383/10. [161] See Lachaud, 'Textiles, Furs and Liveries', 210–17.
[162] E.101/378/6.

and Pentecost.[163] Some members of the household may thus have been excluded from it. In any case, it has been shown that under Edward I, although the accounts of disbursements for the purchase of cloth for robes may give a figure of 190 (in 1300–1) or 300 (in 1305–6), the actual number who received robes in money or kind stood at about 570 persons.[164] We have some evidence for the level of expenditure on robes, but this must also be treated with caution.

In 1289–90, for example, 1,000 l. 6s. 8d. was spent on liveries of robes for the households of the king, queen, and John of Brabant.[165] This represented 1.6% of the total wardrobe expenditure.[166] By 1305–6, expenses incurred on the purchase of textiles and furs reached about 9.6% of total wardrobe expenditure.[167] Although the king's and queen's households themselves have been the subject of a number of studies, much less has been written about the lesser or dependent households of the king's children, his wards, and of those foreign princes maintained and educated at the English court.[168] In many ways, these lesser households provide better grounds for comparison with some of the smaller princely households of continental Europe than the royal establishment itself. The provision of robes to the members of dependent households was undertaken by the king's wardrobe and formed an additional source of expenditure, although it could sometimes be only a temporary one. Royal children tended to marry and therefore leave the immediate orbit of the king's household, although some might return to it as widows—Edward I's daughter Elizabeth, countess of Holland, was an expensive item for the crown after her return to England on the premature death of her husband in 1299.[169] For example, in December 1297, the king's other daughter Margaret, duchess of Brabant, was issued with liveries of robes for her household servants, largely in red and green cloth, on the eve of her

---

[163] E.101/387/14: livery roll, 1334–6.

[164] E.101/368/6, 27; 369/11; Lachaud, 'Textiles, Furs and Liveries', 214.

[165] C.47/4/5, fo. 38r; Table 15(a).

[166] Tout, *Chapters*, vi. 81, but note the cautionary comments on p. 73.

[167] E.101/369/11, fo. 166v; Lachaud, 'Textiles, Furs and Liveries', 217, and the cautionary remarks on pp. 210–17.

[168] See Tout, *Chapters*, ii. 131–50; Parsons (ed.), *The Court and Household of Eleanor of Castile*, 127–32; but see also H. Johnstone, 'The wardrobe and household of Henry, son of Edward I', *BJRL* 7 (1923), 384–420; K. Staniland, 'Welcome, Royal Babe! The birth of Thomas of Brotherton in 1300', *Costume* 19 (1985), 1–13. See above, pp. 49–51. Also Appendix I (a)–(d).

[169] See, for Elizabeth, the accounts for her expenses in E.101/371/8/131; 624/12; 371/8/88; 365/20; 366/30 (1300–5). Also see Appendix V (b).

voyage to Brabant after her marriage to duke John II.[170] Margaret did not suffer premature widowhood, remaining in Brabant as duchess and, apart from the occasional gift or subsidy, was no longer any burden upon her father's finances.

The king's two infant sons by his second marriage—Thomas (b.1300) and Edmund (b.1301)—also had their own separate joint household, whose members received robes at Christmas, Easter, and All Saints (1 November) at a modest total cost of 35 l. 13s. in 1301–2.[171] The two boys, however, were fitted out with 12 ells of the finest woollen cloth *de colore* at Christmas 1301, with tiny miniver hoods, and a further 11 ells of medley (woollen cloth woven with wools of two colours), also with furs and hoods, at the feast of St Edward the Confessor (18 March). The choice of this particular English saint's day may be significant. These amounts would have made a large number of separate garments for such young children. Their livery was said to be *de secta Regine*, that is of the same kind and quality as the liveries of the queen's household.[172] Some degree of uniformity was thus imposed on the entourages of the queen and her youngest children. By 1303–4, the liveries issued to the household of Thomas and Edmund absorbed a grand total of 240 l. 16s. 1d., and the furs cost more than the scarlet, rayed (striped), and other cloth which was provided.[173] Their household servants in 1305–6 were relatively cheaply clothed, however, in robes costing 13s 4d each for valets of the chamber and offices, and 10s each for minstrels and *garciones* of the hall and stable.[174] The silk provided in liveries for Thomas and Edmund at Ascension 1306 alone, however, cost 5 l. 10s. Together with liveries of footwear (*calciamenta*), these thirty-two servants cost the wardrobe a mere 24 l. 5s.[175] Spectacularly higher costs were incurred for cloths of gold offered at certain shrines, and for expensive liveries of cloth (fourteen ells per livery) and furs given to the two five- and six-year-old boys and their sister Eleanor at Christmas, Easter, Ascension, Michaelmas, and All Saints.[176] All their robes were furred with miniver, and the finest scarlet, green cloth (*viridus*), and silk were given to them. There was therefore a considerable imbalance in expenditure within the household. The visible difference between the quality of cloth and furs issued to the princes—and their higher-ranking officers—and those provided for the

[170] E.101/372/12/1. For these marriages see Prestwich, *Edward I*, 127–9.
[171] E.101/360/28, mm. 4r–5r. See also Appendix III.   [172] E.101/360/11, m. 5r.
[173] E.101/366/15.   [174] E.101/368/12, fo. 6r.   [175] Ibid., fo. 7r.
[176] Ibid., fo. 8v.

familia or *maisnie* (that is, the service household) made a clear social and hierarchical point.

The obligation laid upon kings and princes to appear clothed in garments of a fineness and quality superior to those of their entourages is reflected in the extant accounting material. It is also found in some of the theoretical literature of government and princely rule. In a copy of the pseudo-Aristotelian *Secreta Secretorum* made for the young Edward III in *c.*1326–7 and intended by Walter de Milemete to serve as a companion volume to his treatise *De nobilitatibus, sapientiis, et prudentiis regum,* an illumination (Pl. 5)—with a top border decoration showing two grotesque man/beasts playing a courtly game of chess—depicts a king enthroned, before whom three knights kneel, carrying furs of miniver over their arms.[177] This may represent the giving of liveries of fur and cloth by a prince.[178] A frame or rack at the rear of the picture space is hung with furs and textiles. The accompanying text, however, concerns itself with the dress of the prince, who must appear in public clad in 'costly, beautiful and exotic (*extraneis*) garments', surpassing all others in quality.[179] Edward III, judging from the accounts of his wardrobe and household, did his best to follow this injunction.[180] In the text of the *Secreta* much play is made with the notion of princely magnificence, and an anecdote is told about the semi-legendary courts of India, where the ruler appeared in spectacular garments and distributed gifts once a year.[181] The section of the text illustrated by the illumination reads: 'Multum convenit regie maiestati sive dignitati honorifice indui, et semper pulcro apparatu apparere, et excellere alios in decore vestium'[182] ['It very much behoves royal majesty and dignity to be dressed honourably, and always to appear beautifully apparelled, and to exceed all others in the fineness of clothing']. Whether or not the miniature actually shows a livery distribution, its emphasis upon the significance of fine garments, and the materials from which they were made, as an expression of rank and status, is very clear.

In 1311–12, when Thomas and Edmund were now brothers, rather than infant sons, of the reigning king (Edward II), the size of their household had expanded to fifty-three members, and the wardrobe book for

---

[177] BL, Add. MS 47680, fo. 17v.

[178] Lachaud, 'Textiles, Furs and Liveries', 196–7, 414–15, and Plate I.

[179] BL, Add. MS 47680, fo. 17v and *Opera . . . Rogeri Baconi, v. Secreta Secretorum,* ed. R. Steele (Oxford, 1920), 48.

[180] See Vale, *Edward III and Chivalry,* 65, 69–71, 175.

[181] See *Secreta Secretorum,* ed. Steele, 49.   [182] BL, Add. MS 47680, fo. 17v.

that year reveals a more fully-fledged establishment.[183] The total expenditure on cloth and furs for liveries at All Saints, Christmas, Easter, and Pentecost amounted to 135 l. 2s. This represented a fall, however, from the sum expended in 1303–4, although the cost of cloths remained comparable (95 l. as against 101 l. in 1303–4).[184] The cost of furs in 1311–12 had, however, fallen drastically (41 l. 6s. 10d. as against 139 l. 6s. 8d). The cloths were bought from Peter Livisshe, a London cloth merchant, while the silk (*sindon*) used to line the summer liveries of the two brothers, their four knights, and the keeper of their wardrobe was purchased from Giovanni Vanne and his fellow members of the society of the Bellardi of Lucca.[185] The livery account is worth citing in some detail. A strict hierarchy of social status was maintained: the four household knights, headed by the seneschal John de Weston, received cloth of various colours for mi-parti robes, that is, robes divided into two equal, differently coloured, parts, at Christmas; medley and striped cloth at Pentecost. The four clerks, headed by the keeper of the princes' wardrobe, Master John de Claxton, received cloths of medium or dark blue (*bluetto azur'*) at Christmas; at Pentecost, only two clerks were included on the livery list—Claxton and Ambrose de Newburgh, both of whom received cloth *de colore*, but with silk lining for Claxton and lambswool for Newburgh.[186]

Eighteen squires were retained to serve the two ten- and eleven-year-old boys in this small household. At Christmas, their squires were issued with liveries of variously coloured cloth with which to make mi-parti liveries; at Pentecost, medley and rayed cloth. Now these cloths were identical in both type and cost to those received by the four knights. But squires were distinguished from knights by the materials provided for the lining of their garments: superior quality furs at Christmas for the knights, lambswool for the squires; silk at Pentecost for the knights, lambswool (possibly of a lighter variety) for the squires. This pattern repeated itself into the lower reaches of the household. The twenty-three valets of the chamber and various offices received rayed (striped) cloth and lambswool for linings at Christmas; but at Pentecost, no liveries were given to them. The four *garciones* also received striped cloth at Christmas; nothing at Pentecost. But, alone among the rest of the household, both valets and *garciones* were given footwear for both winter and summer use, admittedly at a total cost of only 9 l.[187] But it was perhaps here that the greatest wear and tear in dress among the lower orders took place. Their

[183] E.101/374/19.   [184] Ibid., fos. 13r–v, and see above, pp. 105–6.
[185] E.101/374/19, fo. 13v.   [186] Ibid., fo. 15v.   [187] Ibid., fos. 11r, 15r–v.

liveries of cloth, moreover, were of exactly the same quantity as those delivered to other members of the household (6½ ells each) and probably served to make a number of garments for both winter and summer use. But the contrast with the two young princes could hardly have been greater. Resplendent in liveries given them four times in the year, at All Saints, Christmas, Easter and Pentecost, each comprising 17 ells of cloth (rather than 14, as in 1305–6), adjusted to their age and size, subtly differentiated from those worn by their knights, Edward II's brothers kept up a state of appropriately princely magnificence.[188]

That it was incumbent upon a royal, or noble, house to keep its household servants, clients, and retainers in a decently clothed state is apparent from a number of sources. The treatise known as the *Rules of St Robert*, probably drawn up as an ordinance for the household of Robert Grosseteste, bishop of Lincoln, and then revised in the 1240s for that of Hawise de Quincy, countess of Lincoln, included the injunction that her knights, and all those who took livery of robes from her, should not wear 'old tabards, dirty surcoats nor *cuntrefetes curtepies*' [short jackets] at meals or in her presence.[189] Decent clothing for an entourage, usually supplied in the form of liveries at the lord's or lady's expense, was essential for the maintenance of social status and of the dignity of lordship. Shabby or even filthy household knights, squires, or servants did nothing to promote deference or recognition of rank and position. The authority and status of a prince was reflected in the outward appearance of his following. While excess was to be avoided, the external aspect of a household was to be appropriate to the status of its master.[190] In March 1301, for example, Edward I ordered the keeper of his wardrobe to issue a special livery of cloth to sixteen extremely badly dressed valets from the garrison of Stirling castle who were following his court on the road every day.[191] The cloth was to be of the same *suite* or suit, so that a uniform appearance would be achieved. Otherwise, such people were a disgrace and an affront to majesty.

On some occasions, moreover, crises could occur which rendered such measures even more pressing. At Berwick, on 28 June 1314, when Edward II's household was reeling from the shock of defeat at the hands

---

[188] E.101/374/19., fo. 15v.

[189] *Walter of Henley*, ed. D. Oschinsky (Oxford, 1971), 402.

[190] For adverse comments on Edward II's excesses see e.g. the *Gesta* of the canon of Bridlington, in *Chronicles of the Reigns of Edward I and Edward II*, ed. W. Stubbs (RS, London, 1883), ii. 91.

[191] C.47/22/4/50; cited Lachaud, 'Textiles, Furs and Liveries', 191.

of the Scots at Bannockburn, the keeper of the queen's wardrobe had to
lend the king money for such purposes. Edward had reached Berwick,
accompanied by his fleeing army, which included a small group of
German or Netherlandish knights (*militibus Alemannie*).[192] They had
appeared, in their distress, dressed—or perhaps disguised—as paupers
(*in pauperibus vesturis indutis*) and were given a special livery of 40 marks
to buy themselves new clothes.[193] Even at times of acute crisis, appearances had to be kept up. But by February 1316, Edward's battered and
depleted household had recovered from the worst effects of the setback,
and the surviving roll 'of the great livery made . . . in the ninth year' of his
reign made lavish provision for the display of fittingly regal majesty.[194]

The issue of liveries recorded on the roll was confined to the king and
queen, their immediate family, a few knights, and some of the clerical
members of their households. But we know that liveries were also given to
the knights and other secular members of the household. Between July
1315 and February 1316, a total of 627 l. had been paid to provide robes
for the seven bannerets, forty-five simple knights, and all other members
of the household.[195] The livery roll for February to July 1316 reveals a
lavish outlay of cloth, most of it dyed in the wool (*pannus in grana*), and
of furs for an even smaller circle. The Easter livery for 1316 was, appropriately for the season, of green cloth, trimmed and lined with miniver,
issued to the king, queen, prince Edward, the countesses of Hereford,
Warwick, and Cornwall, and Lady Despenser.[196] At Pentecost, the king,
queen, and prince received robes lined with silk (*sindon*), while the king's
confessor and other clerks had cloth of *burnet* and *camel*. His brother,
Thomas of Brotherton, now a youth of sixteen years, and earl marshal,
was given scarlet and silk to have a tunic and cloak made for Pentecost.
His two knights bachelor received woollen cloth, to be lined with silk.
One of the largest issues was, however, the Pentecost livery of 162 ells
of variously coloured cloth plus furs to the boys, or wards, in the king's
custody. Edward also gave a 'private livery' of eleven green cloths dyed in

[192] E.101//375/9, fo. 19r: 'Domino Rege, de prestito per manum domini Johannis de
Reffeseyt et sociis suis, militibus Alemannie, venientibus cum dicto Rege de conflictu
Strivelyn in pauperibus vesturis indutis, in denariis liberatis eisdem de garderobe Regine
de dono eiusdem Regis, ad novam vesturam eisdem emendam . . .'
[193] The 'Johannes de Reffeseyt' mentioned in the account may be identified as a
member of the family of Ryfferscheid, from the county of Juliers. See G. Nijsten, *Het hof
van Gelre* (Kampen, 1992), 298 n. 8, 371. I owe this reference to the kindness of Dr Gerard
Nijsten.
[194] E.101/376/22.   [195] E.101/376/7, fos. 54r–v, 86r–94r.
[196] E.101/376/22, m. 1r.

the wool, plus furs, to his household knights at a date unconnected with the distribution of general liveries. Such evidence warns us that the practice of giving regular or 'full' liveries (*pleine* in the continental sense) was not the only means whereby a ruler might both reward and sustain his entourage in this form.[197] Occasional grants, or gifts, always lay at his disposal. The fact that the livery given to the knights in 1316 was of a uniform colour also raises the question of how far a distinctive and clearly recognizable 'system' of liveries had developed by the end of the second decade of the fourteenth century. The role of heraldic insignia in that process also has to be considered.

The issue of liveries of identical cloth—and of clothing made up from lengths of fabric of the same quality and colour (*de una secta, d'une suite*)—to members of the English royal household and its dependents was partly determined by a desire to maintain and regulate standards of dress. It was not confined to England.[198] Factors such as the availability of cloth for purchase and ease of access to sources of supply must also be taken into account. Under Edward I, for instance, the clothing of the king's falconers in cloth 'de la seute de eux qi sont demorauntz a la court' enabled them to be uniformly dressed and recognized.[199] Examples could be multiplied almost endlessly. Each category of the household—and of dependent households—could be given liveries of the same quality and colour, although the practice was by no means universally or consistently applied under Edward I. Later evidence, however, points in the direction of greater uniformity—in 1331–2, queen Philippa gave a gift of 'striped cloth of Ghent, *de secta vallettorum stabuli*' ['of the suit', or cut, 'of the valets of the stable'].[200] The livery rolls of 1316, 1334–6, and 1337–9 refer not only to standard types and colours of cloth, but also to the cut and style of some of the garments which were to be made from the fabric.[201] Thus Edward II himself received 16 ells of green medley for two sleeved tunics and two tabards in 1316, while three of his household knights had 12 ells 'for their tunics' (*ad jupas suas*).[202] By 1334–6 the documentation is even more specific, listing the number of garments to be made in each 'robe' issued and referring to items such as tunics *ad*

---

[197] E.101/376/22, mm. 2r, 3r.

[198] For evidence from Flanders and Hainault-Holland, see below, pp. 116, 123, 132, 134–5. See also Table 15(c).

[199] E.101/359/4 and see Lachaud, 'Textiles, Furs and Liveries', 49–87, for discussion of the supply of textiles to the court of Edward I.

[200] E.101/383/2.   [201] See E.101/376/22 (1316); 387/14 (1334–6); 388/8 (1337–9).

[202] E.101/376/22, m. 1r.

modum Almanie ['in the German fashion'].[203] A uniform issue of coloured cloth, to be combined with rayed (striped) cloth in mi-parti *supertunicas*, was made to Edward III's valets of the offices as their summer livery.[204] All this evidence combines to suggest that changes had taken place in the 'system' of costume at the English court over the first three decades of the fourteenth century.

The precise nature and significance of those changes is not easy to describe nor demonstrate, because many anomalies can be found. But the material examined so far suggests that visual identification of an individual's status and function was far more feasible by 1340 than it had been in 1270. The beginnings of what might be called colour-coding of liveries at the English court can be traced to the reign of Edward I. It has been shown that the king's clerks, wards, and knights of his household were often issued with uniform liveries, although the choice of colour could vary from time to time according to market conditions and the availability of cloth.[205] Dependent and lesser households also seem to have had their own means of identification. Hence a series of livery accounts, apparently for the Clare household, between 1291 and 1304, speak of the issue of *reies a ses esquiers* ['striped cloths for his [Gilbert de Clare's] squires'], *reies de Gant aleus ses esquiers, reie de meme le seute, draps de raye a esquiers*, and of white *camelin* for liveries.[206] Although not standard practice, the provision of uniform liveries of the same colour to some categories of Edward I's household between 1300 and 1303 is also revealing.[207] The king's chaplains received blue cloth (of varying shades or hues); the knights predominantly green cloths; and the squires and valets striped cloths (ray).

The later evidence, from the livery rolls and accounts of Edward II's and Edward III's reigns, tends to support the hypothesis that blue, green, and ray (sometimes in mi-parti combinations) had become associated with the clerks/chaplains, knights, squires, and valets respectively of the royal household. Squires could be distinguished from valets only by the quality, trimming, lining (and perhaps cut) of their striped garments. Blue was the dominant colour for clerical liveries under Edward I and this continued under his successors.[208] Analysis of the material for the years

---

[203] E.101/387/14, m. 1r.   [204] Ibid., m. 2r.

[205] See, for an analysis of the evidence for Edward I's livery distributions, Lachaud, 'Textiles, Furs and Liveries', 229–33.

[206] E.101/353/8, mm. 10, 11, 13, 18, 21; 363/17/17 and 20.

[207] See Table 15(c) and C.47/4/5.

[208] See Lachaud, 'Textiles, Furs and Liveries', 221–2, and her table XXVIII.

from 1299 to 1307 has shown that green was the dominant colour for knights, although whether this applied to the wearing of livery on an everyday basis, as well as on solemn occasions, is a matter for speculation.[209] Rayed and mi-parti clothing remained largely confined to the squires, valets, and other servants. It could be given as charitable alms to paupers on Good Friday.[210] Clerks appear not to have been issued with rayed cloth. This was not because of some assumed association between striped cloth and the diabolical, but was determined by considerations of cost, in turn directly related to social and professional (or vocational) status.[211] A clerk might, however, be given a livery of scarlet, as was John de Droxford, keeper of the wardrobe, no doubt as a recognition of his exceptional and privileged position.[212] The ebb and flow of fashion has also to be taken into the reckoning in any analysis of the significance of changes in the choice of colour and pattern. In any discussion of liveries, moreover, technical questions—such as the ability of cloth-making techniques to achieve new effects, or the availability and properties of dyestuffs—have to be taken into account. If new (or improved) techniques became available to weavers, dyers, and finishers of cloth, it would be odd if they were not applied to the creation of new products and effects which might, in turn, have wider implications.

The technical developments in cloth production of the second half of the thirteenth century led to a greater output of two major products: fine quality woollens, largely for the aristocratic and upper bourgeois market; and rayed or striped cloth, which was very popular, above all at the lower end of the market.[213] A shift away from the manufacture of traditional monochrome cloths towards the production of striped cloth has been detected in many cloth-making centres from the 1280s onwards.[214] Improved dyeing techniques also enabled colours to become

---

[209] See Lachaud, 'Textiles, Furs and Liveries', table XXIX.

[210] E.101/376/22, m. 1r (1316).

[211] Cf. M. Pastoureau, *L'Étoffe du diable: une histoire des rayures et des tissus rayés* (Paris, 1991), 17–24, and his 'L'église et la couleur des origines à la Reforme', *BEC* 147 (1989), 227–8.

[212] E.101/357/26; 358/13/23.

[213] See A. Derville, 'Les draperies flamandes et artésiennes vers 1250–1350: quelques considérations critiques et problemmatiques', *RN* 54 (1972), 353–70; P. Chorley, 'The cloth exports of Flanders and Northern France during the XIIIth century: a luxury trade?', *EcHR* 2nd ser. 40 (1987), 349–79; R–H. Bautier, 'La place de la draperie brabançonne et plus particulièrement bruxelloise dans l'industrie textile du moyen âge', *Annales de la Société Royale d'Archéologie de Bruxelles*, 51 (1966), 31–63.

[214] See Derville, 'Les draperies flamandes et artésiennes', 366–9; Chorley, 'The cloth exports of Flanders and Northern France', 360–2.

more standardized and stable. These developments enabled the cloth industry to produce both striped and banded cloth on a much larger scale. Cloth woven in horizontal strips of different colours could produce a *barré* effect, while vertical, or diagonal stripes were characteristic of *rayé* cloths, which could resemble a *pale* pattern (frontispiece).[215] To produce cloth which was readily adaptable, if so desired, to heraldic use, cheaply and in large quantities, may have had wider implications. The basic elements of armorial design—bands, bars, pales, chequers, and chevrons—could now be reproduced with relative ease, sometimes in combination, by the cloth-worker. Mi-parti clothing could also simulate the impaling—and even quartering—of coats of arms, whereby one colour was juxtaposed to another. This must, however, remain a speculative argument until further study is made of the subject.

Whatever the case, it is clear that improvements in cloth-making and dyeing techniques, whereby multi-coloured and striped cloths could be more easily and successfully produced, had some impact upon the rise of liveries as a means of identification. 'It is probable that cloths of ray had specific colours, and that it was the diffusion of rays that made possible the use of colour-coding on costume. The later history of liveries . . . suggests that ray cloth played a major role in the diffusion of liveries using recognizable colours. This also explains why stripes came to be seen as a symbol of service and allegiance.'[216] While it could also be argued that the origin of such tendencies might be found in the use of monochrome cloths—often of greater depth and stability of colour as a result of improved dyeing techniques—to clothe a given status-group or category of household servants, the argument is well founded. It was apparent that by the end of the first quarter of the fourteenth century, the wearing of liveries had assumed certain additional connotations. The colours and patterns of cloth worn by members of some households—not only the royal household—in England seem to have become cognizances, or means of recognition, which sometimes carried social and political overtones. In March 1322, for example, Thomas, earl of Lancaster, defeated after his rebellion against Edward II, was stripped of his armour and dressed in the livery which, the chronicler tells us, he had given to his squires—that is, of rayed or striped cloth.[217] This was seen as a sign of his ignominy, not because rayed cloth was (as Michel Pastoureau and Ruth

---

[215] See the representation of the members of Alexander's court at a feast, wearing striped and banded costume, in Bodleian Library, MS Bodley 264, fo. 188v (1338–44).

[216] Lachaud, 'Textiles, Furs and Liveries', 239.

[217] See *The Brut*, ed. F. W. D. Brie, *EETS* orig. ser. 131 (1906), 219.

Mellinkoff appear to believe) evil or diabolical in its associations, but because Lancaster was deemed unworthy of his exalted rank.[218] He was thus symbolically demoted to the non-knightly rank of squire.[219] It has been shown that the surviving wardrobe acounts for the Lancaster household for 1313–14, for instance, confirm that the summer livery for the squires was indeed of rayed cloth.[220] It would be surprising if this was not the case in 1322. Livery was by this date clearly equated with rank.

As livery became a species of device or cognizance, heraldic elements of an emblematic kind were soon added to it. It is not the purpose of this study to investigate the origins of so-called livery and maintenance, nor the early development of 'bastard feudalism' in England.[221] But the emergence of what one might call 'heraldic costume' in a courtly setting appears to have accompanied the trends in the nature and functions of livery which have been outlined above. It has been argued that the thirteenth century witnessed a marked extension of heraldic decoration to garments in the form of pendants, embroidery, and so on (Pl. 6).[222] Evidence for the use of heraldic devices and insignia on both civil and military dress becomes more plentiful by the 1240s and 1250s. Heraldic elements had probably been introduced into royal costume at the Plantagenet court at an earlier date. The practice was thus very well established when, at Pentecost 1306, for the Feast of the Swans at Westminster, Prince Edward received garments which may have alluded to the tinctures of his coat of arms—red (*gules*) for the field, yellow (*or*) for the lions or leopards, and purple (*pourpre*) for the label indicating his position as eldest son.[223] As king, in April 1316, he had a livery of two tunics, both bearing his heraldic arms. Six ells of scarlet were provided for the tunics, and two ells of yellow cloth for the leopards which were sewn on to

---

[218] Cf. Pastoureau, *L'Étoffe du diable*, 17–24; R. Mellinkoff, *Outcasts: Signs of Otherness in Northern European Art of the Late Middle Ages*, i (Berkeley, 1993), 167–84.

[219] The execution of the Gascon noble Jourdain de l'Isle for his crimes in May 1323, dressed in the pope's livery (he was a kinsman of John XXII) was reported in the *Grandes Chroniques de France*, ed. J. Viard, ix (Paris, 1939), 17–18, and see Vale, *Origins of the Hundred Years War*, 137–8.

[220] See J. F. Baldwin, 'The household administration of Henry Lacy and Thomas of Lancaster', *EHR* 47 (1927), 198–9.

[221] For a recent discussion see P. R. Coss, 'Bastard feudalism revised', *P&P* 125 (1989), 27–64, and D. Crouch, D. A. Carpenter, and P. R. Coss, 'Debate: Bastard feudalism revised', *P&P* 131 (1991), 165–203.

[222] See J. Cherry, 'Heraldry as decoration in the thirteenth century', in W. M. Ormrod (ed.), *Harlaxton Medieval Studies*, i. *England in the Thirteenth Century*, 123–34.

[223] C.47/3/30, m. 1r.

them.[224] He also received more scarlet for the making of two bags or purses (*malas*). The rest of his household received monochrome or striped cloths for their liveries, so that the king stood out from his entourage in this respect. By the reign of Edward III, the provision of heraldic costume for the sovereign, and also for his household, becomes more common—the king's Christmas livery was often of scarlet, providing a ground for appropriate heraldic decoration.[225] By the 1380s and 1390s, the English royal household had adopted Richard II's red and white livery, with emblems of a white hart upon it.[226] As early as the 1340s, however, a profusion of cognizances and devices, associated with costume, were already found in the wardrobe and household accounts of Edward III.[227] This may suggest that a transition from the use of livery as a distinguishing mark of social, functional, or status-groups to use as a means whereby dynastic, political, and personal affiliation and allegiance could be expressed, had already taken place in England. The position concerning this development in other parts of north-west Europe will now be considered.

b. Flanders, Artois, and Hainault-Holland

The Flemish evidence for distribution of cloth and furs as liveries is derived mainly from the household accounts and supporting documentation which survive for the household and entourage of Guy de Dampierre (1278–1305) and his successors. The accounts refer to liveries from the winter of 1268 onwards, but the practice of distributing cloth was clearly of long standing.[228] Grants by the count of *vestes sive robas* [clothes or robes] for life to faithful servants, such as Pierre, *prévôt* of the church of Béthune, are found, in which he was also said to be 'of our household and our council, and that of our heirs'.[229] A total of 267 l. 17s. 7d. was expended *pour les dras des varles diver* and *pour les dras dou Nouel* ['for the cloths of various valets' and 'for Christmas cloths'] in 1268. During Guy's Tunis expedition with Louis IX in 1270–1, his clerk Jean Makiel distributed liveries to his knights and others *pour leur dras de ii termes* ['for their cloths at two terms'] and noted that the count owed

[224] E.101/376/22, m. 1r.   [225] E.101/387/14 (1334).

[226] See D. Gordon, *Making and Meaning: The Wilton Diptych* (London, 1993), 12–24.

[227] See J. Vale, *Edward III and Chivalry*, 64–71; Saul, *Richard II*, 265–6.

[228] RAG, Wyffels, (chron. suppl.) 35.

[229] ADN, B.893, no. 1691: 2 May 1270; and B.3229, no. 3126a for his quittance for winter and Easter robes, 23 Feb. 1290.

42 l. 10s.t. for a large quantity—85 ells—of 'English scarlet', received at
Tunis.[230] The account also listed the thirty-three names of those of his
valets who received cloths, both within and outside the household.[231] In
1272–3, the costs of carriage of liveries of cloth for the household servants
and for the count himself, the countess, her *damoiselles*, and his knights
and serjeants were recorded.[232] The association of squires and valets with
striped cloth was already made in Flanders by 1275, when the valets of the
lord of Mortagne received four *dras piers roies* ['dark blue striped cloths'],
and fur, for their Easter liveries.[233] At the court of Flanders, livery distributions appear to have taken place at All Saints, Christmas, and Easter:
in April 1277, five green cloths and 15 ells of blue cloth were bought for
the count's knights at a cost of 67 l. 16s. 4d. and further expenditure was
incurred on Christmas and All Saints liveries.[234] A continuous series
of references to liveries of cloth are found in the Flemish household
accounts (for both the count and countess) throughout the 1270s and
1280s. The practice was clearly very well established by that date.

The survival of very full and detailed livery rolls from the 1290s and
early 1300s reveals an extensive use of distributions of cloth and furs at
the court of Flanders. In 1293–4, for example, the countess distributed a
large quantity of medley (*dras melles*) for the robes of her *damoiselles* at
Pentecost 1294.[235] A uniform appearance must have been given to this
group of women, headed by the countess herself, also in a robe of medley.
A further issue of medley to the *petis enfans me dame de Flandres* ['small
children of my lady of Flanders'] at Pentecost 1296 suggests that this type
of cloth may have been a regular Pentecost livery.[236] It also appears to have
been a comital practice to send liveries of cloth to those who qualified for
them, even when they were abroad. Hence in the spring of 1304 one of the
count's household marshals was sent to England 'with the cloths of the
lords of Picquigny and of Gavre'.[237] Knights and nobles retained as
clients or *alliés* of the count also received the wherewithal to clothe themselves. In February 1290, Waléran, lord of Fauquemont and Montjoie,
petitioned Guy de Dampierre for payment of 200 l.p. *en dras et en pennes*
['in cloth and furs'] to be bought by his agent, and which Waléran would

---

[230] See *Het Memoriaal van Jehan Makiel*, ed. Buntinx, 81, 104, 107.
[231] Ibid. 129–30.
[232] Ibid. 144–5. The cloth was brought from Douai and Lille to Male.
[233] See above, pp. 112–14, and RAG, Wyffels, (chron. suppl.) 65*bis*.
[234] RAG, St-Genois 209.   [235] RAG, Gaillard 52, m. 10r.
[236] RAG, Gaillard 58, m. 2r.   [237] RAG, Wyffels, (chron. suppl.) 411.

acknowledge at the following Pentecost.[238] But the most comprehensive pieces of evidence for liveries at the court of Flanders are a livery roll of November 1307 and the receiver's account for the year 1308–9.[239] In 1307, the distribution took place at All Saints (6 November) when both furs (graded according to rank) and cloths were issued to Robert de Béthune's household. Both cloth and fur were bought in bulk from the cloth merchant Gossuin of Ghent.[240] The count's clerks received blue cloth or medley; he and his knights green cloth; his squires ray and *gaude* (mottled) cloth for mi-parti robes, and the domestic *maisnie* cloths of various colours. Again, the issue of rayed cloth to the squires confirms a more general practice, and its connotations of service and dependence were also exemplified by the record of a remnant of ray *de maisnies* among the goods found in the possession of Guy de Dampierre on his death in 1305.[241] The lord of Ghistelles, as hereditary chamberlain of Flanders, received his accustomed three *mantiaus* of fur at Christmas and Pentecost (in other words, fur with which to line the cloaks in which he and his knights performed their service before the count). Livery distribution had therefore developed a certain degree of sophistication in Flanders, and its functions appear to have been very close to those outlined above for the English court.[242]

Expenditure on liveries formed a substantial item in the comital budget. In 1307, they accounted for a grand total of 4,651 l.flandr. (*monnaie forte*).[243] In 1309, the total bill for liveries of cloth and furs was 4,190 l. 14s. 5d.flandr. although the final figure was higher (6,687 l. 16s. 5d. flandr.) because Robert de Béthune, as an imperial vassal, had attended the coronation of Henry of Luxemburg as king of the Romans.[244] This involved the fitting out of Robert's retinue, consisting of knights banneret and bachelors, including the count of Nevers, with very expensive dark blue cloth (*piers*) and scarlet, miniver and *gros vair*, and included the

---

[238] ADN, B.4047, no. 145235: 23 Feb. 1290.

[239] RAG, Gaillard 64, 65; AGR, CC, R.1, and Table 15(c), see also Appendix X for the livery roll of 1307.

[240] RAG, Gaillard 64, m. 1r: The roll is headed 'Cest li livrisons des pennes de le Toussains prisses a Goisson de Kolemghien de Gand le lundi apres le Saint Martin en yvier lan 1307'. Further payments to Gossuin for cloth are recorded and a payment 'pour les despens Andriu [le tailleur] a le maison Gossuin de Kalenghien et pour ouvrages de valles'. See Appendix X and Table 15(c).

[241] RAG, Gaillard 746, m. 2r: 'Item, 1 remanant de roie de maisnies'. For his testamentary legacies see Table 18.

[242] See above, pp. 110–12.   [243] RAG, Gaillard 64, 65. See Table 15(c).

[244] AGR, CC, R.1, m. 18r.

replacement of the furs bought for Nevers with pelts of finer quality. They also took silken banners and pennons with them.[245] The cost of 'ordinary' liveries in 1309—excluding the cost of the coronation liveries—was therefore about 16.5% of total expenditure during that year.[246] Colour-coding was also clearly applied to these carefully graded issues of livery. The count's knights received medley; the clerks (apparently) *pers* or blue; the count, his son and daughter, light blue cloth (*cler bleu*); the *damosielles* of his daughter superior quality *pers*; the squires white camelin and ray, to be (as in 1307) divided into mi-parti robes. The count's *maisnie*, or service household, received ray , while the *garçons* at the bottom of the functional and social hierarchy were given cloth of Ypres of unspecified colour or colours. Further liveries were given to individuals: the count, his daughter, and Florent, lord of Beersel, received a distinctive issue of white cloth *a cendal* (taffeta silk) which was to be lined with crimson silk (*cendals vermaus*), no doubt achieving a striking sartorial effect. The count's confessor, almoner, the clerk of his chapel, the chamberlain, the *saussier*, the *sommelier*, and Jean, lord of Bailleul, all received their own personal liveries of cloth.

Distribution of furs followed a similarly hierarchical pattern. As in 1307, miniver (white fur) ranked highest in the pecking order and was given to the count and his immediate family. It was mixed with a livery of *gros vair* (grey fur) for the knights banneret, while the bachelors got *kierkes*, or complete pelts, of unspecified fur, costing $6\frac{1}{2}$d.*d'or* (a single miniver fur cost 5d.*d'or*).[247] The clerks, interestingly, not only received both miniver and *gros vair*, but *kierkes* of exactly the same quality and price as the knights bachelor, while the squires had lambswool furs costing $\frac{1}{2}$d.*d'or* each. Individuals such as the chamberlain and the almoner were provided with their normal allowances. The *maisnie* received no liveries of furs at all. This omission, and other aspects of these very detailed livery accounts, puts livery distribution at the court of Flanders into an ambivalent relationship with the sumptuary legislation of 1279 and 1294 in the kingdom of France.[248] Liveries to the household —as in Hainault—certainly conformed in some respects to the social and

---

[245] AGR, CC, R.1, m. 16v, and m. 16r: 'Pour 2 fourures a caperon cangies pour plus fines pour mon seigneur de Nevers'.

[246] Ibid., m. 25r and, for what follows, mm. 16v–17r. Cf. Table 15(c).

[247] See above, p. 117, and RAG, Gaillard 64, m. 1r.

[248] See Duplès Agier, 'Une ordonnance somptuaire inédite', 176–81.

material criteria set out in the royal *ordonnances*.[249] The restriction of the wearing of miniver, *gros vair, gris*, and ermine to the nobility was borne out by the Flemish evidence in 1307 and 1308–9. The count's squires, for example, were not issued with such furs.[250] But the issue of furs of miniver and *gros vair* to the clerks of the comital household—unless they were all beneficed, which was unlikely—appears to be in direct contravention of the *ordonnances*, and the value of many of the liveries given in 1307 and 1309 would not correspond, even allowing for monetary movements in the interim, with the maximum prices for clothing allowed in 1294.[251]

The very high level of expenditure on liveries—and on the comital household as a whole—became an object of grave concern to the count's chief advisers under Louis de Nevers (1322–46).[252] But the count continued to adopt his predecessors' practices and retained knights, squires, and others with fees and robes. Before his accession, for example, he had given life grants to men such as Wautier Vilain, one of his *varlets*, of *nos draps a sa vie tels que nous donrons et devons a nos escuiers* ['our cloths, for his lifetime, such as we give and owe to our squires'] in October 1312.[253] Reforms or no reforms, this practice was continued throughout his reign. A series of letters of life retainder confirms this inescapable obligation. In October 1332, Guy of Flanders, lord of Riquebourg, was retained as a knight banneret of Louis's household, *chargie et montei selonc nostre estat* ['equipped and mounted according to our estate'] at the count's expense.[254] In September 1338, moreover, Jean de Saint-Quentin was retained for life as a knight bachelor of the household (*de nostre hostel et mesnage*) with livery of robes as given to other knights bachelor (*nos robes teles que nous liverons a nos autres chevaliers bachelers*).[255] But the level of expenditure incurred by the receiver of Flanders on household expenses was, as we have seen, deemed to be unsupportable in 1332. The question of

---

[249] For Hainault-Holland, see below, pp. 129–30; also *Ordonnances des Rois de France*, i. 541–3.

[250] See RAG, Gaillard 64, m. IV (1307); AGR, CC, R.I, m. 17v (1309).

[251] See Duplès Agier, 'Une ordonnance somptuaire inédite', 179–80; Lachaud, 'Textiles, Furs and Liveries', table XII.

[252] See above, pp. 88–93 and Tables 2, 3.

[253] ADN, B.4062, no. 145522: 16 Oct. 1312.

[254] ADN, B.499, no. 6521: 29 Oct. 1332; a similar contract with Rogier, lord of Hangest, is found in B.4065, no. 145579 (Nov. 1333).

[255] ADN, B.4065, no. 145584: 2 and 4 Sept. 1338. For a similar grant to Geoffroi de Weis, knight, of 'nos robes teles et tantefois comme les donrons a noz autres chevaliers' see B.4065, no. 145585 (15 and 16 Jan. 1342).

liveries was, moreover, broached in the memorandum of advice given by Guillaume d'Auxonne and his colleagues.

They considered the 4,500 l.p. spent on the 'ordinary' livery distributions to be acceptable, but thought the 2,000 l.p. for 'extraordinary' liveries to be at least 1,000 l.p. too high.[256] The excessive amount spent was, they warned, much talked about.[257] As it was, the ordinary livery accounted for over 31% of total daily household expenditure. The recommended figure tallied well with actual disbursements: 4,651 l. in 1307, 4,190 l. in 1309, 4,910 l. in 1335.[258] To keep within the parameters laid down (that is, about 4,500 l. per year on ordinary liveries, 1,000 l. on extraordinary liveries and personal clothing for the count and countess) meant that the numbers in receipt of them had to be kept down, and that distribution should take place only once per year.[259] The evidence of the livery rolls after 1332 is of considerable interest from this point of view. Economies were clearly being attempted: the receiver's account for September 1335 to November 1336 included a receipt for cloth, including two *draps de gens de mestiers* ['two cloths for people of household offices'] and one cloth of *royet des escuiers* ['ray for squires'], remaining from the previous All Saints livery in November 1334.[260] A comparison between the quantities of cloths purchased for the All Saints livery of 1335 and the list of liveries given out in 1330, drawn up by the count's advisers in 1332, is instructive. In 1330, liveries of cloth had been given as follows:[261]

Dras de banerez	36 *chevaliers*	
Dras de chevaliers	61	
Dras de granz clers	10 *de consel*	
Dras dautres clers	32	
Dras de petiz clers	10	
Dras descuiers	180	
Dras de mestier	61	
Dras petiz	41	
Dras de dames	3	
Dras de demisseles	7	
Total liveries	441	

---

[256] ADN, B.1569, fo. 69r, and see above, pp. 90–3, and Table 2.
[257] ADN, B.1569, fo. 71v.
[258] See above, p. 90, and AGR, CC, R.5, mm. 11r–12r.
[259] ADN, B.1569, fo. 71v.   [260] AGR, CC, R.5, m. 9r.
[261] ADN, B.1569, fo. 94r.

At the feast of All Saints (6 November) 1335, the following liveries were issued by Nicholas Gaidouche, receiver of Flanders:

Draps melles de grans clers	34
Draps melles de chevaliers	36
Draps royes pour petis valles	15
Draps melles de graine pour grans clers	2
Draps royes de grainne pour chevaliers	3
Draps royes pour chevaliers	29
Draps royes pour escuiers	36
[Draps] blans pour escuiers	36
Draps royes pour gens de mestier	11
Draps bleus	12
Draps melles pour damosielles de chambre	4
Drap melle pour petis clers	1
Total liveries	219[262]

Further distribution of furs followed, including 6 *livrées* for *grans banne-rez*, 14 for *bannerez*, 104 for knights bachelor, and 72 pelts of lamb's fur. The materials for liveries had been purchased in Flanders, France, Nevers, and Rethel. The two lists are, perhaps, not strictly comparable. While the list of 1330 seems to refer to the number of persons receiving liveries, the 1335 account speaks in terms of types and amounts of cloth given to each category within the household. Some of these cloths were clearly intended for mi-parti costumes—certainly in the case of the 36 rays and 36 white cloths for squires, possibly in the case of the knights (36 cloths of medley and 29 rays). But whatever the case, the two lists empha-size the more uniform nature of fourteenth-century livery distributions and a stricter equation between status and type and quality of cloth. The association of rayed cloth with the valets and *gens de métier* was again very marked, although the knights may also have had mi-parti robes of ray and medley.

After the mid-1340s, the evidence for livery distributions at the court of Flanders becomes scantier as a result of the loss of documents. But there can be no doubt that it continued on a similar, if not larger, scale under Louis de Male (1346–84). Between 28 September and 13 December 1348, for example—a period in which the All Saints livery fell—the receiver's account makes no specific reference to an itemized cost of liveries, but gives a globalized total of 3,633 l. 10s. 2d.flandr. for all

[262] AGR, CC, R.5, mm. 11r–12r.

household expenditure during that time.[263] This must have included the cost of liveries, and was below the figure recommended by Louis de Nevers's advisers in 1332. But an additional sum of 284 l. 12s. was expended on cloth and furs *hors livrée* ['apart from the livery'].[264] This included the purchase from Walter Schinkel, draper of Bruges, of 36 ells of scarlet, of which 27 ells were crimson and the remaining nine were of *sanguine escarlate*, to make *cote-hardies*, with lined hoods, for Louis de Male and eight of his knights. A further length of scarlet ray—no doubt, given its high cost, of the finest quality—was bought from Guillaume Hooft for the count and three of his companions to wear at the All Saints feast in 1348. Expensive miniver was also bought, to trim and line the scarlet ray garments. By 1378–9, our knowledge of actual clothing worn by the count is much fuller. The very detailed account of Jean de Namur for furs, cloth, and tailoring expenses records the purchase of very large quantities of fur (1,724 pelts, for example) used to trim and line one of Louis de Male's winter cloaks (of blue cloth) and a scarlet *houpelande*, as well as the costs of repairing and renewing the collars and sleeves of other garments with fur during the winter.[265] Although full livery accounts do not appear to survive for the rest of Louis's reign, occasional references to the clothing of his household servants (and the accounts and contracts for retaining of knights and esquires) make it clear that the annual distributions still took place, supplemented by special provision for individuals. In June 1379, for instance, the count's three *maîtres d'hôtel* recognized that a fur dealer, Woutre Inghel, was owed money for the supply of

ii fourrures de vair, donnez en ce mois de juing . . . lune donnee atout la livree de monditseigneur au chastellain de Berghes, et lautre a messire Pierre de Delft . . . non contenues es comptes de la livree de monditseigneur donnee le premier jour de janvier 1378 precedent, ne depuis en nuls autres comptes, pour ce quil ne furent point adonc ordonnez a la livree de chevaliers de lostel de mondit-seigneur.[266]

[Two furs of squirrel, given in this month of June . . . one given with the livery of my lord to the castellan of Berghes, and the other to *messire* Peter of Delft . . . not recorded in the accounts for my lord's livery given on the preceding first day of January 1378, nor in any subsequent accounts, because they were not then included in the livery of my lord's household knights.]

[263] ADN, B.4066, no. 145592, and AGR, CC, R.6 for a duplicate copy.
[264] B.4066, no. 145592, m. 4r.
[265] B.4067, no. 21,057 (10 Feb. 1379).
[266] B.3232, no. 111716 (14 June 1379).

It seems that by this date the All Saints livery was supplemented by a January distribution. The recommendations of 1332 were perhaps a thing of the past, as household expenses escalated and court life assumed a more luxurious aspect during the last years of Louis de Male.[267] But it can be argued that, by the 1330s, the counts of Flanders were already incurring substantial costs on the provision of liveries to as many as 400 members of both their 'broader' and 'narrower' court. Graded according to social status, and also expressive of function within the household, these increasingly uniform liveries of cloth and furs were closely comparable with those given at the English court. The abundant commercial and mercantile resources of Flanders and Brabant, moreover, were brought to bear on the effective provision of materials for the court—a topic in economic history which still awaits its historian.

At the court of Artois the practice of livery distribution was well established by the time that archival records begin in the later thirteenth century. Cloth, furs, footwear, and saddles were given as liveries to the count's household and entourage. In 1292, Gautier de Bruxelles bought twenty-six saddles for the Pentecost livery which Robert II gave to his knights at Genoa, when he was supporting Charles of Anjou's Italian campaigns.[268] The saddles were decorated with Charles's arms, covered in velvet and silk, with the fleurs-de-lis of goldsmith's work. General liveries of cloth took place at All Saints, Christmas, Easter, and Pentecost—a more liberal provision than was the case in Flanders. In December 1295, the clothing entrepreneur Salomon Boinebroke of Douai was paid 1,077 l.p. at Paris for the supply of cloth *pour nous et pour nostre gent a vestir* ['to clothe ourself and our men'] at the previous feast of All Saints (1 November 1295).[269] During the count's expedition to fight the English in Gascony in April 1296, Boinebroke was recompensed for the cost of having cloths made

pour nous et pour nos chevaliers, et pour toute nostre autre gent, les ques nous deussiesmes avoir eus a Pasches darrenement passees, pour nostre viestir, sieles, lorains et autres chose necessaires faites pour nous et pour nostre gent de nostre commandement, prendes et recheues.[270]

[for us and for our knights, and for all our other people, which we ought to have had last Easter, for our clothing, saddles, harness and other necessary things made for us and our people by our order, taken and received.]

---

[267] See below, pp. 270–2. [268] ADPC, A.132, no. 3. See below, p. 277.

[269] ADPC, A.139, no. 61: 28 Dec. 1295. For Boinebroke see Espinas, 'Jehan Boine Broke, bourgeois et drapier douaisien', 224–48, and above, pp. 75–6.

[270] ADPC, A.140, no. 30: 30 Apr. 1296; and no. 40: 15 May 1296.

The liveries were to be sent to the count in south-west France, an order which had been carried out by 15 May 1296. Christmas liveries were provided on a regular basis: in December 1298, the *bailli* of Arras paid 24 l.p. to a female cloth-dealer for cloth to make long robes and surcoats for the count's huntsmen.[271] Our knowledge of livery distribution at the court of Artois is rendered fuller by a concentration of surviving household material for the last few months of Robert of Artois's life before his sudden death in battle at Kortrijk against the Flemings on 11 July 1302. Thus Jean de la Halle, *bourgeois* of Saint-Omer, was paid a total sum of 2,101 l. 4s.p. by the *bailli* of the town for the Easter liveries of cloth in 1302.[272] The count's Easter robe consisted of five garments, of *pers* (blue) cloth, lined with plain cloth and provided with 'false purses' or pockets.[273] The general livery for All Saints 1302—which Robert did not live to distribute—was, again, ordered from another member of the de La Halle family—Guillaume, merchant and *bourgeois* of Saint-Omer. He was paid 1,000 l.p. for the cloth in December 1302.[274] The count appears to have personally inspected samples of the cloth to be used for the liveries: on 4 June 1302, his tailor, Pierre de Bourges, was paid to go to Saint-Omer and bring back *lesamplaire* of the All Saints livery to the count at Pont-de-l'Arche.[275] He was also sent to Saint-Omer to take delivery of hunting surcoats (*cotes hardies a bois*) for the count and his huntsmen, as part of their livery, and bring them back to Hesdin and Arras. Some of the court of Artois was at Domfront, in Normandy, engaged in the hunt, and Robert was with them for part of the time. Evidently a substantial proportion of the *maisnie* were there, because the robes of the valets *de mestier* were packed up at Paris and transported there in June.[276]

No expense was spared on the count's dress during his last year, especially when he was with the king in Paris during the spring and early summer. Another robe of *pers* was made for him, together with a surcoat of camelin and a hunting jacket, while an elaborate hat, embroidered with silk, cloth of gold, and *sendal* (taffeta), studded with pearls, with 100 little rosettes on its laces, was worked on by five Parisian women embroiderers and seamstresses.[277] Proximity to the French royal line, and frequent residence in the city at the *hôtel d'Artois*, made the court of Artois more attuned to Parisian fashion and more prone to satisfy its needs there than

[271] ADPC, A.145, no. 28: 2 Dec. 1298.
[272] A.183, no. 66: at Paris, 12 Mar. 1302; A.184, no. 98: 29 June 1302.
[273] A.178, fo. 73v.   [274] A.186, no. 93: 26 Dec. 1302.
[275] A.178, fo. 73v.   [276] A.178, fos. 73v, 75r.
[277] A.178, fo. 73v; A.187, m. 2r.

some other princely households. Thus the count was indebted to two Breton furriers in Paris to the tune of 2,208 l. 16s. for the All Saints livery of 1301, owed the Italian banking firm of Scotti 800 l. for a loan, and 300 l.t. to Gautier de Bruxelles (who also dealt with the court of Flanders) for another loan.[278] Gautier had not been paid anything, it was noted, since the Easter livery of 1302. A high level of indebtedness to Parisian—or Paris-based—merchants, traders, artisans, and bankers was quite normal for the Artois household at this time.

Although the household of Artois disintegrated on Robert's death in July 1302—and some of its members perished, with their horses, in the carnage at Courtrai—the costs of the previous year's expenditure were still being paid off after his death.[279] His daughter Mahaut maintained a fitting level of expenditure upon display and upon the giving of liveries, although the character of the court of Artois inevitably underwent some changes during her lifetime.[280] A large quantity of evidence for livery distributions survives for her reign, but one livery account may be selected to illustrate the dominant tendencies of the period after Robert of Artois's death. In 1313 the All Saints livery of cloth and furs consisted of the following items:

19 *dras vermaus pour ma dame et pour ses chevaliers*
19 *dras melles vermaus pour clers*
19 *dras roiies de Gant pour esquyers a 1 camp marbre*
 6 *dras de valles de mestier*
 4 *dras roiies pour petis valles*[281]

The livery of cloth cost 55 l. 10s.t. without allowances for the expense of buying it (and furs) at Louvain, Ghent, and Bruges and of having it dyed. The furs included expensive miniver for the countess's robe and hood, and other lower quality furs for the household, totalling 28 l. 8s. 2d.t. without costs of purchase, transport, tolls, and so on. The grand total for the November livery of 1313 was 87 l. 19s. $10\frac{1}{2}$d.t. It is striking that the detail of type, quality, and colour of cloth accords very well with the evidence so far analysed from England and Flanders.[282] A uniform appearance was clearly given to each status- or functional group in the household of Artois, with the knights in crimson robes, the clerks

[278] A.181, no. 5.
[279] A.179, A.189, A.183 for arrears. Also Table 21.
[280] See Richard, 'Une petite-nièce de St-Louis', 87–102; and below, pp. 277–82.
[281] ADPC, A.1015, fos. 32r–33r.   [282] See above, pp. 99–115, 115–21.

(interestingly) in crimson medley, the squires in stripes (ray) with one 'field' or ground of marbled effect (*marbre*), the servants of the household offices (*de mestier*) in unspecified cloth—probably ray, judging by its price—and the menial servants also in ray. Price differentials confirmed the hierarchical gradations of the liveries. Each cloth provided for the household knights cost 23 s.t.; each cloth for the *petis valles* cost 11s.t.[283] Equivalences between livery, status, and function could hardly be closer.

As in England, the expense of fitting out dependent households was borne by the ruler's treasury in Artois. Thus a series of household and diet accounts for Robert, son of Mahaut d'Artois, and his younger brother Guillaume survive from 1309 onwards for periods when they were not in the countess's company.[284] They were provided with furred robes (of three garments), silk, cendal, silver-gilt buttons, and hose.[285] Their five valets also received hose. Liveries were apparently given to them at All Saints (1 November) and on Ascension Day (8 May), and the household account for May to November 1309 ran between those feast days.[286] This evidence may also reveal something about the impact of cloth-making techniques upon the production and dissemination of uniform liveries. Among the *mises extraordinaires* for 1314, there is mention of the making and supply of yellow silk and yellow cloth with which to make little escutcheons to mount on one of the tunics made for Robert of Artois.[287] A crimson silk tunic was also provided, with yellow silk for the escutcheons. Heraldic costume was being supplied here, and the movement towards the wearing of badges or devices was clearly in motion (Pl. 6).[288] Close-fitting jackets for arming himself were also made for Robert, which were said to be mi-parti, consisting partly of green worsted.[289] The technical developments outlined above may here have contributed to the provision of both military costume and civilian liveries.

The provision of liveries of cloth and furs to members of the household of the counts of Hainault pre-dated the thirteenth century. The incident recorded by Gislebert of Mons in his chronicle, when the hereditary

[283] ADPC, A.1015, fo. 32r.
[284] The accounts are found in ADPC, A.247, A.254, and A.321.
[285] A.247, fo. 27r: Feb.–Apr. 1309.
[286] A.254, esp. fo. 40r. The account for the year 1314 ran between the same feast days: A.321. fo. 1r.
[287] A.321, fo. 35r.   [288] See above, pp. 114–15.
[289] A.321, fo. 35v: 4 'dras destains, queus dras vers . . . furent faiz corses mipartis pour armer'.

officers of the household refused service to Baldwin V at the imperial diets of Hagenau and Mainz in 1184, *propter defectum vestium* ['for lack of clothing'], had produced a ruling that they were to receive their clothing and liveries (*vestes . . . et liberationes*) in the same manner as did the count's household knights.[290] By the early fourteenth century, when surviving records commence, the practice of livery distribution was evidently conducted on a regular, seasonal basis. In 1306, the countess—Philippa of Luxemburg—gave Easter liveries: one of the first liveries for which a detailed record is extant. The distribution was as follows:

Pour Jehan de Haynnau 11 *royes de grainne*
Pour escuiers 12 *roies*
Pour maisnies 9 *roies*
3 *roies pour cottes*
9 *blans camelins . . . pour chevaliers, demiseles et priestres*
2 *. . . melles pour petis clers*
2 *mesles ki furent donnet en France a aucunnes gens pour avancher les besoingnes monsigneur*[291]

The preponderance of ray given is noteworthy. The cloths were graded on a scale which went from 15 florins per piece for Jean of Hainault, 10 florins for the squires, to 7 florins for the *maisnie* and $6\frac{1}{2}$ florins for each of the coats (*cottes*) which were to be supplied to unspecified individuals.[292] The total cost of the distribution of cloths, including the gifts to those who could advance the count's cause in France (presumably at Paris) was 1,634 l.t. The countess, like the counts of Artois, was also giving livery of saddles: in 1307, she gave seven saddles in three liveries to her knights at a cost of 56 l. (8 l. per saddle).[293] Her daughter also received a saddle, costing 50 l., and the bishop of Cambrai one of 20 l. As in England, provision for the ruling house and its immediate following was clearly lavish, setting it well above the knightly members of the household. The giving of saddles and harness was obviously a long-standing habit at the court of Hainault, stemming from much earlier manifestations of lordship. At Easter 1303, twenty-seven knights received saddles

---

[290] Gislebert, *Chronique*, 343. See above, pp. 37–8, and Gislebert, *Chronique*, 151–2, 155–63. For the feast at Mainz in 1184 see also Bumke, *Courtly Culture*, 203–7. When Baldwin VI of Hainault was knighted at Speyer in 1189, the count distributed gifts, including 'precious cloths' to his household knights, clerks, and servants ('militibus et clericis curie et servientibus' (Gislebert, *Chronique*, 237).

[291] AEM, Trésorerie, Cartulaires 20, fos. 155v–157r. See Table 15(c).

[292] AEM, Trésorerie, Cartulaires 20, fo. 156r.   [293] Ibid., fos. 157r, 172r.

from Jean I of Hainault, at a cost of 5 l.t. each.[294] The total saddlery bill for the period from 21 September 1302 to 17 January 1304 totalled 1,848 l. 6s. 2d.t.[295] The entourage clearly expected to enjoy its traditional rewards.

The comital house of Hainault, independent of Flanders after 1280 and enjoying just as much ease of access to the textile market of the Low Countries as the Flemish counts, was an affluent dynasty, increasing in wealth and power with its acquisition of the counties of Holland and Zeeland in 1299.[296] The prestigious marriages of William III's daughters reflected—and furthered—the already much-enhanced position of the house. Thus the inventories of goods and such sources as the executors' accounts for the sale of some of the possessions of the countess Philippa, after her death in April 1311, reveal the value and variety of textiles in her wardrobe and treasury.[297] Clothing such as a complete robe of *camelot marbreit* (consisting of coat, surcoat, and *wardecors*) and two *cotes de tartaire* (one green, one crimson) were in her possession, as well as complete lengths of cloth, including 12 ells of black scarlet, three complete rays, and one piece of *vert drap roiiet de Poperinghe* in Flanders.[298] Another robe *de taneit*, consisting of coat, surcoat, *wardecors*, and cape, furred with miniver, was sold for the high figure of 55 l.t.[299] Eight pieces of velours (*velviiaulz*) in crimson and ray fetched 12 l. 10s. each, a total of 100 l.t. Three black *velours* were sold for 30 l.t. Hoods, robes, including one of white, undyed scarlet, as well as quantities of green, crimson, and black sendal, were put up for sale, and the countess's daughter Margaret acquired a robe of black *camelot*, furred with black sendal, with coat, surcoat, and *wardecors* for 15 l.t.[300] Lotard, the receiver of Hainault, and Jakemon the clerk, also responsible for household accounting, figured quite prominently among those purchasing lengths of cloth, perhaps with

[294] See *De rekeningen*, ed. Smit, i. 27.   [295] Ibid., i. 28.

[296] See A. Janse, 'Jean d'Avesnes, comte de Hollande (1299–1304): les villes, la noblesse, le pouvoir', in *700 ans de franchises à Mons: les privilèges de Jean d'Avesnes (1295)*, *Annales du Cercle Archéologique de Mons* 77 (1996), 207–24; M.-A. Arnould, 'L'industrie drapière dans le Comté de Hainaut au moyen âge', in J.-M. Duvosquel and A. Dierkens (eds.), *Villes et campagnes au moyen âge* (Liège, 1991), 51–70.

[297] AEM, Trésorerie: Recueils 20, no. 40; Chartrier, no. 470; Recueils 74, nos. 32, 34; *Documents*, i. 195–8. For cutlery (including forks) for her household, see Appendix VIII (b) (1307).

[298] See AEM, Trésorerie, Recueils 34, m. 1r; Chartrier, no. 470, mm. 1r, 2r, 4r; Recueils 74, no. 34, m. 1r.

[299] AEM. Trésorerie, Recueils 74, no. 34, m. 5r and, for what follows, m. 6r.

[300] Ibid., no. 32, m. 4r.

an eye to bargains, and to sources of the next term's liveries. A notable feature of the system of livery distribution at the court of Hainault (as elsewhere in the Low Countries) is the apparent lack of money payments to members of the household for the purchase of cloth and furs with which to make liveries. Unlike practice at the contemporary English court, liveries seem to have been made very largely, if not exclusively, in kind— perhaps a reflection of the ready availability of good quality raw materials and easy access to them.[301]

The surviving household accounts after 1311 largely concern the countess's establishment until they come to an abrupt end in 1336. Incidental entries for the purchase of cloth and furs for liveries are found, amid very substantial expenditure on textiles for the personal use of Jeanne de Valois and her immediate family. In July 1328, therefore, thirty furs for the *gens de mestiers* were bought, at a total cost of 30 l. 4s.t.[302] The fact that the servants of the offices (*métiers*) received furs to line their liveries of cloth is in itself noteworthy. This was to be forbidden to all members of a *maisnie*, servant, varlet, or *mesquine* (female servant) by a comital ordinance of 1354, which prevented them from wearing clothes with silk or sendal linings, as well as furred surcoats.[303] But such measures were more often broken than observed. Regular receipt of liveries of footwear (*caucement*) were also recorded.[304] Service to the Hainault household may therefore have carried more material advantages (probably of a traditional kind) than elsewhere.

As was the case with the house of Artois, close familial ties with the French royal family led to an association between the household of Jeanne of Valois, as countess of Hainault, and the household of the French queen at Paris. In April 1331, Colard de Montreuil brought to La Neuville-en-Hez, between Beauvais and Clermont, the 'cloths of the livery of the queen of France for the term of Pentecost' which he had received at Paris.[305] Jeanne de Valois and her entourage were on their way back to

---

[301] See Derville, 'Les draperies flamandes et artésiennes', 364–70; Chorley, 'The cloth exports of Flanders and Northern France', 352–6.

[302] *De rekeningen*, ed. Smit, i. 406.

[303] See *Cartulaire des comtes de Hainaut*, ed. Devillers, i. 410–16, no. 260: 'Item que nulles maisnies, servans, varlet ne mesquines ne puissent mettre ne faire mettre a leur vestures ne capperons estoffes de soye ne de cendaul, ne ossi les mesquines servans estoffez a leur sourcos, ne cottes hardies qui soient de vair, d'iermin ne de laitices . . .' Also see below, pp. 132–3.

[304] See *De rekeningen*, ed. Smit, i. 645, 647, 648.

[305] Ibid., i. 517–18: 27 Apr. 1331.

Hainault after a stay of over seven months in France.[306] The officers of the court of Hainault were evidently as well acquainted with the Parisian market as their colleagues in Flanders and Artois, and Colard de Montreuil also received at the same time (25 April 1331) a consignment of green and crimson sendal for the countess, at a cost of 50 l. 15s.t.[307] He was dealing at Paris with the Lombard supplier Lauda di Bologna, who also acted as purveyor of luxury textiles to Mahaut of Artois.[308] But the network of supply for the Hainault court extended much further—cloths and fine textiles were purchased at Valenciennes itself, Compiègne, Malines, Brussels, Ghent, Tournai, Cambrai, Liège, and Namur, as well as from towns such as Dordrecht and Delft within the Dutch territories of the counts.[309]

Although full livery accounts or rolls do not survive for this period, casual references in the household accounts demonstrate that the practice of livery distribution was a constant feature of the Hainault court. In June 1335, for instance, the countess's *damoiselle* Christine was given money to buy 'cloths for Alice the *bueresse* (butter-maker) which she did not receive at the last Easter livery'.[310] Jeanne de Valois continued to receive livery from Jeanne of Burgundy, queen of France, as she did at All Saints 1335.[311] Similarly, dynastic connections through marriage were expressed by the giving of livery to William, son of count William III of Hainault, by John III of Brabant, whose daughter Joanna he had married in 1331.[312] The livery was also given in summer, for on 22 July 1332, Henkin *de le taillerie* received money for making up the duke of Brabant's livery at The Hague.[313] It seems that the Brabançon gift was given, always well in advance, for All Saints, Christmas, Easter, and Pentecost—a lavish provision of 23 ells per livery.

In the autumn of 1332, however, the knighting ceremony of Jean de France (the future king Jean the Good), eldest son of Philip VI, was to take place at Paris, but William of Hainault was unable to attend, apparently because of illness. Preparations had nonetheless been made for

---

[306] *De rekeningen*, ed. Smit, i. 488.

[307] Ibid., i. 517. For Flanders and Artois, see above, pp. 115–23, 124–6.

[308] See Richard, 'Une petite-nièce de St-Louis', 203–7. See also Appendix VII (b) for her textiles.

[309] For the wide-ranging supply network for princely courts in northern France and the Low Countries see below, pp. 125, 128.

[310] *De rekeningen*, ed. Smit, i. 605.   [311] Ibid., i. 611.

[312] Ibid., i. 625: 15 Jan. 1332, payment to William's chamberlain 'pour fachon de dras del livree le duc de Brabanth et pour ses despens parmi 3 jours, pour soie, fil et cendal'.

[313] Ibid., i. 633, 635, 640.

his attendance.[314] On 25 September a messenger arrived from Brabant bearing the livery (18 ells) of William's father-in-law which he was to wear at the *fieste de France*.[315] His household was given a special livery for the occasion—on 23 September, 64 ells of cloth (the equivalent of two liveries) were finished and prepared for tailoring *pour le fieste de France*, together with 32 more ells for William's Christmas livery to his household. Despite William's non-appearance at Paris, he received Jean de France's livery consisting of three pairs of cloths and a surcoat (*cotte hardie*), possibly with Jean's heraldic insignia.[316] Cloth for William's own liveries was also bought at The Hague by his chamberlain, who was paid for the purchase of 16 ells of grey cloth 'that William gave for winter coats (*cottes de hyvier*).[317] The amount bought bears close comparison with provision for the household of Flanders.[318]

Further liveries of cloth were made at Pentecost 1333, when 44 ells of cloth were brought from Malines to The Hague on 15 June, prepared and made up into clothing by local *tondeurs* and tailors, including one Alice Sceredochter.[319] There was clearly no lack of skilled expertise in The Hague at this time, nor of sources of textile supply. The often-mentioned 'Sclapelake' was a frequent supplier of cloth and luxury products, such as silk thread and ribbon. Cheaper cloth was also readily available in the Dutch territories of the house of Hainault—on 15 June 1333, William's chamberlain bought one full length of medley cloth which was to be made up into seven *wardecors* as livery to his *gens de mestier*.[320] As will be argued later, the possession of Holland and Zeeland offered considerable benefits to the counts of Hainault, and it cannot be argued that they ignored or neglected these territories in any way at this period.[321]

Apart from scattered references to the purchase of cloth to be given to individuals, or to William himself, our major surviving source of evidence for livery distribution within the court milieu of Hainault in the 1330s is a series of payments for the winter liveries given by William in 1333.[322] The distribution was as follows:

37 ells of *gris drap* for 7 *cottes d'yvier* to *li escuyer Willaume*
17 ells of *blanket* to line the same

---

[314] Ibid., i. 636: 'pour che que il fu dehaities'. He also seems to have had a tertiary fever in Apr. 1333: i. 645.

[315] Ibid., i. 632, 635–40.

[316] Ibid., i. 635, 640, and 646: 24 Apr. 1333, received at The Hague.

[317] Ibid., i. 633–4: 22 July 1332.   [318] See above, pp. 115–18.

[319] *De rekeningen*, ed. Smit, i. 649.   [320] Ibid., i. 649–50.

[321] See below, pp. 160–1.   [322] See *De rekeningen*, ed. Smit, i. 672–6.

    3 ells of same for Jean de Laire, squire
    1 lining of black fur
    7 ells of fine cloth (*ieraigne*) to line 8 hoods
    1 complete *gris* for 8 *cottes pour les gens de mestier Willaume*
  31 ells of *voiderlake*
    1 complete *drap gris pour garchons de l'estaule Willaume* for 6 *cottes et 6 paires de cauches*

Pour le fachon de 6 cottes pour les garchons Willaume (listed above)
Pour le caucement de 6 garchons

Apart from these disbursements, the *tondage* of 52 ells of cloth for William and his 'companions', paid for at The Hague on 31 October 1333, when he left Holland for Hainault via his father-in-law's court at Brussels, may represent a further All Saints livery to his entourage.[323] Otherwise, provision of cloth and clothing for individual members of his household was listed separately in the accounts, apart from the more general livery distributions. But the evidence, so far as it exists, demonstrates at least one major characteristic of these Hainault liveries: the uniformity of provision to the members of William of Hainault's domestic household. His squires, his *gens de métier*, and his *garçons* all received grey cloth. But status distinctions were closely observed within this small group. The grey coats provided for the squires cost 1 l. 1s.t. each; those given to the *gens de métier* 14s. 5d.t. each; the *garçons de l'estaule* (stable) received both coats and hose, but the cloth allowed for this purpose cost 2 l. 5s. 6d.t. less than that given to the *gens de métier*.[324] The fact that the squires' coats were lined with cloth (blanket) rather than fur is also noteworthy. The very cheap *voiderlake*—costing 2 l.10s. 4½d.t. for 31 ells—may also have been for the lining of the coats worn by servants in the lower reaches of the hierarchy. If this were so, it would in fact accord well with the subsequent comital ordinance of 1354, forbidding servants to wear silk-lined clothes and furred hoods.[325] This household, then, in its grey liveries, must have given a very uniform—if not sombre—appearance when gathered together.

With the accession of William, as count William V, to the counties of Hainault and Holland, some measures of reorganization appear to have been introduced into the comital household.[326] The surviving household 'ordinance' of May 1354 and the accompanying list of those in receipt of livery from the count and countess provide information not only about

[323] *De rekeningen*, ed. Smit, i. 662–3, 676.   [324] Ibid., i. 672–3.
[325] See above, n. 191; De *rekeningen*, ed. Smit, i. 673.
[326] See Van Riemsdijk, *De Tresorie en Kanselarij*, 254–60.

the size of the households but some rough outline at least of who was given livery, and of what sort.[327] Excluding the count and countess themselves, 6 bannerets (one of them an Englishman), 12 knights, 11 clerks (including one Englishman), 38 squires, 23 *garçons*, 16 valets (*knechte*, one of them English), 2 ladies, and 4 *damoiselles* (two of them English) were entitled to liveries of cloth. The bannerets—including the Englishman, Bartholomew de Burgersh—each received a half-length of Ghent cloth, while the countess, Maud of Lancaster, and her two ladies received two-and-a-half lengths of Brussels cloth, plus linings for their robes. The countess's four *damoiselles*—who included two Englishwomen, Joan Hastings and Joan of Hereford—were given approximately two lengths of Brussels cloth.[328]

In toto the list tells us that 115 members of the households of Hainault-Holland were in receipt of liveries of cloth in 1354. This was a considerably smaller number than the liveried members of the households of Flanders in 1330 (440 names) or, of course, of England (600 or more names even under Edward I between 1285 and 1307).[329] The counsels of moderation emanating from men in the comital entourage such as Philip of Leyden evidently had some impact.[330] Such examples of largesse would, Philip declared, make his subjects more directly dependent upon the prince. According to Philip, the giving of liveries of cloth was to be confined to the prince, as it posed a problem to public order if magnates and nobles gave them to anyone outside their own *familia*, and hence derogated from the prince's authority.[331] This was a counsel of perfection, soon to be disregarded in the outbreak of internecine feuding between Hoeks and Kabeljauws in Holland and Zeeland.

By the 1380s, however, under the Bavarian counts, the recipients of livery from the Hainault-Holland household had substantially increased, and very detailed accounts for some aspects of its livery survive.[332] Large

[327] See above, pp. 52–6; ARA, Den Haag, arch. graven van Holland, inv.nr.221, fos. 75r-v; Van Riemsdijk, *De Tresorie en Kanselarij*, 399–400.

[328] ARA, Den Haag, arch.graven van Holland, inv. nr. 221, fos. 75r, 75v.

[329] See above, pp. 55, 104, 120.

[330] Philip of Leyden, *De Cura*, 89–90, 116: on 'dona pecuniaria, stipendia et vestimentorum'; 327: on distribution of gifts of cloth, when the prince 'vestiat nobiles et virtute probatos . . . Operatur namque in multis libera et oblata stabilis robarum oblatio, quod redituum grandis et multiplex exhibitio desinit adimplere . . .' Compare the *Secreta Secretorum* cited above, p. 106.

[331] Philip of Leyden, *De Cura*, 294: 'ut nulli praeter principem extra familiam suam liceat liberalitatem vestium exhibere'; also 327.

[332] See the material published in *Cartulaire des comtes de Hainaut*, ed. Devillers, esp. vol. v.

quantities of footwear and hose were distributed both to the comital household and to that of the count of Ostrevant.[333] Some of the items purchased were in the uniform livery colours of the house, such as the pattens (clogs) in white and green bought for one of the count's children or the complete liveries of white and green cloth which were made for the pages, chamberlains, and others of the Ostrevant household throughout the 1390s.[334] Some of these were decorated with badges and devices of metalwork (Pl. 6). A fully fledged armorial and heraldic livery system was now in operation, readily comparable with those at other princely courts of the time. But, as we have seen, the evolution had been a gradual one, beginning in the later thirteenth century.

The extent to which the increasing prevalence of uniform, regularly distributed liveries of cloth and furs enabled members of princely house-holds to be immediately recognized outside the narrower circle of the court must remain questionable. To the initiated, the colour—or the quality of the cloth and furs—associated with a given set of garments from the 'suit' or *secta* worn by a particular rank or household department would evid-ently aid recognition and identification. But outside the court circle, such niceties might not be understood. It was only when liveries were distin-guished by emblematic means, with the adoption of heraldic colours, badges (often in metal, precious or otherwise), pendants, devices, mottoes, and other cognizances, that the king's, prince's, duke's, or count's 'man' might be picked out from the generalized mass of lords' retainers and servants. Their status and function might then be determined without undue difficulty. It is from the second and third decades of the fourteenth century, however, that we begin to find the first clear documentary refer-ences to recognizable heraldic devices on civilian liveries and, less fre-quently, to the wearing of colours related to the fields (*champs*) of princes' and nobles' coats of arms.[335] A simple colour-, texture- or pattern-coding, —both social and functional—was, however, already emerging at an earlier date.[336]

The choice of cloth for distribution as livery was in part determined by such considerations, as well as by market conditions, price, and availab-ility, and the extent to which intensity and durability of colour could be achieved. The ability of weavers and dyers to produce chequered, mi-parti,

---

[333] See AEM, Trésorerie, Recueils 70, nos. 7–8, 23, 72; 73, nos. 7, 24; 74, nos. 81, 88–92.

[334] Ibid. 74, no. 81 (pattens); 70, no. 72; 71, nos. 12, 17; 74, no. 102 (complete liveries).

[335] See above, pp. 112–13.   [336] See above, pp. 113–15.

and striped clothing, however, meant that a very basic uniformity of type, colour, and pattern of livery was already present in the late thirteenth century. By the mid-fourteenth century, distinctive costumes—some of them personalized to suit individual taste—displayed a prince's livery colours and insignia and achieved a uniform appearance which could clearly be both impressive and, in some notorious cases, overpowering.[337] The court now wore the prince's livery not only as a mark of status and function within the household but as a sign of dynastic and personal allegiance. Not only did the giving of liveries reflect perceptions of social position within an ordered hierarchy, but their style and form signalled dynastic, political, and personal bonds and affinities. The appearance of distinctive livery colours, which were not necessarily related to the tinctures of the hereditary or personal armorial bearings of a prince, was a marked feature of fifteenth-century political life in many regions of Europe. They began to assume a greater permanence and fixity, less subject to ephemeral changes than had been the case at an earlier period. The liveried retainer, bearing the immediately recognizable colours of his lord—green and white; red and white; red, white, and green; and so on— had arrived on the scene. The flexible, random, and erratic character of earlier livery distributions was largely at an end. But the path leading towards the rise of the king's or prince's affinity had already been laid down in the later thirteenth century.

[337] See Saul, *Richard II*, 375.

Chapter 4

THE TRAVELLING COURT

The convoy was made up of two kitchen waggons, a third with the larder, a fourth for the bakers, a fifth with the cellar, carrying drink and vessels, the sixth with the pastry-cooks, a seventh with the confectioners, the eighth with the coffee-makers, a ninth with the buttery and other supplies, the tenth with the physician and his dispensary, the eleventh with the tableware, the twelfth with the smith and the wheelwright, the thirteenth and fourteenth with the bakery, the fifteenth and sixteenth carried the trunks and belongings of the courtiers who rode in the Prince's carriages, the seventeenth the Prince's garderobe, and the eighteenth the tents. Each was a covered waggon drawn by seven horses . . . Behind them three mounted stable-boys . . . led six camels, covered in beautiful drapes of worked cloth, bearing large chests which contained the library. Behind this caravan . . . came two or three large carriages, and a number of light ones . . . At least eight spare horses for the Prince were led along by an equerry and a stable-hand . . . When the Prince rode a horse, he was followed by a light buggy with a change of clothes, in which rode his valet and barber . . . who carried a soaping-dish and razors in his cartridge-case.[1]

With the exception of the camels, this description might well have been that of a particularly grand later medieval household in transit. Exotic beasts were, in fact, by no means absent from such convoys in the later thirteenth and fourteenth centuries—witness the lions, wolves, bears, monkeys, and other animals which accompanied kings and princes on their travels.[2] But the baggage train of Prince Adam Kazimierz

---

[1] Description of the travelling household of Prince Adam Kazimierz Czartoryski, Palatine of Podolia, *c.*1760, cited in A. Zamoyski, *The Polish Way: A Thousand-Year History of the Poles and their Culture* (New York, 1996), 199–200.

[2] For Edward I of England's travelling lions see J. P. Trabut-Cussac, 'Itinéraire d'Edouard Ier en France, 1286–1289', *BIHR* 25 (1952), 170–200. During one of his visits to Gascony compensation was paid for animals killed by royal lions. See, for instance, PRO, E.36/201, 61: payment of 18s. 9d. to 'Ernaldo Purpoynter de Oleron pro uno

Czartoryski was exceptional by any standards, representing the apex of extravagant display in an aristocratic society where 'money . . . had no investment role . . . and all surplus went into movable property of the most demonstrative kind'.[3] The later Middle Ages were not immune from such manifestations of conspicuous consumption, as we shall see at a later stage. But the material infrastructures of travel, transport, and lodging were of as much concern to a ruler's household officers at this time as they were in eighteenth-century Poland.

1. Transport and logistics

The study of the later medieval court has tended to focus more upon its political, cultural, and (to a far lesser extent) social aspects than upon the sheer logistical problems posed by such itinerant establishments.[4] Similarly, less than adequate attention has been paid to the economic underpinnings of court society and to the nexus established between the court and those who supplied, supported, and serviced it.[5] This chapter does not aim to embark upon a detailed account of such questions, but merely to sketch some of the implications of these issues. It also seeks to assess the extent to which itinerant courts both exerted some impact upon the surrounding economy and society and were, in turn, influenced by these environmental considerations. Cultural contacts and relations between courts and cities or, rather, between 'courtly' and 'civic' culture, will be treated later.[6] But the ubiquitous context of well-nigh constant movement, in which most courts operated, and the special needs created by that phenomenon, demand some attention. The peripatetic pattern of existence shared by most rulers hardly changed at all during this period— despite claims that the growth of more 'centralized' administrations led inevitably to tendencies towards longer residence at a given place, and towards permanent centres of court life.[7] It could be argued that any

equo interfecto per leonem Regis et acquietato, de dono Regis . . .' Also see below, pp. 142–3.

[3] Zamoyski, *The Polish Way*, 198. See below, pp. 168–70.

[4] See above, pp. 34–40, 42–56.

[5] But now see W. Blockmans, A. Janse, H. Kruse, and R. Stein, 'From territorial courts to one residence: the Low Countries in the late Middle Ages', in M. Aymard and M. Romani (eds.), *La Cour comme institution économique*, (Paris, 1999), 17–28.

[6] See below, pp. 247–9, 262.

[7] For one view of the importance of the 'stationary court' see Bumke, *Courtly Culture*, 52–5.

discernible trends towards longer periods of residence were determined
by factors as unremarkable as the process of ageing (which could have the
effect of slowing down the pace and scope of a ruler's travels) or as seemingly fickle as the desire to engage in hunting and hawking to the fullest
possible extent. But many exceptions can be found: the sick and aged
Edward I of England did not let his incapacities in any way prevent him
from campaigning against the Scots until—literally—his dying day.[8] The
rise of permanent administrative centres and capital cities, moreover,
harbouring departments of state such as chanceries, exchequers, *chambres
des comptes*, and so forth, did not necessarily mean that the court followed
suit and set itself up on a permanent basis in one, fixed location. The
example of England is an outstanding instance of this tendency of
the court to remain peripatetic.[9] 'Centralization' and permanency of
residence were not yet dominant features in the evolution of royal and
princely courts.

In England, the royal Chancery, Exchequer, major courts of law, and
so forth became permanently located and settled at London and Westminster during this period. Yet the court continued to itinerate, returning
to Westminster for some—but by no means all—of the liturgical feast
days and other solemn occasions in the life of the ruling house.[10] Changes
were certainly taking place, however, by the 1340s: London had achieved
increasing dominance as the economic and administrative 'capital' of the
kingdom. It was the country's only major city, with an estimated population
of 30,000–40,000 inhabitants, comparable with European cities such as
Paris or Ghent.[11] Bristol, Norwich, or York stood well behind it in size
and influence. But the city was also gradually becoming the kingdom's
major 'focal point of political and social life'.[12] Although this tendency
must not be exaggerated—as regional and provincial 'capitals' also existed
in England—this meant that, as on the European continent, a marked
habit of gravitating towards a major city such as London, while not necessarily residing in it, became a characteristic of the English court and
household. Sheer practicalities had for a long time dictated the evolution

    [8] See M. Prestwich, *Edward I*, 556–7.
    [9] See J. Gillingham, 'Crisis or continuity? The structure of royal authority in England,
1369–1422', in *Das spätmittelalterliche Königtum in Europäischen Vergleich* (Sigmaringen,
1987), 64–70. The development of capital cities in the later Middle Ages is discussed in
Guenée, *States and Rulers*, 126–36.
    [10] See e.g. C. H. Hartshorne, 'An Itinerary of King Edward I', *Collectanea Archaeologica*,
2 (London, 1871), 115–36, 311–41.
    [11] See L. Genicot, 'Les grandes villes de l'occident en 1300', in *Economies et sociétés au
moyen âge: Mélanges offerts à Edouard Perroy*, ed. J. Schneider (Paris, 1973), 199–219.
    [12] Gillingham, 'Crisis or continuity?', 68.

of a more sedentary administrative machinery, distinct from the king's court, for the kingdom. Even in the twelfth century, it was proving difficult for a ruler of England to carry his entire apparatus of government and administration around with him as if it were part of his baggage-train. The nature of Angevin and Plantagenet government has also always to be borne in mind—these kings were not only monarchs of England, but continued to hold continental territories through which they and their households travelled.[13]

There had therefore always been a need in England, since the Norman Conquest, for an administrative machinery which could function effectively during the king's many absences.[14] This pattern was temporarily interrupted as a result of the loss of much of the so-called Angevin Empire during the thirteenth century, but was to some extent restored as a result of the active prosecution of the French wars by Edward III and Henry V. As we have already seen, the Chancery had 'gone out of court' by the late thirteenth century, and the Exchequer was already Westminster-based in the mid-twelfth century.[15] After 1340 it never left Westminster. The court of King's Bench, formerly an itinerant institution, joined the Court of Common Pleas at London on a permanent basis from the mid-fourteenth century.[16] Parliament began to meet more often at Westminster than anywhere else in the kingdom—a very different pattern from the past century or so. Between the political crisis of 1339–40 and 1371, for example, all Edward III's Parliaments were summoned to Westminster.[17] With the Tower of London as the king's major armoury and arsenal, which also housed the royal mint, and with the great storehouse of the Wardrobe at the premises known as La Reole in Vintry ward, the material resources of the monarchy were increasingly concentrated in the city. Furthermore, as a centre of Plantagenet dynastic sentiment, with the shrine of a saintly ancestor and a royal mausoleum within its abbey, Westminster had gained an unchallenged superiority over all other possible locations.[18] But the court did not set itself up on a permanent basis there. In the later years of Edward III's reign (c.1369–77) the greater part

[13] See J. Gillingham, *The Angevin Empire* (London, 1984), 47–64; Vale, *Origins of the Hundred Years War*, 9–14, 63–79.

[14] For some observations on this issue see R. W. Southern, 'England's first entry into Europe', in *Medieval Humanism and Other Studies* (Oxford, 1970), 32–40.

[15] See above, pp. 24–5.

[16] See T. F. Tout, 'The beginnings of a modern capital', in his *Collected Papers*, iii (Manchester, 1934), 249–75.

[17] Ibid., iii. 250–4; Gillingham, 'Crisis or continuity?', 68.

[18] Most recently, see P. Binski, *Westminster Abbey and the Plantagenets: Kingship and the Representation of Power, 1200–1400* (New Haven and London, 1995), 1–9, 90–120.

of the household tended to reside at Windsor, not Westminster, while the king spent his time at manors and smaller palaces in the 'home counties' or near London: Eltham, Sheen, King's Langley, Havering-atte-Bower, and so on.[19] During these years, ultimately marked by his dotage, Edward's small immediate *familia* and the core of the court (including so-called 'favourites') went with him. To some extent, this may represent a regressive tendency, exacerbated under Richard II (1377–99) and already (by 1376) productive of severe political crises.[20]

Nor could it be argued that the later Capetians in France displayed more sedentary tendencies, leading them to reside more often at Paris— Vincennes, Poissy, and Fontainebleau were as frequently visited by their court as the Louvre or the Île-de-la-Cité.[21] The princes of the Low Countries were no exception to this rule. Power ultimately lay with and around the ruler, and that was where the court was—bureaucratic departments of state notwithstanding. If the ruler was hunting, for instance, the court—or at least its nucleus—was with him.[22] All courts therefore travelled. They were essentially mobile, moving from one location to another. This did not end with the Middle Ages: a particularly striking case of the extremely mobile nature of a court is that of Wilhelmine Germany. A former member of the German imperial court observed in 1914 that 'Royalties, especially German Royalties, spend a large portion of their existence in travelling'.[23] Kaiser Wilhelm II had a habit of suddenly leaving one residence for another, upon hearing of an outbreak of even the most minor infection there, causing acute disruption to the court. Of one such occasion, the English governess of his children observed: 'except for the moral support afforded by the white kid gloves and fan, to which we clung convulsively through that long chaos, we should with difficulty have been able to preserve the decent atmosphere proper to a court'.[24]

Such constant journeying presumed that accommodation for a prince and his entourage—the court—would be readily available, both inside

[19] See Given-Wilson, *The Royal Household and the King's Affinity*, 28–39; Gillingham, 'Crisis or continuity?', 64–70.

[20] Gillingham, 'Crisis or continuity?', 65–6; Saul, *Richard II*, 391–2, 454.

[21] See above, pp. 16, 35; Lalou, 'Vincennes dans les itinéraires de Philippe le Bel et de ses trois fils', 192–7.

[22] See below, pp. 179–84.

[23] A. Topham, *Memories of the Kaiser's Court* (London, 1914), 106. See also Röhl, *The Kaiser and his Court*, 75–7.

[24] Topham, *Memories of the Kaiser's Court*, 222.

and outside his dominions. The ancient rights of *hospitia* and *gîte* were still exercised in the thirteenth century, but increasingly to a lesser extent than previously.[25] Residence in monastic houses—a common feature of earlier medieval rulership—became less frequent, particularly as princely establishments grew larger and their demands became more complex and elaborate. These essentially secular courts, with growing numbers of laymen in attendance upon the ruler, as well as the traditional body of clerks, exerted a demand for lodgings in both town and countryside which sometimes came close to exceeding the capacity of a given region to provide for them. Clearly, princely residences were a first line of defence in this respect.

This tendency to move from residence to residence, sometimes at very short notice, remained a characteristic of European court societies for a very long time. In 1913, for example, Rudolf Martin, a former offical of the Reich Office of the Interior under Kaiser Wilhelm II, wrote that 'the Kaiser personally owns three castles in Berlin [Königliches Schloss, Bellevue, and Monbijou], thirteen in Potsdam and environs [including the Neues Palais and Sans-Souci] and in all more than forty castles . . . which together represent a very high value'.[26] The Kaiser's journeyings were to take on a character not dissimilar to those of Henry II, as described by Walter Map.[27] Wilhelm II came to spend less than half a year *in toto* at Berlin and Potsdam—the so-called 'centres' of Prussian imperial court society—and preferred to set up court at far-flung residences throughout his lands. These 'alternative courts' were often sited at retreats and hunting lodges such as Schloss Wilhelmshohe, Donaueschingen, Celle, or Rominten, or at spas such as Bad Homburg.[28] With a body of court officials and servants (many of them noble) totalling about 2,000 people, the Hohenzollern court in some ways represented the apogee of the court society. But its later medieval predecessors—although their personnel are to be reckoned, with the possible exception of the court of Burgundy, in hundreds rather than thousands—bore some similarities to it in both principle and practice.[29] When, for example, the English

---

[25] See J. Richard, 'Les itinéraires de Saint Louis en Île-de-France', in *Vincennes aux origines de l'état moderne*, 166–70.

[26] R. Martin, *Jahrbuch des Vermögens und Einkommens der Millionäre in Berlin* (Berlin, 1913), introduction, cited in Röhl, *The Kaiser and his Court*, p. 75.

[27] See above, pp. 35–6.

[28] See Röhl, *The Kaiser and his Court*, 96–7; T. A. Kohut, *Wilhelm and the Germans: A Study in Leadership* (Oxford, 1961), 235–47.

[29] See Paravicini, 'The court of the dukes of Burgundy: a model for Europe?', 76–7.

governess of the Kaiser's children arrived at Bad Homburg in 1902 she was greeted at the palace by the court official known as the *Hof-fourrier*, a direct descendant of those *fourriers* or quartermasters who had been responsible for the lodging arrangements of later medieval households.[30] The continuities of court life down to 1914 were very striking.

From Carolingian times onwards, rulers had journeyed ceaselessly from one *palatium* or *villa* to another, enjoying rights of *prise* (requisition or purveyance) and *gîte* (lodging or hospitality) over their vassals and tenants.[31] By the thirteenth century, many of these rights had been commuted for money payments, or were simply not exercised. Louis IX was taking such payments from both religious houses and *bourgeois* as late as 1264.[32] But far greater reliance was now being placed on the ruler's ability to pay at normal market rates for what his entourage consumed and used. In 1239, for example, Louis IX's *itinera* (journeys) accounted for about 16% of his total expenditure, incurred very largely in the Île-de-France.[33] Plantagenet travelling was far more wide-ranging, and Edward I covered many thousands of miles during his reign—from Berwick to Bayonne, and from Anglesey to Abbeville.[34] The English kings had more directly held territory in which to itinerate—in the British Isles, Aquitaine, and Ponthieu—than their Capetian contemporaries. The itinerant mode of life adopted by the Plantagenets has been the subject of studies by Tout and his pupils, among others, and the role of officers such as the royal harbingers and quartermasters described. Tout spoke of the propensity of the royal household to terrorize the countryside and to inflict damage upon the king's subjects.[35] This is spelt out in the wardrobe and household accounts.[36] Not only did the king's household cause damage and injury, such as the inadvertent burning-down of a house at Winchester in 1290 by the king's apothecary, but dependent establishments, such as those of his children, did likewise.[37] In October 1301, compensation was paid to one Nicholas de Winterburn for losses sustained by him when his houses at Devizes were set on fire by Master Ralph, physician to the two

[30] See Topham, *Memories of the Kaiser's Court*, 3–4, and below, pp. 153–4.

[31] See Richard, 'Les itinéraires', 166–7.   [32] See *RHF* 21 (1841), 397–413.

[33] Richard, 'Les Itinéraires', 170.

[34] See E. W. Safford, 'Itinerary of Edward I, 1272–1290' (unpublished list, London, Public Record Office, 1935), *passim*. Also *Records of the Wardrobe and Household, 1285–1286*, ed. Byerly, pp. xxvii–xxxvii.

[35] See above, p. 59.

[36] See Trabut-Cussac, 'Itinéraire d'Edouard Ier en France', 175 n. 47, 180 nn. 62–3, 181 n. 65, 183 n. 72.

[37] PRO, C.47/4/5, fo. 51v (1290).

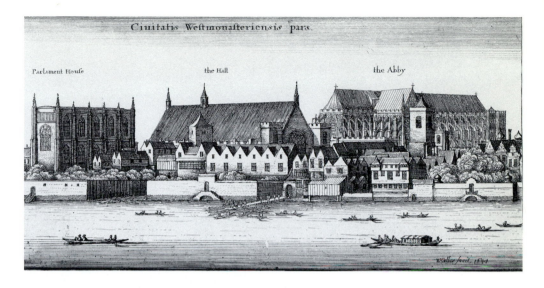

Ciuitatis Westmonasteriensis pars.

Parlament Houfe   the Hall   the Abby

1. The Palace and the Abbey of Westminster, engraving by Wenceslas Hollar, 1647.

2. The Knights' Hall (*Ridderzaal*) of the counts of Holland in the Binnenhof, The Hague. The building, perhaps influenced by Westminster Hall, was constructed during the reign of Floris V (1256-96).

3. The Painted Chamber in the Palace of Westminster, looking east, watercolour by William Capon, 1799. The Chamber was decorated under Henry III and Edward I with wall paintings, but was destroyed in the great Westminster fire of 1834.

La submission que cil de la ville de Bruges fisent au Roy de france et p̃ lan tore de. Tous ceaux qui ces lettres verront et oiront. Nous bourgmaistres Eschevins Conseil et toute la communalte de la ville de Bruges faisons savoir et publiquement confessons et ate nous obligons que de tout ce que depuis la barranne pris fure a aiques avons mespris ou mesfait en quelanques manere que ce soit encontre le Roy de france come contre nosegneur souverain. Nous nous en soumetons et demetons de haut bas a sa volente dit ou ordenance sans iamais aler alencontre. Et en ceste mesme forme et manere. Nous soumectons nous et demetons en no chier naturel et droiturier segneur le conte de flaundres et de Nevers de tout ce que mespris ou mesfait avons depuis la dite pris en quelanques autre manere que ce soit. Et pour ce promectons nous sans delai a Baillier et adonner hostages tant et tels come illeur plaira aprendre en la dite ville et desorenavant barder et tenir envers eaux bone foy come obeissance come bon subget. par le tesmoinng de ces dites seellees durqune seel dela ville de Bruges qui furent fures et donnees le jour me dune en septembre lan de Grace mil cccc vint huit. Et est assavoir q̃ ce ste le est double.

4. Chancery register of privileges and other documents concerning the towns and other possessions of the counts of Flanders, c.1335. The upper border of this folio depicts the submission of
the town of Bruges to the count in 1328, and the lower border has a scene of courtly dancing.

5. Three knights, holding their robes of Livery, kneel before a ruler, with a rack carrying further liveries in the background. Pseudo-Aristotle, *Secreta Secretorum*, *c*.1327-8.

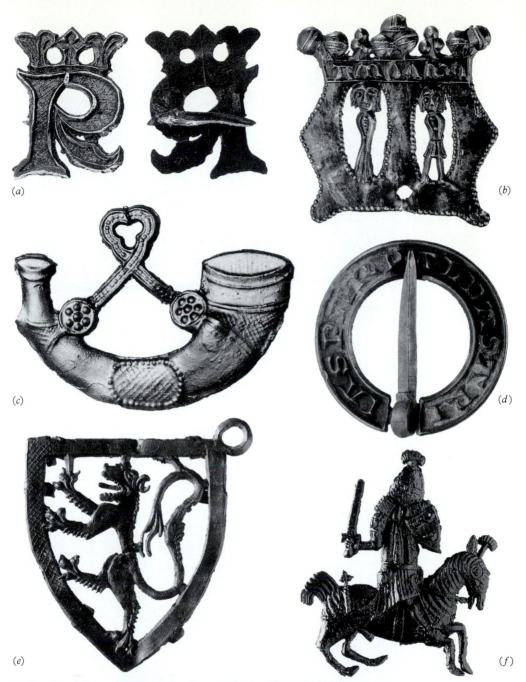

(a)

(b)

(c)

(d)

(e)

(f)

6. Lead and Pewter badges worn by members of households.
a. Clasp in the form of a Crowned letter 'R', *c*.1375-1425. *b*. Clasp in the form of a crowned letter 'm', with male and female figures, inscribed 'AMOVRS' (Love), *c*.1375-1425. *c*. Pendant in the form of a horn, perhaps to be worn by a huntsman as a badge, or as a device of the Hoorn family *c*.1400. *d*. Clasp, with surviving traces of red paint, inscribed 'IASPAR DALDASARI' (IASPAR-BALTHAZAR), *c*.1375-1425. The allusion to two of the three kings may mean that this is a New Year's gift (*étrennes*). *e*. Heraldic pendant in the form of a shield, with lion rampant, *c*.1375-1425 (arms of the counts of Holland?). *f*. Clasp in the form of a mounted knight, *c*.1375-1425 or earlier. The knight bears a shield with the arms of the counts of Hoorn.

7. The count's castle (*Graven-steen*), Ghent. The fortress dates from the reign of Count Philip of Alsace (1168-91), but was extensively rebuilt in the twentieth century.

8. The *Prinsenhof* (count's palace) at Ghent. This residence began as the house known as Ten Walle in the fourteenth century. Engraving from A. Sanderus, *Flandria Illustrata*, 1641.

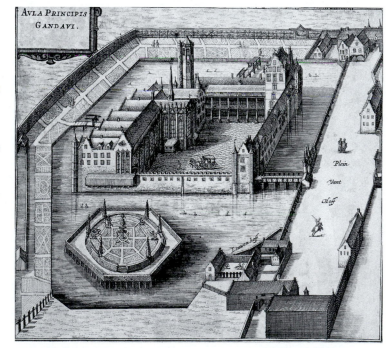

9a. Westminster Abbey, nave and choir, looking east.

9b. Amiens Cathedral, nave and choir, looking east.

(a)

(c)

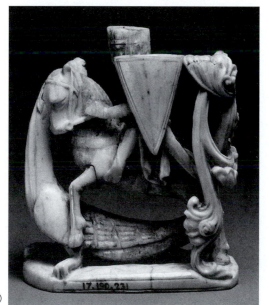

(b)

10. Ivory Chessmen.

a. Knight, in walrus ivory with traces of green paint and gilding, mid-thirteenth century.
b. Knight, in walrus ivory, mid-thirteenth century.
c. Knight, in walrus ivory, mid-thirteenth century.

(a)

11. The game of chess and its imagery.

a. Pewter pendant in the form of a chessboard, c.1375-1425.
b. Casket, decorated with a scene of wildmen and a lady playing chess, c.1380.

(b)

12. Lid of an ivory casket, decorated with scenes of a tournament, the siege of the Castle of Love, and themes from romance, Paris *c.*1325-50.

13. Ivory mirror case, Paris, *c.*1325-50, with a lady presenting a sword to her lover

14. Chess-playing scence from a manuscript of Jacques de Longuyon, *Les Voeux du paon* and Jean Brisebarre, *Le Restor du paon*, illuminated in the Low Countries, *c.*1340–50.

15. Monumental brass to Robert Braunche, burgess of Lynn, and two wives, 1364. St Margaret, King's Lynn, Norfolk.

a. The complete brass.
b. The peacock feast (detail), showing *damoiselles* bringing the meat, accompanied by minstrels.

(a)

(b)

16. Monumental brass to Gottfried and Friedrich von Bülow, Flemish, c.1380, showing wildmen and their king at a feast. This scene parodies those of court feasts found in manuscript illumination of the period. Schwerin Cathedral.

17. The Newport chest, late thirteenth century, with nineteenth-century additions. This travelling chest also served as a portable altar, and the lid is painted with an image of the crucifixion, flanked by figures of the Virgin, St John, St Peter, and St Paul. St Mary's, Newport, Essex.

18. Portable psalter, in small format, Liège or Cambrai, c.1250-75. The calendar pages include the feast days of English saints, some added later. This folio has a representation of the Annuniciation.

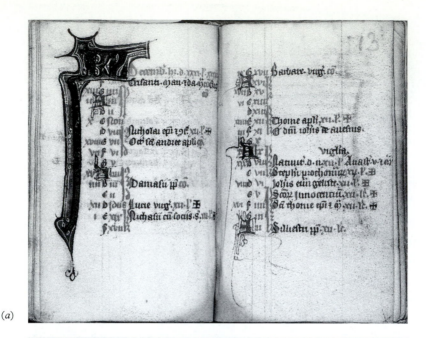

(a)

(b)

19. Portable diurnal, in very small format, Cistercian, northern France, c.1268–70.

a. This page (fo. 13r) records the date on which prayer (obitus) was ordained for the soul of Jean d'Avesnes (d. 24 Dec. 1254), father of Jean I, count of Hainault-Holland (d. 1304)

b. Annunciation page (fos. 2ᵛ–3ʳ). The border grotesque shows a man jousting with a half-beast, half-bird, and carrying a shield with unidentified arms of *argent, a chevron sable.*

infants Thomas and Edmund.[38] The preparation of remedies and cures, involving quasi-chemical experiments by court apothecaries and doctors, could clearly be hazardous undertakings and perhaps lay behind these incidents.

The building works set in train at English royal residences, which provided accommodation during journeys, have been fully described and a pattern of increasing expenditure upon domestic comfort and convenience has been identified.[39] But, as on the European continent, the habit of descending upon religious houses died hard. St Alban's, Bury St Edmunds, Newburgh, Lanercost, and many other monastic houses experienced the presence of the household at quite frequent intervals.[40] Sometimes the arrival of the king and his entourage necessitated hasty adaptations and alterations to existing buildings. In January 1297, for instance, when the court descended on Ipswich and Harwich, near to the east coast, for the events connected with the Brabançon and Dutch marriages of Edward's daughters Margaret and Elizabeth, a sudden surge of works took place. At the house of one William Frank outside Harwich, where the king and his children were to stay, a new chapel was constructed, while general repairs and refurbishments were hurriedly carried out.[41] Similarly, at Ipswich, another new chapel was made for the king next to his chamber in the priory of St Peter, just before his arrival, in December 1296.[42] The works included the provision of linen cloth (*pannum lineum*) with which to cover the large windows of the chapel. Minor expenses on furnishings were part and parcel of itinerant rulership, however, and Elizabeth, countess of Holland, was buying red and green silk (*sindon*) for curtains in her bedchamber (she was newly wed) at Ghent, *en route* for Holland in 1297.[43]

The need to transport bulky goods and furnishings, moreover, meant that a constant supply of horses and waggons had to be ensured—in 1297, the wardrobe of Margaret, as new duchess of Brabant, required a cart drawn by five horses to carry it from London to her embarkation at Harwich.[44] It took a total of eighteen days for all her goods to be carried from the capital to Ipswich. Carts and horses were sometimes provided

---

[38] E.101/360/28: 'occasione combustione domorum suarum apud Devis' facti per magistrum Radulphum fisicum' (Oct. 1301).

[39] See Colvin *et al.*, *The King's Works*, ii, *passim*, for the king's castles and houses and works undertaken upon them.

[40] E.101/368/30; 369/1; Prestwich, *Edward I*, 164–5.

[41] See BL, Add. MS 7965, fo. 14v.   [42] BL, Add. MS 7965, fos. 14v–15r.

[43] C.47/3/48, no. 23. See also Appendix V (a), (b).   [44] E.101/372/12/1.

by means of purveyance, both in England itself and in the continental possessions of the English crown, such as Ponthieu, during royal visits to northern France.[45] Mishaps were frequent occurrences—in July 1313, for example, the carriage, in which the *damoiselles* of Queen Isabella's chamber were returning to England through northern France, broke down between Beauvais and Boulogne, and they were forced to remain overnight at Neufchâtel, awaiting repairs.[46] The demands of the royal household and its dependents were constant, and they severely taxed the resources of the marshalsea and wardrobe. In July 1302, three carts and fifteen horses were required to carry the portable chapel, its furniture, and the wardrobe of Thomas and Edmund from Devizes castle to Windsor. When they stayed at Windsor in November, their wardrobe was transported by water from Westminster to Staines.[47] In 1313–14, the queen's wardrobe alone required between three and six carts for its transport, while the countess Warenne and Lady Despenser needed two carts and one cart each respectively for their total effects.[48]

It was often far less time-consuming and troublesome to convey the king and his court, where feasible, by water. The Thames was a major thoroughfare at this period, linking together points within London. River transport also reduced the time taken by journeys overland, especially from parts of Kent and from the continent.[49] In June–July 1297, therefore, Edward I was travelling by barge on the Thames from Gravesend to Westminster, when his barge-master, Fulk le Coupere, was paid for 'remaining with the said barge by the king's order at the bridge (*pontem*) of the Palace of Westminster, and taking the king from the same bridge to the court (*curia*) of the archbishop of York'.[50] He then took the king to Rotherhithe, to speak with the queen of Navarre, thence to Westminster via the 'hospital next to the Tower of London', and finally back to the archbishop's court at Westminster.[51] This kind of water taxi- or gondola-service was a commonplace routine in the daily timetables of the Plantagenets. The watergates at Westminster and the Tower gave easy access to such mooring points as Queenshithe and Rotherhithe, whereby journeys within the capital could be more speedily undertaken.[52] Some

---

[45] E.101/375/9, fo. 26v: account book for the queen's household, 1313–14.

[46] E.101/375/8, fo. 21r.

[47] E.101/360/28, m. 4r. For Thomas's chapel furniture see Appendix III (1301).

[48] E.101/375/9, fo. 25r.

[49] For access to the continent from Kent see Vale, *Origins of the Hundred Years War*, 30.

[50] BL, Add. MS 7965, fo. 19r.   [51] Ibid., fos. 19r–v.

[52] See J. Stowe, *A Survey of London*, ed. C. L. Kingsford, 2 vols. (Oxford, 1908), i. 40–4, ii. 5–10, and the map appended to vol. ii. Stowe described Queen's Hythe as the 'verie chiefe and principall watergate of this citie' (i. 41).

idea of the extent of the river's use can be gained from the account of Edward and his entourage's transport from Gravesend (they had been at Canterbury) to Westminster between 26 and 28 July 1299.[53] Fulk le Coupere and Absalom of Greenwich, with twenty-six other barge-masters and 115 bargees, were paid their wages for bringing a flotilla of twenty-eight barges, carrying the king, his *familia*, and the greater part of their effects up the Thames. The large scale of the enterprise is clear. Edward II was to continue this intensive use of water navigation and, as we shall see, was also to transform it into a major leisure activity.[54]

In the Low Countries, there was less need for a logistical operation which involved the frequent use of sea passages, although water transport (in Flanders, Holland, and Zeeland, for example) was very common.[55] The Flemish accounting material enables us to form some estimate of the numbers retained in the comital household from 1270 onwards and of the costs of its transport. The fact that the counts of Flanders also held Hainault until 1280 meant that their itinerary tended to be rather wider in range before that date than it was to become later. Frequent visits to Paris, however, were a consistent feature of their travelling.[56] In the 1270s, Guy de Dampierre journeyed through his domains with a relatively small household. In January 1270, he was at Mons with a body of twenty-three named individuals, including his son Guillaume, the lord of Marbais, Pierre, *prévôt* of Béthune, Master Henri de Furnes, Gérard the chaplain, Jaquemon the chamberlain, and a group of unnamed household servants—falconers, messengers, *sommeliers*, and so forth.[57] This means that it is possible only to estimate the total numbers in his household. By 26 January, he was at Viesville, staying there for thirteen nights with a larger household in attendance. There were fifty-three named individuals in the diet account—including a number of nobles and knights from both Flanders and Hainault such as Gossuin de Heripont, Felin de Poul, Barthélemy de Houthem, Michel d'Auchy, Fastre de Werchin, the lords of Hauterive, and Sombreffe, and Rasse de Gavre, lord of

[53] E.101/355/18, m. 6r.   [54] E.101/375/8; 380/4.

[55] See, for the counts of Hainault-Holland and their itineraries, J. G. Smit, 'De reisroutes van de graven van Holland, Zeeland en Henegouwen door hun gebieden', in *Vorst en onderdaan: Studies over Holland en Zeeland in de late middeleeuwen* (Louvain, 1995), 28–64 and map 1. Also id., 'De Graven van Holland en Zeeland op reis: Het grafelijk itinerarium van het begin van de veertiende eeuw tot 1425', in *Holland in Wording: De ontstaansgeschiedenis van het graafschap Holland tot het begin van de vijftiende eeuw* (Hilversum, 1991), 91–124.

[56] See below, pp. 148–9, 151–2. See Table 16.

[57] RAG, Wyffels (chron. suppl.) 38: Mons, 22 Jan. 1270.

Liedekerke.[58] Wages were also paid to unspecified falconers, dog-keepers (*braconiers*), messengers, cooks, *sommeliers*, and to the *menus maisnie* as a body. The wage bill had been just over 13 l. 14s. at Mons; it reached 32 l. 17s. at Viesville. By January 1278, when the count was at Male, the numbers paid wages in his household were again around twenty named individuals—including the knights Huon de Halluin, Sohier de Bailleul, Henri de Ristune, and the lord of Auchy, plus the unspecified cooks, *panetiers*, *bouteillers*, chamberlains, ushers, falconers, *sommeliers*, and *maisnie*.[59] The records do not permit us to estimate the number of carts and horses required for their transport, as some of these were undoubtedly derived from purveyance (*pourvéance*) and never entered the accounts.[60]

A comprehensive picture of the movements of the Flemish household can be established for the seven weeks between 8 January and 25 February 1278.[61] The itinerary was as follows:

8 Jan.	Male
11 Jan.	Male—Wijnendaal
12 Jan.	Wijnendaal—Warneton
13 Jan.	Lille
15 Jan.	Lille—Flines
16 Jan.	Marke-en-Pèvre—Menin
17 Jan.	Rouliers—Male
25 Jan.	Male—Menin
26 Jan.	Menin—Lille—Flines
27 Jan.	Flines—Valenciennes
28 Jan.	Cofontaines—Binche
29 Jan.	Binche—Viesville
30 Jan.	Viesville—Namur
31 Jan.	Namur
13 Feb.	Genappe (at the expense of duke of Brabant)
15 Feb.	Genappe—Brussels—Alost
16 Feb.	Ghent (at the expense of abbot of St Peter's)—Male
19 Feb.	Male—Wijnendaal—Menin
20 Feb.	Menin—Lesquin—Flines
21 Feb.	Flines—Crèvecoeur
22 Feb.	Crèvecoeur—Rosnel—Ham
23 Feb.	Ham—Le Bac—La Verberie
24 Feb.	La Verberie—Louvres
25 Feb.	Louvres—Paris

[58] RAG, Wyffels (chron. suppl.) 38, m. iv.   [59] RAG, St-Genois 237: 8 Jan. 1278.
[60] See, for examples of the accounting procedure, RAG, Gaillard 24 and Gaillard 27.
[61] RAG, St-Genois 237, mm. 1–6.

Of these forty-nine days, a total of fifteen (30.6%) were spent at Male, which provided a kind of home base—and a much-favoured comital residence—to which the household periodically returned.[62] It was kept in good order, and had a number of amenities, including gardens and fish-ponds.[63] As we have seen, however, Paris served as a magnet for the Flemish court, involving heavy expenditure and lavish entertainment of guests at the count's Parisian *hôtel*.[64]

But Guy de Dampierre travelled more widely in the 1280s than merely within his Flemish and northern French sphere. He had of course been a participant in Louis IX's Tunis crusade.[65] Between October 1280 and February 1281 he was in south-west France, visiting shrines, as a pilgrim, with his entourage.[66] He visited Moissac, where he spent Christmas, and Rocamadour, as well as Toulouse, where he spent three weeks, dining with the bishop on one occasion. The members of his itinerant household who are named (in late October and early November 1280) constituted an apparent norm of around twenty individuals:[67] among them were the lords of Ghistelle and Auchy, Guillaume, lord of Mortagne, Gautier de Morslede, and Jean, the count's chaplain.[68] A list of unnamed officers and servants was also included. The total bill for wages stood at 74 l. 2s. On his return journey—in February 1281—Guy visited his relative the countess of Blois at Millesmes, while his household remained at Romorantin (3 February). By 8 February the Flemish party of pilgrims were at Paris, reaching Lille early in March, continuing to Warneton on 11 March. By 16 March, Guy was at Ypres, spending the beginning of Lent there—strictly observed, given the very large quantities of herrings (7,900 both white and red) provided by purveyance for his household.[69] This degree of abstinence was sustained at Wijnendaal after 2 April, when a further 2,700 herrings were consumed by the household during the following week. Yet again, the region around Male, Wijnendaal, and Pettenghien (Petegem) acted as a kind of reference point for the Flemish court, to which they would often—although not invariably—return at the time of the major liturgical feasts.

[62] For the castle and residence at Male see above, p. 64.
[63] AGR, CC, R.2091: account for works at Male, 27 May 1308–24 June 1309.
[64] See above, p. 145.
[65] See *Het Memoriaal van Jehan Makiel*, pp. xxvi–xxviii, 74–82.
[66] RAG, Wyffels (chron. suppl.) 107*bis*: 28 Oct. 1280–7 Apr. 1281.
[67] For the problems of establishing numbers in princely households of this period see above, pp. 52–6.
[68] RAG, Wyffels (chron. suppl.) 107*bis*, mm. 2v, 5v, 8v.
[69] For the very large quantities of herrings consumed during Lent by the Hainault-Holland household see below, p. 161.

Some of the most complete evidence for the itinerant life of the Flemish court is found in a diet account roll for Guy de Dampierre's household from 10 June 1293 to 26 June 1294.[70] This enables us to reconstruct the count's itinerary over a twelve-month period, apart from a small gap in the sequence from 6 March to 12 May 1294 (see Table 16, p. 326). The pattern which emerges from this sequence is one of a relatively restricted itinerary, following well-trodden paths, with regular visits along a fixed route to and from Paris. Of the fifty-four weeks, nine (16.6%) were spent at Paris, while the bulk of the remaining time was taken up in travelling from one Flemish (and sometimes Brabançon or Namurois) location to another. In terms of the number of stays made, the most frequently visited places in Flanders were Wijnendaal (9 visits), Lille (8), Kortrijk (8), Petegem (5), and Male (3), although points on the route to and from Paris such as Senlis and Compiègne were clearly important in the comital itinerary. It is noteworthy that no more than three days were spent in the city of Ghent, and during the entire year only one dinner was eaten by the count and his household at Bruges.[71] The preference was to stay outside the cities of Flemish-speaking Flanders—at Wijnendaal, Petegem, or Male. In *Flandre gallicante*, or French-speaking Flanders, however, more time was spent in the towns, and the Salle-le-Comte at Lille and his residence at Kortrijk received the count on almost as many occasions as his castle at Wijnendaal. It is also worth noting that sixteen days *in toto* were spent at Namur, by virtue of the countess Isabella's title to that county.

A pattern of above-average expenditure can also be traced, revolving around the presence of guests in the household and the cycle of liturgical feast days. For example, on 11–12 June 1293, the Salle-le-Comte at Lille received the countess of Luxemburg, the count of Nevers, the lady of Beaumont, Guillaume of Flanders and his wife, and

grant plente de boene gent, et menga li cuens et si chevaliers avoec les Jacopins, et me dame al'abbiete, et li maisnie menga a lostel et pluseur autre jusques bien a 140 persones.[72]

---

[70] RAG, Wyffels (chron. suppl.) 188 and 314*bis* (10 June 1293–26 June 1294). Also see above, pp. 83, 85; Figs. 10, 14, Table 16.

[71] For the spasmodically turbulent relations between the counts of Flanders and Bruges see J. M. Murray, 'The liturgy of the Count's entry to Bruges, from Galbert to Van Eyck', in B. A. Hanawalt and K. L. Reyerson (eds.), *City and Spectacle in Medieval Europe* (Minneapolis, 1994), 137–40; and A. Brown, 'Bruges and the Burgundian "Theatre-State": Charles the Bold and Our Lady of the Snow', *History*, 84 (1999), 573–6.

[72] RAG, Wyffels (chron. suppl.) 188, m. 7r.

[a large number of worthy people, and the count and his knights dined with the Franciscans, and my lady at the abbey, and the *maisnie* in the household, and many others up to at least 140 people.]

Total expenses (not including *pourvance* or wages to the household) reached 52 l. 12s. 6d. on 11 June, when the lowest sum recorded for daily expenditure stood at about 11 l. The division of the household for dining is of interest, demonstrating that the religious houses of Flanders (in this case, the Franciscans and the abbey of St Peter's) still extended hospitality to the court, although a distinction was made between the households of the count and countess. The *maisnie* ate in the 'household' (*hostel*), that is, within the Salle-le-Comte. Higher rates of expenditure than usual were also incurred at Ypres on 30 July, Lille on 23 August (the eve of St Bartholomew) and 29 August (*decollatio* of John the Baptist), when the countess ate *en le nouvele abbiette* with the countess of Luxemburg's daughter who entered the convent there at that time,[73] while the following few days were spent visiting the other religious houses of the area— Flines, Furnes, Dunes, Berghes—at their expense.[74] A large gathering assembled at Douai on 26 September, including Philip of Flanders and his wife, the *damoiselle* of Luxemburg (now a novice), the abbess of Pontrouwart, the lady of Mortagne, the castellan of Lille, the bishop of Cambrai, the lady of Juliers, and others, sending daily expenditure up to over 54 l.[75] By early October, the comital entourage had reached Paris, and on St-Remy's day (4 October)

disna li cuens avoec le Roy au matin, et me dame avoec le Royne, et au sopir a leur osteil, et i furent li cuens de Nevers, me sires Willaumes, et Philippes de Flandres, ma dame de Thiete, Loys de Nevers, no demoisel et moult de boines gens.[76]

[the count dined with the king in the morning, and my lady with the queen, and in their household for supper, where there were the count of Nevers, my lord William, Philip of Flanders, my lady of Thiete, Louis of Nevers, our *damoiselle* and many worthy people.]

The king and queen presumably met the expenses of both count and countess, as the total daily expenditure was not high. The comital following was clearly substantial at this time: as many as 180 horses were stabled for the count in Paris (6 October 1293).[77] The grand total of expenditure for the twelve days spent there was 576 l. 18s. 3d., well above the average. As with the household of Hainault when it visited Paris, virtually all

---

[73] Ibid., mm. 8r, 9r.   [74] Ibid., m. 10r.   [75] Ibid., m. 11r.
[76] Ibid., m. 13r.   [77] Ibid.

expenses had to be met by cash payment, as *pourvances* were apparently not taken outside the count's own territories.[78] To maintain a presence at Paris was therefore a considerable source of expense to these princely houses.[79] Guy de Dampierre was normally accompanied by a large retinue when he and the countess made these journeys outside their own lands to visit other princes. On 20–1 November 1293, for instance, they were at Brussels visiting Jean I of Brabant, with 200 horses in their train. On 21 November

disna me sire li cuens au bos avoec le duc [de Brabant] u il alerent kacier au senglier, et me dame disna et li hosteus a Brouxele, et demorerent me sire et me dame cele nuit a Bouchefort avoec le duc, et le maisnie vinrent gesir a Wavre.[80]

[my lord the count dined in the woods with the duke, where they were hunting wild boar, and my lady dined with the household at Brussels, and my lord and lady stayed that night at Bouchefort with the duke, and the *maisnie* went to lodge at Wavre.]

The attraction of the hunt for wild boar was here apparent, especially in the forest of Soignes on the outskirts of Brussels, where the duke of Brabant had hunting lodges such as Tervuren which were much frequented.[81] The days following this visit saw an even larger gathering of Netherlandish princes, hosted by Guy de Dampierre at Namur on 1–2 December 1293. The political situation was no doubt a major item of business at that time—England and France were moving towards war, and Guy's negotiations for an English marriage for his daughter Philippine were a potential *casus belli*.[82] The duke of Brabant, the counts of Guelders, Loos, and Luxemburg, and *grant plente de boene gent* ['a large gathering of worthy people'] were present, and the comital costs were partly met by *pourvances*, as Namur was within the count's domains. Thus the total expenditure for fifteen days at Namur, including *pourvances* (mainly of fish) and wages stood at 690 l.—comparable with the level sustained at Paris earlier in the year.[83]

The high point of expenditure for the whole year was, however, attained at Christmas and Epiphany 1293–4.[84] The comital household

---

[78] For the Hainault household see below, pp. 159–62.
[79] See above, pp. 124–5, 148–9.   [80] RAG, Wyffels (chron. suppl.) 188, m. 17r.
[81] See J. E. Davidts, *Tervuren in de Brabantse geschiedenis vanaf 1200 tot 1450* (Tervuren, 1975), 38–52.
[82] See Strayer, *The Reign of Philip the Fair*, 320–1, 328.
[83] See above, p. 149.   [84] See Fig. 14.

was at Lille for the feast of St Thomas (21 December), with *plente de boene gent*, stabling 229 horses, and with *grant plente de gent* on 22 December. Expenditure for the two days ran at an average of 62 l. per day, well above the norm. On 23 December, at Kortrijk, the company was smaller (*moult de boene gent* with 170 horses) but, on Christmas eve, the household assembled with guests at Petegem for the feast itself. Petegem was a relatively recent acquisition of the Dampierre, who had bought the *maison*, woods, water-courses, meadows, homages, rents, and dues for 5,000 l. flandr. from the lord of Cysoing, on behalf of Guy's son Guy de Namur, in 1286.[85] It was there that 'tint li cuens court, et i eut grant plente de chevaliers, de dames et dautre gent', and 990 horses were stabled over the three days of the feast.[86] Preparations had evidently been made well in advance, for payment was recorded to 'those who came ahead to prepare for Christmas' (*ceaus ki vinrent avant pour aparellier pour le Noeil*).[87] Most of the expense was met by *pourvances*, which included 13 sides of bacons, 8 oxen, 16 sheep, 159 capons, and 18,000 loaves of bread. A grand total of 415 l. 14s. 10d.p. was spent over the three days, giving an average daily sum of 138 l. 5s.p.—at least double the highest figure recorded elsewhere in the accounts.[88] The gathering remained at Petegem until 5 January, celebrating New Year's Day there, although the number of horses stabled had fallen to 140, with the count and countess of Guelders still present as guests.[89] On the eve of Epiphany (5 January 1294), they moved to Lille, with 171 horses, and celebrated the feast there and (in the evening) at Seclin, when expenses stood at 51 l. 11s. 4d.p.[90] Expenditure never reached this Christmas figure for the rest of the accounting year.

The immediate post-Epiphany period was marked by an eight-week visit to Paris, which the count and countess reached, with 197 horses, on 12 January.[91] Candlemas eve (1 February 1294) was celebrated at the Parisian *hôtel* of the count, with the duke of Brabant, and the count and countess of Blois, while Candlemas itself was enlivened by dinner (at mid-day) with Philip the Fair, followed by supper at the *hôtel* with the same guests and the count and countess of Luxemburg. Again, the

---

[85] The documents relating to its purchase were included in the chancery register of *c.*1330 (see Pl. 4) which also contained urban privileges: The Hague, KB, MS 75 D 7, fos. 314r–316r.

[86] RAG, Wyffels (chron. suppl.) 188, m. 21r.   [87] Ibid.

[88] See Figs. 8, 11, 14; and above, pp. 149–50.

[89] RAG, Wyffels (chron. suppl.) 188, m. 22r.

[90] Ibid., mm. 22–3.   [91] Ibid., m. 24r.

approaching political crisis may have been influential in bringing this group of magnates together. Whatever the case, total expenditure for the eight weeks spent in Paris reached 3,497 l. 7s.p., including the household's wages, a daily average of 62 l. 7s.[92] Parisian *séjours* were necessary but expensive and, given the ensuing humiliation and imprisonment of Guy de Dampierre, of two of his sons, and of his daughter by Philip the Fair, the count's family and entourage could only have viewed the obligation and accompanying outlay with resentment.[93] A further short visit to Paris was made between 11 and 13 June 1294, after the outbreak of the Anglo-French war, with the count of Nevers, his children, and the count of Guelders. By 14 June, at Senlis, negotiations for Philippine's proposed marriage to the future Edward II of England were clearly under way, as Edward I's envoy in the Low Countries—the lord of Cuijk—was mentioned in the account.[94] Guy de Dampierre's need to consult his subjects was indicated by the presence there on 17–19 June of the *échevins* of Flanders and also those of Valenciennes (Hainault).[95] By late August and early September 1294, the crisis had escalated significantly. Much toing and froing had taken place, with the household of Flanders divided between locations on a number of occasions—on 28 August, for example, part was at Petegem, with the count, the rest at Oudenaarde.[96] By 17 September, the count and his immediate family were again at Paris, as virtual prisoners of Philip the Fair. But, even after the *débâcle* of the years 1294–7, a periodic presence at Paris was essential for the counts of Flanders, and Robert de Béthune differed little in this respect from his father.[97] This pattern of residence at Paris was to remain a constant feature of the itineraries of the counts of Flanders well into the Burgundian period, until the political crisis of 1419–20 ended that practice once and for all.[98]

[92] RAG, Wyffels (chron. suppl.) 188, m. 25r.

[93] See Funck-Bretano, *Philippe le Bel en Flandre*, 350–9; Nicholas, *Medieval Flanders*, 187–8.

[94] RAG, Wyffels (chron. suppl.) 314*bis*, m. 2r.: 'Parties Ghizelin envoie au segneur de Kuyc—8s'.

[95] Ibid., m. 3r.

[96] RAG, St-Genois 735, m. 1r (household account for one of Guy de Dampierre's sons, 12 Aug.–17 Sept. 1294).

[97] See RAG, Gaillard 66 and 67: expenditure at Paris in 1308 averaged 98–120 l.p. per day.

[98] See below, p. 159, and W. Blockmans and W. Prevenier, *The Promised Lands: The Low Countries under Burgundian Rule, 1369–1530* (Philadelphia, 1999), 37–44, 61–3.

2. Residences and lodgings

It worth concentrating on these details of the itinerary of the counts of Flanders, because it provides a basis for consideration of the demands made on a princely household by constant travel. One of the salient features of the period from c.1270 to 1380 was the increasing extent to which the Flemish comital entourage and *maisnie* could not be satisfactorily accommodated in the existing residences which the counts maintained in their domains.[99] The situation became even more acute when the count travelled outside his own lands, with the exception of his periods of residence at his Parisian *hôtel*. Expansion of the travelling household necessitated recourse to other sources of lodging and stabling. The household accounts contain occasional references to provision of accommodation, sometimes in the houses of private individuals, for members of the entourage or *maisnie*. Thus in 1334, Gerard de Steenhuize was lodged, with stabling, at the house of Ghiselbrecht van den Hecke of Ghent.[100] But the most common means of providing for the household when there was insufficient accommodation in the precincts of the ruler's residence was to lodge them in taverns and inns. When Louis de Nevers was at Brussels in December 1345, his *fourrerie* found billets in a number of hostelries in the city: the *Etoile* (Star), the *Clef* (Key), the *Echiquier* (Chessboard), the *Faucon* (Falcon), the *Rouge Ecu* (Red Shield), and the *Pourcelet* (Piglet).[101] This was also the practice of the counts of Hainault.[102] The court was beginning to overflow into the city, bringing some of its members into daily contact with urban dwellers—contact which was sometimes unwelcome, especially given the practice of billeting them in taverns.

Although the time at which Olivier de la Marche wrote about the problems of lodging the much larger Burgundian court (c.1474–7) was still about two centuries ahead, his concerns were not unfamiliar to the quartermasters of the counts of Flanders and Hainault from the later thirteenth century onwards. La Marche, in his description of the household of Charles the Bold (1474) tells us that 'although the duke of Burgundy is prince and lord of the finest towns in the world, his

---

[99] See W. Paravicini, 'Die Residenzen der Herzöge von Burgund, 1363–1477', in H. Patze and W. Paravicini (eds.), *Fürstliche Residenzen im Spätmittelalterlichen Europe* (Sigmaringen, 1991), 215–20.

[100] AGR, CC, R.4, m. 6r (1334).

[101] ADN, B.3232, no. 111703 (16–22 Dec. 1345).   [102] See below, p. 161.

establishment (*état*) is always so great that one finds few towns where they can all lodge'.[103] There was, he wrote, a constant overflow into neighbouring towns and even villages, where lodgings of all kinds (including billets in taverns and hostelries) were secured by the ducal quarter-masters (*fourriers*).[104] Members of the household proper—the principal officers, the squires of pantry and buttery, the carving squires, and the squires of the stable—were all provided with food, drink, and beds by the duke, as far as possible within the confines of the palace or residence.[105] Others, such as visiting princes, nobles, ambassadors, papal nuncios, and other envoys, were to be found quarters of a kind appropriate to their status out of court, generally in the *hôtels* of great nobles, bishops, or abbots.[106] Thus the townhouses of the Gruuthuse, the Ravenstein, the Egmont, the Nassau, or the Croy were brought into use for the housing of ducal guests.[107]

A further measure increasingly adopted by princes was simply to increase the size and facilities of the princely residence itself. In 1361–2, Louis de Male undertook an extensive programme of repairs and modifications to the late twelfth-century comital castle, or Gravensteen, at Ghent (Pl. 7).[108] The building materials purchased included 101,500 bricks, the roofs of both the great hall (*le grande sale*) and chapel were re-clad in lead, new windows were made, with columns, capitals, and sills, and extensive tiling operations took place.[109] A grand total of 5,766 l. 10s 8d. was spent on the works. But the Gravensteen was not to remain the sole comital residence at Ghent throughout the fourteenth century. Under Louis de Male (1346–84) two other sites were purchased, developed and modified according to the count's needs. First, the *hôtel* of *La Posterne* (*De Posteerne*) which, as its name implies, was situated close to one of

[103] La Marche, *Mémoires*, iv. 77–8: 'Et combien que le duc de Bourgoingne soit prince et seigneur des plus belles villes du monde, toutesfois est son estat si grant que l'on trouve peu de villes la ou ilz puissent tous logier.'

[104] La Marche, *Mémoires*, iv. 78: 'et fault souvent adjunctions de villes et de villaiges'.

[105] See M. Sommé, 'Les déplacements d'Isabelle de Portugal et la circulation dans les Pays-Bas bourguignons au milieu du xvᵉ siècle', *RN* 52 (1970), 183–97.

[106] See Paravicini, 'Die Residenzen der Herzöge von Burgund', 243–4: 'in Brussel gibt es in unmittelbarer Nähe des Herzogshofes die Hôtels d'Auxy, de Croy, Kleve-Ravenstein (erhalten), Jacques de Villers, Boquet de Lattre, Souillot, Molenbaix . . . ' (243).

[107] The extensive work of Saintenoy is valuable in this respect: see P. Saintenoy, *Les Arts et les artistes à la cour de Bruxelles*, i. *Leur rôle dans la construction du château ducal de Brabant sur le Coudenberg de 1120 à 1400 et dans la formation du Parc de Bruxelles* (Brussels, 1932).

[108] AGR, CC, R.2090: 23 Apr. 1361–23 Apr. 1362; partially edited in *Documents*, i. 438.

[109] AGR, CC, R.2090, mm. 1r, 2r.

the city's gates, was acquired by the count. It consisted of a complex of buildings, including a hall called the *vielle sale de Flandres*, a chapel, gardens, stables, and other offices, as well as two large townhouses— the *hostelz d'Artois et de Flandres*.[110] It also housed a building known as *Bretagne*, so named because Louis de Male had lodged his relative Jean IV de Montfort, duke of Brittany, there from 1377 to 1379.[111] It has been pointed out that the location of the *Posteerne*, on the west side of Ghent, away from the 'political centre', the marketplace, and close to the Bruges gate, made it a convenient point from which to escape from the turbulent city.[112] Between 1371 and 1377, Louis de Male bought up rented properties around the *Posteerne* so that it could be extended. It served him well as a favoured residence where his many amorous affairs could be discreetly conducted.[113] The extent of these activities was apparent from the terms of one draft of his will, in which his illegitimate children were provided for, including the stipulation:

se aucuns de nos filz ou fillez bastardes *qui encores ne sont venu a cognoissance*, ne fussent par nous en nostre plaine vie pourveu de biens ou rentes selonc ce que bon nous sambleroit, nous volons et ordenons que a chascun fil bastard soit donne et assis bon et souffisant a sa vie. Et a chascune fille bastarde a sa vie tant si avant *quil seroit prouve et cognissable a nos dis executeurs quil fussent nostre* et que nous y fussent tenus en bonne foy.[114]

[if any of our bastard sons or daughters who are not yet known are not provided by us during our lifetime with goods or rents as seems good to us, we wish and ordain that to each bastard son shall be given a good and sufficient sum for his life. And to each bastard daughter for her lifetime, as long as it shall be proven and recognized by our said executors that they are ours, and that we are held to it in good faith.]

Problems of identifying the count's bastards means that their precise number will never be known but, as under his successor Philip the Good of Burgundy, provision for their welfare was a major item of expenditure.

Secondly, a further purchase was made in 1349, when Louis obtained the luxurious and well-furbished *hôtel* known as the *Cour de le Walle* (*Ten*

[110] See M. Boone and T. de Hemptinne, 'Espace urbain et ambitions princières: les présences matérielles de l'autorité princière dans le Gand médiéval (12ᵉ siècle–1540)', in Paravicini (ed.), *Zeremoniell und Raum*, 284–6.

[111] B. Pocquet du Haut-Jusse, *Deux féodaux: Bourgogne et Bretagne (1363–1491)* (Paris, 1935), 24–5.

[112] Boone and de Hemptinne, 'Espace urbain et ambitions princières', 284.

[113] See F. De Potter, *Gent van den oudsten tijd tot heden*, viii (Ghent, 1901), 29–30.

[114] ADN, B.455, no. 11324*bis* (29 Jan. 1384). Italics mine.

Walle) from his Italian creditor and banker Simon de Mirabello, formerly receiver-general of Flanders under Louis de Nevers.[115] Mirabello had bought this desirable property in 1323. It was an attractive residence, with handsome private chambers, including a *chambre verte*, surrounded by moats (*douves*), and, despite its urban location, had some of the character of a rural chateau or *maison de plaisance* about it (Pl. 8).[116] It also lay in the north-west part of the city, away from areas of tension, and might have become one of the count's favourite dwellings had it not been for the positively dangerous nature of Ghent as a comital residence. As it was, the *hôtel Ten Walle* later became known as the *Prinsenhof*, birthplace of the Emperor Charles V in February 1500.[117] The risks involved in residing at Ghent were spelt out during the period of extremely stormy relations, marked by the ascendancy of Philip van Artevelde, between city and count in 1379–84.[118] In May 1380, for instance, all the stallions and mares of the comital stud were kept *au séjour*, not in Flanders, but in the Dampierres' other lordship of Rethel, far away from Flemish conflict, *pour le doubte du comun* ('for fear of the common people' [of Ghent]).[119] Both *Ten Walle* and the *Posteerne* were in a bad state in 1379–80. Not only were the gutters along the passage (*allée*) between the *hostelz d'Artois et de Flandres* at the *Posteerne* broken and leaking rainwater, causing roof timber to rot but, even worse, the *maître du séjour* was shown further damage by Jean la Pont, master of the works, who took him

ou gardin empries la chambre la madame Dartois a acostumee a gisir, et li monstra que une grande partie du mur [du]dit gardin estoit cheus, et les commune gens y entroyent par tout en les gardins, si que pour mieux fait que laissiet par le conseil du dit Jehan la Pont, Jehan le Marissal [*maître du séjour*] le fist resouder, remachoner et refaire.[120]

[into the garden next to the chamber where my lady of Artois is accustomed to reside, and showed him that a large section of the garden wall had fallen down, and the common people had entered all parts of the garden from there, in such a way that, by the advice of the said Jehan la Pont, Jehan le Marissal had it joined up, rebuilt and remade.]

---

[115] Boone and de Hemptinne, 'Espace urbain et ambitions princières', 287.

[116] For an illustration of the residence see the engraving in A. Sanderus, *Flandria Illustrata* (1641) reproduced in W. Prevenier and W. Blockmans, *The Burgundian Netherlands* (Cambridge, 1986), fig. 104.

[117] See *Keizer tussen stroppendragers: Karel V, 1500–1558* (Leuven, 1990), 1–4.

[118] See D. M. Nicholas, *The van Arteveldes of Ghent: the Varieties of Vendetta and the Hero in History* (Ithaca, NY, London, and Leiden, 1988), 120–59, and his *The Metamorphosis of a Medieval City: Ghent in the Age of the Arteveldes, 1302–1390* (Leiden, 1987), 1–17.

[119] AGR, CC.1779, fo. 9r.   [120] Ibid., fo. 13r.

The Ghent rebels had evidently broken into the gardens of the *Posteerne*, having demolished part of the garden wall of what must have been the *hostel d'Artois*.[121] During the disturbances, property had been stolen, including plate and jewels belonging to the lady of Eine, bastard daughter of Louis de Male, from the *maison d'Eine* at Ghent.[122] One of the most active periods of building under Louis de Male was therefore the late 1370s and early 1380s. From July 1379 to June 1380, extensive repairs and alterations were made to both the *hôtel Ten Walle* and the *Posteerne* at Ghent.[123]

During the civil war which broke out in 1379, the comital household was put on a war footing. Accommodation had to be provided for the count's 110 knights and 52 valets *qui continuellement ont este au sejour*.[124] Stabling had also to be provided for their horses, and this absorbed the large sum of 1,309 l. The forge at the *hôtel Ten Walle* produced 2,720 horseshoes, but when the court was forced to move to Bruges in September 1379, insufficient accommodation was available for the *grans chivalers* (that is, the bannerets) and their valets. It was a period of disaffection among the great towns and 56 l.12s. was spent on the lodging of '14 grans chivalers et de 14 varles que Jehan le Maressal avoit mis sur les abbies environ Bruges, et pour le doubte du comun de Gand'.[125] ['fourteen great knights and fourteen valets that Jehan le Maressal had quartered in the abbeys around Bruges, for fear of the common people of Ghent']. The situation then improved, and room was found for them in the count's *hôtel* at Bruges, but conditions in west Flanders had become so difficult by February 1380 that Louis ordered all his knights *grans et petis* to come to the safer haven of Lille, in *Flandre gallicante*, so that he could 'les . . . veier et ordener a son plaisir la ou il les envoieroit et ainsi quil volloit que les grans chevaux furent as joustes a Lespinete'[126] ['review them and ordain at his pleasure where he would send them and also because he wished that the great horses were at the jousts of the *Epinette*']. The comital household evidently still participated in the civic jousts of the *Epinette* at Lille at this time, and the stables of the Salle-le-Comte had to be adapted to meet this invasion. A team of carpenters were set to work preparing for their descent. It appears that Louis was permanently retaining a total of thirty-five knights in his household at this time: they

---

[121] See above, p. 155.   [122] AGR, CC.28579, fo. 3r.
[123] See Boone and de Hemptinne, 'Espace urbain et ambitions princières', 284–8; AGR, CC.1799.
[124] AGR, CC.1799, fo. 1r.
[125] Ibid., fo. 6v; and see Nicholas, *Medieval Flanders*, 228–31.
[126] AGR, CC.1799, fo. 6v.

came to Lille, where their horses were stabled partly at the Salle, and partly in the *hôtel* of the count of St-Pol there (9–26 February 1380). But this put such a burden on resources that the religious houses of the area were again brought into play—the household knights remained at Lille for some days 'ordener es quels abbies on les poroit envoier pour le mieux'.[127] The final distribution was:

St-Pierre at Ghent: 2 *grans chivalers*, 2 *valets*
St-Bavon at Ghent: 2 *grans chivalers*, 2 *valets*
Tronchines: 1 *gran chivaler*, 1 *valet*
St-Winoc at Berghes: 2 *grans chivalers*, 2 *valets*
Abbey of Le Conte and St-André-les-Bruges; St-Martin at Ypres; abbeys of Dunes and Furnes: 27 *chivalers* and *valets*.

The abbeys and other convents of Flanders clearly contributed their share to the support of the count's household, especially in times of disorder. But this was not apparently a comital right, comparable with that of *gîte*. In his will, dated 29 January 1384 at St-Omer, Louis de Male acknowledged this by stating:

Item, cognoissans que ce que nous avons mis nos grans chevaulz et nos chiens aucune fois sur les abbaies de nostre pays, et que on les y a gardes et norris, et fait encores, a este par prisere et de grace, et non mie de droit. Et ne voloms mie que leglise en puist estre aucunement grevee en possession ou en ses drois et libertes, ne que nous ou nostre hoir puissons dire que aucun droit nouvel nous soit par ce aquis, ou a euls en aucun temps advenir.[128]

[Item, we recognize that we have sometimes imposed our great horses and our dogs on the abbeys of our land, and that they have been kept and fed there, and still are, and this has been by requisition and of grace, not by right. And we do not wish that the Church should in any way be harmed in possession of its rights and liberties, nor that we nor our heirs can say that any new right has been acquired by us in this way, nor by them in time to come.]

The accounts confirm this: in January 1382, the *écoutête* of Bruges was given 5 l. 8s.p. with which to purchase grey cloth for the covering of 'un de nos destriers [warhorses] estans en labbeye de Du[n]es'.[129] It was increasingly obvious that the growth in the size of the comital household had rendered much of the pre-existing accommodation provided in residences such as the Gravensteen at Ghent and the Salle-le-Comte at Lille inadequate and unsuitable. Rising expectations of domestic comfort must also have played some part in this process. By 1384, when Philip

---

[127] For this and for what follows see AGR, CC.1799, fo. 7v.
[128] ADN, B.455, no. 11324*bis*.   [129] ADN, B.3240, no. 111898: 12 Jan. 1382.

the Bold of Burgundy succeeded to the *comtés* of Flanders and Artois, a network of castles, *maisons de plaisance*, *hôtels*, and other residences certainly existed for his use there, but they could not meet the needs of the complete household and *maisnie*. Philip spent little time in his Flemish dominions—six months during his reign of twenty years—and preferred to live in Paris.[130] The traditional pattern of itinerary followed by successive Dampierre counts of Flanders was broken once and for all.

The evidence from the court of Hainault-Holland is readily comparable with that from Flanders. The itinerant household—or rather, households, of count and countess—adopted similar procedures and habits on their journeying through the comital dominions. The surviving material for the household of the countess Jeanne de Valois (from 1319 to 1336) is more plentiful than for that of the count.[131] But the impression given by Avesnes Hainault closely resembles that of Dampierre Flanders. It is notable that the countess was often receiving the count and his entourage in her own household, and sometimes meeting the cost.[132] A steady stream of guests and visitors largely accounted for the rise and fall in household expenditure, culminating in the lavish outlay incurred by the Avesnes as a result of the betrothal and marriage of their younger daughter Philippa to the future Edward III of England in 1326–7.[133] In December 1326–January 1327, for example, total monthly expenditure (without *pourvanches*) reached 1,198 l.t., when the average monthly total for the rest of the accounting year stood at 289 l.t.[134] The first meeting of Edward and Philippa took place at this time, and coincided with the visit of Jeanne de Valois and her daughter to Paris to pay their last respects to her father, the dying Charles de Valois.[135]

[130] See Blockmans and Prevenier, *The Promised Lands*, 14–37; Paravicini, 'Die Residenzen der Herzöge von Burgund', 216–17.

[131] See *De rekeningen*, ed. Smit, iii. 1–133 for a detailed discussion of the accounting material; for the accounts of the countess's household see i. 32–615. The countess and her officers were responsible for the count's expenses when he, and members of his own household and council, were with her. The itineraries of the counts and countesses are set out and discussed in J. G. Smit, 'De graven van Holland en Zeeland op reis', 94–101.

[132] See *De rekeningen*, i. 140–1, 169 where it was recorded that the count had been in the countess's household 'par pluizeurs fies' for 87 days during the year from 25 Aug. 1325 to 24 Aug. 1326, while part of his household and council had resided there for 113 days. These were maintained at the countess's expense. There are many other examples of this practice in the accounts.

[133] See Tables 23, 24.   [134] See Table 24.

[135] See Table 22, and *De rekeningen*, ed. Smit, i. 145–53.

As was the case for Flanders, regular visits to Paris by the Hainault household imposed a heavy strain on revenues, which the Avesnes, however, were easily able to bear. Philippa's nuptial ceremonies themselves were celebrated amidst a succession of visits from distinguished guests, from England and elsewhere, during the period from October to December 1327. Hence the total annual household expenditure for the accounting year 1327–8 reached the very large sum of 11,487 l. 10s.t.— the figures for 1326–7 and 1328–9 were 7,718 l. 17s. 5d. and 8,874 l. 4s. 4d.t. respectively.[136] As in Flanders, however, the early 1330s seem to have been a time of retrenchment in expenditure for the Avesnes, and the countess's total annual household expenses for 1332–3 (4,849 l.t.)[137] stood at a similar level to those incurred in 1319–21 (4,829 l.t.) It was often necessary to divide the household for purposes of lodging—for example, in January 1319, the countess and her *damoiselles* lodged at Dordrecht, while a part of the *maisnie* were at Schiedam, and the rest accompanied the count's son William to The Hague.[138]

The possession of Holland and Zeeland by the Avesnes extended their itineraries, and their northern territories were in no way neglected.[139] In 1319–20, for instance, the countess spent almost seven months—from July 1319 to January 1320—in Holland and Zeeland, mainly at Dordrecht and The Hague.[140] The Binnenhof there (Pl. 2) witnessed a series of 'courtly' events and occasions at this time—in July 1319, the count of Guelders and other notables came to The Hague for jousts; in August the countess received Louis of Évreux and Mahaut d'Artois there; and Christmas was celebrated in lavish style, when Dutch nobles and officers such as the lady of Voorne, the castellan of Leiden, and *autre pluseur chevalier et autres* were at court.[141] The provisions supplied to the court by *pourvanche* included 336 quarters of salt mutton, 105 sides of bacon, 23 pigs, 158 hens, and 49 swans for the Christmas and New year festivities.[142] On 20 January, in the evening, the court left for Hainault, and its personnel included Dutch members such as the lord and lady of Voorne. A ten-day journey took them to Binche by 30 January 1320, whence they travelled to Mons on 20 February.[143] Lent was enlivened by the presence of a succession of guests and visitors, reaching a peak on 21 and 22 March when 450 people were accounted for by the receiver, including the

---

[136] See Table 24.　　[137] Ibid.
[138] *De Rekeningen*, i. 42. There are many other examples in the accounts.
[139] See above, p. 131.　　[140] *De Rekeningen*, ed. Smit, i. 33–52.
[141] Ibid., i. 35, 37, 49–50.　　[142] Ibid., i. 51–2.　　[143] Ibid., i. 52, 54, 56.

entourage of John of Luxemburg, king of Bohemia, the *consuls* of Tournai and Hainault, as well as a large number of the count's household.[144] Fish provided by *pourvanche* (during Lenten abstinence from meat-eating) included 875 carp, 26 breem, 2.5 tuns of herrings, and 7 salt salmon. One of the incidental benefits which accrued to the Avesnes through their possession of Holland and Zeeland was a ready supply of Lenten herrings, which they gained by *pourvanches* levied on their territories and for which they paid nothing.[145] It seems that they were able to feed their entire household from this source during Lent. In April 1321, for example, the receiver accounted for no less than 22,000 smoked and salted herrings, as well as a further consignment of 12 tuns of 'white' herrings.[146] These were provided by Henri de Malines, the receivers of South-Holland and Frisia, the abbot of Cambron, and one Ghijsbrecht Pauwelzoon, a fish merchant of Dordrecht, who supplied luxury items for the upper reaches of the court including a *porc de mer*, 17 salmon, and 83 shads. On Easter Day, meat returned to the comital table in the Salle-le-Comte at Valenciennes in the form of bacon, pigs, *grosses biestes*, sheep, bullocks, and veal.[147] This pattern of consumption was repeated year after year and examples could be multiplied endlessly.

The increasing size of the Hainault household led to their quartering in taverns and inns, as was the practice in Flanders and Brabant.[148] At Mons, Binche, and Valenciennes, members of the household were lodged at inns such as those displaying the signs of the Ostrich, the Three Kings, the Pewter Pot (*pot d'Etain*), the Shield of St George (*Ecu de St-Georges*), and the Helm (*Heaume*) at Mons; the Star, the Peacock, the Swan, and the Crown at Binche; and the Key (*Clef*), the Cauldron, the Salmon, the Hearth (*Cheminee*), the Sheep (*Mouton*), and the Helm at Valenciennes.[149] While the count or countess and their entourages resided in the comital castle or residence, the rest of the household were spread over the town. Extensions to the Salle-le-Comte at Valenciennes enabled more of the household to be accommodated within the precincts of the prince's residence, but this proved inadequate to their needs.[150]

[144] Ibid., i. 59.   [145] Ibid., i. 97–8 (1321).   [146] Ibid., i. 97–8.
[147] Ibid., i. 98–9.   [148] See above, p. 153.
[149] See AEM, Trésorerie, Recueils 69, no. 79 (1378); 70, no. 19 (1384); 72, no. 54; 74, no. 93. For Brabant see AGR, CC.46922 (Genappe, Aug. 1371); 46925 (Mons, Binche, Brussels, 1372–9).
[150] See *Documents*, i. 275–6.

The picture of the travelling court which is given by this evidence appears to hold good for all the major principalities of the Low Countries. Analysis of the large volume of accounting and other material which survives enables us to trace common patterns in these neighbouring territories. A relatively restricted itinerary, revolving around fixed nodal points, which were visited on the major feast-days of the liturgical calendar, and where 'full' or 'solemn' courts were held, provided the norm. There was little sign at this date of any slackening of the pace of itineration—although the households of rulers' wives and kinswomen often tended to reside for longer periods at a given location—nor of the 'centralization' of courts in any one place. The development of the court was here moving in a rather different direction from that assumed by a ruler's principal legal, financial, and administrative institutions. But it was at court that real power lay.

Part Two

CULTURE

Chapter 5

COURT LIFE AND COURT CULTURE

1. Luxury, display, and the arts

In previous chapters we have seen how the material infrastructure of courts developed from the later thirteenth century onwards. The following chapters attempt to describe and analyse the superstructure—that is, the cultural forms and artistic expression—of court life. Nevertheless, just as the religious and secular features of the court can never be entirely separated, so its material and non-material aspects can never be completely divorced from each other. There was a symbiotic relationship between the two, and one sphere constantly overlapped and impinged upon the other. Moreover, as we shall see in a subsequent chapter, it is necessary to adopt a much broader definition of court 'culture' than has sometimes been the case. Thus the following chapters seek to integrate the arts, both 'fine' and applied, into a more general cultural context in which as much emphasis is placed upon use and function as upon style and aesthetic response. The elaborate panoply of ritual and display, of liturgy and ceremony, was supported by—and to some extent embodied in—the visual and other arts. It is evident that during this period painting, sculpture, literature, music, dance, drama, and the applied arts could serve many purposes. But, in a courtly setting, they could convey specific messages about the nature and representation of power, the role of devotional religion, and the forms of behaviour appropriate to a social milieu in which concepts such as *courtoisie* and *debonaireté* were increasingly gaining ground.[1] Art at court is therefore treated here as both a symptom and an agent of cultural change—as an active as well as a passive index of the evolution of taste, of the representation of power, and the development of dynastic ideologies.

[1] See Vale, *Origins of the Hundred Years War*, 23–5.

It has been said that the art and artefacts produced by a given civilization not only illustrate and shape our understanding of its culture but
'substantially . . . form that culture'.[2] The influence of both Marxist
and postmodernist criticism in literature, anthropology, and the visual
arts has prompted a revision of accepted views of 'court' culture. A great
building such as Westminster abbey (Pls. 1, 9a, 24), with its monastic
foundation, shrine, and palace, is now seen not merely as an 'illustration
of the beliefs and principles of a certain type of political culture, but as
a practical incorporation of those beliefs and principles'.[3] According to
this interpretation, the thirteenth- and fourteenth-century abbey rightly
becomes a *Gesamtkunstwerk*, uniting many art-forms within its precincts,
but as a corporate embodiment of a formative political ideology: the
ideology of dynastic kingship rooted (for the first time) in a specifically
English location. The very fact that its location was English, not French,
is highly significant. By transferring their burial place from Fontevrault
in Anjou (the original heartland of the dynasty) to Westminster the
Plantagenets were not only accepting thirteenth-century political realities
but making a political and ideological point.[4] But it has been argued that
the manner in which that point was expressed did not stem from any kind
of singularity of outlook, embodied in a unitary artistic style.[5] Although
Westminster conformed to the general conventions of thirteenth-century
Gothic, it was not conceived as a unified, homogeneous, architectural
and artistic commission, unlike the public buildings and prestige projects
of more recent regimes. There was no Albert Speer in thirteenth- and
fourteenth-century England to create an ideologically charged architecture expressive of a particular kind of regime and its aims.[6] As we shall
see, eclecticism was the hallmark of later medieval court patronage, and
Westminster was no exception to this rule. The major constituents of
the eclectic Plantagenet 'programme' for the abbey church and palace at
Westminster were thus composed of Gothic architectural forms deriving
largely from France (Pls. 9a, 9b); English wall and panel-paintings

---

[2] Binski, *Westminster Abbey and the Plantagenets*, 8.　　　[3] Ibid., p. vii.

[4] See T. S. R. Boase, 'Fontevrault and the Plantagenets', *Journal of the British
Archaeological Association*, 3rd ser. 34 (1971), 1–10; Vale, *Origins of the Hundred Years War*,
9–10. For criticism, from an anthropological viewpoint, of functionalist interpretations
of culture as an 'ideological artifice' see M. Sahlins, 'Two or three things that I know
about culture', *Journal of the Royal Anthropological Society*, 5 (1999), 404–7.

[5] Binski, *Westminster Abbey*, 44–5.

[6] See the catalogue of the exhibition *Art and Power: Europe under the Dictators, 1930–45*
(Hayward Gallery, London, 1995), 322–9.

(Pls. 3, 22a, 22b), influenced by both northern and southern European styles; English liturgical textiles and embroidery; English, Parisian, and Limousin goldsmiths' and enamellers' work (Pl. 23); and Italian mosaic paving.[7]

Such eclecticism also characterized the practice and aesthetics of display in the rest of north-west Europe at this time. But this had social and devotional, as well as political, connotations. The so-called 'meaning-systems', of which buildings and artefacts are said to form a part, are seen to take on specific, localized forms, although these ultimately derived from a limited number of 'formal archetypes'.[8] Among those archetypes, the abbey of St-Denis, the Sainte-Chapelle (Pl. 21), and the cathedrals of Amiens (Pl. 9b) and Rheims provided models for Westminster. But the functionalist argument which lies behind such views can be overstated. A reductionist interpretation of works of art and architecture merely as political propaganda tends to exaggerate one feature at the expense of others. These forms reflected or embodied not only the supposed political or ideological aims of rulers and their agents, but literally enshrined local devotional traditions (such as the cults of specific saints and martyrs, whose relics they often preserved) and had specific liturgical purposes within a court milieu. In a courtly setting, form could also be related to function outside a strictly artistic and architectural context. The practice, for example, of gift-giving and exchange could partially determine the production, purchase, and valuation of plate and jewels in court societies.[9] The needs of the court could thus influence and shape the ebb and flow of artistic production, as well as the selection and acquisition of objects and artefacts by rulers, their advisers, and the middlemen appointed to purchase such items.

Similarly, the episodic and occasional nature of courtly display could mould its aesthetic expression—the use of heraldic achievements, luxury textiles, and the whole apparatus of ritual and ceremony had something, but by no means everything, in common with drama and the medieval

---

[7] There is a detailed survey of the abbey, its monuments and decoration in *Royal Commission on Historical Monuments. England*, i. *Westminster Abbey* (London, 1924); see also, for a plan of the monuments to 1307, Binski, *Westminster Abbey*, 112, fig. 151.

[8] Binski, *Westminster Abbey*, 44: 'the use of much court art was precisely its uselessness, its ability to promote an aesthetic realm of functionless irresponsibility to ideological ends ... Permanent structures ... were formed not only with reference to stable archetypes but also to this less stable, and essentially political, aesthetic of display ...'

[9] See below, pp. 267–8. Also Appendices II, IV, V.

stage.[10] Specific ceremonies had their own scenery, properties, stage directions, and choreography: the rituals of coronations, baptisms, marriages, churchings, funerals, initiations into knighthood, and tournaments could all employ the visual arts, speech, drama, and music to mark their passage and to celebrate dynastic pride and well-being. Yet it is easy to speak of such manifestations—in a later medieval context—as examples merely of 'pageantry', largely devoid of inner meaning and significance, conforming to much more recent notions of outward show. The conscious, contrived revival—or invention—of rituals of all kinds, especially from the latter part of the nineteenth century onwards, has perhaps led to fundamental misinterpretations of medieval practices.[11] Compounded by the influence of reductionism, this tendency to deprive ritual of its content, and to speak in terms only of 'theatre' and 'pageant'[12] denies much of its intrinsic and underlying power to later medieval ceremony. Huizinga's thesis of the role of the ludic in culture may be open to many objections, but his stress upon the inner meaning and significance of later medieval liturgical, heraldic, and chivalric ritual still carries some weight.[13]

Yet luxury and display had their other face. 'Ostentatious display conferred significance upon its denial'[14]—the more lavish the display, the more effective was any gesture whereby it was renounced. Louis IX of France (1226–70) had set the tone for all subsequent manifestations of kingly denial. As a virtuoso in the arts of self-denial and self-mortification, Louis provided a model for other rulers to follow. None achieved his exalted levels of ostentatious humility (expressed, for example, through the regular washing of monks' and paupers' feet), of penitential discipline (administered to him with a cane or switch by his confessor), or of rigorous self-abnegation (symbolized by the wearing of hairshirts

[10] See below, pp. 204–7, 243–6. For the construction of a 'stage' for the coronation ceremony in the choir at Westminster see Colvin et al., King's Works, ii, 1044 n. 40 (1307–11).

[11] For the contribution of the late nineteenth and early twentieth centuries to the 'invention of tradition' see D. Cannadine, 'The context, performance and meaning of ritual: the British monarchy and the "invention of tradition", c.1820–1977', in E. Hobsbawn and T. Ranger (eds.), The Invention of Tradition (Cambridge, 1983), 101–64, and B. S. Cohn, 'Representing authority in Victorian India' ibid. 165–209.

[12] See, for instances of this tendency, R. Barber and J. Barker, Tournaments (Woodbridge, 1989), 1–2, and, for a less reductive view, M. H. Keen, Chivalry (New Haven and London, 1982), 200–1, 216–18.

[13] See J. Huizinga, Homo Ludens (London, 1970), 125–6.

[14] Binski, Westminster Abbey, 44.

and by fasting).[15] But, paradoxically, the greater the level of conspicuous consumption and extravagant display practised by a ruler, the greater the impact created by its conscious and purposeful rejection. It was incumbent upon later medieval rulers to indulge in the maximum degree of display which their resources and incomes would allow. A cult of magnificence—closely associated with munificence—was developing in the court societies of this period. But denial of that luxury and extravagance—during Lent, or at times of self-imposed austerity, often associated with the making of vows—was all the more impressive, and more efficacious for the health of the soul, if it stood in stark contrast with great luxury. A cycle of indulgence and denial—the latter sometimes practised vicariously through monks and friars—therefore formed a kind of counterpoint to the liturgical rhythmn of the year dictated by the feasts of the Church. In this process, the role of the mendicant orders was crucial.[16] It is no coincidence that the confessors and chaplains of kings and princes were often drawn from the ranks of either the austere (non-mendicant) Cistercians or the (mendicant) Dominicans and Franciscans at this time.[17] The essential sub-text to mendicant culture, which alone made it meaningful, was furnished by material affluence and its rejection.[18] And it was, as we have seen, at courts that material affluence was often most visible. Display and its denial thus formed the seemingly paradoxical qualifications for virtuous and pious rulership.[19]

To study luxury and display in a courtly context involves, above all, a consideration of conspicuous consumption and its material expression. We have already seen how the provision and distribution of liveries in cloth and furs, and the consumption of food and drink at table, marked court societies off from many others.[20] Among the inmates of courts, it was also customary to engage in hunting and hawking; to participate in tournaments; to play games of both skill and chance, involving the wagering of sums of money; and to acquire and enjoy certain luxuries unknown

---

[15] See J. Le Goff, *Saint Louis* (Paris, 1996), 757–60, 869–70; J. Richard, *Saint Louis: Crusader King of France*, ed. S. Lloyd, tr. J. Birrell (Cambridge, 1992), 237–44.

[16] See L. K. Little, 'St Louis' involvement with the friars', *Church History*, 33 (1962), 125–48; Le Goff, *Saint Louis*, 746–51.

[17] See Richard, *Saint Louis*, 237–40; *Le Somme Le Roy*, attributed to the Parisian miniaturist Honoré, ed. E. G. Millar (Oxford, Roxburghe Club, 1953), 1–4.

[18] See L. K. Little, *Religious Poverty and the Profit Economy in Medieval Europe* (London, 1978), 4–12, 25–40.

[19] See above, pp. 73–4; E. Kantorowicz, *The King's Two Bodies: A Study in Medieval Political Theology* (Princeton, 1966), 45–61.

[20] See above, pp. 95–6.

to other ranks of society. All these activities could carry symbolic over-tones, expressive of status and function in the hierarchical society of a court. It is the purpose of the following section to examine some of these forms of court life and to assess their cultural meaning.

2. Courtly pursuits

a. Games and gambling

One expression of aristocratic lifestyles and mentalities which found especial favour at courts was the ubiquitous habit of gambling and of playing games of both skill and chance. Those members of society who had both leisure and, so they believed, surplus funds available engaged enthusiastically in such activities. The two favourite chamber games of the period were chess (Pl. 10) and *tables* (*tabulae, taules*). Chess was norm-ally considered the superior of the two forms, but *tables* or 'tables'(like 'cards' today) was the generic name for as many as twenty-five different games 'only linked together by the use of a common apparatus for play'.[21] The common apparatus which gave its name to these pastimes was not in fact the board upon which the games were played, but the flat, circular counters (*tabula, tabulae*), resembling modern draughts or backgammon tokens, which formed the pieces or 'men' employed. From *tables*, the word *tabularium, tablier*, or *taulier* was derived: that is, the board on which all these games were played.[22] In practice, chess and 'tables' were often associated together—the chessboard often formed one half of the hinged box which could also contain the *tabularium*.[23] English fourteenth-century sources can thus refer to 'pairs of tables' divided into inner and outer boards, each board sub-divided into six 'points', including ace-points and sice-points. All forms of 'tables' were played with dice, so that there was an aleatoric, or chance element in all of them. All involved two sides, or teams, of fifteen men or pieces, and the object of the exercise was to run a race along a track provided by the board.[24] Men could be captured and taken, and there were rules about the doubling and piling of pieces.

In many cultures, dicing and fighting have had certain affinities, some of them very ancient.[25] The game of 'tables' was not entirely unlike the

---

[21] H. J. R. Murray, 'The Medieval game of tables', *Medium Aevum*, 10 (1941), 58.
[22] Ibid. 58–9.   [23] See below, pp. 172–3.
[24] Murray, 'Medieval game of tables', 62.   [25] Huizinga, *Homo Ludens*, 77.

mêlée-style of tournament, with a *dedans* and *dehors* side, in which the winner succeeded in capturing his opponents' men and pushing them off the board. The capture and ransom of opponents and their horses, and the winning of the field by one side, in the team encounters of a *mêlée* had a certain affinity with the game. Although based upon the Roman *alea*, the medieval game had many variants. 'The chief differences are the number of dice used, the existence or not of an initial arrangement of the men, the direction of the course prescribed for each player, the restriction of the right to pile men in particular parts of the board, and the value attached to certain forms of victory.'[26] There could thus be a combination of chance and skill in most forms of the game. As with the game of chess, a literature of problem-books grew up, composed for the purposes of wagering, involving either the use of dice or the prior choice of throws (*ludi optativi*). 'Tables' could make intellectual demands, often resembling mathematical problem-solving, and should not be dismissed out of hand nor compared unfavourably to the skills required by chess.

The rapid diffusion of games from the Islamic world across western Europe in the course of the twelfth century led to their incorporation into knightly styles of life: in the *Disciplina Clericalis* of Petrus Alfonsi (*c.*1100–25) ability at chess was listed among the seven skills to be acquired by a good knight.[27] Such techniques were learnt and transmitted, often by clerks, in a household setting—they were part of the educative function of household culture. The future Edward II of England, for instance, was already an experienced player of games of skill and chance in July 1299, when he was given 40s. by his father to meet the costs of his wagering in *diversos ludos*.[28] The habit began at an early age—his brothers Thomas and Edmund were receiving sums of money from their wardrobe clerk in 1311–12, when they were aged 10 and 11 respectively, for playing dice (*taxillos*), chess (*scaccarium*), and 'tables' (*tabulas*).[29] Christmas was a particularly popular time for gambling, and Edward II and his entourage were often playing at 'tables' on Christmas eve.[30] The king's

[26] Murray, 'Medieval game of tables', 62.

[27] See R. Eales, 'The game of chess: an aspect of medieval knightly culture' in C. Harper-Bill and R. Harvey (eds.), *The Ideals and Practice of Medieval Knighthood* (Woodbridge, 1986), 15. Also R. Eales, *Chess: A History of a Game* (London, 1985), 3–10.

[28] PRO, E.101/355/18, m. 5r; H. Johnstone, *Edward of Carnarvon, 1284–1307* (Manchester, 1946), 45.

[29] E.101/374/19, fos. 4r, 5v; Murray, 'Medieval game of tables', 57–69.

[30] E.101/374/7, fo. 26v: prest to Piers Gaveston *ad ludendum*, 25 Dec. 1310; 376/7, fo. 41r: prest to the king to play *ad taulos* on Christmas eve, 25 Dec. 1314.

gambling debts were high—he must have played for high stakes, receiving a total of over 80 l.st. on two occasions in 1307–8.[31]

That chess should be played for money—despite ecclesiastical censure and opposition—was in no way uncommon or exceptional at this time. True to form, Louis IX—in thrall, his critics claimed, to the friars—attempted to ban the practice in his *ordonnance* against gambling at dice and tables in 1254.[32] His action was a total failure. Household accounts and inventories give the lie to any notion that anyone paid any attention whatsoever to such unenforceable edicts. Chess—like that other pro-hibited activity, the tournament—was inordinately popular, especially in a courtly milieu. The value set upon the game, not only in monetary terms, is evident from the very finely made and valuable chessboards and chess-sets which survive, or are recorded in inventories (Pls. 10, 11, 14).[33] It was socially highly prestigious—the nobleman's game *par excellence*—and could serve to mark off a member of the nobility, however poor, from the rest of society.[34] Thus Edward I's second wife Margaret of France had in a casket:

Unum scaccarium de jaspide et cristallo cum imaginibus in cristallo argento munitis, et cum familia de jaspide et cristallo . . . Unum scaccarium de jaspide rubeo et viridi argento deaurato munitum, cum familia de jaspide et cristallo . . . Unum tabularium de nucibus muscadis cum ligneis de metallo, et familia ad idem de zinzibere et nucibus muscadis argento ligatis cum taleis argentis.[35]

[A chessboard of jasper and crystal with crystal images bound with silver, and with the pieces of jasper and crystal . . . A chessboard of red and green jasper bound with silver-gilt, with the pieces of jasper and crystal . . . A set of tables of nutmeg with metal stems, and the pieces for the same [made] of ginger and nutmeg bound with silver and with silver tallies.]

These elaborately wrought board-games, made of green and red jasper, crystal, and even of carved nutmeg and ginger-stems and roots, all mounted with silver, were valued at the high price of 40 l.st. each.[36]

[31]   E.101/373/15, fos. 9r, 9v.   [32]   *Ordonnances des rois de France*, i. 70, 74.

[33]   See N. Stratford, 'Gothic Ivory Carving in England', in Alexander and Binski (eds.), *Age of Chivalry*, 107–13, esp. 109.

[34]   Eales, 'The game of chess', 12–13; for the possession of a chessboard as a mark of noble status see E. Perroy, 'Social mobility among the French *noblesse* in the later Middle Ages', in his *Études d'histoire médiévale*, ed. R. Fossier (Paris, 1979), 229 (originally published in *P&P*, 21 (1962), 25–38). Also H. J. R. Murray, *A History of Chess* (Oxford, 1913), pp. 5–9.

[35]   BL, Add. MS 7966A, fo. 2r: wardrobe book for 1300–2.

[36]   Cf. *Liber Contrarotulatoris Garderobiae, 1299–1300*, ed. J. Topham *et al.* (London, 1787), 351: 'una familia pro scaccario de jaspide et cristallo in uno coffro' (1299–300).

Some five years earlier, an inventory of Edward's plate and jewels referred to a box or chest containing a chess-set (*familia*) of jasper and crystal, together with some books, including two liturgical songbooks.[37] This may have been one of those listed in the queen's possession in 1300, and the use of the term *familia* to describe the pieces is noteworthy. A similar usage obtained in the game of 'tables'.[38] This use of *familia* corresponded to the French *maisnie* or *mesnie*, which was in current usage to describe chessmen in thirteenth-century vernacular wills, accounts, and inventories. Hence inventories such as those of the goods of Beatrice, lady of Kortrijk (d.1288) listed an *eschekier qui est dou testament monsigneur Rogier* [de Mortagne, d.1275] *et est li maisnie aveuc*[39] ['A chessboard which is from the testament of my lord Rogier and the chessmen are with it']. The overtones of rank and hierarchy implicit in such usages applied especially well in a courtly or household context. The terms *familia* or *maisnie* conventionally described the domestic household or permanent establishment around a ruler or noble.[40]

By the mid-twelfth century, a representative tradition had developed whereby the pieces of a chess-set were depicted as kings, queens, bishops, knights, and men-at-arms (Pl. 10).[41] The lowliest member of the *maisnie*—the pawn—was still a non-representational piece. By the later thirteenth century, however, the pawn had become the *pedes, pedinus*, or footman, with associations of both fighting on foot and domestic service. The origins of the names found for chessmen in the Islamic world lay in the terminology of the ancient Indian and Persian army. But the medieval game in Western Europe departed from the 'purely military symbolism' of its Indian and Muslim origins: 'the appearance of unwarlike figures: the queen, and sometimes bishops, counts or counsellors as well, make it resemble a picture of a state in miniature rather than an army in the

---

[37] See E.101/353/30, m. IV : 'in i cofino est i familia pro scaccario de jaspide et cristallo' (1295–6). The inventory of 1295–6 also listed 'una familia de ebore ad scaccarium' (m. 3r).

[38] See e.g. the English treatise on the game of chess (*c*.1330) in BL, MS Royal 13 A. xviii, fos. 158–60.

[39] RAG, St-Genois 517; cf. ADN, B.446, no. 1872: testament of Rogier de Mortagne, lord of Espierre, in which Béatrice de Kortrijk is listed as an executor, and which bears her seal: 14 Mar. 1275.

[40] See above, pp. 23, 49, 56, and Vale, 'Provisioning princely households', 37 nn. 30, 31.

[41] A well-known example are the pieces known as the Lewis chessmen of *c*.1150–70. See Eales, *Chess*, pl. 2.

field'.[42] Yet such a shift could also bring the symbolism of the pieces closer to that of the court or household. A comparison of the Arabic and Latin Christian terms for chessmen reveals the following broad equivalences:[43]

Arabic	Latin	English
shah	*rex*	king
firz (vizir)	*regina*	queen
al-fil (elephant)	*episcopus/stultus/canis/*	bishop/fool/dog/
	comes/senex/calvus	count/counsellor
faras (horse)	*miles/eques*	knight
rukh (chariot)	*rochus/marchio*	rook/margrave
baidaq (footman/ footsoldier)	*pedes/pedinus*	pawn

The shift whereby the *al-fil* (Arabic: elephant) became the count, counsellor, bishop, dog, or fool in western terminology points to the capacity of chess to adapt itself to the cultures and societies into which it was absorbed. A late tenth or early eleventh-century poem from Einsiedeln (the so-called 'Einsiedeln Verses') describes the piece as a *canis* (dog), but it becomes the bishop in the twelfth century and could also be known as the *stultus* (fool) in the thirteenth.[44] This seems to confirm the status of chess as an essentially courtly and aristocratic pastime—one piece now represents the fool or jester, as an essential member of the household, retinue, or *maisnie*. The employment of the term *canis* to describe the same chessman is also suggestive—in classical Latin, the word for 'dog' could also describe the worst throw at dice. In Alfonso X's treatise, moreover, one variety of 'tables' is called *Los doze canes* ('The Twelve Dogs') played with twelve pieces on each side, in which any throw a player cannot use is lost.[45] Here is perhaps the origin of the joker in the later pack of cards. The chess-set could thus be perceived as a miniature household, or entourage, as well as a more general 'symbolic representation of society'.[46] Although the pieces had originally been non-representational, remaining close to their Muslim models, they soon began to assume representational and

---

[42] Eales, *Chess*, 46.

[43] The table is derived, with some additions, from Eales, 'The game of chess', 17, and *Chess*, 23, 45.

[44] See Eales, 'The game of chess', 13–15.

[45] Murray, 'Medieval game of tables', 60, 67.   [46] Eales, *Chess*, 67.

symbolic form in western societies.[47] Surviving examples demonstrate
the adaptability of the game to the knightly and courtly culture in which
it thrived (Pl. 10).[48]

Both surviving examples and documentary sources show that the
normal materials from which chessboards and their *maisnies* (men) were
made were ivory and ebony: in 1295–6, for example, a large chest identified under the letter 'F' in Edward I's wardrobe inventory contained *una
familia de ebore ad scaccarium* ['a set of ivory chessmen'], together with a
jasper cup, crystal pitcher, and a silver-gilt image.[49] Similarly, in February
1300, Robert II of Artois's *eschequetier*, called Biertaut, was paid at Paris
for his work on a 'great chess-set for my lord, and for eight ivory pawns'.[50]
Some chess-sets were, however, of less monetary value, and could be
bought for sums of around 1 or 2 l.p.: in March 1277, a board and set were
bought at Paris for 52s.p. for the Flemish household.[51] In 1309, similarly,
a chessboard and pieces were bought for the young Robert of Artois for
20s., plus a birdcage for his little birds and 4s. 8d.p. in cash for gaming
was also recorded.[52] The counts of Hainault, moreover, not only had
board- and table-games in their possession but manuals and problem-
books: in December 1304, for example, an inventory of the count's goods
included a book *de parchons* (a game involving the casting of lots) and
de taules ('tables') covered in cloth of gold; a book *en assielles* (wooden
boards) concerning chess; and two others, relating to both chess and
taules, one covered in red leather, the other concerning only the game of
chess, in velvet.[53]

Now the earliest treatises on chess were of Arabic origin, disseminated
via the Iberian peninsula to the West. By the later thirteenth century,
a substantial literature on the game existed, some of it in the form of
books and manuals of game-problems. The Italian *Bonus Socius* collection (*c.*1280–1300), and a number of verse manuscripts, survive from the

---

[47] Eales, 'The game of chess', 19.
[48] For exceptionally fine examples dating from [?] *c.*1220–40 and [?] 1240–50, see
N. Stratford, in *Age of Chivalry*, cat. nos. 145–8, pp. 252–4: 'these small-scale sculptures
[of knights] are among the most vivid surviving expressions of the taste of the feudal aristocracy of Henry III's reign'.
[49] E.101/353/30, m. 3r, and above, n. 37.   [50] ADPC, A.162, fo. 37v (Feb. 1300).
[51] RAG, St-Genois 209: for 'un jiu desches et un eskechier par Joffroi': 7 Mar. 1277; also
41s.p. were paid for 'taules, tauliers et pour esches divoire par Joffroi' at Paris on 12
Mar. 1277.
[52] ADPC, A.254, fo. 39r: 'pour un eschequier et pour les esches pour Robert'.
[53] AEM, Trésorerie, Cartulaires 19, fo. 120r: 4 Dec. 1304.

period, as well as Alfonso X of Castile's *Libro del Acedrex* (1283)—a book of chess and other game-problems deriving from Arabic sources.[54] By this date, the game of chess had also given rise to a symbolic and allegorical literature, best expressed by Jacobus de Cessolis' *Liber de moribus hominum et officiis nobilium*, of which no fewer than 200 manuscripts survive.[55] The association of chess with calculation and ruse gave rise to literary *topoi* employing the game as a source of metaphors for behaviour in war and love. Its courtly affinities made it an ideal setting for lovers' encounters, instanced by romance narratives and their artistic expression (Pls. 11b, 12, 14).[56] Yet the element of intellectual dexterity and calculating skill demanded by chess was to some extent paralleled in other, less complex, courtly games.

Games of chance enjoyed a wide vogue and attracted much wagering of money. They appealed to the highly-developed sense of uncertainty and its accompanying tension which Huizinga saw as the primary reason for the popularity of gambling games.[57] Payments *pour jeuer, pour juer as taules, pour juer as des* (dice), and so on, for example, are scattered throughout the surviving Hainault-Holland household accounts from 1319 to 1336.[58] The women of the Hainault court, including Jeanne de Valois and her daughters, were as active in gaming as the men, while the young William of Hainault (the future count William V) received constant supplies of small change with which to gamble.[59] As in England, the elaborate nature of the equipment provided for some of these board-games testified to the value placed upon them. A later fourteenth-century Hainault account records payments to Jacquemart Manceus, a minstrel, for making chessboards and chessmen, including a *jeu deskies*

[54] See Murray, *A History of Chess*, 619 ff., 643 ff., 701–2; Eales, 'The game of chess', 19; also the facsimile edition of *Das spanische Schachzabelbuch des Königs Alfons des Weisen*, ed. F. Hiersemann (Leipzig, 1913).

[55] Eales, 'The game of chess', 33.

[56] See the numerous representations on caskets and mirror-cases of Tristan and Isolde or Lancelot and Guinevere playing chess: e.g. London, Victoria and Albert Museum, cat. nos. A.563–1891 and 803–1891.

[57] Huizinga, *Homo Ludens*, 29, 68.

[58] See *De rekeningen*, ed. Smit, i. 320, 321, 322–4, 418, 423, 523–4, 613, 670; ADN, B.7860, fo. 43r: payment to William of Hainault to 'juer as taules contre Colart de Mal Ausnoy' (16 Nov. 1334); and to 'nos demisieles de Haynau pour juer as des le nuit Sainte Katerine' (24 Nov. 1334).

[59] For one example among many see *De rekeningen*, ed. Smit, i. 670 'en le bourse Willaume qui juoit contre monsigneur Simon de Bentem en le cambre medemiselle': 30 Aug. 1333.

appartenans a un tablier divoire me dame Dostrevant ['a chess set belonging to an ivory set of tables of my lady of Ostrevant'] which was regilded and repainted, while the *tables et eskies appartenans au dit tablier* ['tables and chess set belonging to the said set of tables'] were painted brown and green, for a total cost of 32 l. 15s. 7d.[60] These items were relatively expensive, though less so than Queen Margaret of England's green and red chess-sets in jasper and crystal at the end of the previous century.[61] But the immense popularity of both chess and 'tables' continued unabated into the fifteenth century.

Apart from the hope of monetary winnings, games of both skill and chance appealed to the instinctive risk-taking and love of wagering found in many societies. An English fourteenth-century treatise on 'tables' described the positions and problems which players faced as *jupertiae*, which 'put them in jeopardy'.[62] But in the courtly context of the later thirteenth and fourteenth centuries, the playing of such games was also one index of well-bred behaviour and good 'nurture'. Gambling could also be 'an aspect of upper-class social relations, a disguised form of patronage and largesse', especially when it led to the magnanimous giving away of winnings and their distribution among others.[63] The structures, rules, and conventions of these games also reflected and symbolized certain aspects of contemporary society. Hierarchy clearly ruled the chessboard, and the chessmen formed miniature households—with knightly, clerical, and domestic personnel. Literary texts began to adopt metaphors and allegories drawn from gaming, particularly from chess, and could refer to human predicaments in love and war by terms such as 'check' or 'mate'. Sermons and homilies 'moralized' the game of chess, stressing the mutual relationships of the social orders and their respective obligations.[64] The terminology of these games also employed the contemporary language of love and courtesy, and of campaign and castle. Some terms had amorous or erotic overtones—treatises and problem-books composed about the game of 'tables' contain such words as *aditus*, *intrare* (entry, to enter), *nudare* or *denudare* (to bare, or leave a point empty), *nudus* (a blot, or blank piece), or *ablatio* (bearing, playing a piece off the board).[65] The term for 'taking' in chess, or 'bearing a piece' in games of 'tables', was *ablatio*—deriving from Lat. *aufero* (to bear off) but also meaning 'abduction' (cf. Dutch: *schaken*—to play chess, to abduct [a

---

[60] AEM, Trésorerie, Recueils 74, no. 81. [61] See above, nn. 35–7, 49.
[62] BL, MS Royal A.xviii, fo. 159v (*c.*1330). [63] See Eales, 'The game of chess', 29.
[64] Eales, *Chess*, 38–41. [65] Murray, 'Medieval game of tables', 64–6.

girl]; *schaker*—chess-player, abductor). The vocabulary of war was also, of course, in constant use, especially in chess, but even 'tables' dealt in terms such as *ferire* (to strike or take), *firmare* or *facere punctum* (hold a point by piling men on it), *homo captus* (captured man), and *jactus* (throw of the dice), as a spear or javelin might be thrown.[66]

The liking for games was not confined to the gaming tables. A propensity for sports—some played for money—also characterized courtly society. Tennis was popular, and sometimes took place in unexpected surroundings. Thus in September 1314, at St-Omer, the young Robert of Artois was reimbursed for the 10s. 'which he had lost at the game of tennis at St-Bertin' (*que il a perdu au giu de la paume a St Bertin*).[67] It seems that the abbey of St-Bertin must have possessed a tennis court, just as the secular residences of princes did.[68] In 1376, duke Wenceslas of Brabant was playing ball-games at Brussels 'before the gate of Caemberghe, such as *le cache*'.[69] The *jeu de quilles*, or skittles, was also popular, played either indoors or in the open. In November 1382, for example, Wenceslas was wagering on skittles, and lost one florin 'in the new wood outside the gate of Brussels . . . in the game called *metten cloten*'.[70] Here, as in other respects, 'popular' culture met that of the court. Throughout the court societies of this period, a common taste for risk-taking, and for the playing of games for stakes, both high and low, was marked. At the end of the fourteenth century, games of 'cards' began to emerge. Playing cards seem to have been relatively expensive and confined to a very limited clientele when they first appeared.[71] They posed no serious rivalry to either chess or 'tables' until the sixteenth century.

The enduring strength of these games among the upper ranks of later medieval society was in part a product of their appeal to aristocratic values and to their adaptability. The chameleon-like nature of many of them was clearly apparent, as they evolved and were adapted to the western court societies in which they flourished. A recent authority has concluded that chess retained its appeal as the most prestigious and essentially aristocratic pastime throughout the later Middle Ages: it was

[66] See the lists in Murray, 'Medieval game of tables', 64–9.

[67] ADPC, A.321, fo. 35v: 6 Sept. 1314.

[68] The tennis court at the *Prinsenhof* of Bruges was depicted in later engravings. See the reproduction from Sanderus' *Flandria Illustrata* (1641) in Prevenier and Blockmans, *The Burgundian Netherlands*, fig. 102, p. 131.

[69] See A. Pinchart, 'La cour de Jeanne et de Wenceslas et les arts en Brabant, pendant la seconde moitié du xive siècle', *Revue trimestrielle*, 6 (1855), 31.

[70] Ibid. 31.   [71] Eales, *Chess*, 48–9, 58, 79.

the aristocrat of games.[72] But beside it there co-existed other forms of gaming, some crude and 'popular', some more complex and sophisticated, which also commended themselves to a courtly and aristocratic audience. The playing of games in the courts and households of the great thus formed an essential part of the courtly tradition, inherited from the past yet moulded and shaped by the preoccupations and concerns of the present.

b. Hunting: the cult of the chase

The pursuit of the chase had been an aristocratic habit from a very early date. By the mid-thirteenth century, an extensive literature on the art of falconry had grown up, culminating in the Emperor Frederick II's treatise, *De arte venandi*. The art of hunting with dogs had to wait until Gaston Fébus of Foix-Béarn's *Livre de Chasse* (1387) for its definitive work.[73] In a courtly setting, the maintenance of a hunting establishment was a constant—but necessary—source of expenditure, while the location of forests and other areas suitable for hunting could determine both royal and princely itineraries. The surviving evidence for the permanent retaining of huntsmen, dogs, falcons, and their handlers varies in both quantity and quality from household to household. We have already seen something of the position of hereditary officers responsible for the hunting establishments of princely households.[74] Some of the most revealing material is to be found, however, in the household account rolls, registers, and subsidiary documents, dating from 1290 to 1302, conserved in the archives of the counts of Artois.

The sums spent by the counts on the upkeep of their hunting and hawking establishments were substantial. Between 19 September and 24 October 1300, for example, Robert II of Artois spent 82. l.p. (an average of 16 l. 10s.p. per week) on expenses incurred for birds and dogs.[75] The upkeep of his hunting dogs was evidently a subject close to the count's heart: in April 1302, for instance, he ordered his receiver to deliver 100 l.p. to Coquelet, his huntsman (*veneur*). If the receiver did not have the

---

[72] Ibid. 58.

[73] See P. Tucoo-Chala, *Gaston Fébus: Un grand prince d'Occident au xiv* siècle* (Pau, 1976), 163–89. For editions of the *Livre*, see *Le Livre de Chasse de Gaston Fébus*, ed. G. Tilander, [*Cynegetica* 18], (Karlehouven, 1971) and *Le Livre de Chasse de Gaston-Phoebus (trad. en français moderne)*, ed. A. and R. Bossuat (Paris, 1931).

[74] See above, pp. 37–40 for the hereditary *veneur* of Hainault. For the retaining of huntsmen at the court of Flanders see Appendix VI.

[75] ADPC, A.161, no. 38, and cf. the expenses listed in Figs. 15, 16.

money to hand, he was to borrow it, and make sure that it was repaid from the very next sum he received (*de la premiere nostre monnoie que vous receverez*). He was further enjoined, in terms mildly reminiscent of some of Edward I of England's more peremptory missives to his officers:

ce ne laissiex en nule maniere, si chier comme vous avez nostre amour, par coy nostre veneour et nostre chien ne perdent ceste presente saison par defaute de monnoie.[76]

[Do not fail to do this in any manner, as you hold our love dear, so that our huntsmen and dogs do not sustain loss this season through lack of money.]

Personal participation in hunting was general among these princes. This extended to the use of the crossbow as a hunting weapon—thus in June 1300, a fine cloth cover (*tartaise*) for Robert of Artois's crossbow was sent from Paris to La Verberie where he was hunting.[77] In similar fashion, Edward II of England was shooting with the bow in his park at Hatfield in June 1312: on 4 June, two weeks before the death of Piers Gaveston, he gave a gift of 20s. to one William de la Paneterie, a *valletus* of Aymer de Valence, who lent him his bow and arrows there.[78]

   The passion for the chase meant that a permanent body of dogs and their handlers was retained by the Artois household. The dogs were divided into a number of categories: greyhounds (*levriers*), 'running dogs' (*chiens courans*), and *braces* (ordinary hounds) trained, handled, and cared for by *valets des chiens* and *braçonniers* (hound-handlers). At full strength, there were about forty-five or fifty dogs kennelled at any one time.[79] The greyhounds received an allowance of 4d.p. per day for their upkeep; while the *chiens courans* got 3d. per day. The names of some of the dogs, especially the greyhounds, were recorded: in May 1302, a collar was bought at Amiens for one of the count's greyhounds called 'Desraine'.[80] The hounds were normally kept at the castle and summer residence of Hesdin (Artois), where the park provided plenty of good hunting for both stags and boar, but some of the year was spent on the count's Norman estates near Domfront, where the hunting establishment was retained *pour faire courre auz cer[f]s*[81] ['to pursue stags']. The chases there were evidently close to the sea-coast. On at least two occasions stags or hinds were driven into the sea by the hounds, and had to be 'fished out'; while on another,

---

   [76] ADPC, A.184, no. 1: 4 Apr. 1302.   [77] A.162, fo. 44v: 18 June 1300.
   [78] E.101/375/8, fo. 25r; Chaplais, *Piers Gaveston*, 88.
   [79] ADPC, A.178, fo. 76v: 47 dogs, Apr.–May 1302; fo. 77r: 46 dogs, May–Aug. 1302; A.183, no. 7: 45 *chiens courans*, Mar.–Apr. 1302; A.186, no. 90: 22 dogs, Dec. 1302.
   [80] A.178, fo. 74r: 29 May 1302.   [81] A.178, fo. 76v: May–Aug. 1302.

boats were hired to retrieve some of the hounds from the water when they had pursued a stag into a river.[82]

The practice of hunting at this time was not without its practical and beneficial effects. Oscar Wilde's dictum on the foxhunting habits of the English aristocracy and gentry at the end of the nineteenth century—'the unspeakable in pursuit of the uneatable'—did not apply to the medieval hunt. Venison was hunted to be eaten, and the costs of salting it recur throughout the Artois accounts; wild boar were also much prized at table. The costs of aristocratic hunting to the peasantry could, however, be high. Compensation payments were regularly made to them for damages and losses sustained during the hunting season. In June 1302, a sum of 4s.p. was given on the count's order to 'un povre homme de Montfort sus Ruile pour ce que on li avoit foule son ble quant monsigneur chacoit et pris le cerf dedens son ble'[83] ['a poor man of Montfort sus Ruile because his corn had been trampled down when my lord hunted and took a stag in his corn'].

The trampling of corn by dogs, horses, huntsmen, and their prey was paralleled by the occasional killing of peasants' animals by over-eager hounds running amok. A sum of 8s. was thus paid out for the loss of four ewes killed by the hunting dogs in the forest of Oucret in May 1302.[84] More dangerous than the whole hunting establishment put together, however, was the wolf which was kept by the count. The comital menagerie included 'wild cats' at Hesdin and monkeys.[85] But the depredations committed by the wolf (le leu) were legion. Ostensibly kept by a servant called Guillot, the animal slaughtered livestock on every side and was apparently allowed to do so with impunity. In April 1300, it was killing birds as well as sheep at Hesdin; in March–May 1302 it killed eighteen sheep, two lambs, two calves, and three geese, the owners of which were all paid compensation.[86] Some measure of control over the animal was no doubt afforded by the provision of a collar (24 June 1300) and warning of its whereabouts and approach was perhaps given by the clappers and bells bought for it on 11 June 1302.[87] But the taste of the animal for live prey continued to be fed by such indulgence. Like the hunting rights and privileges of the counts of Artois, it was an

---

[82] A.178, fos. 34r, 77r; A.183, no. 7.   [83] A.178, fo. 76r: 7 June 1302.

[84] A.178, fo. 76v: 'que li chien estrainglerent en la forest Doucret'.

[85] A.162, fo. 20v: 'chats sauvages' (18 May 1300); fo. 40v: payment to Jeannot de la Garde Robe 'qui demoura a Tornehem avec le singe' (6 May 1300); fo. 44r: for sugar and other items 'quil pris pour le singe monsigneur' (20 June 1300).

[86] A.162, fos. 40r, 41r; A.178, fos. 68v, 69v, 70v, 74r.   [87] A.178, fo. 76r.

aspect of princely behaviour and power which no one could apparently gainsay.

The addiction to the hunt was ubiquitous among the inmates of the royal and princely households of the later Middle Ages. The wills and testaments of princes and nobles give an impression that the huntsmen—especially the falconers—retained by them in their households enjoyed an especially privileged status. They were in receipt of liveries of cloth and footwear, and were sometimes indentifiable by the badges which they wore (Pl. 6c). Thus Robert of Flanders, lord of Cassel, left 20 l.t. to his chief falconer, and the horse which he rode 'with my birds which he has in his keeping'.[88] In his will of February 1336, William III, count of Hainault-Holland, gave all his household officers and servants (*tous nos gens doffisses et de mestiers*) the use of their horses, while his falconers kept not only their horses but their birds as well (*a tous nos fauconniers leurs chevaus et leur oisiaus*).[89] Members of the hunting establishment were among the best-rewarded household officers and servants of Robert of Artois after his death in July 1302, receiving 'restitutions' for their service. Hence Guillot *le veneur* received 40 l.t., and Coquelet *le veneur* 60 l.t.—a sum identical to that given to the count's chaplain.[90]

The most striking (and in some ways most deplorable) instance of an addiction to the hunt carried to extreme lengths was that of Louis XI of France. In his last few months (in 1483), such was the passion of the bed-ridden king for the delights of the chase that he appears to have imported stoats, weasels, ermine, and other predators into his chamber at Plessis-lez-Tours. They were released to kill smaller animals such as mice while he enjoyed the spectacle.[91] Moreover, even the saintly Louis IX was apparently not immune from the attractions of hunting as a young man, frequenting the royal forests of the Île-de-France. But his biographers say nothing of such habits during his maturity and later years.[92] His grandson, Philip the Fair (1285–1314) was, however, particularly noted by contemporaries for his fondness for the chase, and his itinerary reflects that preoccupation.[93] The king resided at Saint-Germain-en-Laye on

[88] ADN, B.451, no. 5879: 'et son cheval que il chevauche avoeques mes osiaus que il a en sa garde': 1 Sept. 1331.

[89] Ibid., no. 7069/3: 22 Feb. 1336.

[90] ADPC, A.185, nos. 28, 32, 41; A.186, nos. 25, 27, 31; and see Table 21.

[91] See Philippe de Commynes, *Mémoires*, ed. J. Calmette and G. Durville, ii (Paris, 1925), 325–6.

[92] See J. Richard, 'Les itinéraires de St-Louis en Île-de-France', 168.

[93] See R.-H. Bautier, 'Diplomatique et histoire politique: ce que la critique diplomatique nous apprend sur la personnalité de Philippe le Bel', *RH* 259 (1978), 3–27.

forty-two occasions during his reign; at Fontainebleau on forty-one occasions; at Montargis on thirty occasions.[94] All these places were located in, or close to, the royal forests of Laye, Biere, and Paucourt. This record was almost equalled by his son Charles IV (1322–8) who spent much of his reign journeying from one hunting lodge to another—set in the forests of Halatte, Lyons, Laye, Les Loges, and so on.[95] Louis XI simply continued this habit in the fifteenth century.

A similar pattern of itineration can be established for the dukes of Brabant, whose domains—together with those of the counts of Hainault-Holland—comprised some of the best chases in the Low Countries. The great forests of Brabant, such as that of Soigne around Brussels, led the dukes to reside—and entertain their guests—at hunting lodges such as Tervuren or Boisfort. In November 1293, for example, Guy de Dampierre was at Brussels, with ninety horses stabled there, dining with Jean I 'in the forest . . . where they went to hunt wild boar'.[96] The counts of Flanders, moreover, had a particular liking for falconry, flying their birds in the forests around Male and Wijnendaal.[97] Like the Avesnes counts of Hainault, so the Dampierre of Flanders retained a *veneur* to oversee their hunting establishment. An agreement, probably drawn up in 1299, survives between the count and Gillion Roussel, *nostre veneur*.[98] He was to receive an annual pension of 100 l.flandr., paid at Christmas, Easter, and the Nativity of John the Baptist; receive two pairs of robes 'just as we give to our serjeants' (as at the court of Hainault); gain an allowance of firewood; and to keep thirty-two hunting dogs and six greyhounds, together with their attendant *braçonniers* and a *garçon*. The establishment was retained to hunt in the *comtés* of both Flanders and Namur, and the count agreed to maintain all hunting lodges and kennels in the forests.

The practice of hunting with dogs, and of falconry, was thus universal among princes and their entourages. It appealed primarily to the love of pursuit and the risks of the sport, as well as to the satisfaction derived from a good and successful 'kill'. This was to be a lasting feature of

---

[94] See Lalou, 'Vincennes dans les itinéraires de Philippe le Bel et de ses trois fils', 192–3.

[95] Ibid. 196–7.

[96] RAG, Wyffels (chron. Suppl.) 188: 'au bos avoec le duc u il alerent cacier au senglier': 21 Nov. 1293. For continuity of hunting practice in Brabant (and elsewhere in the Low Countries) during the Burgundian period see C. Niedermann, *Das Jagdwesen am Hofe Herzog Philipps des Guten von Burgund* (Brussels, 1995), 227–57.

[97] RAG, Wyffels (chron. Suppl.) 105: *c.*1280. See also, for later Burgundian practice, Niedermann, *Das Jagdwesen*, 231–3.

[98] ADN, B.3230, no. 4300; see Appendix VI.

western European aristocracies.[99] An imaginative literature of the hunt also evolved, alongside the treatises on the subject, and some of the most vivid descriptions of the chase are to be found in fourteenth-century epics and romances.[100] As with games, hunting provided a source of symbolism, analogy, and allegory in literary texts. So familiar was the cry of the hounds and call of the falcons that no later medieval aristocratic household of any substance was without its pack and its flight. But the hunt also provided food, and hunting rights yielded a good return among the assets of any ruler: the enjoyment of *pourvanches* or *pourvéances* by the counts of Flanders and Hainault-Holland was partly derived from the pursuit of prey from the excellent chases within their domains. From the world of the chase, with its emphasis on the joys and skills of horsemanship, it was only a short step to the world of the tournament.

c. *The tournament*

Among the relatively neglected subjects to which recent medieval and Renaissance scholarship has turned its attention, the tournament bulks quite large. What was once largely an untilled field has become relatively well cultivated in recent years. Yet the role and function of tournaments in a specifically courtly setting has received rather less attention. More work has perhaps been done on the tournament at the English and

---

[99] In the Court Precedence Regulation of Kaiser Wilhelm II (19 January 1878), for instance, the Principal Hunt-Master (*Der Oberst-Jägermeister*) ranked very highly—seventh in the list of 62 officers at the imperial court (Röhl, *The Kaiser and his Court*, 87–90). Such was the Kaiser's love of hunting that one of his aristocratic hosts 'felt obliged . . . to provide 20,000 pheasants to be shot down by the monarch and his entourage' (97). For a remarkably detailed account of King George V's hunting activities as Emperor of India see J. Fortescue, *Narrative of the Visit to India of their Majesties King George V and Queen Mary and of the Coronation Durbar held at Delhi, 12th December 1911* (London, 1912), 190–203. The 'total bag for the ten days was 39 tigers, 18 rhinoceros, of which the King killed eight, and four bears, of which the king killed one' (201). He dispatched a total of 21 tigers in the course of the visit.

[100] The most celebrated descriptions are found in works such as the Middle English *Sir Gawain and the Green Knight* and in Froissart's *Meliador*. See *Sir Gawain and the Green Knight*, ed. J. R. R. Tolkien and E. V. Gordon, 2nd edn., rev. N. Davis (Oxford, 1967), esp. ll. 1319–71, 1412–75, 1601–21, 1893–1921. See also M. Thiebaut, *The Stag of Love: The Chase in Medieval Literature* (Ithaca, NY, and London, 1974), 17–58, 71–88. For the medieval French literature of falconry see B. van den Abeele, *La Fauconnerie dans les lettres françaises du xiie au xve siècle* (Leuven, 1990), esp. 249–60. Hunting scenes often illustrated the calendar page for the month of May in psalters and books of hours. See e.g. BR, MS 10607, fo. 3: psalter of Gui de Dampierre (*c.*1280–97).

German courts than elsewhere.[101] The study of the licensing (and also the prohibition) of tournaments by English kings, and the political, social, and cultural role of such events, has been taken further during the last twenty years than it had ever been before. For thirty or so years after N. Denholm-Young's article of 1948 on the tournament in the thirteenth century, little interest was evinced by historians in the subject.[102] Only Ruth Harvey's *Moriz von Craûn and the Chivalric World* (Oxford, 1961)—the work of a scholar of German medieval literature—took the topic substantially further. The fundamental part played by the tournament—in its various forms—as a political, social, and cultural phenomenon now receives widespread recognition.[103]

In England, the piecing-together of information about the later thirteenth- and fourteenth-century tournament, from chroniclers' narratives (which are often laconic), financial accounts, indentures, documents recording the payment of compensation for loss of horses, letters and petitions, has transformed our knowledge.[104] Study of Edward III's activities in this respect has been particularly illuminating. But in a continental context, the centrality of such chivalric encounters to both court—and civic—life and culture has not always been sufficiently stressed. Many tournaments which took place in the setting of a court were directly associated with major events in court life—they might coincide with the holding of 'full' or 'solemn' courts at the major liturgical festivals. Or they might form part of the festivities celebrating particularly significant

[101] Among a large body of recent literature see esp. J. Barker, *The Tournament in England, 1100–1400* (Woodbridge, 1986); J. Vale, *Edward III and Chivalry* (Woodbridge, 1982), esp. chs. 1 and 2; M. H. Keen, *Chivalry* (New Haven and London, 1984), ch. 5; R. Barber and J. Barker, *Tournaments* (Woodbridge, 1989); H. Watanabe-O'Kelly, *Triumphall Shews: Tournaments at German-speaking Courts in their European Context, 1560–1730* (Munich, 1992); M. Vale, *War and Chivalry* (London, 1981), ch. 3, and 'Le tournoi dans la France du Nord, l'Angleterre et les Pays-Bas (1280–1400)', in *Actes du 115e Congrès National des Sociétés Savantes (Avignon, 1990)* (Paris, 1991), 263–71; and the collection of essays published in J. Fleckenstein (ed.), *Das ritterliche Turnier im Mittelalter* (Göttingen, 1985).

[102] N. Denholm-Young, 'The Tournament in the Thirteenth Century', in R. W. Hunt, W. A. Pantin, and R. W. Southern (eds.), *Studies presented to F. M. Powicke* (Oxford, 1948), 204–68.

[103] See R. Harvey, *Moriz von Craûn and the Chivalric World* (Oxford, 1961)—an excellent work which deserves to be more widely known. For a recent examination of the wider social aspects of the tournament see J. Vale, 'Violence and the Tournament', in R. W. Kaeuper (ed.), *Violence in Medieval Society* (Woodbridge, 2000), 143–58.

[104] See J. Vale, *Edward III and Chivalry*, 57–9; Barker, *The Tournament in England*, 112–36.

occasions in the life of a royal or princely house—a birth, baptism, marriage, churching, treaty of alliance, or other event. But there were many tournaments for which the accounting officers of princely households disbursed sums of money which bore no apparent relation to such occasions. They were a normal part of everyday aristocratic existence. Moreover, the tradition of civically sponsored tournaments in northern France and the Low Countries (documented from the later thirteenth century onwards) also provided occasions for princes, nobles, and the upper echelons of urban society to engage in (and aspire to) common aristocratic and chivalric pursuits.[105] Some of the best, and earliest, evidence for tournament activity is, again, derived from the court of Artois during the last quarter of the thirteenth century.

Compensation for their tournament losses, which could be quite heavy, was regularly paid to his household knights by Robert II of Artois. In January 1274, for example, Baudouin de Roulencourt was given 132 l.p. *pro deperditis torniamentorum Siclini et pro vadiis suis apud Meduncam* ['for losses at the tournaments of Seclin and for his wages at Mantes'].[106] Losses normally involved horses—Baudouin de Savonnières, knight, thus received compensation for a horse lost (or ransomed by his opponents) at a Lenten tournament at Senlis in 1274.[107] A series of letters of recompense charts the distribution of these payments by Robert of Artois during the years from 1275 to 1282.[108] Some were granted for losses while serving in the count's team or company, and the extent to which the conventions of tournament practice went beyond the immediate household circle of a prince can be glimpsed in the record of a payment of 3,387 l. 15s.p. to Robert de Béthune, eldest son of Guy de Dampierre, count of Flanders. Robert had served, with his knights, in Robert of Artois's company in a tournament at Creil in July 1281.[109] This very large sum was to be repaid in instalments, and the count pledged all his lands in the *bailliage* of Artois as security for the payment. It appears from such

---

[105] See J. Vale, *Edward III and Chivalry*, ch. 2; D. Nicholas, 'In the pit of the Burgundian theater-state: urban traditions and princely ambitions in Ghent, 1360–1420', in B. A. Hanawalt and K. L. Reyerson (eds.), *City and Spectacle in Medieval Europe* (Minneapolis, 1994), 271–95; E. van den Neste, *Tournois, joûtes, pas d'armes dans les villes de la Flandre à la fin du moyen âge (1300–1486)* (Paris, 1996); and the observations in A. Brown, 'Bruges and the Burgundian "Theatre-state": Charles the Bold and Our Lady of the Snow', *History*, 84 (1999), 573–89.

[106] ADPC, A.22, no. 2: 16 Jan. 1274.   [107] A.22, no. 5: 15 Feb. 1274.

[108] A.22, no. 29; A.26, nos. 5, 6, 13; A.27, nos. 36, 52, 57; A.28, nos. 1, 15.

[109] A.27, no. 36: 17 July 1281.

evidence that the composition of a tournament team at this time was not necessarily confined to the immediate entourage and vassals of a given noble.[110] Teams could be made up from neighbouring prince's retinues so that numbers could be equalized, and the balance between *dedans* and *dehors* 'sides' maintained.

At this time, the *mêlée*-style tournament, pitting two teams against each other, who fought in mounted units, normally with the sword, was considered the superior form of chivalric encounter.[111] But the coupling of collective *mêlée* with individual joust is also visible in the Artois sources at this date. In May 1298, the valets of the count's stable brought horses from Hesdin to Paris *pour les joustes*, and a further ten horses came from Hesdin to jousts at Arras on 2 June.[112] Towns such as Compiègne were freqent tournament venues, and often hosted large and spectacular events: thus in June 1300, bread was bought for the count's household *quant le grant tournoy fu a Compiegne*.[113] Tournaments were expensive, and members of the Artois household—as well as the count—found themselves in debt as a result. Hence in June 1302, Guillaume de Béthune, knight, lord of Locres acknowledged a debt of 16 l.t. to Biertremin Aubiert, merchant and citizen of Siena, and to *damoiselle* Isabelle de Ribestiel, for expenses at 'the tournament of Cambrai'.[114] He also waived and renounced all exemptions that he enjoyed by virtue of taking a crusader's vow and through privileges granted him by the king of France and other princes. Again, the repayment—although the sum in this case was small—was to be made in instalments. He agreed to honour the contract and 'tenir, warder et acomplir sour me loyaute et sour me chevalerie, sour le foi de men cors et sour le fei ke je doi a tous mes signeurs terriens'.[115] The pledging of personal 'loyalty' and 'knighthood' in a financial transaction was part and parcel of knightly assumptions and style of life. A common form of guarantee on which to secure a bond given by a knight was *par ma loyauté de chevalerie* or some similar formula.[116] The

---

[110] See, for evidence from the tournament held at Chauvency in 1285, J. Vale, *Edward III and Chivalry*, 10–12.

[111] See Keen, *Chivalry*, 94, 99–101. [112] ADPC, A.1015, fo. 4r.

[113] ADPC, A.162, fo. 41v. [114] ADPC, A.184, no. 109.

[115] He thus confirmed the contract and agreed to 'hold, keep and accomplish [it] on my loyalty and knighthood, on the faith of my body and that which I owe to all my earthly lords' (A.184, no. 109).

[116] See e.g. ADN, B.4065, no. 145585: confirmation of a contract between Louis de Nevers, count of Flanders and Godefroi de Weis, knight: 16 Jan. 1342. See also below, pp. 189–91.

conventions of *courtoisie* were observed in these mundane matters, for honour was too important in this milieu to be set aside or impugned, even in dealings with merchants and financiers.

Participation in tournaments by knights in the allegiance of the French crown, especially within the kingdom of France, was hampered by a series of prohibitions emanating from the monarchy from the reign of Louis IX onwards.[117] Hence members of the courts of northern France and the Low Countries often took part in tournaments on the marches of the kingdom, or in neighbouring lordships. This partly explains the popularity of the borders of Bar, Lorraine, and the *pays d'Outremeuse*, that is, in Limburg and Brabant 'beyond the Meuse', as a venue for such events. An undated letter from Jeanne de Chauvigny, lady of Châteauroux, to her aunt Béatrice de Kortrijk in about 1280 reported that her husband 'has been at these tournaments, but is still under the king's ban, and my brother Jacques is with him, and we have heard news from them that they are going to a tournament at Bois-le-Duc'.[118] A tournament at Bois-le-Duc, in Brabant, was of course well outside the prohibited limits. Within the kingdom—and within some of the more directly held fiefs—it was, however, sometimes possible to proclaim tournaments under the guise of 'hastiludes' or 'behourts', in which jousting took place, but no *mêlée*. This may have been the case in February 1294, when Guy de Dampierre, count of Flanders, was at Paris with the count of Nevers, other Netherlandish and French lords, *et aucun tournoier*.[119] February jousts were a common event at this season of the year, during the period after the feast of the Purification.

The counts of Flanders were also in the habit of retaining household knights under contracts which specifically referred to service at tournaments. English examples of this practice also survive.[120] Hence in October 1332, Louis de Nevers, count of Flanders, retained Guy of Flanders, lord of Riquebourg, by a contract in which Guy recognized that he had become Louis's liegeman (*homs liges*) for life, in receipt of an annual fief-rente of 500 l.flandr. Guy undertook to serve as a knight banneret, with another knight in his company

---

[117] See R. W. Kaeuper, *War, Justice and Public Order: England and France in the later Middle Ages* (Oxford, 1988), 198–205.

[118] RAG, St-Genois 522, printed in *Oorkondenboek van Noord-Brabant tot 1312*, ed. H. P. H. Camps, i (The Hague, 1979), 538, no. 434.

[119] RAG, Wyffels (chron. suppl.) 188: 2–4 Feb. 1294.

[120] For retaining contracts in England which included tournament service see Barker, *The Tournament in England*, 27–8, 120–3.

contre tous hommes et en tous lieus a la guerre *et au tournoy*, nous autre a baniere, chargie et montei selonc nostre estat, le quel compagnon a baniere et nous aussi noz diz . . . sires doit delivrer de tous coustz et de tous frais. Et li ferons compaignie en son hostel, et en alant aval le pays toutes foiz quil le nous mandera.[121]

[against all men and in all places at war and tournament, we and another banneret, armed and mounted according to our rank, which companion banneret and we ourselves should also have all costs and expenses paid. And we shall keep him company in his household, journeying through the land at all times that he so orders us.]

The blending of service in war, tournament, and the household is here complete, marking a synthesis of chivalric and courtly activities and obligations. As we saw in Chapter 3, Louis of Nevers's liking for the tournament and for extravagant display was well known—especially to his financial advisers—and a series of surviving letters of retainder bear this out. In November 1333, Rogier, lord of Hangest, was retained by the count with an annual fief-rente of 200 l.p. Rogier was to serve in both war and tournament *devant tous et encontre tous* ['before all and against all'] except his liege-lord the king of France *et les besoignes touchans la coronne de France*, ['and the needs touching the crown of France'], while Louis agreed

a le guerre monter le dit sire de Hangest, et mener de tous cou[t]s et de tous frais, et le devons monter *au tournoi* bien et souffiss[antement], et donner 40s. par[isis] tous les jours de gages, alant et venant, et rendre restor pour ses compaignons, as autres 100 l. par[isis], et 16s. par[isis] tous les jours de gages, alans et venans, et 60 l. par[isis] pour les bachelers seuls, et 12s. par[isis] tous les jours alans et venans.[122]

[to mount the said lord of Hangest for war, and bear all costs and expenses, and we should mount him well and sufficiently for the tournament, and give him 40s.p. as daily wages, coming and going, and provide *restaur* for his companions, to the others 100 l.p. and 16s.p. every day as wages, coming and going, and 60 l.p. for the bachelors alone, and 12s.p. every day, coming and going.]

These were generous terms, which were echoed in a subsequent contract with Jean du Tramet de Noyelles, knight bachelor, in April 1338. Jean was retained by Louis de Nevers *aveuques nous et de nostre mesnage* for life, with an annual fief-rente of 60 l.flandr., secured on the revenues of Menin. He was to serve

---

[121] ADN, B.499, no. 6521: at Nevers, 29 Oct. 1332. Italics mine.
[122] ADN, B.4065, no. 145579: at Male, 6 and 8 Nov. 1333.

a la guerre *et au tournoy, en joustes et en toutes autres choses appartenans a chevalier a fere . . .* et se doit monter pour la guerre *et pour le tournoy* par tele condicion que pour le restor de le montee du tournoy nous li renderons tels somme dargent comme a noz autres chevaliers.[123]

[in war and tournament, in jousts and in all other matters pertaining to a knight . . . and he should be mounted for war and tournament in such a way that we shall give him such a sum of money for the *restaur* of his tournament horse as we give to our other knights.]

Loss of his warhorse was to be compensated at a price agreed with the count's marshal, and he was to be paid 12 *gros tournois* to cover his daily expenses when summoned to a tournament *en alant, venant et demorant* ['in coming, going and staying']. The distinction made between tournament and joust is revealing, and it is also spelt out in contemporary treatises such as Geoffroi de Charny's *Livre de Chevalerie*.[124] It seems that the joust was considered as part of the more personal, individualized accomplishments of a knight at this time, while service in war and in tournament (that is, the *mêlée*) were perceived as closely related obligations, in which participation as a member of a team or unit was paramount. During his attendance at tournaments, Jean du Tramet was to be 'en nostre hostel toute fois quil y sera, a delivrance pour 3 chevauls, et soit delivrez ensi que a bacheler appartient'[125] ['in our household every time he is there, with the cost of three horses paid, and he shall be supported as is fitting for a knight bachelor']. Jean was also retained to serve Louis's son, the future count Louis de Male, after his father's death. The connection between household membership and tournament was also borne out in a similar contract, dated September 1338, by which Louis de Nevers retained Jean de Saint-Quentin, knight, as *de nostre hostel et mesnage*, with a fief-rente for life of 40 l.flandr. secured on the castellany of Ypres. He was, like Jean du Tramet, to enjoy

delivrance de 3 chevals toutes les fois que nous le manderons, et que il sera entour nous. Et li avons octroie et octroions nos robes teles que nous liverons a nos autres chevaliers bachelers. Item, toutes les fois que il nous servira a la guerre et au tournoy, monture selonc son estat.[126]

---

[123] ADN, B.4065, no. 145583: at Bruges, 25 Apr. 1338. Italics mine.

[124] See *The Book of Chivalry of Geoffroi de Charny: Text, Context and Translation*, ed. R. W. Kaeuper and E. Kennedy (Philadelphia, 1996), 33, 84, 86, 88, 100.

[125] ADN, B.4065, no. 145583. See also above, n. 123.

[126] ADN, B.4065, no. 145584: at Male, 2 and 4 Sept. 1338.

[provision for three horses every time we command him, and that he will be with us. And we have granted and grant him our robes as we give them to our other knights bachelor. Item, every time when he will serve us in war and tournament, a mount according to his rank.]

The provision of horses and robes strengthened the ties of dependence between man and lord, both in war and tournament—the two still cannot be forced apart at this period. Louis de Nevers, moreover, actively enshrined the union of war and tournament in a grant which he made, but apparently never fulfilled, in 1346. According to a later letter of his son, Louis de Male, dated November 1349, the older Louis had promised to endow his cousin Louis of Namur with 1,000 l.t. for life

au jour que la bataille fu a Cressi . . . tant pour les bons serviches que il lui avoit fais en nostre compaignie, comme pour son estat acroistre de lever baniere.[127]

[on the day when the battle took place at Crécy . . . as much for the good services which he performed in our company, as for the increase of his estate to enable him to raise a banner.]

Louis de Namur was to serve the count *en tous estas a la guerre et a la jouste et au tournoy* ['in all conditions, in war, joust and tournament']. The habit of battlefield promotion from knight bachelor to banneret was by no means confined to the counts of Flanders at Crécy: the Black Prince gave a dramatic demonstration of the practice at Nájera in 1367, when he simply created Sir John Chandos a banneret by cutting the tail off Chandos's pennon, thereby transforming it into the square banner of a knight banneret.[128] Louis de Male fulfilled his father's wishes by acting in this manner, securing the grant on land within the *comté* of Rethel. And there was no question of separating service in war from service in both tournament and joust—all three, as Charny observed, were integral to knightly existence in the mid-fourteenth century.[129]

The counts of Hainault also played an active role in promoting and participating in tournaments within both a courtly and civic context. A long-standing chivalric tradition, represented by such figures as Baudouin d'Avesnes or the crusading hero Gilles de Chin, characterized the comital house and nobility of Hainault. This was to be perpetuated in

---

[127] Ibid., no. 145590: at Male, 20 Nov. 1349.

[128] See Froissart, *Oeuvres*, ed. Kervyn de Lettenhove, vii. 195–6.

[129] *The Book of Chivalry of Geoffroi de Charny*, 86, 100, 102: 'je ne tieng qu'il soit nul petit fait d'armes fors que tous bons et grans, combien que li un des fais d'armes vaille miex que li autre' (86).

the fifteenth century by men such as Jacques de Lalaing, the celebrated jouster, and other members of his family.[130] Mons and Valenciennes were important and popular tournament venues, and the *comté* benefited from its location as a cross-roads, easy of access, bordering the kingdom of France, the *comtés* of Flanders and Artois, the duchy of Brabant, and the bishoprics of Cambrai, Tournai, and Liège.[131] Here, as elsewhere, the tournament was an expensive pursuit: in 1311, an account drawn up for the estate of Philippa, countess of Hainault, after her death, included a debt of 100 florins to Lothart le Mercier, lent by her to John of Hainault *et envoie apres lui au tornoi au Castiel en Cambresis*[132] ['and sent after him to the tournament at Câteau-Cambrésis']. Câteau-Cambrésis lay just outside the *comté* of Hainault, in the bishopric of Cambrai, and was a staging-post on the road (often taken by the countess and her household) to Paris.[133]

The acquisition of the counties of Holland and Zeeland by the comital house of Hainault meant that they also patronized chivalric activities at the court of Holland.[134] Dutch contacts with England were especially marked—Floris V, John I, and their nobles were often in the company of members of the English court, and dynastic marriages were arranged.[135] An active tournament tradition clearly existed in Holland by this time: the Dutch nobility had undergone important changes in the second half of the thirteenth century.[136] These rendered it much more readily comparable with neighbouring nobilities in the southern Netherlands. A knightly lifestyle was cultivated, including participation in the tournament. By the second quarter of the fourteenth century, the surviving evidence for tournaments in Holland and Zeeland becomes more extensive—

---

[130] See Vale, *War and Chivalry*, 98–9.

[131] See below, pp. 194–5 and, for the economic significance of Hainault's role as a *carrefour* see G. Sivery, *Les Comtes de Hainaut et le commerce du vin au xive siècle et au début du xve siècle* (Lille, 1969). The political importance of Hainault in the early to mid-fourteenth century is emphasized in Lucas, *The Low Countries and the Hundred Years War*, 47–51. For Mons as a tournament venue, see A. de Behault de Dornon, 'Le tournoi de Mons de 1310', *Annales du Cercle archéologique de Mons*, 38 (1909), 103–256.

[132] AEM, Trésorerie, Recueils 20, no. 41.

[133] See above, pp. 159–60; Table 22.

[134] See De Boer *et al.*, *Wi Florens* (Utrecht, 1996), 154–72, 252–6.

[135] See above, pp. 63–4, 104–5; *Wi Florens*, 264; Prestwich, *Edward I*, 388–9.

[136] See A. Janse, 'Adel en ridderschap in de tweede helf van de dertiende eeuw', in *Wi Florens*, 158–60 and 169: 'the nobility was transformed into a class of well-born [*welge-borenen*] consisting of knights and esquires and their offspring in direct male descent. The legal and formal distinction between the old nobility and knightly newcomers had disappeared.'

in February 1327, for instance, William, son of count William III of Hainault-Holland, received payments for expenses incurred 'at the jousts at 's-Gravenzande' (*as joustes au Savelon-le-Conte*).[137] Although the Avesnes counts themselves appear to have maintained a highly itinerant lifestyle, their children and kinswomen seem to have resided for longer periods at a given place, sometimes in Holland or Zeeland. Their Dutch territories were thus in no way neglected, or considered unduly remote, by members of the comital court and family.[138]

In September 1333, therefore, the days before Michaelmas were marked by the holding of a 'Round Table' by the count's son William (later William IV) at Haarlem. The practice of staging such events was common among princes and nobles of the time and only serves to demonstrate that the Dutch nobility were well integrated into the chivalric world of the early to mid-fourteenth century.[139] Hence, on Sunday 26 September 1333, William left The Hague for Rijnsberg *pour aler as joustes a Herlem*, reaching Helighem for dinner on Monday 27th, and arriving in time for supper at Haarlem.[140] This was the communal meal of the *feste*, where the assembled knights and ladies—no doubt playing Arthurian roles—gathered ('pour despens fais a Herlem le lundy . . . que Willaumes donna a souper les chevaliers de le taule ronde et les dames').[141] Among those listed as present were both Dutch and Hainault nobles: the lords of Arkel and Steenhuizen, and Florens de Heemstede, knight, among the Dutch, and Thierry de Walcourt among the Hainaulters.[142] William was supplied with a special horse for the jousts, brought to Haarlem by a valet, and the total expenditure incurred on the Round Table stood at 118 l. 10s. 4d.t. (=72 l. 18s. 8d.holl.), without *pourvanches*.[143] Further jousts were held at 's-Gravenzande on 4 October 1333, where William received money *en le bourse* to make offerings to Our Lady.[144] Payments were also made to one of the (Dutch) lord of Voorne's pages, who brought William a horse called *Ghistelle*, owned by his master, and a saddle for it. Money was also paid to the Lombards at 's-Gravenzande for beds and bedcovers. Dutch and Hainault nobles thus jointly took part in chivalric events under Avesnes patronage within the county of Holland at this time.

[137] *De rekeningen*, ed. Smit, i. 323.
[138] See the itineraries above, pp. 160–2; Table 22.
[139] See Keen, *Chivalry*, 98, 99, 190–2; J. Vale, 'Arthur in English society', in W. R. J. Barron (ed.), *The Arthur of the English* (Cardiff, 1999), 187, 191–4, 348 n. 60.
[140] *De rekeningen*, ed. Smit, i. 661.   [141] Ibid., i. 654.
[142] Ibid., i. 661; Froissart, *Ouevres*, ed. Kervyn de Lettenhove, xxiii. 269 ff.
[143] *De rekeningen*, ed. Smit, i. 672, 654, 662.   [144] Ibid., i. 674.

This pattern was continued after the accession of the house of Bavaria to the counties of Hainault and Holland in the mid-fourteenth century. The receivers' accounts include recurrent issues of cash for tournament expenses—Mons was a popular venue, especially after the Purification and during Lent. Thus on 3 and 4 February 1361, the duke Albert of Bavaria was jousting at Mons, and gave 20 *moutons* to the minstrels of the count of Flanders and duke of Brabant.[145] Two years later, a *behourt* (joust) was held at Mons, at which the lady of Werchin was a spectator, receiving her expenses on 18 February 1363, and the duke distributed 100 florins to the minstrels and heralds present there on the same day.[146] The events, which lasted from 11 to 19 February, were described as *le fieste de joustes et behourt as quaresmiaus* [following Quadragesima Sunday] and evidently took place annually—Lenten jousts were also proclaimed by the Hainault court at Le Quesnoy.[147]

The Mons Shrovetide tournament was evidently a major event in the court life of the Low Countries at this time, as were Lenten tournaments at the courts of England and France. In February 1379, for instance, the entire households of the duke and duchess of Brabant attended the *feste* at Mons, including the lords of Berg, Gruuthuse (who, although Flemish, had Brabançon lands, and had recently served as seneschal to the Brabançon court) Bouchot, Cuijk, Diest, Rotselaar, and Schoonvorst.[148] Among other nobles attending were Jacques de Bourbon, the count of Salm, Guillaume de Namur, Gerard de Berghes, the duchess of Guelders, and Jean, duke of Berry. They were lodged in the hostelries (*hospicia*) of Mons, such as the *Ecu St-Georges* (the Shield of St George), the *Paon* (Peacock), and the *Trois Rois* (the Three Kings, or Magi). By 24 February, the participants were lodging at Binche, on their return from Mons, again in the town's inns.[149] Binche was in fact part of the Brabançon dominions at this time, as the lordship formed part of the *douaire* of the duchess Jeanne, daughter of Jean III of Brabant, deriving from her previous

---

[145] *Cartulaire des comtes de Hainaut*, ed. Devillers, v. 554.   [146] Ibid., v. 574.

[147] Ibid., v. 574, 592: 'pour les pourvanches del hostel monseigneur et de le fieste des joustes qui fu au Caisnoit as quaresmiaus': 30 Jan. 1366. For the more general context of Shrovetide festivities in the Low Countries and Germany see M. de Roos, 'Een ezel kent men aan zijn oren: Charivaresk drama op de grens van middeleeuwen en nieuwe tijd', in *Volkskundig Bulletin: Tijschrift voor Nederlandse cultuur wetenschap*, 15 (1989), 316–34, esp. 323–30 and n. 32.

[148] AGR, CC.5462 printed in *Chartes de Brabant: Inventaire*, ed. A. Verkooren, viii (Renaix, 1922), 20–1; below, p. 196.

[149] AGR, CC.5463; *Chartes de Brabant*, viii. 22–3.

marriage to William of Hainault-Holland.[150] On such occasions, court met city—the distribution of tournament participants over the inns and hostelries of a town, where their banners, pennons, shields, and crests were 'fenestrated', gave an urban dimension to such chivalric encounters which could only have an impact on the life of the citizens.[151] Citizens watched the events from stands, *loges*, and the upper windows of their houses and, as Juliet Vale has shown, civic ordinances were constantly reissued to ensure a minimal degree of law and order during the festivities.[152]

Mons was no exception to a general trend at this time—before the accession of the Burgundian dynasty to Flanders and Artois, and its subsequent rise to hegemony in the Low Countries, the princes of the region acted both individually and jointly to promote the tournament in a civic setting. Although it had no equivalent of the *Epinette* at Lille, or the *Ours Blanc* at Bruges, and was 'not a center of secular culture', even the turbulent and episodically rebellious city of Ghent witnessed the staging of jousts and tournaments.[153] Both Louis de Male and his son-in-law, Philip the Bold of Burgundy (even before he succeeded to Flanders and Artois in 1384), actively patronized the civic tournament and often assisted in its financing.[154] It has been said that 'Philip the Bold tried to promote concord with the Flemish cities before 1379 by staging spectacles in them, hoping thereby to make his accession to the countship [of Flanders] smoother'[155]—a policy that apparently came to an end with the war between the count and Ghent in 1379–85. In May 1375, four years before the renewed outbreak of disaffection and subsequent open warfare in the city, Philip was in Ghent, promoting a tournament. A company of

---

[150] See Pinchart, 'La cour de Jeanne et de Wenceslas', *Revue trimestrielle*, 6 (1855), 11–14.

[151] See the depiction of 'fenestrated' banners and arms in the *Livre des Tournois* of René of Anjou: René d'Anjou, *Traité des Tournois: Dresden, Sächsische Landesbibliothek, Mscr. Dresd. Oc 58* [Edition microfiche couleurs], ed. J. Heers and F. Robin (Munich, 1993), 23, 28 (fo. 17v of the Dresden manuscript).

[152] See J. Vale, *Edward III and Chivalry*, 27–8, and 'Violence and the Tournament', esp. 155–8; van den Neste, *Tournois, joûtes, pas d'armes dans les villes de Flandre*, 39–52; A. Brown, 'Urban jousts in the later Middle Ages: the White Bear of Bruges' (forthcoming); Nicholas, 'In the pit', esp. 274.

[153] See Nicholas, 'In the pit', 272, 273, 275–7, 290–1. For urban jousts and tournaments in the duchy of Guelders see G. Nijsten, 'The duke and his towns', in B. A. Hanawalt and K. L. Reyerson (eds.), *City and Spectacle in Medieval Europe* (Minneapolis and London, 1994), 240–2.

[154] Nicholas, 'In the pit', 273, for Philip the Bold's contribution towards the cost of jousts at his wedding festivities in June 1369.

[155] Nicholas, 'In the pit', 290.

household knights from Hainault took part in these *joustes a Ghant*, using the comital domain and residence at Ath in Hainault as a staging-post on their journey to Ghent.[156] They lodged at Ath on 12 May with twenty horses, and the castellan there also paid the valets who brought cloth for horse-trappers and *houches* to be used in the jousts. The lord of Lalaing, hereditary seneschal of Hainault, lodged separately and stabled four horses, while silver plate for the knights' use was sent on ahead to Ghent for the festivities. Despite the city's stormy reputation, the civic authorities at Ghent clearly provided a location—usually either the Friday Market square or the Kouter—and facilities for the tournament at this time.[157]

Less turbulent towns, however, served as a more regular venue for chivalric encounters of this kind. In October 1377, for example, at the time of the feast of St Luke (18 October), Jeanne and Wenceslas of Brabant were again at Mons for the jousts there.[158] Lodgings were again secured by the quartermasters of the court of Hainault in the town's inns—Wenceslas of Brabant had forty-seven horses stabled at the *Ange* (Angel), and another thirty-two at the *Couronne* (Crown). John II, lord of Gruuthuse stayed at the *Miroir*, the lord of Schoonvorst at the *St-George*. The Flemish Gruuthuse represented the court of Brabant at this time, where he was serving as seneschal, having been slighted, as he saw it, by his 'natural' lord, Louis de Male of Flanders, in a family dispute.[159] It seems that the innkeepers at Mons were also responsible for lodging minstrels and messengers—thus the *Hermite*'s landlord was paid for this task in 1377.[160] Spectators watched the jousts from stands and from the windows of houses around the marketplace in which they took place. Thus one Moise le Barbier was paid for the hire of his *loge* to accommo-

---

[156] AEM, Trésorerie, Recueils 69, no. 55; Nicholas, 'In the pit', 274.

[157] See M. Boone, 'Destroying and reconstructing the city: the inculcation and arrogation of princely power in the Burgundian-Habsburg Netherlands (14th to 16th Centuries)', in M. Gosman, A. Vanderjagt, and J. Veenstra (eds.), *The Propagation of Power in the Medieval West* (Groningen, 1997), 1–33; P. Arnade, *Realms of Ritual: Burgundian Ceremony and Civic Life in Late Medieval Ghent* (New York, 1996), 200–24; Nicholas, 'In the pit', 275–80.

[158] AGR, CC.46925, fos. 12r–15r: 'as joustes de Mons a le Saint Luc lan 1377'.

[159] For Gruuthuse see T. Leuridan, 'Statistique féodale du département du Nord, iv. Le Ferrain', *Bulletin de la commission historique du Nord*, 17 (1886), 118; *Inventaire des chartes et cartulaires des duchés de Brabant et de Limbourg et des pays d'Outre-Meuse. Deuxieme partie: Cartulaires*, 2 vols. (Brussels, 1861), ii. 173. Gruuthuse had returned to Louis de Male's service by 1379.

[160] AGR, CC.46925, fo. 15r.

date courtly spectators. The practice of 'fenestration' of arms may lie behind a payment to the patron of the *Ange* 'for 3 sendals [taffetas] and for the making of the *houches* for the shields'.[161] The apparatus of the tournament was thus a highly visible feature of town life during this period.

Evidence of this kind also makes it clear that the feasts of the liturgical year offered a structure and rhythm for the proclamation and staging of tournaments, with their attendant feasts and entertainments. Epiphany, Shrovetide, Pentecost, St Luke's day, and so forth were marked by such encounters. The month of February was clearly among the most important for jousting, and the Hainault-Holland household often participated in jousts at Brussels, in the neighbouring duchy of Brabant. On 9 February 1360, for example, two valets were paid by the receiver of Hainault for bringing horses and jousting harness from Mons to Enghien, en route for the *joustes a Brouxelles*.[162] Similarly, in February 1361, Albert of Bavaria appeared at the Brussels jousts in a surcoat of *argent* and *azur* cloth (the tinctures of the Bavarian arms) and won the first prize.[163] There was evidently a reciprocal arrangement between Brabant and Hainault-Holland, whereby attendance at jousts within their respective lands formed part of the rythmn of court life. Pentecost jousts were also staged at Brussels—in May 1376, Albert was issuing warrants for household expenditure 'in our *hôtel* and at Brussels during the feast of jousts held there'.[164]

So close were the connections between the ruling houses of the Low Countries that joint participation in tournaments, despite political differences, continued to be a major feature of court life. It has been estimated—and this is a conservative estimate—that at least seventy-nine tournaments were proclaimed by the princes of the Netherlands between 1360 and 1383, an average of somewhat more than three a year.[165] A series of letters proclaiming Shrovetide jousts at Brussels, patronized by Wenceslas of Brabant, Albert of Bavaria, Louis de Male, the count of Blois, and others offer evidence of common chivalric preoccupations among them.[166] The *feste* at Brussels in 1377 began on the eighth day of

---

[161] Ibid., fo. 14r.   [162] ADN, B.7882, fo. 51v.

[163] *Cartulaire des comtes de Hainaut*, ed. Devillers, v. 555: 30 *moutons* given to the heralds there 'pour chou que ledis messires li dux en eut le prix des joustes'.

[164] *Cartulaire*, v. 627: 'en no hostel et a Brouscelle a le fieste de joustes qui la furent'.

[165] See Pinchart, 'La cour de Jeanne et de Wenceslas', *Revue trimestrielle*, 6 (1855), 14, and 13 (1857), 29–30.

[166] See the accounts of the receivers of Binche in AGR, CC.8765–8772 (1372–80). At this period the receipts from Binche—a fief of the counts of Hainault—formed part of the dowry of the duchess Jeanne of Brabant. See Bautier and Sornay, *Sources de l'Histoire Economique et Sociale*, i.2, 575–6.

February (Quinquagesima Sunday that year), and lasted for one week.
The duke and duchess of Brabant were particularly exercised by the
question of female participants. The *prévôt* of Binche, with Gérard de
Beaufort, knight, was thus ordered to ride to Mons and Maubeuge in
Hainault, taking the ducal letters, and requesting the presence of

demiselles de Mons et de Maubuoege . . . et pryes de par nous les demoiselles
dont les lettres vous envoions que venir vuellent deles nous a nostredicte feste. Et
se vus savez aucunes austres belles, si les escrisies sus les lettres que nous vous
envoions sans superscripcion, et les priies quelles y vuellent venir.[167]

[*damoiselles* of Mons and Maubeuge . . . and request, on our behalf, the *damoiselles* for whom we send you letters that they will come to us at our said *feste*. And
if you know any others who are good-looking, send them the letters which we
send you, without superscription, and request them to come.]

Transport was to be provided, and all expenses paid. The central importance of the attendance of *damoiselles* at the joust in the later fourteenth
century could hardly be more clearly illustrated. Further orders to ducal
officers required them to invite other *damoiselles*, from Nivelles and
Maubeuge, and the wives and daughters of nobles, such as the two sisters
of Aigremont, the ladies of Saussoit and Espinoy, the daughter of the
lord of Trazégnies, and the wife of Gérard de Beaufort.[168] That these
summonses were obeyed is evident from the record of payments for the
expenses of four *damoiselles* of Mons and five of Maubeuge, incurred at
Mons, Maubeuge, Binche, and Brussels

et en oultre de ce qui leur fu delivreit a court le terme que lidicte fieste dura,
parmy forge, carlerie, scellerie quil falli pour les cars desdictes demiselles.[169]

[and also for what was given to them at court during the said *feste*, including
smithery, cartage, and saddlery necessary for the carts of the said *damoiselles*.]

In a courtly setting, the evidence from Hainault and Brabant thus
demonstrated the extent to which jousts continued to be occasions for
festivities and entertainments demanding the company and participation
of women, especially of young women. As such, they perpetuated a tendency already found a century or more earlier, witnessed by such descriptions as the verse narratives of the tournaments at Le Hem (1278) and

---

[167] Pinchart, *Rev. trimestrielle*, 6: 12.

[168] Ibid., 6: 12–13, 24–5, n. 32: 25 Jan. and 12 Feb. 1377. Pinchart's reading (12) of these
letters as requiring the attendance of young nuns and canonesses from the convents of
Mons and Maubeuge cannot be sustained.

[169] Ibid., 13: 2 n. 34.

Chauvency (1285). The dancing and other social activity that habitually accompanied such events had clearly assumed such a significance that the proclamation of jousts was now followed by virtual summonses to aristocratic women within—and even outside—a ruler's domains. It was on these occasions that a court society came together, as well as at the 'full' and 'solemn' courts of the year.

Yet, however secular they may have been, jousts and tournaments in a courtly context still tended to take place at the times of the great religious feasts. The Shrovetide carnival tradition, similarly linked to the liturgical calendar, also brought court and city together.[170] Members of the patriciates and nobilities of these regions still joined together as participants in civic jousts and tournaments. Before the Burgundian acquisition of Hainault in 1428, for example, it was customary for members of the comital house to take part in such events as the annual civic procession dedicated to St George at Mons. In April 1393, William of Ostrevant thus rode in the cortège dressed in a *houppelande* adorned with silver and silver-gilt ornaments.[171] With the advent of the house of Burgundy, however, an increasing tendency to greater exclusiveness, rather than a continuation of the inclusive character of the *feste*, may have become more marked.[172] Civic *festes* certainly continued to be staged in the Low Countries. But at Ghent, it is argued, jousts became less frequent after about 1385 because 'the counts, who liked them, tended to avoid the city, sending their relatives and councillors instead'.[173] Once again, the very limited period of residence by Philip the Bold of Burgundy (d.1404) in his Flemish domains—a mere six months in all during a twenty-year reign—was to contribute to an increasing sense of separation between Burgundian court society and the urban context in which it lived.

The tournament thus remained what it had long been—an event or occasion at which and around which other activities clustered. In a courtly context, it provided opportunities for a particular kind of display and

[170] See M. de Roos cited in n. 147 above. Also, for Guelders, Nijsten, 'The duke and his towns', 239–41.

[171] AEM, Trésorerie, Recueils 71, no. 17: account for *orfevrerie* supplied by Jacques de le Kiese: 'Item, pour le hupelande de monseigneur quil eut de le fierte Saint Jorge a le prociession de Mons, u il eut 4 onces de bouillons dargent, moities blancs, moities dores.'

[172] Further investigation is required. A contrary tendency seems to have been at work in the duchy of Guelders where 'in the fourteenth century [tournaments] were strictly a matter for the nobility but shifted to the towns in the fifteenth century . . . Gradually the monopoly of the nobility over tournaments was broken' (Nijsten, 'The duke and his towns', 241).

[173] For Ghent see Nicholas, 'In the pit', 290–1.

spectacle, with its own rules, rituals, and quasi-theatrical modes of behaviour. It could mark seasonal changes, which were in turn reflected in the rhythms of the liturgical year, and it had a fundamental part to play in the rites of passage celebrated by ruling houses. As such, it was an intrinsic and ineradicable part of the life of court societies, and remained so for a long time. There is therefore no evidence from this period for anything approaching decline or decay in this expression of chivalric mentalities in a courtly setting.

3. Ritual and ceremony

a. How power was expressed: secular rituals

The study of power and its representation in the Middle Ages has attracted much recent interest. Not only has the iconography of rulers and their environment been the subject of a number of recent studies but, under the influence of social and cultural anthropology, historians have viewed power-structures as symbolized and expressed in ritualized and ceremonial forms.[174] The example of African and Asian societies, for instance, can sometimes illuminate the practice of Western courts. The clear and obvious differences in culture, politics, and society between these cases, such as the differing role of kinship patterns, religious beliefs and practices, or institutional development (and non-development), have always to be borne in mind.[175] Yet there appears to be sufficient common ground—in principle—for some mutually illuminating parallels to be drawn. No one would contend that the functions of ritual and ceremony in these vastly different contexts were identical. Ritual has been defined as 'action wrapped in a web of symbolism', and its purpose,

[174] For a good example, in which 'traditional procedures' are said to be 'characterized by textual scrutiny and iconographical analysis', whereas 'new questions and novel methods' are represented by 'modes of inquiry elaborated in the social sciences' see J. M. Bak (ed.), *Coronations: Medieval and Early Modern Monarchic Ritual* (Berkeley, Los Angeles, and Oxford, 1990), 2. The application of notions derived from the social sciences to the later medieval Low Countries is well illustrated in P. Arnade, *Realms of Ritual: Burgundian Ceremony and Civic Life in Late Medieval Ghent* (New York, 1996). There is a useful discussion (by Wim Blockmans) of the recent literature of 'symbolic communication in late-medieval society' in Blockmans and Janse (eds.), *Showing Status*, 1–16.

[175] See the perceptive comments on the idea of a Burgundian 'theatre-state'—a term borrowed from the work of the anthropologist Clifford Geertz on Balinese society—in A. Brown, 'Bruges and the Burgundian "Theatre-state"', 574–5. See also C. Geertz, *Negara: The Theatre-State in Nineteenth-Century Bali* (Princeton, 1981), esp. 10–18, 102–5.

function, and meaning necessarily differed according to time and place.[176] Yet parallels can be found which suggest similar assumptions and pre-occupations among court societies.

The medieval royal court of Ethiopia—to take just one single instance—had developed ceremonial functions which, by the fifteenth century, were laid down in written ordinances, stemming originally from oral tradition. As was to be the practice in western Europe, two kinds of household ordinances developed: the practical body of regulations governing the functions of the lower offices in the king's household; and the ceremonial ordinances concerned with ritual and protocol.[177] The scale of the Ethiopian establishment was, however, very different from its Western counterparts, with some 30,000 to 40,000 people attending banquets at the mobile royal court.[178] In this African context, the function of ritual and ceremony was linked to fixed points of the year, such as the great banquets which marked the special councils at which the location of the court at the onset of the rainy season was established. A strict hierarchical order was observed in the nature of the food and drink served, strikingly similar to that prevailing at the court of Majorca.[179] The banquet also coincided with the taking of tribute from subjects by the Ethiopian kings, paralleled by the homage and oath-taking ceremonies of Western medieval courts. The rituals of royalty therefore shared common characteristics across continents, a tendency also reflected in the practice of non-royal courts. The importance of household office was such that it

[176] See D. I. Kertzer, *Rituals, Politics and Power* (New Haven and London, 1988), 9. As Brown points out, in its journey from Bali to Burgundy, the 'theatre-state' has undergone a significant change of meaning: in Bali, 'power served pomp'; in Burgundy, we are told, pomp served power ('Bruges and the Burgundian "Theatre-state"', 575). The Balinese ceremonies served to represent and locate the ruler and his subjects within a supernatural order, but—quite unlike the Burgundian 'theatre-state'—had no general nor specific political end in view. Much recent writing on the subject appears to be a transposition of an old, traditional theme of Netherlandish historiography—'centralizing' and authoritarian princes imposing their will upon urban liberties—into the world of the 'new history'. For an excellent example, see Boone, 'Destroying and reconstructing the City', esp. 1–8, 31–3.

[177] See M. Kropp, 'A mirror view of daily life at the Ethiopian royal court in the Middle Ages', *North-East African Studies*, 2–3 (1988), 51–87; cf. the *Leges Palatinae* of Majorca in *Aragonische Hofordnungen im 13. und 14. Jahrhundert*, ed. K. Schwarz (Berlin and Leipzig, 1914), esp. 142–4, and the household ordinances for the Dauphiné in *Mémoires pour servir à l'histoire du Dauphiné* ed. M. Valbonnais (Paris, 1711), 200–21, 407–26). See also above, pp. 42–5.

[178] See Kropp, 'A mirror view', 62 n. 26.

[179] Cf. Leçoy de La Marche, *Les Relations politiques de la France avec le royaume de Majorque*, ii. 23–4.

was said of the Ethiopian case that 'the court is, with its organisation and regulated life and functions, a microcosm of the [Ethiopian] Empire; the Empire itself is nothing but a projection of the royal court and household . . .'[180] In so far as it was a microcosm of empire, it bore a closer resemblance to early medieval imperial establishments—such as the Carolingian and Ottonian courts—than to their later medieval princely successors. Yet, as we have seen, the continued significance of household office—especially hereditary office-holding—in the later medieval kingdoms and principalities of north-west Europe bore witness to similar patterns of evolution.[181] There too, it was at 'full' courts that a ruler was seen at his most symbolically 'powerful'. Political reality may sometimes have given the lie to the expression of power—or the semblance of power—but it none the less remained a potent symbol of the dignity and superiority of the prince. Whether expressive of distance between ruler and ruled, or of companionship within a patriarchal style of household, ritual and ceremony in a courtly setting deserve close attention.

A fundamental point must above all be emphasized. As we have seen, limitations are imposed on our knowledge of pre-fifteenth-century court rituals by the nature of our sources. There is, for example, no equivalent for north-west Europe between *c.*1270 and 1400 of the Byzantine *Book of Ceremonies*, let alone the prescriptive and descriptive sources for Oriental courts. Surviving household ordinances do not generally deal with etiquette and protocol.[182] The exceptions to this rule are found in the Iberian peninsula and, remarkably, in the minor southern French principality of the Dauphiné. The household regulations contained in the *Siete partidas* of Alfonso the Wise of Castile (1284), and the *Leges palatinae* of James II of Majorca (1337), reissued in revised form by Pedro IV of Aragon (1344) concern themselves, in part, with ritual and ceremony. The *Leges palatinae*, promulgated at Palma on 9 May 1337, set out in seven sub-divided parts, are the most elaborate set of ordinances to survive from this period.[183] They address the issue of defining the functions and duties of the four great officers of the household: the *majordome* or *maître d'hôtel*, the *camerlingue* (great chamberlain), the chancellor, and the *maître des comptes* or *maître rational*.[184] Although the chamberlain and his subordinate

---

[180] Kropp, 'A mirror view', 53.   [181] See above, pp. 42–8.

[182] See above, p. 201. Also W. Paravicini, 'Europäische Hofordungen als Gattung und Quelle', in Kruse and Paravicini (eds.), *Hofe und Hofordnungen, 1200–1600*, 13–20.

[183] See *Acta Sanctorum*, ed. van Papenbrock, *Junii*, iii (Venice, 1743), 1–7, for the *Leges palatinae*, and see above, Ch. 2, nn. 129–31.

[184] See Leçoy de La Marche, *Relations politiques*, ii. 22–4.

knights, esquires, and non-noble valets possessed some ceremonial functions, the *majordome* was responsible for the observance of protocol in all matters relating to court rituals. Above all, his supervision of the king's table was comparable to that exercised by the later *grand maître d'hôtel* at the court of Valois (and later Habsburg) Burgundy.[185] Earlier models of court life and organization have thus to be considered as important influences upon the evolution of the Burgundian and other later courts. For its detailed account of how the more practical aspects of household management merged with the ceremonial dimension of court life in the first half of the fourteenth century, the Majorcan ordinance represents a rare survival.

At the Majorcan court, both the *majordome* and the chamberlain were to be nobles by birth. The *majordome* played a visually prominent role in court ceremonial—he preceded the ruler, bearing his verge or rod of office, when he came to dine and when he left the table. The verge (as at the English court) denoted his jurisdictional authority over the household.[186] He was served by two sub-*majordomes*, both noble, who were in turn set over four esquires, of handsome appearance, who served drink and who kept the drinking vessels clean. The tableware in use was also graded according to the status of the drinker—drinking vessels were either silver gilt or plain silver. Tasting was a vital part of the *majordome*'s duties, a practice, as Olivier de La Marche described it, which was also to be found in the Burgundian household.[187] One of the king's two doctors was also always present near to the ruler at meals. The correct manner of bringing the various *plats*, or courses, to a meal, was laid down: a further four esquires, one of whom was noble, were to carry the *plats*, but had no authority to put them on the table. This was done by their superiors, after tasting. The number of *plats* was strictly determined: two for ordinary meals, three for feast days, plus an unspecified number of *petits plats*. Dessert was already part of the meal, and consisted of two types of fruit, or cheese, if fruit was scarce. The revised version of the *Leges palatinae* drawn up by Pedro IV of Aragon gave wider currency to the Majorcan

---

[185] See Paravicini, 'The court of the Dukes of Burgundy: a model for Europe?', in *Princes, Patronage and the Nobility*, 98–101. The fundamental importance of the *maestro di casa*, an officer closely comparable to the *majordome* or *maître d'hôtel* elsewhere, is evident from the ordinances for the household of the dukes of Urbino (c.1482–90). See *Ordine et officij de casa*, 22–5.

[186] See above, pp. 24, 35.

[187] See La Marche, 'Estat de la maison', 13, 23, 33. For the relationship between status and gifts of tableware see Appendix II (a).

ordinance by translating it into Latin.[188] Emphasis was placed in the preamble on the need of a ruler to appoint suitable officers *gradu debito et decenti ordine* ['of due rank and appropriate order'] so that 'majoribus minores obediant et majores minores in eo, in quo deficerent aut possent deficere, corrigant et emendent'[189] ['the lesser obey the greater and the greater correct and amend the lesser in those things in which they are lacking or could be lacking'].

A near-identical advocacy of strict hierarchical obedience was found in the *De cura* of Philip of Leyden (*c*.1350).[190] Yet the Aragonese ordinance also expatiated on what might be called the more aesthetic aspects of court ceremonial. A pleasing and harmonious image of the ruler and his regime (however at odds with reality) was to be presented by the court. The ordinance observed that pluralism was to be avoided as

officiorum varietas et in diversis personis facta distributio nobilitatem et pulcritudinem in presidentium regimine representat, quam pulcra et placens dispocio regiminis reputatur, quando singula officia singulis distribuuntur personis *ad instar humani corporis*, in quo varietas membrorum ad diversa officia deputatorum resultat tocius corporis pulcritudinem elegantem.[191]

[the diversity of offices and the distribution made to various people displays the nobility and beauty of the ruler, as the nature of a government is reckoned fair, when single offices are distributed to individuals, in the image of the human body, in which the variety of members deputed to various offices produces the elegance of the whole body.]

An anthropomorphic analogy was here employed to support the notion that the body politic of the court was enhanced in its 'elegant beauty' by the variety of offices which were appropriately distributed to individuals by the prince. The multiple functions of the various members of the body contributed to its handsome nature, and so it should be in a ruler's court and household. We are thus confronted with what is in effect a kind of corporeal propaganda on behalf of the ruler. The harmonious and elegant impression given by a well-ordered establishment might be at odds with the realities of power-relationships within a given area (and the kingdom of Aragon was not without its political problems), but it represented a perception of the role of the court which was to become even more significant in the future. The semblance, rather than the reality of power, could be just as potent a force in the creation and sustenance of princely ideology as the 'rise of absolutism' or the advent of the modern state.

[188] *Aragonische Hofordnungen*, 142–4.   [189] Ibid. 142.
[190] Philip of Leyden, *De Cura*, 106–7.
[191] *Aragonische Hofordnungen*, 144. Italics mine.

Ceremonial ordinances do not, as we have seen, survive for the larger, royal households before the fifteenth century. The survival of another early *état de la maison* which predates Olivier de la Marche's late fifteenth-century description of the Burgundian household (1476) by 150 years emanates from an unexpected source. In 1336, the Dauphin Humbert de Vienne was at Crémieu, progressing through his lands to receive his vassals' homages. As was apparently the case elsewhere, such occasions provided the opportunity on which to draw up regulations for the conduct of the prince's household.[192] Why such elaborate and detailed prescriptions for protocol, as well as household management, should stem from the relatively minor principality of Dauphiné is not clear. But its close geographical proximity to the papal court at Avignon at this time might have played some part. The *Ordinatio in qua varia officiorum genera disponuntur* ['Ordinance in which various kinds of offices are assigned'] thus provides us with an account of the functions of the delphinal household officers, including their ceremonial duties.[193] It was apparently the work of the proto-notary Amblard de Beaumont, and listed the chancery staff and delphinal council as essentially household departments. As in England, regulations were made limiting the rights of members of household departments to common table or *bouche de court* and to live within the household.[194] As in the Majorcan and Aragonese ordinances, moreover, detailed stipulations were included concerning the conduct of meals at the court of Dauphiné. Members of the household were seated at table according to their office, and elaborate regulations prescribed the quantities and quality of food to be served. The ordinance also gave instructions on the manner of receiving guests and 'strangers'. Rank could be reflected in the type and quantity of food and drink served—thus the prince himself in effect received a surfeit, of which the residue was to be distributed to the poor.[195]

[192] For Flemish evidence of an analogous kind see above, pp. 47–8. For Dauphiné, see Valbonnais, *Mémoires pour servir à l'histoire du Dauphiné*, esp. 200–1, 206–12.

[193] Valbonnais, *Mémoires pour servir à l'histoire du Dauphiné*, 407–26. For the papal court at Avignon see B. Schimmelpfennig, 'Der Palast als Stadersatz: Funktionale und zeremonielle Bedeutung der Papstpalaste in Avignon und im Vatikan', in Paravicini, *Zeremoniell und Raum*, 239–56, and 'Papal Coronations in Avignon' in Bak (ed.), *Coronations*, 179–96.

[194] For England, see above pp. 19–21, 23–4; for Dauphiné, *Mémoires pour servir à l'histoire du Dauphiné*, 200, 202.

[195] See Bumke, *Courtly Culture*, 195, for evidence for overfilling of the plates of lord, lady, and court so that alms might be given from the residue, and Valbonnais, *Mémoires pour servir à l'histoire du Dauphiné*, 211, 421–2.

It is striking that no such ordinance survives for the royal court of France, and that our knowledge is so much more detailed for such lesser courts. The glimpses afforded of ceremony at the French court are fleeting and insubstantial. The household ordinance of Philip the Fair and his queen, issued at Vincennes in January 1286, for example, lists its personnel and some of their rights and duties, but says little about the forms of ritual which accompanied court life.[196] We can, however, glean some impression of the state in which Philip held court from incidental details recorded amid the list of personnel. The three *panetiers* were to find and serve bread at table, while the four *échancons* (cup-bearers) were to buy wine and 'servir en et estre au traire mesmement aus grans festes' ['serve and be there to carry it at the great feasts']. Among the staff of the *paneterie* was Galeran des Nappes, who 'prepared the king's place' (*qui fait le siege du roy*)—a hint at the special position of the monarch at table. Similarly, the staff of the *fruiterie* were to serve fruit at the king's and his brothers' table 'except in Lent, when only figs, nuts, and dates were to be served to them'.[197] That the king received more light to eat by than his brothers—the princes of the blood—was evident from the fact that the *fruitiers*—responsible also for the supply of wax and candles—were to provide him with twelve *grans torches*, while his brothers received only four. The fact that the ordinance categorically states that both clerks of the chapel and knights of the household were only entitled to receive their liveries of cloaks, robes, and furs at Easter and All Saints 'if they are at the feast at court, and not otherwise' (*se il sont a la feste a court, et non autre*) suggests the possibility of a ritualized distribution on those occasions.[198]

There is therefore a considerable degree of imbalance in our knowledge of royal and princely ceremony before the fifteenth century. We certainly know about rituals such as coronations because formal ordinances and treatises survive which describe (and prescribe) their conduct.[199] Similarly, initiation ceremonies, such as dubbings to knighthood and other rites of passage, such as marriages and funerals, have left a substantial

---

[196] See *Histoire de S. Louys IX du nom, roy de France, ecrite par Jean, sire de Joinville, senechal de Champagne*, ed. C. Du Fresne, sieur du Cange (Paris, 1668), 112–15. For a description and discussion of French royal household ordinances of this period see, most recently, E. Lalou, 'Les ordonnances de l'hôtel des derniers Capetiens directs', in Kruse and Paravicini (eds.), *Höfe und Hofordnungen, 1200–1600*, 91–101.

[197] See *Histoire de S. Louys*, 113.   [198] Ibid. 113, 114.

[199] For recent examples see J. Le Goff, 'A coronation program for the age of Saint Louis: the Ordo of 1250', in Bak (ed.), *Coronations*, 46–57; also R. A. Jackson, 'The *Traité du sacre* of Jean Golein', *Proceedings of the American Philosophical Society* (1969), 113–14, 305–24; and *The Coronation Book of Charles V of France*, ed. E. S. Dewick (London, 1899).

deposit of material. But the rituals observed at the great feasts of the liturgical year and, even more so, in the everyday business of court life at this
period, are very difficult to discern. It is therefore to didactic, literary, and
narrative sources—treatises, romances, and chronicles—that historians
have tended to turn in order to fill these gaps in our knowledge. But the
accounts of feasts, banquets, and other events found in these sources
can be misleading. They can reflect imaginary perceptions rather than
reality, exaggerating for rhetorical, satirical, or critical effect the nature
and scale of such festivities. As we have seen, it has been argued, largely
from this type of evidence, that a truly 'courtly' manner of behaviour
was only apparent on such occasions.[200] The feast at court provided an
opportunity, in life as in literature, for the projection of a ruler's self-
image, as well as that of aristocratic society as a whole. Hence Bumke
argues that the lengthy descriptions of feasts in an Arthurian setting,
often at Pentecost, found in the epics and romances, 'reflect the modern
character of contemporary court life in many details of material culture
and courtly etiquette'.[201] This may well be so, and literary works such the
Roman des comtes d'Anjou or the interpolations to the *Fauvel*, composed
by a writer familiar with French court life, also contain elaborate descriptions of feasts at courts.[202] Yet the historian has other types of evidence
that can be brought to bear, such as household accounts and the more
formal documents of royal and princely administration, to shed some
light on reality.

Nevertheless, the evidence offered by the chroniclers and romancers
can be compelling, and can sometimes animate the dry bones of some—if
by no means all—types of archival documentation. The accounts of incidents at great feasts are often highly revealing. These include such passages
as the descriptions in Gislebert de Mons's chronicle of the dispute
between the count of Hainault and some of his hereditary household
officers at the Pentecost feast staged by the Hohenstaufen emperor at
Mainz in 1184; or Ottokar von Steiermark's account in his *Reimchronik* of
the argument which broke out over seating order at another imperial feast
—the homage-taking ceremony on the election of Albert I of Habsburg
at Nuremberg in 1298, when the ecclesiastical electors of Mainz and

---

[200] See Bumke, *Courtly Culture*, 4, and above pp. 28–9.

[201] Bumke, *Courtly Culture*, 4 and 203–73 for court feasts.

[202] See N. F. Regalado, 'The *Chronique métrique* and the moral design of BN fr.146:
Feasts of Good and Evil', in Bent and Wathey (eds.), *Fauvel Studies*, 466–94, esp. 476–80.
The interpolator of the *Fauvel* text and the author of the *Chronique métrique* 'were writing
for an audience that delighted in descriptions of feasts' (481).

Cologne and their vassals disrupted the events.[203] The occasion was also marked by Wenceslas of Bohemia's refusal to perform the service of imperial cup-bearer, while his peers—the other three princes of the Empire—acted as seneschal, chamberlain, and marshal of the household respectively.[204] Apart from such instances of *rapportage* of the exceptional, many narrative and literary accounts of court feasts have a formulaic quality, in which near-identical schemata are employed. Yet the emphasis which these sources place upon display and open-handed generosity endorses a fundamental point—the desire of princes to impress vassals, guests, and rivals with the material means at their disposition was a common phenomenon.[205] The timing of such occasions was quite deliberate. The taking of homages, renewal of oaths, and forming of alliances were to some degree affirmed and cemented by such ceremonial occasions. A further dimension was, moreover, added to the feast at rulers' courts during this period by the advent of formal and elaborate vowing rituals which took place, it seems, exclusively in this festive setting.

Evidence for the taking of vows at court feasts is to be found in both the documentary and literary sources of the first half of the fourteenth century. Yet the practice can be traced back to very ancient origins. Vowing rituals can be found in the Celtic *Geis*, the Germanic *Gab* or battle-boast, and in many Asian and African customs.[206] True to form, Huizinga saw the later medieval vow as an archaic survival from a former culture: 'The chivalrous vow exists . . . under an individual and occasional form. Here the barbarous character, testifying that chivalry has its roots in primitive civilization, comes to the surface.'[207] Barbarous or not, the practice certainly became a part of the more sophisticated court culture of the later Middle Ages. Like the Celtic *Geis*, the later medieval secular vow could prohibit a person from, or enjoin him to, certain acts, such as not to sleep or eat, or to observe certain lines of conduct. Thus the Celtic hero Murough vowed not to 'sleep two nights on the same bed, nor to eat

---

[203] See Bumke, *Courtly Culture*, 203–7; *Österreichische Reimkronik*, ed. J. Seemüller, 2 vols. (Vienna, 1890–3), ll. 73604–22.

[204] Bumke, *Courtly Culture*, 189; see also A. Legner (ed.), *Die Parler und der Schöne Stil, 1350–1400: Europäische Kunst unter den Luxemburgern*, ii (Cologne, 1978), 748–9, for a manuscript of 1400, containing the Golden Bull of the Emperor Charles IV, in which the imperial electors are depicted as officers of the imperial household.

[205] See below, pp. 258–60.

[206] See J. R. Reinhard, *The Survival of the Geis in Medieval Romance* (Halle, 1933), 3–4, 316–24; and 'Some illustrations of the medieval *Gab*', *University of Michigan Publications: Language and Literature*, 8 (Ann Arbor, 1932), 27–57.

[207] Huizinga, *Waning of the Middle Ages*, 86.

two meals of meat at the same table' until he had accomplished certain aims.[208] Similarly Edward II of England vowed not to sleep in the same bed on consecutive nights in 1306, and, at Philip the Good's Feast of the Pheasant at Lille in 1454, a Burgundian noble expressed his intention not to sleep on Saturday nights until he had engaged the Turk in single combat.[209] The Germanic battle-boast or *Gab* must also have influenced such vows. By the mid-twelfth century, such boasting or bragging had become associated with courtly conviviality. The more outrageous boasting and vowing usually accompanied feasting, and became more extreme and exaggerated as the participants became more intoxicated.[210] What had been customary in the halls of warband-leaders in Germanic societies now took place in rulers' and nobles' courts and households. Incorporated into the romances, the 'primitive' vow gained a further lease of life. In Chrétien de Troyes' *Perceval* (*c.*1180) Perceval vowed not to sleep two nights in the same lodging until he knew whom the Grail served and why the lance bled.[211] Bizarre vows could be made, sometimes by women: thus in *Le Vengeance Raguidel* the heroine vows to wear her clothes inside out until her lover's death is avenged.[212] Other undertakings involved not cutting hair or beards. But what is of particular concern here is the practice of collective vowing by groups of individuals in a more formal setting. Arthurian romance provided good examples: in the prose *Lancelot* (*c.*1214–37), for instance, the story of Bohort and Brangoire includes outrageous bids by a company of knights on a formal occasion to perform feats for Brangoire's daughter.[213] But, apart from the fictitious world of the romances, evidence survives for the reality of collective vowing rituals in the high and later Middle Ages.

It is obvious, for example, that the secular vowings which accompanied certain court festivities of the early fourteenth century owed something to the crusaders' vows to take the cross. It has been shown that the

[208] Reinhard, *Survival of the Geis*, 317–19, and nn. 209, 211 below.

[209] See C. Bullock-Davies, *Menestrellorum Multitudo: Minstrels at a Royal Feast* (Cardiff, 1978), p. xxx, for Prince Edward's vow; for the vows of the Pheasant see R. Vaughan, *Philip the Good* (London, 1970), 297–8.

[210] See Reinhard, 'Some illustrations of the medieval *Gab*', 28–9, citing Gaimar's *Lestorie des Engles* of *c.*1150.

[211] Chrétien de Troyes, *Der Percevalroman (Li Contes del Graal)*, ed. A. Hilka (Tübingen, 1958), ll. 4728–9: 'Qu'il ne girra an un ostel / Deus nuiz au trestot son aage . . .'

[212] *Le Vengeance Raguidel*, ed. M. Friedwanger (Halle, 1901), ll. 5166–71.

[213] See Reinhard, 'Some illustrations of the medieval *Gab*', 44–7; Chrétien de Troyes, *Percevalroman*, ll. 4718–46; *Vulgate Version of Arthurian Romances*, ed. H. O. Sommer (Washington, 1909–13), iv. 266–74.

crusader's vow was not wholly distinct from the pilgrim's vow until the late twelfth century. Formal rites appeared, in writing, by that time, and canon law began to define them as 'deliberate commitments made to God to do or not to do certain acts'.[214] Cross-taking rituals therefore had some affinity with the ancient practices already described. Although, as we have seen, vows made in a secular context long pre-dated crusading commitments, it may be no coincidence that crises were experienced in the crusading idea during the later thirteenth century, and these may have contributed to the emergence of formal, collective vowing rituals at court feasts. These reflected secular concerns and could take fantastic and bizarre forms. Huizinga memorably characterized such vowings as 'supplying romantic and erotic needs and degenerating into an amusement and a theme for raillery'.[215] But did such episodes have any deeper purpose or significance, and what did their symbolic and allegorical character actually convey? Can such rituals be related to the representation and expression of a ruler's authority? A sequence of what can be called 'vow-narratives'—both fictional and factual—survives from the early fourteenth century onwards. These all concern collective vows sworn on birds. They stem from northern French, English, and Italian contexts. They begin with Edward I of England's Feast and Vows of the Swans (1306), and include the Vows of the *Épervier* (Sparrowhawk, 1310), *Paon* (Peacock, *c.*1310–12), and Heron (1338). Philip the Good of Burgundy's Vows of the Pheasant (1454) were clearly influenced by these fourteenth-century precursors but also—unlike them—had a crusading inspiration.

Of the four vowing-ceremonies—two historical and two (in the form in which they survive) fictional—only one is supported by documentary evidence. Edward I's Pentecost feast at Westminster on 22 May 1306 was the subject of extensive preparations and provisioning, documented in the records of the great wardrobe. On 2–3 May, 84 lengths of cloth of various colours were transported from the houses of various merchants in *Tamysestrete et Chepe* and brought to the wardrobe at the Tower of London.[216] Further expenses were incurred by Ralph de Stokes, clerk of the great wardrobe for large purchases of cloth, some of it at the St Ives' fair, including no less than 4,400 ells of *canabii* (canvas), and further coloured cloths *pro liberacione novorum militum contra festum Pentecost'*

---

[214] J. Riley-Smith, *What were the Crusades?* (London and Basingstoke, 1977), 54.

[215] Huizinga, *Waning of the Middle Ages*, 86–7.

[216] E.101/368/30, m. 3r. The events of Pentecost 1306 at Westminster are recounted in detail by Bullock-Davies, *Menestrellorum Multitudo*, pp. ix–xli.

['for the livery of new knights at the feast of Pentecost']. Between 26 April and 12 May, cloth, furs, linen, and canvas were bought at Winchester *pro liberacione facta pro principe et aliis diversis hominibus factis militibus die Pentecost' in comitiva dicti principis* ['for the livery made on behalf of the prince and various others knighted on the day of Pentecost in the said prince's company']. The mass knighting ceremony which was to accompany the Pentecost feast was to be attended by over 300 aspirants to knighthood, and by a number of guests, including Thibaut de Bar, bishop of Liège, kinsman of Edouard, count of Bar, and the count's daughter.[217] The connection with the *comté* of Bar was not without significance, as we shall see, and the ties of kinship between Edward I's court and the Barrois family cemented the alliance between the two dynasties.[218] Apart from the mass knighting, the Pentecost feast was also to become the occasion upon which vows of a decidedly political nature were to be taken by the participants.

Four years later, in late 1310 or early 1311, at Milan, the Emperor Henry VII of Luxemburg and his entourage, campaigning against the Guelfs in Italy, took vows on an *Épervier* (Sparrowhawk) in which the Emperor's political and military ambitions were the subject of collective oath-taking.[219] Henry VII entered Milan on 23 December 1310 and was crowned king of Lombardy there on 6 January 1311.[220] The account of the incident by the Liègois chronicler, Jean d'Outremeuse (1338–99), credited Thibaut de Bar, bishop of Liège, with the instigation of the vows. At about the same time (*c*.1310–12) the most popular fictitious literary description of vowing rituals on birds appeared from the Bar-Lorraine region. In Jacques de Longuyon's version of the *Romance of Alexander*,

---

[217] E.101/368/18: account for her expenses in Kent and at London, rendered at Westminster, 4 May 1306.

[218] See M. Prinet, 'Les armoiries des français dans le poème du siège de Carlaverock', *BEC*, 92 (1931), 347–8, for Jean de Bar, younger son of Thibaut II, count of Bar, at Edward I's siege of Carlaverock in 1300. Also E.101/357/10, m. 4r: gift of a cup (*ciphus*) by Edward I to 'domino Savarico de Beuryon, militi comitis de Bar redeunti cum eodem domino versus partibus propriis' at Berwick, 6 July 1302. For family ties—the count Edouard's mother was Edward's daughter Eleanor (married 1294)—see Collin, 'Le train de vie d'Edouard Ier, comte de Bar', 796–7.

[219] For a prose narrative of the incident see Jean des Preis dit d'Outremeuse, *Le Myreur des Histors*, ed. S. Bormans (Brussels, 1880–7), vi. 133–7; for a verse account, attributed to Simon de Marville, canon and treasurer of the cathedral at Metz, secretary and *nuncio* of the Emperor Henry VII, see 'Les Voeux de l'Epervier', ed. G. Wolfram and F. Bonnardot, *Jahrbuch der Gesellschaft für lothringische Geschichte und Altertumskunde*, 6 (1894), 177–280.

[220] *Grandes Chroniques de France*, ed. J. Viard, viii (SHF, Paris, 1934), 268.

an extended account of a fictitious vowing ceremony during a feast at Alexander's court was included (frontispiece).[221] This episode was the *Voeux du Paon* (Vows of the Peacock), which survives in thirty-five manuscripts, and of which we have documentary evidence at the court of Artois in 1313. A well-known record survives in the shape of a quittance, dated 9 September 1313, from Thomas de Maubeuge, bookseller (*libraire*), for the receipt of 8 *livres parisis* from Master Étienne, treasurer of Mahaut, countess of Artois and Burgundy, as payment 'pour deus romans, lun de la vie des sains, et lautre des veus du paon, rendus et delivres a Madame Dartois et de Bourgogne'[222] ['for two French books, one concerning the life of the saints, and the other concerning the vows of the peacock, rendered and delivered to my lady of Artois and Burgundy']. This manuscript of the *roman* does not survive, but the matter-of-fact nature of the record suggests that the work may already have been well-known and in circulation for some while. The many representations of scenes from it in the visual arts of the period point to its popularity (frontispiece, Pl. 14).[223] A finely carved ivory saddle, for instance, was listed in an inventory (1343–4) of the goods of Raoul de Brienne, constable of France, with scenes from both the *Voeux du Paon* and their *Fulfilment (Accomplissement)* carved upon it.[224] Moreover, Jean d'Outremeuse made a direct connection between the *Voeux du Paon* and the Vows of the *Épervier*, in his account of the latter event in *le Myreur des Histoires*. His narrative describes the episode in terms of an encounter between Waléran de Montjoie, brother of the emperor Henry VII, and Thibaut de Bar, bishop of Liège, in which Waléran's *épervier* breaks free of its leash in the palace where the emperor and the commanders of his army were lodged,

---

[221] See A. Thomas, 'Jacques de Longuyon, trouvère', in *Histoire littéraire de France*, 36 (Paris, 1927), 1–35; D. J. A. Ross, *Alexander historiatus* (London, 1963), 14–17; P. Meyer, *Alexandre le Grand dans la littérature française du moyen âge*, ii (Paris, 1886), 221–2, 267–72, and 'Étude sur les MSS du roman d'Alexandre', *Romania*, 2 (1882), 213–32. For a Scots analogue, and a more general discussion of the texts of the *Voeux du Paon*, see *The Buik of Alexander*, ed. R. L. G. Ritchie (Scottish Text Society, 1925), esp. i. pp. xxxv–xlvi.

[222] ADPC, A.312, no. 56.

[223] See, in particular, the scene of Alexander and his court feasting in Bodleian Library, MS Bodley 264, fo. 188v (dated 1338–44). The illustrations to the Bodley manuscript are reproduced and discussed in M. R. James, *The Romance of Alexander (MS Bodley 264)* (Oxford, 1933). The text, in a Picard dialect, was finished by the scribe on 18 Dec. 1338, and the illuminations were completed on 18 Apr. 1344 (fo. 209r).

[224] See Paris, AN, JJ.269, fo. 6v: 'Item, pour une selle a parer a palefroy, les arconnieres d'ivuire a ij dames et ij roys, un lyon et un petit enfant; et ou siege le[s] Veus du Paon et les Accomplissemens, tout d'ivuire . . .' (account of Geoffroy Le Breton, king's saddler, for the liquidation of Raoul de Brienne's debts, 1343–4).

some of them playing at 'tables', others eating. The bird flew straight to Thibaut de Bar and his companions and, as a result of an exchange between Waléran and Thibaut, in which Waléran made a slighting remark, the sparrowhawk is appropriated by the exceedingly secular (and bellicose) bishop. The author has him tell Waléran 'vos savies comment fut vowiez li pawons par les prinches'[225] ['you know how the peacock was vowed upon by the princes']. This can only mean that at the time the *Myreur* was composed (probably *c*.1370–80) the *Voeux du Paon* were very well-known in aristocratic circles. The story of the incident at Milan in 1310/11—which may be part-fact, part-fiction—is significant as an example of the manner in which vows of this kind were related to the aims of rulers. The thirteen vows listed all concerned imperial policy, which was now combined with personal honour: the participants vowed to capture the city of Brescia, to have Henry VII crowned emperor at Rome, to recover the Holy Sepulchre at Jerusalem, and so on.[226] In the event, the prince-bishop Thibaut de Bar, as aggressively bellicose as any of his secular peers, met his death at the subsequent siege of Brescia.[227] Jean d'Outremeuse also described the attempted fulfilment of at least one of the vows, when Guy of Namur broke lances against the gates of the city and challenged four *Lombars* to single combat.[228] The *Voeux du Paon*, and its subsequent additions such as *Le Parfait du Paon* (1340) by the Hainaulter Jean de le Mote, or *Le Restor du Paon* (*c*.1330–40) by Jean Brisebarre (Pl. 14), was evidently profoundly influential in this courtly milieu.

If the taking of vows on the *Épervier* was inspired by the *Voeux du Paon*, then the poem entitled the *Voeux du Heron* (Vows of the Heron), dating from *c*.1340, set at the court of Edward III in, allegedly, the year 1338 was even more closely related.[229] Its nineteenth-century editor considered it

---

[225] Jean d'Outremeuse, *Myreur*, 133.   [226] Ibid. 133–6.   [227] Ibid. 150.

[228] Ibid. 136–7. The verse narrative of the vows of the Épervier has close analogies with the *Voeux du Paon* (see 'Les Voeux de l'Épervier', esp. ll. 115–19, 135–46).

[229] See the edition of the text in *Political Poems and Songs relating to English History*, ed. T. Wright, 2 vols. (RS, London, 1859–61), i. 1–25. A new critical edition of the poem is badly needed. There is another account, in Latin, of the episode in *Chronographia regum Francorum*, ed. H. Moranville, ii [1328–80] (Paris, 1893), 35–8, where it is more plausibly dated to 1337 and direct allusion is made to the *Voeux du Paon* (36). The French *Chronique des Pays-Bas, de France, d'Angleterre et de Tournai*, ed. J. J. de Smet, *Recueil des chroniques de Flandres* (Brussels, 1856), iii. 147 also describes the incident as taking place 'a uune feste qui estoit en le ville de Londres' where Robert of Artois served a heron before Edward III, on which he and his court vowed 'a maniere que firent jadis li Grisgois au paon, au tamps du grant roy Alisandre'.

'entirely deficient of historical truth', although admitting that 'it is still possible that the ground of the poem may have been some assembly in which king Edward's courtiers took such vows upon them'.[230] The poem shares many common features with the *Voeux du Paon* including, as we shall see, the role of young women (*damoiselles*) and minstrels, and can in many ways be read as a direct parody of the *Paon* texts. In the *Voeux du Heron*, the exiled Robert of Artois plays the part of Alexander's courtier Cassamus from the *Voeux du Paon*, exhorting (and shaming) the participants in a feast to make vows on a bird. With the exception of the entirely fictitous *Voeux du Paon*, all these vowing-rituals were related to the political and military aims and ambitions of contemporary rulers. The secularization of collective vowing ceremonies led not only to 'amusement and raillery' but to the expression of commitment to certain causes and the pursuit of certain obligations to avenge slights and affronts to honour.[231] The very fact that they take place at a ruler's court, whether directly instigated by him or not, suggests that such events were now essentially representative of power and authority, even when (as in the *Voeux du Heron*), a direct challenge to that authority was being issued. It is for that reason that they repay closer examination, not only for their cultural significance, but for the manner in which they illustrate important aspects of the royal and princely court's development.

There was a clear literary pedigree for all these vowing-rituals. But why were they all sworn on birds? A well-established convention whereby certain attributes and qualities were associated with certain birds in lyric poetry came into play here and a literary tradition of allegorical debate poetry, in which birds participate, was also influential. A poem survives from Metz, dated *c*.1324–5, entitled *Le Sermon du Papegai* [*The Sermon of the Parrot*] where a bird-allegory was devised to represent the leading protagonists and their parties in the factional conflicts within the city. The poet urges the appeasement of these internal quarrels among the *bourgeois*, and the poem has been associated with the context from which the earlier vows of the *Épervier* stemmed.[232] The qualities attributed to certain birds in both imaginative and didactic literature were evidently significant in determining the form taken by vows in a courtly setting. In

---

[230] *Political Poems*, ed. Wright, i. pp. xv, xvi.

[231] Huizinga, *Waning of the Middle Ages*, 86–7.

[232] See *La Guerre de Metz en 1324*, ed. E. de Bouteiller (Paris, 1875), 326–34. Also see Bodleian Library, MS Douce 308 for a manuscript of probable Metz origin (*c*.1300–25) which contains the *Voeux du paon*, a *Bestiaire d'Amour*, the verse narrative of the Chauvency tournament (1285), and the *Tournoiement Antechrist*.

1301, Philip IV of France was compared by the dissident Bernard Saisset, bishop of Pamiers, to an owl, because (so Saisset alleged) he merely sat and stared at men, never speaking in public.[233] Saisset's interrogation record referred to a literary origin for such an insulting comparison— the allegorical story of the birds who choose the owl as their ruler. Yet historians have tended to adopt a very cautious view of the symbolism and significance of the birds chosen for the swearing of vows. When describing the Feast of the Swans (1306), Constance Bullock-Davies observed, in a pioneering study, 'why two swans were chosen is anyone's guess', and Maurice Keen concluded that 'a sound literary pedigree and its theatrical potential seem to be the keys to the ritual significance [of these vowings] . . . not any coherent attempt to symbolize or signify'.[234]

Any analysis of the court culture of this period must, however, concern itself with the layers of meaning which such rituals could convey. What may seem to us curious or bizarre can be more readily and fully interpreted if an approach akin to that of iconography in the visual arts is adopted.[235] Contingent sources, such as the bestiaries, heraldic treatises, didactic literature, and poetry of the period, provide plenty of evidence (some of it contradictory and conflicting) for the allegorization and personification of animals and birds, and for their attributes. Why did Edward I choose swans at Pentecost 1306? Why did Thibaut de Bar urge Henry of Luxemburg and his court to vow on a sparrowhawk? Why did Robert of Artois prescribe a heron for Edward III, Philippa of Hainault, and their court? It would not perhaps be entirely irrelevant to allude to the close acquaintance of many rulers and nobles of this period with types of bird, both from the art of falconry and the practice of keeping aviaries.[236] It is known, for instance, that the counts of Bar had an especial liking for exotic and rare birds, witnessed by count Edouard I's keeping of a collection of *oisaulz Monseigneur* and his retaining of a household servant whose function was to trap cranes (*grues*) at the lake of Lachaussée for the comital aviary and, it seems, table. In 1334, for example, cranes were sent to Metz for the Pentecost feast.[237] A clue to the reasons behind the choice

[233] See P. Dupuy, *Histoire du différend d'entre le pape Boniface VIII et Philippes le Bel* (Paris, 1655), 643, 656, 660.

[234] See Bullock-Davies, *Menestrellorum Multitudo*, p. xxxv; Keen, *Chivalry*, 215.

[235] For a good example, see E. Panofsky, *Meaning in the Visual Arts* (Harmondsworth, 1993), esp. 51–81.

[236] See above, pp. 179, 182–4.

[237] See Collin, 'Le train de vie d'Edouard, comte de Bar', 804.

of certain birds for vowing may be found in the *Voeux du Paon*. The peacock, the poem tells us, is the meat of the 'brave and worthy':

> C'on doit faire au paon l'usage du pays,
> Chascuns y doit voer son bon et son avis . . .
> C'est la viande as preux, a ceulz qui ont amie . . .
> Si doit on bien vouer et payer attaie
> Et d'armes et de chevalerie:[238]

> [One must observe the custom of the country towards the peacock,
> Everyone should pledge his goods and inheritance . . .
> It is the food of the brave, of those who have lovers . . .
> Thus one should vow and pay homage
> To arms and knighthood.]

Certain virtues (and vices) were attributed to certain birds and hence to those who ate their meat. The very close parallels between the *Voeux du Paon* and the *Voeux du Heron* are evident here. The latter, possibly of Hainault origin, parodies the former.[239] Edward III's 'cowardice' in not pursuing his rightful claim to the French throne is symbolized by the choice of the heron—it was, says Robert of Artois in the poem, the most cowardly of birds:

> Le plus couart oysel ay prinst, ce mest avis . . .
> Si tost quil voit son umbre il est tous estordis . . .
> A li doivent vouer les gens de cest pais . . .
> C'au plus couart qui soit ne qui oncques fust vis
> Donrrai le hairon, chest Edouart Loeis,
> Deshiretes de Franche, le nobile pais.[240]

> [I have taken the most cowardly bird, I believe . . .
> As soon as it sees its shadow it is all astounded . . .
> The people of this land should make their vows upon it . . .
> To the greatest coward who is or ever was alive
> I shall give the heron, that is Edward Louis,
> Disinherited from France, the noble land.]

Deriving his words from the *Voeux du Paon*, Robert of Artois is made to proclaim at Edward's feast, mockingly:

---

[238] See the edition of the French text, from Paris, BN, MS fr.12565 (late 14th cent.) in *The Buik of Alexander*, ed. Ritchie, iii. ll. 3911–12, 3944–6.

[239] See B. Whiting, 'The Vows of the Heron', *Speculum*, 20 (1945), 261–78, where the poem is seen as a piece of 'anti-war' polemic. For related texts of Hainault origin see *Le parfait du Paon*, ed. R. J. Carey (Chapel Hill, NC, 1972), and J. Brisebarre, *Le restor du Paon*, ed. E. Donkin (London, 1980).

[240] *Political Poems*, ed. Wright, i. 5–6.

Vechi viande as preux, a chiaux qui sont soubgis
As dames amoureuses, qui tant ont cler le vis . . .[241]

[Here is the food of the brave, for those who are subject to amorous ladies, who have such fair complexions . . .]

The text echoes that of the *Paon*: 'C'est la viande as preux, a ceulz qui ont amie'[242] ['It is the food of the brave, for those who have lovers']. The allusion could not have been lost upon the assembly. Similarly, in the poem, Robert of Artois is made to carry the roast heron between two silver dishes, accompanied by singing *damoiselles* and minstrels (see also Pls. 15a, 15b).[243] Although the atmosphere and setting is secular, it is worth noting that all the vows on the heron are made to Christ and the Virgin Mary, or to named saints, such as Saint-Amand, the Hainault patron.[244] This, among other circumstantial details, may suggest that the poem is in fact based on historical reality, however loosely.[245] The text breathes the spirit of Edward III's court in the earlier part of the reign, with its extravagant-sounding vows, culminating in Queen Philippa's vow not to be delivered of her unborn child (in the event, Lionel of Antwerp) unless and until Edward embarked with her on an expedition against

[241] Ibid., i. 5.

[242] *Voeux du Paon*, ll. 3944–6, and see above, n. 65. The relationship between the texts of the *Vows of the Heron* and the various versions of the *Paon* episode merits much further investigation.

[243] *Political Poems*, ed. Wright, i. 5–7; *Voeux du Paon*, ll. 3910–18, 3935–41. The serving of a peacock at a feast, accompanied by *damoiselles* and minstrels, is also represented in a rectangular panel below the figures on the elaborate Flemish (or north-east German?) monumental brass of Robert Braunche, Mayor and merchant of King's Lynn, and his two wives Lettice and Margaret (1364) in St Margaret's, Lynn. See M. Clayton, *Catalogue of Rubbings of Brasses and Incised Slabs* (Victoria and Albert Museum, London, 1968), plate 39, and pp. 3, 4, 20, 22, 53, 79. See also R. le Strange, *A Complete Descriptive Guide to British Monumental Brasses* (London, 1972), 93. The so-called 'King John cup' of King's Lynn (*c.*1340) bears enamels depicting elegant figures generally resembling the participants in the peacock feast on the Braunche brass, but there is no known connection between the two objects. See *Age of Chivalry*, cat. no. 541 (435–6); and H. K. Cameron, 'Fourteenth-century Flemish brasses at King's Lynn', *Archaeological Journal*, 136 (1979), 151–72.

[244] *Political Poems*, ed. Wright, i. 22, 23.

[245] The poem gives a date of September 1338 at London as the time and venue of the incident. Edward III was abroad—at Antwerp and Koblenz—from 16 July 1338 onwards. See Rymer, *Foedera*, ii, II (London, 1821), 1050–62; *CPR, 1338–40*, 189–91. For Robert of Artois's role at this time see G. T. Diller, 'Robert d'Artois et l'historicité des *Chroniques* de Froissart', *MA* 86 (1980), 217–31; Jean Froissart, *Chroniques: Début au premier livre: Edition du manuscrit de Rome Reg. lat. 869*, ed. G. T. Diller (Geneva, 1972), 228–34. Froissart does not recount the episode of vowing on the heron.

France in pursuit of his claim. Political aims are embodied and enshrined within a chivalric ritual, as in other aspects of Edward III's court. Although probably pre-dating the foundation of the Order in 1348, the poem's inclusion of the phrase in Philippa's vowing, 'Et honnis soit li corps qui ja si pensera', bears a striking resemblance to the Garter motto ('Hony soit qui mal [y] pense').[246] Could this be either a source for the motto itself or a parody of it, if the poem was in fact composed after the Garter's foundation? Whatever the case, the Vows of the Heron may be less 'deficient of historical truth' than has been assumed.[247]

If, as has been suggested, the choice of birds upon which vows were taken could possess some symbolic and didactic significance, the problem of the Feast of the Swans (1306) remains. The Arthurian background is, of course, clear. The choice of Pentecost for the feast and mass knighting-ceremony puts the event firmly in the context of Edward I's 'Arthurianism'. Geoffrey of Monmouth's account of Arthur's great Pentecost feast at Carleon lay behind many such occasions.[248] The swans also had an Arthurian connotation in, for example, the Lohengrin legend. But there is no clear connection in Arthurian sources between vowing on swans and their appearance at courtly feasts or other events. It is to the bestiaries and related works that one must turn in order to find evidence for the connotations and associations attached to the swan. Two prominent characteristics emerge from such sources: the swan was perceived essentially as a singing bird, closely associated with music, minstrelsy, and harping; and it was also seen as a harbinger of death, because it was said to sing best in the last year of its life. The swan is made to sing as it dies through roasting in the collection of Latin and Middle High German songs from the monastery of Ottobeuren, made famous through Carl Orff's *Carmina Burana*.[249] In thirteenth-century bestiaries the swan was said to 'pour out sweet song', to fly to the sound of zithers being played, and to sing most sweetly just before its death. In Pierre de Beauvais's bestiary (compiled before 1218) the swan 'delights in singing to the harp', and an illumination to the manuscript shows a swan singing before a

---

[246] *Political Poems*, ed. Wright, i. 23. A version of the poem in Brussels (BR, MS 10.433) renders the phrase as 'Et honnis soit li corps qui ja y pensera' (l. 405) bringing it even closer to the Garter motto.

[247] See above, pp. 213–14.

[248] See Bullock-Davies, *Menestrellorum Multitudo*, 225–9; R. S. Loomis, 'Edward I, Arthurian enthusiast', *Speculum*, 23 (1953), 119–23.

[249] For a discography of *Carmina Burana* see I. March, E. Greenfield, and R. Layton, *The Penguin Guide to Compact Discs* (Harmondsworth, 1999), 1027–9.

harpist.[250] At the 1306 feast, minstrels, including harpers, accompanied the entry of the swans, and music was an integral part of the ritual and ceremony at the feast.[251] If significance is to be attributed to the choice of swans in 1306, it would seem that Edward I may have opted for swans because they were heralds of death—the illness from which he was to die in July 1307 had already taken hold—and because the bird was viewed as a 'sacrificial' creature, upon which vows to fight to the death to avenge Robert Bruce's murder of John Comyn were taken.[252] Lastly, the close family connections between Edward and his kinsmen and kinswomen in the *comté* of Bar and bishopric of Liège may have exerted some influence. Those who took the vows on the swans in 1306, and were knighted, committed themselves to the fulfilment of those vows in the Scots campaigns of both Edward I and Edward II. The writer of the *Flores Historiarum* reported:

Tunc allati sunt in pompatica gloria duo cigni vel olores ante regem, phalerati retibus aureis vel fistulis deauratis, desiderabile spectaculum intuentibus. Quibus visis, rex vovit Dei caeli et cignis se velle profisci in Scotiam, Sanctae Ecclesiae injuriam et mortem Johannis Comyn et fidem laesam Scotorum vindicaturus *mortuus sive vivus*.[253]

[Then two cygnets or swans, ornamented with gold nets or gilded piping, were brought in ostentatious splendour before the king, a desirable spectacle for the onlookers. After he had seen them, the king vowed to God in heaven and to the swans that he proposed to set out for Scotland, to avenge the harm to Holy Church, the death of John Comyn, and the Scots' breach of faith, alive or dead.]

The king's vow was then taken up by others, and the *Flores* stated:

Sponderunt igitur illud votum caeteri magnates, fide bona asserentes se secum paratos esse in vita regis et *post mortem ipsius* cum filio suo principe in Scotiam profisci, votum regium expleturos.[254]

---

[250] See F. McCullock, *Medieval Latin and French Bestiaries* (Chapel Hill, NC, 1960), 176; *Le Bestiaire d'Amour Rimé: poème inédit du xiiie siècle*, ed. A. Thordstein (Lund/Copenhagen, 1941), ll. 221–43; Bod. Lib., MS Douce 308, fos. 89v–90r: 'Car il est i pais ou li cines chantent si bien et si volontiers haut ou harpe devant eux, il sacorde a la harpe tout au teille maniere com li tabors au flajol, et nomeemant an lan kil doit morir . . .'

[251] See Bullock-Davies, *Menestrellorum Multitudo*, pp. xxx, xxxiii; E.101/362/20: covering and description of the swans; E.101/369/8: payments to minstrels, totalling 114 l. 10s., including 'Adinet le harpour' (Adinet le Roi?).

[252] Prestwich, *Edward I*, 505.

[253] *Flores Historiarum*, ed. H. R. Luard, iii (RS, London, 1890), 132. Italics mine.

[254] Ibid., iii. 132. Italics mine.

[Thereupon the other magnates vowed the same vow, affirming in good faith that they were ready to set out for Scotland with him while he lived and, after his death, with his son the prince, thereby fulfilling the regal vow.]

The emphasis on Edward's death appears to bear out the potentially valedictory nature of the occasion. Some of those who vowed in this manner perished in the subsequent conflict. When considered in this light, the chivalric vow-taking of the early to mid-fourteenth century does not immediately suggest that it had degenerated into the frivolous and insincere activity which Huizinga identified. If commitment to a ruler's 'just' cause was endorsed and strengthened by such undertakings, however fantastic or bizarre they may seem, the rituals of vowing in a courtly setting have a secure place among the means whereby power was represented and expressed.

b. The role of the court chapel

The demands of the liturgical year determined many aspects of a later medieval ruler's daily life. In the study of the *Alltag*—the day-to-day existence of courts and households—the primacy of the Church's calendar (the *only* calendar of the medieval year) must always be borne in mind. Just as the canonical hours, inexorably recurring from day to day, regulated the passing of day and night, so the calendar of liturgical feast and fasting days provided both fixed and movable points whereby weeks, months, and seasons were measured and remembered.[255] Although dating by the day of the month was already common by the later thirteenth century, the habit of dating by saints' days and other feasts of the Church was certainly very often used and, in some areas, almost ubiquitous. It was normal to date an event, a transaction, and the document which recorded it, from the day upon which it fell in the liturgical calendar. The need for accurate calculation of movable feasts, and precise knowledge of the fixed festivals of the Church, was therefore imperative. In the context of court culture, it was the court chapel and its personnel who thus served to regulate the rhythms of the court's year.

[255] For the liturgical calendar see, among many works, E. Bishop, *Liturgica Historica* (Oxford, 1918); R. T. Hampson, *Medii aevi kalendarium, or Dates, Charters, and Customs of the Middle Ages*, 2 vols. (London, 1841), containing much valuable information concerning the feasts of the Church and the texts of calendars; also, for a useful short account of the reckoning of time in the Middle Ages, see C. R. Cheney (ed.), *Handbook of Dates for Students of English History* (Cambridge, repr. 1997), 1–11 and, for saints' days and feasts used for dating, 40–2. For a concise account of the measurement of time—and of attitudes towards it—in pre-industrial societies see J. R. Hale, *Renaissance Europe, 1480–1520* (London, 1971), 11–18.

The practice whereby rulers either created their own chapels, or made use of existing foundations, had a long history. Charlemagne's palace chapel at Aachen was, of course, celebrated, and in many respects moulded and shaped the subsequent actions of lesser princes.[256] The foundation of chapels for the saying (and singing) of masses, the commemoration of the dead through obits on the anniversaries of their deaths, and the offering and distribution of alms, was an essential part of devotional religion.[257] Yet the special circumstances of later medieval rulers, like most of their aristocratic contemporaries, profoundly influenced the provision which they made for the observance and celebration of the liturgical offices and the salvation of their (and their family's) souls. In an age of itinerant rulership, a tension naturally arose between the existence, on the one hand, of fixed court chapels, often associated with an existing religious foundation, and the need to provide an apparatus for the satisfaction of spiritual and devotional needs during a ruler's journeys. The portability of liturgical and devotional artefacts was at a premium, and the travelling court or household demanded easily transportable apparatus so that the requirements of both private and collective religious observance could be fulfilled.

At its most fundamental, this devotional requirement was met by the provision of portable altars, and even by the construction of temporary chapels in places of residence visited during a ruler's progress through his, or her, territories.[258] Hence in May 1314, just before her departure to accompany Edward II on the ill-fated Bannockburn campaign, Queen Isabella of England was provided with a wooden altar 'bound with iron bands in the manner of a coffer', which could be trussed up and carried by a sumpter horse. This was 'for the celebration of masses before the

---

[256] See, for Charlemagne's palace chapel, D. Bullough, *The Age of Charlemagne* (London, 1980), 149–53.

[257] Among a vast literature, see especially K. L. Wood-Legh, *Perpetual Chantries in Britain* (Cambridge, 1965); J. Lemaître, *L'Église et la mémoire des Morts dans la France médiévale* (Paris, 1986); J. Chiffoleau, *La Comptabilité de l'au-delà: les hommes, la mort et la religion dans le région d'Avignon à la fin du moyen âge* (Paris, 1980); J. Le Goff, *The Birth of Purgatory* (London, 1984); and most recently—for the architectural expression of commemorative piety—H. M. Colvin, *Architecture and the After-Life* (New Haven and London, 1991), esp. 152–89.

[258] See above, p. 143. For early instances of the grant of papal indults to lay people, permitting them to have portable altars, see *Calendar of Entries in the Papal Registers relating to Great Britain and Ireland: Papal Letters*, i. *1198–1304*, ed. W. H. Bliss (London, 1893), 274 (to the countess of Lincoln, Sept. 1251); 300 (to William de Valence and to Robert, the king's steward, June 1254).

queen during her journeys both in England and Scotland'.[259] A rare surviving example of such an altar chest is the so-called 'Newport chest' (Pl. 17), dating from the late thirteenth century. The lid of the chest can be opened to reveal a painted crucifix flanked by saints, and it is, like Queen Isabella's portable altar, clearly 'bound with iron bands in the manner of a coffer'. Many of the smaller-scale painted retables and altarpieces found in contemporary inventories were intended for similar purposes. Everything pertaining to the itinerant court chapel—plate, vestments, textiles, and service books—had to be easily packed for transport, often in oiled cloth. Books had to be securely bound.[260] The very small size of some surviving service books, and the signs of wear which they reveal, bears witness to the fact of constant itineration (Pls. 19a, 19b).[261] A late fourteenth-century inventory of goods, drawn up at the court of Hainault-Holland, vividly makes the point: it included 'a missal which the clerk of the chapel carried at his saddle-bow' and 'one-half of a breviary, with notation, for summertime'.[262] In this travelling society, which was constantly on the move, the need for portable, durable devotional artefacts was keenly felt and could not fail to exert its influence on the visual and applied arts of the age.

A further conclusion, based on the assumption that longer periods of residence in fixed locations were becoming a more frequent occurrence in the lives of rulers and their dependents, has been drawn by literary historians. The distinction between the stationary court and the itinerant household has been assumed to have acted as a fundamental influence upon court culture.[263] Stress has been laid upon the rise of permanent chanceries and the emergence of fixed places of residence which, it is argued, provided the necessary infrastructure for the development of princely courts as centres of literary production.[264] But the chancery was

---

[259] PRO, E.101/375/9, fo. 24r: payment to John Fraunceys of London for his labour, 26s. 8d. (7 May 1314). For the 'Newport chest' see P. Eames, *Furniture in England, France and the Netherlands from the Twelfth to the Fifteenth Centuries* (London, 1977), 134 and pls. 64b, 65.

[260] See C.47/22/3, no. 79: expenses of transporting the king's chapel and the binding of its books, Oct. 1304; also Lachaud, 'Textiles, Furs and Liveries', 167–9.

[261] See e.g. The Hague, KB, MS 74 G 31: Diurnal, in tiny, portable format, 59 × 43 mm., northern French/southern Netherlandish, c.1268–70; MS 135 G 18: psalter *non feriatum*, in similar format, 86 × 62 mm., Netherlandish, c.1260–75.

[262] AEM, Trésorerie, Recueils 74, no. 33: 'un missel que le clerc de la chapelle portoit a larcon de sa selle . . . Item, le moitie dun breviaire note du temps deste'. The missal was valued at 30 l., the breviary at 10 l.

[263] See Bumke, *Courtly Culture*, 16–17, 52–5; Van Oostrom, *Court and Culture*, 8–9, 16.

[264] Bumke, *Courtly Culture*, 54–5, and see below, pp. 226–7.

not the only source of literate, educated personnel. Tutors, confessors, and clerks were also drawn from the chapel. As a 'cultural' as well as liturgical institution, the ruler's chapel deserves rather more attention.[265] As we shall see, palace chapels developed as increasingly independent entities during the later Middle Ages, often detaching themselves from the religious foundation—cathedral, abbey, or monastery—of which they had formerly been an integral part. The proprietary status of lay patrons—that common later medieval phenomenon—was thus expressed in a courtly context.[266]

The rise of the palace chapel also represented a natural development of the role of the castle chapel in the liturgical organization of earlier medieval households. The creation of collegiate foundations with a body of resident canons had been a common feature of devotional practice from an early date.[267] The later Middle Ages saw a proliferation of such institutions, with increasingly large numbers of chaplainries, canonries, and prebends attached to them. In the ladder of ecclesiastical preferment, tenure of such a position often served to advance a clerk's career.[268] A canon of a collegiate foundation such as the chapel of St Nicholas in the royal castle at Wallingford (Pl. 20), or even a principal chaplain at the much smaller castle chapel of Le Quesnoy in Hainault, had excellent prospects of promotion.[269] Such places did not provide 'centralized' residences for rulers, but formed regularly visited points on the itineraries of the kings of England and counts of Hainault (and their families). Yet the later Middle Ages witnessed a distinct tendency for certain institutions to assume the character of the *Eigenkloster*, or private foundation, of an earlier period.[270] The chapels in the castles and palaces of rulers at Westminster (St Stephen's), Paris (Ste-Chapelle), Brussels, The Hague,

---

[265] See Binski, *Westminster Abbey*, 176–7, 183–5.

[266] See A. Martindale, 'Patrons and minders: the intrusion of the secular into sacred spaces in the late Middle Ages', in D. Wood (ed.), *The Church and the Arts: Studies in Church History* (London, 1992), 171–86.

[267] See, for the significance of collegiate foundations in the eleventh and twelfth centuries, G. Duby, 'Les chanoines réguliers et la vie économique des xie et xiie siècles' in his *Hommes et Structures du Moyen Age. Recueil d'articles* (Paris and The Hague, 1973), 203–12.

[268] See H. Millet, 'Les chanoines au service de l'état; bilan d'une étude comparative' in J.- P. Genet (ed.), *L'État moderne: Genèse. Bilans et perspectives* (Paris, 1990), 137–46.

[269] For the foundation at Wallingford see the cartulary in St John's College, Oxford, Munim. III.1. For Le Quesnoy, *Cartulaire des comtes de Hainaut*, ed. Devillers, vi. 237–41: Mar. 1353, and below, pp. 235–6.

[270] See Binski, *Westminster Abbey*, 46–7.

or Prague provide clear instances of this tendency (Pls. 21, 22).[271] As a supreme example of the trend towards separation from 'parent' institutions, the Emperor Charles IV's series of sumptuously decorated chapels in his castle of Karlstejn (Karlstein, c.1344–70) represent the independent castle chapel in its most elaborate form.[272] The fitting-out and decoration of court chapels thus played a highly significant part in the evolution of court culture.

An important stage in the process whereby certain fixed locations became not only the power-centres of a ruler's territories, but also representative of the ideology of his (and his dynasty's) rule, was reached during this period. It has thus been argued that the complex of abbey and palace at Westminster (Pl. 1, Map 3) formed an 'embodiment . . . of a formative political culture', part of a process 'whereby state, government and the persona and mythology of the king obtained a location'.[273] In this development, the religious foundation established there, with the palace chapel, played a vital role. If, as was increasingly the case, an abbey church, monastery, or collegiate foundation became a dynastic mausoleum, the sense of identification with a dynasty or ruling line became even more intense. Westminster and St-Denis were to become the mausoleums of Plantagenets, Capetians, and Valois, but the process was not an entirely smooth nor rapid one.[274] Westminster only emerged as the exclusive burial-place of the English monarchs in 1377, and it had more in common with such family burial churches as Royaumont (for the Capetians) or the monastery of Las Huelgas, near Burgos (for the Castilian kings) than with the abbey church of St-Denis.[275] Not only were the crowned sovereigns themselves buried at Westminster, but many of their kinsmen and kinswomen, clustering around the east end of the

[271] See C. Billot, 'Les Saintes Chapelles (xiiie–xvie siècles): approche comparée de fondations dynastiques', Revue d'histoire de l'église de France, 73 (1987), 64–86. The forthcoming proceedings (ed. J. Fajt et al.) of the international symposium on 'Court Chapels of the High and Late Middle Ages and their Artistic Decoration' (Prague, 23–5 Sept. 1998) will take our knowledge of the subject substantially further.

[272] See V. Dvorakova et al., Gothic Mural Painting in Bohemia and Moravia, 1300–1378 (London, 1964), 51–65, 80–100, 114–21; and also F. Kavka, 'The role and function of Karlstejn Castle as documented in records from the reign of Charles IV', and L. Gottfried, 'Selection of archival source materials on the history of Karlstejn Castle and its artistic decoration', in J. Fajt (ed.), Magister Theodoricus: Court Painter to Emperor Charles IV (Prague, 1998), 15–28 and 29–33.

[273] Binski, Westminster Abbey, 1, 4.

[274] See ibid., 90–120, esp. 116–20.

[275] See M. Gomez-Moreno, El panteon réal de las Huelgas de Burgos (Madrid, 1946), 10–35; E. A. R. Brown, The Monarchy of Capetian France and Royal ceremonial (Aldershot, 1991), 241–66; Binski, Westminster Abbey, 92–3.

abbey (Pls. 23–7).[276] At St-Denis, the thirteenth-century projects of tomb-building and re-housing led to the reservation of burial in the abbey to those anointed as kings at Rheims.[277] At Westminster there was no such exclusivity.

The only visible tendency towards discrimination according to status was the positioning of the tombs of highly ranking members of the court milieu (Pls. 23–7) close to the high altar and to the shrine of St Edward the Confessor. William de Valence (d.1296) (Pl. 23), Edmund of Lancaster (d.1296))(Pls. 24–6), Aymer de Valence (d.1326) (Pl. 24), and John of Eltham (d.1339) (Pl. 27) were gathered together at the east end of the abbey as a kind of curial elite.[278] The concentration of royal and 'curial' tombs, some of them with high-status gilt bronze effigies, around the Cosmati pavement, the shrine of St Edward, and the chapel of St Edmund represented the court's appropriation of sacred space within the abbey church.[279]

The rituals of court funerals and burials will be discussed later, but the choice of Westminster or St-Denis as dynastic mausoleums was highly significant in the process whereby ruling houses and their courts were identified with the cults of certain saints. In the gradual shift towards an anglo-centric monarchy in England, the mid- and late thirteenth century was a critical and seminal period.[280] The cult of Edward the Confessor began to rival that of St Denis, although the fourteenth century was to

[276] W. H. St John Hope, 'On the funeral effigies of the kings and queens of England, with special reference to those in the abbey church at Westminster', *Archaeologia*, 60 (1907), 517–70; Colvin *et al., King's Works*, i. 147–50; F. H. Crossley, *English Church Monuments, 1150–1550* (London, 1921), 54–9. Evidence for specific royal wishes that near-kinsmen be buried close to the sovereign at Westminster is found in a letter of Edward III to the abbot and convent in which he orders that 'selonc la esleccion et le devis de nostre . . . mere Isabel, Royne Dengleterre, vueilletz ordiner et suffrir que le corps de nostre trescher frere Jehan, jadis counte de Cornewaill' [John of Eltham] peusse estre remuez et translatez du lieu ou il gist jusques a autre plus covenable entre les Roials, faisant toutefoitz reserver et garder les places les plus honourables illoeques pour le gisir et la sepulture de nous et de noz heirs . . .' (WAM, 6300*, at Brussels, 24 Aug. 1339).

[277] See A. Erlande-Brandenburg, *Le Roi est mort: étude sur les funérailles, les sépultures et les tombeaux des rois de France jusqu'à la fin du xiiie siècle* (Geneva and Paris, 1975), 68–86.

[278] See Binski, *Westminster Abbey*, 107–8; RCHM, *England*, i. *Westminster Abbey* (London, 1924), 102–6.

[279] See Martindale, 'Patrons and minders', 171–9; H. J. Plenderleith and H. Maryon, 'The royal bronze effigies in Westminster abbey', *Antiquaries Journal*, 39 (1959), 87–90. For the higher status accorded to bronze, see *CCR, 1242–47*, 293: Henry III orders two leopards on each side of his stall (*sedes*) at Westminster to be made from bronze (*leopardos eneos*) rather than of incised or sculpted stone, as it was more 'sumptuous' (*parum plus erit sumptuosum*) on 13 Mar. 1245.

[280] See J. Gillingham, *The Angevin Empire*, 82–5; Vale, *Origins of the Hundred Years War*, 1–6, 10–11, 266–9.

witness a further shift in England towards the military St George.[281] There were obvious differences between the English and French monarchies in this respect: whereas so much of the apparatus of dynastic ideology was concentrated at Westminster, in France it was more dispersed. By the early fourteenth century, the 'sacred spaces' associated with the Capetians were distributed across the city of Paris and the heartlands of their dynasty—at St-Denis, the Île-de-la-Cité, Notre Dame, Rheims, Royaumont, Poissy, and so on. The division of the body of Louis IX into many parts, to be lodged in a number of different locations is entirely indicative of this phenomenon.[282] Although Philip the Fair could refer to the Sainte-Chapelle as the *caput regni* ('head of the kingdom') when St Louis's head was transferred there in 1306, there was no one fixed centre of Capetian (or Valois) identity.[283] The contrast with England should not, however, be overdrawn.[284] Westminster was by no means the only complex of ecclesiastical and secular buildings with a special significance for the Plantagenets. Canterbury, York, Windsor (from the reign of Edward III onwards), and the many religious foundations and pious endowments initiated by individual kings, their relatives and households, served as important centres whereby the crown extended its influence—and consequently the influence of the court—in the kingdom at large.[285] It is, moreover, difficult to see the building campaigns and decorative schemes initiated at Westminster from the 1240s onwards as 'evidence of England's priority in developing symbolic notions of the centralized state'.[286] The

[281] See D. A. L. Morgan, 'The Cult of St George *c.*1500: national and international connotations' in *Publications du Centre Européen d'études Bourguignonnes (xiv*ᵉ*–xvi*ᵉ *siècles)*, 35 (1995), 152–4; Binski, *Westminster Abbey*, 52–3.

[282] R. Branner, 'The Montjoies of St Louis', in D. Fraser, H. Hibbard, and M. Lewine (eds.), *Essays in the History of Architecture presented to Rudolf Wittkower* (London, 1967), 13–26; E. A. R. Brown, 'Death and the human body in the Middle Ages: the legislation of Boniface VIII on the division of the corpse', *Viator*, 12 (1981), 221–70. Queen Isabella of England also wished her body to be divided and buried in three churches of her choice. See *Calendar of . . . Papal Registers: Papal Letters*, ii. *1305–1342*, 235 (Dec. 1323).

[283] See *Vitae Paparum Avenionensium*, ed. G. Mollat, iii (Paris, 1921), 63–4: letter of Philip the Fair to Clement V where reference is made to the Sainte-Chapelle as 'capellam eamdem, quam caput totius regni Francie per stricti districtionem examinis appellamus' (after 17 May 1306).

[284] Cf. Binski, *Westminster Abbey*, 5: 'Westminster was ostensibly an act of piety . . . Yet it was also, in a deeper sense, an acknowledgement of the political centralization of the kingdom . . .'

[285] See e.g. the evidence for endowment and building works in Colvin *et al.*, *King's Works*, i. 248–57 (Vale Royal); ii. 972–3 (King's Langley); 872–3 (St George's, Windsor).

[286] Binski, *Westminster Abbey*, 5; cf. R. Branner, *St Louis and the Court Style in Gothic Architecture* (London, 1965), 4–6, 10–11.

constant itineration of the monarchy, and the establishment of alternative centres of government and administration—for example, York—may give the lie to premature assumptions about English 'centralization' in this respect.[287] The essentially mobile nature of the court—as a travelling household—in many ways cut across these centralizing and nucleating tendencies. Although the departments of state—Chancery, Exchequer, Wardrobe, courts of law—became fixed at London, the true centre of power often lay elsewhere, with the king in the midst of his court.[288]

The court chapel—or rather, chapels—reflected such characteristics of English government and the infrastructures of power. By the mid- to late thirteenth century the palatine chapel *strictu sensu* was the king's private chapel of St Stephen within the palace of Westminster (Pls. 1, 22).[289] Its role under Henry III was limited to serving the devotional needs (which were many) of the king.[290] Its later, more public function was not yet apparent. But its internal decor and organization was not neglected. For example, on 7 February 1245, Henry wrote to Edward fitz Odo, his goldsmith, painter, and gilder:

In exteriori parte sedis regis in capella Sancti Stephani Westmonasterii, sicut intratur in capella decendendo de aula, bene depingi faciat pulcram et decentem imaginem Sancte Marie, et ex alia parte cancelli versus hostium gardini, imagines regis et regine, ita quod parate sint et bene depicte in proximo adventu regis ibidem.[291]

[On the outer part of the king's seat in the chapel of St Stephen at Westminster, as it is entered by descending from the hall, he shall have had painted a fine and handsome image of St Mary, and on the other side of the chancel towards the garden, images of the king and queen, so that they shall be ready and well painted for the king's next coming.]

Such works were evidently of close personal concern to the king, for the chapel was very much a part of his domestic enviroment, adjacent to his hall and near to the Painted Chamber (Map 3).[292] At this date, however, the chapel was clearly not equivalent to the Sainte-Chapelle, and bore few signs of acting as a reliquary chapel or more public vehicle for the

---

[287] See T. F. Tout, 'The beginnings of a modern capital: London and Westminster in the fourteenth century', in *Collected Papers*, iii (Manchester, 1934), 249–75. Also see above, pp. 138–40.

[288] See Gillingham, 'Crisis or continuity?', 64–6.

[289] See Binski, *The Painted Chamber*, 20–4; Cherry and Stratford, *Westminster Kings*, 28–49.

[290] Binski, *The Painted Chamber*, 9, 16.   [291] *CCR, 1242–47*, 287.

[292] Binski, *The Painted Chamber*, fig. 1.

display of relics.[293] Under Edward I, however, works undertaken in St Stephen's after 1292 suggest that its status had begun to rise, and it has been claimed that its increasing separation from the devotional and cultural life of the abbey church made it 'a major foyer of innovation independent of the abbey'.[294] But it was under Edward III that St Stephen's became a palatine chapel in the grander, more public sense. Between 1348 and the 1360s the chapel became a collegiate foundation with a body of canons, analogous to the king's college at Windsor and, sumptuously decorated (Pls. 22a, 22b) with paintings and stained glass, more nearly comparable with its French counterpart (Pl. 21).[295]

Although patronage of the visual arts in a court context will be discussed in a later chapter, the decorative schemes found in court chapels are important evidence for the image which rulers wished to project and for the function of such foundations in that process. The evidence from Artois, Flanders, and England illuminates such concerns. In the substantial body of archival documentation which survives for works at the count of Artois's castle and park at Hesdin, the chapel—or chapels—bulk large.[296] The castle included at least two chapels—the *grant capele* and the *noeve capele*—by the end of the thirteenth century. Between July and November 1299, a campaign of works at Hesdin revolved around the decoration and fitting-out of the chapels, as well as works to the *nueve sale* (new hall), the *paveillon* on the Marais there, and various chambers.[297] A sculpted image of the recently canonized St Louis was provided for the countess's oratory, worked on in the *grant capele* by Jean de St-Omer and painted by Guissins the painter.[298] The Artois household had been quick to venerate the newly created saint—a payment for writing and 'noting' (in other words, with musical notation) the sixteen *offices* of St Louis was made on 13 December 1298.[299] The works in 1299 included the provision of what was evidently an elaborate painted crucifix for the chapel, new columns and capitals (representing angels, which were also painted), and 105 feet of stained glass (*vairre paint dimagerie*) at 2s. per foot, transported from Arras and installed by 'Master Oste'.[300] The scale of the works may have been to some extent influenced by a royal visit—Philip

[293] Branner, *St Louis and the Court Style*, 56–7; Binski, *Westminster Abbey*, 145–6.

[294] Binski, *Westminster Abbey*, 176.

[295] See Cherry and Stratford, *Westminster Kings*, 28–49, esp. 44–9.

[296] See A. van Buren, 'Reality and romance in the parc of Hesdin', in *Medieval Gardens* (Dumbarton Oaks, 1986), 117–34.

[297] ADPC, A.147 (1 July–30 Nov. 1299).

[298] A.147, m. 1r: 19 Sept. and 10 Oct. 1299.   [299] A.145, no. 32.

[300] A.147, mm. 1, 3, 4, 5.

the Fair was at Hesdin at this time.[301] Similarly, at the time of Edward II
of England's stay at Hesdin in July 1313, measures were taken to ensure
that the Artois establishment appeared at its best. A team of painters were
paid for 'washing the paintings of the great chapel . . . and the vaulted
chapel'.[302] The account entries were followed by further payments *contre
le venue du roy Dengleterre*.[303] The paintings in the 'great chapel' were
the subject of constant attention, and in June 1302 Raoul Lengles
(L'Anglais), painter and his valets had been paid for painting 'the length
of the great chapel' and for 're-varnishing . . . the paintings of the said
chapel', using *mauvres couleurs*, ochre and brown, as well as for washing
the 'old paintings of the great chapel'.[304] The colours in which the chapel
was to be painted also included vermillion, *orpuinet* (yellow), and *fine inde*
(purple or indigo), transported in sacks from Arras. This evidence suggests that the counts (and countesses) of Artois perceived their chapels
at Hesdin not only as private places of devotion, but as integral parts
of the complex of spaces into which their guests and visitors might be
introduced. Their apparently close (and early) identification with the
cult of St Louis—to whom, of course, they were very closely related—
emphasized their Capetian loyalties. Robert II of Artois was to meet his
death while discharging his obligations to the dynasty, as a prince of the
blood (at Kortrijk in July 1302).

While the Dampierre counts of Flanders certainly had chapels in their
castles of Male, Pettegem, and elsewhere, there is less evidence for
activity on the scale of the counts of Artois. No one chapel emerges as
possessing greater significance than others until the later years of Louis
de Male (1370–84). Even then, the favoured institution did not lie
within one of the comital castles or residences but was located within an
existing religious foundation. This was consistent with the pious wishes
and intentions of previous counts. Guy de Dampierre (d.1305) had especially favoured the abbey of Beaulieu near Pettegem, where he elected to be
buried. His testament provided for burial in the abbey 'qui est del ordene
Sainte Clare, que je et Yzabeaus me chiere compaigne, jadis contesse de
Flandr' et de Namur, avons fondee, ou quel lieu je estaulis une capelerie
perpetuele'[305] ['which is of the order of St Clare, which I and Isabella, my
dear companion, late countess of Flanders and Namur, have founded, in

---

[301] A.147, m. 5: payment of 20s. 'pour toile dont on fist verrieres as fenestres du mares
quant li Rois i fu', Oct. 1299.

[302] A.309: 'pour laver les paintures de le grant capele . . . et de le capele de voutes',
23 June, 7 and 17 July 1313.

[303] A.309: 14 July 1313.   [304] A.180, no. 3, m. 4: 9 June 1302.

[305] ADN, B.449, nos. 4181a and 4181b.

which place I establish a perpetual chapelry']. In 1372, Louis de Male founded a chapel in the collegiate church of Notre Dame at Kortrijk (Pl. 28). He had originally elected to be buried there, in the chapel *que en icelle eglise nous avons de nouvel fait faire et edifier*[306] ['that we have newly had made and built in the same church']. Immediately before his death, however, he had revoked this clause and chosen the chapel of Notre Dame de la Traille in the collegiate church of St Pierre at Lille. But the chapel at Kortrijk appears to have been conceived as a means of commemorating and celebrating the Dampierre counts and their predecessors. The public expression of this intention took the form of a series of wall-paintings (Pl. 28) depicting the counts of Flanders back to the legendary Lideric le Forestier in ancient times. Louis de Male's painter Jan van Hasselt was responsible for the series, which was completed in 1374.[307] These were full-length figures of the counts, with inscriptions recording the dates of their reigns and their burial places (where known), and depictions of their (sometimes legendary) coats of arms.[308] It is very striking that the inscriptions (which survived in fragmentary form into the nineteenth century) were in Flemish, not French or Latin, suggesting that at this date there was a degree of bilingualism at the court of Flanders (Pl. 28). The inscriptions could also have served to instruct the counts' Flemish-speaking subjects in the history of the comital line—further evidence of the more public uses to which court chapels might be put. As such, the portrait series might be compared with the more elaborate, but near-contemporary, cycle of paintings representing the Emperor Charles IV and his ancestors at the Karlstejn.[309] There was also a Flemish precedent for such a series in the magistrates' chamber at Ypres, dating from 1323.[310]

The chapel at Kortrijk also housed another portrait of Louis de Male, on the wall of his pew or oratory, where he was depicted in the presence

---

[306] ADN, B.455, no. 11, 323: revised testament, 28 Jan. 1384.

[307] See F. Vandeputte, 'La chapelle des comtes de Flandre à Courtrai', *Annales de la Société d'Émulation de Bruges*, 10 (1875), 189–282; L. Devliegher, *De Onze-Lieve-Vrouwkerk te Kortrijk* [Kunstpatrimonium van West-Vlaanderen, vi] (Lannoo-Tielt-Utrecht, 1973), 72–3, pls. 198–215.

[308] L. Campbell, *Renaissance Portraits* (New Haven and London, 1990), 41–2.

[309] See Dvorakova *et al.*, *Gothic Mural Painting in Bohemia and Moravia*, 53–6, 63–6, 134 and pls. 62–70; A. Martindale, *Heroes, Ancestors, Relatives and the Birth of the Portrait* (The Hague, 1988), 5–9.

[310] A. Vandenpeereboom, *Ypriana*, ii. *La Chambre des échevins* (Bruges, 1879); E. de Busscher, 'Recherches sur les anciens peintres gantois', *Le Messager des sciences historiques* (1859), 149–50, for a similar series at Ghent.

of the infant Christ.[311] This painting may have had some similarities to the representation of Edward III and his family in St Stephen's chapel (Pl. 22a).[312] The Magi-like depiction of rulers at this time was very influential on the development of royal and princely iconography—and court ceremony and ritual also had its part to play. It has been rightly observed that contemporary court ceremonial and 'the images of themselves propagated by princes in portraits and at public appearances unquestionably influenced the ways in which painters visualized Biblical narrative', especially the Adoration of the Magi.[313] This was thus a two-way process— the representation of princes and that of certain biblical episodes were in a state of mutual interaction in the court art of the later fourteenth century. The sheer sumptuousness of St Stephen's chapel after its re-foundation by Edward III as a collegiate body in 1348 provokes comparisons with the Sainte-Chapelle (Pls. 21, 22). Like its Parisian predecessor, St Stephen's served as a 'vessel for figurative stained glass', but much of its internal decoration was of a military and chivalric character.[314] The figures of twenty-six soldier-saints and martyrs painted on the walls, and the devotion to St George, represented by his presence on the east wall as patron and intercessor for the king's family, marked something of a departure from the traditional role of St Edward and St Edmund in Plantagenet iconography. But this was a hallmark of the 1340s and 1350s. The palatine chapel now both celebrated and consecrated the military achievements of the ruler, yet also made a statement about the functions and expectations of kingship which had a more universal and timeless significance.

Whatever dynastic, political, or ideological role it might serve, the primary function of the court or palace chapel was of course devotional and liturgical. There can be little doubt of the concern of rulers of this period for the state—past, present, and future—of their souls and those of their kin, their forebears and others among the living with whom they had particular connections. The plethora of papal indults permitting the use of portable altars (Pl. 17), the celebration of mass before daybreak, or in places under interdict, testifies to this concern, however much it may have been a product of pre-conditioning and the prompting of

---

[311] Vandeputte, 'La chapelle des comtes de Flandre', 217.

[312] See Cherry and Stratford, *Westminster Kings*, 44–8.

[313] Campbell, *Renaissance Portraits*, 103.

[314] Binski, *Westminster Abbey*, 183; Cherry and Stratford, *Westminster Kings*, 39, for a later engraving of the representation of the soldier-saints Mercurius and Eustache in St Stephen's chapel.

confessors and chaplains. To take but one example, Clement VI had granted William IV, count of Hainault, the right to hear mass before dawn in March 1345, and a similar indult was issued by Innocent VI, in favour of Margaret, countess of Hainault, in December 1353. The pope replied to her supplication by commending her piety and devotion, and gave her permission to hear mass before daybreak, although this was not canonically approved 'quia cum in altaris officio immoletur dominus noster Dei filius Jhesus Christus, qui candor est lucius eterne, congruit hoc non in noctis tenebris fieri sed in luce'[315] ['because when our lord Jesus Christ, the Son of God, who is the dazzling whiteness of eternal light, is sacrificed in the rite at the altar, it is fitting that it should be done not in the darkness of night but in the light']. Christ was the light of the world, and the Eucharistic sacrifice could only be performed in the light. But the constraints of princely and aristocratic life, including departures on military campaigns before dawn, or the demands of constant itineration, made such conditions of sacramental observance difficult—if not impossible—to fulfil.[316] The random nature of sentences of interdict and excommunication also made it impossible to predict whether the route of an itinerary might lie within areas thus affected. Hence the petitioning by princes and nobles for exemption from the effects of interdict: Margaret of Hainault gained an indult to that effect on 10 December 1353, which stated:

si forsan ad loca ecclesiastica interdicto supposita te contigerit declinare, liceat tibi in illis, clausis januis, excommunicatis et interdictis exclusis, non pulsatis campanis, ac submissa voce, tibi et familiaribus tuis domesticis missam et alia divina officia facere celebrari.[317]

[if perchance it should happen that you pass near to places under ecclesiastical interdict, it shall be lawful for you, in those places, behind closed doors, excluded from excommunication and interdict, without ringing of bells, and with subdued voice, to have mass and other divine offices celebrated for yourself and the members of your household.]

The inclusion of the countess's household (*familiares tuos domesticos*) in the indult points to the spiritual needs of all members of the travelling court, some of whom were clearly present when mass and other offices were celebrated in a ruler's presence.

---

[315] *Cartulaire des comtes de Hainaut*, ed. Devillers, i. 390.

[316] For examples of the many papal indults to this effect see *Calendar of . . . Papal Registers: Papal Letters*, i. *(1198–1304)*, 527 (to Edmund of Lancaster and his wife Blanche, Mar. 1291); also *Calendar of . . . Papal Registers. Papal Letters*, ii. *(1305–42)*, 367 (Marie de Saint-Pol, countess of Pembroke, 1331), 368 (Sir Oliver Ingham, 1332).

[317] *Cartulaire des comtes de Hainaut*, ed. Devillers, i. 389.

Not only was the health of the souls of the living maintained by the continual, cyclical celebration and administration of the sacraments, but also that of the dead. The foundation of *chapellenies* or what were, in effect, chantry chapels by princes, their relatives, advisers, and other members of their entourages, was a common practice. These could be additions to existing institutions, or entirely new foundations. At their most elaborate they took the form of self-sufficient chantries, while many were harboured within abbey, cathedral, and collegiate churches, or in court chapels themselves.[318] The motives for their creation were often the product of specific circumstances or events in a ruler's life. Thus, in September 1357, the mentally unstable William (V) of Bavaria, count of Hainault, Holland, and Zeeland, founded a *chapellenie* in his court chapel at The Hague (*in Haga, nostra curia*) for the celebration of masses for his soul, his wife's, those of his ancestors, relatives, and successors, and especially for the soul of the Dutch noble Gerard van der Wateringen (*et precipue pro memoria anime Gherardi de Watheringe*).[319] William had, it seems, already begun to display the first signs of the mental illness which was to lead to his removal from power in favour of Albert of Bavaria. He had been personally responsible for the death of Gerard van der Wateringen, and the *chapellenie* was in part a penitential act.[320] But most foundations were the product of less dramatic and unusual circumstances.[321] Sometimes, however, a *curialis* in a prince's service would himself institute anniversary masses for the souls of his patrons and protectors in a church with which he was associated. Hence Jakemes de Maubeuge, canon of Cambrai, founded an *obit anniversaire* for the counts and countesses of Hainault-Holland in the cathedral there in May 1347.[322] The clerical *curiales* of a ruler might also create such commemorative *chapellenies* within palace or castle chapels. In September 1323, Adam

---

[318] See, from a voluminous literature, K. Edwards, *The English Secular Cathedrals in the Middle Ages* (Manchester, 1949), esp. 291–308; J. T. Rosenthal, *The Purchase of Paradise: The Social Function of Aristocratic Benevolence, 1307–1485* (London and Toronto, 1972), esp. 53–80; Wood-Legh, *Perpetual Chantries*, esp. 1–25.

[319] See *Groot charterboek der graaven van Holland, van Zeeland en heeren van Vriesland*, 4 vols. (Leiden, 1753–6), iii. 29; *Cartulaire des comtes de Hainaut*, ed. Devillers, i. 514: 30 Sept. 1357. Gerard van der Wateringen was listed in the *ordinacie* of the comital household in 1354 as master squire. See ARA, Den Haag, Arch. grav. van Holland, inv. nr. 221, fos. 76r–77r; Van Riemsdijk, *De Tresorie*, 403; and above, pp. 53–5.

[320] See Van Oostrom, *Court and Culture*, 2–3; H. M. Brokken, *Het onstaan van de Hoekse en Kabeljauwse twisten* (Zutphen, 1982), 105–8.

[321] See Rosenthal, *Purchase of Paradise*, 40–52.

[322] *Cartulaire des comtes de Hainaut*, ed. Devillers, i. 166–7.

Huret, treasurer of St-Ame at Douai and chaplain to William III of Hainault, established a foundation of this kind in the count's castle chapel at Le Quesnoy with an annual rent of 100 l.t. which he had purchased from the count.[323] Such chapels were particularly privileged, as they were very much part of the fabric of a ruler's devotional life, and it is from grants of rights and privileges to their personnel that we can often find evidence of how they functioned.

In February 1291, Floris V, count of Holland, provided for the sustenance of his four chaplains who served as 'ministers of the altar' at the court chapel of The Hague.[324] As no suitable ecclesiastical benefices were currently available, the four chaplains were granted 50 l.holl. from the count's annual revenues, half at the feast of St Odulph and the rest on the feast of St Martin *hiemali*. This was to assist them in their functions

tam ad horas canonicas quam ad divinum officium deputatos, vita et moribus commendandos . . . ut ipsi proinde nostri et nostrorum parentum jugem habeant memoriam in canone ac in aliis horis divinis et pro nobis ad Dominum fundant preces.[325]

[entrusted with both the canonical hours and divine office, commended in life and behaviour . . . that they therefore have us and our kin remembered in the canon and in other divine services, and pour out prayers to the Lord for us.]

The perpetual offering of masses and prayers for both the living and the dead demanded endowment, through presentation to benefices in a ruler's gift or through the grant of rents and other revenues. A further supplement to Floris V's grant—revenues from land at Dordrecht—was made on the same date, and the endowment was confirmed by his successor, John I, in July 1297.[326] The comital chapel in the Binnenhof at The Hague was a well-endowed institution by the mid-fourteenth century, when it—like St Stephen's at Westminster and many others—became a collegiate body, largely through the counsel and persuasion of Master Gerard of Leiden.[327] Philip of Leyden urged the counts of Holland to follow the example of greater princes (*maiores*, cas. 44, 45) in this respect, as in others.[328] An inventory of the chapel's liturgical

---

[323] *Cartulaire*, vi. 237 n. 1: *vidimus* dated 27 Sept. 1342 of letters of 27 Sept. 1323.

[324] *Oorkondenboek van Holland en Zeeland tot 1299*, iv. 974–5, nr. 2561: 2 Feb. 1291.

[325] Ibid., iv. 975. For a later copy of the lost original see ARA, archief kappitel Sint Marie op het Hof te 's Gravenhage, nr. 59, fo. 4v: *c*.1381.

[326] Ibid., iv. 975–6, nr. 2562.   [327] Philip of Leyden, *De Cura*, 314 (cas. lxxv).

[328] Ibid. 184.

equipment, probably dating from June–July 1307, lists three altars, for which six chalices and other items were provided.[329]

The counts of Hainault-Holland possessed a number of chapels in their residences—at The Hague, Valenciennes, Mons, Binche, and Le Quesnoy. At the latter, an enquiry into the rights and privileges of the principal chaplain was undertaken in March 1353. The chaplain, Jakemon Hughelin, had petitioned the countess Margaret for continued enjoyment of the rents, dues, and offerings made to the chapel 'en quel-conques lieus deven le compris [precinct] de nodit castiel ... soit a lautel, u en crois aourer, ou en obis faire' ['in certain places within the precinct of our said castle ... whether at the altar, or in veneration of the cross, or for the performance of anniversary masses'].[330] The close relationship of the chapel to the court was indicated by his claim to dine at table 'whenever the household is housed in our said castle' (*li tauvle toutes fois hon tient hostel en nodit castiel*).[331] The subsequent enquiry heard a number of informed witnesses, including previous chaplains, of whom the most distinguished and successful was clearly Pierron Fueillet, dean of the canons of Notre-Dame de la Salle (that is, of the comital palace) in the church of Saint-Géry at Valenciennes. He affirmed that the principal chaplain was permitted to dine with the household:

Sur l'article de le tauvle en lostel du seigneur u de le dame, dist que ainsy l'a-il veu maintenir et user, nonobstant ordonnanche au contraire faicte en l'hostel et le gouvernanche des seigneurs, car li dit capellain y estoient tantost rapiellet et especiaument li possesseres.[332]

[On the article concerning the table in the lord's or lady's household, he says that he has seen it maintained and used thus, notwithstanding the ordinance to the contrary made in the household and the lord's jurisdiction, for the said chaplain was often summoned there and especially the current incumbent.]

In effect, the principal chaplains of the castle chapel at Le Quesnoy enjoyed the equivalent of *bouche de court* when the household lodged there. Their proximity to the court meant that they were well placed on the ladder of preferment, and could expect promotion to a canonry, a deanship, or even higher office, through the patronage of the count or countess. Jakemon Hughelin also referred in his petition to the offerings and alms

[329] AEM, Trésorerie, Cartulaire 20, fos. 174v–175r. See Appendix XI (a).
[330] *Cartulaire des comtes de Hainaut*, ed. Devillers, vi. 238: 15 Mar. 1353. For the chapel at Binche, see Appendix XI (b).
[331] *Cartulaire des comtes de Hainaut*, ed. Devillers, vi. 238.   [332] Ibid., vi. 239–40.

given in and around the castle chapel at Le Quesnoy. It is to this important aspect of the court chapel and its functions that we must now turn.

The giving of alms formed a major part of the devotional life of any
layman or lay woman of any substance. As we have seen, affluence and
indulgence were offset by obligation—the doctrine of justification (and
redemption) by good works made alms-giving imperative.[333] Rulers had
their almoners, responsible for the receipt and distribution of offerings,
from alms-dishes and purses, to the poor and other worthy causes (Pl. 37).
As clerks—literate members of princely households—almoners could also
play a part in the literary life of a court.[334] The annual cycle of alms-
giving can be charted for the English court as a result of the surviving wardrobe and household accounts. Between November 1301 and
November 1302, for instance, alms offered at masses celebrated for the
household of Edward I amounted to 657 l. 9s. 3d.[335] The accounts enable
weekly totals to be calculated. Offertories reached their highest point
during the week which included the feasts of All Saints and All Souls
(1 and 4 November), when the *communis participatio* at masses totalled
53 l. 16s. 7d. The second highest sum was reached during the week from
17 to 23 June, when Trinity Sunday and the feasts of St Botolph and St
Edward (*translatio secunda* on 20 June) brought offerings of 44 l. 19s. 11d.
The two weeks from 24 December 1301 to 6 January 1302 provided
sums of 27 l. 18s. 3d. and 24 l. 3s. 3d. respectively, and included not only
Christmas and Epiphany but the feast days of St Thomas of Canterbury
(29 December) and the *depositio* of St Edward (5 January). It seems that
the number of saints' days and feasts within a week determined the level
of alms and offerings. For weeks in which only a single such day was
recorded, a sum of between 5 l. and 10 l. was given. None of these were
enormous sums, and it is to the occasional outlay at specific moments in
the liturgical calendar that one should look for more lavish displays of
charitable giving. Hence the senior chaplain of Edward II's chapel was
paid 7d. per day for the daily oblations of the king from 8 July 1315 to 31

---

[333] See above, pp. 168–9.

[334] See J. van der Meulen, 'De panter en de aalmoezenier: Dichtkunst rond het
Hollands-Hennegouwse hof', in F. Willaert (ed.), *Een zoet akkoord: Middeleeuwse lyriek in
de Lage Landen* (Amsterdam, 1992), 93–108, 343–8.

[335] For this, and for what follows, see PRO, E.101/361/21, and below, Table 14. Also
A. J. Taylor, 'Royal alms and oblations in the later thirteenth century: an analysis of the
alms roll of 12 Edward I (1283–4)', in F. Emmison and R. Stephens (eds.), *Tribute to an
Antiquary: Essays Presented to Marc Fitch by Some of his Friends* (London, 1976), 93–125;
M. Prestwich, 'The piety of Edward I', in W. M. Ormrod (ed.), *England in the Thirteenth
Century: Proceedings of the 1984 Harlaxton Symposium* (Harlaxton, 1985), 120–8.

January 1316, 'except for the day of Epiphany when the king offered gold, frankincense, and myrrh'.[336] The queen's chaplain also received the same daily sum, except for alms given at three Marian feasts—the Assumption, Nativity, and Conception of the Virgin—when Isabella offered gold. In terms of outlay, however, the provision of masses, rather than the giving of alms and oblations, took the lion's share of royal benefaction. In the same year, Edward II thus gave 38 l. 6s. 8d. (over six times the total sum spent on daily oblations) to the Carmelites at Sheen for celebrating divine service 'for the souls of the king's ancestors' from 2 July 1315 to 31 January 1316.[337] But such sums were even smaller when compared with the outlay on gifts to secular members of the court, which totalled 334 l. 18s. 11d. in New Year's gifts (*étrennes*) alone.[338] To take the figures for the day-to-day giving of oblations at masses on their own, however, tends to distort the complete picture, for the large sums expended on particularly favoured religious houses or foundations—and the spontaneous acts of pious largesse to which rulers were prone—need always to be taken into account.[339]

Besides the formal, conventional alms-giving at the perpetual round of masses said or sung in court chapels, members of the court elite were especially exposed to the solicitations of paupers, hermits, anchorites, mendicants, widows, orphans, and other indigent people as they travelled, often in considerable state, through a ruler's domains and outside them. Robert II of Artois was particularly subject to both spontaneous and more contrived displays of charitable giving.[340] Just as Louis IX regularly washed the feet of paupers, so Robert of Artois did likewise on Maundy Thursday. In April 1300, the paupers whose feet were washed by the count at Hesdin received 42s. 3d.p. in alms and a further 8 l.p. on Good Friday. In Holy Week 1302, thirteen paupers came at the count's order to Ste-Mande, where they received 31s. 2d.p., and a further 48s. on Ash Wednesday.[341] Not only did rulers perform such quasi-penitential duties, but young princes such as Edward II's brothers Thomas and Edmund, aged 10 and 11 years respectively on Maundy Thursday 1312. They washed the feet of the poor at Winchester, and provided them with clothing

---

[336] E.101/376/7, fo. 5r.   [337] Ibid., fo. 5v. For the total of alms given see Table 7.

[338] E.101/376/7, fos. 99r–v.

[339] See Prestwich, 'Piety of Edward I', 4–6; W. M. Ormrod, 'The personal religion of Edward III', *Speculum*, 64 (1989), 849–77.

[340] For Robert II of Artois's charitable gifts to paupers, recluses, poor children, and indigent women during his campaign in Gascony in 1296–7 see ADPC, A.144, mm. 3–5; *CR* iii, nos. 30229, 30239–40, 30241, 30245, 30222, 30231, 30257. See also Fig. 15.

[341] ADPC, A.162, fo. 19v; A.178, fo. 30v.

and footwear at a cost of 4 l. 15s. 8d.[342] When members of a ruling family journeyed over longer distances, often through the territories of other rulers, their alms-giving could become very frequent. In May 1332, Edward III's sister Eleanor travelled with an impressive entourage from London to Nijmegen for her marriage to Reinhoud, count of Guelders.[343] At Dover, on 5 May, just before she set sail, she gave oblations of 1d. each to twenty-four paupers who sought her alms, and also gave a 'special' gift to a hermit there of 6s. 8d.[344] On the other side of the English channel, another group—of forty paupers—met her as she disembarked at Sluys on 10 May, each receiving the same sum of 1d.[345] Such offerings may well have been associated with prayers for a safe crossing and thanksgiving for it. They clearly required some degree of preparation and planning— the role of the almoner was crucial here—and we know that Eleanor's alms were distributed from a silver *olla* (pot) for which a case, covered in black leather, was supplied by John le Hanaper of Woodstreet in London before her departure for Guelders at a cost of 6s. 8d.[346] For less formal and solemn distributions, two buckets (*bukettorum*) were supplied by her almoner, and *magni denarii* (alms pennies, or maundy money) were also struck for her oblations. Although she was now to be set over a foreign court, Eleanor observed some English customs—she gave five gold Florentine florins in oblation 'on the day when she went to church with her candle, after the solemnization of her marriage, according to the English use . . . in the castle chapel at Nijmegen' (*die quo ipsa ivit ad ecclesiam cum candela sua post solempnitatem nupciarum secundum modum Anglie . . . in capella Castri de Novi Magi*).[347]

The celebration of marriages in a courtly setting differed only in scale from those of other members of the social aristocracy. As we shall see later, royal and princely wedding festivities were accompanied by lavish entertainments in which music played an important part. But the nuptial ceremony itself was also marked by rituals which were not strictly liturgical. The custom of throwing coins at the entrance or threshold of the church was well-established. This was a literally open-handed means of distributing alms and largesse. In January 1297, a marriage ceremony took place when the English court was at Ipswich for the marriage of

---

[342] E.101/374/19, fo. 3r.
[343] E.101/386/7, printed by E. W. Safford in *Archaeologia*, 77 (1928), 111–40; see Tables 11–13 for her gifts.
[344] E.101/386/7, fo. 2r.   [345] Ibid., fo. 2v.
[346] Ibid., fo. 3r.   [347] Ibid., fo. 2v.

Edward I's daughter Elizabeth to John I, count of Holland.[348] A payment
was made from the king's wardrobe of coin (*specie*) 'both placed on the
book as well as thrown over the men standing at the porch at the entrance
to the church of the same priory where lord Thomas de Multon espoused
the said Eleanor with a ring'.[349] (Thomas de Multon, knight, had shortly
before been married to Eleanor de Burgh in the priory church of St Peter
at Ipswich.) A similar custom was followed at the wedding of John of
Holland and Elizabeth—but, as befitted the status of the couple, the sum
given was 3 l. rather than 2 l. 0s. 10d. Further oblations followed—12s.
for offerings at the nuptial mass and other sums to friars on the 8 January
'on which day lady Elizabeth . . . was given in wedlock'.[350] It seems that
the practice of throwing coins was a normal marriage custom, and on 1
November 1307 (All Saints) Edward II received the relatively large sum
of 7 l. 10s. 6d. in coin at Berkhamstead which was to be thrown 'in the
porch of the church over the heads of lord Peter [that is, Piers Gaveston,
the king's favourite] and his wife . . . at their entrance into the said
church'.[351] In this instance, the favourite was clearly being treated in a
princely fashion.

Among the rituals which marked the passage of time, linked to the
liturgical calendar, one recurrent practice at the English court took place
on Easter Monday. It was the custom for the queen's ladies and *damoiselles*
to surprise the king in his bedchamber and fine him for a breach of his
own (the king's) peace.[352] The origins of the custom are obscure, but may
lie in pagan tradition, associated with springtime cults. It was certainly
in regular use under Edward I and Edward II. On Easter Monday 1290,
for example, Edward I was taken from his bed and fined by seven ladies
and *damoiselles* of the queen's chamber; a substantial sum of 14 l. was paid
on the king's behalf by Hugh de Cerne, an esquire of John de Weston,
steward of the household.[353] Other instances of the king being put in his
own mercy and fined are singularly rare. But there was one occasion
on which Edward I was himself fined and which possessed no ludic or

---

[348] For the marriages see Prestwich, *Edward I*, 128–9, 317, and above, pp. 143–4. Also
Rymer, *Foedera*, i, II. 658, 853. See also Appendix V (a) for her father's gift of plate to John.

[349] BL, Add. MS 7965, fo. 6v: 7 Jan. 1297.   [350] Ibid., fos. 6v–7r.

[351] E.101/373/15, fo. 22r: 1 Nov. 1307; Chaplais, *Piers Gaveston*, 34.

[352] See Prestwich, *Edward I*, 111; Chaplais, *Piers Gaveston*, 8; for the possible origins of
the custom see C. Hole, *Easter and its Customs* (London, 1961), 52–3.

[353] C.47/4/5, m. 45v: payment to 'Domine de camera Regine' who 'ceperunt dominum
Regem in lecto suo in crastino Pasche, et ipsum fecerunt finire versus eas pro pace Regis':
15 May 1290. Also see the references cited in Chaplais, *Piers Gaveston*, 9 nn. 18–20.

playful character. At the wedding festivities of another of his daughters—Margaret—with John of Brabant, in July 1290, the king hit John de Blaundyn, a squire in the prior of Beaumont's household, with a rod (*virga*) and was fined 13 l. 6s. 8d. so that amends could be made. We do not know the reasons for the assault, but the squire's name may suggest a Netherlandish origin (?Blandijn).[354] The marriages of his daughters were evidently of considerable personal concern to Edward and such behaviour could well have been related to sudden surges of anger in the heat of an emotional moment.[355]

Other rites of passage, such as funerals and burials, took place as the court moved around, in many churches and burial-places. The court chapel no doubt performed its liturgical services on behalf of the deceased, but the wishes of testators often specified particular locations for their obsequies, or masses and prayers to be offered by particular kinds of religious foundation or order. When the king died, however, the full panoply of funeral and burial ritual was unfurled. We know that Edward I was buried at Westminster in a very plain and austere tomb, without any effigy, but his *exequiae*, or funeral rites, were not simple.[356] Edward died on 7 July 1307, campaigning to his last breath against the Scots, and his body lay in state at Burgh-on-Sands, many hundreds of miles from Westminster.[357] It was the duty of the seneschal and treasurer of the king's household to devise the appropriate accoutrements for the king's body.[358] These included banners, pennons, and crests, and the seneschal and treasurer bought red cendal at Carlisle, and *or file pour ses armes batre* ['gold thread with which to work his [heraldic] arms']. A team of forty artisans worked for one week on the gold and cloth required. Edward's body was then transported to his manor of Blyth (Northants) for his

---

[354] C.47/4/5, fo. 47v: 'pro emendacione quasi facta pro delicto Regis versus eundem scutiferum de dono Regis'.

[355] See P. Chaplais, 'Some private letters of Edward I', *EHR* 77 (1962), 79–80.

[356] See P. Binski and J. Blair, 'The tomb of Edward I and early London brass production', *Transactions of the Monumental Brass Society*, 14 (1988), 234–40. For other, near-contemporary, austere royal tombs see J. Gardner, 'The Cosmati at Westminster: some Anglo-Italian reflexions', in J. Garms and A. M. Romanini (eds.), *Skulptur und Grabmal des Spätmittelalters in Rom und Italien* (Vienna, 1990), 212–15.

[357] See Prestwich, *Edward I*, 556–8.

[358] E.101/373/8: 'Ce sunt les parceles qui touchent Elys de Wodeberes, tailleur, et Thomas Cokerel, pur les armes le Roy Edward . . . les queux furent devises par le seneschal et le tresor[ier] que les le deveroyent faire dement[er]s que le corps i eust a Bourgh' sur Sablonu, la ou nostre dit seignour morust.'

exequiae, for which large quantities of wax (totalling 838 lb.) were bought by the wardrobe in order to make candles to burn around the corpse as it rested there.[359] On its journey south, the cortège, attended by the court, reached Nottingham on 7 August, where cloths of gold from St Botolph's fair were placed over the body. Such practices were repeated, on a less lavish scale, for members of the household—their funerals and burials were normally at the king's expense. Hence the costs of the obsequies of Walter de Beauchamp, knight, seneschal of the king's household (1298–1303) were borne by the wardrobe.[360] They are representative of the kind of rituals which accompanied the passing of a high-ranking member of the household. A hearse (*hercie*) was made to support the 300 candles placed around and over the body; two horses were obtained to bear the deceased's arms before his body; and marble was bought to provide the tomb. The bells of the city of London tolled, as was the city's custom, again at the wardrobe's expense.[361] Similar outlay was incurred in July 1320 for the funeral and burial expenses of John de Knokyn by Robert de Driffield, Edward II's confessor, including a 'marble stone and its working', three cloths of gold, and sums paid for the tolling of bells throughout the city of London.[362] The burial of this household member was attended by no less than 157 friars of various orders, all of whom received alms from the wardrobe for their services. Given the normal costs of this rite of passage, members of the household—and their families and executors—were certainly privileged in this respect.

The funeral ceremonies of princes and nobles from the latter part of the fourteenth century are well known and often remarked upon for their chivalric and heraldic nature.[363] Yet earlier instances may be found. The Dampierre predecessors of Louis de Male (d.1384)—whose obsequies were recorded in detail and copied in many chivalric and heraldic miscellanies—elected to be accompanied to their last resting places by the apparatus of war and tournament. Thus Guy de Dampierre, in his testament and its codicil (15 April 1299 and 4 May 1304), chose to be buried in the abbey of Beaulieu near Pettegem, and stated:

si doins au liu devant dit [Beaulieu] men plus riche destrier tout couviert de mes millieurs couvertures de fier, et toutes mes milleurs armeures de wiere,

---

[359] E.101/373/8; E.101/373/9 for purchases of wax.   [360] E.101/507/4.
[361] Ibid., m. iv.
[362] E.101/377/19: 'ad excitandum populum ut orarent pro anima defuncti'.
[363] See Vale, *War and Chivalry*, 88–95.

et quanque il affiert au cors dun chevalier armer pour mener et chevauchier, la endroit devant men cors quant on me portera a le sepulture.[364]

[thus I give to the aforesaid place [Beaulieu] my richest warhorse, all covered with my best horse armour, and all my best weapons of war, and whatever is necessary to arm a knight to lead and ride it, going before my body when I shall be taken for burial.]

The instruction that his best warhorse should be led before his body in the funeral procession, fully equipped and armoured, was echoed by his son's testamentary request in September 1322 that 200 l.p. should be allowed for

loffrande des chevax et des armures que on menra devant mon corps et que on offera ou lieu et au jour de me sepulture et que ce soit a lordenance et devise de mes testamenteurs . . . tout ce qui sera entour mon corps au jour et au lieu de me sepulture, soit en dras dor, en chierges, ou en autres choses, excepte les chevax et les armures, demeure au lieu la ou mes corps sera ensevelis.[365]

[the offering of horses and equipment that shall be carried before my body, and that will be offered in the place and on the day of my burial, shall be at the order and devising of my executors . . . all that shall be around my body on the day and at the place of my burial, whether cloth of gold, torches, or other items, except for the horses and the equipment, shall remain in the place where my body shall be interred.]

The horse and the armour of his father's will has now become plural, and Robert de Béthune's will represents a further step along the road towards the more elaborate heraldic funerals of the later fourteenth and fifteenth centuries.[366] We can get a glimpse of what was provided from a surviving inventory of the dead count's goods, dated 27 September 1322.[367] These included two tournament saddles for the obsequies, and four banneret's saddles (*seles de baniere*); four sets of gilded reins for warhorses (*grans chevaus*); one saddle with reins and bridle for war; and horse-trappers of velvet, with the heraldic arms of Flanders, to put over the horse-armour. Four banners of the count's arms of diaspered gold and one 'old banner

[364] ADN, B.449, nos. 4181a and 4181b. For a useful survey of princely testaments from the southern Low Countries, 1195–1441, see P. Godding, 'Le testament princier dans les Pays-Bas méridionaux (12ᵉ–15ᵉ siècles): acte privé et instrument politique', *TRG* 64 (1993), 217–35.

[365] ADN, B.448, no. 5473: 5 Sept. 1322.

[366] See Vale, *War and Chivalry*, 89–93; for one of the most lavish of these ceremonies see A. F. Sutton, L. Visser-Fuchs, and P. W. Hammond, *The Reburial of Richard, Duke of York, 21–30 July 1476* (London, 1996), 1–10.

[367] ADN, B.3231, no. 5475; *Documents*, i. 238–48.

batue dor' completed the funeral apparatus. It therefore appears that four warhorses, ridden by knights bearing the count's banners, and two tournament horses, made up the military and heraldic equipment needed for the funeral. The multiple offerings of horses, weapons, and heraldic achievements at the funeral of Louis de Male in 1384 thus had sound precedent.[368]

From the second half of the thirteenth century onwards, as in so many other areas of aristocratic life, the funeral ceremony was to become increasingly elaborate and subject to the demands of heraldic and chivalric display.[369] Beginning among the higher echelons of noble society, including the court elites, such practices soon filtered down to the middle and lower ranks. Although excessive pomp—and, in some instances, any pomp at all—could always be renounced and forbidden by testators, the more elaborate later medieval practices profoundly influenced subsequent developments. In some regions, these customs survived for a very long time. The evidence from England in the sixteenth and early seventeenth centuries is clear: the heralds had gained control of the funeral rites of both nobility and gentry and, although the arms and achievements carried in procession were now specially made for that occasion, their symbolic purpose remained the same.[370] Later medieval rituals survived, in the most exaggerated and theatrical form, in parts of central and eastern Europe. In Poland they flourished well into the eighteenth century. Such was the dramatic character of Polish mourning that an *archimimus*, representing the deceased, not only rode into the church but contrived to fall off the horse beside the catafalque, thus symbolizing the mortality of the dead nobleman.[371] Weapons, banners, rods of office,

[368] See AGR, CC.100, fos. 4r–7v; BR, MS 16381–90, fos. 1r–9v; and the edition of one version of the account printed in L. van Praet, *Recherches sur Louis de Bruges* (Paris, 1831), 257–9.

[369] See M. Vale, 'A Burgundian funeral ceremony: Olivier de La Marche and the obsequies of Adolf of Cleves, Lord of Ravenstein', *EHR* 111 (1996), 920–38.

[370] See R. Marks and A. Payne (eds.), *British Heraldry: From its Origins to c.1800* (London, British Museum, 1978), 44–5 and cat. no. 80 for the achievements borne in the funeral procession of Queen Elizabeth I (1603). See also *Herald's Commemorative Exhibition, 1484–1934: Enlarged and Illustrated Catalogue* (2nd edn., London, 1970), 31–2, 65, 78–9, and plate XV. For earlier examples of helms hung over the tombs of knights and nobles see J. S. Gardner, *Armour in England* (London, 1898), 59–65, figs. 22–4, 26.

[371] See M. Bogucka, *The Lost World of the 'Sarmatians'* (Warsaw, 1996), 85–6 and fig. 28, showing the development of the later medieval hearse into the *Castrum Doloris* of the 18th century. Also J. Chroscicki, *Pompa funebris* (Warsaw, 1974), 141–56. For the *castrum doloris* or *chapelle ardente* used in funeral ceremonies in the later Middle Ages see P. van Dael, 'Wegwerparchitectuur: Het castrum doloris in de geschiedenis', *Kunstlicht*, 9 (1983), 22–8.

and heraldic achievements were not merely presented in the church, but ritually broken or torn. A French visitor to Poland in the mid-seventeenth century could have been describing later medieval funerary rituals when he wrote:

In Poland funerals are celebrated with great pomp, as festivities rather for the living than for the dead. The corpse in the highly ornate coffin is put on a bier, drawn by six horses in black cloth. The coffin is covered by a large velvet pall adorned with a cross of red satin. Six or more servants, dressed in deep mourning, hold the edges of the pall. The bier is preceded by priests, monks and other people carrying burning wax candles. Three riders on large black horses carry the weapons of the deceased: his sword, his lance, his spear. The procession proceeds very slowly and arrives at the church only after many hours. After the liturgical ceremony the horsemen ride into the church to break the weapons of the deceased on his coffin . . .[372]

The theatrical dimension to the liturgy—which had always been present to a greater or lesser degree—was thus extended, elaborated, and formalized during the later Middle Ages to encompass and embody commemorative practices rooted in the secular world. Yet there were other manifestations of this tendency besides the rise of heraldic and chivalric display at the funeral ceremony.

As we have seen, the feast days of the liturgical calendar provided occasions for secular solemnities and festivities—crown-wearings, 'full' courts, feasts—in the courts and households of the great.[373] These might involve dramatic and musical performances, normally of a secular kind. But the liturgy had also its own drama, and what were in effect theatrical performances were contained within it. We can take one example. The feast of St Nicholas, bishop of Myra (6 December) was traditionally an occasion for celebrations which, in part, subverted (or rather, inverted) the natural order of things.[374] The miracles performed by St Nicholas, such as his resuscitation of the three boys, made him the natural patron saint of children. The custom of appointing a boy bishop (*episcopus*

---

[372] *Cudzoziemcy o Polsce: Relacie i opinie*, ed. J. Gintel (Krakow, 1971), i. 326, cited in Bogucka, *Lost World*, 48–9.

[373] See above, pp. 28, 32–3.

[374] The life of St Nicholas is found in J. de Voragine, *La Légende Dorée*, tr. and ed. T. de Wyzewa (Paris, 1910), 18–27; see also D. Attwater, *A Dictionary of Saints* (Harmondsworth, 1965), 250–1. For the liturgical celebration of his feast day see Bishop, *Liturgica Historica*, 236–40. For anthropological studies of inversion rituals and of 'transgressive hybridity' see P. Stallybrass and A. White, *The Politics and Poetics of Transgression* (New York, 1986), and M. Bakhtin, *Rabelais and his World* (Bloomington, Ind., 1984).

puerorum) on the feast of St Nicholas was well established by the later Middle Ages. It was regularly observed at princely courts and in court chapels. In December 1294, for example, Edward I's wardrobe was at Chester, where a livery of cloth of gold was issued on the king's order for the making of 'an episcopal choir cope for the service of boys (*servicio puerorum*) in the same town as long as it shall last'.[375] The arrival of two young male children in Edward's household, from his second marriage to Margaret of France, made provision for the celebration of St Nicholas's day all the more necessary.

In December 1303, the two boys—Thomas of Brotherton and Edmund of Woodstock—were at Windsor, where they witnessed a boy performing the office of bishop in the castle chapel on St Nicholas's day. The boy, accompanied by John of London, constable of the castle, then came 'with his companions, singing a canticle', to the boys' chamber, where they received alms.[376] Thomas and Edmund were aged 2 and 3 years respectively. The pattern was repeated in following years: in December 1305, the boy who played the bishop's part was named. William de Clere performed the role at the vigil and on the day of St Nicholas in the boys' chapel at Windsor and received the same sum in alms (5s.) as previously given.[377] When they had reached the ages of 9 and 10, the custom continued—on 6 December 1311, at Stroguil castle in Scotland, they witnessed the boy bishop and his 'accomplices' (*cum complicibus suis*) performing the office and singing a canticle in the castle chapel.[378] Yet the celebration and enactment of the story of St Nicholas at court was not confined to occasions upon which royal children were present. On 6 December 1314 a boy named Robert, son of Geoffrey Tyeis of Edenstowe, was boy bishop in Edward II's and Queen Isabella's chapel, and received alms of 40s. through the hands of Robert de Upton, chaplain of the parish there.[379]

The practice was observed at other courts. The court of Hainault celebrated the feast of St Nicholas, sometimes on behalf of its younger members. On 6 December 1332, William, son of count William III, received alms to give to the 'clerchons de St-Nycolai' and gifts were also

[375] E.36/202, p. 106: 6 Dec. 1294. The cloth was supplied by the king's almoner.
[376] E.101/366/15, m. 1r: 'Cuidam puero . . . ministranti officium episcopi die Sancti Nicolai . . . psallenti unum canticum in honore dicti sancti in camera ipsorum filiorum' (6 Dec. 1303).
[377] E.101/368/12, fo. 2r: 6 Dec. 1305.
[378] E.101/374/19, fo. 3r: alms of 3s.: 6 Dec. 1311.
[379] E.101/376/7, fo. 41r: 6 Dec. 1314.

made to them on 8 November 1332 (at Maubeuge) and 9 November 1333 (at Mons), when 5s. 5d. was put into William's purse 'to give to the clerks of St Nicholas' (*a donner as clers de St-Nycolai*).[380] Perhaps these related to the celebration of St Nicholas's legendary arrival in north-west Europe. But the cult was clearly firmly established, providing occasions and opportunities for both liturgical (and less formal) commemoration and enactment of stories and episodes from the saint's life. The court chapel, in this as in other ways, served as a focus for such activity and, by reason of its functions in the receipt and distribution of alms, enabled such observances to take place in a court context.

[380] See *De rekeningen*, ed. Smit, i. 637, 639, 678.

Chapter 6

ART AT COURT: INVESTMENT IN CULTURE?

1. Court art and court style

With the increasing development of the French royal court into a sharply distinguished social elite formation, court society developed a special culture as a natural part of its special social existence. Early forms of this elite culture in gestures, speech, love-making and taste . . . had existed not only at royal courts but even, and especially, at the courts of territorial lords as early as the Middle Ages.[1]

Norbert Elias's admission that the 'elite culture' of courts—albeit in an 'early form'—existed before the sixteenth and seventeenth centuries is noteworthy. The close correlation which he perceived between the rise of a court society and culture, on one hand, and the centralized state on the other, cannot therefore be fully sustained. If the courts of medieval 'territorial lords' witnessed the development of an elite court culture, quite independently of the rise of the state, other explanations for its emergence are necessary. Elias sketched out a possible blueprint for further analysis when he wrote that 'if one took the trouble, one could trace precisely how what may be called "court culture" gradually grows out of the social field as a distinct elite formation'.[2] Some attempts have subsequently been made to take the question further, and art historians such as Martin Warnke have argued for the development of a specifically 'court' art, freed from market constraints, which made later medieval and Renaissance courts havens of artistic innovation and change.[3] Court culture expressed itself through court art, which was 'liberated' from

---

[1] Elias, *The Court Society*, 186.   [2] Ibid. 187.
[3] M. Warnke, *The Court Artist: On the Ancestry of the Modern Artist*, tr. D. McLintock (Cambridge and Paris, 1993), 2–5.

civic and guild restrictions and which was not subject to normal market conditions.[4]

An eighteenth-century analogy from the world of another art form—music—may be apposite here. It could be argued, for example, that the innovatory symphonic and other forms developed by Josef Haydn in the service of Count Miklos Esterhazy were a product of the freedom allowed to the court composer by an enlightened patron.[5] The Viennese—or any other—public would not, it is claimed, have tolerated such *avant-garde* tendencies. Nor, indeed, it could be objected, would many princely patrons, less 'enlightened' than Esterhazy. The contrast between court and other forms of patronage can clearly be overdrawn. There was no obvious reason why originality, experiment, and innovation should not have been possible with sponsorship from an equally, if not more, enlightened patrician or upper bourgeois patron. The analogy also breaks down when applied to a later medieval context. To isolate the court completely from the rest of society, especially from urban society, makes little sense in the later thirteenth and fourteenth centuries.[6] Westminster, Paris, Prague, Brussels, even Windsor, Hesdin, or Male—the 'seats' of later medieval courts—were not as physically remote from urban life as the palace of Esterhaza (Fertod) in the Transdanubian plain. But the shadow of Louis XIV's Versailles, or Frederick the Great's Potsdam, lies heavily over many analyses of 'court culture' and the 'court artist'.[7] A more convincing point of view has recently been advanced, however, represented by such work as that of T. Da Costa Kaufmann on the cultural history of central and eastern Europe.[8] Although courts could certainly act as

[4] Warnke, *The Court Artist*, 2–3.

[5] See H. C. Robbins Landon, *Haydn: Chronicle and Works*, ii. *Haydn at Eszterhaza, 1766–1790* (Bloomington, 1978); F. K. and M. G. Grave, *Franz Joseph Haydn: A Guide to Research* (New York and London, 1990), 6–9; for comparisons with Mozart's situation see R. V. Dawson, 'Haydn and Mozart', *The Musical Quarterly*, 16 (1930), 498–509.

[6] See above, pp. 137–40.

[7] See Elias, *The Court Society*, 35–6, 146–213; Warnke, *The Court Artist*, 4–9. The influence of Versailles and Potsdam seems to have informed the views expressed (by A. G. Dickens) in A. G. Dickens (ed.), *The Courts of Europe: Politics, Patronage and Royalty, 1400–1800* (London, 1977), 7: 'A court did not serve merely as the home and governmental headquarters of a ruler', but 'as the nucleus of a ruling class, as a planned monumental environment, as a prime focus of culture . . . A court naturally tried to become a permanent pageant . . .' For another, more recent view, which stresses the diversity of 'courtly' influences on culture—and of courts themselves—see J. Adamson, 'The making of the ancien-régime court, 1500–1700', in id. (ed.), *The Princely Courts of Europe*, esp. 7–10.

[8] T. Da Costa Kaufmann, *Court, Cloister and City: The Art and Culture of Central Europe, 1450–1800* (London, 1995), esp. 51–73.

initiators of stylistic and other change, they were not alone in this respect. By adopting a socio-political interpretation, that sees 'high' culture as a product of commissions and purchases not merely by the courts, but by the higher clergy and the *haute bourgeoisie*, a more plausible explanation of artistic and stylistic innovation becomes possible. 'High-status' patronage was thus not confined to the courts and their inmates—clerical and civic activity were an essential part of the infrastructure of 'high' culture and none of these spheres of patronage were, in turn, entirely isolated from the beliefs and concerns of 'low' culture (for example, cults of saints, pilgrimages, and magic).[9]

Schematic oversimplification has to a certain extent dogged the study of 'court culture'. The impact of Marxism, and of politically determined and often teleological interpretations of 'court' and 'bourgeois' culture, have left their mark on many studies. For north-western Europe in the later Middle Ages, however, court art and court culture have been until recently identified almost exclusively with French culture. The rise of other vernacular languages as vehicles of literary production has often been linked to reactions against French-speaking princes and their courts.[10] This, too, as we shall see, is an oversimplified view. The historians of 'early democracies' and movements of revolt in the Low Countries also tended to stigmatize court culture as the product of foreign influences on, and intervention in, the indigenous vernacular culture of a Netherlandish-speaking populace.[11] In England, the king's court has likewise been seen as a francophone, cosmopolitan, and therefore an 'un-English' agent of cultural and artistic development.[12] Nationalist movements, with their undeniable influence upon the writing of history, have also (since the later nineteenth century) introduced assumptions and attitudes towards

[9] Kaufmann, *Court, Cloister and City*, 22–3; see also P. Cinzelbacher, 'Volkskultur und Hochkultur im Spätmittelalter', in P. C. and H. D. Muck (eds.), *Volkskultur des europäischen Spätmittelalters* (Stuttgart, 1987), 1–14.

[10] See below, pp. 283, 288–90.

[11] See H. Pirenne, *Early Democracies in the Low Countries: Urban Society and Political Conflict in the Middle Ages and the Renaissance* (New York, 1963), esp. 25–40. For some important observations from a literary point of view see F. van Oostrom, 'Middle Dutch literature at court', in Kooper (ed.), *Medieval Dutch Literature in its European Context*, 30–1, 33–5. For francophone culture at courts see below, pp. 284–8.

[12] See e.g. Genet, 'La monarchie anglaise: une image brouillée', 100–1, where Richard II is said to have been inspired by the 'French model' to 'create a court, the increasing importance of which seems precisely to have been one of the major complaints levelled against him by his enemies'. Edward IV, it is argued, was also 'inspired by the Burgundian model' (101). See also above, pp. 17–18.

cultural developments that make little or no sense in later medieval terms.[13] The desire to differentiate artistic production by means of its supposed 'Englishness', 'Dutchness', or 'Frenchness' is more often than not doomed to fail. Courts were cosmopolitan places, accustomed to receiving a constant stream of envoys, guests, visitors, entertainers and performers of all kinds. It would be surprising if their 'culture' did not embody and express that cosmopolitanism.

The idea of a common fund of Gothic artistic styles, drawn upon by artists of varying geographical origins, patronized by those who could afford to do so from a number of higher social and professional groups, has recently been put forward in relation to discussion of a 'court' style in the later thirteenth century. Paul Binski has argued that, during the last third of the century, both the English court and high-status patrons in Paris engaged in a 'mutual and roughly concurrent participation in a reservoir of styles'.[14] This did not imply submission or acquiescence to Paris or to some kind of French (or Capetian) cultural hegemony.[15] The difficulties of distinguishing between French, southern Netherlandish, and English provenance at this time in, for example, both manuscript illumination and panel painting, have long been recognized. William Morris, in 1902, saw the period from about 1275 to 1300 as coming 'close to the climax of illumination' when 'nothing can exceed the grace, elegance, and beauty of drawing and loveliness of colour . . . in the best-executed books'.[16] But it was, he claimed, impossible to identify 'English' or 'French' work at this time. Morris wrote:

As to relations between England and France, it must be said that, although there is a difference between them, it is somewhat subtle, and may be put thus: of some books you may say, This is French; of others, this is English; but of the greater part you can say nothing more than, This belongs to the French-English School. Of those that can be differentiated with something like certainty, the French excel specially in a dainty and orderly elegance, the English especially in a love of life and nature, and there is more of rude humour in them than in their French contemporaries, but he must be at once a fastidious and an absolute man who could say the French is better than the English, or the English than the French.[17]

[13] See T. F. Tout, *France and England: Their Relations in the Middle Ages and Now* (Manchester and London, 1922), 1–6, 35–6, 157–62.

[14] Binski, *Westminster Abbey*, 165–6, 171–4.   [15] See below, pp. 251–2, 288.

[16] W. Morris, *Some Notes on the Illuminated Books of the Middle Ages* (New Rochelle, 1902), 3–4.

[17] Ibid. 4.

Yet, fastidious and absolute or not, art historians have devoted considerable energy to attempting to make such distinctions and, in many
respects, rightly so. But it is evident from such artefacts as the Arundel,
Alfonso, Queen Mary, and Tenison psalters, or the Douce Apocalypse,
that many English works share common features with contemporary
French and southern Netherlandish production.[18] An even more striking
case of mutual interaction can be found in the breviary of Renaud de Bar,
bishop of Metz.[19] Much the same can be said for both architecture
and panel painting. Westminster abbey owed much to both Rheims and
Amiens, and the Westminster retable has clear French exemplars behind
it (Pls. 9a, 9b, 30).[20] Such evidence points up the essential artificiality
behind any attempt to identify 'national' schools of painting or 'national'
styles during this period. It has been argued that court art—that is, the art
and artefacts produced for high-status patrons in the orbit, ambiance,
or milieu of a court—was in essence eclectic in its nature, drawing upon a
multiplicity of forms, styles, and sources. The implications of this notion
are worth pursuing.

'Eclecticism rather than singularity of outlook'—such is the conclusion
reached by a recent study of patronage in and around the English court
between 1240 and 1400.[21] Diverse, atomized, even 'federal' in character,
high-status patronage and its audience, it is argued, did not promote
anything which could meaningfully be called a 'court style'.[22] This may
well be true, but it does not necessarily follow that because there was no
'unified court culture' a common culture might not be shared by royal
and princely courts during this period.[23] Eclecticism of styles and diversity of taste were not incompatible with a broadly shared acceptance of
cultural norms, in which the reception and adaptation of French Gothic

[18] Binski, *The Painted Chamber*, 81–2, 86–90.

[19] See P. M. de Winter, 'Une réalisation exceptionnelle d'enlumineurs français et
anglais vers 1300: le bréviaire de Renaud de Bar, évêque de Metz', *Actes du 103ᵉ Congrès
National des Sociétés Savantes (1978)* (Paris, 1980), 27–62. For relations between England
and Bar, see above, pp. 211–13.

[20] Binski, *Westminster Abbey*, 40–3, 160–1.

[21] Ibid. 44, and *The Painted Chamber*, 105–12.

[22] Cf. Branner, *St Louis and the Court Style*, 112; J. Bony, *The English Decorated Style:
Gothic Architecture Transformed* (Oxford, 1979), 2–3; for critiques see H. M. Colvin, 'The
"court style" in medieval English architecture: a review' in V. J. Scattergood and J. W.
Sherborne (eds.), *English Court Culture in the Later Middle Ages* (London, 1983), 129–40;
Binski, *Westminster Abbey*, pp. vii, 44–51.

[23] Cf. P. Brieger et al. (eds.), *Art and the Courts: France and England from 1259 to 1328*, 2
vols. (Ottawa, 1972), i. 8–21; Vale, *Origins of the Hundred Years War*, 21–47.

styles in all art forms, together with an appreciation of their qualities and characteristics, provided a common norm. There may well not have been a unitary court style, but that did not preclude the existence of a court culture. The art produced in and around courts could thus be 'progressive' or 'atavistic', modernizing or archaic, according to the taste, preoccupations, and predilections of individual patrons within that milieu.[24] It has rightly been said that 'the social character of the court was itself federal, its constituents being the households of the ruling dynasty and the thoroughly mobile population of the court and administration at large', and this may explain why courts could promote 'several aesthetics'.[25] Later, anachronistic assumptions about an equation between royal or princely power and an 'official', centrally determined and dictated court art, are out of place in this setting.[26] Beyond the confines of the later medieval court, moreover, networks of patronage and influence could operate to spread these diverse styles of painting, tomb sculpture, or modes of building—the clerical network of curial and civil servant bishops, king's clerks and envoys, or the secular network formed by members of the household—king's knights and squires—which extended 'court' and metropolitan styles into the countryside.[27] Yet, even if we accept this degree of pluralism and co-existence of styles and aesthetics within a court milieu, can any distinguishing features of 'court art' be identified?

[24] See Warnke, *The Court Artist*, 2–3; Binski, *Westminster Abbey*, 9.

[25] Binski, *Westminster Abbey*, 45. This 'thoroughly mobile population' consisted of 'the constituent members of the royal family, the queen, the royal children, the favourites, the highly placed and frequently clerical administrators, and the floating population of adherents'. The secular officers and members of the household, and the ever-present guests and visitors, should also be included.

[26] See A. Hauser, *The Social History of Art*, ii. *Renaissance, Mannerism and Baroque* (London, 1962), 174–9, 186–9.

[27] For architecture, see Colvin, 'The "court style" in medieval English architecture', esp. 130–9; for the clergy see B. Smalley, *English Friars and Antiquity in the Early Fourteenth Century* (Oxford, 1960), 70–84; for the extension of the 'Composed London Style' in tomb sculpture into the countryside through tomb sculpture during the later thirteenth century, see H. A. Tummers, *Early Secular Effigies in England: The Thirteenth Century* (Leiden, 1980), 86–95. See also L. Stone, *Sculpture in Britain: The Middle Ages* (Harmondsworth, 1955), 133–5, and esp. 141–9, 159–67. For affinities between such artefacts as the monumental brass of Sir Hugh Hastings (d.1347), steward of Queen Philippa's household, at Elsing, Norfolk, and Westminster tombs such as that of Aymer de Valence (d.1324) see J. Page-Phillips (ed.), *Witness in Brass* (Victoria and Albert Museum, London, 1987), 25, cat. no. 123. See also, for the Hastings brass, P. Binski, 'The Coronation of the Virgin on the Hastings brass at Elsing, Norfolk', *Journal of the Church Monuments Society*, 1 (1985), 1–9, where the representation of the Coronation of the Virgin on the brass is related to the Parisian style of Jean Pucelle (d.1334).

Recent studies of the Sienese painter Simone Martini (d.1344) have given rise to reconsideration of the question. Simone was in close contact with northern art, partly as a result of his residence at the papal court at Avignon (1334/5–44).[28] Hence Italian reactions and responses to modes and idioms deriving from northern European courts are, it is argued, highly important as determinants of Simone's style (Pls. 29a, 29b).[29] This has led to the somewhat paradoxical observation that 'Simone, who spent most of his working life in republican Siena, was in a curious way, a court artist *par excellence*'.[30] If courts promoted 'several aesthetics' then the appreciation of, and demand for, works expressing those qualities was obviously not confined to a 'courtly' audience or milieu. Simone, it has been argued, 'brought to the developing Gothic style in Italy an appreciation of the obvious features of court art—finesse, dexterity in the handling of detail, an appreciation of secular pomp and grandeur, an eye for costume and fashion and, on occasion, ability as a painter of heraldry and portraits (Pls. 29a, 29b)'.[31] These are indeed all qualities which we can perceive in the extant works of art associated with princely patrons or those who served them. From Simone's St Louis of Toulouse altarpiece for Robert of Anjou (*c*.1317) to Richard II of England's Wilton Diptych (*c*.1394–6), a series of works clearly displays many of these qualities.

A further characteristic discernible in court art, from the later thirteenth century onwards, was the degree to which artifice began to be employed to achieve more naturalistic effects. The more representational idioms found in both painting and sculpture of the later thirteenth and early fourteenth centuries demanded skills from the artist in which *ars superbat materiam* (artifice conquers the material). For example, more animated and 'life-like' freestone and alabaster effigies (Pls. 23–7); altarpieces and other devotional artefacts in which the display of precious stones and metals began to be subordinated to the expressive (and impressive) depiction of sacred events, and the figurative representation of doctrines; and manuscripts in which the border decoration began to

---

[28] A. Martindale, *Simone Martini: Complete Edition* (Oxford, 1988), 45.

[29] J. Stubblebine, 'French Gothic elements in Simone Martini's *Maesta*', *Gesta*, 29 (1990), 139–52; Martindale, *Simone Martini*, 9–13, 65–8.

[30] A. Martindale, *Gothic Art* (London, 1967), 200: 'His work was certainly popular outside Tuscany, and it may be safely assumed that, for its grace and elegance, it would have been acceptable in Paris.'

[31] Loc. cit. For affinities between Simone's painting, the Westminster retable, and the decorative features of the tomb of Edmund of Lancaster (d.1296) at Westminster see Martindale, *Simone Martini*, 65–6 and also Binski, *The Painted Chamber*, 56–63.

include more 'realistic', lively images of the natural world—all put a premium upon creative talent and the mastery of materials (frontispiece, Pls. 4, 32).[32] In an English context, it has been concluded (with especial reference to the Westminster retable of *c.*1290) that 'artifice of this character was obviously a rare commodity, and since such methods (for example, *aurum battutum* hemlines) appear also to have been used in the Westminster Palace's wall-paintings, we may legitimately think of them as courtly' (Pl. 30).[33] Named artists, many of whom could work in a number of different media, such as Edward Fitz Odo or Edward of Westminster under Henry III, or Michael of Canterbury, Adam the Goldsmith, William Torel, or Alexander of Abingdon under Edward I, received the patronage of the great, both ecclesiastical and secular.[34] It can also be argued that the appearance of greater subtlety of tonal gradation in panel painting, a liking for shiny, highly reflective surfaces (sometimes achieved by the employment of non-precious stones) on altarpieces, and the application of polychrome decoration to render sculptures and tomb effigies more life-like, became hallmarks of court art (Pls. 23, 24, 25). Appreciation of such qualities was shared by high-status patrons in England, France, and the Low Countries, as both surviving works and documentary sources indicate. Yet, within this broader frame, diversity and eclecticism held sway.

As we shall see, modern, post-Enlightenment ideas of 'high' art are not always applicable to the art forms, idioms, and modes of representation with which we have to deal during this period. Eclecticism was a natural consequence of the functions of the visual and applied arts and of the needs which they met. Court art served a number of purposes: first, the imperatives of display, whereby formal models and exemplars were adapted to meet specific requirements—political, ideological, or dynastic —induced rulers and those who served them to patronize a broad spectrum of art forms.[35] Secondly, later medieval princes and their agents did

[32] See Tummers, *Early Secular Effigies*, 114–17; Stone, *Sculpture in Britain*, 149–51; W. Sauerlander, 'Die Naumburger Stifterfiguren: Ruckblick und Fragen', in R. Hausherr and C. Vaterlein (eds.), *Die Zeit der Staufer*, Württembergisches Landesmuseum, Stuttgart, 1977), v. 169–245; L. F. Sandler, *Gothic Manuscripts 1285–1385: A Survey of Manuscripts Illuminated in the British Isles*, 2 vols. (1986), ii. 118–21, and figs. 274–8, 280, 282 for the Luttrell Psalter's (*c.*1325–35) virtuoso rendering of naturalistic effects.

[33] Binski, *Westminster Abbey*, 160; *The Painted Chamber*, 63–9, 109. For *aurum battutum* see above, p. 240: works for Edward I's *exequia* include provision of 'or file pour ses armes batre' (E.101/373/8).

[34] Binski, *Westminster Abbey*, 172.

[35] The 'aesthetic of display' and its relation to the 'contingencies of royal decorum' are ably analysed by Binski, ibid. 44–5.

not generally commission and purchase art and artefacts for art's sake alone.[36] Form was often expressive of function—the requirements of the table thus determined the style of much goldsmith's work. Devotional needs dictated the form in which wall paintings and altarpieces were created, sometimes housing tabernacles containing the sacrament, while the liturgical functions of textiles, as vestments and as altar furniture, shaped much of the embroiderer's work. Thirdly, the desire to commemorate, linked as it was to the offering of masses for the souls of the dead, infused so much of the sculpture and its integral heraldic display that one is tempted to characterize much 'court' art of this period as that of the mausoleum and necropolis.[37]

Display developed its own aesthetic but it was an essentially transient activity—it could mark rites of passage, giving meaning and significance to what were transitory events in the life of any ruling dynasty: births, baptisms, churchings of women, marriages, dubbings to knighthood, holding of 'full' or 'solemn' courts, and, perhaps above all, deaths.[38] It is no coincidence that court art, in the form of sepulchral monuments, reflected an increasing consciousness of the transience of worldly things, best expressed in such surviving sources as the epitaph on the tomb chest of Edward the Black Prince (d.1376) at Canterbury.[39] Funerary rituals also had their effect on figuration and modes of representation—hence the incorporation of figures along each side of the tomb chest from which the motif of 'weepers' or mourners was to stem.[40] Tombs such as that of Edmund of Lancaster (d.1296) (Pls. 24–6) or Aymer de Valence (d.1324)

[36] Cf. Kaufmann, *Court, Cloister and City*, 26: after the 'reception of the Renaissance' in central Europe 'art consciously became an area for social distinction, a consciously chosen site for leisure activity and self-definition'.

[37] See Colvin, *Architecture and the After-Life*, 147–51, for 'funerary fantasy' in tomb construction; E. Panofsky, *Tomb Sculpture* (New York, 1964), 149–84; Binski, *Westminster Abbey*, 112–20; E. A. Wendebourg, *Westminster Abbey als königliche Grablege zwischen 1250 und 1400* (Worms, 1986), 92–102, 125–35, 136–50.

[38] See e.g. Binski, *Westminster Abbey*, 44: 'styles and images changed freely, even radically, with the changing currents of royal mythology'.

[39] For the epitaph see *La Vie du Prince Noir by Chandos Herald*, ed. D. B. Tyson (Tübingen, 1975), 165–6 and ll. 4253–80: 'Cy ensuit la scripture fait sur la tumbe du tres noble Prince devant nomie'. Also id., 'The epitaph of Edward the Black Prince', *Medium Aevum*, 46 (1977), 98–104. For the Prince's will, giving the epitaph and funerary instructions, *Collections of All the Wills Extant of Kings and Queens of England*, ed. J. Nichols (London, 1780), 166–70.

[40] L. L. Gee, ' "Ciborium" tombs in England, 1290–1330', *Journal of the British Archaeological Association*, 3rd ser. 132 (1979), 29–41; Tummers, *Early Secular Effigies*, 29–31.

(Pl. 24) in Westminster abbey depicted the relatives and companions-in-arms of the deceased (identifiable by their heraldic achievements) as carved and/or painted figurines on the tomb chest (Pl. 26).[41] Representations of the cortège began to form around the mortal body and would soon include both kinswomen as well as kinsmen, attired in mourning.[42] However 'closed' the aesthetic of some kinds of court art may have been, the canopied tomb, set either between columns or within a wall-niche, was to prove enormously influential. It may well have had its origins in the refurbishing of St-Denis under Louis IX, but it was soon to be found—in various adaptations and forms—all over north-west Europe.[43]

The need and desire to commemorate—in words as well as images—was thus a fundamental determinant of the forms taken by court art. It could take both secular and devotional form. Although the concept of *Gedechtnus* (*Gedächtnis*) or remembrance was actively promoted by the Habsburg Emperor Maximilian I (d.1519), it was not an entirely novel idea.[44] Many features of the art and literature produced for and by his itinerant court, despite their 'Renaissance' character and inspiration, would not have been out of place two hundred years earlier. Eclecticism and diversity were again dominant characteristics, and the blend of classical and medieval elements simply furthered those tendencies within court art.[45] Maximilian's tomb at Innsbruck blended these elements,

[41]   The ten knightly figures painted on the side of Edmund of Lancaster's tomb-chest at Westminster are recorded in a framed sketch, made by John Carter in July 1782, in Westminster Abbey Muniments. The figures included Edmund's male relatives and comrades such as William de Valence, William de Forz, John de Warenne, and Roger de Clifford. All stand on hillocks, holding lances with rectangular banners. See also Binski, *Westminster Abbey*, 118 and fig. 161.

[42]   Stone, *Sculpture in Britain*, 145–7, 159–60. For a general survey of the 'weepers' theme see P. Quarré, *Les Pleurants dans l'art du moyen âge en Europe* (Dijon, 1971).

[43]   See Erlande-Brandenbourg, *Le Roi est mort*, 81–4, 116–17. For the 'closed aesthetic order' represented by Westminster see Binski, *Westminster Abbey*, 51, where it is argued that its influence could only be disseminated through its 'fragmentation into component parts'—of which tomb architecture and sculpture were presumably one.

[44]   Maximilian wrote that 'He who creates no remembrance (*gedachtnus*) for himself during his lifetime has no remembrance after his death, and such a man is just forgotten with his funeral bell, and so the money I spend on remembrance is not wasted . . .' ('wer ime in seinem leben kain gedachtnus macht, der hat nach seinem tod kain gedachtnus und desselben menschen wird mit dem glockendon vergessen, und darumb so wird das gelt, so ich auf die gedechtnus ausgib, nit verloren': A. Schultz, 'Der Weisskunig', *Jahrbuch der kunsthistorischen Sammlungen des allerhöchsten Kaisershauses*, 6 (1888), 66). See also, for a general survey, J. D. Müller, *Gedechtnus: Literatur und Hofgesellschaft um Maximilian I* (Munich, 1982).

[45]   Kaufmann, *Court, Cloister and City*, 67–9.

representing his real and supposed ancestors (including King Arthur), combining an 'ancient tomb with a funeral procession' in which later medieval precedents were clearly visible.[46] The example of central and eastern Europe in the Renaissance offers further analogies with north-western Europe in the later Middle Ages. In Hungary, Bohemia, Poland, and Russia, the reception of Renaissance (above all, Italian) styles and idioms led to stylistic change, often initiated at rulers' courts.[47] But these Italianate and humanistic forms were adapted, moulded, and sometimes transformed through transmission. So it was with French Gothic idioms in the later thirteenth and fourteenth century, as they were received elsewhere in Europe including, of course, Italy.[48] In this process, the court played a significant role: the court patronage of the Plantagenets, the Luxemburgs, and the Wittelsbachs can be compared with that of the later Habsburgs or Jagiellonians.

Hence Jagiellonian court art in Poland around 1500 was highly eclectic, promoted by a dynasty with quasi-imperial attitudes, combining Gothic and Renaissance elements.[49] As king of Bohemia, moreover, the desire of Vladislav Jagiellon to commemorate his ancestors was in part spurred by a need to re-establish dynastic and cultural continuity with previous royal houses who ruled the kingdom across the breach created by the Hussite period. But east-central European courts of this period all displayed multi-national, multi-ethnic, and eclectic tendencies in their art patron-age, as in other respects.[50] In this, they were no different from some of their predecessors in other regions of Europe. If Italian Renaissance styles, modes, and fashions enjoyed international currency in the fifteenth and sixteenth centuries, then French Gothic played a similar role at an earlier period. The very notion of an 'International Gothic' style (or rather, styles) can be challenged, but it may possess a certain validity when applied to court art.[51] Yet it was never unitary nor uniform— adaptation and transformation as a result of contact with other traditions,

---

[46] See E. Egg, *Die Hofkirche in Innsbruck: Das Grabdenkmal Kaiser Maximilian I* (Innsbruck, Vienna, and Munich, 1974). Also see Kaufmann, *Court, Cloister and City*, 70–1.

[47] See J. Bialostocki, *The Art of the Renaissance in Eastern Europe* (Ithaca, NY, and Oxford, 1976), 21–3.

[48] See above, pp. 249–51. Also see Martindale, *Simone Martini*, 65–8.

[49] See Kaufmann, *Court, Cloister and City*, 59–64.

[50] Bialostocki, *The Art of the Renaissance in Eastern Europe*, 23.

[51] For some pertinent observations see Martindale, *Gothic Art*, 265: 'Many major cen-tres of art, particularly those dominated by a court, shared similarities of taste and fashion. In general terms, there was a synthesis of a figure-style originating in Paris with a command of form and structure originating in Italy . . .'

idioms, techniques, and workshop practices meant that court art remained multi-faceted and eclectic.

If a definition of court art is hard to formulate, court culture—in an aesthetic sense—is even more resistant to definition. It is probably inappropriate to look for evidence of creative originality, as some have done, or of 'enlightenment and excellence of taste in the arts and . . . the humanities' among the princes of later medieval Europe and those who made up their courts.[52] We are not yet in the world of a Frederick the Great or a Josef II. It was not part of a ruler's function to 'patronize the arts' in the sense understood by the Enlightenment and later movements.[53] The Aristotelian and Thomist concept of 'magnificence' (*megaloprepeia*) certainly informed and influenced the behaviour of later medieval rulers, prompted by their tutors and counsellors, and the formative role of works such as the *Tresor* of Brunetto Latini and the *Secreta Secretorum* cannot be neglected.[54] Yet the arts (visual, plastic, and applied) fulfilled other purposes—liturgical, devotional, didactic, decorative, and ideological. It has been concluded that one 'cannot find signs of original artistic taste consciously fostered and promoted either by Edward III or Richard II, nor evidence of royal leadership which laid the foundations for the emergence of a coherent growth of courtly taste'.[55] But such notions seem to be products of much later concepts of taste and patronage which cannot be convincingly applied to this period. As will be argued later, to identify court culture requires consideration of patterns of behaviour, styles of life, and levels of material consumption which kings and princes were both expected and able to adopt. It has as much to do with the use and functions of textiles, plate, and jewellery, the role of ritual and ceremony, and the distribution of alms and oblations, as with

---

[52] See Sherborne, 'Aspects of English court culture in the later fourteenth century', in Scattergood and Sherborne (eds.), *English Court Culture*, 7.

[53] For patronage under Josef II see *Österreich zur Zeit Kaiser Josephs II* (exhib. cat., Melk, 1980) and, for Frederick the Great and lesser rulers, A. Fauchier-Magnan, *The Small German Courts in the Eighteenth Century* (London, 1958), esp. 29–32.

[54] See *Three Prose Versions of the Secreta Secretorum*, ed. R. Steele (EETS, extra ser. 74, London, 1898); for an excellent example of a *de luxe* manuscript miscellany containing (among other works) the *Livre du Trésor*, the *Secreta Secretorum*, and (now lost) the *Gouvernement des Princes* of Giles of Rome, see BN, MS fr. 571 (c.1325–30). The manuscript appears to have been presented to the young Edward III by Philippa of Hainault, on their betrothal in 1326. See M. A. Michael, 'A manuscript wedding gift from Philippa of Hainault to Edward III', *Burl. Mag.* 127 (1985), 582–98; Sandler, *Gothic Manuscripts*, ii. 103–5, fig. 246.

[55] Sherborne, 'Aspects of English court culture', 7.

books, panel and wall paintings, music, and the other arts. 'High' art was so often an integral part of these activities that it makes little sense to consider it apart from them. Distinctions, valid for later periods, cannot convincingly be drawn between 'high' culture and more popular modes of expression at this time. Court culture was more diverse, multi-faceted, and eclectic in nature than has often been assumed. As such, it closely resembled court art.[56]

The patronage and acquisition of 'cultural' artefacts and objects in a court context was thus a facet of consumption which could carry social, political, and religious meanings. The meaningful use of those artefacts and objects was both mental and material, and could reflect the identities of the status-groups that consumed them in distinctive ways. Consumption was accompanied by investment in cultural artefacts of many kinds. But to invest implies a hope of gaining a return on that investment. It could be claimed that, at its most rudimentary, the endowment of masses, accompanied by the commissioning or purchase of altarpieces and liturgical artefacts, was a form of investment for the salvation of the soul. The return expected from investment in secular art was less easily defined and could take many forms. The functions of consumption and display in pre-industrial societies, in which art patronage played a major part, have been, of course, the subject of a number of celebrated studies. Max Weber concluded that ' "Luxury" in the sense of rejecting the purposive-rational control of consumption is, for the dominant feudal strata, nothing "superfluous": it is a means of social self-assertion'.[57] Later medieval rulers and those who served them added political to social self-assertion and, as Veblen pointed out, 'conspicuous consumption' was one means whereby rivals might be kept at bay and overawed by the display of treasure and riches in many forms.[58] The court could provide a stage, or arena, for such display. Yet the extent to which the court, as an institution, acted as an agent of patronage—let alone of innovation—in the visual and applied arts, has not been satisfactorily established for the

---

[56] See Binski, *The Painted Chamber*, 105–9, and, for the eclecticism and structures of 'court' patronage see below, p. 282; for textiles, plate, and jewellery see Appendices II, IV, V, VII (b).

[57] M. Weber, *Economy and Society: An Outline of Interpretive Sociology*, ed. G. Roth and C. Wittich, 3 vols. (New York, 1968), 1106; Elias, *The Court Society*, 37. For more recent anthropological interpretations of consumption see P. Bourdieu, *Distinction* (London, 1984); A. Appadurai (ed.), *The Social Life of Things: Commodities in Cultural Perspective* (Cambridge, 1986).

[58] See T. Veblen, *The Theory of the Leisure Class* (London, 1899), 65–78.

period with which we are concerned. It is to the forms, structures, and mechanisms of patronage that we must now turn.

2. The structures of court patronage

Studies of the rise of the artist in western culture have tended to put considerable emphasis upon the urban civilization of Renaissance Italy as the major factor responsible for far-reaching changes in both status and functions.[59] The urban context in which so many Italian artists of the fifteenth and sixteenth centuries worked was thought to both recognize and release creativity in ways unknown to the courts of rulers, especially those of northern Europe. Romantic notions of the independence of the artist, and the autonomy of his mind, fuelled by Vasari's *Lives*, prematurely dated that phenomenon to the Renaissance. The study of Florence —a republic—as a centre of artistic patronage and production dominated much art-historical writing, and the role of Italian princely courts as sources of sponsorship and support for the visual arts was relatively neglected.[60] Recent movements in scholarship have reacted against such tendencies. Martin Warnke has perhaps formulated the most thoroughgoing challenge to the thesis that the town was the primary agent of artistic innovation and change.[61] He sees the princely court, rather than the city, as a 'liberating' agent, where the artist was privileged, escaping the constraints of guild and corporate regulation, and enjoying the subventions and regular salaries which a ruler could offer.[62] The court was, he argues, an institution which both conserved and transmitted traditions, but it also initiated artistic innovation through the greater freedom offered to artists in a prince's service. The 'modern artist', we are told, thus emerged for the first time in the court culture of the Italian Renaissance. Yet the origins of patronage structures and mechanisms found in the fifteenth century and later can, Warnke admits, be traced to the mid-thirteenth century.[63]

---

[59] See A. Martindale, *The Rise of the Artist in the Middle Ages and the Early Renaissance* (New York, 1972), 232–45; Warnke, *The Court Artist*, 2–3; G. Henderson, *Gothic* (Harmondsworth, 1967), 15–42.

[60] See A. Cole, *Art of the Italian Renaissance Courts: Virtue and Magnificence* (London, 1995), 7–14.

[61] Warnke, *The Court Artist*, 1–6; cf. Le Goff, 'The town as an agent of civilisation', 71–95.

[62] Warnke, *The Court Artist*, 2–3, 12–26.   [63] Ibid. 4–5; also above, pp. 247–8.

An argument employed by literary scholars in their analysis of court culture is applied to the visual arts by Warnke. From the mid-thirteenth century, he writes, western European monarchs 'consolidated their power and established fixed administrative centres'.[64] Just as the rise of permanent chanceries and other institutions of administration are thought to have fostered the literary culture of courts, so the visual arts are linked to alleged 'centralizing processes' and power-consolidation.[65] 'Only through the establishment of large royal and ducal households could a stable court culture flourish, with a sophisticated audience permanently present and a much larger public at hand for regular celebrations and performances.'[66] This was undoubtedly true, but an increase in household size was, however, not necessarily a consequence of bureaucratic growth within the household. Indeed, the reverse was sometimes the case. The tendency of some bureaucratic departments of state—chanceries, treasuries, exchequers, *chambres des comptes*—to 'go out of court' and establish themselves in fixed locations apart from the main residences of the ruler (as we have noticed earlier) hardly supports this argument.[67] Nor does the record of much royal and princely itineration, which remained constant throughout the period. Such 'fixed administrative centres' as existed were staffed by busy officials and clerks whose contribution to 'courtly' activity was largely confined to (generally occasional) literary composition.[68] Patronage of the visual and applied arts was not particularly prominent among their activities. Of course there were preferred and favoured residences which princes adopted but, again, they did not always coincide with the location of important administrative departments. In the Burgundian period, for example, while Philip the Good might favour Brussels as his residence, the chief accounting office for the Burgundian lands—the *chambre des comptes*—

---

[64] Ibid. 10.

[65] See above, pp. 137–8. For a contrasting view of early modern courts and their 'culture' see Adamson, 'The making of the ancien-régime court', 10–15, 33–9. A 'new court history' is there outlined, taking the form of 'an attempt to emancipate . . . court culture from crudely functionalist modes of analysis and the equally distorting concept of "propaganda"'. It also questions 'the analysis of European *ancien régimes* in terms of "state-building", in which the importance of early modern institutions is gauged according to the extent that they "anticipate" modern structures of bureaucratic power' (40). A similar approach could profitably be applied to the later Middle Ages. See above, pp. 222–3 and below, pp. 262–3.

[66] Van Oostrom, *Court and Culture*, 8; also above, pp. 222–3.

[67] See above, pp. 24, 137–8. [68] See Tout, *Chapters*, v. 104–10.

remained at Lille.[69] At an earlier date, neither the English nor the French royal chanceries—from the reigns of Edward I or Philip the Fair and his sons onwards—were located within the precincts of their most frequently visited 'permanent' residences: the palaces of Westminster and the Louvre respectively. Yet, by gravitating towards the towns of their domains, many rulers ensured that the infrastructure of court patronage could be sustained within those towns as they and their courts travelled, despite the peripatetic nature of their lives. Clearly some 'fixed administrative centres' played a greater role than others in the promotion of court art— Westminster and Paris provide the best instances. The contribution of the city and its resources, rather than the simple concentration of bureaucratic government, to this process has always to be taken into account. It might also be suggested that one reason why we 'see the relations between artists and courts more clearly' from the mid-thirteenth century onwards lies in the fact that a far greater volume of written documentation (in the form of accounts, inventories, contracts, and so on) survives from that period.[70] It is in this sense that the growing bureaucratization of government played an important role in the infrastructures of patronage.

The mere fact of archival survival, and the developments in accounting procedures and record-keeping which marked the mid- to late thirteenth century, mean that we possess a far greater body of artists' and craftmens' names than for preceding periods. This may lend a rather distorted perspective to notions of artistic 'individuality', especially when names—in much greater numbers—can be associated with surviving works of art.[71] Yet it is quite true, as Warnke observes, that monastic and clerical workshops were being steadily superseded by lay establishments, a process which accelerated in the second half of the thirteenth century.[72] Thus, in England, France, and—to take a particularly well-documented example

---

[69] See D. Clauzel, *Finances et politique à Lille pendant la période bourguignonne* (Dunkirk, 1982), 21–5; A. Smolar-Meynart, 'The establishment of the court of Philip the Good and the institutions of government in Brussels: a city becomes a capital' in *Rogier van der Weyden* (exhib. cat., Brussels, 1979), 15–23.

[70] See Warnke, *The Court Artist*, 9, and above, pp. 72–5, 80.

[71] The names of Master Honoré, Jean Pucelle, Melchior Broederlaam, the Malouels, the Limburgs, André Beauneveu, Claus Sluter, and so on can all be attached to surviving works dating from the period *c*.1280–1384. See C. Dehaisnes, *Histoire de l'art dans la Flandre, l'Artois et le Hainaut avant le xve siècle* (Lille, 1886), 350–2.

[72] See R. K. Lancaster, 'Artists, suppliers and clerks: the human factors in the art patronage of King Henry III', *JWCI* 35 (1972), 81–107; Warnke, *The Court Artist*, 10. For a detailed and comprehensive survey of artistic production and the status of the artist see X. Baral I Altet (ed.), *Artistes, artisans et production artistique au moyen âge*, 2 vols. (Paris, 1986).

—the kingdom of Naples under the Angevins, named individuals received the title (in formal documents and accounts) of *magister pictor, pictor regis, familiaris,* or *familiaris et fidelis*.[73] Painters and workers in other media, such as goldsmiths and masons, appear as members of household pay-rolls, in regular employment, with liveries, salaries, and more formal titles.[74] But whether or not rulers and their courts enjoyed the exclusive services of such men is a matter for debate. The case of Simone Martini, working for republican Siena as well as for the pope, cardinals, and secular princes, suggests otherwise.[75] The evidence is best treated by considering each of our group of northern European courts in turn.

a. England

The sheer bulk of surviving documentation makes England somewhat exceptional. Without the substantial archive formed by the Chancery Rolls, Pipe Rolls, Wardrobe and Household accounts, and other classes of record, our knowledge of court patronage of the visual and applied arts would rest upon a relatively small number of surviving works. Yet an imaginative leap has to be taken to visualize the nature of some of the works which are mentioned in the documentary sources, but have perished. We can, however, establish the identity of many artists and craftsmen and the manner in which they were employed. Under Henry III (1216–72) the shift towards the employment of increasingly large numbers of laymen and their workshops becomes apparent.[76] From the 1240s—the time which saw the onset of Henry's building and decorating campaigns at Westminster—men such as Edward of Westminster, goldsmith, Edward Fitz Odo, goldsmith, painter, and gilder (son of Odo the goldsmith), Walter and Thomas of Durham, painters, and Peter of Spain, painter, appear in the Chancery and Exchequer records.[77] They were in receipt of liveries, appeared on the payroll of those paid wages by the household,

---

[73] See Warnke, *The Court Artist,* 10–13; F. Bologna, *I pittori alla corte angioina di Napoli, 1266–1414* (Rome, 1969), 25–68; J. Gardner, 'Saint Louis of Toulouse, Robert of Anjou and Simone Martini', *Zeitschrift für Kunstgeschichte,* 39 (1976), 10–25.

[74] See Lancaster, 'Artists, suppliers and clerks', 92–104; also below, pp. 265–7, 271, 276, 280–2.

[75] See Martindale, *Simone Martini,* 37–44, 66–7.

[76] See Binski, *The Painted Chamber,* 106–9; J. G. Noppen, 'The Westminster school and its influence', *Burl. Mag.* 57 (1930), 72–81; 'Westminster paintings and Master Peter', *Burl. Mag.* 91 (1949), 305–9.

[77] See Binski, *Westminster Abbey,* 34, 45, 47, 84, 135–6, 138, 164; *The Painted Chamber,* 47–9. For the properties owned by Odo the Goldsmith at Westminster, and his affluence, see G. Rosser, *Medieval Westminster, 1200–1540* (Oxford, 1989), 26–7.

and some began to be described as *pictor* or *pictor regis*. There can be little doubt that Henry III was nothing if not an active—and discriminating—patron. His letters and orders to craftsmen in his service, and to the financial officers responsible for their payment, bear this out. For example, in October 1243, he ordered Edward Fitz Odo

quod in camera regis apud Westmonasterium depingi faciat bonis et decentibus coloribus, ita quod imago Sancti Johannis Ewangeliste depingatur in orientali parte camere illius, Sancti Mathei in occidentali, Sancti Luce in australi, Sancti Marci in boriali et . . . in camera regine et in cameris vicinis eidem camere, et eciam in camere Edwardi, ubi Scaccarium residere consuevit.[78]

[that he shall have the king's chamber at Westminster painted, in good and fitting colours, so that an image of St John the Evangelist shall be depicted in the eastern part of the same chamber, St Matthew in the western part, St Luke in the southern part, St Mark in the northern part and . . . in the queen's chamber, and the chamber next to it, and in Edward's chambers, where the Exchequer was accustomed to reside.]

Edward Fitz Odo was also to 'make ready the king's hall and other of the king's houses at Westminster, for the king's arrival' and would be paid when the king knew the cost of all these works. Henry could be peremptory and demanding in his mandates, as could his son.[79] But artists and craftsmen were not the only recipients of such commands. In February 1244, Henry told his treasurer and Edward Fitz Odo to finish a chamber at Westminster *ad opus militum* ('for the use of the knights') in time for Easter (a 'full' court) even if it needed a thousand workers per day.[80] Another mandate to Edward was very specific in its requirements for a porch (*porticum*) at the palace of Westminster. He told Fitz Odo:

porticum illum que tanto palacio conveniat fieri faciat inter lotorium ante coquinas regis et hostium per quod intratur in aulam minorem, ita quod rex in ea descendere possit de palefrido suo ad honestam frontem et sub ea iri possit inter predictum hostium et lotorium predictum, et etiam a coquina regis et camera militum, et eam plumbo predicto cooperiri faciat.[81]

[he shall have an entrance which befits such a palace made between the washing-place in front of the king's kitchens and the doorway through which the lesser hall is entered, so that the king may dismount from his palfry with dignity and make his way beneath it between the said entrance and washing-place, and thence to

[78] *CCR, 1242–7*, 45 (1 Oct. 1243), and see J. G. Noppen, 'Building by King Henry III and Edward, son of Odo', *Antiquaries Journal*, 28 (1948), 138–48; 29 (1949), 13–25.
[79] See Chaplais, 'Some private letters of Edward I', 79–81.
[80] *CCR, 1242–7*, 160 (16 Feb. 1244. Easter fell on 3 April).
[81] Ibid. 273 (2 Dec. 1244).

the king's kitchen and the knights' chamber, and he shall have it covered with lead.]

This was evidently to be done before the Christmas feast and we have here one instance of the manner in which the rhythm of the court's year could determine the structure and pace of artistic and architectural patronage. This was indeed court patronage, with an active part played by the ruler. A goldsmith, moreover, was in effect operating as a clerk of works, clearly conversant with other media and with the organization of a labour force.[82] As a general factotum responsible for supplying labour and materials, as well as a skilled craftsman, Edward Fitz Odo hardly resembles the 'modern' artist. He was also required by Henry III to provide wax tapers (*cereos*) for such liturgical events as the feast of St Edward the Confessor. The king desired that

contra adventum regis apud Westmonasterium fieri faciat tot cereos quot ad festum Sancti Edwardi solent poni in ecclesia de Westmonasterium, et ibidem ardeant in adventu regis, et provideat quod magnum lampadarium, quod est in ecclesia predicta, tunc accendetur et ardeat.[83]

[in time for the king's arrival at Westminster he shall have as many candles made as are wont to be placed at the feast of St Edward in the church at Westminster, and to burn there at the king's coming, and he shall make sure the great candelabra, which is in the said church, shall then be lit and shall burn.]

A further order, to William de Hawkeswell, the king's treasurer, specified the making of four silver candelabra to replace those 'which are around the shrine of the blessed Edward at Westminster' in readiness for the feast day.[84] Once again, provision for the king's next coming determines the nature of 'cultural' activity in a courtly setting. This was an inevitable consequence of itinerant rulership and was not confined to England. As became even more markedly the case under his son, Henry III's style of kingship—peripatetic and therefore exceedingly demanding for members of his household and administration—had a distinct effect upon the structure and organization of patronage. Of course longer-term, more stable projects existed (such as the protracted, centuries-long work on Westminster abbey and palace), but the demands made by an episodically resident court were paramount.

Under Edward I and Edward II, the evidence grows, and larger numbers of named artists and craftsmen can be identified, some in

---

[82] See Noppen, 'Building by King Henry III and Edward, son of Odo', 138–42.
[83] *CCR, 1242–7*, 41 (at Bordeaux, 30 Aug. 1243).   [84] Ibid. 42 (30 Aug. 1243).

connection with surviving works. Thus William Torel, a London gold-smith, was commissioned to make the gilt bronze effigies of Henry III and Eleanor of Castile in 1290.[85] Adam the Goldsmith, again a London burgess, was employed by Edward I from the 1290s onwards in many capacities, including the making and purchase of jewels and plate for a series of court functions. The throne which was to have been made from copper alloy and then gilded was one of the (abandoned) projects upon which he worked, and the so-called 'coronation chair' was the work of the painter Master Walter of Durham.[86] Both Alexander of Abingdon and Michael of Canterbury worked extensively as painters for the court circle in the latter part of the reign—it is perhaps no coincidence that their names (together with Walter and Thomas of Durham) may link them to centres of ecclesiastical patronage, both monastic and secular.[87] Abbots of Abingdon, archbishops of Canterbury (and priors of Christ Church there), and bishops of Durham required the services of such men for their own short- and long-term purposes. The network of high-status clerical patronage may have brought them into royal service. Sometimes the entries in wardrobe and household accounts reveal little about the nature of the works produced—in October 1310, for example, Alexander le Ymagenour was paid a prest for making 'an image for the king' (*ymag-inum*).[88] But fuller details are often recorded: in December 1311, Adam de Garstrete, *pictor*, was paid for three images—of the Virgin, St Catherine, and St Margaret—bought from him for the chapel of Edward II's two younger brothers, Thomas and Edmund, at the manor of 'Hamstede', and 'placed in the same by his own hand'.[89] These were presumably panels, mounted on an altar by the painter himself. Yet few of such men could be described as 'court artists' in the formal sense. They were not retained on the household payroll, nor given liveries, but operated from their workshops in London and Westminster, working for many other clients and patrons than the court alone.[90] A few were granted more

---

[85] See Plenderleith and Maryon, 'The royal bronze effigies in Westminster Abbey', 87–90.

[86] PRO, E.101/355/18, m. 6r: 1 Aug. 1299. The payment was in the form of a prest 'super quamdam cathedram pingend' of 100s. For Walter's long career (*c*.1265–*c*.1305) as 'king's painter' (*pictor regis*) see Binski, *The Painted Chamber*, 17–21, 48. He was succeeded by Thomas of Westminster, probably his son. See Appendix II.

[87] Binski, *Westminster Abbey*, 107–9, 171; Colvin *et al.*, *King's Works*, i. 483–4.

[88] E.101/373/26, fo. 43r: 13 Oct. 1310.   [89] E.101/374/19, fo. 4r: 31 Dec. 1311.

[90] See Rosser, *Medieval Westminster*, 145–55, 158–61; Lancaster, 'Artists, suppliers and clerks', 89–107. A similar situation prevailed in Paris.

permanent positions and paid wages over longer periods of time. Such was Master Thomas of Westminster, who took daily wages for a whole year from the wardrobe, except for twenty-six days when he was absent from the court.[91] But the employment of London craftsmen—or those from other towns if the court was at York, Berwick, or elsewhere—on a piecework, non-salaried basis, appears to have constituted the norm. The exercise of patronage remained flexible—the arts and crafts were not easily susceptible to 'centralized' organization at this time. Work was often commissioned and ordered by means of intermediaries. Hence in 1296, a payment was made from the wardrobe to John de Bitterle, monk of Westminster

pro una virga argentea per ipsum empta, super quam pom[um] Regis Scocie, per Regem oblatam ad feretrum Sancti Edwardi in ecclesia eiusdem abbathie, affigitur super idem feretrum per preceptum Regis, et pro deauracione eiusdem virge et pomi, et pro clavis argenteis per ipsum emptis pro corona et septro Scocie firmand' super feretrum, et pro stipendio unius aurifabri operantis circa omnia predicta firmanda super feretrum ut predicitur.[92]

[for a rod of silver bought by him, on which the orb of the Scottish king, oblated by the king to the shrine of St Edward in the church of the same abbey, has been fixed by the king's command, and for the gilding of the same rod and orb, and for silver keys bought by him to secure the crown and sceptre of Scotland to the shrine, and for the stipend of a goldsmith working to secure all the above things to the shrine as stated above.]

Edward I's offering of the insignia of the Scottish crown to the shrine of St Edward at Westminster, whereby the orb (*pomum*), crown, and sceptre of Scotland were integrated into it, was therefore implemented through a monk of the abbey. The work was done by a goldsmith, with no known relationship to the king's household, who had been contracted for the purpose by John de Bitterle. With the exception of Adam, who is sometimes styled 'the king's goldsmith', most of the named (and unnamed) goldsmiths who appear in the records seem to have been recruited, commissioned, and sub-contracted from the large reservoir of craftsmen

---

[91] E.101/374/5, fo. 34r: 1310–11. He was repairing defects in the wall-paintings of the Painted Chamber and elsewhere in 1307–8 (E.101/468/21, fo. 72r) but declined to accept weekly wages during that time, receiving expenses, as *magistrum in officio pictorie* for his time of residence within the palace of Westminster. See also Binski, *The Painted Chamber*, 107–8, for his terms of service and the fluid relationship between the court and the king's painters.

[92] BL, Add. MS 7965, fo. 23r.

in the city of London.[93] Adam was thus employed, like others who worked
for the court, in many capacities: between 1293 and 1295 he made vases
(*vasa*) on three occasions from silver bars brought from the mines in
Devon.[94] He also acted as a purchasing agent for the king—in the late
summer of 1299 he was sent to Paris to buy 245 items of gold, silver,
and silver gilt plate and jewels for the king's forthcoming marriage to
Margaret of France (Pl. 34).[95] Among those who ministered to the needs
of English rulers and their courts, therefore, specialization of function
was exceptional, and we should picture most of the 'masters' among the
artists and craftsmen who worked for the English court as contractors
and sub-contractors, rather than as individuals exercising artistic and
creative autonomy. Individualistic and creative they may have been, but
workshop methods and organization made court art just as dependent
upon collective workmanship as any other.

b. Flanders

The Flemish evidence for this period is not comparable in volume with
that emanating from the English court and household. It is confined to
scattered references in household accounts and inventories to artists and
craftsmen in the pay of the count, countess, and members of their
family.[96] There appears to be no clear evidence of specifically designated
comital painters or other craftsmen until 1365, when Jan van Hasselt is
mentioned as Louis de Male's painter in a warrant assigning him wages
and establishing a prior claim on his services.[97] Yet the early household
accounts are not devoid of payments, especially to book illuminators,
notators of antiphoners and tropers, and goldsmiths. Between 1273
and 1279, payments were made to one Baudouin le Clerc, who can be

---

[93] E.101/355/18, m. 5r: payment of 4s. to Adam *aurifaber Regis* for 'denariis per ipsum
solutis pro argento per ipsum apposito circa emendacionem unius ciphi et picheri argenti,
et pro stipendio unius aurifabri dictos ciphum et picherum emendantium' (July 1293).
For Adam, see also Appendix II (a), (b).

[94] E.36/202, p. 54: payment of 344 l. 17s. 7d. 'in platis de exitu minere Devon' recepti de
magistro Willelmo de Wymundham . . . ad vasa inde faciendum'.

[95] E.101/355/23; 355/22; 355/24–6: items intended as gifts for those attending the celebrations at Canterbury in Sept. 1299. The total cost of items bought at Paris from six
Parisian goldsmiths was 10,519 l. 8s. 6d. (E.101/355/24). See below, Appendix II.

[96] See e.g. *Documents*, i. 61–72, 169–72, 174–5, 194–5, 212–13, 238–48, 282–3, 434–6,
444, 458; ii. 522–4, 569, 573–95. For the patronage of literature by the counts of Flanders
see M. D. Stanger, 'Literary patronage at the medieval court of Flanders', *French Studies*,
11 (1957), 214–29. See also below, pp. 288, 292.

[97] ADN, B.1566, fo. 56v; printed *Documents*, i. 458.

identified with Baudouin l'Enlumineur.[98] In 1273 he illuminated an unspecified *romans* (possibly a romance, or simply a book in French) for which he received 12 l., and in 1278 he wrote a troper for the countess's chapel.[99] He formed part of the team which produced a breviary for the countess in 1278–9. The notation of the summer section of the *breviares me dame de le capele* had begun in October 1278, parchment for that part was bought on 5 November, and an unnamed clerk was paid for writing 'both parts' on 9 December.[100] Production of such liturgical books was a protracted process, and it was not until 7 June 1279 that Baudouin was paid for the illumination of the summer section of the breviary.[101] The binder of that part was paid on 7 September. Baudouin received the same sum—12 l.—for the breviary as he had for the 'romance' six years earlier. He was the best paid of any of the team of craftsmen who worked on the breviary. The payments were made by the receiver at Male or Wijnendaal but it seems that the books were written and illuminated elsewhere. Between October 1272 and May 1273, for instance, Jean Makiel's account recorded a payment 'for going to Male for a scribe (*escrivent*) who my lady of Namur had ordered to [go to] Lille in order to write her breviary'.[102] This suggests urban workshop production.

The receiver also bought the raw materials for artistic activity, and on 15 July 1285 disbursed the relatively large sum of 24 l. 15s. 9d. *pour pointures, couleurs*.[103] Images could also be purchased ready-made—thus on 16 October 1277 'a painted image offered at Aardenburg for my *damosielle* Jeanne' was bought.[104] Occasionally accidental losses of liturgical books necessitated their rapid replacement—on 23 October 1293, one of the countess's chaplains, frère Jean, was given 10 l. 'to buy a breviary when she lost hers on the journey to Ghent'.[105] In such circumstances, there was no alternative but to buy ready-made books on the open market. Few of the books—as far as they can be identified—owned by the counts and countesses of Flanders have survived. Guy de Dampierre's psalter, however, bears the proprietary marks of the comital family and has medallions depicting the shields of the count and his immediate kin (Pl. 31).[106] The psalter bears a family resemblance to manuscripts emanating from

[98] RAG, Gaillard 29: 7 June 1279.
[99] *Het Memoriaal van Jehan Makiel*, 101; RAG, Gaillard 28: 4 Oct. 1278.
[100] RAG, Gaillard 28.   [101] Ibid. 29.
[102] *Het Memoriaal van Jehan Makiel*, 143.   [103] RAG, St-Genois 384.
[104] RAG, Gaillard 27.   [105] Ibid. 52, m. 7r.
[106] BR, MS 10607, fos. 7v–r, 84v; C. Gaspar and F. Lyna, *Les principaux MSS à peintures de la Bibliothèque Royale de Belgique*, i (Brussels, 1937), 219–28 and pl. xlv.

Artois, especially from the St-Omer area.[107] This suggests that books might be written and illuminated for a Flemish ruler outside his immediate domains. The patronage of the counts was thus eclectic and in no way constrained by rigid structures confining the choice of artists and craftsmen to any one centre of production. Different parts of manuscript books could be written and illuminated in various workshops, giving a composite quality to them, and additions could be made to them at a later date.[108] A 'courtly' provenance or background can only be posited or suggested for some surviving books. Hence a register containing grants of privileges and other documents from the *comté* of Flanders (issued during the period 1252 to 1335) may well have been the product of court patronage, and may have been kept in the comital chancery.[109] Pride of place is given to the charter of submission issued by the town of Bruges (September 1328), and the document (Pl. 4) is, exceptionally, adorned with an elaborate illuminated initial and border decoration (fo. 3v). These represent the burgomaster and echevins of Bruges on their knees, while a document inscribed *Carte de Brugg'* is exhibited to them from the battlements of a castle. In the lower border, scenes of 'courtly' celebration take place—trumpeters sound while men and women join hands in a round, or ring, dance. The men all have purses and daggers at their belts, while the side borders contain birds and grotesques making music—a wildman with a vielle, a stag with a portative organ, more dancers, and a bagpiper. Such features bear comparison with other, more lavish manuscripts of courtly origin (frontispiece).[110]

The reign of Louis de Male (d.1384) is better documented than those of his immediate predecessors, and his missal, breviary, and antiphoner (1360–5) all survive (Pl. 32). His missal has a representation of Louis and his wife, Margaret of Brabant, praying at the foot of the cross, flanked by the Virgin and St John.[111] The count and countess have banderolles issuing from their praying hands reading *Nunc Arbor nos defende* (Louis) and *Crucis ambos* (Margaret). Although probably illuminated in or near Ghent, the manuscript bears signs of English influence.[112] Louis's breviary

[107] Bod. Lib., MS Douce, 5, 6.

[108] See e.g. Bute MS 150, of which part dates from c.1270–80, part from c.1330, illuminated at Cambrai and (?) Paris, esp. fo. 266r.

[109] Den Haag, KB, MS 75 D 7, 393 folios, dating from c.1330–40. The decorated charter is on fo. 3v.

[110] See, for a good example, Bod. Lib., MS Bodley 264, fo. 173, where the lower border depicts minstrels (1338–44). See also above, pp. 253–4.

[111] BR, MS 9217, fo. 115v; Gaspar and Lyna, *Les principaux MSS*, i. pl. lxxiv and 344–6, 346–9.

[112] Gaspar and Lyna, *Les principaux MSS*, i. 346–9.

Donacio et concessio cuiusdam annualis redditus
exeunt de terris in Warberew et Stillingford

Ciant presentes et futuri qd nos Ed
mundus filius quondam Ricardi regis Ale
mannie et comes Cornub. Dedimus
concessimus et presenti carta nostra confir
mauimus deo Beate marie et Capelle sancti Nicholai
in Castro nostro Wallingford ac Rogero de drayton
decano dicte capelle et successoribus suis decanis p nos
et heredes nostros ibidem substituendis ad sustentacio
nem. Sex Capellanorum. Sex Cliroz et quatuor
Ceropherarioz in eadem Capella deo seruientiam et
seruituroz impetim pro salute anime nostre et ania ȝ
Ricardi quondam Regis alemannie patris nostri
Senenchie Matris nostre Beatrici Regis Anglie anima
li nostri. et p salute anime domini. Edwardi illustri
tres Regis Anglie. et p animabus omnium fidelium defunctoz
Quadraginta libras sterlingoz anni redditus in
in Warberew et stillingford cum omnibus suis ptinen
cijs p manus Senescall nostroz subscriptoz in dicte
villis annuatim ad duos anni terminos percipiendas
videlicet in octauis sancti Michis viginti libras
et in octauis pasche viginti libras. Videlicet p ma
nus abbatis de dorkcester se veisu ad Reynald Johis

20. Cartulary of the college and chapel of St Nicholas in the castle of Wallingford, early
sixteenth century, recording the foundation deeds of the collegiate establishment, 1282.

21. Sainte-Chapelle, Paris. Interior of upper chapel.

(a)

(b)

22. St Stephen's chapel in the Palace of Westminster.

a. Wall painting on the north half of the altar-wall, showing Edward III and his sons with St George (lower register) and the Adoration of the Magi (upper register). Tempera and gold leaf on paper, by Richard Smirke, *c.*1800-11.

b. Artist's impression of the chapel *c.*1360-70, varnished watercolour on paper, by Adam Lee, *c.*1820-30. Although highly imaginative, the perspective view conveys an impression of great richness of decoration.

23. Westminster Abbey, tomb of William de Valence (d. 1296), Limoges enamel, copper and wood, on a stone base.

24. Westminster Abbey, tombs of Aveline de Forz (d. 1273), Aymer de Valence (d. 1324), and Edmund of Lancaster (d. 1296).

25. Westminster Abbey, gable figure (north side) from the tomb of Edmund of Lancaster (d. 1296).

26. Sketch by John Carter (dated July 1782) of armed figures painted on the base of Edmund of Lancaster's tomb in Westminster Abbey. They include members of the families of Valence, Warenne, Bigod, and Clifford. All wear armorial surcoats and hold lances bearing small rectangular banners.

27. Westminster Abbey, tomb of John of Eltham (d. 1336) in St Edmund's chapel. A royal writ of 1339 survives ordering the abbot and monks to move John's body from a temporary grave to its present location 'amongst the royals'.

28. Wall paintings of the counts and countesses of Flanders, in the comital chapel, 1374. Kortrijk, Notre Dame.

29a. Simone Martini, Musicians, from the chapel of St Martin, c.1312-19. Assisi, S. Francesco.

29b. Simone Martini, St Martin's renunciation of arms in the imperial camp. Assisi, S. Francesco.

30. The Westminster retable: central section with the Virgin, Christ, and St John, *c*.1280-90.

31. Psalter of Guy de Dampierre, count of Flanders, *c.*1270, with roundels displaying the arms of Flanders and Namur.

32. Missal of Louis de Male, count of Flanders, Flemish, *c.*1360. The count, wearing a tunic lined with miniver, and countess kneel at the foot of the cross, with banderolles issuing from their praying hands, and symbols of the four Evangelists in medallions at each corner of the page.

33. Ewer, rock crystal and silver gilt., Paris, *c.*1350.

34. Casket, silver-gilt, with the arms of England and France, *c*.1299-1307. The arms represent the marriages of Edward I to Margaret of France (1299) and of Edward , Prince of Wales (later Edward II) to Isabella of France (1307).

35. Enamelled ewer, silver-gilt, Paris, *c.*1320-30. Decorated with grotesques and, around the neck, scenes of games.

37. Alms-purse (*aumônière*), velvet and silk, embroidered, mid-fourteenth century. The embroideries represent the hunting of the unicorn.

36. Reliquary-statuette of St James, silver-gilt and enamel, Paris, *c*.1321. Geoffroi Coquatrix, burgess of Paris and financial officer of the French crown, gave it to the cathedral of St James at Compostella, as the Latin inscription records.

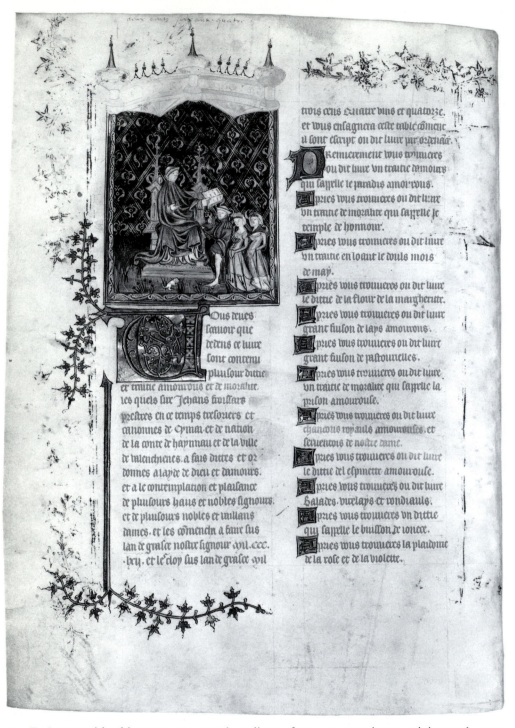

38. Froissart reciting his poems to a courtly audience, from a manuscript containing works composed by him between 1362 and 1394.

bears the marks of ownership by representing the arms of Flanders on five separate folios, and the illumination suggests a similar provenance to that of the missal.[113] The years immediately following the production of these liturgical books for Louis de Male offer evidence for a more formal organization of the arts at his court. Jan van Hasselt is found as 'count's painter', working on a series of projects, including the comital chapel at Kortrijk in 1372–4 (Pl. 28).[114] In 1380–1 he was decorating textiles and banners and in receipt of a pension from the count.[115] In January 1381, a painter whose high-quality work can be identified—Master André Beauneveu—received 60 l.p. through Henri de Douzy, the count's chamberlain, when he was at Ghent 'by reason of our *images*'.[116] By September 1381, 'Melsior le poyntre monseigneur' (that is, Melchior Broederlaam) is found painting five of the count's *caiieres* (*chaises* or seats) and upholstering them *de son mestier*, for the sum of 44 l.p.[117] Despite the political upheavals and civil war—especially in and around Ghent—of his last four years, Louis de Male was engaging in lavish patronage of many art forms, particularly of goldsmiths' work from named craftsmen such as Joris van Tielt, Jan van Ruddervorde, Claas van Haren, Jan Stommelin, and Jan van Brabant.[118] Philip the Bold of Burgundy, as the new count of Flanders, simply inherited his father-in-law's structures of patronage—and his debts. The artists who had served Louis went on to serve Philip—Beauneveu and Broederlaam, in particular, found regular employment in Burgundian service. But their early careers had included service in Flanders in far less auspicious political circumstances than those in the duchy and county of Burgundy after 1384. Civil war could certainly have a deleterious effect upon some of the luxury trades. The Ghenters were responsible for the pillage of comital plate and jewels, such as the four great silver pots, two ewers (Pls. 33, 35), and twenty-four saucers (*escales*) of which the goldsmith Jan van Ruddervorde was robbed at Bruges in April 1382.[119] Turbulent Flanders may have been, but it did not entirely preclude comital patronage of the arts on a princely scale. The count

---

[113] BR, MS 9427, fos. 14r, 43r, 81v, 100v, 124r; and see below, pp. 291–2. The manuscript includes vernacular proverbs (in Dutch) and scenes derived from *fabliaux*.

[114] See above, pp. 230–1.   [115] *Documents*, ii. 569.

[116] ADN, B.3236, no. 111758: at Bruges, 5 Jan. 1381.

[117] ADN, B.3239, no. 111865; *Documents*, ii. 573–4: at Bruges, 5 Sept. 1381; also no. 111829 for upholstery, 900 latten nails, fringes, leather and wire for the *caiieres*, Apr. 1380.

[118] ADN, B.3239, nos. 111856, 111864, 111866b, 111880 (schedule of expenses, in Dutch), 111888; B.3240, no. 111927; B.3241, no. 111975: Nov. 1380–May 1382.

[119] ADN, B.3241, no. 111975: 'les quellz furent desrobz a Bruges de ceulz de Gand dessoubz les mains dudit Jehan' and valued at 317 l. For the depredations of the Ghent rebels see also above, pp. 256–7.

could always retire to his *bonnes villes* of Lille, or even Bruges, when the Ghent rebellion was at its height.[120] Political stability was certainly not a prerequisite for the flourishing of artistic creativity and for lavish investment in a wide range of art forms.

c. Hainault-Holland

The counts of Hainault were noted for a long tradition of literacy and of literary patronage, which they had promoted since the twelfth century.[121] The first inventories, dating from the early fourteenth century, of their collections of books in French (*li romanch*) suggest a broad acquaintance with a range of devotional and secular works.[122] Some of William III's (1304–37) books were quite highly valued—of nineteen books, three were worth 30 l., one was valued at 20 l., and the rest at sums ranging from 15 l. to 30s.[123] The three most valuable manuscripts were a *Lancelot*, and two parts of a French Bible, and the next most valuable was a *romanch de Merlin*. This suggests a certain level of de luxe patronage of a discriminating kind. If the valuations of these French books are compared with the liturgical books in the count's chapel at the same time, they appear to be generally higher. The highest price put upon a liturgical book was 16 l. for a large two-volume antiphoner for winter and summer, which was 'almost new'.[124] The next most valuable book was valued at 10 l. However, the most highly priced liturgical books were listed with the plate, vestments, and other fine textiles in the chapel. These were two books, valued at 60 l., of which the bindings were in effect goldsmith's work—adorned with raised images in gold and silver, no doubt resembling surviving Gospel books.[125] Books were cared for and prized at the court

---

[120] See D. Nicholas, *The van Arteveldes of Ghent: the Varieties of Vendetta and the Hero in History* (Ithaca, NY, London, and Leiden, 1988), 120–75; R. Demuynck, 'De Gentse oorlog (1379–1385): Oorzaken en karakter', *Handelingen der Maatschappij voor Geschiedenis en Oudheidkunde te Gent*, n.s. 5 (1951), 305–18; J. M. Murray, 'The liturgy of the Count's Advent in Bruges, from Galbert to Van Eyck', in *City and Spectacle in Medieval Europe*, 138–52, esp. 139–40, 147–8.

[121] See e.g. Jacques de Guyse, *Annales Hannoniae*, ed. E. Sackur, *MGH, Scriptores*, 30 (1896), 224–26, for the important literary interests of Baldwin V of Hainault.

[122] AEM, Trésorerie, Cartulaires 19, fo. 120r–v (4 Dec. 1304), printed *Documents*, i. 156–7; AEM, Recueils 115, no. 2 (?1311). See Appendix VIII (a). Janet van der Meulen (Leiden University) is preparing a study of literature and patronage at the court of Hainault-Holland under the Avesnes dynasty.

[123] AEM, Trésorerie, Recueils 115, no. 2.

[124] Ibid., no. 2: 'pour yvier et pour estet assez nuef'.

[125] Ibid., no. 2: 'Item, 2 livres a aisselles ymageriez dehors dymagerie eslevee dor et dargent'. See also Appendix XI (a), (b).

of Hainault—in November 1325, for example, the future William IV was provided with a *layette* in which to keep his books, bought by Jean le Clerc.[126] Some of the books acquired by the Hainault court came from Paris—in March 1328, Colard de Monstreuil was given 10s. to give to the carrier who brought 'a romance from Paris', and in December 1332, Jean the chaplain was given 22s.t. for 'a little portable missal of common masses bought at Paris'.[127] Otherwise, workshops at Valenciennes and Mons produced illuminated books for the comital milieu.[128] Many books appear not to have been illuminated or decorated in any way—the workaday character of some of them is evident from their relatively low cost. Thus in July 1335, a *livre de saint Loys* was acquired through Guillaume Foullet, a noble member of the countess's household, for 32s. 6d.[129] Two years earlier a *livret d'Ensegnemens saint Loys* was copied for the future William IV for the very small sum of 5s.[130] As at other princely courts, patronage of book production and illumination was thus eclectic and diverse in nature.

Much the same can be said of the acquisition by the counts and countesses of goldsmiths' work. Liturgical plate was often obtained from local craftsmen working at or near the court's place of residence at a particular time—thus in May 1327, when the countess and her household were at The Hague, Jan, goldsmith of Delft, was paid for his labour on a *vaissiel dargent et de cristal pour le jour dou Sacrement, mis a le capielle de Le Haye* (Pl. 33)[131] ['a vessel of silver and crystal for the day of the sacrament, placed in the chapel at The Hague']. But the increasingly lavish expenditure on conspicuous consumption and display by the Avesnes family, as Hainault moved into the centre stage of European politics in the second quarter of the fourteenth century, led to the patronage of some of the best goldsmiths of their time (Pls. 35, 36).[132] These were such men as Simon de Lille or Adam de St-Quentin, both of whom supplied William III and Jeanne de Valois with plate and jewels. Adam, living at Bruges (outside the comital domains) was paid for 'rings, precious stones, and jewels' in August 1326, and again in April 1328, when he sold the countess eighty oriental pearls, and other jewels, including a cameo.[133] Simon de Lille, one of the richest men among the merchant class of Paris, himself a

---

[126] *De rekeningen*, ed. Smit, i. 215.   [127] Ibid., i. 403, 640.

[128] See *Documents*, i. 295, 304.

[129] *De rekeningen*, ed. Smit, i. 606; for Guillaume Foullet see Riemsdijk, *De Tresorie*, 393.

[130] *De rekeningen*, ed. Smit, i. 668.

[131] Ibid., i. 297: 22 May 1327.   [132] See above, pp. 86–7.

[133] *De rekeningen*, ed. Smit, i. 292, 403–4.

patron of literature and the arts, supplied the count and countess with goods worth a total of almost 3,000 l.t. in July 1328, including a diamond worth 12 l.t., and various rings, brooches, and *croisettes* for the countess, worth 84 l.p.[134] These suppliers of luxury items were to some extent specialists. But the normal patterns of trade and craft organization tended to mean that, as in England, certain regular purveyors supplied a variety of raw materials, finished products, and labour under contract. Hence in 1311–13, the raw materials for the tomb of Jean I and his wife Philippine were supplied by Robert le Cochon, but he was also responsible for providing cloths of gold and wax for the first anniversary of the countess's obsequies (*a Robert le Cochon pour le tombe monseigneur et me dame, pour les pieres, pour ovraiges et fierures et pour le huge dont li tombe est couverte*, 6 April 1311)[135] ['to Robert le Cochon for the tomb of my lord and lady, for stone, for stonework and metalwork, and for the canopy with which the tomb is covered']. The tomb was worked upon by 'Master Gilbert' and his team, while Jean Severin painted it. Collective, workshop production was here, once again, the rule.

The mechanisms for patronage of panel and wall painting—and of interior decoration—were similarly broadly based, although the appearance in 1334–5 of '*Mastre Gillebert lymageneur*', retained by the count with an annuity for life indicates a more formal and permanent provision for the arts.[136] Yet there can be little doubt of the richness of some of the artefacts possessed by the comital family. In 1311, the chapel inventory included what was evidently a diptych, representing the Virgin and the Crucifixion, of 'Greek work' (perhaps Italian?) valued at the high price of 20 l.[137] Artists and craftsmen from many sources were regularly employed—in April 1331, the countess Jeanne bought two *tabliaus d'or* from Guillaume of Arras, possibly to be identified as Guillaume Acart the Arras painter.[138] The many residences maintained by the counts and countesses—in Holland as well as Hainault—required the services of teams of painters,

---

[134] *De rekeningen*, ed. Smit, i. 404, 407; for Simon de Lille see R. Lightbown, *Medieval European Jewellery, with a Catalogue of the Collection in the Victoria and Albert Museum* (London, 1992), 362–3. In 1338 Simon had provided a jewelled hat for Louis de Nevers, count of Flanders, priced at 8,000 *écus d'or*, of which only half had been paid by 1385.

[135] *Documents*, i. 195–8.

[136] ADN, B.7860, fo. 38v: payment of 73 l. 11s. 10d.t. to 'Maistre Gillebert lymageneur pour rente quil tient a sa vie des rentes monseigneur'.

[137] AEM, Trésorerie, Recueil 115, no. 2: 'Item, 2 tabliaus de pointure ensanle, cloans, del ouvrage de gressce, et i a une ymagerie de nostre Dame en lun, et en lautre un crucifiement'.

[138] *De rekeningen*, ed. Smit, i. 516: payment of 12 l. 4s. 8d.p. on 29 Apr. 1331.

gilders, metal workers, and glass-makers, as well as the carpenters, plas-
terers, tilers, and other labourers who populate the building accounts
in such numbers. Between November 1326 and January 1327, the
countess's oratory in the chapel of the Binnenhof at The Hague was
painted by Jan 'the painter of Delft'.[139] A further payment, simply to 'the
painter who painted the oratory of my lady'(Jan van Delft?) listed the
raw materials used: 2,100 leaves of gold, 4 pounds of azure pigment, $7\frac{1}{2}$
pounds of *blanke coleur*, 7 pounds of green, $\frac{1}{2}$ pound of *sinople* (purple),
1 pound of vermilion, 5 pounds of varnish, oil, and *fause coleur*, amount-
ing to a total of 20 l. 16s.[140] Once again, local labour from a nearby town—
The Hague was still only a very small settlement, not even comparable
with Delft at this time—was drawn upon. Works at other, secular, buildings
similarly demanded the labour of painters, for both wall painting and for
the heraldic display which such residences always required. In 1359–60,
a campaign of works on the count's castle at Escaudoeuvres included
payment to *maistre Clays le paigneur de Valenchiennes* for painting a banner
of the count's arms which flew from 'the tower covered with slate'. Clays
painted the banner, another craftsman made it, but payment was made to
the painter, perhaps suggesting sub-contracting.[141] Similar works were
undertaken in an extensive refurbishment of the Salle-le-Comte at
Valenciennes between 1374 and 1376, when wall paintings, decorative
ironwork, and glass were installed.[142] With substantial residences at
Valenciennes, Mons, Binche, Le Quesnoy, Dordrecht, and The Hague,
the counts of Hainault-Holland were inevitably important patrons of
domestic architecture and all that went with it—the interior of the residence was, to judge from the surviving records, receiving considerably
more attention as styles of aristocratic life became more elaborate and
expectations of a prince's 'estate' grew.

But this was a common characteristic of the principalities of northern
France and the Low Countries in the second half of the fourteenth
century, some of which were soon to be absorbed into the Burgundian
dominions. Yet, without the legacy bequeathed to it by the counts of
Hainault-Holland, the cultural climate of the court of Burgundy might
have been very different. Hainault-Holland formed a kind of prefigura-
tion—on a smaller scale—of the composite dominions of the house of

---

[139] Ibid., i. 292: to 'Jehan le pingeur de Delf, ki penist l'oratore medame'
(28 Nov. 1326).
[140] Ibid., i. 295: 11 Jan. 1327.   [141] ADN, B.7882, fo. 115r.
[142] *Documents*, ii. 526–7, 533, 538.

Burgundy, in which romance and Germanic cultures met.[143] A French-speaking, French-cultured dynasty—the Avesnes—held court, or courts, throughout their domains in Hainault, Holland, and Zeeland. The structures of court patronage of the arts closely resembled those prevalent in neighbouring principalities—indeed, those principalities provided some of the artists and craftsmen who served the counts and countesses. Flexibility and freedom of choice were allowed to them by reason of Hainault-Holland's wealth and its key position in the dynastic and marital strategies of the German Empire and the English kingdom during the second quarter of the fourteenth century. The advent of the Bavarian dynasty after 1358 did not radically change this position, and Albert of Bavaria and William of Ostrevant continued many of the practices of their Avesnes predecessors.[144] The *orfevrerie*, for instance, purchased by William of Ostrevant from Jacques de le Kiese in April 1393 for the St George festivities at Mons would not have been out of place in the time of William IV or William V.[145] The constant demand for heraldic painting, whether of shields of arms, banners, pennons, or war, jousting, and tournament equipment, kept Jean de Louvain, painter, of Mons; Louis, painter, 'our *ouvrier* of Valenciennes'; Jacquemart, painter, of Mons; and Jean the painter, in regular employment by the Bavarian dukes (May 1366, Dec. 1373, May 1380, Feb. 1395, and Aug. 1396).[146] A long tradition of cultural patronage lay behind the activities of a house that was to give the world such treasures as the famous group portrait of the court of Hainault-Holland at a fishing party or, although its provenance is not beyond doubt, the Turin-Milan Hours.[147] It should also be remembered that Jan van Eyck was in the employment of the house of Hainault-Holland-Bavaria at The Hague before he entered the service of Philip the Good of Burgundy.

[143] See C. A. J. Armstrong, 'The language question in the Low Countries: the use of French and Dutch by the Dukes of Burgundy and their administration', in J. Hale, B. Smalley, and R. Highfield (eds.), *Europe in the Late Middle Ages* (London, 1965), 386–409.

[144] See *Documents*, i. 389, 414–15, 419, 450; ii. 526–7, 533, 538; Van Oostrom, *Courts and Culture*, 22, esp. nn. 44, 45. See also above, pp. 133–4, 199–200.

[145] AEM, Trésorerie, Recueil 71, no. 17.

[146] See *Cartulaire des comtes de Hainaut*, ed. Devillers, iii. 635; v. 594, 619, 646, 727.

[147] The group portrait is in Paris, Musée du Louvre, Cabinet des Dessins no. 20674; see O. Kurz, 'A fishing party at the court of William VI, count of Holland, Zeeland and Hainault: notes on a drawing in the Louvre', *Oud-Holland*, 71 (1956), 117–31. For the Turin-Milan Hours and for Jan van Eyck's service at the court of Holland see A. Châtelet, *Early Dutch Painting* (New York, 1981), 27–46, 194.

d. Artois

The counts of Artois, like their cousins of Flanders and Hainault, were often drawn to Paris as a prime source of high-quality works of art and of artefacts, especially under Robert II and the countess Mahaut.[148] Paris was a natural magnet for a house which was of the royal blood of France, and whose members—with one notable exception—were foremost among the pillars of Capetian and Valois monarchy. Communications with the Île-de-France were relatively easy, and close links between the households of the king and queen, on the one hand, and the counts and countesses of Artois, on the other, can be observed. Such connections were exemplified in the dual roles played by some members of the comital entourage, such as Gautier de Bruxelles, *bourgeois* of Paris, who was not only a royal *panetier* (pantler) of Philip the Fair, but an *échanson* (cupbearer) in the household of Robert II of Artois.[149] He supplied the Artois court with a wide range of items—around Candlemas 1292, for example, he provided saddles, trumpet banners, heraldic escutcheons for the count's messengers, penoncels, and horse trappers. The richness of their heraldic decoration made the saddles particularly noteworthy (and costly), especially because some of them incorporated the arms of other princes: three saddles bore the 'new arms of . . . the duke of Brabant' (presumably including the arms of Limburg, gained by the duke in 1288), another carried on its samite covering two shields of Charles of Anjou's arms, another was covered with black camois, embroidered with the 'arms of the counts of Burgundy and Brittany', and a 'great saddle' was purchased for Robert II 'made and worked with his arms . . . of velvet, silk and the fleur-de-lis of *orfevrerie*. And with the arms of . . . the duke of Brabant embroidered on samite . . .'[150] The alliances and kinship bonds between the house of Artois and its peers were here being displayed.

'Court patronage' by the counts was channelled in a number of directions, but the provision of richly decorated artefacts intended for everyday use—and therefore for frequent display—absorbed their apparently ample funds and characterized Robert II's style of living. In the month before Robert II's sudden death in the carnage at Kortrijk in 1302, the count's receiver accounted with Baude de Croissilles, *bourgeois* of Arras, for a single horse-trapper for Robert II, at a total cost of 63 l. 17s. 10d.p.,

[148] See J.-M. Richard, *Une petite-nièce de St Louis*, 48–52, 79–84; *Documents*, i. 123, 165, 173, 182–3.

[149] ADPC, A.132, no. 3 (1292); A.136, no. 159 (Nov. 1294).

[150] A.132, no. 3. Total expenditure stood at 39 l. 10s.p.

when the household was on a war footing.[151] Something of the panoply with which Robert of Artois embarked upon the ill-fated Kortrijk campaign may be glimpsed from such lavish and dispendious provision.

Baude de Croissilles of Arras was a purveyor of a multiplicity of goods and services to the court of Artois.[152] They ranged from the recruitment of minstrels and players to the purchase of hay and straw for the count's horses. Specialization was not in evidence here. But the costliness of the 'covering for a great horse made for my lord' in June 1302 was an index of Robert II's status and wealth. Parchment was provided for backing, four pieces of crimson sendal, four of blue sendal, and four ells of vermilion sendal 'to make the labels' (on the count's coat of arms) were bought, plus 2,500 leaves of 'fine gold', 43 ells of silk for fringes for the trapper, saffron and other dyes, and labour costs above all this. A colour scheme of crimson (*gules*), blue (*azure*), and yellow (*or*) formed the arms of Artois.[153] Heraldic painters were also employed—witness the payments to Jacquemin, *paintre*, Poytevin, *paintre*, and a female painter—Maroie Lescussiere ('the escutcheoness'?) working for eight and five days respectively. Two armourers and two tailors (*cousturiers*) were also employed on this extremely expensive operation, which cost 63 l. 17s. 10d. in total, of which 52 l. 8s. were accounted for by the sendal cloth and gold leaf alone.[154] Was this 'art' patronage? In the context of court life, the answer has to be framed in terms of the function of the arts, as essential accompaniments to a style of behaviour and public display which was expected of princes. Heraldic and other decoration remained part of an artist's functions—however fine his panels or wall-paintings might be—for a long time.

Like their other princely contemporaries, the counts and countesses of Artois acquired illuminated and other books from a range of sources—from Paris, Arras, and other centres. In the 1290s, intermediaries were clearly in use for this purpose. The countess thus made payments for the writing and, perhaps, illumination of her 'breviaries' on a number of occasions through a chaplain, brother Thierry de la Croix, and a *damoiselle*

---

[151] ADPC, A.179, m. 4r. The account ran from 16 June 1302 onwards. See above, pp. 124–5.

[152] For his role in provision for court festivities see Appendix VII (a).

[153] ADPC, A.321, fo. 37v: purchase of 10 ells of 'soie bleu, jaune et vermele dont on fist 12 escus pour la grande tent' of Robert of Artois, Sept. 1314.

[154] A.132, no. 3; A.179, no. 4*bis*: provision of a horse crupper, covered in sendal, for the count, and payment of 40 l.p. 'pour le dit hernoys batre et armoier des armes monseigneur, les fleurs de lis enlevees de fin or'.

of her household.[155] Although illuminated books could be purchased at Arras, Parisian workshops were clearly favoured by the Artois family.[156] In April 1302, for instance, a number of books were referred to in the household account: on 11 April, the concierge of the count's Parisian *hôtel*, the appropriately named dame Bienvenue, supplied a 'cover of gold and silk . . . by the count's command for the book of the queen of France' at a cost of 50s.[157] On 13 April, two 'books of the art of astronomy in which there is the new calendar' were purchased through the medium of Simonnet le Clerc.[158] An anonymous illuminator (*enlumineur*) who illuminated 'the book of my lady' (the countess) was paid 40s. on 25 April, this time through the medium of Master Thierry d'Hérisson.[159] The interest of Mahaut, countess of Artois, in books is well known, and we know that she bought a copy of the *Voeux du Paon* for 8 l.p. from Thomas of Maubeuge, a bookseller (*librare*) in September 1313.[160] In 1310 she acquired a *Tristan* and Thierry d'Hérisson's accounts refer to a *Roman de Troye* in Latin in 1321.[161] In the same year, the alienated Robert of Artois, plotting against her, stole a number of books from Mahaut's collection at Hesdin.[162] There can be no doubt of the strong literary interest at the court of Artois at this time.[163]

But the constant, and predominant source of interest and expenditure was the comital castle, park, gardens, pavilion, and *marais* at Hesdin.[164] This equivalent of later rulers' summer palaces absorbed substantial annual sums of the counts' and countesses' income. We have already seen something of the works carried out on the chapel (or chapels) there, but the other, secular, buildings and attractions necessitated constant outlay.[165] The famous *engins* housed in a pavilion on the *marais* at Hesdin were celebrated, and their water-works, plumbing, and internal decoration

[155] A.144, no. 3, m. 1r: payments of 30 l.p. and 6 l.p. respectively.

[156] A.162, fo. 40r: payment of 8 l.p. 'pour 1 livre paint que monseigneur aceta a Arraz' (17 Apr. 1300).

[157] A.178, fo. 70r; A.187, no. 1, m. 2: payment of 50s. for 'une couverture dor et de soie au livre la Roine par monseigneur'.

[158] A. 178, fo. 70v.   [159] Ibid., fo. 71v.   [160] A.312, no. 56; *Documents*, i. 207.

[161] ADPC, A.275, and *Documents*, i. 191; A.850 and *Documents*, i. 237. The *Tristan* was acquired at Arras for 7 l.

[162] AN, KK.393, fos. 44r–45v; *Documents*, i. 235–6.

[163] ADPC, A.458; *Documents*, i. 272 (1327); A.482, no. 25; *Documents*, i. 276; and see above, p. 212.

[164] See Van Buren, 'Reality and romance in the parc of Hesdin', 117–34. Professor Van Buren's extensive study of the park at Hesdin is forthcoming.

[165] See above, pp. 228–9.

were constantly undergoing repair and refurbishment. These had been installed under the supervision of Master Regnaud Coignet (Rinaldo Cognetto) who had come from Naples in the service of Robert of Artois where the count had been campaigning on behalf of Charles of Anjou. A works account for July–November 1299 included expenditure on *les engiens du paveillon raparelier*.[166] The ingenious devices, whereby guests were surprised by the sudden eruption of water-squirts, sprays, and deluges, flour, soot, and other unexpected happenings, required regular attention and between June and October 1300, the 'engines' were strung with new cords, and the lead pipes which brought the water to the pavilion were cleaned and repaired.[167] But the other parts of the complex at Hesdin also demanded regular maintenance—thus in 1299 the *bailli* of Hesdin accounted for work by Master Jean de Boulogne and seven other painters on the *gloriete* (summer-house or arbour), as well as the payment of the large sum of 120 l.p. to Michel de Boulogne for 'painting the new *salle* and the chamber sown with shields of my lord's arms'.[168] This was evidently heraldic wall painting of high quality, and its upkeep demanded subsequent expenditure on a regular basis. In the summer of 1313, on the occasion of Edward II of England's visit to Hesdin, all the wall paintings were cleaned by teams of painters—in the *salle d'Inde* (Indian chamber), the *gloriete*, the *cambre aus cauchans au mares* (chamber of pigs [?] in the Marais), and the *sale as escus* (hall of shields).[169] Once again the demands of the court calendar were making themselves felt.

The practice of making payments to artists and craftsmen through intermediaries—chaplains, household members, officers, or contractors— means that we know all too little about the identity of many of those employed by the counts and countesses of Artois at this time. But sometimes names such Jean and Michel de Boulogne, or Tassins de Rollincourt, emerge from the anonymous mass of painters.[170] Under the countess Mahaut, more artists can be identified, such as Master Evrart d'Orléans, responsible for works at Mahaut's *hôtel* at Paris, for 'having a tomb made' for Eudes, count of Burgundy and, as *Everart Lymagier* for unspecified 'works' for the countess.[171] Evrart's seal, appended to his quittances, bore the image of a tower or gateway, perhaps indicating that his *imagerie* was essentially contained within an architectural setting. For the extensive programme of wall paintings ('a huille', in other words,

---

[166] ADPC, A.147, m. 1r.   [167] A.157, no. 2.   [168] A.147, mm. 1r, 3r, 5r.
[169] A.309: May–July 1313.   [170] A.147, mm. 3r, 5r; A.309.
[171] A.312, nos. 12: 15 June 1313; 51: 21 Aug. 1313.

in oils) in a gallery at her residence—the *hôtel d'Artois*—at Conflans, depicting scenes from the life and chivalrous deeds of her father, Robert II, Mahaut contracted with Pierre de Brossielles, 'painter living at Paris', in June 1320.[172] The contract between Mahaut and the painter referred to a 'roll' in which the content of the *images* and *estoires* was set out. The heraldic arms borne by all the knights included in the paintings during their lifetime were also to be ascertained. Pierre de Brossielles was paid 16 l.p. in advance, and the rest (32 l.p.) was to be paid on completion. The agreement was secured by oath:

Et promist ledit Pierres pardevant nous par son serment a bien et loyaument faire, en la maniere que dit est, les choses desus devisees et a rendre et poier touz couz et domages que l'en auroit en ce cas par sa deffaute. En obligeant quant a ce, a la dite madame la contesse, soy, ses hoirs, touz ses biens et de ses hoirs, meubles et non meubles, presenz et avenir.[173]

[And the said Pierre promised before us on oath to accomplish well and truly, in the agreed manner, the things set out above, and to render and pay all costs and damages that might be sustained by his default in this matter. In this respect he pledged himself, his heirs and all his movable and immovable goods, and those of his heirs, to the said lady the countess.]

The court patronage of the house of Artois was among the most wide-ranging of any of its time, and the counts enjoyed relative proximity to Paris, as well as ready and easy access to the resources of their own and their neighbours' territories. The countess was thus employing both Spinon de Nivelles, goldsmith of the count of Hainault, and Mathieu, goldsmith of Arras, simultaneously in 1298. Spinon had worked on various unspecified assignments, while Mathieu supplied her with a crown and a *tressour*.[174] The names of some of the goldsmiths with whom the counts and countesses dealt are revealing—Jacquemin de Lille or Master Jean de Douai, again giving further grounds for emphasizing the diversity and eclectic nature of 'court' patronage.[175]

High-quality workmanship was evidently prized, and the house of Artois had the resources with which to obtain it. The castle at Hesdin and its bizarre machinery were to be inherited by both Louis de Male, as count of Flanders and Artois, and by Philip the Bold of Burgundy,

---

[172] A.388: contract drawn up before the *prévôt* of Paris, 20 June 1320; *Documents*, i. 229–30.

[173] ADPC, A.388; *Documents*, i. 229–30.

[174] ADPC, A.144, no. 3, m. 1r; Lightbown, *Medieval European Jewellery*, 118–29.

[175] ADPC, A.178, fo. 64r: 4 Jan. 1302; A.184, no. 95: 27 June 1302.

by virtue of the same titles.[176] The assumption that the *engins*, the puppet-monkeys who waved to approaching visitors from a bridge over the Marais, the sound and light effects in the pavilion, or the hydraulic devices there were a product of 'Burgundian' culture is unfounded. Philip the Good of Burgundy may well have undertaken an extensive programme of repairs to the *engins* and their housing in 1433—on his personal order—but repairs they were, and not products of Burgundian origin or initiative.[177] The machinery at Hesdin ultimately derived its inspiration from Byzantine and Sicilian models, but evidently owed something to more local sources—the creators and producers of stage scenery, properties, and 'effects' for both liturgical and secular drama at Arras. A strong tradition of cultural patronage—of both 'high' and less high culture—often associated with, and dependent upon, the flourishing urban resources upon which the counts of Artois could draw, was therefore taken up and absorbed by the Burgundian court. As with the counts of Hainault, its French—and francophone—background made the process of absorption of Artois and its cultural legacy by the Valois dukes of Burgundy considerably easier. There may well have been no 'unified court culture', but the independent principalities of northern France and the Low Countries in the later thirteenth and fourteenth centuries had much in common. Structures of court patronage were strikingly similar among them, and they drew upon a common reservoir not only of styles, but of urban artists, craftsmen, and suppliers (often through middlemen), who met their demands across a very wide range of art forms.

3. A francophone culture?

The question of language has tended to figure prominently in accounts and analyses of medieval court culture.[178] If there *was* a common 'court

[176] See R. Vaughan, *Philip the Bold* (London, 1962), 205–6 (for the office of 'peintre du chastel de Hesdin et maistre des engiens d'esbattements' and Melchior Broederlam's supervision of the repair of the *engins* and painting of the gallery there); and *Philip the Good* (London, 1970), 137–8.

[177] See *Inventaire sommaire des archives départementales du Nord. Série B*, ed. A le Glay *et al.*, 10 vols. (Lille, 1863–1906), iv. 123–4. An extract from the 1433 account is translated and printed in Vaughan, *Philip the Good*, 138–9.

[178] See Scattergood, 'Literary culture at the court of Richard II', in *English Court Culture*, 36: 'the available lists of books suggests that the culture of the court [of Richard II] was still overwhelmingly Latin and French, and French of a somewhat old-fashioned sort too . . .

culture', to what extent was it expressed, transmitted, and cemented by means of a *lingua franca*? The later Middle Ages witnessed the steady growth and spread of vernacular languages which began to vie with French—allegedly the primary medium of courtly and aristocratic culture—as acceptable and accepted means and media of expression among the upper echelons of society. The pace at which indigenous vernacular languages, such as Middle English or Middle Dutch, gained ground differed from one region to another. Middle Dutch, for example, developed and spread relatively rapidly during the second half of the thirteenth century in the Low Countries, while Middle English emerged rather more slowly and at a later date in England. But by the last quarter of the fourteenth century the phenomenon was widespread throughout north-west Europe.[179]

Further questions are posed by this marked, and novel, characteristic of the period from *c.* 1270 to 1380: was there, for instance, an inherent tension between the rise of vernacular literature and speech in the courts of the Low Countries and England and the cosmopolitanism of court culture? Or was vernacular literature—in Middle English, Middle Dutch, and Middle High German—largely intended not for a 'courtly' or 'noble' audience, but for burghers who were advancing their power and their status—political, social, and economic—in the thirteenth century?[180] Whatever the case, the rise of vernaculars to acceptability as vehicles of 'court' literature poses important questions about the nature of court culture. A number of assumptions have been made about the role of language in that culture. Some of them have been influenced by later notions—especially of conflict between princes and towns, or between nobilities and townsmen, and by nineteenth-century attempts to equate

English evidently had to go far before it acquired any sort of prestige.' Also see A. I. Doyle, 'English books in and out of court from Edward III to Henry VII', ibid. 163–81; Bumke, *Courtly Culture*, 452–75.

[179] See W. Prevenier, 'Court and city culture in the Low Countries from 1100 to 1530', in Kooper (ed.), *Medieval Dutch Literature*, 16–20. For a general account of the rise and spread of literary vernaculars at this time see N. Havely, 'Literature in Italian, French and English: uses and muses of the vernacular', in Jones (ed.), *New Cambridge Medieval History*, vi. (Cambridge, 2000) 257–70. The role of translation in furthering the development of vernacular prose is discussed in R. Copeland, *Rhetoric, Hermeneutics and Translation in the Middle Ages: Academic Traditions and Vernacular Texts* (Cambridge, 1991), esp. ch. 5.

[180] See e.g. R. Meyer, *Literature of the Low Countries: A Short History of Dutch Literature in the Netherlands and Belgium* (The Hague and Boston, 1978), 22–6; cf. Prevenier, 'Court and city culture', 14–18.

the use of vernacular languages with the rise of national sentiment and identity.[181]

One of the most common of these assumptions is that the pre-eminently 'courtly' culture of western Europe—not only in the later Middle Ages—was French, and that all other courts (with the possible exception of that of Burgundy) were overshadowed, or even eclipsed, by that—or those—of France. Joachim Bumke can thus write that, in German-speaking lands, 'the courtly ideal of society did not grow gradually, but was adopted . . . as a literary import from France'.[182] The thirteenth century has been seen by French historians as 'the century of St Louis', and the ascent of the Capetian monarchy to European dominance after the collapse of the German Hohenstaufen emperors in 1250 has led some to speak of a French hegemony which lasted until the crises and humiliations at the hands of the English in the 1340s and 1350s.[183] In cultural terms, the eulogization of Louis IX by subsequent generations perhaps conferred undue significance upon his reign when, it is claimed, a 'court style'—in architecture and manuscript illumination—was born.[184] The justifiable admiration of later historians for the cultural and intellectual life of Paris in the thirteenth century has also set the tone of much subsequent scholarship.[185] It is hardly surprising that something of a reaction to this kind of view should have taken place, especially among Belgian and Dutch scholars. Furthermore, European courtly literature, from the later twelfth century onwards, is often considered to be either exclusively French—in both language and inspiration—or so heavily influenced by French models and exemplars that it is almost entirely derivative and lacking in originality.[186]

The adoption, in court circles, of a common French literary language which also differed from the romance variations which proliferated around it is revealing. Although it could be heavily influenced by dialectal

---

[181] See the pertinent comments in Van Oostrom, 'Middle Dutch literature at court', 39–40.

[182] Bumke, *Courtly Culture*, 276.

[183] See, for a good instance of this tendency, J. Le Goff, *Saint Louis*, 13–14, 892.

[184] See Branner, *St Louis and the Court Style*, esp. 85–137.

[185] See A. Henry, *L'Oeuvre lyrique d'Henri III, duc de Brabant* (Bruges, 1948), 25: 'le xiiie siècle, le grand siècle, consacra la France et, singulièrement, Paris comme centre intellectuel de l'univers'.

[186] See Bumke, *Courtly Culture*, 458–74. For an analogous critical reaction against French 'supremacy' in the visual arts see Binski, *Westminster Abbey*, 161–7, esp. 166: 'we must be wary of the deeper chauvinisms of art history, the resistant beliefs in the supremacy of Parisian art over French, of French art over English, or of Italian art over both'.

forms—Picard or Walloon, for example—the language known as *francois*, or *francien*, was based upon that of the Île-de-France, especially from the region around Paris and Pontoise. Adenet le Roi, when in the service of Henri III of Brabant, wrote in his *Berte aus grans pies* that the king and queen of Hungary, as well as Berthe, knew 'le francois de Paris' very well:

> Com se il fussent ne au bourc a Saint Denis,
> Car li rois de Hongrie fu en France norris.[187]

> [As if they had been born at St-Denis,
> For the king of Hungary had been brought up in France.]

Similarly, Philippe de Beaumanoir, in his *Jean de Dammartin et Blonde d'Oxford* (*c.*1280) spoke of the English-born heroine of his romance in glowing terms, while commenting:

> Un peu paroit a son langage
> Que ne fu pas nee a Pontoise.[188]

> [It was just a little apparent from her speech
> That she had not been born at Pontoise.]

Chaucer took up the distinction between Anglo-Norman and Parisian French, for comic effect, in his frequently cited depiction of the well-born Prioress in the *General Prologue* to the *Canterbury Tales*:

> And Frensch she spak ful faire and fetisly,
> After the scole of Stratford atte Bowe,
> For Frensch of Parys was to hire unknowe.[189]

The distinction made at this time between the terms *francois* (or *francien*) and *roman* in French-language sources is also noteworthy. The generic term *roman* was clearly distinct from the more precise *francien*, meaning the French of the Île-de-France and the Paris basin. The international currency of the latter language was a primary characteristic of court

---

[187] Adenet le Roi, *Oeuvres*, ed. A. Scheler (Brussels, 1874), ll. 150–1.

[188] P. de Beaumanoir, *Oeuvres Poétiques*, ed. H. Suchier, 2 vols. (Paris, 1885), ii. 14, ll. 358–9; P. Rickard, *Britain in Medieval French Literature, 1100–1500* (Cambridge, 1956), 125–9, 170–3.

[189] G. Chaucer, *The Canterbury Tales*, ed. A. C. Cawley (London, 1975), ll. 124–6. See also W. Rothwell, 'Stratford atte Bowe and Paris', *Modern Language Review*, 80 (1985), 40–2, 54. For the teaching of French in England see B. Merrilees, 'Donatus and the teaching of French in medieval England', in I. Short (ed.), *Anglo-Norman Anniversary Essays* (London, 1993), 273–91, and W. Rothwell, 'A mis-judged author and a mis-used text: Walter of Bibbesworth and his "Tretiz"', *Modern Language Review*, 77 (1982), 282–93. By the late fourteenth/early fifteenth century English compilers of Donatus and other treatises refer to 'Donait soloum douce franceis de Paris' [Donatus according to the fair French of Paris] (Merrilees, 'Donatus', 283–91).

society and—like clerical Latin—it was gradually becoming a true *lingua franca* of secular discourse. From the late twelfth century onwards, the dialect of the Paris region was seen by many as superior, at least in its written form, to the other northern French variants with which it was surrounded.[190] In England, the use of French, in its Anglo-Norman form, was widespread among the upper and middle strata of society until the rise of London English in the age of Chaucer. The Anglo-Norman modes in which the French language was cast could therefore give rise to derision and mockery among the more 'courtly' practitioners of Île-de-France French, as did other regional variations of the language within France itself.[191]

But it would be misleading to draw too sharp a contrast between 'insular' (English) and 'continental' French—there were also marked differences between Parisian French and neighbouring forms such as Picard, Norman, and Walloon. But the book- and letter-collections of English princes and nobles, and the manuscripts presented to them, also suggest some degree of familiarity with the 'best' literary French.[192] It was thought to be both desirable, and necessary for social ascent, to learn French—the evidence of a rhyming chronicle composed, in Middle English, between *c*.1294 and 1300 by Robert, a monk of St Peter's abbey, Gloucester, is clear on this point. Despite his robust English patriotism, Robert wrote that in England since the Norman Conquest of 1066

---

[190] For Parisian French and its status see Rothwell, 'Stratford atte Bowe and Paris', 42; for French in England, H. Suggett, 'The use of French in England in the later Middle Ages', *TRHS* 4th ser. 28 (1946), 60–83; M. T. Clanchy, *From Memory to Written Record* (London, 1979), 151–4, 197–201. For more recent surveys see A. J. Minnis (ed.), *Latin and Vernacular: Studies in Late-Medieval Texts and Manuscripts* (Cambridge, 1988), and J. Coleman, *Public Reading and the Reading Public in Late Medieval England and France* (Cambridge, 1996).

[191] Beaumanoir, *Oeuvres poétiques*, ii. 83 (ll. 2635–6, 2639–40); 84 (ll. 2658–9). For the active role of Anglo-Norman in England in the later thirteenth and fourteenth centuries see W. Rothwell, 'The "Faus Franceis d'Angleterre": later Anglo-Norman', in I. Short (ed.), *Anglo-Norman Anniversary Essays* (London, 1993), 309–26. Rothwell observes that in England, by the fourteenth century, French—in its more strictly *francien* form—'must have become increasingly a written language, perpetuated . . . by an educated class whose members had either French blood, had studied in France, or had learned French in England to further their careers' (323). The wider use of Anglo-Norman, however, among other social groups, and its development as a living language, revealed divergences akin to those found in France itself between Parisian and other forms of French.

[192] See M. Blaess, 'L'abbaye de Bordesley et les livres de Guy de Beauchamp', *Romania*, 78 (1957), 511–18; Vale, 'England, France and the Origins of the Hundred Years War', in Jones and Vale (eds.), *England and her Neighbours*, 212–13.

The Normans spoke nought but their own speech,
And spoke French . . . and did their children teach;
So that high men of this land, that of their blood came,
All speak this tongue, that they took from the same,
For unless he speaks French, a man's worth is less,
As low men holden to English, and their own speech confess.[193]

The monk considered it best to know both English and French 'as the more a man knows, the more worth he is'.[194] To attain status and 'worthiness' in English society at the end of the thirteenth century it was thus still necessary to learn French, at least in its Anglo-Norman form. Court society refined this linguistic requirement further, but the existence of an independent Anglo-Norman literature in English court circles again indicates the significance of important linguistic variations within French-speaking regions.[195] Nevertheless, the existence of a common French literary language, comprehensible throughout the courts of north-west Europe, cannot be denied. The court, as a focus and forum of literary activity therefore functioned as both a centre and a vehicle for the reception and dissemination of primarily French literary themes and genres, in both written and oral form.

Orality, aurality, and literacy—if they were to enable a largely non-Latinate laity to communicate across regional and national boundaries—had to find a common tongue and a common medium. Since the second half of the twelfth century, French had been the language of much vernacular literature outside France—in Italy and England, for example—and of much aristocratic and clerical discourse as well as everyday speech.[196] But there is also evidence that the courts of Dutch-speaking

---

[193] *The Metrical Chronicle of Robert of Gloucester*, ed. W. A. Wright, 2 vols. (RS, London, 1887), ii. ll. 7537–43. For his patriotism see i. ll. 1–5. Italics mine.

[194] Ibid., ii. l. 7547: 'vor the more that a man can. the more worthe he is . . .'

[195] See M. D. Legge, *Anglo-Norman Literature and its Background* (Oxford, 1963), 3–6, 162–75, 278–310; also *La Vie du Prince Noir by Chandos Herald*, ed. Tyson, 24–37; Rothwell, 'The "Faus Franceis d'Angleterre" ', 321–6; and his 'The missing link in English etymology: Anglo-French', *Medium Aevum*, 60 (1991), 173–96. For recent work in historical linguistics, emphasizing the importance of variation, see J. Milroy, *Linguistic Change and Variation* (Oxford, 1992), 124–8, 154–7. Anglo-Norman historical writing is discussed in J. C. Thiolier (ed.), *Édition critique et commentée de Pierre de Langtoft, Le Règne d'Édouard Ier*, i (Paris, 1989), 9–30.

[196] For the popularity of one influential Old French text in both France and Italy see L.-F. Flutre, *Li Fait des Romains dans les littératures française et italienne du xiiie au xvie siècle* (Paris, 1932); P. Meyer, 'De l'Expansion de la langue française en Italie pendant le moyen âge', *Atti del Congresso Internazionale di Scienze Storiche, Roma, 1903*, iv (Rome, 1904), 61–104. For French and Provençal courtly literature and the notion of *cortesia* in Italy

Brabant and Holland were conversant with literature in French and with the use of French as a spoken as well as a written language. Four surviving pieces of admittedly undistinguished lyric verse in French have been attributed to Henri III of Brabant (1248–61), while Floris V of Holland (1256–96) was said to have been taught both French and Dutch (*walsch ende dietsch*) in his childhood.[197] In England, bilingualism prevailed among the upper and middle social strata—and in towns with close economic and other connections with continental Europe—until the end of the fourteenth century and, in the case of legal French, well beyond.[198] The court stood at the apex of this linguistic pyramid. The fact that John Gower (*c.*1330–1408) wrote both English and French prose and poetry, as well as Latin, in which he was fluent and practised, for a courtly audience, using English and French for different purposes and in different contexts, is striking. Gower's *Cinkante Balades* (*c.*1399–1400) represent the end of a tradition of Anglo-Norman lyric verse which had already lost ground to the increasingly pervasive influence of Middle English.[199] The francophone hegemony was, in England, slowly but perceptibly beginning to wane.

Yet to see *francophonie* (in its modern sense) as both a symptom and an instrument of some form of French cultural imperialism distorts the evidence. It has, for example, been argued that a strong sense of 'regnal solidarity', or of national or regional identity, was in no way incompatible with the use of French, nor of one of its many dialects or variants, among people for whom the Capetian or Valois crown meant little or nothing.[200] Nor do the mixed, multilingual courts of the Low Countries, especially of Flanders, Holland, and Brabant, conform to a monoglot pattern. Netherlandish language had been introduced as a literary tongue at the court of Flanders between 1238 and 1244 (with the Dutch version of the romance *Aiol* for countess Joanna); of Brabant between 1267 and 1294 (under Duke John I); and of Holland between 1266 and 1296 (under Count Floris V).[201] The role of Dutch as a court language in the duchy of Brabant was demonstrated by the composition of the *Rijmkroniek van*

---

see, for a succint account, J. Larner, *Italy in the Age of Dante and Petrarch, 1216–1380* (London, 1980), 95–102.

[197] See Henry, *L'Oeuvre lyrique d'Henri III*, 27, 36–40.

[198] See Legge, *Anglo-Norman Literature*, 330, 360–1; W. Rothwell, 'From Latin to Modern French: fifty years on', *Bulletin of the John Rylands Library*, 68 (1985), 193–4.

[199] Legge, *Anglo-Norman Literature*, 357–8; also see D. Pearsall, 'Gower's Latin in the *Confessio Amantis*', in Minnis (ed.), *Latin and Vernacular*, 12–26.

[200] See Gillingham, 'Crisis or continuity?', 65–7.

[201] See Prevenier, 'Court and city culture', 16.

Woeringen (1290) by Jan van Heelu, a Brabançon friar of the Teutonic Order, and its dedication to Margaret, daughter of Edward I of England, the new bride of John, the duke's son. This verse narrative of John I of Brabant's victory at Woeringen (1288) was presented to Margaret so that she might learn Dutch:

> Vrouwe Margriete van Inghelant,
> Die seker hevet van Brabant
> Tshertoghen Jans sone Jan,
> Want si dietsche tale niet en can
> Daer bi willic haer ene gichte
> Sinden van dietschen gedichte,
> Daer si dietsch in leeren moghe;
> Van haren sweer, den hertoghe,
> Sindic haer daer bi beschreven—
> Want en mach niet scoenres geven—
> Van ridderscape grote dade.[202]

[As lady Margaret of England, who is betrothed to the duke of Brabant's son John, does not understand Dutch speech, I wish to send her a present of Dutch poetry, so that she may learn Dutch; and besides I send her an account—as I can give nothing more beautiful—of her father-in-law the duke's fine deeds of knighthood.]

The Brabançon court thus fostered vernacular Dutch literature, and Margaret might also—as future duchess of Brabant—find a knowledge of Dutch valuable in communicating with the Netherlandish-speaking elements among her subjects. But there can also be no doubt of the familiarity of the rulers of these principalities—and the members of their courts—with French as both a literary and everyday, spoken and written language. One language never completely displaced the other.

The co-existence of Dutch and French at the court of Holland in the later thirteenth century, for instance, is well documented. The reign of Floris V (1256–96) saw the increasing acceptance and use of Middle Dutch as a literary language.[203] The work of the Fleming, Jacob van Maerlant, culminating in his verse *Spiegel historiael*, a Dutch version of Vincent of Beauvais's *Speculum*, of *c.*1281–8, was patronized largely by Dutch nobles in the circle around the young Floris V.[204] It was continued by the Brabançon Lodewijk van Velthem who produced a fourth and fifth

---

[202] Jan van Heelu, *Rymkronyk van Jan van Heelu betreffende den slag van Woeringen van het jaar 1288*, ed. J. F. Willems (Brussels, 1836), ll. 1–11.

[203] Van Oostrom, 'Middle Dutch literature at court', 31–2; Prevenier, 'Court and city culture', 16–17.

[204] F. Van Oostrom, *Maerlants Wereld* (Amsterdam, 1996), 307–10, 416–20.

book of the *Spiegel* taking it up to 1316.[205] The acceptability of Dutch as a vehicle of courtly discourse and literary production was furthered by the work of Melis Stoke, chancery clerk at the court of Holland, serving—it should be stressed—under both the Dutch-speaking and French-speaking counts (c.1278–1310). The manuscripts of his verse chronicle, the *Rijmkroniek van Holland*, bear dedications to both Floris V and William III of Hainault-Holland.[206] It has thus been concluded that 'the [Middle Dutch] verse chronicle functions primarily in courtly surroundings'.[207] It was certainly not confined to an audience of burghers. Similarly, recent work on Middle Dutch literature in general has led to such conclusions as 'a simple polarization (French equals nobility; Middle Dutch equals other estates) will not do . . . In actual fact, there seems to have been extensive multilingualism . . . Middle Dutch and French to a very large extent co-existed at court, with successive shifts in priority'.[208]

The multilingualism of the Dutch court—in which Latin, French, and Dutch co-existed—is evident from a number of sources. Among them is a letter which Floris V sent to Edward I of England, probably between January and May 1290. The letter was drawn up by a clerk of Floris's chancery, in French.[209] The count wrote that he was sending the king a falcon (*un ostoir des mieudres de mon pais par Williame mon vallet ki warde mes ostoirs*) ['one of the best falcons of my land by means of William, my valet who keeps my falcons']. This clerk has been identified as the writer of a number of other surviving letters, all in Dutch, dating from 1281 to 1293.[210] The bi- (or multi-) lingual skills of Dutch chancery and other clerks suggest a familiarity with both Latin and the vernacular

[205] Lodewijk van Velthem, *Voorzetting van den Spiegel Historiael*, ed. H. van der Linden, P. de Keyser, and A. van Loey, 3 vols. (Brussels, 1906–38), esp. vol. iii; for a brief biographical summary see Kooper (ed.), *Medieval Dutch Literature*, 313.

[206] See F. W. N. Hugenholtz, 'Melis Stoke en Jacob van Maerlant', in D. De Boer and J. W. Marsilje (eds.), *De Nederlanden in de late middeleeuwen* (Utrecht, 1987), 18–26, and the biographical sketch in *Medieval Dutch Literature*, 313. For Melis Stoke as a clerk in William III's service (1305) see *De rekeningen*, ed. Smit, iii. 77.

[207] A. Hage, *Sonder Favele, Sonder Lieghen: Onderzoek naar vorm en functie van de Middelnederlandse rijmkroniek als historiografisch genre* (Utrecht, 1990), 274 and ch. 6.

[208] Van Oostrom, 'Middle Dutch Literature at Court', 31.

[209] PRO, SC.1/18/118; printed in *Oorkondenboek van Holland en Zeeland*, iv. no. 2499 [p. 865]. See Appendix IX.

[210] See J. W. J. Burgers, *De Paleografie van de documentaire bronnen in Holland en Zeeland in de dertiende eeuw*, iii (Leiden, 1995), 112–19: 'hand N of the comital chancery'. Also *Ooorkondenboek van Holland en Zeeland*, iv. nos. 1974, 2022, 2244, 2429, 2457, 2481, 2504, for other letters written by the same scribe.

languages which reflected, and to some extent promoted, the cosmopolitanism of court society. This degree of conversance with more than one written language can also be found in the household administrations of the counts of Hainault-Holland and of Flanders under the Avesnes and Dampierre houses respectively. Although some of the Dutch-speaking clerks in the service of the Avesnes counts of Hainault-Holland were not apparently fully competent in French, there is evidence for extensive bilingualism.[211] Sometimes a tell-tale slip or scribal error in an account can be very revealing. Thus in September 1333, the clerk who wrote the household account of William, son of William III of Hainault-Holland, recorded the payment of 4 *estrelins* to the receiver, Sandrin, for a sum lent by him 'pour un esprevier Wuillaume reprins en le *tune* d'une povre femme' ('for one of William's sparrowhawks recovered in a poor woman's garden').[212] The clerk must have been thinking of the Dutch word *tuin* (for *jardin*, garden) when he wrote this entry. The original quittance that he could have been registering may have been in Dutch, so that he slipped into that language.

As we have already seen, the joint participation of Dutch and Hainaulter nobles in such events as tournaments and Round Tables must have given currency to the use of French among them.[213] Similarly, in the *comté* of Flanders, the close juxtaposition of francophone and Flemish-speaking areas led to extensive bi-lingualism. This was expressed by the patronage and ownership of Flemish books, including collections of secular poetry and musical settings, among members of the count's court and household.[214] The familiarity of the Flemish clerks of the *Chambre des*

---

[211] See *De rekeningen*, ed. Smit, iii. 219–20. In 1344, a Dutch officer of the count, Ysebaut van Asperen, was assisted by French-speaking ('Walsche') clerks at Binche to draw up his accounts in French and, in 1345, four of his accounts, drawn up in French, were also copied out in Dutch (ibid. 220).

[212] Ibid., i. 671. Italics mine.

[213] Ibid., i. 654, 661–2, 672: Round Table at Haarlem, Sept. 1333. See also above, pp. 193–4.

[214] The so-called Gruuthuse Songbook (*c.*1390–1400), owned by the Gruuthuse family of Bruges, contains 14 poems and 147 songs, largely in Dutch, with a few verses in French, reflecting the popularity of vernacular lyrics among the upper classes. In 1462 the collection was assembled in its present form, and entitled 'Rhetorijcke ende Ghebeden Bouck van mher Loijs vanden Gruythuijse'. See K. Heeroma and C. W. H. Lindenburg (eds.), *Liederen en gedichten uit het Gruuthuse-handschrift* (Leiden, 1966); K. Vellekoop, 'Gruuthuse-Handschrift', in L. Fischer (ed.), *Die Musik in Geschichte und Gegenwart: Allegemeine Enzyklopädie der Musik begründet von Friedrich Blume*, iii (Kassel, 1995), 1722–3. For recent comment on the relationship between French and Netherlandish lyrics in the Gruuthuse manuscript and other sources, see below, n. 216.

comptes with both French and Dutch meant that both languages could be employed side-by-side within the same piece of accounting material. Hence, under Louis de Male, a schedule of expenses was drawn up in November 1381 which began in Dutch, moved into French, and ended in Dutch. The clerk moved from one language to the other with ease—even if he had simply been copying warrants and quittances on to the roll, there is no sign of any awkwardness or clumsiness in the transcription. The expenses of packing, loading, and carting the count's tapestries (*tapis-series*) at Lille (*te Rijsele*) were thus certified at Bruges in a mixture of juxtaposed Dutch and French entries.[215] When subsidiary documents such as quittances and vouchers could be received by accounting officers in both languages, this kind of duality was common. In an administrative as well as in a literary context, the two languages co-existed.

The common usage of French was reflected in the extreme internationalism of certain art forms. In music, many lyrics were in French—and in its dialects and variants—in order to command an audience across the courts of north-west Europe. England, Flanders, Artois, Hainault, Brabant, and Holland witnessed the constant passage of minstrels and singers from court to court. The French *virelai* and *ballade* were appreciated everywhere, although a hybrid form, the *virelai-ballade* with lyrics in Middle Dutch and Middle High German, continued to be popular in the Low Countries and the Rhineland.[216] But the provenance and identity of visiting minstrels recorded at the English court in the later thirteenth and early fourteenth centuries suggests that French was also the *lingua franca* there of the performing arts.

The marriages of Edward I's daughters Joan and Margaret in the spring and summer of 1290 attracted large numbers of 'foreign' minstrels and other performers. Minstrels came from a wide geographical area—northern France (Champagne, the *comtés* of Aumale and St-Pol, Douai, Artois, Brittany), the Low Countries (Flanders, Brabant, Liège, Holland), and Scotland.[217] They included Adinet 'de Pyrewe' (or 'de

[215] ADN, B.3241, no. 111859: 6 Nov. 1381.

[216] See Willaert in *Middle Dutch Literature*, esp. 173–5. Also, for a survey of Netherlandish lyric poetry and song, and its relationship to the French repertoire, during the period from *c.*1280 to *c.*1400, see F. Willaert, 'Een proefvlucht naar het zwarte gat. De Nederlandse liedkunst tussen Jan I van Brabant en het Gruuthuse-handschrift', in F. Willaert (ed.), *Veelderhande Liedekens: Studies over het Nederlandse lied tot 1600* (Leuven, 1997), 30–46, esp. 40–3. For recent studies of musical forms and performing techniques during this period see C. Page, *Voices and Instruments of the Middle Ages: Instrumental Practice and Songs in France* (London, 1987), and his *Discarding Images: Reflections on Music and Culture in medieval France* (Oxford, 1994).

[217] PRO, C.47/4/5, fos. 45v, 47r, 48v, 49r: May–Sept. 1290.

Perou') minstrel of Guy de Dampierre, count of Flanders, given 66s. 8d. by Joan at her wedding, on the king's special order.[218] He was the highest-paid of any minstrel recorded in the account for the event, and can perhaps be identified with the celebrated Adinet le Roi, then in the service of the count of Flanders. On 11 July 1290, moreover, Walter de Stourton, the king's harper, dispensed payment to no fewer than 426 minstrels 'both English and foreign, on behalf of John, son of the duke of Brabant, on the morrow of the nuptials of lady Margaret, the king's daughter'.[219] On 12 July, Artois, the fool of Robert II of Artois, was rewarded. He had come to the festivities in the company of John I of Brabant and was returning to his home country. Similar evidence could be multiplied on the occasion of other royal weddings—in July 1299, foreign minstrels attended the second marriage of Edward I, to Margaret of France, at Canterbury. They included vielle-players of the bishop of Carcassonne and of Geoffroi de Lusignan, and the father-and-son combination of John *Simphoniste*, senior and junior, as well as twelve other minstrels performing before the king there.[220]

The world of minstrels and other performers was equally mobile and fluid in the Low Countries. Individual singers and players were often associated with particular princes, lords, or towns, and were clearly retained by them, but this in no way prevented them from performing (and, no doubt, composing) at other courts. Between December 1276 and May 1277, for example, the court of Flanders received a constant stream of minstrels—among them, those serving the duke of Brabant ('Tassin', 'Boidin', and 'Estuol le sot'), the count of Holland, the counts of Boulogne, Artois, Rethel, and Champagne, and Nicholas Morel, king-herald and minstrel of Edward I.[221] During this period, at least one minstrel exercised other skills at the Flemish court—on 11 March 1277, when Guy de Dampierre and his household were at Paris, one Gilot le menestrel pulled out teeth as a *traicheur de dens*.[222] Besides the visiting performers, recurrent payments to 'Adam le menestrel', or 'Adan le menestrel' may refer to Adinet le Roi's more permanent position at the court of Flanders.[223] A century later, Louis de Male was supporting both

[218] C.47/4/5, fo. 47r; also BL, Add. MS 35294, fo. 10v; E.101/352/21. On 17 July 1298 he had received 100s. by special order of the queen at Havering.

[219] C.47/4/5, fo. 48r.   [220] E.101/355/18, m. 4r: 13 and 17 July 1299.

[221] RAG, St-Genois 209, mm. 1r–v: 25 Dec. 1276–28 May 1277; Bullock-Davies, *Register of Royal and Baronial domestic Minstrels*, 123–5, for 'Roi Morel'.

[222] RAG, St-Genois 209, m. 1v.

[223] Ibid., mm. 1r, 1v: Dec. 1276; Wyffels (chron. suppl.) 107*bis*, m. 2r: Oct–Nov. 1280; Gaillard 52, m. 2r: July 1292.

francophone and Dutch-speaking minstrels on a lavish scale, including his own *pipere* (*pijper*) Jehanin, as well as visiting performers from the duke of Brittany, the lord of Hondeschout, and those accompanying Anne of Bohemia when she journeyed through Flanders on her way to marry Richard II of England in November 1381. In March 1382, Louis rewarded minstrels from the earl of Hereford, the lord of Couchy, the lord of Hekelsbeke, and the chamberlain of the king of Scotland.[224]

The role of minstrels as poets, reciting verse aloud in a courtly setting, is confirmed by evidence from the court of Hainault-Holland under the Avesnes (Pl. 38). Thus in May 1327, the countess Jeanne of Valois rewarded minstrels who 'recited before my lady at The Hague' (*ki compterent devant medame a Le Haie*) and the count's son William paid a certain Master Jean *conteur de dis* [*dits*] in May 1332.[225] In the following year a *compteur* [*conteur*] called Le Borgne, who was also a herald or pursuivant, received payment at Valenciennes.[226] Thus the herald-minstrel-poet combination could still be found in one person, a tendency continued later in the fourteenth century by such figures as Gelre and Chandos Heralds.[227] Many of such men must have been able to perform in more than one language, as *conteurs*, *sprekers*, and *dichters*.

The world of the performing arts in the courts of north-west Europe at this time was therefore never exclusively francophone. In some regions, Netherlandish and Germanic speech enjoyed a role in literary, theatrical, and musical performance which could rival—but never, it seems, entirely replace—that held by French, in all its variant forms. England provided something of an exception to this tendency. Middle English only gained recognition and acceptance in court circles towards the latter part of the fourteenth century, a good century after Middle Dutch or Middle High German had been received and accepted at some continental European courts. French had to be learned, however, if entry into the international court milieu of the fourteenth century was to be achieved and sustained. This was a fact of cultural life which long outlived the later Middle Ages.

---

[224] ADN, B.3237, no. 111771; B.3238, nos. 111793, 111818, 111866b: minstrels of Anne of Bohemia, the duke of Tessen, the king of Scotland and the duke of Luxemburg, paid a total of 172 l. 5s. 8d.p. on 18 Nov. 1381; B.3240, no. 111931–2: 26 Mar. 1382. For Anne of Bohemia's reception in Flanders see Table 19.

[225] *De rekeningen*, ed. Smit, i. 305–6, 630.   [226] Ibid., i. 643: 3 Feb. 1333.

[227] See the studies of Gelre (Guelders) Herald in W. van Anrooij, *Spiegel van ridderschap: Heraut Gelre en zijn ereredes* (Amsterdam, 1990), esp. 56–77, and G. Nijsten, *Het Hof van Gelre*, esp. 129–43. For Chandos Herald see *La Vie du Prince Noir by Chandos Herald*, ed. Tyson, esp. 4–15.

CONCLUSION

This book has attempted to examine the princely courts of north-west Europe during the later thirteenth and fourteenth centuries from a number of standpoints—political, economic, social, religious, artistic, and more broadly 'cultural'. As such, it inevitably runs a number of risks. Primarily there is the likelihood of encountering criticism from specialists within each of those fields of enquiry. It is inevitable that some areas have received more attention than others. Its geographical range also gives rise to the perfectly justifiable objection that each of the areas chosen should have received more comprehensive, separate treatment before a general, comparative study was undertaken by a single author. Within the frame of broadly comparative discussion, however, efforts have been made to incorporate such an approach, and my conclusions are based upon detailed, free-standing treatments of many aspects of the various courts and households which are the book's concern. However, the connections and affinities between them appeared to justify a study which overrode artificial national, regional, and linguistic boundaries, departed from 'traditional' historiographical approaches and discussed consumption, logistics, and expenditure, as well as artistic and cultural issues, within the same framework. To encompass a geographical area which forms a large part of north-west Europe within a single volume also prompts questions about the extent to which both national and regional 'schools' of historical writing have determined and shaped interpretations of this period, not only in Britain and France, but also in the Low Countries.

The history of princely courts, many of which were essentially cosmopolitan in character, maintained by dynasties which were sometimes 'foreign' to the area and to the people over whom they ruled, is not easy to integrate into interpretations of the later Middle Ages which focus upon the growth of national sentiment and the rise of the 'modern' nation-state. The tendency of both British and French historians to search for signs of state formation and a sense of national identity in their medieval past is well known and needs little further comment. Yet the very different evolution of the state in the Low Countries has not prevented Belgian and Dutch scholars from tracing similar tendencies. Since the creation of the modern states of Belgium and the Netherlands in the second quarter of the nineteenth century, national sentiment has played its part in moulding perceptions of their very different destinies. It has been rightly said that 'the Netherlands and Belgium did not emerge into nationhood through some natural, organic, historical process'.[1] A broadly accepted nineteenth- and twentieth-century view sees the modern state essentially as a unitary nation-state—if there is no nation, it is claimed, then there can be no state capable of survival. Hence historians of both the northern and southern Low Countries have tended to seek out signs of 'national' self-consciousness in, for example, the struggles of the Flemish towns (above all, the city of Ghent) with the medieval counts of Flanders, or the sturdy independence of the Dutch burghers and farmers from princely authority. Foreign rule during the fifteenth and sixteenth centuries—Burgundian and Habsburg—heightened awareness of both national and regional characteristics, or so it is argued, and Netherlandish speech came to symbolize identity, separatism, and dissent.

It should nevertheless be borne in mind that none of the political units of the period studied in this book coincide with modern states or other recognizably modern political or administrative divisions—the kingdom of England was to form only one part of the United Kingdom of Great Britain and Ireland; the kingdom of France possessed different boundaries from the present hexagon, and monarchical authority was not equivalent —nor even comparable—to that of the modern French state; the neighbouring medieval *comtés* of Flanders and Hainault are now internally split between France and Belgium; the *comté* of Artois was not co-terminous with the modern *département* of Pas-de-Calais; and the county of Holland formed only one relatively small, though very important, part of the much-expanded modern Netherlands. Hence an examination of the courts held and maintained by the rulers of these composite political units, often consisting of disparate territories and peoples, tends to emphasize a fundamental characteristic of later medieval (and early modern) polities: the 'states' over which these princes ruled were not clearly defined territorial entities, but communities of subjects and vassals bound together by common dynastic allegiances. Within their dominions, rulers were obliged to observe regional, provincial, and seigneurial privileges—the prince and his court came to the regions, exchanged oaths, endorsed

[1] J. A. Kossmann-Putto and E. H. Kossmann, *The Low Countries: History of the Northern and Southern Netherlands* (Rekkem, 1997), 59.

liberties and immunities, and engaged in dialogue with their representatives. The looser, more federal, structures of authority in this period may have more in common with modern notions of a 'Europe of regions' than with that of the unitary nation-state, with its common linguistic, cultural, and in the most ideologically extreme and alarming instances, ethnic identity.

A fundamental premise of this book is that a common culture prevailed among the court milieux and societies of the later thirteenth and fourteenth centuries. Although a specifically 'court' culture tends to elude definition and identification, while the concept of a 'court style' in the arts is difficult to sustain—let alone demonstrate in practice—sufficient similarities existed between courts for one to argue for a community of shared values, norms, and conventions. Some, but by no means all, forms, modes, styles, and genres in literature and the visual arts may have ultimately derived from French origins, but they were adapted to the context and circumstances in which they were received. The anthropological concept of cultural 'hybridity' is of relevance here, seeing cultures as permeable and porous, constantly borrowing, exchanging, and consuming both ideas and material goods.[2] Constant contact between princely courts thus tended to hold back the emergence of self-contained cultures which, rather, remained eclectic and open to outside influences of many kinds. Furthermore, high status demanded conspicuous consumption, and a passion for hunting, gambling, and the tournament was common to all courts and their members. In terms of their organization, functions, and the assumptions and expectations of those who frequented them, there were striking similarities between them. Dynastic politics, moreover, lubricated by alliances cemented by betrothal and marriage, were conducted in the setting of all these courts, which provided a forum for external relations as well as for dialogue and negotiation between rulers and their nobilities.

If such notions hold good, it could be argued that the history of princely courts departs in several important respects from the patterns and tendencies visible in much historical writing about states and rulers in the later Middle Ages. In the first place, the nationalisms and chauvinisms of the nineteenth and twentieth centuries find little place within it. If princely

---

[2] See M. Sahlins, 'Two or three things that I know about culture', *Journal of the Royal Anthropological Society*, 5 (1999), 411–12. For anthropological discussions and applications of the concept of 'hybridity', see P. Bourdieu, *The Field of Art Production* (Cambridge, 1993), and H. K. Bhabha, *The Location of Culture* (London, 1994).

courts were cosmopolitan, multilingual places, receptive to 'foreign' influences and fashions, their contribution to the rise of the nation-state was, at best, indirect. Perhaps that is one reason why they have been relatively neglected by historians of the modern state.[3] Courts often harboured 'foreign' favourites, were increasingly costly, and open to alien and external influences. They were thus more likely to arouse sentiments of both resentment and xenophobia among some sections of a ruler's subjects, provoking expressions of 'national' sentiment in reaction to their allegedly alien and extravagant nature. The court was a vehicle whereby a degree of internationalism and cosmopolitanism was transmitted to the upper strata—both clerical and lay—of society, in part through the use of a common language. Although the non-French vernacular languages of north-west Europe were certainly spoken and often written at the courts of this period—albeit on varying time-scales—French (and its variations) and Latin were known and used everywhere.[4] The popularity of works such as Froissart's *Chroniques* ensured the survival of his courtly French in court circles. No translation into English, for example, was made until 1524, when Lord Berners rendered the chronicles 'out of Frenche into our maternal englysshe tonge'.[5]

Nor did the court provide a model for 'modern' bureaucratic government. With its backbone furnished by the ruler's household, the court was a power-centre in which formal bureaucratic processes might be by-passed or ignored. The organization of the household gave structure and discipline to the otherwise structureless court, in which it was subsumed. The household departments or offices (*métiers*, *états*) might vary from region to region, but the mechanisms of supply and distribution whereby the needs of the ruler and his entourage were met were remarkably similar. Movement from one court to another was rendered easier by these similarities. Differentiation and stratification within households also became more clearly marked during this period, and the emergence of an upper household, populated by knights and squires, besides the clerks who had traditionally formed the permanent or 'palatine' establishment around a ruler, can be detected. Expenditure on courts and

[3] See, for recent discussion, J. Adamson, 'The making of the ancien-régime court', in id. (ed.), *The Princely Courts of Europe*, 9–10 and esp. 40.

[4] See L. Wright, 'Trade between England and the Low Countries: evidence from Historical Linguistics', in C. Barron and N. Saul (eds.), *England and the Low Countries*, 169–79; Rothwell, 'The "Faus Franceis d'Angleterre"', 310–12.

[5] G. C. Macaulay (ed.), *The Chronicles of Froissart, translated by John Bourchier, Lord Berners* (London, 1908), p. xxvii.

households increased as they grew in size, sometimes triggering criticism and complaint from dissident or excluded subjects. Household ordinances begin to survive in larger quantities, and the more detailed regulation of ceremony and protocol, as well as domestic function, appears from the second quarter of the fourteenth century onwards (Majorca, Dauphiné). The distribution by a ruler of liveries (*livrées*) in cloth, furs, and money had already served to delineate membership of a household, but the beginnings of colour-coded, heraldic, and other means of identifying those in receipt of livery were also found at this time. A ruler's 'affinity', retained, fed, and clothed by him, had become a fixed element in the courts of the later fourteenth century.

The later medieval court certainly influenced aristocratic and patrician attitudes and lifestyles and was, in turn, influenced by them. But it would be erroneous to see the court, in crudely functionalist terms, as an instrument whereby princes and their agents deployed forms of propaganda designed merely to bolster their authority. The centralization and bureaucratization of government was undoubtedly taking place, but courts did not necessarily form part of that process, nor did they develop centralized and bureaucratic functions at the same pace as other, more strictly administrative institutions. Although certain locations might be preferred, and fixed reference points for ruling houses were emerging (such as favoured burial places for their members), the court of this period remained what it had been for a long time: an assemblage of itinerant and peripatetic households. Polycentric, eclectic in its cultural and artistic tastes, albeit often drawn from a common reservoir of styles, the court was not a monolithic institution. Eclecticism characterized much of the artistic production which emanated from court milieux. The artists and craftsmen who worked for rulers and the members of their courts were not exclusively contracted to court service. Although some were retained for long-term service to a court, the notion that 'court artists' enjoyed a favoured position, allowing them greater freedom than that offered by urban guilds, or by other kinds of patron, cannot be sustained. High-status patrons of many sorts, mercantile, civic, and ecclesiastical, thus drew upon a wide range of talent and expertise, which was in no sense monopolized by the princely court.

Twelfth-century writers had referred to the court as a 'market', or *entrepôt*, in which trading of all kinds was carried on.[6] Power-broking, power-sharing, and the provision of points of contact between rulers and

[6] See Map, *De Nugis*, 242; also Lalou, 'Le fonctionnement de l'hôtel du roi', 146.

ruled, both formal and informal, whether through the celebration of the great liturgical feasts or through less overt, public means—these characteristics of the court were of enduring significance. So also was the role of religious and devotional activity at courts. The court's calendar was determined and regulated by liturgical observance, feasting, and fasting, and the court chapel played an increasingly significant part in the ritualization of everyday life. The evolution of the ruler's residence which harboured—or was adjacent to—a conventual house of monks, friars, or canons had already begun. The thirteenth-century palace-monastery at Westminster could be seen as a precursor of the sixteenth-century Escorial. The later Middle Ages have sometimes been portrayed as a period which saw the increasing secularization of the sacred. But they may also be seen as one which witnessed the increasing sacralization of the secular. A more formal, ritualized element gradually invaded the domestic life of princely courts, receiving its most marked—and often extravagant—expression at court feasts in which vows were taken, elaborate interludes and *entremets* introduced, and a more dramatic and theatrical dimension brought to the holding of 'full' or 'solemn' courts. Yet such developments were built on existing foundations, many of them reaching back into a distant past. The history of European courts can never exclude or ignore change, but it remains essentially a study of continuities.

Tables and Figures

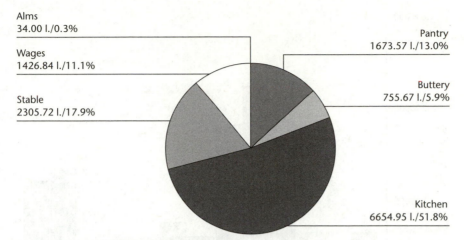

Alms
34.00 l./0.3%

Pantry
1673.57 l./13.0%

Wages
1426.84 l./11.1%

Buttery
755.67 l./5.9%

Stable
2305.72 l./17.9%

Kitchen
6654.95 l./51.8%

Total annual household expenditure = 12866.75 l. st.

FIG. 1 England: Total household expenditure, Nov. 1304–Nov. 1305

Source: PRO, E.101/367/15.

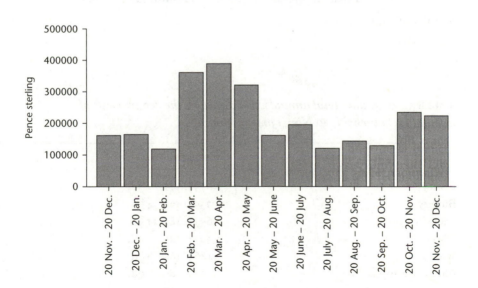

FIG. 2 England: Monthly totals for household expenditure, 1304–1305

Source: PRO, E.101/367/15.

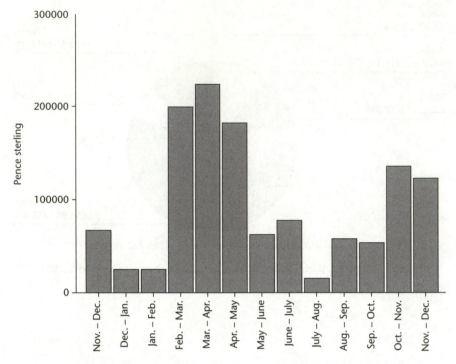

FIG. 3 England: Monthly kitchen expenditure, 1304–1305

Source: PRO, E.101/367/15.

TABLE 5. *England: Total annual expenditure on the departments of Edward I's household, 20 Nov. 1304–19 Nov. 1305*

Office or heading	Total expenditure
Pantry	1,673 l. 11s. 5d.
Buttery	755 l. 13s. $4\frac{1}{2}$ d.
Kitchen	6,654 l. 18s. 11$\frac{1}{2}$ d.
Stable	2,305 l. 14s. 4d.
Wages	1,426 l. 16s. $8\frac{1}{2}$ d.
Alms & oblations	34 l. 0s. 0d.
Grand Total:	12,866 l. 14s. $9\frac{1}{2}$ d.

Source: PRO, E.101/367/15.

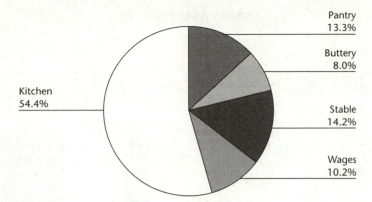

FIG. 4 England: Household expenditure, 20 Nov. 1306–7 July 1307

Source: PRO, E.101/370/8.

TABLE 6. *Expenditure on Edward II's household, 8 July 1307–7 July 1308*

	Sum spent
Prests (advances) to household members & offices	306 l. 19s. 10½d.
Gifts	1,194 l. 16s. 2d.
Messengers	40 l. 12s. 4d.
Kitchen	967 l. 6s. 8d.
Hall & Chamber	30 l. 16s. 6½d.
	665 l. 19s. 2½d.
	83 l. 12s. 10½d.
Total:	780 l. 8s. 7½d.
Marshalsea	310 l. 18s. 2½d.
	542 l. 18s. 11d.
Total:	853 l. 17s. 11 d.
Pantry & Buttery	473 l. 12s. 5d.
Oblations	18 l. 4s. 0d.
Expenses of salsaria	34 l. 16s. 0½d.
Prests to knights	274 l. 8s. 8½d.
Horses purchased	1,183 l. 4s. 7d.
Cloth purchased	93 l. 13s. 4d.
Wax, furs, saddles etc.	522 l. 15s. 7d.
GRAND TOTAL of expenditure:	20,241 l. 15s. 1½d.

Source: PRO, E.101/373/15.

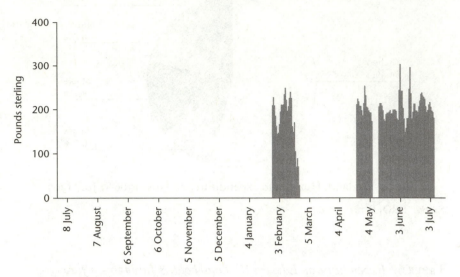

FIG. 5 Total household expenses of the future Edward III, 1312–1313
(running averages, from surviving accounts)

Source: PRO, E.101/375/3.

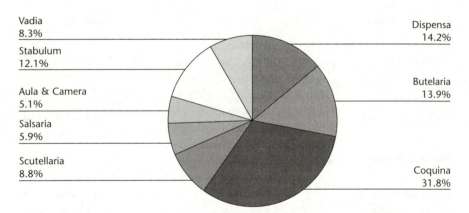

FIG. 6 Distribution of daily expenses for the future Edward III, 1312–1313

Source: PRO, E.101/375/3.

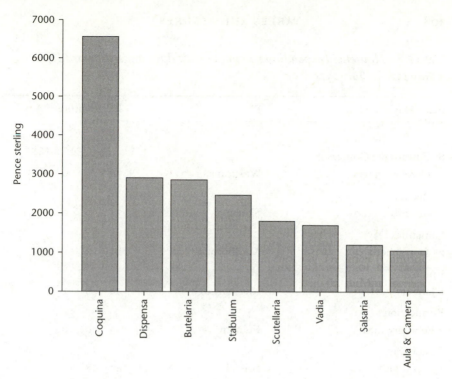

FIG. 7 Distribution of daily expenses for the future Edward III, 1312–1313

Source: PRO, E.101/375/3.

TABLE 7. *Expenditure on Edward II's household, 8 July 1315–7 July 1316*

Department or heading	Expenditure		
	l.	s.	d.
Alms	194	11	11
Necessaria	4,644	12	0½
Victualia	887	14	1
Wages of some servants	146	15	10½
Calciamenta	43	3	4
Dona	3,018	14	8
Knights' fees	196	13	4
Wages of war	9,958	0	1
Roba	627	0	0
Jocalia	334	18	11
Wine purchase	1,160	13	9
GRAND TOTAL:	21,212	17	11

Source: PRO, E.101/376/7.

TABLE 8. *Household expenditure on major feast days under Edward II, 8 July 1320–7 July 1321*

Feast Day and Date	Place	Expenditure		
		l.	s.	d.
St Edward the Confessor 13 October 1320	Westminster	33	8	0½
All Saints 1 November 1320	Sheen	35	0	0½
Christmas Day 25 December 1320	Marlborough	41	12	11
Epiphany 6 January 1321	Marlborough	18	6	1½
Purification 2 February 1321	Fulham	33	0	10½
Easter Day 19 April 1321	Bristol	40	18	6
Ascension 28 May 1321	Westminster	21	15	9
Pentecost 7 June 1321	Faversham	42	9	0½
Nativity of St John Baptist 24 June 1321	Dover	21	18	6
Total expenditure on feast days:		288	9	9½ (5.6%)
Total household expenditure:		5,099	2	8

Source: PRO, E.101/378/10.

TABLE 9. *Household expenditure on major feast days under Edward II,*
8 July 1321–30 Apr. 1322

Feast Day and Date	Place	Expenditure		
		l.	s.	d.
[Creation of Edmund, the king's brother, as earl of Kent, 26 July 1321]	Westminster	31	14	7
Michaelmas Day 29 September 1321	Tower of London	25	18	2
All Saints 1 November 1321	Leeds castle	59	10	8
Christmas Day 25 December 1321	Cirencester	87	13	$7\frac{1}{2}$
Epiphany 6 January 1322	Cirencester	25	17	4
Purification 2 February 1322	Hereford	35	13	$4\frac{1}{2}$
Easter Day 11 April 1322	Pontefract	82	7	3
Total expenditure on feast days:		348	15	0 (5.2%)
Total household expenditure:		6,657	3	$10\frac{1}{2}$

Source: PRO, E.101/378/11.

TABLE 10. *Household expenditure on major feast days under Edward II and Edward III, 1 Nov. 1326–24 Jan. 1328*

Feast Day and date	Place	Expenditure		
		l.	s.	d.
Christmas Day 25 December 1326	Wallingford	142	0	$11\frac{1}{2}$
Epiphany 6 January 1327	Westminster	58	4	8
[Coronation of Edward III, 1 February 1327]	Westminster	1,323	0	$7\frac{3}{4}$
Purification 2 February 1327	Westminster	47	2	9
Easter Day 12 April 1327	York	58	17	$7\frac{3}{4}$
Pentecost 31 May 1327	York	102	18	$6\frac{1}{4}$
Nativity of St John Baptist 24 June 1327	Carlisle	42	6	4
Christmas Day 25 December 1327	Worcester	116	19	$5\frac{3}{4}$

Source: PRO, E.101/382/9.

Note: These figures represent the addition of expenditure on the *hospicium* and the *expensa forinseca*, where appropriate, as recorded in the wardrobe account. Annual totals are not given, as the *expensa forinseca* include payment of wages of war by the wardrobe and therefore distort the figures for household expenditure.

TABLE 11. *Itinerary and expenses of the household of Eleanor, sister of Edward III of England, on her marriage to Reinhoud, count of Guelders, at Nijmegen, 26 Apr. 1332–11 June 1332*

Headed: Rotulus expensarum hospicii domine Alienore, sororis domini . . . Regis Anglie, tam in partibus Anglie quam in partibus Flandrie, Brabancie et Almanie, una cum expensis familie eiusdem domine *pro solempnitate nupciarum inter dominum comitem Gerlens' et ipsam initarum per . . . Regem assign' redeunt' de partibus supradictis usque London', tempore domini Roberti de Tong, locumtenentis custodis Garderobe eiusdem domine a [26 Apr. 6 Ed III–11 June 6 Ed III].*

Lists initial expenses of household departments at London [cf. E.101/386/7, fo. 2a]: i.e. of *dispensaria* [pantry], *butillaria, garderoba, coquina, scutillaria, salsaria, aula, elemosina, stabulum & vadia.*

Itinerary		Weekly total expenditure		
26 Apr.–1 May 1332	London			
1 May	Dartford	87 l.	18s.	6d.
2 May	Rochester & Canterbury			
3 May–5 May	Dover			
6 May–9 May	Sluys	167 l.	3s.	5d.
9 May–16 May	Bruges–Ghent–Denremonde– Malines–Leyre–Turnhout	68 l.	13s.	8d.
17 May–26 May	Bois-le-Duc–Grave–Nijmegen	56 l.	11s.	9d.
27 May–30 May	Grave–Bois-le- Duc–Tornhout– Malines	74 l.	15s.	$9\frac{1}{2}$d.
m. 2: 30 May–6 June	Tenremonde–Junius/Ghent– Bruges–Aardenberg–Dunkirk– Calais–Wissant	81 l.	9s.	$7\frac{1}{4}$d.
7 June–11 June	Wissant–Dover–Canterbury– Ospringe–Rochester–Dartford– London	41 l.	7s.	$3\frac{3}{4}$d.
	Total expenses:	569 l.	2s.	$1\frac{3}{4}$d.

Source: PRO, E.101/624/27, m. 1.

Note: Cf. E.101/386/7: account book of similar expenses, for 18 Apr.–26 July 1332; pub. *Archaeologia*, 77 (1928), 111–40.

TABLE 12. *Horses received and distributed by Robert de Tonge, treasurer of Eleanor, countess of Guelders, at the time of her marriage, Apr.–June 1332*

Horses received

Source	Horses
Master Robert de Ayleston, king's treasurer	8 *dextrarii*
Same	1 palfrey
Same	12 sumpterhorses
Same	8 carthorses
Purchase by Robert de Tonge	7 sumpterhorses
Eleanor, countess of Guelders	5 *dextrarii*
	6 palfreys
	9 carthorses
Total:	56 horses

Horses given

Recipient	Horses
Count of Guelders	11 warhorses (*dextrarii*)
Hospice of St John of Jerusalem (at Nijmegen)	1 *dextrarium carvannum*
Bishop of Winchester	1 *dextrarium*
Henry de Lancaster	1 palfrey
Knight (unnamed) for his fee	1 palfrey
Joan de Seynton, damoiselle of countess's chamber	1 palfrey
Matilda de Wilmington, damoiselle of same	1 palfrey
Ev[n?]a de Wilmington, damoiselle of same	1 palfrey
Count of Guelders (at Roosendael)	2 palfreys
Otelin Lalmaund	1 sumpterhorse
Count of Guelders	6 sumpterhorses
Nicholas Touk, almoner	1 sumpterhorse
Nicholas de Barneby, senior chaplain	1 sumpterhorse
John Perrot	1 sumpterhorse
Hugh Burglion	1 sumpterhorse
John de Cliseseby	1 sumpterhorse
Count of Guelders	6 carthorses
Richard Fisher, carter	1 carthorse
Béguine of Malines	1 carthorse *carvannum*
Total horses given:	13 *dextrarii*
	7 palfreys
	13 sumpterhorses
	8 carthorses
Total:	41 horses

Source: PRO, E.101/386/7, fo. 10v.

TABLE 13. *Gifts given by Eleanor, countess of Guelders, on her marriage, 17–20 May 1332*

Name of recipient	Gift(s)
Edward de Bohun, knight banneret	Each:
William de Bohun, knight	1 gold clasp with jewels;
Ralph de Neville, knight, king's seneschal	1 silk belt garnished with pearls;
William La Zouche Mortimer, knight	1 ell of silk embroidered with
John de Grey, knight	gold thread, sewn with pearls
Hugh de Audley, knight	
John de Cromwell, knight	
John de Verdoun, knight	
Constantine de Mortimer, knight	
Thomas de Bradeston, knight	
Walter de Manny, knight	
[. . .]* banneret 'of Germany', carving @ table before countess on wedding day	
[. . .]* banneret 'of Germany', serving her drink on wedding day	
[. . .]* banneret, tester of food for her on same day	
[. . .]* seneschal of count of Guelders	
[. . .]* chamberlain of count of Guelders	
[. . .]* marshal of count of Guelders	
William de Montacute, knight	Each:
Nicholas de la Beche, knight	1 gold clasp with jewels & pearls
Ralph de Hastings, knight	
Ralph de Cromwell, knight	
William de Cusaunce, knight	
Master Johan Moliard, canon of Arnhem, treasurer of count	1 gold clasp with jewels & pearls
Master Isambert, count's clerk	
John Teysaunt, king's herald & minstrel	1 silk belt with enamels; 1 ell of silk
Total jewels etc. given:	22 clasps and buckles
	19 purses & ells of silk
	19 belts

Source: PRO, E.101/386/7, fos. 10r–10v.

Note: * Names lacking in the original document.

TABLE 14. *Alms given and masses celebrated by the English court: 1301–1302*

Week	Saints' and Feast Days	Sums spent
19–25 Nov. 1301	St Edmund (20 Nov.) St Cecilia (22 Nov.) St Clement (23 Nov.) St Catherine (25 Nov.)	25 l. 8s. 2d.
26 Nov.–2 Dec.	St Andrew (30 Nov.)	10 l. 8s. 3d.
3–9 Dec.	St Nicholas (6 Dec.) BVM, *conceptio* (8 Dec.)	18 l. 10s. 9d.
10–16 Dec.	St Lucy (13 Dec.)	8 l. 10s. 9d.
17–23 Dec.	St Thomas the Apostle (21 Dec.)	8 l. 10s. 9d.
24–30 Dec.	Christmas Day (25 Dec.) St Stephen (26 Dec.) St John Evangelist (27 Dec.) Holy Innocents (28 Dec.) St Thomas of Canterbury (29 Dec.)	27 l. 18s. 3d.
31 Dec. 1301–6 Jan. 1302	St Silvester (31 Dec.) Circumcision (1 Jan.) St Edward, *depositio* (5 Jan.) Epiphany (6 Jan.)	24 l. 3s. 3d.
7–13 Jan.	St Hilary (13 Jan.)	6 l. 0s. 9d.
14–20 Jan.	St Maur (15 Jan.) St Wulfstan (19 Jan.) SS Fabian & Sebastian (20 Jan.)	15 l. 8s. 3d.
21–7 Jan.	St Agnes (21 Jan.) St Vincent (22 Jan.) St Paul, *conversio* (25 Jan.)	14 l. 15s. 9d.
28 Jan.–3 Feb.	St Agnes, *secundo* (21 Jan.) St Brigida (1 Feb.) BVM, *purificatio* (2 Feb.) St Blaise (3 Feb.)	15 l. 8s. 3d.
4–10 Feb.	St Agatha (5 Feb.) St Scholastica (10 Feb.)	8 l. 3s. 3d.

TABLE 14. *Continued*

Week	Saints' and Feast Days	Sums spent
11–17 Feb.	St Valentine (14 Feb.)	5 l. 0s. 9d.
18–24 Feb.	St Peter *in cathedra* (22 Feb.) St Matthew the apostle (24 Feb.)	11 l. 13s. 3d.
25 Feb.–3 Mar.	St David (1 Mar.)	5 l. 8s. 3d.
4–10 Mar.	—	—
11–17 Mar.	St Gregory (12 Mar.)	4 l. 3s. 3d.
18–24 Mar.	St Edward, king & martyr (18 Mar.) St Cuthbert (20 Mar.) St Benedict (21 Mar.)	7 l. 18s. 3d.
25–31 Mar.	BVM, *annunciatio* (25 Mar.)	12 l. 5s. 9d.
1–7 Apr.	St Richard, bishop St Ambrose	6 l. 5s. 9d.
8–14 Apr.	—	4 l. 3s. 3d.
15–21 Apr.	Monday of Holy Week Tuesday of Holy Week Wednesday of Holy Week	8 l. 10s. 9d.
22–8 Apr.	Easter Day (22 Apr.) St George (23 Apr.) St Mark (25 Apr.)	17 l. 18s. 3d.
29 Apr.–5 May	SS Philip & James (1 May) Holy Cross, *inventio* (3 May)	12 l. 18s. 3d.
6–12 May	St John *ante portam latinam* (6 May)	8 l. 10s. 9d.
13–19 May	St Dunstan (19 May)	5 l. 0s. 9d.
20–6 May	St Aldhelm (25 May) St Augustine of Canterbury (26 May)	6 l. 18s. 3d.
27 May–2 June	Ascension (31 May)	8 l. 10s. 9d.
3–9 June	St Wulfstan, *translatio* (7 June) St Edmund, *translatio* (9 June)	9 l. 3s. 3d.

Table 14. *Continued*

Week	Saints' and Feast Days	Sums spent
10–16 June	Pentecost (10 June) St Barnabas (11 June) St Richard, *translatio* (16 June)	14 l. 15s. 9d.
17–23 June	Trinity Sunday (17 June) St Botolph (17 June) St Edward, *translatio secunda* (20 June) & *communis participatio* <div align="right">Total:</div>	 24 l. 3s. 3d. 20 l. 16s. 8d. 44 l. 19s. 11d.
24–30 June	St John Baptist, *nativitas* (24 June) SS John & Paul (26 June) SS Peter & Paul (29 June) St Paul, *commemoratio* (30 June)	16 l. 18s. 3d.
1–7 July	St Swithin (2 July) St Martin, *translatio* (4 July) St Thomas of Canterbury, *translatio* (7 July)	13 l. 3s. 3d.
8–14 July	SS *Septem fratres* (10 July) St Benedict, *translatio* (11 July)	5 l. 13s. 3d.
15–21 July	St Swithin, *translatio* (15 July) St Kenelm (17 July) St Arnulf (18 July)	12 l. 3s. 3d.
22–8 July	St Mary Magdalene (22 July) St James, Apostle (25 July) SS *Septem dormientes* (27 July) St Sampson (28 July)	18 l. 8s. 3d.
29 July–4 Aug.	St Peter *ad vincula* (1 Aug.) St Stephen, *inventio* (3 Aug.)	14 l. 15s. 9d.
5–11 Aug.	St Oswald (5 Aug.) St Laurence (10 Aug.) St Tiburtius (11 Aug.)	12 l. 10s. 9d.
12–18 Aug.	St Hypolitus (13 Aug.) BVM, *assumptio* (15 Aug.)	13 l. 10s. 9d.

TABLE 14. *Continued*

Week	Saints' and Feast Days	Sums spent
19–25 Aug.	St Magnus (19 Aug.) St Bartholomew (24 Aug.)	13 l. 10s. 9d.
26 Aug.–8 Sept.	St Augustine, bishop & doctor (28 Aug.) St John Baptist, *decollatio* (29 Aug.) St Giles (1 Sept.)	16 l. 0s. 9d.
9–15 Sept.	Holy Cross, *exaltatio* (14 Sept.)	8 l. 10s. 10d.
16–22 Sept.	St Edith (16 Sept.) St Matthew (21 Sept.) St Maurice (22 Sept.)	16 l. 0s. 9d.
23–9 Sept.	St Firminus (25 Sept) SS Cosmas & Damian (27 Sept.) St Michael (29 Sept.)	11 l. 13s. 3d.
30 Sept.–6 Oct.	St Jerome (30 Sept.) St Remigius (1 Oct.) St Francis (4 Oct.) St Faith (6 Oct.)	8 l. 8s. 3d.
7–13 Oct.	St Hugh, *translatio* (7 Oct.) St Denis (9 Oct.) St [?Ethelburga] (11 Oct.) St Edward, *translatio* (13 Oct.)	
14–20 Oct.	St Michael *in Monte Tumba* St Lukle (18 Oct.)	11 l. 13s. 3d.
21–7 Oct.	11,000 Virgins (21 Oct.) St John of Beverley, *translatio* (25 Oct.)	5 l. 13s. 9d.
28 Oct.–4 Nov.	SS Simon & Jude (28 Oct.) All Saints (1 Nov.) & *communis* *participatio* All Souls (4 Nov.) & *communis* *participatio*	 20 l. 16s. 8d. 12 l. 3s. 3d. 20 l. 16s. 8d.
	Total:	53 l. 16s. 7d.

TABLE 14. *Continued*

Week	Saints' and Feast Days	Sums spent
5–10 Nov.	St Leonard (6 Nov.) 4 *coronati martyres* (8 Nov.)	10 l. 12s.
11–17 Nov.	St Martin (11 Nov.) St Bricius (13 Nov.) St Machutus (15 Nov.) St Edmund, archbishop (16 Nov.) St Hugh, bishop (17 Nov.) Anniversary of king Henry III (16 Nov.)	18 l. 5s. 9d.
18–19 Nov.	Pittances for 90 & 23 paupers *de custuma antiqua*	
	Grand Total:	634 l. 17s. 10d.

Source: PRO, E.101/361/21.

TABLE 15 (a). *Liveries of money for robes paid to Edward I's household, Nov. 1289–Nov. 1290*

Annual amount for livery		Rank	Total
Winter	Summer		
5 l. 6s. 8d.	5 l. 6s. 8d.	Banneret	10 l. 13s. 4d.
2 l. 13s. 4d.	2 l. 13s. 4d.	Simple knight	5 l. 6s. 8d.
2 l. 13s. 4d.	2 l. 13s. 4d.	Wardrobe clerk	5 l. 6s. 8d.
2 l. 13s. 4d.	2 l. 13s. 4d.	King's surgeon	5 l. 6s. 8d.
2 l. 13s. 4d.	2 l. 13s. 4d.	Chaplains of king's chapel	5 l. 6s. 8d.
2 l. 13s. 4d.	2 l. 13s. 4d.	Merchants of Lucca	5 l. 6s. 8d.
1 l. 13s. 4d.	1 l. 13s. 4d.	Clerks of household offices	2 l. 6s. 8d.
1 l. 13s. 4d.	1 l. 13s. 4d.	Serjeants-at-arms	2 l. 6s. 8d.
1 l. 13s. 4d.	1 l. 13s. 4d.	King's huntsmen	2 l. 6s. 8d.
1 l.	1 l.	Squires of king's Chamber	2 l.
1 l.	1 l.	Falconers with 2 horses	2 l.
1 l.	1 l.	Minstrels	2 l.
1 l.	1 l.	Trumpeters	2 l.
10s.	10s.	Sub-clerks, falconers with 1 horse	1 l.
6s. 8d.	6s. 8d.	Messengers, valets, keeper of king's bear in Tower of London	13s. 4d.
5s.	5s.	Sumpters & palfreymen	10s.
3s. 4d.	3s. 4d.	Other sumpters	6s. 8d.
2s. 6d.	2s. 6d.	Other palfreymen	5s.

Sources: PRO, E.101/352/24 and C.47/4/5; and F. Lachaud, 'Textiles, Furs, and Liveries', table XXIII.

TABLE 15 (b). *Liveries for English knighting ceremonies, 1301–1302 and 1327–1328*

Rank	Livery of cloth	Quantity
1301–1302		
Bannerets	Cloth of gold *in serico*	2 cloths
Simple knights	Cloth of gold *in canabo*	2 cloths
Sons of barons	Cloth of *tarse*	2 cloths
1327–1328		
Earls (2)	Cloth of gold *in serico dyasprum*	2 cloths
	Cloth for robe of scarlet	12 ells
	Cloth for robe of green	13 ells
Bannerets (5)	Cloth of *camoca* (silk)	12 ells
	Cloth for robe of scarlet	11 ells
	Cloth for robe of green	11 ells
Bannerets (1)	Cloth of *tarse* with gold ray	6 ells
	Cloth for robe of scarlet	11 ells
	Cloth for robe of green	11 ells
Simple knights (10)	Cloth of *tarse*	6 ells
	Cloth for 2 robes of azure	
	bluett and green	21 ells

Sources: PRO, E.101/361/17; 371/21/60, 61, 88, 90; E.101/383/4; and Lachaud, 'Textiles, Furs, and Liveries', table XXXII.

TABLE 15 (c). *Colours of cloth and types of fur worn by members of princely households*

Flanders: count's household, All Saints, 1307

Rank	Colour of cloth	Fur
Clerks	blue*/medley (7 cloths)	miniver, *gros vair*
Knights	green (14 cloths)	miniver, *gros vair*
Squires	ray*/*gaude* (33 cloths)	*unspecified*
Maisnie	various (13 cloths)	*lambswool*

England: king's household, 1300–1303

	1300–1	1301–2	1302–3
King's chaplains	dark blue	*paonaz* (blues)	blue
Clerks	various	various	various
Knights	green*	green*	ray/*de colore*
Squires	ray, camelin/ ray, green/ ray	ray*	ray*
Valets	ray	ray	ray
Minstrels	ray	mi-parti	—

* predominant colour

Hainault: countess's household, 1306

Rank	Colour of cloth
Knights, *damoiselles*, ordained clerks	white camelin
Lesser clerks	medley
Squires	ray (12 cloths at 10 *florins* each)
Maisnie	ray (9 cloths at 7 florins and 1 *abenghe* each)

Sources: Flanders: RAG, Inv. Gaillard, 64, 65; England: PRO, C.47/4/5, and Lachand 'Textiles, Furs, and Liveries', tables XXVII–XXIX; Hainault: AEM, Cartulaire 20, fos. 155v–157r.

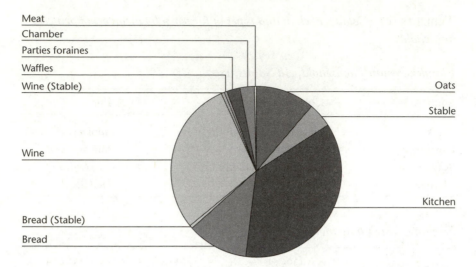

FIG. 8 Count of Flanders: Household expenses, 20 May–1 June 1293

Source: RAG, Wyffels 188.

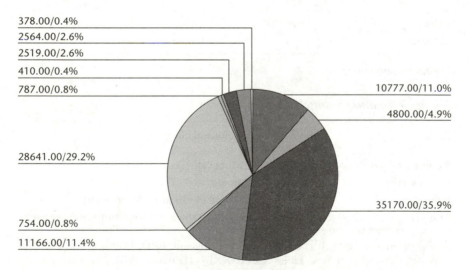

FIG. 9 Count of Flanders: Household expenses, 20 May–1 June 1293
(in *deniers parisis*)

Source: RAG, Wyffels 188.

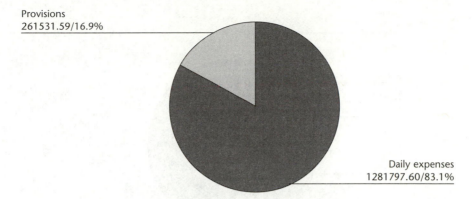

Provisions
261531.59/16.9%

Daily expenses
1281797.60/83.1%

FIG. 10 Count of Flanders: Household account, 1293–1294 (in *deniers parisis*)

Source: RAG, Wyffels 188, 314*bis*.

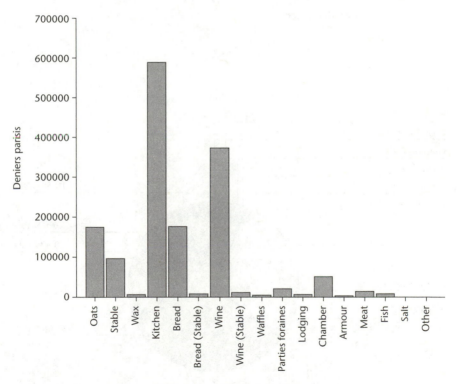

FIG. 11 Count of Flanders: Household account, 1293–1294

Source: RAG, Wyffels 188, 314*bis*.

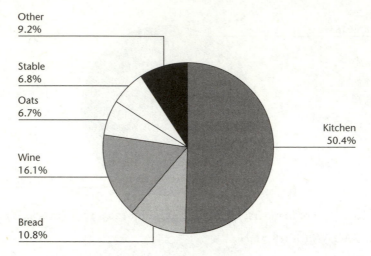

FIG. 12 Count of Flanders: Expenditure for the count's household,
1293–1294

Source: RAG, Wyffels 188, 314*bis*.

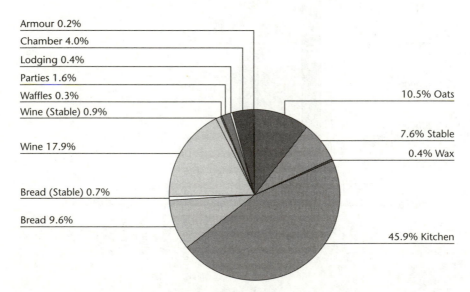

FIG. 13 Count of Flanders: Daily expenses, 1293–1294

Source: RAG, Wyffels 188, 314*bis*.

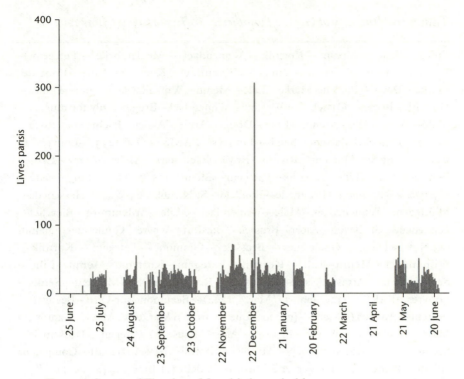

FIG. 14 Count of Flanders: Monthly household expenses, 1293–1294

Source: RAG, Wyffels 188, 314*bis*.

TABLE 16. *Itinerary of Guy de Dampierre, 10 June 1293–25 June 1294*

Ypres — Lille — Menin — Kortrijk — Wijnendael — Meulembeke — Petegem — Kortrijk—Lille—Kortrijk—Ypres—Wijnendael—Kortrijk—Lille—Pont-de-Marke—Douai—Pont-de-Marke—Lille—Menin—Wijnendael—Furnes—Dunes—Dunkirk—Berges—Cassel—Le Wastine—Wijnendael—Bruges [only for dinner]—Male—Wijnendael—Menin—Lille—Douai—Arras—Assiet—Esclusiers—Roye—Risson—Pont-Ste-Maixent—Senlis—Louvres—PARIS (2 Oct. 1293)—Louvres (14 Oct.)—Pont-Ste-Maixent—Risson—Roye—Esclusiers—Assiet—Arras—Lens—Pont-à-Vendin—Lille—Kortrijk—Petegem—Ghent (25–7 Oct. 1293)—*maison Huon de le Wulstrate* at Hassenede—Boudelo—St Nicholas-en-Waas—Hassenede—Maldegem—Wijnenedael—Male—Wijnendael—Male—Ardemburg—Biervliet—Hassenede—St Bavon—Alost—Brussels—Boisfort—Wavre—Goulesmes—Namur (23 Nov.–9 Dec.) — Goulesmes — Brussels — Gramont — Petegem — Kortrijk — Wijnendael—Menin—Lille—Kortrijk—Petegem—Kortrijk—Menin—Lille—Seclin—Lens—Arras—Assiet—Esclusiers—Roye—Pont-Ste-Maixent—Senlis—Louvres—PARIS (12 Jan.–3 Mar. 1294)—Beaumont-sur-Oise—Beauvais—Breteuil—Amiens (6 Mar.)—[gap in sequence from 6 Mar. to 12 May]—Namur (13 May)—Goulesmes—Wavre—Brussels—Alost—Fauseke—Petegem—Dossemeir—Seclin — Arras — Assiet — [?] — Mieville — le-Roi [?]—Angicourt—Compiègne (16 June Pentecost)—La Verberie—Senlis—PARIS (11 June 1294)—Senlis—[?]—Lihons-en-Santiers — Arras — Le Bassée — Erkenghien — [?] — Zinnebeke—Wijnendael (25 June 1294).

Source: RAG, Wyffels 188, 314*bis*.

TABLE 17. *List of nobles and knights in the service of Guy de Dampierre,*
count of Flanders, and their payment for household residence (c.1299–1300)

Dorse: *Les séjours de [?ceus] del hostel*

Lord of Gavre: [=hereditary *bouteiller* —cf. ADN B.1569, fo. 11r]
Lord of Gavre *avoech lui chevaliers*
Lord of Rodes [=hereditary *panetier*—cf. ADN B.1569, fo. 14r]
Me sire Gerars de Mamines
Rasson, his son
Roger Dysenghien *le fil*
Lord of Landenghien [*bouteiller*—cf. ADN B.1569, fo. 11r]
26 esquires
Total: for 10 days—249 l. 6s 7d.
Also to lord of Gavre: same company for 6 nights—49 l. 13s. 4d.

                                                   Grand total: 298 l. 19s. 11d.

Gerard le Mor, knight:
Gerard le Mor *avoech lui chevaliers*
Sohier de Gand
Gobert de Harleville
Pieron de Utkerke
Total: for 13 days—108 l. 3s. 10d.
Also to him for same company for 7 nights—62 l. 12s.

                                                   Grand total: 170 l. 15s. 10d.

Rogier de Ghistelle, knight:
Rogier de Ghistelle *avoech lui chevaliers*
Castellan of Basce
Lord of Dysenghien
Jehan de Gistelle
Total for 6 nights—56 l. 8s.
Also to him for same company for 7 nights—48 l. 6s.   Grand total: 104 l. 14s.

Gerart de Uterb[w?]assans, knight:
Total for 9 nights—24 l. 19s. 6d.
Also to him for 7 nights—17 l. 7s. 8d.   Grand total: 42 l. 7s. 2d.

Guillaume de Mortagne, knight:
Guillaume de Mortagne *avoech lui chevaliers*
Gerart de Diestre
Gossuin Dypre
Gerard de Potes
Bauduin de Mortagne
Total for 17 days—382 l. 12s. 2d.

TABLE 17. *Continued*

Le vidame d'Amiens:
Vidame d'Amiens *avoech lui chevaliers*
Lord of Fiefes
Pieron Daussi
Lord of Jourin
Renaut de Bouberch
Prévôt of Rosnais
Total for 7 nights—61 l. 11s.
Also to him for same company for 7 nights—90 l. 13s.   Grand total: 152 l. 4s.

Pour les chevaliers Jehan de Douay:
Lord of Ghistelle [*chambellan*—cf. ADN B.1569, fo. 12r–v]
Wautier de Haluin
Jehan de Fourmesulwes [?] *puis kil fut chevaliers*
Total for 10 days—164 l. 13s.
Also to same for 7 nights—86 l. 11s.   Grand total: 251 l. 4s.

Lord of Rane [Raue?]:
Lord of Rane with 1 companion
Lord of Tranlers with 27 *armures de fer*
Total for 10 nights—160 l.
To same for 7 days *et fu avoech eus deus me sire Mahius de
Leval*—49 l.   Grand total: 209 l.

Watervliet *a 7 armures de fer*
Total for 10 nights—39l. 6s.
Also to him for 7 nights—13 l. 9s. 6d.   Grand total: 52 l. 15s. 6d.

Le castelain de Berghes *avoech lui chevaliers*
Lord of Leaune
Lord of Diedon
Lord of Preure
Le Magre de la Viesville
Total for 9 days—170 l.
Also to them for 7 nights—104 l.   Grand total: 274 l.

Monseigneur Robert de Montegni:
7 nights—16 l.

Final Grand Total: 1,944 l. 12s. 6d.

Source: ADN, B.1266, no. 234.

TABLE 18. *Testamentary legacies by Guy de Dampierre, count of Flanders, to his household (*maisnie*), at Wijnendael, 4 May 1304*

Name of recipient	Legacy
Jehan Danets, count's chaplain	80 l.
Master Nicolas de le Piere, count's physician	50 l.
Denis d'Ypres, *écolâtre* of Cassel	*1 hanap dargent a couvercle* or 40 l.
Eullard de Donze, count's valet	100 l.
Guillaume de Berghes, count's *huissier*	80 l.
Coppin, his son	20 l.
Bauduin Maton	60 l.
Symon, count's *panetier*	60 l.
Thierry, count's *bouteiller*	60 l.
Huet, count's barber	40 l.
Jakemon Floket, count's *courretier de vins*, of Compiègne	10 l.
Garsel, count's clerk	40 l.
Andrieu, of count's chamber	40 l.
Haluing, of count's chamber	20 l.
Baudet, of count's *paneterie*	30 l.
Mayhiu, count's cook	20 l.
Casin, count's almoner	16 l.
Collete, keeper of count's palfreys	10 l.
Hele, count's laundress	20 l.
Hannekin, clerk of count's chapel	10 l.
Hannekin de Morebeke, of count's kitchen	10 l.
Blonniekin, his companion	5 l.

Members of his daughters'*maisnies* at Dendermonde:

Brother Byguard	40 l.
Madame du Plaissiet	100 l.
Gillon, count's clerk	60 l.
Lyauebout	30 l.
Cassiel	20 l.
Jehennet de Binch	30 l.
Jehan le Boutillier	30 l.
Thomas le Portier	30 l.
Adam le Keu	30 l.
Flament du fer	20 l.

TABLE 18. *Contiuned*

Name of recipient	Legacy
Wautier le keu	20 l.
Gillekin de Ghelre	30 l.
Jehennet le peskeur	30 l.
Olivier du four	10 l.
Guillaume de Thimes	10 l.
Coppin le clerc	10 l.
Jehennet le bouchier	5 l.
Esthevenet de le cuisine	5 l.
Kokeron	10 l.
Jehan de Douai	10 l.
Jehan le sage	5 l.
Lamnekin	10 l.
Damoiselle Marie de Wais	20 l.
Damoiselle Marie de le Val	60 l.
Maroie du parc	20 l.
Agnes, her sister	10 l.

Total recipients: 48

Total legacies: 1,476 l.

Source: ADN, B.449, no. 4181b.

TABLE 19. *Members of the company of Colard van den Clite conducting Anne of Bohemia, queen of England, on her journey through Flanders, and their expenses, Nov. 1381*

Headed: Che sont les gens messire Colard de le Clitte a eult avoec lui et en se compaignie pour le convoy de le royne Dengleterre . . . Et le trouva entre Audenarde et Courtray. Si le convoya jusques a Bruges ou quel voyage il furent par 7 jours.

Name	Lances (Glaives)	Horses	Men-at-Arms (Panchiers) (with horses)
Messire Colard [van den Clite]	2	7	6
Messire Jan Hauweel	2	4	1
Messire Jean de Beaufremez	2	5	1
Jacques le Bruwere	1	2	1
Guillaume de le Val	1	2	2
Martin le Borgne	2	5	–
Wautier le Bruwere	1	2	2
Robert de la Douve	2	4	1
Pietre Hellin	1	2	1
Willem Vulveric	1	2	1
Jean Carlin	1	2	1
Willem du Ham	1	2	–
Lippin de le Val	1	2	–
Jean de Noeveglise	1	2	–
Jean du Leene	1	2	–
Franse de Comines	1	2	–
Willem de Revermers	1	2	–
Total:	22	49	17

Costs:		
	4 lances with 3 horses:	7 l. 4s.
	18 lances with 2 horses:	25 l. 4s.
11 crossbowmen & archers at 14s. each per day:		7 l. 14s.
6 men-at-arms at 8s. each per day:		2 l. 8s.
	Total:	297 l. 10s.

Source: ADN, B.3240, no. 111908.

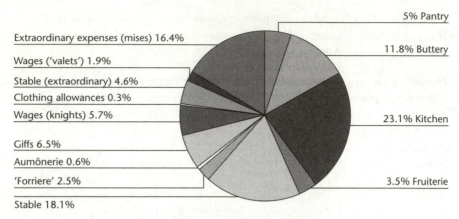

FIG. 15 Count of Artois: Household expenses, 1300

Source: ADPC, A.162.

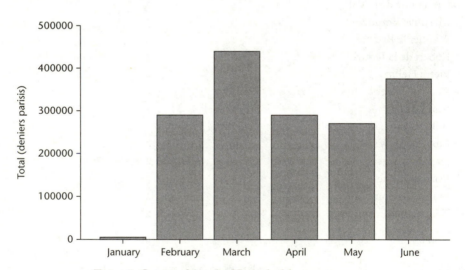

FIG. 16 Count of Artois: Household expenses, 1300

Source: ADPC, A.162.

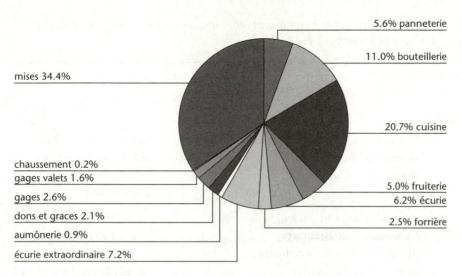

5.6% panneterie

11.0% bouteillerie

mises 34.4%

20.7% cuisine

chaussement 0.2%

gages valets 1.6%

gages 2.6%

5.0% fruiterie

6.2% écurie

dons et graces 2.1%

2.5% forrière

aumônerie 0.9%

écurie extraordinaire 7.2%

FIG. 17 Count of Artois: Household expenditure, 1302

Source: ADPC, A.178.

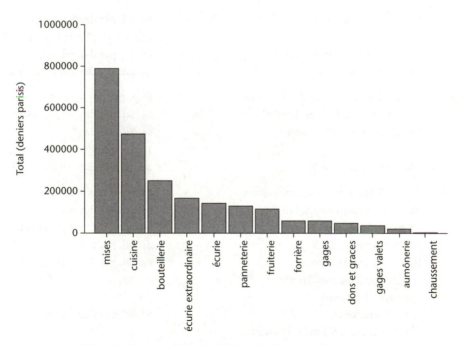

FIG. 18 Count of Artois: Household expenditure, 1302

Source: ADPC, A.178.

TABLE 20. *Monthly wages of knights and other members of household of Robert II, count of Artois, 6 Feb.–28 June 1300*

Month	Recipient	Days absent from household	Sum
Feb. 1300	Master Paumier, count's physician	–	8s.p. per day = 12 l.p.
	Renaud, chamberlain	–	6s. 8d. per day = 10 l.p.
	Pierre de Ste-Croix, knight	4	6s. 8d. per day★ = 10 l. 13s. 4d. 10s. per day★
	Simon de Cinq-Ormes, knight	–	6s. 8d. per day = 10 l. 13s. 4d.
	Monseigneur de Beaumetz [for 38 days in count's company]	–	20s. per day = 38 l.p.
	Master Gautier, clerk	–	4s. 4d per day = 6 l. 13s. 4d.
Mar. 1300	Master Paumier, count's physician	–	8s.p. per day = 12 l.p.
	Pierre de Ste-Croix, knight	10	6s. 8d. per day★ = 11 l. 13s. 4d. 10s. per day★
	Renaud, chamberlain	7	6s. 8d. per day★ 10s. per day★ = 11 l. 3s. 4d.
	Simon de Cinq-Ormes, knight	–	6s. 8d. per day = 10 l.p.
	Master Gautier, clerk	–	4s. 4d. per day = 6 l. 13s. 4d.
Apr. 1300	Master Paumier, count's physician	–	8s.p. per day = 12 l.p.
	Simon de Cinq-Ormes, knight[1]	8	6s. 8d. per day = 17 l. 16s. 7d.
	Pierre de Ste-Croix, knight	18	6s. 8d. per day★ 10s. per day★ = 13 l.p.
	Master Gautier, clerk	–	4s. 4d. per day = 6 l. 13s. 4d.
May 1300	Master Paumier, count's physician	–	8s.p. per day = 12 l.p.
	Simon de Cinq-Ormes, knight	–	6s. 8d. per day = 10 l.p.
	Pierre de Ste-Croix, knight	31	10s. per day★ = 15 l. 6s. od.
	Master Gautier, clerk	–	4s. 4d. per day = 6 l. 13s. 4d.
	Renaud, chamberlain	–	6s. 8d. per day = 10 l.p.
	Hugues de Sapignes, knight (30 days with count)	–	6s. 8d. per day = 10 l.p.
	Wale Paele, knight (24 days in May & June with count)	–	6s. 8d. per day = 8 l.p.

Table 20. *Contiuned*

Month	Recipient	Days absent from household	Sum
June 1300	Master Paumier, count's physician	–	8s.p. per day = 12 l.p.
	Master Gautier, clerk	–	4s. 4d. per day = 6 l. 13s. 4d.
	Renaud, chamberlain	6	6s. 8s. per day*
			10s. per day* = 11 l.p.
June 1300	Simon de Cinq-Ormes, knight[2]	5	6s. 8d. per day = 8 l. 6s. 8d.
	Pierre de Ste-Croix, knight	22	6s. 8d. per day*
			10s. per day* = 13 l. 13s. 4d.
Feb.–June 1300	Master Thierry d'Hérisson (49 days *a la court*)	101	6s. 8d. per day*
			10s. per day* = 66 l. 16s. 8d.

Source: ADPC, A.162, fos. 22r–23r.

Notes: *Daily wages out of court = 10s.p.; in court = 6s. 8d.p.

[1] Fo. 22v: Ou quel mois davril il fu hors de lostel monseigneur en Flandres ou monseigneur lenvoya, pour lui et pour Pierre Sot, et pour 6 chevaliers avec lui, 8 jours, et despendi 10 l. 10s.

[2] Fo. 22v: Dou quel il a este hors de lostel monseigneur pour ses besoignes 5 jours.

TABLE 21. *Members of the household of the late Robert II, count of Artois (died in battle at Kortrijk (Courtrai) 11 July 1302) receiving compensation for their services to him, July–Oct. 1302*

Name [original spelling]	Sum paid in *restitution* [in *livres tournois*]
Robins le clers du Gardemenger	20 l.t.
Jehanot Dipre, dit de l'argent	30 l.t.
Boutegourd	20 l.t.
Le muet	20 l.t.
Gosset	5 l.t.
Perres Seurin	5 l.t.
Guillot du Mont St Eloy	1 l.t.
Jakemin de la paneterie	5 l.t.
Perrot de la sausserie	10 l.t.
Petit	5 l.t.
Gilles de la fruiterie	5 l.t.
Herniset	5 l.t.
Escot	5 l.t.
Le page des palefrois	50 l.t.
Jehan de Paris	5 l.t.
Renaus de la forge	30 l.t.
Jamite le muletier	20 l.t.
Robers de Calabres	5 l.t.
Martin des grans chevaus	3 l.t.
Lombars	1 l.t.
Renaus de Chivreuses	16 s.t.
Guilles de Toulouse	2 l.t.
Loeys de la forge	20 l.t.
Oudin des grans chevaux	3 l.t.
Mikelet le Normand	5 l.t.
Petrole	1 l.t.
Lengles, page des palefrois	5 l.t.
La femme Thebaud de la fourrerie	15 l.t.
Chabot	10 l.t.
Guillaumet de Graveran	5 l.t.
Le Chat	5 l.t.
Rousselet	5 l.t.
Symonnet des Braches	2 l.t.
Geuffrin	1 l.t.

TABLE 21. *Continued*

Name [original spelling]	Sum paid in *restitution* [in *livres tournois*]
Robins le messager	2 l. 10s.t.
Grimeustet	2 l. 10s.t.
Capete	1 l.t.
Le conte de bar [*sic*]	1 l.t.
Jakemars de le Braiele	50 l.t.
Guiot le veneur	40 l.t.
Cokelet le veneur	60 l.t.
Gautiers de Vilaines	80 l.t.
Perre Fol	30 l.t.
Evrard le charetier	5 l.t.
Therris de la fourrerie	20 l.t.
Monsire Jehan Darras	12 l. 10s.t.
Monsire Bouchard	12 l. 10s.t.
Les trois pages des chiens	1 l.t.
Bouchiers le queu	60 l.t.
Jehans de Flouri	10 l.t.
Gautiers le Picars	5 l.t.
Trois pes	20 l.t. *et un cheval du pris de 30 l.t.*
Jehans le barbier	5 l.t. *et un cheval*
Guillot qui fu clers de la chapelle	5 l.t.
Estevenet le messagier	2 l. 10s.t.
Forcaillies	50 l.t.
Jehans de Rebes	10 l.t.
Le prestre de la paneterie	5 l.t.
Guillot de l'aumosne	5 l.t.
Jehanot le page de la fruiterie	3 l.t.
Copin des oysiaus	1 l.t.
Winoc	30 l.t.
Robin des palefrois	40 l.t.
Lorin des chiens	10 l.t.
Guillaumet Lenglet	5 l.t.
Guillaumet le cheveucier	5 l.t.
Samet	5 l.t.
Guillaumet le page	3 l.t.
Jakemins de Lisle	40 l.t.
Guide le muletier	40 l.t.

TABLE 21. *Continued*

Name [original spelling]	Sum paid in *restitution* [in *livres tournois*]
Carvenale muletier	40 l.t.
Gervaise le queu	10 l.t.
Estevene chevalet	5 l.t.
Ernaudon le trompeur	20 l.t.
Bertelot de Pertes	30 l.t.
Guillemins de Roussy	50 l.t.
Jean de Melfe	40 l.t.
Thibe d'Oblaing	30 l.t.
Jehanotin de l'argent	5 l.t.
Jehanot de la sausserie	5 l.t.
Antrongne	30 l.t.
Tiestart	50 l.t.
Maistre Andrieu le Capelain pour lui et sa mere	60 l.t.
Perot de Mitri	20 l.t.
Maistre Jake de Poissi	50 l.t.
Guillaume de Buissieres	50 l.t.
Amauri le marescal	2 l.t.
Pijon de la fruiterie	5 l.t.
Ogier de la boutillerie	5 l.t.
Denissot de la quisine	5 l.t.
Jehanot de la fouriere	4 l.t.
Pieres Darras	1 l.t.
S[imon?] de Bietune	10 l.t.
Garsie de Martegnance	100 l.t.
Jehan de Monchiaus	80 l.t.
Guillemuce	20 l.t.
Gille de Tret	20 l.t.
Henri le Sarasin	5 l.t.

Total names: 102

Total sums paid out: 1,789l. 6s.t.

Source: ADPC, A.185, nos. 28, 32, 41; A.186, nos. 25, 27, 31.

TABLE 22. *Itinerary of Jeanne de Valois, countess of Hainault, and her daughter Philippa, 1 Dec. 1325–19 Jan. 1326*

Sun	1 Dec. 1325:	Valenciennes—Câteau-Cambrésis (expenses met by bishop of Cambrai)
Mon	2 Dec.	Câteau-Cambrésis—Bohain
Tues	3 Dec.	Roupy—Han
Wed	4 Dec.	Noyon—Choisy (near Compiègne)
Thurs	5 Dec.	La Verberie—Senlis
Fri	6 Dec.	Louvres—Paris
Sat	7 Dec.	Paris
Sun	8 Dec.	Paris (BVM, *conceptio*)—Trappes (near Versailles)
Mon	9 Dec.	Trappes—Le Perray (near Rambouillet) [saw Charles de Valois, Jeanne's father, d.16 Dec. 1325]
Tues	10 Dec.	Le Perray
Wed	11 Dec.	Essars-le-Roi—Neauphle-le-Château (cant. Montfort Amaury)
Thurs	12 Dec.	Poissy
Fri	13 Dec.	Paris until Thurs 19 Dec. [16 Dec.: day of Charles de Valois's death]
Fri	20 Dec.	Bourg-la-Reine—Palaiseau [to see body of Charles de Valois]
Sat	21 Dec.	Paris until Thurs 26 Dec. [24 Dec.: *nuit de Noel*; 25 Dec.: *jours de Noel*]
Fri	27 Dec.	St-Denis—Louvres—Vaus-Dierlans—Paris (household divided)
Sat	28 Dec.	La Chapelle-en-Serval (between Louvres and Senlis)—Senlis
Sun	29 Dec.	La Verberie—Choisy
Mon	30 Dec.	Noyon—Margny
Tues	31 Dec.	Roupy—St-Quentin (*nuit del an*)
Wed	1 Jan. 1326:	Bohain
Thurs	2 Jan.	Câteau-Cambrésis [countess with bishop and household in town]
Fri	3 Jan.	Le Quesnoy—Valenciennes
Sat	4 Jan.	Valenciennes—*y furent mesires, medame et leur enfant toute jour*
Sun	5 Jan.	Valenciennes (*nuit des Rois*)
Mon	6 Jan.	Le Quesnoy until Wed 8 Jan.
Thurs	9 Jan.	Bavay
Fri	10 Jan.	Mons
Sat	11 Jan.	Mons [duchess of Brabant there until Sunday after dinner]
Sun	12 Jan.	Mons—St-Gillain [with count's household]
Mon	13 Jan.	Mons—St-Gillain [with count's household]
Tues	14 Jan.	Mons until Sun 19 Jan.

Source: *De rekeningen*, ed. Smit, i. 145–53 [from ADN, B.3270].

TABLE 23. *Total monthly expenses of the household of Jeanne de Valois, countess of Hainault, 25 Aug. 1325–24 Aug. 1326*

Page	Month	Amount
140–1	1st (25 Aug.–22 Sept.1325)	208 l. 3s.t. *sans pourvanches*
142–3	2nd	243 l. 17s. 7d.t.
144	3rd	248 l. 5s. 9d.t. [including *cour sollempnel* at All Saints]
147	4th	418 l. 4s. 9d.t. *sans pourvanches*
151	5th	1,198 l. 1d.t. [including Paris visit]
154	6th	379 l. 7s. 8d.t. *sans pourvanches*
156	7th	175 l. 8s. 5d.t. *sans pourvanches*
158	8th	264 l. 17s.t. *sans pourvanches*
160	9th	348 l. 1s. 3d.t. *sans pourvanches*
162	10th	307 l. 10s. 9d.t. *sans pourvanches*
164	11th	299 l. 11s. 5d.t. *sans pourvanches*
166	12th	313 l. 9s. 3d.t. *sans pourvanches*
168	13th	270 l. 19s. 6d.t. *sans pourvanches*
169	Grand total of all expenses:	5,344 l. 14s. 2d.t.

Source: *De rekeningen*, ed. Smit, i. 107–242 [from ADN, B.3270].

TABLE 24. *Total annual expenses from the household accounts of Jeanne de Valois, Countess of Hainault, 1319–1316*

Year	Grand Total of all expenses and *parties foraines*
1319–21	4,829 l.t. (average p.a.)
1325–26	7,691 l. 8s. 4d.t.
1326–27	7,718 l. 17s. 5d.t.
1327–28	11,487 l. 10s.t.
1328–29	8,874 l. 4s. 4d.t.
1330–31	9,107 l. 15s. 1d.t.
1332–33	4,849 l. 0s. 4d.t.
1335–36	2,035 l. 5s. 1d.t.

Source: *De rekeningen*, ed. Smit, i. [from ADN, B.3270].

TABLE 25. *List of wages paid to members of the household of William, count of Hainault and Holland 9 Dec. 1335–9 June 1336*

Headed: *C'est li estrais des waiges des gens monsgnr, ki commenchierent, depuis c'on ne paia [9 Dec. 1335] . . . et finerent [9 June 1336] . . . C'est pour le terme de 26 semainnes et 2 jours.* [listed in order of apparent status not according to order of original].

Name of recipient	Wages paid		
Monsgr Villain d'Estenkerke	1 l.	1s.	
Monsgnr E[rnoul?] de Boullant (with			
Colard de Hasnoit & Ernoul de Herimes)	32 l.		
Medame le femme monsgnr Wolfart [van Borselen?]	15 l.	10s.	
Monsgnr de Manchicourt	20 l.	5s.	
Monsgnr Richard [p.m. Brisset]	2 l.	1s.	4d.
Monsgnr Richard Pourchiel		17s.	3d.
Monsgnr de Pottes	47 l.	14s.	7d.
Monsgnr Simon le bastard	17 l.	4s.	
Monsgnr Willaume de Fordes	3 l.	2s.	6d.
Monsgnr J. de Lisserueles	5 l.	1s.	6d.
Monsgnr Simon de Bentem	8 l.	9s.	
Maistre Blik	32 l.		
Maistre Hellin	32 l.	12s.	
Monsgnr J. l'aumonnier	19 l.	18s.	8d.
Maistre Clais Stuc	22 l.	4s.	
Maistre Mathix	29 l.	8s.	
Others listed incl: (selection)			
Jehan de Werchin	32 l.	6s.	6d.
Willaume de Ghiselle	11 l.	15s.	
Willekin de Bourbon	5 l.	10s.	
Piere de le Sauch	9 l.	11s.	10d.
Willaume de le Sauch	14 l.	8s.	
Lambert le marissaut	14 l.	8s.	
Pipre	9 l.	13s.	4d.
Piere Courtebaniere	18 l.	8s.	4d.
Gilliet le barbier	13 l.	2s.	4d.
Lotard le barbier	13 l.	11s.	6d.
Jehan Cauffecire	13 l.	19s.	8d.
Ernekin le messagier	3 l.	1s.	4d.

TABLE 25. *Continued*

Name of recipient	Wages paid
Gosset de le quisinne	2 l. 14s.
Candelaire	2 l.
Plumet & Aumone [life annuities]	2 l. 6s. 8d.
Perrot l'arbalestrier	11 l. 13s. 3d.
Mourekin le faukenier	20 l. 9s. 8d.
Gerard le panetier	14 l. 8s. 2d.
Richard le clerck	13 l. 0s. 8d.
Colin dou Gardin	2 l. 6s. 3d.
Jakemin de le forge	2 l. 6s. 3d.
Colart de Malaunoyt	20 l. 12s.
Willekin le tailleur	17 l. 19s.
Hanekin le prouvost	4 l. 14s.
Blanc estrain & Taissiel	2 l. 5s. 6d.
Pietre l'uissier	2 l. 11s.
Coppin l'uissier	2 l. 5s.
Mathix le messagier	7s.
Ouleffart de le Vere	8 l. 8s.
Gerard de le Maletesde	3 l. 0s. 8d.
Willaume de le Poulle	11 l. 4s.
Nicaise l'orfevre	17s. 4d.
Gilkin le portier	7 l. 12s.
Guillot le cambrelent, *qui fu au vesque de Cambray*	15s.
Hanekin le messagier	1 l.
Le dame as gambes	9s. 4d.
L'ostel a le Bourse	8 l. 16s. ⋆
Gerard le fourbissuer	5 l. 4s.
Marghe le corduainiere	16 l. 1s. 2d.
Jehan le Marisaut	10s.
Jakemart le Barbieur, clerk of Le Quesnoy for writing services	2 l.
Gilliet le barbier for J. messagier	1 l. 15s.

p. 393:

 Total names: 121

 Total wages paid: 1,276 l. 17s. 3d.t.

 Sum, paid by letters and in *argent sec*: 329 l. 8s. 8d.t.

⋆Addition: *s'en a un pot d'argent et une escuiele en waiges.*

Source: Van Riemsdijk, *De Tresorie*, 389–93 [from AEM].

TABLE 26. *List of wages for the household of Jeanne de Valois, countess of Hainault, from 3 Dec. 1335–23 June 1336*

Headed: *C'est li estrais de chou ke on doit as gens medame pour leur waiges dou [3 Dec. 1335] . . . jusques au [23 June 1336] . . . C'est pour 28 semainnes.*

Name of recipient	Wages paid
Monsgnr Jehan de Biaumont	53 l. 5s. 10d.
Monsgnr Willaume Foullet	35 l. 4s.
Monsgnr Henri de Braibant	39 l.
Maistre Nicole	37 l. 12s.
Maistre Ernoul	32 l. 1s.
Gobert [le Clerc]	16 l. 17s. 6d.
Jakemon de Benengh	31 l. 18s.
Gerard de Raporst [Raephorst]	13 l.
Thiery de Somaing	17 l. 3s. 2d.
Boulhard	21 l. 0s. 10d.
Jehan de Poullane	17 l. 0s. 2d.
Alard de Lokeron	21 l. 0s. 10d.
Jehan de Quinchi	18 l. 13s. 1d.
Baudry de Roisin	17 l. 2s. 4d.
Pietre de Braibant	31 l. 4s.
Jeham d'Iske	13 l.
Simon Boussut	21 l. 0s. 10d.
Ghisebrecht d'Alblais	11 l. 5s. 4d.
Jakemard le panetier	20 l. 14s. 3d.
Jehan le nain	18 l. 6s. 7d.
Jehan de Maubuege	17 l. 16s. 6d.
Jehan le marissal	18 l. 7s. 6d.
Jehan de Condet [?Jean de Condé]	18 l. 11s. 10d.
Renier le keut	19 l. 16s. 10d.
Willaume d'Ech [d'Ath?]	17 l. 19s. 8d.
Pier le clerk	4 l. 1s. 8d.
Colin le clerk	3 l. 5s. 4d.
Bauduin le panetier	7 l. 7s.
Willaumet le panetier	3 l. 5s. 4d.
Jehan dou four	3 l. 5s. 4d.
Hane Coene	14 l. 5s. 4d.
Stampie	13 l. 6s. 8d.
Hainin d'Anchin	3 l. 5s. 4d.

TABLE 26. *Continued*

Name of recipient	Wages paid		
Jehan Robert	3 l.	3s.	
Sauvage	3 l.	5s.	4d.
Taisin [Caisin] de Roisin	3 l.	5s.	4d.
Jehan des Loges	3 l.	5s.	4d.
Colin le messagier	10 l.	7s.	
Lotin du four	2 l.	9s.	
Trapendit [?Crapendic]	2 l.	4s.	6d.
Gherart Paubiel	2 l.	13s.	8d.
Clais de le quisinne	1 l.	2s.	9d.
Stassin de le Boussiere	2 l.	6s.	8d.
Hanin de Fontenieles		7s.	
Jacot de le cambre	2 l.	9s.	
Le Francois		2s.	4d.
Le Malarde	7 l.	10s.	
Total wages:	678 l.	18s.	
Paid by letters and *en argent*:	201 l.	8s.	9d.t.
Grand total of wages for count and countess:	1,905 l.	14s.	3d.
Payments already made:	530 l.	17s.	5d.t.
Balance due:	1,374 l.	16s.	10d.t.

Source: Van Riemsdijk, *De Tresorie*, 393–5 [from AEM].

Appendices

APPENDIX I

Ordinances for dependent households subsidiary to the English royal household, *c.*1284–1305

(a) *Ordinance for the Household of John of Brabant in England (1284, 1285, 1288–1290, 1292–1294)* (PRO, C.47/3/21, no. 12)

[Indenture]

Cest lordinement del houstel Jehan de Brabant fait devaunt le Roi a Langele le samedy prochein devaunt la [Goulaufin?]

E primes ordene est qe Jehan gisce en court e preigne pour sa chaumbre ceo qe mestier lui sera. E son chaumberlain qi prendra livree. E toute sa autre meignie, hors pris les garzons qi serunt a gages, mangerunt en loustel le Roi.

Item, son chivaler prendra livree de vin e de chaundeille, e quant il gist bien loinz de court prendra viaunde p[or] soper sel[onc] ceo qe reson sera por lui e por les clers e por les esquiers.

Item, les genz de office e les vallez de mestier qi sont a Jehan e ausi com son keu, son taillour, le panetier, le botiller e le mareschal maungirent ausi en la sale le Roi ausi com le gent le Roi meymes.

Item, Jehans prendr[a] livree por tainz de leverers [. . .] puture(?) por taunz des faukuns com il tendra [. . .] Et le garzon qe [. . .] de le [. . .] Jehan prend g[a]ges [. . .] devant dites [. . .] Jehan quant il gist en court cum sa femme [. . .] E [. . .] dis Jehan ne est mie en court mes a son hostel e vodra a loustel mangier, il prend[ra . . .]

Item, Jehans aura por sen cors 3 palefreis e 2 coursiers, 2 somers a livree de fein e de aveine et 8 garzon qi (?) garderent [. . .] qi prendront gages chescun tres mailles le jour. Mon sire Daniel, son chevaller 4 chivaus e 3 garzons. Gah . . . s[on] vallet qi gist en sa chaumbre 1 chival e 1 garzon. Hukelin de Reigny son compaignon 3 chivaus e 2 garzouns. Son prestre e Giles son clerk 3 chivaus e 2 garzouns. Hennekin qi trencha devant Jehan 1 chival e 1 garzon. Deus faukeners 2 chivaus e 2 garzons. G[er]ard le keu 1 chival e 1 garzon.

Item, Jehan eit une bone charette e 3 chivaus lowee por portier le remenant de son herneis et de ses genz.

Le portier e le botiller ⎱
Son chaumberleyn ⎰ chescun prenge 1 [marc?] por sa robbe e sa
Son taillour ⎱ chauseure solom la custume del houstel le Roi
son mareschal ⎰

Les 8 garzons por son cors preignent cheskun dimid.' marc por sa robe e lor chauceure solom ceo qe reson sera. E le garzon qi garde les chiens autresi.

(b) *Household roll of John of Brabant (temp. Edward I)* (very badly damaged) (PRO, C.47/3/46/31)

Brabant

Anfroye de Boum [i.e. Humphrey de Bohun]
Chevaliers Jehan
Chapelains Johan
Hughenins de [?Reigny]
Ses compains
[?Renaut] ki est en Brabant
Henris ki trenche devant Johan
Giles de Wynenghem
Stenes
Gerars li keuz
Addinet
Giles li clers
Pieres de Maubu (?)   ⎫
Willelmes li Loys   ⎬   varlez Anfroy
Varles du chevalier   ⎭

Mestier

Marescaus   ⎫
Boutelliers. panetiers ⎬
Li chamberlins ——— le chamberlain [. . .]
Le taillour [. . .]
Uns garcons de le cuisine e uns de le bouteillerie sont en sale [. . .] a gages [. . .] a cy a gages a son cors par lordenance.
Le barbour fu puis lordenance retrises a Jehan [. . .] par mon segnur [. . .]
Watrelos de Ligne ke Jehans retint en son service puis lordenance e est en lostel par le comant Jehan de ses [?robes]
H [. . .] ke Jehan delivra de prison est en lostel e par le comant Jehan.
Uns garcons ki court apres Jehan en bos e en riviere atout chiens est en lostel par le comant Jehan.
Me sire Jehans de Buz[?] [laisse son?] escuier entour Jehan quant il sen ala atout un cheval e un page en sale, e mist mesire Jehans un page en sale pour aidier a gardeir les soutils Jehan.
E par lui e par [?Mensart?] est uns en sale ki gist tous jours en le garderobe Jehan cousant.
E [. . .] Jehans a un messagier alant e venant en ses besoingnes e a ses robes.

(c) *Ordinance for the household of 'Madame la Nyete'*
(temp. Edward I) (PRO, E.101/171/8/172)

Ma dame la Nyete

Item, une dame et 2 damoiseles et la damoysele la dame.

Un chevaler al ordenance mons.' Johan de [?W/B]arr.' et son vadlet ovesques 3 chevalers et 3 garc[ons] a gages.

2 vadletz cest assaver Johan de la Moillie et aucun autre por servir devant ma dame et lor 3 garc[ons] a gages et chevaux 3 a gages.

Richard Lengleys et un autre por sa chambre. Vadlez a pie de mestier.

4 palefroys por ma dame et les damoiseles et 4 garzons a gages.

Les gentz doffice soient ordenez et bailletz par le seneschal et tresorer.

Cest a saver 1 vadlet de panetr[ie], 1 vadlet de but[lerie], 1 vadlet de quisine, et 1 page, 1 vadlet por esquieler[ie] et sauser[ie].

(d) *Ordinance for the household of John de Warenne*
(temp. Edward I) c.1303–1305 (PRO, E.101/371/8/97)

Cest lordeinement qui est fait por lestat que Johan de Garenne deit avoir en lostel le Roi tant come il serra en garde, le quel ordeinement feut fait par levesque de Cestre, tresour[er] le Roi [1295–1307], mons.' Henri de Percy, mons.' Robert de la Warde, seneschal [1303–7], Johan de Drokenesford, gardeyn de la garderobe [1295–1307], et Jehan de Benstede, contreroulour [1295–1305].

Le dit Johan avera 2 vadletz et un enfaunt trenchant devant li.

Item, il meismes por son corps avera 2 foiz robes par an, dont Esmon de Mortimer serra de sa seute, et les fuiz de tieux grants seigneurs a Noel et a Pasque, et un robe de russet por ivern a la Seynt Michel. Et ses 3 vadletz auront 2 foiz robes par an as dites festes dautre seute, sicome les vadletz denfauntz de garde.

Item, le dit Johan aura 3 vadletz de mestier, cestassavoir un chamberleng, un vadlet de panetr[ie] et buteller[ie] et un vadlet keu, et le dit vadlet de chambre prendra sa liveree come autres chamberlengs, les autres 2 vadletz mangeront en loustiel le Roi.

Item, il aura 2 palefroys et 2 palefriours por les 2 palefreys.

Item, por son corps, 3 somiers et 3 sometiers a gages.

Item, por ses 3 esquiers: 5 chevaux et 3 garzsons a gages.

Item, le dit Johan prendra deniers por ses chevaux et ses garzsons; la somme des chevaux: 10 chevaux, 2s. 6d. le jour; 2 palefriours et 3 sometiers chescun 2d. le jour, 10d. Et les 3 garzsons des vadletz chescun $1\frac{1}{2}$d. le jour, $4\frac{1}{2}$d. La somme de gages por chevaux et garzsons: 3s. $8\frac{1}{2}$d.

Item, por le dyner de meisme celi Johan: 3d., payn, 3 mes de quisine, un picher de vyn et 2 pichers de cervoise.

Item, pour manger quant il mangera hors de sale: 6d., payn, 2 pichers de vyn, 4 pichers de cervoise, 4 mes de quisine ove laferant de poletrie.

Item, por son souper: de payn, 4d., 2 pichers de vyn, 3 pichers de cervoise, et 3 mes de quisine.

Item, de chaundelerie, une torche tant come ele porra durer, 2 torciz, 12 chaundeles et 3 perchers.

[deleted: Item, por Roger de Mortimer, soi treiz a 4 chevaux et 3 garzsons por son corps, et 3 chevaux et 2 garzsons por ses vadletz, et por son corps vestuz 3 foiz par an ove Johan de Garrenne ses vadletz, sicome les autres vadletz denfauntz de garde.]

APPENDIX II

Plate and jewels provided for the marriage celebrations of Edward I and Margaret of France, September 1299

(a) *Plate and jewels bought by Adam the Goldsmith in Paris,*
some of which were given as gifts to those attending the wedding,
September 1299 (PRO, E.101/355/23)

m. 1r:

Jocalia empta Paris' per Adam Aurifabrum Regis et liberata in Garderobe apud
Cantuar' 11 die Sept. anno 27 prout extrahebantur de paneris venientibus de Paris'

12 ciphi auri aimellati
 2 picheri auri
14 ciphi argenti aimellati
23 ciphi argenti aimellati deaurati
49 ciphi argenti deaurati talliati

m. 2r:

12 ciphi argenti deaurati et gravati cum mediis aimellatis
19 ciphi argenti deaurati cum costis quorum aliqui gravati
64 ciphi argenti deaurati plani
16 ciphi argenti deaurati externis plani et interius gravati
 4 ciphi argenti cisillati cum rosettis

m. 2v:

12 ciphi argenti deaurati sive cooperti quorum 8 cisillati et 4 plani
10 par pelvium quorum 4 cum uno biberone
 1 discus argenti pro elemosinis
 3 picheri argenti, quorum unum cum 2 capit'
 1 justa argenti deaurat' nigell' cum dublett'
 1 ciphus argenti deauratus et gravatus interius et exterius cum
 1 pichero ad vinum et alio ad aquam de eodem opere . . .

De veteri thesauro
3 justa argenti deaurata, quorum 1 cum petrar' minut' et 2 aymellat'—[dantur
duci Burgundie, comitisse de Deu et comitisse de Dammart[in]—*deleted*]

[Total = 248 items]

Note (in right-hand margin): ponitur in panerio signato cum cruce +

Gifts given to members of queen's entourage and others

Ciphi auri aimellati

[1] datur duci Burgundie [*deleted*]—val. 280 l. 15d.t. Ponitur in panerio de O.

[2] datur duci Britann' [*deleted*]—val. 284 l. 13s. 9d.t.

[3] datur comitisse de Deu—val. 251 l. 6s. 3d.t.

[4] datur comitisse de Dammartyn—val. 211 l. 10s. 6d.t.

Ciphi argenti aimellati deaurati

[5] datur domino Hugone de Castello, advoc' ven' cum duce Burgundie—val. 41 l. 15d.t.

[6] datur domino de Beumanoir, militi ducis Brittanie—val. 52 l. 7s. 3d.t.

[7] datur vicedomino de Pynkeny—val. 46 l. 14s. 6d.t.

[8] datur domino Brunetto de Vernoil, militi Regine Francie—val. 52 l.t.

[9] datur domino Theobaldo de Corbie, magistro, servienti Regis Francie cum R[egine?]—val. 50 l. 15s. 8d.t.

[10] datur domino de Machetlon, militi ducis Britannie—val. 46 l. 16s.t.

[11] datur domino Thome de Sabaudie, clerico, nepoti comitis Sabaudie—val. 46 l. 7s.t.

[12] datur domino de Layak, militi ducis Britannie—val. 47 l. 0s. 8d.t.

[13] datur domino de Noers, militi ducis Burgundie—val. 58 l. 12s. 6d.t.

[14] datur domino Guillelmo ly Bornes, militi ducis Britannie—val. 45 l. 5s. 4d.t.

[15] datur domino de Rothested, militi ducis Britannie—val. 55 l. 4s. 5d.t.

[16] datur domino Willelmo de Loesy, militi ducis Burgundie—val. 34 l. 3s. 2d.t.

[17] datur domino Galfrido Turnemine, ven' cum Regina—val. 32 l. 3s. 9d.t.

[18] datur domino de Valle Grivaudi, militi ducis Burgundie—val. 35 l. 17s. 3d.t.

[19] datur domino Bernardo de Sorel, militi vicedomini de Pynkeny—val. 20 l. 6s. 3d.t.

[20] datur domino Ottoni de Grandisone ad unum calicem inde facere—val. 28 l. 10s. 4d.t. [for 'i ciphus argenti aimellatus deauratus']

[21] datur domino de Rosers, militi ducis Burgundie—val. 45 l. 11s.t.

Ciphi argenti deaurati talliati

[22] datur domino Petro de Cheyner, militi Regine—val. 42 l. 15s. 5d.t.

[23] datur domino Eustach' de Nova Villa, militi comitisse de Dammartyn—val. 30 l. 9s. 6d.t.

[24] datur domino Guillelmo de Flavencort, magistro hospicii Regis Francie—val. 39 l. 17d.t.

[25] datur domino Petro de Mornay, militi Regine—val. 39 l. 13s.t.

[26] datur domino Johanni de la Brau [?] militi ducis Burgundie—val. 28 l. 4s. 6d.t.

[27] datur domino Godefrido de Malestroyt, militi ducis Britannie—val. 32 l. 16s. 3d.t.

[28] datur domino Anselmo de Montlar, militi ducis Burgundie—val. 32 l. 16s. 3d.t.

[29] datur domino Reginaldo filio vicedomini de Pynkeny—val. 30 l. 9s. 7d.t.

[30] datur magistro Johanni de Forest 16 die Oct. [*deleted*]

[31] datur domino Erardo fratri comitis de Bar 18 die Sept. in recessu suo—val. 38 l. 14s. 8d.t.

[32] datur domino Johanni filio vicedomini de Pynkeny—val. 28 l. 18s. 2d.t.

[33] datur domino Jacobo de Montcheverel, militi comitis de Dammartyn—val. 24 l. 3s. 9d.t.

[34] datur domino castellano de Danemours panetario Regis Francie—val. 25 l. 11s. 9d.t.

[35] datur domino Waltero de Velu—val. 24 l. 8s. 9d.t.

[36] datur magistro Radulpho de Bellomonte magistro coco Regis Francie—val. 22 l. 12s. 11d.t.

[37] datur domino Matheo de Leons—val. 25 l. 7s. 10d.t.

[38] datur domino Willelmo de Beleville, militi ducis Britannie—val. 24 l. 17s.t.

[39] datur Gerardo de Pynkeny filio vicedomini de Pynkeny—val. 23 l. 12s. 6d.t.

[40] datur Elmeline domicelle comitisse Deu—val. 19 l. 17s. 6d.t.

[41] datur Isabelle de Chanes ven' etc in comitiva comitisse Deu—val. 28 l. 19s. 6d.t.

Ciphi argenti deaurati et gravati cum mediis aimellatis

[42] datur domino Bruno de Brunebek, militi comitisse de Deu—val. 38 l. 8s.t.

[43] datur domino Fulconi de Merle—val. 53 l. 15s.t.

[44] datur domino Guidoni de Castello Briani, militi ducis Britannie—val. 29 l. 9s. 9d.t.

[45] datur capellano ducis Burgundie—val. 24 l. 8s. 2d.t.

[46] datur—de Valle de Sestales, elemosinario domine Marie Regine Francie—val. 20 l. 6s. 3d.t.

[47] datur domino Bonables [?] de Rocheford' militi ducis Britannie—val. 28 l. 5s. 8d.t.

[48] datur Emeline de Lasart domicelle comitisse de Dammartyn—val. 15 l. 18s. 9d.t.

Ciphi argenti deaurati plani

[49] datur domino Galfrido de Syan militi ducis Britannie—val. 26 l. 10s. 9d.t.

[50] datur magistro Waltero marescallo Regis Francie—val. 19 l. 6s. 3d.t.

[51] datur Waltero hostiario ven' cum R[egine]—val. 15 l. 12s. 6d.t.

[52] datur Petro de Beaufort servienti ad arma Regis Francie—val. 15 l. 19s. 9d.t.

[53] datur domino Johanni de Katus militi ducis Britannie—val. 19 l. 17s. 6d.t.

[54] datur Johanne de Haye domicelle comitisse de Deu—val. 22 l. 12s. 6d.t.

[55] datur Johanni de Char servienti ad arma Regis Francie—val. 19 l. 13s. 9d.t.

[56] datur per preceptum Regis per dominum Edwardum filium Regis Brunardo Deynill Ville [?] ven' ad eundem dominum Edwardum in nunc' ex parte Regine Francie—val. 21 l. 11s. 3d.t.

[57] datur Galerando magistro but[elario]—val. 16 l. 15s.t.

[58] datur domino Alano de Ponte Albo militi ducis Britannie—val. 18 l. 18s. 9d.t.

[59] datur Gerardo de Lau clerico garderobe Regis Francie—val. 13 l. 10s. 8d.t.

[60] datur Johanni Bastel servienti ad arma regis Francie—val. 17 l. 5s.t.

[61] datur Simoni puletario Regis Francie—val. 15 l. 14s. 2d.t.

[62] datur domino Bridoni de Wermont militi ducis Burgundie per manus comitis Sabaudie—val. 23 l. 7s. 6d.t.

[63] datur Henrico valletto comitisse de Lucenburgh' ven' ad Regem in nunc' eiusdem domine sue ibidem 15 die Spet.—val. 20 l. 9s. 6d.t.

[64] datur Beatrici de Belloponte domicelle comitisse de Danmartyn—val. 18 l. 4s. 5d.t.

[65] datur Johanni de Marcily valletto ven' etc apud Boxle 29 die Sept.—val. 17 l. 0s. 15d.t.

[66] datur Nicholao hostiario Regis Francie—val. 15 l. 10s. 5d.t.

[67] datur domino Henrico de Sancto Lamberto militi Campanie—val. 34 l. 19s. 2d.t.

[68] datur—alteri clerico domini Thome de Sabaudie—val. 18 l. 17s. 6d.t.

[69] datur magistro Galfrido clerico domini Thome de Sabaudie—val. 18 l. 17s. 6d.t.

[70] datur Egidio le Keu, valletto domine Marie regine Francie, redeunti ad eandem dominam suam cum litteris ipsius Regis—val. 18 l. 7s. 6d.t.

[i ciphus venditur domino Ottoni de Grandisone—*interlined*]

[71] datur Regi Manari Regi haraldorum de Campanie ven' etc—val. 18 l. 3s. 9d.t.

[72] datur domino Galfrido de Gleskyn militi ducis Britannie—val. 26 l. 13s. 9d.t.

[73] datur Rogero salsario Regis Francie—val. 17 l. 7s. 9d.t.

[74] datur Guillelmo de Pontoys magistro marescallo Regis Francie—val. 13 l. 15s.t.

[75] datur Artus de Vaer militi ducis Britannie—val. 20 l. 8s. 9d.t.

Ciphi argenti deaurati exterius plani et interius gravati

[76] datur Lamberto cissori Regis Francie ven' cum Regina—val. 29 l. 5s.t.

[77] datur domino Saverico de Beaureyn commilitoni domini Erardi de Bar in recessu suo etc apud Cantuar' 18 die Sept.—val. 25 l.t.

[78] datur Girardo de Mauntepuletario Regis Francie—val. 15 l. 14s. 2d.t.

Ciphi argenti cisillati cum rosettis

[79] datur magistro Johanni de Dys clerico Regis Francie—val. 29 l.t.

[80] datur domino Radulpho de Monteforti militi ducis Britannie—val. 27 l. 12s. 6d.t.

[81] datur domino Radulfo le Visconte militi ducis Britannie—val. 29 l. 2s. 6d.t.

[82] datur Petro Jencian servienti Regis Francie—val. 29 l. 10s.t.

Ciphi argenti deaurati sine cooperculis etc

[83] datur Russello submarescallo Regis Francie—val. 9 l. 15d.t.

[84] datur Saketto valletto de porta Regis francie—val. 9 l. 15d.t.

[85] datur Briano coco Regis Francie ven' cum Regina—val. 8 l. 12s. 5d.t.

[86] datur Guioto de Beaumont coco—val. 9 l. 8s.t.

[87] datur Olivero janitori—val. 10 l. 8s. 6d.t.

[88] datur Guilloto clerico naperie Regis Francie—val. 9 l. 3s. 3d.t.

[89] datur Henrico de Centron valletto domine Marie Regine France ven' ad Regem cum litteris Regis Francie—val. 10 l. 4s 10d.t.

[90] datur Roberto fructuario ven' cum Regina—val. 8 l. 17s. 10d.t.

[91] datur Victori janitori Regis Francie 9 l. 14s 1d.t.

[92] datur Morello janitori valletto de porta Regis Francie—val. 8 l. 17s. 10d.t.

[93] datur Petronille de Vivi domicelle comitisse de Danmartyn—val. 8 l. 14s. 9d.t.

Pelvi

[94] datur comitisse de Danmartyn—val. 54 l. 15s. 8d.t.

[95] datur comitisse de Deu—val. 55 l. 15s. 7d.t.

[96] datur magistro Wide Valenc' phisico Regine red' etc apud West-monasterium 6 die Novembr.—val. 43 l. 8s. 3d.t.

[97] datur vicedomino de Pynkeneye—val. 37 l. 17s.t

[i venditur domino Ottoni de Grandesono—*interlined*]

(b) *Account with Adam the Goldsmith for jewels and plate for the queen, 1299* (PRO, E.101/356/22)

m. 1r:

Ade aurifabro pro 1 firmaculo auri precii 60 l. paris', 2 diamand' prec. 50 l. par., emptis de eodem ad opus Regine in primo adventu suo usque Cantuar' anno 27: 110 l. paris' qui valent in turon' 97 l. 10s. et in sterling: 22 l. 18s. 4d.

Inde recepit 15 pollardorum ante Natale qui valebant in turon' 60 l. Et 15 l. post Natale qui valent 30 l.t.

Summa recepte in turon: 90 l. Et sic debentur ei adhuc 47 l. 10s. qui valent in sterling: 6 l. 18s. 4d.

Eidem pro uno cipho argenti deaurato, 1 cipho argenti albo pond' in toto: 57s. 11d. empt' de eodem ad opus Regine et liberat' Jaketto de Tabarie et Hugoni de Caumbray London' in primo adventu suo ibidem: 104s. 6d.

Eidem pro 4 zonis argenti muniend' et 2 florinis ad deaurandum harnesium dictarum zonarum, et pro factura harnesii predicti 26s.

Eidem pro factura unius firmaculi cum scutis aymellatis et 2 anulis cum ameraldis: 7s. et pro auro et factura unius anuli cum rubetto ad opus eiusdem: 2s. 6d.

         Summa: 9s. 6d.

Eidem pro 5 duodenis butonorum cum aimellatis de armis Francie et Anglie emptis de eodem ad opus Regine ponder' $17\frac{1}{2}$s.:   46s. 6d.

Eidem pro 1 rubetto perforato empto pro quibusdam Paternostres missis per Reginam ad partes Francie per manus Mathei de Montem[er]: 100s. et pro ballesio pendente in paternostres predictis: 40s.   Summa: 7 l.

Summa particularum predictarum: 24 l. 4s. 10d.

APPENDIX III

Indenture recording delivery from the Wardrobe of chapel furniture and liturgical equipment for Thomas of Brotherton, Edward I's son, 7 January 1301 (PRO, E.101/360/15)

m. 1r:

Indentura de diversis ornamentis subscriptis liberatis per dominum Johannem de Drokensford, custodem Garderobe Regis, Roberto de Langeton, clerico Garderobe domini Thome filii Regis, pro capella eiusdem filii Regis apud Westmonasterium [7 Jan. 29 Edward I (1301)] viz:

1   textus cum platis et imaginibus argenti deauratus
1   tabula munita argenti pro pace danda
1   auriculum de panno de tars pro altari
1   frontale brodat' cum perlis
1   cassus pro corporalibus de imaginibus broudatus
2   frontalia broudata maiora et minora de una secta, Casula, tunica et dalmatica de nigro et viridi diapre linat' sindone rubea, Capa chori vetus broud', linata de panno de arista(?)
1   pecten' eburneneti pro capella
1   tualla de albo serico radiata pro altare
1   tualla de albo serico clare in una pecia pro patena
1   Gradale
1   calix argenti deauratus
1   par corporalium in quodam cassa de serico
2   tualle cum uno rocheto
2   panni ad aurum usitat' pro altare
2   fiole argenti
1   tabula plat' munita [argenti deaur'] pro pace danda
4   superp[el]lecia usitata
1   pulvinar' usitat'
1   vas de stagno pro aqua benedicta
3   albe, 3 amice cum parur', 2 stole, 3 fanon' et 1 casula et 1 capa chori

m. 2r:

Ita que secuntur 1 missale, 1 portiphorium, 1 Gradale, 2 [. . . .] pro capella [. . . .] de serico usitat'[. . . .] preci predictorum nescio, 1 thur[. . . .]ulum de [. . . .]nd' una pixi de eodem[. . . .]

Witnessed by Robert de Langton, 10 January 1301.

APPENDIX IV

Indenture recording delivery from the Treasury in the Tower of London of plate, jewels, and relics for Queen Margaret, 28 March 1305 (PRO, E.101/684/56, no. 9)

On 28 Mar. 33 Edward I (1305) John de Droxford, keeper of the wardrobe, extracted the following items from the king's treasury in the Tower of London, in the queen's presence, which were delivered to her cofferer Thomas de Querle:

Quadam crux argenti deaurata cum imagine crucifixi et imaginibus Marie et Johannis ex utraque parte, et cum pede argenti aymellat'.

Item, una imago argenti deaurat' ad modum angeli cum lapidibus preciosis, tenens coronam auri in manu sua, cum 2 imaginibus ad modum angelorum confectis loco cerofer[um].

Item quedam relique de Sanctis Bede, Laurencie, Stephano, Gregorio, Vincentio, Laurenc', et de sudar' Sancte Marie, posite in quadam plata spissa argenti deaurat' superscripsioni dictorum sanctorum in circuitu continenti.

Item, quadam plata auri cum diversis reliquis in quadam bursa de serico viz: de sancto Petro . . . Bartholomeo, . . . Blasio, Meloro, Audoeno, Paulo, Cristoforo, Vincencio, Leodogar', Egidio, Nicholao, Dionisio, Jacobo, Stephano, Margareta, et Agatha, dente Sancti Laurenc', de panno Sancte Eldrede, de ligno domini, de cunabulo domini, de claro domini, et de arundine unde percussus fuit Christi.

Item, diverse relique in 1 vase argenti viz: de capite Sancti Austeri, de capite Sancti Augustini, et de Sanctis Petro Martiri, Augustino Anglorum, appostolo Rumane, confessore, et pontifice Paulino, et Thome, Mauric', Vincent' et de Sancta Edburga virgine.

Item, 1 crux auri cum cathena aurea ad pendend' circa collum hominis, et nescitur quid sit interius.

Item, 1 vas auri quadratum in quo nichil continetur.

Item, de oleo Sancte Katerine in quodam vaso parvo.

Item, quedam relique de Sancto Nicholao in quodam vase de cristallo.

Item, 1 incensarium argenti deaur'.

Item, quodam tabernaculum fere planum cum cruce deaurata et cum bendis argenti deauratis.

Item 1 crux cum 1 cristallo in medio, in qua continetur de ligno domini et de corona Christi.

Item, 1 superaltare cum bendis argenti deauratis.

APPENDIX V

Gifts of plate by Edward I to John, count of Holland, and Elizabeth, countess of Holland, on their marriage, January–August 1297

(a) *Indenture recording plate given by Edward I to John, count of Holland, 17 January 1297* (PRO, E.101/354/15)

Memorandum quod [17 Jan. 25 Edward I] apud Herewicum liberavit dominus Johannes de Drokensford, custos Garderobe domini Regis, per preceptum eiusdem Regis ad opus domini Johannis comitis Holland', transfretantis versus partes proprias in presencia [. . . .]Regina[. . . .] [Guidonis] Ferre, et magistri Ricardi de Havering', domino Cristancio de Keppehorst et Waltero clerico, attornatis dicti comitis ad res ipsas recipiend' per eundem deputatis, diversa jocalia subscripta pro servicio dicti comitis, viz:

[Marginal: Empt' London']

1 ciphum a[rgenti? . . .] cum pede et cooperculo pro ore [. . .] pond' 28s 5d. precii 36s. 5d.
6 ciphos argenti albi cum pedibus sine cooperculis quorum unus ponderat 38s. 4d., alius 3 mar. 15d.

[Marginal: Dengaine st.']

1 picherum argenti pro aqua cum scutis deauratis pond' 51d.
5 picheros argenti albos cum cooperculis quorum 1 ponderat 4 l. 20d., alius ponderat 47s. 6d. [. . .]
1 par pelvium pro aula pond' 9m. 2 unc. 12½d.
1 pelvem pond' 6m. 4s. 6d.
1 pelvem pond' 73s. 7d.
1 lavatorium argenti album pond' 49s.
1 lavatorium argenti deauratum [. . .]
1 salarium argenti album pond' 1m.
24 ciphos argenti albos et platos [. . .]
36 discos argenti albos pond' 43 l. 4s. 6d.
36 salsaria argenti pond' 13 m.
2 discos argenti [pond' . . .] 38s. 11d.

Note: m. = marks
    unc. = ounces

(b) *Plate given by Edward I to his daughter Elizabeth, countess of Holland, on her marriage, 2 August 1297* (PRO, E.101/354/16)

Memorandum quod die veneris secundo die Augusti anno regni regis Edwardi 25 apud Westmonasterium liberavit dominus Johannes de Drokensford, custos Garderobe . . . Regis, per preceptum eiusdem Regis, ad opus domine Elizabeth', filie ipsius Regis, comitisse Holland', transfretanti versus partes proprias, domino Johanni de Weston', militi, attornato eiusdem comitisse, ad jocalia ipsa recipienda per eandem deputato, diversa jocalia subscripta, viz:

Pro capella

1 crucem argenti deaurat' cum imagine Christi pond' 3m. 32d. precii 100s.
1 calicem argenti deaurat' . . . precii 70s.
1 calicem argenti deaurat' . . . precii 21s. 6d.
Unam tabulam ad pacem cum platis argent' et imagine Sancte Trinitatis—precii 50s.
1 coupam argenti deauratam ad inponend' corpus domini—30s. 5d.
2 candelabra argenti—precii 40s. minus 3d.
4 phiolas argenti
2 bacinos . . . qui fuerunt G. de Langele
Unam naviculam argenti ad inponend' thus' et unum coclearum argenti pro eadem pond' 24s.—precii 34s.
1 insensar' argenti deaurat'—4 l. 10s.
1 insensar' argenti album—precii 70s.
1 vas argenti pro aqua benedicta—6m. minus 12d.
1 aspersorum argenti—25s.
1 campanell' argenti—22s.

Pro elemosina

1 discum argenti magnum pro elemosina—8 l. 8s.
1 ollam argenti pro eadem—9m. 6s. 8d.
1 navem argenti—10m. 9d.

Pro panetr'

1 salarium argenti deauratum per partes pond' 17s. 8d.
6 coclear' auri—11s. 4d.
5 duoden' coclearum argenti quorum 12 ponderant 12s. 11d. et 4 duoden' pond' 4m.

Pro But[ellaria]

12 picheros auri pro vina et pro aqua [of which] 2 ponderant 49s. 6d et 48s. 10d.
46 ciphos argenti cum pede sine cooperculo et sine ped'

Pro aula

1 par pelvium argenti cum scutis deauratis pond' 4 l. 11s. 3d.
2 par' pelvium . . .
2 lavatoria argenti alba—4 l. 11s.

Pro coquina

 6 discos magnos pro interfertulis pond. 52s. [each]
98 discos argenti
96 salsaria argenti

Pro speciebus

2 platas pro speciebus
1 platam cum pede pro speciebus
3 coclear' argenti

Quoslibet ciphos cum pede et cooperculo: 55 ciphos
[including]:
  1 ciphum argenti deauratum gravatum cum Babewyns pond' 38s. 6d.
  1 ciphum argenti deauratum qui fuit abbatis de Hida pond' 37s.
  1 ciphum argenti deuratum qui fuit abbatis de Leycestrie pond' 37s. 6d.
  1 ciphum argenti deauratum qui fuit missus ad curiam per abbatem
     Westmonast' pond' 40s. minus 4d.
  1 ciphum argenti deauratum qui fuit abbatis de Sancto Albano pond' 4m. 3s.
  1 ciphum argenti deauratum qui fuit abbatis Cestrie pond' 50s.
  1 zonam cum perlis et 1 bursam cum perlis de armis Regis
  4 nouchia
 16 firmacula

APPENDIX VI

Draft letter of Guy de Dampierre, count of Flanders, concerning the services and rights of his huntsman (veneur), c.1299 (ADN, B.3230, no. 111682)

Dorse: Copie des convenench' faites a Rousel le Veneur par le conte Guy

Nous Guy, etc. que nous avoms a Gillion Rousesel nostre veneur faites tels convenenches qui sensuivent et qui sont contenues en ches presentes lettres, les queles convenenches doivent durer tersci a nostre rapel, ou nostre volontee, et nient avant.

Primers, nous devons et prometons au dit Gillion 100 livres de nostre monnoie de Flandres chascun an de sa pension, tant et si longement que les convenenches duront entre nous et lui, les quels 100 l. par an nous lui prometons a paier et a delivrer as termes qui sensuient, chest asavoir 40 l. de la dite monnoie au jour de le Nativitei Saint Jehan prochainement venant, 40 l. au jour de Noel suivant apres, et 20 l. de la dite monnoie au jour de Pasques apres suivant [deleted: sains moien] et ensi de terme en terme chascun an tant com li dite conveneche nous plaira. Apres nous lui devoms livrer deus kevaus, les quels il doit escoustenger a son frait. [deleted: Apres nous lui octroions tous les ans] Et les doit metre en no service, les quels, se il muerent en no service, ou aucuns deaus, nous lui devons rendre apres, nous lui avoms octroie et octrereons, durans les dites conveneches, deus paire de robes teles com nous les donroms a nos serjands.

Encore lui octreoms nous tous les ans durans les dites convenenches 2 millers de nostre ramit dou bos de Nieppe, et 500 de faiscaus del dit bosch, et lui octreoms que il puist avoir de son droit, les dite convenances durans, en nostre bos de Niepe 4 vaches et 2 veaus.

Et parmi tant il doit tenir 32 kiens de chache et 6 levriers et 2 braconniers et 1 garchon qui wardera les kiens tous a son frait. Et doit li dis Roussiaus venir et aler ca[c]hier tout par tout la il nous plaira, et ou nous lui commanderons en Flandre et en le terre de Namur, tout a son frait sans le nostre. Et toutes les fois que nous le manderoms il doit venir [deleted: a nous] jusques a nous et amener ses kiens tout a son frait. Et quand il eit venus jusques a nous, il doit avoir pour 2 chevaus avaine et dou pain pour ses kiens, et ses convenables frais, ensi come autre veneur qui ont este a nous en nostre hostel ont [deleted: en] usee dusques a ore. [inserted:] Et a savoir que nous devoms soustenir et retenir a no frait les maisons des veneurs et des kiens qui sont au bos desusdit, et dont li dis Roussiaus avoir ses droitures des biestes quil prendera. Et li braconnier ausi leur droiture ensi com il ont usei dusques a ore.

Les queles choses desusdites nous lui prometoms loiaument a tenir en bone foi ensi come elles sont chi desus escriptes.

APPENDIX VII

Festivities and textiles at the court of Artois, *c.*1306–1317

(a) *Provisions and purchases for court festivities ordered by Mahaut,*
countess of Artois [?1306–1307] (ADPC, A.1015, fos. 16r–v)

fo. 16r:

Che sont les parties que me dame Dartoys a commande a faire a Baude de Croisilles

Premierement pour le poiscon et pour le serpent a 3 testes de quoi Robers Dartois issi, et Williames de Vyane, doit on [50?]s. de Parezis

Item, pour toutes les choses qui appartienent a lachevisement dun chevalier, chest a savoir 10 ausnes de toile, pour chascune ausne 18d. paris', sen fist ou couvretures de chevales, et cotes a armer, et manches a bras, et cauchettes, et coiffes, si valent—15 s. par.

Item, pour 2 couronnes le Roy de Navare et le roine, dorees de fin or, et pour le cuevrechief du hyaume—valent 12 s. par.

Item, pour un escu—4 s. par.

Item, pour 1 hyaume et pour le creste et les G[ar]landes—6 s. par.

Item, pour 1 espee et pour les cercles, et pour les chycles, et le boistelet dentour les rains, et pour les claus et pour le teste de cheval—3 s. par.

Item, pour lor et largent, et pour les couleurs de choi les couvretures et les cotes a armer et les brachieres furent batues et paintes—10 s. par.

Item, pour les ouvriers de ches choses chi, pour leur despens et leur journees—7 s. par. pour chascune paire de harnas.

Item, pour le fu a sekier toutes ches choses—16 s. par.

Some pour chascun achevisement de chevalier couste 45 s. par., si en ja 6 chevaliers, si valent 13 l. 10 s. par.

Item, pour les 6 dames ki furent en chele maniere a cheval, et eurent camises en liu de cotes, et manteles four[r]es, et sambues, et testes en liu de hiaumes, et colieres de crespes, pour chascun achesivement—45 s. par. si valent 13 l. 10 s. par.

Item, pour le keval ke Baudes chevaucha pour 5 journees—18 d. par. chascun jour—valent 7s 6d. par.

Item, pour les 10 compaignons ki fisent le ju des vielles, pour leur despens fait a Heyding le nuit Saint Bertremiu ke Denis comanda a Baude—11 s. par.

Item, pour leur recort faire, et iaus assanler a le maison Baude, pour 1 despens dun menger—7 s. par.

Item, pour le despens de ches 10 compaignons, alans et venans Darras a Heyding—25 s. par.

Item, pour fil, pour cole, pour cordes, pour froumage fres, pour bure, pour lait, pour 1 panier et pour 1 chat—4 s. par.

Item, pour les journees de ches 10 compaignons—5 jours chascun alant et venant chascun 5 jours—3 s. 8d. Et valent chil 10 compaignons pour toutes leur journees—36 s. 8d.

    Some de toutes ches parties—35 l. 9 s. 2d. par.

Item, pour le houchete Robert Dartois, pour 13 aunes de cendal, et pour lor et pour les fringes, et pour le capelet—4 l. 13 s. par.

fo. 16v:

Premierement pour une ouce Robert seme descucons de ses armes—4 l.

Item, pour une baleine et 1 serpent a 3 testes—30 d.

Item, pour le harnoys de 6 chevalliers et 6 dames qui tournoierent ensanble—21 l. 12 s.

Item [. . .]ables [. . .]Darras a Hesding—7 s. 6d.

Item, pour les despens des 10 compaignons allans et venans Darras a Heding—25 s.

Item, pour fil, corde, buerre etc et 1 chat—4 s.

    Some—31 l. 13 s. 2d.

Item, pour 1 bacinet pour Robert et unes greves et uns polains—40 s.

Item, pour le fascon dun porpoint, et pour telle et soie, et pour estofer le bacinet—30 s.

Item, pour le cendal

Item, pour 1 aubergon et 1 camalh—50 s.

Item, pour une bourse pour porter le argent Robert—5 s.

(b) *Inventory of textiles and furnishings of Mahaut, countess of Artois, delivered to Colart le Tailleur on 31 December [n.d.] [?c.1313–1317]*
(ADPC, A.1015, fos. 23r–24r)

fo. 23r:

Che sont les joiaux ma dame de la garderobe baillies a Colart le Tailleur le deerrain jour de Decembre.

Premierement, 3 garnimens de samit de flours, mantel, surcot et gardecors dont le mantel est fourre dermine, et les autres 2 pieces de menu ver.

Item, 3 pieces de velvet, coquet, mantel, sourcot et cote fourre de menu ver.

Item, 4 pieches de velvet inde, mantel, surcot et gardecors et cote fourre de dermine.

Item, 2 pieces de bleu samit, surcot, gardecors fourre de menu ver.

Item, 4 pieces de camelot vert, chape, surcot, gardecors, fourre de menu ver.

Item, 3 pieches de jaune samit, mantel, surcot et cote fourre de menu ver.

Item, 4 pieches de saie de Florence, chape, sourcot, gardecors et [cote fourre de sendal—deleted]

Item, 4 pieces de vermeille saie Dillande, chape, sourcot, gardecors et cote fourre de menu ver.

Item, 3 pieces de saie Dirllande, surcot, gardecors, et cote fourre de menu ver.

Item, 1 chape de jaune camoissie et 1 cote sans fourreure.

Item, 1 vert cote camoissie.

Item, une cote de bleu et de vermeill diaspre.

Item, une cote folete camoissie.

Item, ne cote tanee a egletes.

Item, une cote dun vermeill velvet.

Item, une cote blance de louvrage de Flandres.

Item, une cote de jaune samite.

Item, 3 garnemens de soie jaune Dillande, surcot, gardecors et cote fourre de menu ver.

Item, 1 mantel de camelin fourre de menu ver.

Item, 1 fourreure a chape et 1 pelichan sans mances de menu ver.

Item, 1 lit des armes de France, coute pointe, dras de cheues, 5 tapis, 4 pieces de courtines, 12 quarriaus et 1 couvertoir de scarlate fourre de menu ver.

Item, 1 lit des armes Dangleterre . . . [as above] 3 tapis, 4 pieces de courtines vermeilles, et 1 couvertoir de graine fourre de menu ver.

fo. 23v:

Item, 1 drap de fleurs et de bleu a rosetes qui nest mie entier

Item, 2 tapis vers et 3 rouges que len estent par la maison.

Item, 20 coussins alans par lostel.

Item, 1 robe descarllate sanguine de 5 garnemens, chape, mantel, surcot, gardecors,et cote fourre de menu ver.

Item, 1 robe dun vert melle de 5 pieces, chape, mantel, surcot, gardecors et cote fourre de menu ver.

Item, 1 robe de coignet de 5 pieces, chape, mantel, surcot, gardecors et cote dont le mantel est fourre de menu ver et les autres non.

Item, 1 fourreure dun mantel clos de menu ver.

Item, 1 mantel vermeill clos fourre de lievres de 2 pennes blances.

Item, 1 demi couvertoir de gris.

fo. 24r:

Item, 1 lit seme descuchons des armes Dengleterre que la contesse de Bourgoigne donna a madame—couvertoir, coute pointe, 4 pieces de courtines, 4 tapis, 1 cuevrechief fourre de menu ver, 5 quarriaus, 2 orilliers.

Item, 4 orilliers de cendal rouge.

Item, 1 lit a filatieres seme de pluseurs escuchons, coute pointe, couvertoir, fourre de menu ver, drap de ceues, 3 tapis.

Item, 1 couvertoir des armes de France fourre dermine.

Item, 1 esprevier vert.

Item, 1 doublet de cendal jaune.

Item, 1 drap vert entier.

Item, 4 roumans.

Item, 60 aunes de toile.

Item, 40 aunes de napes.

Item, 65 aunes de touailles.

Item, 2 barens de pieces.

Item, 5 paire de linceaus pour le lit madame.

Item, 1 tapis vers et vermeill alant par lostel.

Item, 2 quarriaus des armes Dengleterre et Dalemaigne.

Item, 1 escarlate vermeille dont on a fait une robe pour ma dame.

Item, 1 melle que maistres Thierris donna dont on a fait une robe pour madame.

Item, 1 vert gay dont on a fait une robe pour madame.

Item, 1 vermeille tiretaine de Florence dont on a fait une robe pour madame.

Item, 10 pennes de menu ver, chascun de 8 tir, des queles 10 pennes on a fourre pour ma dame 4 garnemens de vermeille escarlate . . .

APPENDIX VIII

Hainault-Holland inventories

(a) Inventory of books in French (*li romanch*), with valuations, for William III, count of Hainault (?1311) (AEM, Trésorerie, Recueil 115, no. 2)

Che sont li romanch que maistres Jehan de Florence a pris pour monsr le conte et prisiet par avis[1]

Premierement, le romanch de Merlin prisiet—20 l.

Item, j romanch de Lanselot prisiet—30 l.

Item, j romanch de traitier des vertus, comment on aprent bien a morir, couvert dune blanche couverture prisiet—12 l.

Item, j romanch des estoires des romains prisiet—12 l.

Item, une partie de le bible en romanch, si contient le parolle de Salmon, le livre des Ecclesiastes, le cantike de Salmon, le livre de sapience, le livre de ecclesiastie, le livre de Ysaie, et pluseurs autres livres prisiet—30 l.

Item, j livre danchiennes canchons prisiet—100s.

Item, j autre partie de le bible en romanch, si contient pluiseurs livres de le bible, prisiet—30 l.

Item, j autre livre dou traitiet de vertus prisiet—8 l.

Item, j autre romanch des choses de Romme ke on apelle Lukain prisiet—12 l.

Item, j romanch des vies Loherens et des Novials prisiet—15 l.

Item, j romanch con apelle tresor prisiet—12 l.

Item, j livre de canchons prisiet—7 l.

Item, j livre ke on apelle lestitut des empereurs prisiet—40s.

Item, j autre petit romanch prisiet—60s.

Item, j livres con apelle le gouvernement des rois ke freres Gilles Hawescuis fist prisiet—8 l.

Item, j autre livre Dathene prisiet—8 l.

---

[1] Compare the list of books printed in *Documents*, i. 156–7, from AEM, Trésorerie, Cartulaire 19, fos. 120r–v, and dated on the basis of a later note in the cartulary to 4 Dec. 1304.

Item, j livre u il a ymages prisiet—10 l.

Item, j livret des natures des oisiauls prisiet—30s.

Item, j livret des 12 tribulations prisiet—40s.

    Somme de le prisie de ces livres par avis—235 l. 10s.

(b) Inventory of cutlery, with valuations, for the countess of Hainault, 1307 (AEM, Trésorerie, Cartulaire 20, fos. 169r–v)

fo. 169r:

Cest chou ke Biernardins a livreit de coutiaus pour ma dame puis quelle revint en Valenchiennes, jusques a le penthecouste 1307

Premiers 2 paire ke me dame donna a monsr son fill porter en Hollande

Item, 6 paire pour trenchier devant li

Item, 1 paire pour Jehan de Haynnau

    Summa, 9 paire sa en le paire 3 pieches, valent a 50s le pieche—22 l. 10s.t.

Item, 26 paire de petis coutiaus pour me dame, sa en le paire 2 coutiaus et une fourchete, 10s le paire—13 l. noirs t.

Item, 17 petis coutiaus avoec forchetes et poinchons pour me dame—4 l. 5s.t.

Item, 1 grant coutiel ke me dame donna a leveske Dutreich—10s.t.

Item, 4 coutiaus a fort dos ke me dame envoia a monsr en Hollande—40s t. Item, 6 coutiaus grans pour monsr Jehan cui Dieus absoille—60s.t.

Item, 4 annemelles pour me dame de que[quoi] me dame livra les manches—20s.t.

Item, 6 paire ke me dame envoia en Hollande—60s t.

fo. 169v:

Item, 9 coutiaus a forchetes et a poinchons—45 s.t.

Coutiaus fais par la maisnie Bernart 49 petis coutiaus a toutes les forchetes—9 l. 16s.t.

Item, 5 paire de grans coutiaus, 3 pieches en le paire—100s.t.

Item, 1 grant coutiel a fort dos ke me dame donna frere Gerard de Masuny—10s.t.

Item, pour coutiaus ke Bauduins de Biaumont eut—60s.t.

Item, pour coutiaus livreit a me dame le contesse maressalle—40s t.

    Summa, 71 l. 16s t.

Somme des grans coutiaus ke Bernardins a livreit—20 paire

Et 35 paire de petis coutiaus

Et 12 paire de grand coutiaus simples

Et 66 coutiaus petis simples

Et 4 annemelles sans manches

Summa del argent ke li coutial coustent—65 l. 16s.t.

APPENDIX IX

Letter (in French) of Floris V, count of Holland, to
Edward I, probably 1290, between January and June,
sending him the gift of a falcon (PRO, S.C.1/18, no. 118;
and see *Orkondenboek van Holland en Zeeland tot 1299*,
ed. J. G. Kruisheer, iv (Assen, 1997), no. 2499.)

A trehaut prence et tre noble, a mon chier segnor E. le Roy Dengleterre, Florens
cuens de Hollande son cors et quant quil puet a son service tout dis aparellies a
tous ces commandemens et a tous ces plaisiers.

Treschier sire, je vous envoie un ostoir des mieudres de mon pais par Williame
mon vallet ki warde mes ostoirs, et se vous voleis nule chose ke je puisse faire, tre-
dous sire, si le me faichies asavoir, et je le ferai molt volentiers et nostre sires vos
wart et en arme et en cors.

APPENDIX X

Livery Roll of Robert de Béthune, count of Flanders, 13 November 1307 (RAG, Gaillard 64, another copy in Gaillard 65)

[1 membrane; parchment]

m. 1r:

Cest li livrisons des pennes de le Toussains prisses a Goisson de Kolemghie de Gand le lundi apres le Saint Martin en yvier lan 1307

Premiers, pour le cors monsingneur de Flandres 2 fourures de menut vair, de 9 tires le piece, 7 florins dor—valent 14 flor. dor

Item, pour lui mesmes, une fourure de gros vair—vaut 5 flor. dor

Item, pour lui mesmes, 1 pelicon de gris—vaut 6 flor. dor

Item, pour lui mesmes, 1 caperon de menut vair—vaut 1 flor. dor

Item, pour 15 baneres, 15 fourures de menut vair—valent a 6 flor. le piece 90 flor. dor

Item, pour eaus, 15 fourures de gros vair, le piece 5 flor. —valent 75 flor. dor

Item, pour eaus, 15 fourures de caperons—valent 15 flor. dor

Item, pour 5 clers 5 pennes de menut vair, le piece 6 flor.—valent 30 flor. dor

Item, pour eaus, 5 fourures de gros vair, le piece 5 flor.—valent 25 flor. dor

Item, pour eaus, 5 fourures de caperon—valent 5 flor. dor

Item, pour 12 bacelers, 12 kierke, le kierke 7 flor. dor—valent 84 flor. dor

Item, pour 5 clers ki ont kierkes come baceler, le kierke 7 flor.—valent 35 flor. dor

Item, pour nos deus demisieles, 2 pelicons de gris fin, de 2 tires—valent 16 flor. dor

Item, pour elles, 8 fourures de menut vair, de 9 tires, valent le piece 7 flor.—56 flor. dor

Item, pour elles, 4 caperons—valent 8 flor. dor

[deleted: Item, pour 2 cotes hardies pour monsingneur le conte et pour monsingneur Robert son fil de gros vair, le piece 5 flor.—valent 10 flor. dor

Item, pour eaus 2 caperons—valent 2 flor. dor]

Somme . . . 560 flor. dor a le mache

De ce rabat on que les parties furent trop haut contees, 20 flor. dor

Somme . . . 540 flor. dor

Item, lui doit on pour 3 mantiaus pour le singneur de Ghistelle pour le Pentecouste prochain . . . . 18 flor. dor

Somme . . . 558 flor. dor

[Deleted: Item, doit on audit Goss[uin] pour 13 dras pour le maisnie, le piece 8 flor. dor—valent 104 flor. dor

Item, pour 15 dras gaudes pour partir as eschiviers, le piece 14 flor.—valent 210 flor. dor

Item, pour 5 dras piers por les clers, le piece 15 flor.—valent 75 flor. dor

Item, pour 2 dras melles pour les clers, le piece 13 flor.—valent 26 flor. dor]

Somme . . . 415 flor. dor

[Grand total = 973 flor. dor]

m. iv:

Item, pour monsingneur Robert le fil monsingneur, une fourure de 9 tires pour un entredeus—7 flor. dor

Item, pour lui 1 pelican de gris—4 flor. dor

Item, pour le cors monsingneur pour une reube a parer, et pour une autre reube, 6 fourures de menut vair, de 9 tires, le piece 7 flor.—42 flor. dor

Item, pour lui, 1 fourure de gros vair—5 flor. dor

Item, pour lui, 2 caperons, de 5 tires—3 flor. dor

Item, pour lui, 1 pelican de gris—4 flor. dor

Item, pour monsingneur Robert, pour 1 reube a parer, 3 fourures de menut vair, de 9 tires, le piece 7 flor.—valent 24 flor. dor

Item, 1 caperon de 5 tires—1 flor. dor

[Deleted: Item, pour monsingneur Baudewin Denisebroch, 2 fourures de 7 tires et 1 caperon—7 flor. dor]

Item, pour 1 noviel chevalier, 2 fourures de 8 tires de gros vair—8 flor. dor

Item, pour lui 1 caperon—1 flor. dor

Item, pour lui 1 penne de mantel—6 flor. dor

Item, pour 3 mantiaus le singneur de Ghistelle, pour le Noel lan 1307—18 flor. dor

Item, pour Helle, mariee a Dunkerke, 1 penne de mantel—6 flor. dor

Item, pour lui 2 pennes de 8 tires, le piece 4 flor.—8 flor. dor

Item, 1 drap [vert—deleted] pour lui—11 flor. dor

[Partly deleted:]

Item, pour 1 drap marbriet pour monsingneur pour caschun jour—15 flor. dor

Item, pour 1 drap melle pour monsingneur et pour monsingneur Robert a parer—42 flor. dor

Item, pour 18 dras raies pour le parture des eschuiers, le piece 12 flor.—216 flor. dor

Item, pour 14 dras vers por les chevalier de le livre monsingneur, le piece 16 flor.—224 flor. dor

Item, pour 1 vert [. . . ?drap . . .] singneur de Ghistelles, et pour le noviel cevalier—17 flor. dor

Item, pour 2 dras vers de present, dont on ne conte nient, et furent de cestuy livree

Item, pour 120 pennes dagniaus pour les gens monsingneur, le piece 26s. 3d.—valent 157 l. 10s.

Item, pour les despens Andriu a le maison Goss[uin] de Kalenghie[n] et pour ouvrages de valles—12 l.

Item, pour monsingneur Thomas de Savoie, prises par maistre Guillaume . . . son compaingnon

Premiers, 5 fourures de menut vair et 1 fourure de menus popes, et 5 fourures de bacelers pour clers—11 pennes—46 flor. dor

Item, 6 fourures de gros vair et 4 de menut vair a caperons pour 16s. depens' a bonne monnoie—7 flor. et 6s. de bonne monnoie

Item, 10 fourures dagniaus et 1 fourure de cauriaus—14 l. monn. flandr.

Item, 1 penne de gros vair de 8 tires et 1 penne de caperon—5 flor. dor

Item, 7 drap mellet—11 flor. dor

Item, 4 pennes dagniaus—8 l. monn. de flandr.

Somme . . . pour monsingneur Thomas—75 flor. et 5 gros t.

Item, pour le recheveur, pour lui et pour ses freres, 3 dras et 2 pour ses valles—$49\frac{1}{2}$ flor.

Item, presteit a Matiet—7 flor.

Item, pour tondage de drap—55s.

Item, pour 11 ausnes de drap pour Andriu le tailleur que il doit paier—14 l. 11s. 5d.

Somme . . . 61 flor. et 6 gros.

Item, pour 17 pennes et 3 caperons pour le recheveur et ses gens—29 l.

APPENDIX XI

Hainault-Holland: chapel inventories

(a) Inventory of the count of Hainault-Holland's chapel at The Hague, probably June–July 1307 (AEM, Trésorerie, Cartulaire 20, fos. 174v–175r)

[For extracts see E. Gachet, 'Un cartulaire de Guillaume 1er de Hainaut, 1305–1312', *BCRH* 2e sér. 4 (1852), 115–17; Dehaisnes, *Documents et extraits divers conçernant l'histoire de l'art*, i. 180–1].

fo. 174v:

Hec sunt vestimenta capelle de Haga in Holl' . . .

Item, unam ymaginem argenteam feren' pacem

Item, 6 dalmatikas et 6 tunikas de pannis aureis

Item, 2 tuniculas pro pueris . . .

Item, 2 missalia in 4 voluminibus seu peciis

Item, 2 magna gradualia

Item, 1 magnum antiphonarium

Item, 1 breviarium in 2 peciis

Item, 1 psalterium

Item, 2 turribulas argenteos

Item, 1 crucem cum crucifixo partem argenteam et partem cupream

Item, 1 ymaginem eboream de beate virginie

fo. 175r:

Item, 3 pannos aureos, 2 de armis comitis Hollandie, et alterum de crucifixo

Item, 2 coffrellis pro reliquiis

Item, 2 tasselles argenteos pro cappis

(b) Inventory of the count of Hainault-Holland's chapel at Binche, [1] May 1308 (Ibid., fo. 176r)

Ce sont les cozes ki sont a le capelle a Binch le jour de May 1308

Primers un calice et une platine dargent et dor

Item, une petite louchette dargent

Item, 1 messel et 2 greelz noviaulz tous entirs

Item, 1 vies greel

Item, 2 anthiphonniers tous nues, lun destet et lautre diver

Item, 2 kasures et 3 aubes

Item, 3 amis et 2 stoles et 2 phanons

Item, 3 nappes dautel

Item, 1 drap devant lautel dor et de soie

Item, 1 drap de lainne sour lautel

Item, 1 drap devant lautel sour coi li prestres passe

Item, 4 corporalz

Item, 3 sarros et 1 clokette

Item, 2 pochons destain

Item, 1 escrin, et 1 staphil et 1 esamiel

Item, 2 candelers de keuvre

Item, 1 aisselette divoire entaillie pour porter pais

Item, 1 ascouse

Maps

MAP 1. North-West Europe, *c.*1300

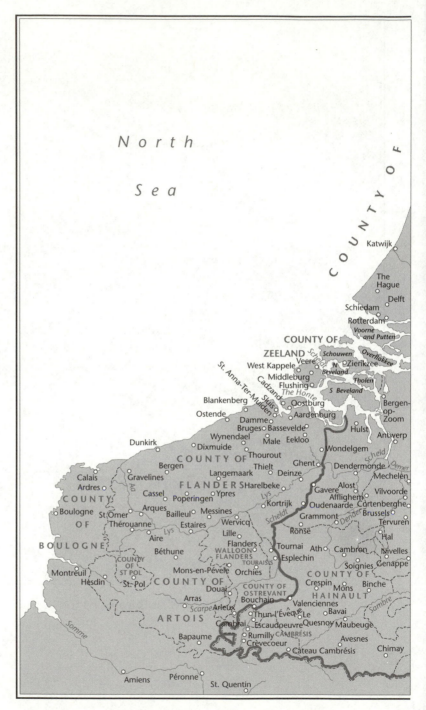

MAP 2. The Low Countries, *c.*1300

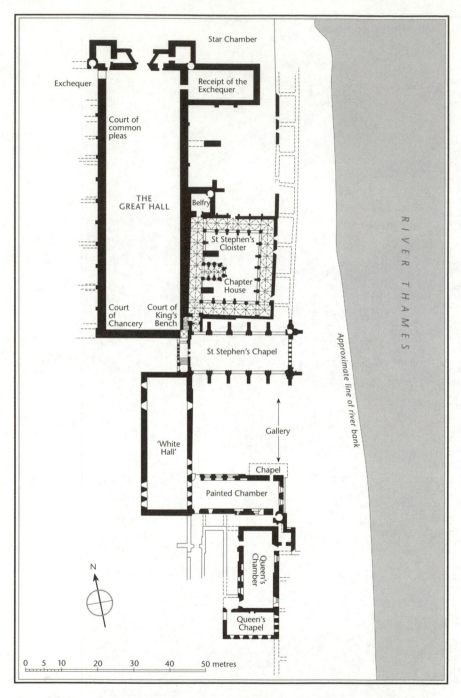

MAP 3. Schematic plan of main Westminster Palace buildings

BIBLIOGRAPHY

I. Manuscript Sources

Note: The following list has been confined to the main classes and categories of archive used in each repository, given the very large number of documents seen. The call numbers of individual archival documents are therefore, with the sole exception of Westminster Abbey muniments, not indicated.

Arras, Archives Départementales de Pas-de-Calais

Série A	Trésor des Chartes des comtes d'Artois

Brussels, Archives Générales du Royaume

CC	Chambre des Comptes, comptabilité
CC, R	Chambre des Comptes, Comptes en rouleaux

Brussels, Bibliothèque Royale

MSS	9217, 9427, 9627–8, 10368, 10607, IV.319, IV.463

Ghent, Rijksarchief

Chartes de Flandre	Inventaire Gaillard
	Inventaire Saint-Genois
	Inventaire Wyffels
	Inventaire Wyffels (chron. suppl.)

The Hague, Koninklijke Bibliotheek

MSS	71 H 39, 73 J 22, 74 G 31, 75 D 7, 76 J 18, 78 D 40, 131 G 37, 135 G 18

The Hague, Algemeen Rijksarchief

Archief Graven van Holland	Inventarissen 90, 218, 219, 221

Lille, Archives Départementales du Nord

Série B	Trésor des Chartes
	Chambre des Comptes

London, British Library

Additional MSS	7965, 7966A, 7966B

London, Public Record Office

C.47	Chancery Miscellanea
E.30	Diplomatic Documents
E.36	Exchequer Books
E.101	King's Remembrancer, Accounts Various
E.361	Wardrobe and Household Accounts
E.364	Foreign Accounts
S.C.1	Ancient Correspondence

London, Westminster Abbey Muniments

| Muniments | 6300, 9464, 12193, 12196, 12214 |
| | Drawing by John Carter, 1782 |

Mons, Archives de l'État

Trésorerie des comtes de Hainaut

Cartulaires 19, 20
Recueils 1–4, 19, 20, 69–71, 76, 83–6

Oxford, Bodleian Library

| MSS | Bodley 264 |
| | Douce 308 |

Paris, Archives Nationales

Serie J	Trésor des Chartes, Layettes
Serie JJ	Trésor des Chartes, Registres
Serie K	Monuments Historiques, Cartons
Serie KK	Monuments Historiques, Registres

II. Primary Sources

Adenet le Roi, *Oeuvres*, ed. A. Henry, 6 vols. (Bruges and Brussels, 1951–71).

Aragonische Hofordnungen im 13. und 14. Jahrhundert, ed. K. Schwarz (Berlin, 1914).

Beaumanoir, P. de, *Oeuvres poétiques*, ed. H. Suchier, 2 vols. (Paris, 1885).

Boendale, Jan van, *De Brabantsche Yeesten*, ed. J. F. Willems, 3 vols. (Brussels, 1839).

A Book of Prests of the King's Wardrobe for 1294–95, ed. E. B. Fryde (Oxford, 1962).

The Book of Chivalry of Geoffroi de Charny: Text, Context and Translation, ed. R. W. Kaeuper and E. Kennedy (Philadelphia, 1996).

Brisebarre, J., *Le Restor du paon*, ed. E. Donkin (London, 1980).

Calendar of Close Rolls.

Calendar of Patent Rolls.

Calendar of Entries in the Papal Registers relating to Great Britain and Ireland: Papal Letters, i. *1198–1304*, ed. W. H. Bliss (London, 1893).

'Un cartulaire de Guillaume Ier, comte de Hainaut, de Hollande et de Zeelande', ed. E. Gachet, *Bulletin de la Commission Royale d'Histoire*, 2nd sér., 4 (1852), 9–118.

Cartulaire de Louis de Male, comte de Flandre: Decreten van den grave Lodewyck van Vlaenderen, 1348 à 1358, ed. T. de Limburg-Stirum, 2 vols. (Bruges, 1898–1904).

'Cartulaires de Hainaut (1071–1310)', ed. F. A. T. de Reiffenberg, in *Monuments pour servir à l'histoire des provinces de Namur, de Hainaut et de Luxembourg*, i (Commission Royale d'Histoire, Brussels, 1844), 309–499.

'Cartulaires de Hainaut (suite) (1310–1347)', ed. L. Devillers, ibid. iii (Commission Royale d'Histoire, Brussels, 1874), 1–469.

'Cartulaires de Hainaut: Supplement (1176–1310)', ed. L. Devillers, ibid. 471–629.

'Cartulaires de Hainaut: Second supplement (1312–1327)', ed. L. Devillers, ibid. 633–772.

Cartulaire des comtes de Hainaut, de l'avènement de Guillaume II à la mort de Jacqueline de Bavière, ed. L. Devillers, 7 vols. (Commission Royale d'Histoire, Brussels, 1881–96).

Chandos Herald, *La Vie du Prince Noir*, ed. D. B. Tyson (Tübingen, 1975).

Chronicles of the Reigns of Edward I and Edward II, ed. W. Stubbs, 2 vols. (Rolls Series, London, 1883).

Chronique artésienne (1295–1304) et Chronique tournaisienne (1296–1314), ed. F. Funck-Brentano (Paris, 1899).

A Collection of Ordinances and Regulations for the Government of the Royal Household (Edward III–William and Mary), 2 vols. (London, 1790).

Collections of All the Wills Extant of Kings and Queens of England, ed. J. Nichols (London, 1780).

'Un compte de l'hôtel du roi sur tablettes de cire, 10 octobre–14 novembre [1350]', ed. E. Lalou, *BEC* 152 (1994), 91–127.

Le Compte général du receveur d'Artois pour 1303–1304: Edition précédée d'une introduction à l'étude des institutions financières de l'Artois aux xiiie et xive siècles, ed. B. Delmaire (Commission Royale d'Histoire, Brussels, 1977).

Comptes de l'argenterie des rois de France au xive siècle, ed. L. Douet-d'Arcq (Paris, 1851).

Nouveau recueil de comptes de l'argenterie des rois de France, ed. L. Douet-d'Arcq (Paris, 1874).

Comptes de l'hôtel des rois de France aux xive et xve siècles, ed. L. Douet-d'Arcq (Paris, 1865).

Comptes du Trésor (1296, 1316, 1384, 1477), ed. R. Fawtier (Paris, 1930).

Comptes royaux (1285–1314), ed. R. Fawtier and F. Maillard, 3 vols. (Paris, 1953–6).

Les Comptes sur tablettes de cire de la Chambre aux deniers de Philippe III le Hardi et de Philippe IV le Bel (1282–1309), ed. E. Lalou (Paris, 1994).

'Constitutio Domus Regis', in *Dialogus de Scaccario*, ed. C. Johnson (rev. edn., Oxford, 1983).

'Documents des xiii⁰ et xiv⁰ siècles relatifs à l'hôtel de Bourgogne (ancien hôtel d'Artois) tirés du Trésor des Chartes d'Artois', ed. J.-M. Richard, *Bulletin de la Société historique de Paris et Île-de-France*, 17 (1890), 137–59.

Documents et extraits divers concernant l'histoire de l'art dans la Flandre, l'Artois et le Hainaut avant le xv⁰ siècle, ed. C. Dehaisnes, 2 vols. (Lille, 1886).

Extraits de comptes relatifs au Hainaut antérieurs à l'avènement de Philippe le Bon, ed. A. Pinchart (Mons, 1884).

Fiscal Accounts of Catalonia under the Early Count-Kings (1151–1213), ed. T. N. Bisson, 2 vols. (London, 1984).

Flores Historiarum, ed. H. R. Luard, 3 vols. (Rolls Series, London, 1890).

Froissart, J., *Oeuvres*, ed. Kervyn de Lettenhove, 26 vols. (Brussels, 1867–77).

—— *Chroniques: Début au premier livre: Édition du manuscrit de Rome Reg. lat. 869*, ed. G. T. Diller (Geneva, 1972).

Histoire de S. Louys IX du nom, roy de France, ecrite par Jean, sire de Joinville, senechal de Champagne, ed. C. Du Fresne, sieur du Cange (Paris, 1668).

The Household of Edward IV: The Black Book and the Ordinance of 1478, ed. A. R. Myers (Manchester, 1959).

Household Accounts from Medieval England, ed. C. M. Woolgar, i (Oxford, 1992).

The Household Book of Queen Isabella of England for the Fifth Regnal Year of Edward II, ed. F. D. Blackley and G. Hermansen (Edmonton, 1971).

Les Journaux du Trésor de Charles IV le Bel, ed. J. Viard (Paris, 1917).

Les Journaux du Trésor de Philippe IV le Bel, ed. J. Viard (Paris, 1940).

La Marche, Olivier de, 'Estat de la maison du duc Charles de Bourgoigne, dit le Hardy', in *Mémoires d'Olivier de la Marche*, ed. H. Beaune and J. d'Arbaumont, iv (Paris, 1888).

Le Bel, Jean, *Chronique*, ed. J. Viard and E. Deprez, 2 vols. (Paris, 1904–5).

Leyden, Philip of, *De Cura Reipublicae et Sorte Principantis*, ed. R. Fruin and P. C. Molhuysen (The Hague, 1915).

Liber Contrarotulatoris Garderobiae, 1299–1300, ed. J. Topham *et al.* (London, 1787).

Liber Regie Capelle: A Manuscript in the Bibliotheca Publica, Evora, ed. W. Ullmann (London, 1961).

Liederen en gedichten uit het Gruuthuse-handschrift, ed. K. Heeroma and C. W. H. Lindenburg (Leiden, 1966).

Le Livre de Chasse de Gaston Fébus, ed. G. Tilander [Cynegetica 18] (Karlehouven, 1971).

Map, Walter, *De Nugis Curialium*, ed. M. R. James (Oxford, 1914).

Mémoires pour servir à l'histoire du Dauphiné, ed. M. Valbonnais (Paris, 1711).

Het memoriaal van Jehan Makiel, klerk en ontvanger van Gwijde van Dampierre (1270–1275), ed. J. Buntinx (Commission Royale d'Histoire, Brussels, 1944).

The Metrical Chronicle of Robert of Gloucester, ed. W. A. Wright, 2 vols. (Rolls Series, London, 1887).

Mons, Gislebert de, *Chronicon Hanoniense*, ed. L. Vanderkindere (Commission Royale d'Histoire, Brussels, 1904).

Oorkondenboek van Holland en Zeeland tot 1299, iv *(1278–1291)*, ed. J. G. Kruisheer (Assen, 1997).

Oorkondenboek van Noord-Brabant tot 1312, ed. H. P. H. Camps, i (The Hague, 1979).

Ordine et officij de casa de lo Illustrissimo Signor Duca de Urbino, ed. S. Eiche (Urbino, 1999).

Ordonnances des rois de France de la troisième race, ed. J. de Laurière, i (Paris, 1723).

Österreichische Reimkronik, ed. J. Seemüller, 2 vols. (Vienna, 1890–3).

Panégyriques des comtes de Hainaut et de Hollande Guillaume I et Guillaume II, ed. C. Potvin (Mons, 1863).

Le Parfait du Paon, ed. R. J. Carey (Chapel Hill, NC, 1972).

Paris, Matthew, *Chronica Majora*, ed. H. R. Luard, 7 vols. (Rolls Series, London, 1872–84).

Preis, Jean des, dit d'Outremeuse, *Le Myreur des Histors*, ed. S. Bormans, 6 vols. (Brussels, 1880–7).

Records of the Wardrobe and Household, 1285–1286, ed. B. F. and C. R. Byerly (London, 1977).

Records of the Wardrobe and Household, 1286–1289, ed. B. F. and C. R. Byerly (London, 1986).

'Die Reiserechnungen des Bischofs Wolfger von Passau', in *Beiträge zur Geschichte der deutschen Sprache und Litteratur*, 17 (1893), 441–549.

De rekeningen der grafelijkheid van Holland onder het Henegouwsche huis, ed. H. G. Hamaker, 3 vols. (Werken van het Historisch Genootschap, gevestigd te Utrecht, n.s. xxi, xxiv, xxvi, Utrecht, 1875–8).

De rekeningen der grafelijkheid van Zeeland onder het Henegouwsche huis, ed. H. G. Hamaker, 2 vols. (Werken van het Historisch Genootschap, gevestigd te Utrecht, n.s. xxix, xxx, Utrecht, 1879–80).

De rekeningen der graven en gravinnen uit het Henegouwsche huis, ed. J. Smit, 3 vols. (Werken van het Historisch Genootschap, gevestigd te Utrecht, 3rd ser. xlvi, liv, lxix, Amsterdam and Utrecht, 1924–39).

Roll of Divers Accounts for the Early Years of the Reign of Henry III, ed. F. A. Cazel (Pipe Roll Society, n.s. xliv, 1982), 93–102.

The Romance of Alexander (MS Bodley 264), ed. M. R. James (Oxford, 1933).

Rotuli de Liberate ac de Misis et Praestitis Regnante Johanne, ed. T. D. Hardy (London, 1844).

Rymer, T., *Foedera, Conventiones, Litterae etc.*, 20 vols. (London, 1727–35).

—— ed. A. G. Clarke and F. Holbrooke, i–iii (Record Commission, London, 1816–30).

Sanderus, A., *Flandria Illustrata* (The Hague, 1641).

Le Somme le Roy, attributed to the Parisian miniaturist Honoré, ed E. G. Millar (Roxburghe Club, Oxford, 1953).

Stowe, J., *A Survey of London*, ed. C. L. Kingsford, 2 vols. (Oxford, 1908).

Velthem, Lodewijk van, *Voorzetting van de Spiegel Historiael (1248–1316)*, ed. H. Vanderlinden, W. de Vreese, and P. de Keyser (Commission Royale d'Histoire, Brussels, 1906–38).

'Les Voeux de l'Épervier', ed. G. Wolfram and F. Bonnardot, *Jahrbuch der Gesellschaft für lothringische Geschichte und Altertumskunde*, 6 (1894), 177–280.

'Les Voeux du paon', in *The Buik of Alexander*, ed. R. L. G. Ritchie, 3 vols. (Scottish Text Society, 1925).

'The Vows of the Heron', in *Political Poems and Songs relating to English History*, ed. T. Wright, 2 vols. (Rolls Series, London, 1859–61).

Walter of Henley and other Treatises on Estate Management and Accounting, ed. D. Oschinsky (Oxford, 1971).

III. Secondary Sources

Adamson, J. (ed.), *The Princely Courts of Europe: Ritual, Politics and Culture under the Ancien Régime, 1500–1750* (London, 1999).

Alexander, J. J. G., 'Painting and manuscript illumination for royal patrons in the later Middle Ages', in Scattergood, V. J., and Sherborne, J. W. (eds.), *English Court Culture in the Later Middle Ages* (London, 1983), 141–62.

—— and Binski, P. (eds.), *Age of Chivalry: Art in Plantagenet England, 1200–1400* (exhib. catal., London, 1987).

Alquier, G., 'Les grands charges du Hainaut', *Revue du Nord*, 21 (1935), 5–31.

Appelt, H. (ed.), *Adelige Sachkultur des Spätmittelalters. Internationaler Kongress, Krems an der Donau, 22. bis 25. September 1980* (Vienna, 1982).

—— (ed.), *Terminologie and Typologie mittelalterlicher Sachguter: Das Beispiel der Kleidung* (Vienna, 1988).

Armstrong, C. A. J., 'The language question in the Low Countries: the use of French and Dutch by the Dukes of Burgundy and their administration' in Hale, J., Highfield, R., and Smalley, B. (eds.), *Europe in the Late Middle Ages* (London, 1965), 386–409.

—— 'The Golden Age of Burgundy: dukes that outdid kings', in Dickens, A. G. (ed.), *The Courts of Europe* (London, 1977), 54–75.

Arnade, P., *Realms of Ritual: Burgundian Ceremony and Civic Life in Late Medieval Ghent* (New York, 1996).

Arnould, M.-A., 'L'industrie drapière dans le Comté de Hainaut au moyen âge', in Duvosquel, J. M., and Dierkens, A. (eds.), *Villes et campagnes au moyen age* (Liège, 1991), 51–70.

Asch, R. G., and Birke, A. M. (eds.), *Princes, Patronage and the Nobility: The Court at the Beginning of the Modern Age, c.1450–1650* (London and Oxford, 1991).

Avril, F., *Manuscript Painting at the Court of France: The Fourteenth Century* (London, 1978).

Bak, J. M. (ed.), *Coronations: Medieval and Early Modern Monarchic Ritual* (Berkeley, 1990).

Baldwin, J. F., 'The household administration of Henry Lacy and Thomas of Lancaster', *EHR* 47 (1927), 180–200.

Baral I Altet, X. (ed.), *Artistes, artisans et production artistique au moyen âge*, 2 vols. (Paris, 1986).

Barber, R., and Barker, J., *Tournaments* (Woodbridge, 1989).

Barker, J., *The Tournament in England, 1100–1400* (Woodbridge, 1986).

Barnes, P. M. (ed.), *List of Documents Relating to the Household and Wardrobe, John to Edward I* (Public Record Office Handbooks, vii, London, 1964).

Baron, F. (ed.), *Les Fastes du gothique: le siècle de Charles V* (exhib. catal., Paris, 1981).

Bartlett, R., *The Making of Europe: Conquest, Colonization and Cultural Change, 950–1350* (Harmondsworth, 1994).

Bautier, R.-H., 'La place de la draperie brabançonne et plus particulièrement bruxelloise dans l'industrie textile du moyen âge', *Annales de la Société Royale d'Archéologie de Bruxelles*, 51 (1966), 31–63.

—— 'Diplomatique et histoire politique: ce que la critique diplomatique nous apprend sur la personnalité de Philippe le Bel', *RH* 259 (1978), 3–27.

—— Sornay, J., and Muret, F. (eds.), *Les Sources de l'histoire économique et sociale du moyen âge: les états de la maison de Bourgogne*, i. *Archives des principautés territoriales*, 2. *Les principautés du Nord* (Paris, 1984).

Beaune, Colette, 'Costume et pouvoir en France à la fin du moyen âge: les devises royales vers 1400', *Revue des sciences humaines*, 55 (1981), 125–46.

Bedos-Rezak, B., 'The social implications of the art of chivalry: the sigillographic evidence (France, 1050–1250)', in Haymes, E. R. (ed.), *The Medieval Court in Europe* (Munich, 1986), 142–75.

Bennert, U., 'Art et propagande sous Philippe le Bel: le cycle des rois de France dans la Grand' Salle de la Cité', *Revue de l'art*, 97 (1992), 46–59.

Bent, M., and Wathey, A. (eds.), *Fauvel Studies: Allegory, Chronicle, Music and Image in Paris* (Oxford, 1998).

Berger, R., *Litterature et société arrageoise au xiiie siècle: les chansons et dits artésiens* (Arras, 1981).

Berings, G., *Tervuren in de middeleeuwen: Aspecten van de Brabantse geschiedenis* (Tervuren, 1984).

Bialostocki, J., *The Art of the Renaissance in Eastern Europe* (Ithaca, NY, and Oxford, 1976).

Bigwood, G., 'Un relevé de recettes tenu par le personnel de Thomas Fini, receveur général de Flandre', in *Mélanges d'histoire offerts à Henri Pirenne*, i (Brussels, 1926), 31–42.

Billot, C., 'Les Saintes Chapelles (xiiie–xvie siècles): approche comparée de fondations dynastiques', *Revue d'histoire de l'église de France*, 73 (1987), 64–86.

Binski, P., *The Painted Chamber at Westminster* (Society of Antiquaries Occasional Paper, n.s. 9, London, 1986).

Binski, P., 'The cosmati at Westminster and the English court style', *Art Bulletin*, 72 (1990), 5–34.
—— *Westminster Abbey and the Plantagenets: Kingship and the Representation of Power, 1200–1400* (New Haven and London, 1995).
—— and Blair, J., 'The tomb of Edward I and early London brass production', *Bulletin of the International Society for the Study of Church Monuments*, 8 (1983), 161–4.
Blaess, M., 'L'abbaye de Bordesley et les livres de Guy de Beauchamp', *Romania*, 78 (1957), 511–18.
Blanc, O., 'Historiographie du vêtement: un bilan', in *Le Vêtement: histoire, archéologie et symbolique vestimentaires au moyen âge*, Cahiers du Léopard d'Or, i (Paris, 1989), 7–33.
Blockmans, W., Prevenier, W., and Janse, A. (eds.) *Showing Status: Representations of Social Positions in the Late Middle Ages* (Turnhout, 1999).
—— Janse, A., Kruse, H., and Stein, R., 'From territorial courts to one residence: the Low Countries in the late Middle Ages', in Aymard, M., and Romani, M. (eds.), *La Cour comme institution économique* (Paris, 1999), 17–28.
—— *The Promised Lands: The Low Countries under Burgundian Rule, 1369–1530* (Philadelphia, 1999).
Boase, T. S. R., 'Fontevrault and the Plantagenets', *Journal of the British Archaeological Association*, 3rd ser. 34 (1971), 1–10.
Bogucka, M., *The Lost World of the 'Sarmatians'* (Warsaw, 1996).
Bologna, F., *I pittori alla corte angioina di Napoli, 1266–1414* (Rome, 1969).
Boone, M., 'Destroying and reconstructing the city: the inculcation and arrogation of princely power in the Burgundian-Habsburg Netherlands (14th to 16th centuries)', in Gosman, M., Vanderjagt, A., and Veenstra, J. (eds.), *The Propagation of Power in the Medieval West* (Groningen, 1997), 1–33.
—— and De Hemptinne, T., 'Espace urbain et ambitions princières: les présences matérielles de l'autorité princière dans le Gand médiéval (12ᵉ siècle–1540)', in Paravicini, W. (ed.), *Zeremoniell und Raum* (Sigmaringen, 1997), 279–304.
Borenius, T., 'The cycle of images in the palaces and castles of Henry III', *JWCI* 6 (1943), 40–50.
Bougard, P., 'La fortune et les comptes de Thierry d'Hérisson (+1328)', *BEC* 123 (1965), 126–78.
Branner, R., *St Louis and the Court Style in Gothic Architecture* (London, 1965).
—— 'The Montjoies of St Louis', in Fraser, D., Hibbard, H., and Lewine, M. (eds.), *Essays in the History of Architecture presented to Rudolf Wittkower* (London, 1967), 13–26.
Brieger, P., *English Art, 1216–1307* (Oxford, 1968).
—— Verdier, P., and Montpetit, M. F. (eds.), *Art and the Courts: France and England from 1259 to 1328*, 2 vols. (Ottawa, 1972).
Brokken, H. M., 'Het Hof in Den Haage: grafelijke residentie en centrum van bestuur', in Van Pelt, R. J., and Tiethoff-Spliethoff, M. E., *Het Binnenhof: Van grafelijke residentie tot regeringscentrum* (Dieren, 1984), 13–20.

Brown, A., 'Bruges and the Burgundian "Theatre-State": Charles the Bold and Our Lady of the Snow', *History*, 84 (1999), 573–89.

Brown, E. A. R., 'Death and the human body in the Middle Ages: the legislation of Boniface VIII on the division of the corpse', *Viator*, 12 (1981), 221–70.

—— *The Monarchy of Capetian France and Royal Ceremonial* (Aldershot, 1991).

Brush, K., 'The "Recepta jocalium" in the Wardrobe Book of William de Norwell, 12 July 1338 to 27 May 1340', *Journal of Medieval History*, 10 (1984), 249–70.

Bruwier, M., 'Un conflit d'administration au xive siècle: les droits du veneur de Hainaut', *MA* 69 (1963), 541–53.

Bullock-Davies, C., *Menestrellorum Multitudo: Minstrels at a Royal Feast* (Cardiff, 1978).

—— *A Register of Royal and Baronial Domestic Minstrels, 1272–1327* (Woodbridge, 1986).

Bumke, J., *Mazene in Mittelalter: Die Gönner und Auftraggeber der höfischen Literatur in Deutschland, 1150–1300* (Munich, 1979).

—— *Courtly Culture: Literature and Society in the High Middle Ages*, tr. T. Dunlop (Berkeley, Los Angeles, and Oxford, 1991).

Cafmeyer, M., 'Het kasteel van Male', *Annales de la Société d'Émulation de Bruges*, 83 (1940–6), 112–32.

Caillebaut, D., 'Le château des Comtes à Gand', *Château Gaillard: Études de Castellogie médiévale*, xi (1983), 45–54.

Calkoen, C. G., 'Het binnenhof van 1247–1747', *Jaarboek Die Haghe*, (1902), 35–181.

Campbell, L., *Renaissance Portraits* (New Haven and London, 1990).

Chaplais, P., 'Some private letters of Edward I', *EHR* 77 (1962), 79–86.

—— *Piers Gaveston: Edward II's Adoptive Brother* (Oxford, 1994).

Châtelet, A., *Early Dutch Painting* (New York, 1981).

Cherry, J., 'Heraldry as decoration in the thirteenth century', in Ormrod, W. M. (ed.), *Harlaxton Medieval Studies*, i. *England in the Thirteenth Century* (Stamford, 1991), 123–34.

—— and Stratford, N., *Westminster Kings and the Medieval Palace of Westminster* (British Museum Occasional Paper 115, London, 1995).

Chevalier, A., 'Les Fêtes à la cour de Brabant sous les ducs de la branche cadette de Bourgogne-Valois (1406–1430)' (unpub. thesis, Université Libre de Bruxelles, 1991).

Chorley, P., 'The cloth exports of Flanders and Northern France during the XIIIth century: a luxury trade?', *EcHR* 2nd ser. 40 (1987), 349–79.

Chroscicki, J., *Pompa funebris* (Warsaw, 1974).

Cinzelbacher, P., 'Volkskultur und Hochkultur im Spätmittelalter', in Muck, P. C. and H. D. (eds.), *Volkskultur des europäischen Spätmittelalters* (Stuttgart, 1987), 1–14.

Clanchy, M. T., *From Memory to Written Record: England 1066–1307* (London, 1979).

Clauzel, D., *Finances et politique à Lille pendant la période bourguignonne* (Dunkirk, 1982).

Cole, A., *Art of the Italian Renaissance Courts: Virtue and Magnificence* (London, 1995).

Collin, H., 'Le train de vie d'Edouard Ier, comte de Bar (1302–36)', *BHPCTHS* (1969), 793–817.

Colvin, H. M. *et al.* (eds.), *A History of the King's Works*, 6 vols. (London, 1963–82).

—— 'The "court style" in medieval English architecture: a review', in Scattergood, V. J., and Sherborne, J. W. (eds.), *English Court Culture in the Later Middle Ages* (London, 1983), 129–39.

—— *Architecture and the After-Life* (New Haven and London, 1991).

Crossley, F. H., *English Church Monuments, 1150–1550* (London, 1921).

Davidts, J. E., *Tervuren in de Brabantse geschiedenis vanaf 1200–1450* (Tervuren, 1975).

Davies, R. R., 'Baronial accounts, incomes and arrears in the later Middle Ages', *EcHR* 2nd ser. 21 (1968), 211–29.

De Boer, D. E. H., Cordfunke, E. H. P., and Sarfatij, H., *Wi Florens: De Hollandse graaf Floris V in de samenleving van de dertiende eeuw* (Utrecht, 1996).

Dehaisnes, C., *Histoire de l'art dans la Flandre, l'Artois et le Hainaut avant le xve siècle* (Lille, 1886).

Delcambre, E., *Les Relations entre la France et le Hainaut (1280–97)*, 2 vols. (Mons, 1927).

De Loisne, A., comte, 'Itinéraire de Robert II, comte d'Artois', *BPHCTHS* (1913), 362–83.

—— 'Une cour féodale vers la fin du xiiie siècle: "L'hôtel" de Robert II, comte d'Artois', *BPHCTHS* (1918), 84–143.

Delort, R., *Le Commerce des fourrures en Occident à la fin du moyen âge (vers 1300–vers 1450)*, 2 vols. (Rome, 1978).

—— 'Note sur les livrées en milieu de cour au xive siècle' in Schnerb, B. (ed.), *Commerce, Finances et Société, xie–xvie siècles: Mélanges H. Dubois* (Paris, 1993), 361–8.

Denholm-Young, N., 'The Tournament in the Thirteenth Century', in Hunt, R. W., Pantin, W. A., and Southern, R. W. (eds.), *Studies presented to F. M. Powicke* (Oxford, 1948), 204–68.

Derville, A., 'Les draperies flamandes et artésiennes vers 1250–1350: quelques considérations critiques et problematiques', *Revue du Nord*, 44 (1972), 353–70.

Devillers, L., 'Notice sur un cartulaire de Guillaume Ier, comte de Hainaut, de Hollande, de Zélande et seigneur de Frise', *BCRH* 3e sér. 7 (1865), 351–82.

—— 'Sur le mort de Guillaume le Bon, comte de Hainaut, de Hollande, de Zélande, et seigneur de Frise', *BCRH* 4e sér. 5 (1878), 409–23.

—— 'Sur les expéditions des comtes de Hainaut et de Hollande en Prusse', *BCRH* 4e sér. 5 (1878), 127–44.

Devliegher, P., *Les Maisons à Bruges* (Liège, 1975).

Dickens, A. G. (ed.), *The Courts of Europe: Politics, Patronage and Royalty, 1400–1800* (London, 1977).

Diller, G. T., 'Robert d'Artois et l'historicité des *Chroniques* de Froissart', *MA* 86 (1980), 217–31.

Dornon, A. de Behault de, 'Un tournoi à Mons au xive siècle', *Annales du Cercle archéologique de Mons*, 19 (1886), 385–411.

—— 'Le tournoi de Mons de 1310', *Annales du Cercle archéologique de Mons*, 38 (1909), 103–256.

Duindam, J., *Myths of Power: Norbert Elias and the Early Modern European Court* (Amsterdam, 1995).

Duplès Agier, H., 'Une ordonnance somptuaire inédite de Philippe le Hardi', *BEC* 15 (1854), 176–81.

Dvorakova, V. *et al.*, *Gothic Mural Painting in Bohemia and Moravia, 1300–1378* (London, 1964).

Eales, R., *Chess: A History of a Game* (London, 1985).

—— 'The game of chess: an aspect of medieval knightly culture', in Harper-Bill, C., and Harvey, R. (eds.), *The Ideals and Practice of Medieval Knighthood* (Woodbridge, 1986).

Eames, P., *Furniture in England, France and the Netherlands from the Twelfth to the Fifteenth Century* (London, 1977).

Elias, N., *The Court Society* (Oxford, 1983).

Erlande-Brandenbourg, A., *Le Roi est mort: études sur les funérailles, les sépultures et les tombeaux des rois de France jusqu'à la fin du xiiie siècle* (Geneva, 1975).

Espinas, G., 'Jehan Boine Broke, bourgeois et drapier douaisien [?–1310 environ]', *Vierteljahrschrift für Sozial- und Wirtschaftsgeschichte*, 2 (1904), 34–121, 219–53, 282–412.

Eyton, R. W., *Court, Household and Itinerary of King Henry III* (New York, 1974).

Fajt, J. (ed.), *Magister Theodoricus: Court Painter to Emperor Charles IV* (Prague, 1998).

Favier, J., *Un conseiller de Philippe le Bel: Enguerran de Marigny* (Paris, 1963).

Finot, J., 'L'hôtel des comtes et comtesses de Hainaut', *BHPCTHS* (1891), 188–209.

—— 'Introduction', in *Inventaire sommaire des archives départementales antérieurs à 1790. Nord: archives civiles—série B*, vii (Lille, 1892), pp. i–cxii.

Fleckenstein, J. (ed.), *Das ritterliche Turnier im Mittelalter* (Göttingen, 1985).

—— (ed.), *Curialitas: Studien zu Grundfragen der höfisch-ritterlichen Kultur* (Göttingen, 1990).

Fris, V., 'Thomas Fin, receveur de Flandre', *BCRH* 5e ser. 10 (1900), 8–20.

Fryde, E. B., 'Financial resources of Edward I in the Netherlands, 1294–98: main problems and some comparisons with Edward III in 1337–40', *RBPH* 40 (1962), 1168–87.

—— 'Financial resources of Edward III in the Netherlands, 1337–40', *RBPH* 45 (1967), 1142–93.

Fryde, N., 'Antonio Pessagno of Genoa, king's merchant of Edward II of England', in *Studi in memoria de Federigo Melis*, ii (Naples, 1978), 159–78.

Funck-Brentano, F., *Les Origines de la Guerre de Cent Ans: Philippe le Bel en Flandre* (Paris, 1897).

Galesloot, L., *Recherches sur la maison de chasse des ducs de Brabant et l'ancienne cour de Bruxelles* (Brussels and Leipzig, 1854).

Gardner, J., 'Saint Louis of Toulouse, Robert of Anjou and Simone Martini', *Zeitschrift für Kunstgeschichte*, 39 (1976), 10–25.

—— 'The French connection: thoughts about French patrons and Italian art, *c.*1250–1300', in Rosenberg, C. M. (ed.), *Art and Politics in later medieval and early Renaissance Italy, 1250–1500* (Notre-Dame and London, 1990), 81–102.

—— 'The Cosmati at Westminster: some Anglo-Italian reflexions' in Garms, J., and Romanini, A. M. (eds.), *Skulptur und Grabmal des Spätmittelalters in Rom und Italien* (Vienna, Österreichische Akademie der Wissenschaften, 1990), 201–15.

Gaspar, C., and Lyna, F., *Les principaux MSS à peintures de la Bibliothèque Royale de Belgique*, i (Brussels, 1937).

Gee, L. L., '"Ciborium" tombs in England, 1290–1330', *Journal of the British Archaeological Association*, 3rd ser. 132 (1979), 29–41.

Genet, J.-P., 'La monarchie anglaise: une image brouillée', in Blanchard, J. (ed.), *Représentation, pouvoir et royauté à la fin du moyen âge* (Paris, 1995), 93–107.

Gerritsen, W. P., 'Wat voor boeken zou Floris V gelezen hebben?', in *Floris V: Leven, wonen en werken in Holland aan het einde van de dertiende eeuw* (The Hague, 1979), 71–86.

Gillingham, J., *The Angevin Empire* (London, 1984).

—— 'Crisis or continuity? The structure of royal authority in England, 1369–1422', in *Das spätmittelalterliche Königtum in Europäischen Vergleich* (Sigmaringen, 1987), 64–70.

Given-Wilson, C., 'The merger of Edward III's and queen Philippa's Households, 1360–1369', *BIHR* 51 (1978), 183–7.

—— *The Royal Household and the King's Affinity: Service, Politics and Finance in England, 1360–1413* (New Haven and London, 1986).

Godding, P., 'Le testament princier dans les Pays-Bas méridionaux (12ᵉ–15ᵉ siècles): acte privé et instrument politique', *TRG*, 64 (1993), 217–35.

Gomez-Moreno, M., *El panteón real de las Huelgas de Burgos* (Madrid, 1946).

Gordon, D., *Making and Meaning: The Wilton Diptych* (London, 1993).

—— Monnas, L., and Elam, C., *The Regal Image of Richard II and the Wilton Diptych* (London, 1997).

Green, R. F., *Poets and Princepleasers: Literature and the English Court in the Late Middle Ages* (Toronto, Buffalo, and London, 1980).

Griffiths, R. A., 'The king's court during the Wars of the Roses: continuities in an age of discontinuities', in Asch, R. G., and Birke, A. M. (eds.), *Princes, Patronage and the Nobility: The Court at the Beginning of the Modern Age, c.1450–1650* (London and Oxford, 1991).

Guenée, B., *States and Rulers in Later Medieval Europe*, tr. J. Vale (Oxford, 1985).

Giuseppi, M. S., 'The wardrobe and household of Bogo de Clare, 1284–6', *Archaeologia*, 70 (1920), 1–56.

Hage, A., *Sonder Favele, Sonder Lieghen: Onderzoek naar vorm en functie van de Middelnederlandse rijmkroniek als historiografisch genre* (Utrecht, 1990).

Hallam, E. M., 'Royal burial and the cult of kingship in France and England, 1066–1330', *Journal of Medieval History*, 8 (1982), 359–80.

Hanawalt, B. A., and Reyerson, K. L. (eds.), *City and Spectacle in Medieval Europe* (Minneapolis and London, 1994).

Harvey, R., *Moriz von Craûn and the Chivalric World* (Oxford, 1961).

Heers, J., *Fêtes, jeux et joûtes dans les sociétés d'Occident à la fin du moyen âge* (Montreal and Paris, 1971).

—— 'La cour de Mahaut d'Artois en 1327–1328: solidarités humaines, livrées et mesnies', *Anales de historia antigua y medieval*, 2 (1977–9), 7–43.

Henderson, G., *Gothic* (Harmondsworth, 1967).

Henry, A., *L'Oeuvre lyrique d'Henri III, duc de Brabant* (Bruges, 1948).

Hobsbawn, E., and Ranger, T. (eds.), *The Invention of Tradition* (Cambridge, 1983).

Horrox, R., 'Caterpillars of the commonwealth? Courtiers in late medieval England', in Archer, R. E., and Walker, S. (eds.), *Rulers and Ruled in Late Medieval England: Essays presented to Gerald Harriss* (London, 1995), 1–15.

Hugenholtz, F. W. N., 'Melis Stoke en Jacob van Maerlant', in De Boer, D., and Marsilje, J. W., *De Nederlanden in de late middeleeuwen* (Utrecht, 1987), 18–26.

Huizinga, J., *The Waning of the Middle Ages*, tr. F. Hopman (Harmondsworth, 1965).

—— *Homo Ludens* (London, 1970).

—— *The Autumn of the Middle Ages*, ed. and tr. R. J. Payton, and U. Mammitzsch (Chicago, 1996).

—— *Herfsttij der Middeleeuwen*, ed. A. van der Lem (Amsterdam, 1997).

Jaeger, C. S., *The Origins of Courtliness: Civilizing Trends and the Formation of Courtly Ideals, 939–1210* (Philadelphia, 1985).

—— 'Cathedral schools and humanist learning, 950–1150', *Deutsche Vierteljahrsschrift für Literaturwissenschaft und Geistesgeschichte*, 61 (1987), 569–616.

Janse, A., 'De hoofse liedcultuur aan het Hollands-Beierse hof omstreeks 1400', in Willaert, F. (ed.), *Een zoet akkoord: Middeleeuwse lyriek in de Lage Landen* (Amsterdam, 1992), 109–15.

—— 'Het muziekleven aan het hof van Albrecht van Beieren (1358–1404)', *Tijdschrift van de vereniging voor Nederlande muziekgeschiedenis*, 26 (1986), 136–57.

—— 'Jean d'Avesnes, comte de Hollande (1299–1304): les villes, la noblesse, le pouvoir', *Annales du Cercle Archéologique de Mons*, 77 (1996), 207–24.

Johnson, C. H., 'The system of account in the wardrobe of Edward I', *TRHS* 4th ser. 6 (1923), 50–72.

—— 'The system of account in the wardrobe of Edward II', *TRHS* 4th ser. 12 (1929), 75–104.

Johnstone, H., 'The wardrobe and household of Henry, son of Edward I', *Bulletin of the John Rylands Library*, 7 (1923), 384–420.

Johnstone, H., 'The wardrobe and household accounts of the sons of Edward I', *BIHR* 2 (1924), 36–45.

—— *Edward of Carnarvon, 1284–1307* (Manchester, 1946).

Jones, M., and Vale, M. (eds.), *England and her Neighbours: Essays in Honour of Pierre Chaplais* (London, 1989).

Jones, W. R., 'The Court of the Verge: the jurisdiction of the steward and marshal of the household in later medieval England', *Journal of British Studies*, 10 (1970–1), 1–29.

Kaeuper, R. W., *Bankers to the Crown: The Riccardi of Lucca and Edward I* (Princeton, 1973).

—— *War, Justice and Public Order: England and France in the Later Middle Ages* (Oxford, 1988).

Kaiser-Guyot, M.-T., 'Manger et boire au moyen âge: un thème à la recherche de son histoire', *Francia: Forschungen zur westeuropäischen Geschichte*, 15 (1987), 793–800.

Kantorowicz, E., *The King's Two Bodies: A Study in Medieval Political Theology* (Princeton, 1966).

Kaufmann, T. da Costa, *Court, Cloister and City: The Art and Culture of Central Europe, 1450–1800* (London, 1995).

Kavka, F., *Am Hofe Karls IV* (Stuttgart, 1990).

Keen, M. H., *Chivalry* (New Haven and London, 1982).

Kerling, N. J. M., *Commercial Relations of Holland and Zeeland with England from the Late Thirteenth Century to the Close of the Middle Ages* (Leiden, 1954).

Kerscher, G., 'Die Perspektive des Potentaten: Differenzierung von "Privat-trakt" bzw. Appartement und Zeremonialraümen im spätmittelalterlichen Palastbau', in Paravicini, W. (ed.), *Zeremoniell und Raum* (Sigmaringen, 1997), 155–86.

Kittell, E., *From Ad Hoc to Routine: A Case Study in Medieval Bureaucracy* (Philadelphia, 1991).

Kooper, E. (ed.), *Medieval Dutch Literature in its European Context* (Cambridge and New York, 1994).

Kort, J. C., *Het archief van de graven van Holland*, 3 vols. (The Hague, 1981).

Kossmann-Putto, J. A., and Kossmann, E. H., *The Low Countries: History of the Northern and Southern Netherlands* (Rekkem, 1997).

Kovacs, E., 'L'orfèvrerie parisienne et ses sources', *Revue de l'art*, 28 (1975), 25–33.

Kropp, M., 'A mirror view of daily life at the Ethiopian royal court in the Middle Ages', *North-East African Studies*, 2–3 (1988), 51–87.

Krul, W., 'In the mirror of Van Eyck: Johan Huizinga's *Autumn of the Middle Ages*', *Journal of Medieval and Early Modern Studies*, 27 (1997), 353–84.

Kruse, H., and Paravicini, W. (eds.), *Hofe und Hofordnungen, 1200–1600* (Sigmaringen, 1999).

Kuile, E. H. ter, 'De bouwgeschiedenis van het grafelijk paleis op het Binnenhof', *Holland*, 10 (1978), 313–28.

Kurz, O., 'A fishing party at the court of William VI, count of Holland, Zeeland and Hainault: notes on a drawing in the Louvre', *Oud-Holland*, 71 (1956), 117–31.

Lachaud, F., 'Textiles, Furs and Liveries: a Study of the Material Culture of the Court of Edward I (1272–1307)' (unpub. Oxford D.Phil. thesis, 1992).

—— 'An aristocratic wardrobe of the late thirteenth century: the confiscation of the goods of Osbert de Spaldington in 1298', *Historical Research*, 67 (1993), 91–100.

—— 'Liveries of robes in England, *c.*1200–*c.*1330', *EHR* 111 (1996), 279–98.

—— 'Order and disorder at court: the ordinances of the royal household in England in the twelfth and thirteenth centuries', in Kruse, H., and Paravicini, W. (eds.), *Höfe und Hofordnungen, 1200–1600* (Sigmaringen, 1999), 103–16.

Lacroix, A., 'Inventaire de l'armure de Guillaume II, comte de Hainaut, qui existait au château de Mons en 1358', *Annales du Cercle Archéologique de Mons*, 9 (1869), 145–50.

Lalou, E., 'Les tablettes de cire médiévales', *BEC* 147 (1989), 123–40.

—— *Les Comptes sur tablettes de cire de la Chambre aux deniers de Philippe III le Hardi et de Philippe IV le Bel (1282–1309)* (Paris, 1994).

—— 'Un compte de l'hôtel du roi sur tablettes de cire, 10 octobre–14 novembre 1350', *BEC* 152 (1994), 91–127.

—— 'Le fonctionnement de l'hôtel du roi du milieu du xiiie au milieu du xive siècle' in Chapelot, J., and Lalou, E. (eds.), *Vincennes: aux origines de l'état moderne* (Paris, 1996), 145–55.

—— 'Vincennes dans les itinéraires de Philippe le Bel et de ses trois fils (1285–1328)', ibid. 191–212.

Lancaster, R. K., 'Artists, suppliers and clerks: the human factors in the art patronage of King Henry III', *JWCI* 35 (1972), 81–107.

Larner, J., *Italy in the Age of Dante and Petrarch, 1216–1380* (London, 1980).

Leçoy de la Marche, A., *Les relations politiques de la France avec le royaume de Majorque*, 2 vols. (Paris, 1892).

Legge, M. D., *Anglo-Norman Literature and its Background* (Oxford, 1963).

Legner, A. (ed.), *Die Parler und der Schöne Stil, 1350–1400: Europäische Kunst unter den Luxemburgen*, 3 vols. (exhib. catal., Cologne, 1978).

Le Goff, J., 'The town as an agent of civilisation', in Cipolla, C. M. (ed.), *The Fontana Economic History of Europe: The Middle Ages* (London, 1973), 77–86.

—— *Saint Louis* (Paris, 1996).

Lehugeur, P., *De hospitio regis et secretiore Consilio, ineunte quarto decimo saeculo, praesertim regnante Philippo Longo* (Paris, 1897).

—— *Philippe V, le mécanisme du gouvernement* (Paris, 1931).

Lestocquoy, J., *Patriciens du moyen âge: les dynasties bourgeoises d'Arras du xie au xve siècle* (Arras, 1945).

—— *Aux origines de la bourgeoisie: les villes de Flandre et d'Italie sous le gouvernement des patriciens* (Paris, 1952).

Leupen, P., *Philip of Leyden: A Fourteenth-Century Jurist: A Study of his Life and Treatise 'De Cura Reipublicae et Sorte Principantis'* (Leiden, 1981).

Lightbown, R. W., 'Les origines de la peinture en émail sur or', *Revue de l'art*, 22 (1969), 46–53.

—— *Medieval European Jewellery, with a Catalogue of the Collection in the Victoria and Albert Museum* (London, 1992).

Limburg-Stirum, T., *La Cour des comtes de Flandres: leurs officiers héréditaires*, i. *Le Chambellan et les sires de Ghistelles* (Ghent, 1868).

Little, L. K., *Religious Poverty and the Profit Economy in Medieval Europe* (London, 1978).

Loomis, R. S., 'Edward I, Arthurian enthusiast', *Speculum*, 28 (1953), 114–27.

Lucas, H. S., *The Low Countries and the Hundred Years War, 1326–1347* (Ann Arbor, 1929, repr. Philadelphia, 1976).

Lyon, B., and Verhulst, A. E., *Medieval Finance: A Comparison of Financial Institutions in Northwestern Europe* (Bruges and Providence, RI, 1967).

Maddicott, J. R., *Thomas of Lancaster, 1307–1322* (Oxford, 1970).

Marks, R., and Payne, A. (eds.), *British Heraldry: From its Origins to c.1800* (London, British Museum, 1978).

Martindale, A., *Gothic Art* (London, 1967).

—— *The Rise of the Artist in the Middle Ages and the Early Renaissance* (New York, 1972).

—— *Simone Martini: Complete Edition* (Oxford, 1988).

—— *Heroes, Ancestors, Relatives and the Birth of the Portrait* (The Hague, 1988).

—— 'Patrons and minders: the intrusion of the secular into sacred spaces in the late Middle Ages', in D. Wood (ed.), *The Church and the Arts: Studies in Church History* (London, 1992), 171–86.

Matthew, G., *The Court of Richard II* (London, 1968).

Mayhew, N. J. (ed.), *Coinage in the Low Countries (880–1500): The Third Oxford Symposium on Coinage and Monetary History* (British Archaeological Reports, International Series 54, Oxford, 1979).

—— and Walker, D. R., 'Crockards and Pollards: imitation and the problem of fineness in a silver coinage', in Mayhew, N. J. (ed.), *Edwardian Monetary Affairs, 1279–1344* (British Archaeological Report 36, Oxford, 1977), 125–37.

Meyer, R. P., *Literature of the Low Countries: A Short History of Dutch Literature in the Netherlands and Belgium* (The Hague and Boston, 1978).

Michael, M. A., 'A manuscript wedding gift from Philippa of Hainault to Edward III', *Burlington Magazine*, 20 (1985), 582–9.

Millet, H., 'Les chanoines au service de l'état: bilan d'une étude comparative' in Genet, J.-P. (ed.), *L'État moderne: Genèse. Bilans et perspectives* (Paris, 1990), 137–46.

Monier, R., *Les Institutions financiers du comté de Flandre du xiᵉ siècle à 1384* (Paris and Lille, 1948).

Morgan, D. A. L., 'The king's affinity in the polity of Yorkist England', *TRHS* 5th ser. 23 (1973), 1–25.

—— 'The house of policy: the political role of the late Plantagenet household, 1422–1485', in D. Starkey (ed.), *The English Court: from the Wars of the Roses to the Civil War* (London and New York, 1987), 25–41.

Müller, J. D., *Gedechtnus: Literatur und Hofgesellschaft um Maximilian I* (Munich, 1982).

Müller, P. L., *Regesta Hannonensia: Lijst van oorkonden betreffende Holland en Zeeland, 1299–1345* (The Hague, 1882).

Munro, J. H., 'The medieval scarlet and the economics of sartorial Splendour' in Harte, N. B., and Ponting, K. G. (eds.), *Cloth and Clothing in Medieval Europe* (London, 1983), 13–70.

Murray, H. J. R., *A History of Chess* (Oxford, 1913).

—— 'The medieval game of tables', *Medium Aevum*, 10 (1941), 57–69.

Murray, J. M., 'The liturgy of the Count's entry to Bruges, from Galbert to Van Eyck', in Hanawalt, B. A., and Reyerson, K. L. (eds.), *City and Spectacle in Medieval Europe* (Minneapolis and London, 1994), 137–40.

Myers, A. R. (ed.), *The Household of Edward IV: The Black Book and the Ordinance of 1478* (Manchester, 1959).

Newton, S. M., *Fashion in the Age of the Black Prince: A Study of the years 1340–1365* (Woodbridge, 1980).

Nicholas, D. M., *The Metamorphosis of a Medieval City: Ghent in the Age of the Arteveldes, 1302–1390* (Leiden, 1987).

—— *The van Arteveldes of Ghent: The Varieties of Vendetta and the Hero in History* (Ithaca, NY, London, and Leiden, 1988).

—— *Medieval Flanders* (London, 1992).

—— 'In the pit of the Burgundian theater-state: urban traditions and princely ambitions in Ghent, 1360–1420', in Hanawalt, B. A., and Reyerson, K. L., *City and Spectacle in Medieval Europe* (Minneapolis and London, 1994), 271–95.

Niedermann, C., *Das Jagdwesen am Hofe Philipps des Guten von Burgund* (Brussels, 1995).

Nijsten, G., *Het hof van Gelre: Cultuur ten tijde van de hertogen uit het Gulikse en Egmondse huis (1371–1473)* (Kampen, 1992).

Noppen, J. G., 'The Westminster school and its influence', *Burlington Magazine*, 57 (1930), 72–81.

—— 'Building by King Henry III and Edward, son of Odo', *Antiquaries Journal*, 28 (1948), 138–48; 29 (1949), 13–25.

—— 'Westminster paintings and Master Peter', *Burlington Magazine*, 91 (1949), 305–9.

Orme, N., 'The education of the courtier', in Scattergood, V. J., and Sherborne, J. W. (eds.), *English Court Culture in the Later Middle Ages* (London, 1983), 63–85.

Ormrod, W. M., 'The personal religion of Edward III', *Speculum*, 64 (1989), 849–77.

—— *The Reign of Edward III: Crown and Political Society in England, 1327–1377* (New Haven and London, 1990).

Page, A., *Vêtir le prince: tissus et couleurs à la cour de Savoie, 1427–1447* (Lausanne, 1993).

Panofsky, E., *Tomb Sculpture* (New York, 1964).

Paravicini, W., 'Die residenzen der Herzöge von Burgund, 1363–1477', in Patze, H., and Paravicini, W. (eds.), *Fürstliche Residenzen im spätmittelalterlichen Europa* (Sigmaringen, 1991), 207–63.

—— 'The Court of the Dukes of Burgundy: A Model for Europe', in Asch, R. G., and Birke, A. M. (eds.), *Princes, Patronage and the Nobility: The Court at the Beginning of the Modern Age, c.1450–1650* (London and Oxford, 1991), 69–102.

—— *Die ritterlich-höfische Kultur des Mittelalters* (Munich, 1994).

—— (ed.), *Alltag bei Hofe: 3. Symposium der Residenzen-Kommission der Akademie der Wissenschaften in Göttingen* (Sigmaringen, 1995).

—— (ed.), *Zeremoniell und Raum* (Sigmaringen, 1997).

Parsons, J. C., *The Court and Household of Eleanor of Castile in 1290* (Toronto, 1977).

—— 'Piety, power and the reputation of two thirteenth-century English queens', in Vann, T. (ed.), *Queens, Regents and Potentates: Women of Power*, i (Cambridge, 1993), 107–23.

—— (ed.), *Medieval Queenship* (New York, 1993).

Pastoureau, M., *L'Étoffe du diable: une histoire des rayures et des tissus rayés* (Paris, 1991).

Pinchart, A., 'La cour de Jeanne et de Wenceslas et les arts en Brabant pendant la seconde moitié du xive siècle', *Revue trimestrielle*, 6 (1855), 5–31; 13 (1857), 25–67.

Piponnier, F., *Costume et vie sociale: la cour d'Anjou, xive–xve siècle* (Paris and The Hague, 1970).

Pirenne, H., *Early Democracies in the Low Countries: Urban Society and Political Conflict in the Middle Ages and the Renaissance* (New York, 1963).

Plenderleith, H. J., and Maryon, H., 'The royal bronze effigies in Westminster abbey', *Antiquaries Journal*, 39 (1959), 87–90.

Prestwich, J. O., 'The military household of the Norman kings', *EHR* 96 (1981), 1–35.

—— 'The place of the royal household in English history, 1066–1307', *Medieval History*, 1 (1991), 37–52.

Prestwich, M., 'The piety of Edward I', in W. M. Ormrod (ed.), *England in the Thirteenth Century: Proceedings of the 1984 Harlaxton Symposium* (Woodbridge, 1985).

—— *Edward I* (London, 1988).

Prevenier, W., 'En marge de l'assistance aux pauvres: l'aumônerie des comtes de Flandre et des ducs de Bourgogne (13e–début 16e siècle)', in *Recht en instellingen in de Oude Nederlanden tijdens de Middeleeuwen en de Nieuwe Tijd: Liber amicorum Jan Buntinx* (Louvain, 1981), 97–138.

—— 'Court and city culture in the Low Countries from 1100 to 1530', in Kooper, E. (ed.), *Medieval Dutch Literature in its European Context* (Cambridge and New York, 1994), 11–29.

—— 'The Low Countries, 1290–1415', in Jones, M. (ed.), *The New Cambridge Medieval History*, vi. c.*1300*–c.*1415* (Cambridge, 2000), 570–94.

—— and Blockmans, W., *The Burgundian Netherlands* (Cambridge, 1986).

Prinet, M., 'Les armoiries des français dans le poéme du siège de Carlaverock', *BEC* 92 (1931), 345–52.

Prost, B., 'Recherches sur les "peintres du roi" antérieurs au règne de Charles VI', in *Études d'histoire du moyen âge dédiées à Gabriel Monod* (Paris, 1896), 389–403.

Quarré, P., *Les Pleurants dans l'art du moyen âge en Europe* (Dijon, 1971).

Queller, D. E., and Kittell, E. E., 'Jakemon of Deinze, general receiver of Flanders, 1292–1300', *RBPH* 61 (1983), 286–321.

Quicke, F., *Les Pays-Bas à la veille de la période bourguignonne, 1356–84* (Brussels, 1947).

Raveschot, P., and Caillebaut, D., *Het Gravensteen te Gent* (Ghent, 1986).

Rhodes, W. E., 'The inventory of the jewels and wardrobe of Queen Isabella (1307–8)', *EHR* 12 (1897), 517–21.

Richard, J., 'Les itinéraires de Saint Louis en Île-de-France', in Chapelot, J., and Lalou, E., *Vincennes aux origines de l'état moderne* (Paris, 1996), 163–70.

Richard, J.-M., *Inventaire sommaire des archives départementales antérieures à 1790. Pas-de-Calais: Archives civiles, série A*, 2 vols. (Arras, 1878–85).

—— *Une petite-nièce de Saint Louis: Mahaut, comtesse d'Artois et de Bourgogne (1302–1329). Étude sur la vie privée, les arts et l'industrie en Artois et à Paris au commencement du xive siècle* (Paris, 1887).

Robin, F., 'Le luxe de la table dans les cours princiers (1360–1480)', *Gazette des Beaux-Arts* (1975), 105–31.

—— 'Art, luxe et culture: l'orfèvrerie et ses décors à la cour d'Anjou (1378–80)', *Bulletin monumental*, 141 (1983), 337–74.

Röhl, J. C. G., *The Kaiser and his Court: Wilhelm II and the Government of Germany* (Cambridge, 1994).

Roover, R. de, 'The commercial revolution of the thirteenth century', *Bulletin of the Business History Society*, 16 (1942), 34–9; repr. in Lane, F. C., and Riemersma, J. C. (eds.), *Enterprise and Secular Change* (London, 1953), 80–95.

Rosenthal, J. T., *The Purchase of Paradise: The Social Function of Aristocratic Benevolence, 1307–1485* (London and Toronto, 1972).

Rosser, G., *Medieval Westminster, 1200–1540* (Oxford, 1989).

Rothwell, W., 'From Latin to Modern French: fifty years on', *Bulletin of the John Rylands Library*, 68 (1985), 193–4.

—— 'The missing link in English etymology: French', *Medium Aevum*, 60 (1991), 173–96.

—— 'The "Faus Franceis d'Angleterre": later Anglo-Norman', in Short, I. (ed.), *Anglo-Norman Anniversary Essays* (London, 1993), 309–26.

Ruiz, T. F., 'Festivités, couleurs et symboles du pouvoir en Castille au xve siècle: Les célébrations de mai 1428', *Annales*, 46 (1991), 521–46.

Saffroy, G., *Bibliographie généalogique, heraldique et nobiliaire de la France des origines à nos jours, imprimés et manuscrits*, 4 vols. (Paris, 1968–79).

St John Hope, W. H., 'On the funeral effigies of the kings and queens of England, with special reference to those in the abbey church at Westminster', *Archaeologia*, 60 (1907), 517–70.

Saintenoy, P., *Les Arts et les artistes à la cour de Bruxelles*, i. *Leur rôle dans la construction du château ducal de Brabant sur le Coudenberg de 1120 à 1400 et dans la formation du Parc de Bruxelles* (Brussels, 1932).

Sandler, L. F., *Gothic Manuscripts, 1285–1385: A Survey of Manuscripts Illuminated in the British Isles*, 2 vols. (London, 1986).

Saul, N., *Richard II* (London, 1997).

Scaglione, A., *Knights at Court: Courtliness, Chivalry, and Courtesy from Ottonian Germany to the Italian Renaissance* (Berkeley, Los Angeles, and Oxford, 1991).

Scattergood, V. J., 'Literary culture at the court of Richard II', in Scattergood, V. J., and Sherborne, J. W. (eds.), *English Court Culture in the Later Middle Ages* (London, 1983), 29–43.

—— and Sherborne, J. W. (eds.), *English Court Culture in the Later Middle Ages* (London, 1983).

Scott, M., *Late Gothic Europe, 1400–1500* (History of Dress Series, London, 1980).

Sivéry, G., 'L'évolution des documents comptables dans l'administration hennuyère de 1287 à 1360 environ', *BCRH* 141 (1975), 133–235.

—— 'L'influence des techniques comptables italiennes dans les comptabilités administratives de l'Europe du Nord-Ouest vers 1300', in *Studi in memoria di Federigo Melis*, i (1978), 543–52.

Sleiderink, R., 'Dichters aan het Brabantse hof (1356–1406)', *De nieuwe taalgids*, 86 (1993), 1–16.

—— 'Pykini's parrot: music at the court of Brabant', in Haagh, B., Daelemans, F., and Vanrie, A. (eds.), *Musicology and Archival Research*, special issue *Archief- en Bibliotheekwezen in Belgie* (1994), 358–91.

Smit, H. J., 'Het begin van de regeering der Henegouwsche graven (1299–1320)', *Bijdragen voor vaderlandsche geschiedenis en oudheidkunde*, 7 (1932), 29–71.

Smit, J. G., *Vorst en onderdaam: Studies over Holland en Zeeland in de late middeleeuwen* (Louvain, 1995).

—— 'De Graven van Holland en Zeeland op reis: Het grafelijk itinerarium van het begin van de veertiende eeuw tot 1425', in Van Anrooij, W. *et al.*, *Holland in Wording: De onstaansgeschedenis van het grafschap Holland tot het begin van de vijftiende eeuw* (Hilversum, 1991), 91–124.

Smolar-Meynart, A., 'The establishment of the court of Philip the Good and the institutions of government in Brussels: a city becomes a capital', in *Rogier van der Weyden* (exhib. catal., Brussels, 1979), 15–23.

Sommé, M., 'L'alimentation quotidienne à la cour de Bourgogne au milieu du xve siècle', *BPHCTHS* (1968), 103–17.

—— 'Les déplacements d'Isabelle de Portugal et la circulation dans les Pays-Bas bourguignons au milieu du xvᵉ siècle', *RN* 52 (1970), 183–97.

Spufford, P., *Money and its Use in Medieval Europe* (Cambridge, 1988).

Stanger, M. D., 'Literary patronage at the medieval court of Flanders', *French Studies*, 11 (1957), 214–29.

Staniland, K., 'Welcome, Royal Babe! The birth of Thomas of Brotherton in 1300', *Costume*, 19 (1985), 1–13.

Starkey, D. (ed.), *The English Court: from the Wars of the Roses to the Civil War* (London and New York, 1987).

Stone, L., *Sculpture in Britain: The Middle Ages* (Harmondsworth, 1955).

Strayer, J. R., *The Reign of Philip the Fair* (Princeton, 1980).

Strohm, R., *Music in Late Medieval Bruges* (Oxford, 1990).

Stubblebine, J., 'French Gothic elements in Simone Martini's *Maesta*', *Gesta*, 29 (1990), 139–52.

Sturler, J. de, *Les Relations politiques et les échanges commerciaux entre le duché de Brabant et l'Angleterre au moyen âge* (Paris, 1936).

Suggett, H., 'The use of French in England in the later Middle Ages', *TRHS* 4th ser. 28 (1946), 60–83.

Sutton, A. F., Visser-Fuchs, L., and Hammond, P. W., *The Reburial of Richard, Duke of York, 21–30 July 1476* (London, 1996).

Taylor, A. J., 'Royal alms and oblations in the later thirteenth century: an analysis of the alms roll of 12 Edward I (1283–4)', in Emmison, F., and Stephens, R. (eds.), *Tribute to an Antiquary: Essays presented to March Fitch by Some of his Friends* (London, 1976), 93–125.

—— 'Count Amadeus of Savoy's visit to England in 1292', *Archaeologia*, 106 (1979), 123–32.

Terroine, A., 'Le Roi des ribauds de l'hôtel du roi et les prostituées parisiennes', *Revue historique de droit français et étranger*, 56 (1978), 253–67.

Thiebaut, M., *The Stag of Love: The Chase in Medieval Literature* (Ithaca, NY, and London, 1974).

Thomas, P. 'Une source nouvelle pour l'histoire administrative de la Flandre: le registre de Guillaume d'Auxonne, chancelier de Louis de Nevers, comte de Flandre', *RN* 10 (1924), 5–38.

Topham, A., *Memories of the Kaiser's Court* (London, 1914).

Tout, T. F., *Chapters in the Administrative History of Medieval England: the Wardrobe, the Chamber and the Small Seals*, 6 vols. (Manchester, 1920–33).

—— *France and England: Their Relations in the Middle Ages and Now* (Manchester and London, 1922).

—— 'The beginnings of a modern capital: London and Westminster in the fourteenth century', in *Collected Papers*, iii (Manchester, 1934), 249–75.

—— *The Place of the Reign of Edward II in English History* (2nd edn., Manchester, 1936).

Trabut-Cussac, J. P., 'Itinéraire d'Edouard Ier en France, 1286–1289', *BIHR* 25 (1952), 170–200.

Tucoo-Chala, P., *Gaston Fébus: un grand prince d'Occident au xive siècle* (Pau, 1976).

Tummers, H. A., *Early Secular Effigies in England: The Thirteenth Century* (Leiden, 1980).

Tyson, D. B., 'The epitaph of Edward the Black Prince', *Medium Aevum*, 46 (1977), 98–104.

Uyttebrouck, A., *Le Gouvernment du duché de Brabant à la fin du moyen âge* (Brussels, 1975).

—— 'Les résidences des ducs de Brabant, 1355–1430', in Patze, H., and Paravicini, W. (eds.), *Fürstliche Residenzen im spätmittelalterlichen Europa* (Sigmaringen, 1991), 189–205.

—— 'La cour de Brabant sous les ducs de la branche cadette de Bourgogne-Valois (1406–30)' in *Actes des journées internationales Claus Sluter* (Dijon, 1992), 311–35.

Vale, J., *Edward III and Chivalry: Chivalric Society and its Context, 1270–1350* (Woodbridge, 1982).

—— 'Arthur in English society', in Barron, W. R. J. (ed.), *The Arthur of the English* (Cardiff, 1999), 185–96.

—— 'Violence and the Tournament', in Kaeuper, R. (ed.), *Violence in Medieval Society* (Woodbridge, 2000), 143–58.

Vale, M., *War and Chivalry: Warfare and Aristocratic Culture in England, France and Burgundy at the End of the Middle Ages* (London, 1981).

—— 'Le tournoi dans la France du Nord, l'Angleterre et les Pays-Bas (1280–1400)', in *Actes du 115e Congrès National des Sociétés Savantes (Avignon, 1990)*, (Paris, 1991), 263–71.

—— 'Provisioning princely households in the Low Countries during the pre-Burgundian period, *c.*1280–1380', in Paravicini, W. (ed.), *Alltag bei Hofe* (Sigmaringen, 1995), 33–40.

—— *The Origins of the Hundred Years War: The Angevin Legacy, 1250–1340* (Oxford, 1996).

—— 'A Burgundian funeral ceremony: Olivier de la Marche and the obsequies of Adolf of Cleves, lord of Ravenstein', *EHR* 111 (1996), 920–38.

—— 'The world of the courts', in M. Bent and A. Wathey (eds.), *Fauvel Studies: Allegory, Chronicle, Music and Image in Paris, Bibliothèque Nationale, MS francais 146* (Oxford, 1998), 591–8.

Van Anrooij, W., *Spiegel van ridderschap: Heraut Gelre en zijn ereredes* (Amsterdam, 1990).

Van Buren, A., 'Reality and romance in the parc of Hesdin', in *Medieval Gardens* (Dumbarton Oaks, 1986), 117–34.

Van Dael, P., 'Wegwerparchitectuur: Het castrum doloris in de geschiedenis', *Kunstlicht*, 9 (1983), 22–8.

Vandaele, B., 'L'Alimentation de l'hôtel comtal de Hainaut au xive et au début du xve siècles' (unpub. thesis, Université de Lille III, 1975).

Van den Abeele, B., *La Fauconnerie dans les lettres françaises du xiie au xve siècle* (Louvain, 1990).

Van den Neste, E., *Tournois, joûtes, pas d'armes dans les villes de la Flandre à la fin du moyen âge (1300–1486)* (Paris, 1996).

Vandeputte, F., 'La chapelle des comtes de Flandre à Courtrai', *Annales de la Société d'Émulation de Bruges*, 10 (1875), 189–282.

Van der Essen, L., 'Les grands féodaux de Brabant et la "maisnie" ducale au xiiie siècle', in *Tablettes du Brabant*, i (1956), 29–32.

Vandermaesen, M., 'Het slot van Rupelmonde als centraal archiefdepot van het graafschap Vlaanderen (midden 13e–14d^e e.)', *Handelingen van de Koninklijke Commissie voor Geschiedenis*, 136 (1970), 273–317.

Van der Meulen, J. F., 'De panter en de aalmoezenier: Dichtkunst rond het Hollands-Henegouwse hof', in Willaert, F. (ed.), *Een zoet akoord: Middeleeuwse lyriek in de Lage Landen* (Amsterdam, 1992), 93–108.

Vanderwoude, K., 'De hofhouding van de laatse Vlaamse graaf en de eerste Bourgondische hertog (ca.1380–1404): Bijdrage tot de kennis van het hotel van Filips de Stoute als centrale instelling', 2 vols. (unpub. thesis, Ghent).

Van Marle, R., 'L'iconographie de la décoration profane des demeures princières en France et en Italie aux xive et xve siècles', *GBA* (1926), 163–82, 249–74.

Van Oostrom, F. P., *Court and Culture: Dutch Literature, 1350–1450* (Berkeley, Los Angeles, and Oxford, 1992).

—— 'Middle Dutch literature at court (with special reference to the court of Holland-Bavaria)', in Kooper, E. (ed.), *Medieval Dutch Literature in its European Context* (Cambridge and New York, 1994), 30–45.

—— *Maerlants Wereld* (Amsterdam, 1996).

Van Praet, L., *Recherches sur Louis de Bruges* (Paris, 1831).

Van Riemsdijk, T., *De Tresorie en Kanselarij van de graven van Holland en Zeeland uit het Henegouwsche en Beyersche huis* (The Hague, 1908).

Van Uytven, R., 'Cloth in medieval literature of western Europe', in Harte, N. B., and Ponting, K. G. (eds.), *Cloth and Clothing in Medieval Europe: Essays in Memory of Professor E. M. Carus-Wilson* (London, 1983), 151–83.

—— 'Rood-wit-zwart: kleuren-symboliek en kleursignalen in de Middeleeuwen', *Tijdschrift voor Geschiedenis*, 97 (1984), 447–70.

—— 'Showing off one's rank in the Middle Ages', in Blockmans, W., and Janse, A. (eds.), *Showing Status: Representations of Social Positions in the Late Middle Ages* (Turnhout, 1999), 29–34.

Vaughan, R., *Philip the Bold: The Formation of the Burgundian State* (London, 1962).

Vellekoop, C., 'Muziek en hoofse cultuur', in Stuip, R., and Vellekoop, C. (eds.), *Hoofse cultuur: Studies over een aspect van de middeleeuwse cultuur* (Utrecht, 1983), 87–117.

—— 'Gruuthuse-Handschrift', in Fischer, L. (ed.), *Die Musik in Geschichte und Gegenwart: Allegemeine Enzyklopedie der Musik begründet von Friedrich Blume*, iii (Kassel, 1995), 1722–3.

Viard, J., 'L'hôtel de Philippe de Valois', *BEC* 55 (1894), 465–87.

Warlop, E., *The Flemish Nobility before 1300*, 4 vols. (Kortrijk, 1975–6).

Warnke, M., *The Court Artist: On the Ancestry of the Modern Artist*, tr. D. McLintock (Cambridge and Paris, 1993).

Wendebourg, E., *Westminster Abbey als königliche Grablege zwischen 1250 und 1400* (Worms, 1986).

Whiting, B. J., 'The Vows of the Heron', *Speculum*, 20 (1945), 261–78.

Willaert, F., 'Entre trouvères et Minnesanger: La poésie de Jean Ier, duc de Brabant', in Busby, K., and Kooper, E. (eds.), *Courtly Literature: Culture and Context* (Amsterdam, 1990), 585–94.

—— '*Hovedans*: fourteenth-century dancing songs in the Rhine and Meuse area', in Kooper, E. (ed.), *Medieval Dutch Literature in its European Context* (Cambridge, UK, and New York, 1994), 168–87.

—— 'Een proefvlucht naar het zwarte gat: de Nederlandse liedkunst tussen Jan I van Brabant en het Gruuthuse-handschrift', in Willaert, F. (ed.), *Veelderhande Liedekens: Studies over het Nederlandse lied tot 1600* (Leiden, 1997), 30–46.

Willard, J. F., Morris, W. A., Strayer, J. R., and Dunham, H. (eds.), *The English Government at Work, 1327–1336*, 3 vols. (Cambridge, Mass., 1940–50).

Wilkins, N., *Music in the Age of Chaucer* (Cambridge, 1979).

—— 'A pattern of patronage: Machaut, Froissart and the houses of Luxembourg and Bohemia in the fourteenth century', *French Studies: A quarterly review*, 37 (1983), 257–84.

Zamoyski, A., *The Polish Way: A Thousand-Year History of the Poles and their Culture* (New York, 1996).

INDEX